D0166430

10,000 YEARS OF Pottery

WITHDRAWN

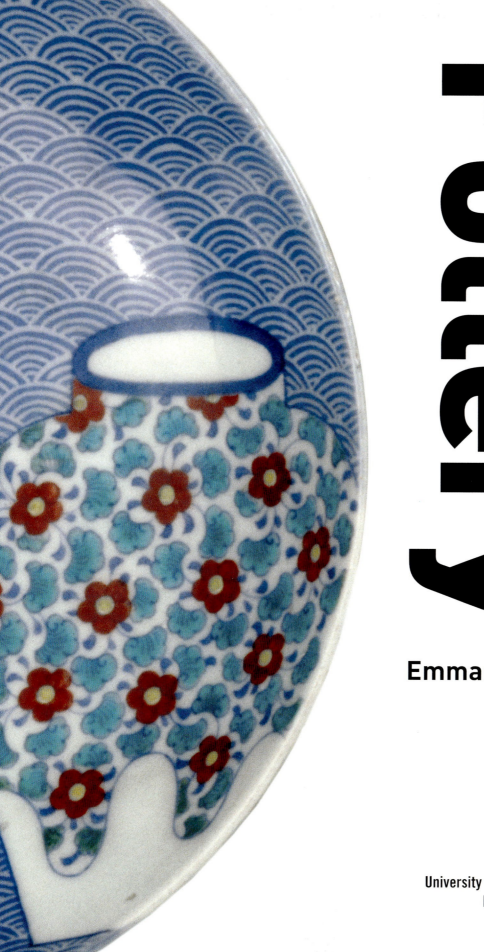

10,000 YEARS OF Pottery

Emmanuel Cooper

University of Pennsylvania Press
Philadelphia

AUTHOR'S ACKNOWLEDGEMENTS

Many people have been of great help in reading drafts, directing me to the latest literature and generally offering support and practical suggestions for this edition. In particular I would like to acknowledge the advice and practical help, often far beyond the call of duty, of curatorial, photographic and administrative staff at The British Museum, especially the patient and generous guidance given by Aileen Dawson and Dr David Gaimster. My thanks are also due to Andrew Watts for bringing new information to my attention and to the many potters who responded so positively to requests for photographs. I have also received constant support from David Horbury, Simon Watney, Jeffrey Weeks, the staff at *Ceramic Review* and, last but by no means least, Nina Shandloff, Jemima Scott-Holland and the editorial team at British Museum Press.

HALF-TITLE PAGE: Kirsten Coelho, *Two Jars*, 2009 (© Kirsten Coelho). FRONTISPIECE: Nabeshima dish, Japan, Edo period, 18th–19th century AD. (© The Trustees of the British Museum) RIGHT: Virgil Ortiz, vase, 2005 (© Virgil Ortiz)

First published 1972 as
A History of World Pottery
Second edition 1981
Third edition 1988
Fourth edition 2000

First published in paperback 2002 by
The British Museum Press
A division of The British Museum Company Ltd

Paperback first published in the USA 2010 by
University of Pennsylvania Press
3905 Spruce Street
Philadelphia, Pennsylvania 19104

A catalogue record for this book is available
from the Library of Congress

ISBN 978-0-8122-2140-4

The papers used in this book are natural, renewable and recyclable products and the manufacturing processes are expected to conform to the environmental regulations of the country of origin.

Designed and typeset in Garamond and Trade Gothic by Bobby Birchall. Additional typesetting by Helen Robertson. Maps by Technical Art.
Printed in China.

Contents

Introduction

EMMANUEL COOPER

Pottery is one of the oldest activities of humankind, shedding light on the cultures within which it was made and revealing technological and artistic achievements as well as being an art form in its own right. New discoveries are constantly being made. Ten thousand years, though a vast period, remains a conservative estimate of the time in which pottery has been made, and as more pottery is found so the earliest activities are pushed even further back in time. One of the most recent archaeological finds was made in the caves of Tuc d'Audobert, where beautifully preserved clay bison have been found that are estimated to be 12,000 years old.

The power of fire to transform soft, malleable clay into a robust and durable material was recognized 25,000 years ago, but the first appearance of pottery vessels came much later, coinciding with the development of more settled communities. The Jomon culture of Japan produced some of the earliest pottery for which there is clear archaeological and scientific evidence. Since then clay has taken many forms, from fired bricks and votive figures thrown into flames as part of fertility rituals to the most sophisticated and technically accomplished pots produced within the ceramic industry. Research into superconductors, ceramic automotive parts and spaceship cladding indicates that ceramics remain at the forefront of technological development. *Ten Thousand Years of Pottery* is intended to serve as a general introduction to the art and craft of pottery. By definition it cannot hope to be exhaustive, but I have sought to make it as representative as possible, indicating in broad strokes the major movements and technical and artistic developments.

Since the late 1950s there has been a move away from regarding pottery solely as a means of dating, whereby different pottery types are related to chronological change, towards a desire to understand the nature and processes of its production as a key to social context, economic organization and trade, and technical virtuosity. In looking at areas both geographically and chronologically, this book attempts not to construct a linear, unproblematic line of development but to set out the kind of pottery made during each particular period, while taking into account the social, economic, technical and artistic ideas that informed it.

This book looks at the progression of pottery-making, starting from its earliest manifestation in ancient civilizations and moving right up to the present day. Major countries and regions are dealt with more or less as a whole, and pottery developments are followed roughly chronologically. A brief outline of the basic pottery processes is given in chapter 1, and thereafter different techniques are explained as they occurred and related to those that existed elsewhere at the same time. The book traces the stylistic and technological developments through ancient Greece and Rome and the Far East as well as dealing with the distinctive pottery produced within the Islamic world. It looks at the ceramics of the Renaissance period, the tin-glazed and decorated earthenwares, and the high-fired salt-glazed wares.

The book also chronicles the rapid development of ceramics during the eighteenth century, a period that heralded the growth of the pottery industry and the production of fine porcelains in the West. It traces the use of clay for more decorative purposes in the nineteenth century, either in the form of ornaments or as elements of decorative mouldings and architectural motifs, and details the response of the Arts and Crafts movement to growing industrialization. The final two chapters look in detail at the work of artist-potters around the world in the twentieth century, discussing their involvement with industry and the growth of pottery as a 'medium of expression'. Ceramics in

Clay bison from the cave of Tuc d'Audobert, Hautes-Pyrénées, France.

the twentieth century are dealt with both thematically and, where appropriate, by country. Today there is a great interest in the art and craft of pottery throughout the world. Historically, ceramics have been a focus for major exhibitions, while the production of studio ceramics has been encouraged by the activities of government-sponsored bodies such as the Crafts Council in the United Kingdom and the American Crafts Council and the National Endowment for the Arts in the United States. The appearance of magazines devoted to ceramics has also served to increase awareness of and interest in new work, improving communication between potters and the public.

In one sense there is no history of pottery, in that techniques, shapes, kilns and glazes were developed in different countries at different times; there have been many jumps in time and place, for a variety of reasons. However, there are threads that can be followed, which link countries and people in a fascinating way, and these I have attempted to identify.

Sufficient detail has been included in this book to interest the more knowledgeable reader, yet it is essentially an introduction to one of our oldest and most exciting art forms, and as such will, I hope, serve as a springboard for further research and investigation.

Early Beginnings

With Earth's first Clay

They did the Last Man knead

EDWARD FITZGERALD

Jomon vessels with cord markings and incised lines from Hokkaido, final phase, first millennium BC. Height (tallest) 24.4 cm (9.75 in).

Two jugs with relief decoration. Early Bronze Age, c. 2700–1500 BC. Western Anatolia, from cemeteries in the Yortan area. Black burnished handmade jugs with cutaway spouts and varied decoration are typical of the period. Red burnished jugs became common in the second millennium BC. Height (tallest) 30 cm (12 in).

The discovery that clay was plastic, that it could be modelled and shaped, dried and then baked in a fire to transform it into ceramic, was made many thousands of years ago. The type of pottery made is dependent on a large number of factors: the availability of particular raw materials such as clay, the fuel used for the kiln, the techniques practised and the demands of the society within which it is produced. The first appearance of pottery vessels generally seems to coincide with the development of less nomadic, more settled or sedentary ways of life. From relatively humble beginnings, clay forms became more accomplished, ambitious and sophisticated. As firing techniques developed, so the objects could be made more robust and increasingly ornate in form and decoration. Kiln design grew more efficient at retaining heat and eventually the objects could be protected from the direct flame, enabling ever more refined results to be achieved. In parallel with developments in glass technology, glazes were developed, which provided a smooth and hygienic surface that could also be colourful and attractive. This chapter describes the basic processes of pottery, and their use and development in early civilizations.

BASIC MATERIALS AND PROCESSES

It is not difficult to see why the plastic qualities of clay appealed to early farmers, who shaped simple pots and modelled small figures. The Jomon culture of Japan, a hunter-gatherer society, was making pottery over 12,000 years ago, and pottery became a fundamental part of the first sedentary communities along the Middle Nile Valley some 9000 years ago. Early farmers needed means of storing grain and other produce, including liquids, and pottery containers could be made more efficiently than those fashioned out of animal skins, bark, basketware or hollowed-out stone or wood. Pottery vessels could also be used for cooking and processing cultivated foods. Whether soft and malleable or dry and hard, clay also offered great scope for elaboration and decoration. Many early societies – such as the European Beaker culture, that of Predynastic Egypt and the American-Indian culture – developed specialized vessels for funerary use.

In general, pottery production was a part-time seasonal activity combined with agricultural work. It was often women who were the potters, as the hand-building methods used meant that the work cycle was regularly interrupted to give the part-built vessels time to stiffen and strengthen before being completed, and this fitted in well with women's domestic role in such societies. In Mesopotamia, by the time of the Halaf culture (c. 6000–5000 BC) more advanced levels of production had developed, bringing a measure of craft specialization. Turning pots on a potter's wheel was regarded as more skilled than hand-building and was probably done

by men. As the population continued to expand and more stable settlements arose, so production became more sophisticated. The communal lifestyle stimulated technological innovation. The introduction of the fast-rotating wheel enabled potters to produce a wider range of pottery intended for specific purposes, more quickly and efficiently than hitherto. Records of the Ur III period (2100–2000 BC) refer to pottery workshops of between two and ten people working on a seasonal basis under a supervisor, the remainder of the year being devoted to agricultural work.

It is not known how the discovery was made that dried clay subjected to dull red heat (about 600°C) changes its chemical and physical structure to become hard and thus not liable to disintegrate in water. It is likely that the idea developed over time and there are many theories as to its origin. The first and perhaps most valid is the hearth theory. Fire was a valuable and vital resource for early societies; it provided warmth and

Coffin from Crete, painted with flowers. Minoan, 1400–1200 BC. Earthenware, hand-built. Length 9.8 cm (24.5 in).

light, helped to frighten away animals and was used for cooking food. A fire would have to be carefully tended and maintained. Holes made in the ground could well have been lined with clay to keep water out, and in such a hearth the fire would bake the clay, resulting in a crude vessel.

Another theory is that baskets (or even birds' nests) may have been smeared with clay to render them waterproof. As the clay dried out, the object could be placed as a cooking vessel in the fire, where it would subsequently be found to have been baked hard. Such a theory presupposes the existence of basketry, however, and while in some early cultures basket-making pre-dated pottery, in others it arose later. Alternatively, the discovery may have been made by placing figures modelled in clay into the fire, perhaps as part of some ritual or ceremony, and finding them to be altered by the heat. From early times myth and magic played an important part in the life of many communities and it is more than likely that some of the modelled clay symbolic figures that have been found were made for use in such ceremonies.

The plastic qualities of clay that make it so workable and responsive are largely the result of its physical and chemical structure. Clay is made up of tiny particles that are flat and plate-like, each

Terracotta foundation cylinder of Nabonidus, c. 555–540 BC, from the temple of Shamash, Sippar, recording the king's pious reconstruction of temples to the moon and sun gods. 22.5 cm (9 in) x 9 cm (3.6 in).

carrying an electrical charge, which causes them to cling together. The presence of water enables the particles to slide over one another without breaking apart. Too much water results in a formless mass, known as slurry, or even mud, while too little prevents any movement and pressure may cause the clay to crack apart. As the water in the clay evaporates, the clay shrinks and becomes hard and brittle, but it will soften and disintegrate if placed in water. Depending on the amount of water present, clay can take the form of a dry, powdery solid, a sticky but plastic mass or a lumpy liquid. All these states are useful to the potter in different ways, but it is in the plastic state that clay responds most quickly to the potter's hands.

Unlike materials such as wood or ivory that have a grain, clay has no defining internal structure. This 'structureless' quality of clay means that, unlike most other materials, it has few limitations and technically can be shaped into virtually any form. Nevertheless, some shapes are better suited to clay, and easier to make with it, than others. It would be possible, for example, to make a pair of scissors in clay, but the blades would have little mechanical strength. The versatility of clay has been one of its greatest assets, enabling a wide variety of forms and shapes to be produced by different techniques: modelled as sculptural pieces, fashioned into bricks for architecture or thrown on the potter's wheel.

The forms and shapes of ceramic objects are largely determined by the method of manufacture. For instance, pots thrown on the potter's wheel are hollow and rounded while those built from slabs of clay tend to be flat or curved and sit on a flattened base. Objects or containers produced by pressing clay into or over moulds such as shells or gourds take on these forms, while hand-building by methods such as coiling or pinching out a ball of clay can create a great variety of shapes and sizes. All these methods have been used for thousands of years. The introduction of more industrial methods of manufacture such as slip-casting liquid clay into plaster moulds, or a more mechanical process such as the jigger and jolly, further extended the range of forms made and increased the speed of manufacture.

As a generalization, most pots are rounded, and even before the wheel was invented the majority took this shape, largely as a result of the method of making rather than the demands of the clay. It is much easier, for example, to squeeze out a round rather than a square pinch pot, or to coil a rounded vessel as opposed to a square or rectangular one. Nevertheless, there are many surviving containers that are rectangular or oval, and some from Crete are fashioned in the form of troughs divided into partitions or coffins with lids.

Not only has clay no defining structure, but it has little or no intrinsic value, although clay objects have often been made to imitate the form and appearance of more costly or highly regarded materials such as bronze, gold, silver, glass and jade. In addition to aping the appearance of more precious inorganic materials, clay has also been used to copy the shapes of natural forms and materials such as gourds, ostrich eggs, bamboo and even animals, as well as basketry, wooden trays and leather bags and bottles.

Early discoveries

It is likely that clay was used for a whole variety of purposes before the discovery was made that it could be transformed by fire. For example, clays of different colours, mixed with water to form pigments, were used for cave paintings as well as probably for building or strengthening shelters. In the ancient Near East during the eighth millennium BC clay was used to make sun-dried or lightly baked figurines and 'tokens', and also to build architectural structures. Only with the discovery

Terracotta female figurine. Parthian. Height 88 cm (35 in).

Earthenware pot in the form of a bird. Its head acts as a stopper. Basuto. Height 12.5 cm (5 in).

Earthenware pots from Haçilar, Turkey. Central Anatolia, *c.* 5000 BC. Hand-built with painted decoration. The jar is modelled in the form of a female figure. Height (tallest) 11.5 cm (4.6 in).

that heat transforms clay into ceramic does the history of pottery begin.

The use of clay seems to have arisen independently in different parts of the world. Nomadic societies had little time to make or opportunity to transport or use pottery and so it is with the beginnings of the more settled life of the New Stone Age that the making of pots can be identified. Before then, images of men, women and animals were modelled in clay and probably used for magical or ritual purposes. So-called mother goddesses, with enlarged sexual organs and exaggerated female features, have been excavated in various parts of the world, including Anatolia (modern-day Turkey) and the Levant. These figures date to prehistoric times and are thought to be related to religious cults encouraging human fertility and successful harvests. Some of the earliest surviving baked clay female figurines, dating to about 6000 BC, have been found at Çatal Hüyük, Haçilar, in Anatolia. These appear to have been placed in grain bins. Also made in this area was a group of painted wares, dating from around 5000 BC. The majority have geometrical designs painted in red pigment on to a cream slip applied to the pots after firing,

possibly reflecting an interest in contemporary wall painting. The surfaces of these pots are burnished, giving them a rich effect.

As tribes settled, their ritual figures and objects began to be hardened in the fire, thereby surviving to provide information about the societies that made them. It is possible also that such figures could have been used for trade, along with shells and coloured stones.

Clay preparation

Clay occurs naturally over much of the earth's surface and, while it may vary in colour and be more or less plastic and malleable and capable of higher- or lower-temperature firing, the basic working qualities are much the same. Since early times good usable clay has been highly valued, and some groups travelled many miles to collect more workable clay or clay of a particular colour. Much of the technical success of the Athenian and Corinthian potters of ancient Greece can be attributed to their use of the fine, smooth clays that were readily available. The Pueblo potters of Zuni in the south-western mesas of North America carried clay from the top of a mountain because of its workable qualities. In ancient Egypt the smooth Nile clays resulted in fine wares with thin, strong walls. During the seventeenth century clay was taken from East Anglia in England to Holland to be used by potters in Delft because it was particularly suited to the needs of fine white maiolica. In the modern world clays are transported from Devon and Cornwall to potteries in many parts of Britain and to many other countries.

As pottery-making became a more specialist activity, the availability of suitable clays became a major determining factor in the success of the industry. Good clay had to be easily accessible, relatively clean, free from impurities or foreign matter such as stones or vegetation, and of a suitable colour. It also had to be sufficiently plastic to enable it to be moulded and worked, and able to withstand the heat of the fire without collapsing. The art of clay preparation was brought to perfection by the ceramic industry that developed in Britain in the second part of the eighteenth century. This depended not only on highly skilled manufacturing processes but also on the ability to devise a body that was fine, white and smooth as well as tough; clays from different regions of the country were carefully blended and virtually all iron impurities were eliminated to produce such bodies.

All clays, whether for the ceramic industry or for hand-building, have to be carefully prepared. Any stones or other foreign bodies that could cause the pot to crack as it dries or to explode during the firing need to be removed and the clay body made even or homogeneous by a process called wedging. This combination of banging and kneading can be carried out with either the feet or the hands. If large pots are to be made, some sort of filler may need to be added to the body to improve its working qualities, open it and make it easier to control when modelling. This has traditionally taken the form of broken shells, sand, grit, chaff, straw or (later on) grog made from ground-up fired clay. For cooking pots refractory clay is required – that is, a clay more capable of withstanding the rapid expansion known as thermal shock that takes place when a fired pot is exposed to direct heat.

Making methods
Before the invention of the wheel, pottery was built entirely by hand using one of several methods, either alone or in combination:

1. Pinching or squeezing small lumps of clay between the fingers. Some potters in Japan continue to employ this method for tea bowls because the qualities it offers are quite different from those of wheel-thrown ware; the process is also used by some modern studio potters (see chapter 14).

2. Constructing vessels from coils or rings of clay. These are placed on top of each other, joined by pushing one into the other, then smoothed over. This method enables larger pots to be made than would normally be possible on the wheel. Building pots from small overlapping pats of clay is an alternative technique.

3. Employing moulds or a former of some sort to enable objects to be made in quantity, relatively quickly and with great accuracy. The clay can be used in a variety of forms. Soft clay can be smeared over natural forms such as gourds, coils can be pressed in or over the mould, or clay can be rolled or cut into a slab and laid in or over the mould, which requires a flat surface.

Terracotta pilgrim flask with stamped scene of St Menas. Alexandria, 5th–7th century. Height 15.2 cm (6 in).

Coffin lid from the site of Lachish in Israel, thought to have been used by the Sea Peoples of Aegean origin, who served with the Egyptians and made slipper-shaped coffins with lids modelled with human features. 1400–1150 BC.

Pottery stand from Ur, in Mesopotamia, 2100–2000 BC. The invention of the potter's wheel during the fourth millennium BC led to increased mass-production, including the making of more specialized objects such as fruit-stands. Height 43.75 cm (17.5 in).

4. Constructing containers from flat slabs of clay. These are made by cutting, slicing or beating a solid block of clay and can be built up to form flat-sided 'troughs' or other angular forms.

5. Beating out a lump of clay using a beater on the outside and a mushroom-shaped support inside enables vessels with thin, strong walls to be formed. These tools, sometimes known

respectively as the paddle and anvil, were and still are in use in several parts of the world. This method may also be employed to complete the form of a pot built by coiling or thrown on the wheel.

Most early potters worked sitting on the ground. They may have used their inner thighs to support the pot or rested it on a disc or mat in front of them, which would have allowed the pot to be turned round much more easily; the potter's wheel was developed in Mesopotamia some time around 4000–3000 BC. The earliest examples – often known as slow wheels – were constructed with a stone or wooden wheelhead pivoted in the ground. As the mechanism of the wheel improved, so it revolved more smoothly and faster, enabling more refined forms to be produced at greater speed. The wheel was either pushed or kicked round with the foot. Making pots on the wheel meant that the clay had to be more carefully prepared so that any stones or irregularities would not impede the throwing process, and the potter had to acquire the necessary throwing skills. The wheel also had a strong influence on the form, as pots made by this method were round, with no sharp corners or angles. Decoration, too, was influenced by the development of the wheel; horizontal bands could be drawn quickly and easily on the revolving pots and this method of decoration came to predominate. This completely new technique not only speeded up production but, because pottery was now regarded as highly skilled, it also changed the status of the potter.

As the efficiency of the machine increased, the wheel became even smoother and faster, and in some areas it was propelled by a stick placed in a hole on the wheelhead. The earliest archaeologically attested wheels, dating to about 3000 BC or later, were used in Japan and were pushed clockwise. Later the pivot supporting the wheelhead was improved and eventually a shaft was fitted to the wheelhead and a flywheel added at the base, so enabling a faster, smoother continuous action. The biggest development came with the invention of the crank, which converted a kicking action into a spinning movement. On this sort of wheel the potter was able to sit up and power the wheel by kicking on a treadle. Today most potter's wheels are mechanically operated, usually by an electric motor, which ensures both speed and control.

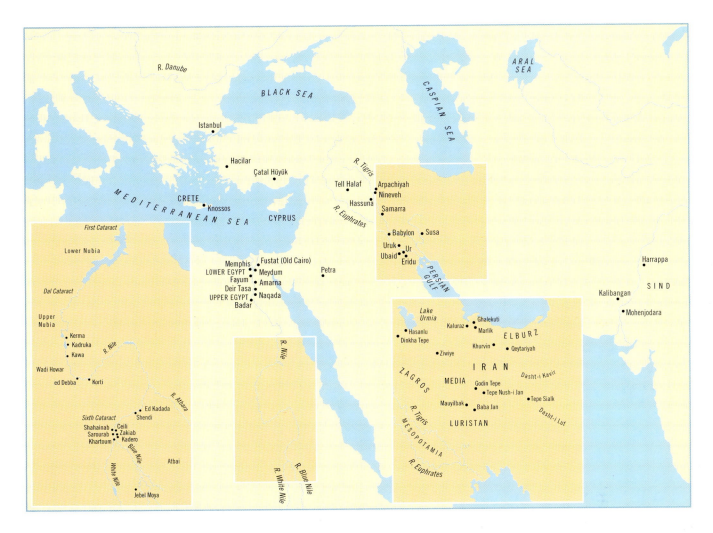

Map of the ancient Near East, with sites of early civilizations in Mesopotamia, Iran, Egypt and the Indus Valley.

Finishing the pots

Pottery fired to the relatively low temperatures obtainable in bonfire firings – which are still in use in various parts of the world today – was remarkably effective, and, although porous, the pots so made are reasonably strong and efficient. Porosity is a desirable feature of pots intended to contain water in a hot climate, as the constant evaporation from the outside helps keep the contents cool. Until waterproof glassy glazes came into widespread use other methods were devised to render the pottery impervious, increase its strength and make the surface smoother. One common method was to burnish the surface of the clay before it was fully dry by rubbing with a smooth stone or pebble; this presses the clay particles flat, giving the surface a dull but attractive shine and rendering it less porous. The shine remains after firing. Patterns could also be produced by burnishing. An alternative method of producing a smooth, shiny surface was to cover it with a slip of finely levigated clay. This was prepared by making a watery clay mixture, allowing the larger particles to sink and decanting off the fine ones left in suspension, which were used for the slip. It was a technique used to great effect by the Greeks on their red and black painted ware to give a decorated as well as a smooth surface.

On other pots a vegetable 'glaze' was painted or splashed on to the surface of the pot while it was still hot from the firing. The 'glaze' was made by boiling vegetation such as special leaves or bark until a strong solution was obtained, and although the results were not as permanent as a true glaze, the pot would be more waterproof. Some potters in Africa still use this method. Asphalt was also applied to the inside of vessels to make them waterproof. Manipulation of the firing by controlling the smoke and flame was another method that could help reduce porosity and increase strength. This process could blacken the surface of the pot to make it more attractive, and some pots made in ancient Egypt were fired so that one half of the pot was black, the other red. Another method of blackening the surface was to cover the vessel with wet leaves towards the end of the firing, which produced smoke that penetrated the pores and made the pot a black colour – a process known as 'carbon smoking'.

Kilns and firing

Clay is changed into ceramic by heating it as evenly as possible to dull red heat (about 600°C) and above. The earliest firings were probably carried out in the domestic hearth, although open bonfires would also have been used – a method that can still be seen in parts of South America, Africa and the Middle and Far East. In this process the fire is slowly started round the thin-walled and round-shaped pots, the heat gradually built up, and then the whole covered with material such as grass, reeds or cattle dung to protect the contents from cooler air and to serve as fuel. The comparatively low temperature obtained by this type of firing is sufficient to turn the usually fine-grained red clay into ceramic. The use of glaze is rare in such firing. The colour of the pots is affected by the flames and smoke, giving uneven but often attractive markings.

Kilns evolved slowly, the earliest most probably consisting of little more than a shallow hole in the ground with some sort of temporary structure built to contain the pots. In the Near East early kilns were circular up-draught kilns with sunken fireboxes. Pots were stacked inside from the top and probably covered over with broken pots, mud or earth, leaving a small hole for the smoke to escape. Even a simple kiln such as this gave much more control than an open bonfire; it retained the heat, allowed for a controllable draught and kept the pots together in one place. Such kilns eventually evolved so that the pots could be separated from the flames of the kiln. Increased control involved the careful direction of the flow of the flame either by the use of a perforated grate (the most common method) or, eventually, by placing the pots in ceramic saggars such as were used in the ceramics industry in Stoke-on-Trent in the large bottle kilns.

In the Far East simple up-draught kilns were constructed in the side of a hill. The fire was made at the base and the flames passed through the structure, which acted as a chimney and had a narrow opening at the top to conserve the heat. Potters later made use of greater knowledge of refractories and temperature control to develop more sophisticated kilns, which ensured that the flames stayed inside longer by directing them first to the top and then to the exit flue at the bottom. Down-draught kilns such as these have the advantage of retaining heat for longer periods, enabling the higher temperatures required for stoneware and porcelain to be reached.

MESOPOTAMIA

The earliest civilizations in the Middle East developed in the fertile land between the rivers Tigris and Euphrates – the region known as Mesopotamia (sometimes called 'the land between the two rivers') – before 8000 BC. Mesopotamia's diverse geographical regions include lowlands, upland plains, mountains and desert, with the various cultures reflected in their respective ceramic traditions. It embraced the ancient kingdoms of Assyria and Babylonia (modern-day Iraq and eastern Syria). The earliest urban centres arose in the lowlands, an area characterized by deposits of highly plastic clays left by annual floods. To some extent this influenced the great variety of clay production, which ranged from the making of bricks for the construction of buildings to a variety of ceramic containers as well as slabs used for hieroglyphics.

Prehistoric wares

The earliest pots were hand-built, low-fired, undecorated and made from reddish-brown clays. Proto-Hassuna ware dates to the seventh millennium BC and consists of handmade, low-fired coarse wares, often with a lightly burnished surface. Decoration is limited to reddish-brown banded lines and modelled additions such as small knobs, animals and schematic human figures. Slab-built keel-shaped jars and four-footed vessels are characteristic of this ware; larger storage jars were sunk into floors as fixed storage containers.

In early settlements, in what is known as the Hassuna period, people lived in farmhouses, cultivated crops, kept cattle and sheep, wove materials and made pots. The pots were relatively well fired compared with earlier ceramics and the earliest identifiable kilns date to this period. Globular jars

Painted bowls from Samarra. Hand-built, *c.* 6300–6000 BC. Height (tallest) 6.3 cm (2.5 in).

and open bowls were decorated with chevron and herringbone patterns, possibly inspired by basketry, by incision, with red or black pigment added, or by a combination of techniques. Straight-sided oval trays with scored walls and flat corrugated-base interiors may have been employed as 'husking trays' used in the production of flour. Large jars were used for grain storage. Kilns were clustered within enclosures, implying the separation of ceramic production from household activities.

The Samarran culture flourished from *c.* 6300 to 6000 BC, mainly in the Tigris and Euphrates river valleys of central Mesopotamia. The number of known kilns suggests that each settlement may have been largely self-sufficient in ceramics. Bowls and wide-mouthed jars are painted with bold geometric reddish-brown designs recalling woven patterns. Occasionally semi-stylized natural motifs of animals as well as swastikas and human faces

were incorporated into the designs. Painted signs on the bases may represent potters' marks, which suggests manufacture for a market beyond immediate household needs; sporadic finds of Samarran painted wares have been made at sites across Mesopotamia, implying limited trade.

The Halaf culture

In the Halaf culture (*c.* 6000–5000 BC), new farming villages were founded in the dry upland plains of northern Mesopotamia. Here distinctive pottery and figurines were produced. Significant technological developments such as the more careful preparation of clays affected the quality of the wares produced. Fine clays were used for thin-walled vessels, coarser clays for jars and cooking ware. Pottery became increasingly varied and complex in form: thin-walled bowls, jars with rounded rims and sharply curved sides and a variety of round-bottomed vessels indicate the range of shapes. Red and black pigments derived from natural ocherous earths were painted on to the pots before they were fired. Modelled female figures have also been found.

At Arpachiyah vessels were carefully wet-smoothed, obscuring traces of the forming method and leaving a covering of fine slip. A major feature of these ceramics is the use of painted decoration. A bull's head was a popular decorative motif, and is taken as evidence of stock-rearing or bull cults. Occasionally snakes, leopards and human figures are shown, but patterns of chequers, stipples and floral designs are more common. The use of sophisticated kilns enabled pots to be decorated with painted designs before they had been fired, and to retain their

The Ubaid culture

The Ubaid culture (*c.* 6000–4000 BC) arose in the alluvial plains of lower Mesopotamia. Despite the size of the region there is a notable degree of homogeneity of ceramic style, particularly during the late phase. Pottery was clearly important. Within a single house at Tell Madhhur as many as seventy-eight ceramic vessels have been found. The vessels were handmade and may have been finished on a slow wheel of some sort, with wet-smoothing carried out during the final stages. Gypsum discs may have been used as bases on which to turn the pot.

Ubaid ceramics range from shallow, medium-sized and deep bowls to closed forms and lugged jars capable of holding twelve to thirty litres. There are also spouted vessels with basket handles and

Two finely made and painted beakers from Susa in Iran, 5th–4th century BC. Height (tallest) 15.5 cm (6.2 in).

clear colours during the firing. In earlier kilns pots came into contact with the flame and smoke, which coloured them red, black and brown, largely obscuring any painted decoration. Circular up-draught kilns continued to be used, attaining temperatures of approximately 950°C.

thin-walled 'tortoise' vessels with trumpet spouts. Painted decoration is common; it varies according to period and site and may have been executed on the slow wheel with such pigments as iron and manganese oxides, often quite thickly applied. Naturalistic decoration is rare, although there are representations of birds, felines, human figures, bulls' heads and scorpions. In addition to vessels, potters also produced reaping hooks held in the left hand, known as 'sickles', axe-heads and figurines.

Improvements in kiln design increased the temperature range to between 1050°C and 1200°C, although coarse wares were fired to lower temperatures. The development of the slow wheel and the improved kiln temperatures fundamentally affected the entire production of pottery. Clay had now to be more carefully prepared than for hand-building, or a smoother clay had to be selected. The local, plastic clays fired a characteristic pale olive-green colour, and occasionally tempers of various kinds were added to open the body.

The Uruk period

Far-reaching changes took place within Mesopotamian society during the fourth millennium, in what is known as the Uruk period, after the site of the same name. These included the building of fortified cities, large constructions, the development of writing and art, long-distance trade and new crafts and industries. Such changes inevitably affected ceramics. During this time the potter's wheel was developed, leading to the greater mass-production of pots, although some hand-built coarse wares continued to be made. Pottery was generally red or grey burnished, although a northern variety was painted. During the Late Uruk period hand-painted decoration was largely replaced by the more rapid process of incising designs, although some vessels were left plain. Sand was commonly added to the body to improve its working qualities. New forms included conical beakers, tall jars with short, upright spouts, droopy-spouted wine jars and globular storage jars with perforated vertical lugs, sometimes with burnished red slip or incised decoration. The lugs may have been used to secure 'lids' of cloth or skin with tightly bound string.

Towards the end of the period new regional styles of painted wares were briefly popular. Polychrome painted, burnished, red-slipped jars were made in central Mesopotamia and traded, perhaps because of their unusual and attractive decoration.

Early Dynastic period

During the third millennium the region was a patchwork of independent city-states, each with its own gods and kings, with the Sumerians dominating southern Mesopotamia. The arts, trade, early writing and monumental architecture flourished under a high degree of patronage, a particularly spectacular example being a rich group of 'Royal Tombs' at Ur.

As pottery-making became more specialized, workshops began to be sited near the edges of towns. The reasons for this were the low social status of the craft, easier access to clays and fuel supplies, and the fire risk posed by the kilns. A more sophisticated ceramic technology developed in northern Mesopotamia in the Early Dynastic and Akkadian periods. Vessels were thrown on a

Oval glazed coffin lid. Uruk, southern Mesopotamia. The moulded decoration shows a standing figure with a bushy hairstyle, wearing a sword on his left thigh. The lid originally fitted on the end of a long glazed coffin, also decorated in relief. Associated grave goods included glass vessels, figurines, bone 'handles' and coins. Height *c.* 85 cm (34 in).

fast wheel from highly plastic clays, and polished or spiral-burnished in imitation of metalwares. Greater kiln control enabled temperatures of 950–1050°C to be maintained to yield grey, olive green or red stoneware jars and thin-walled streaky self-slipped beakers and bowls, some of which were

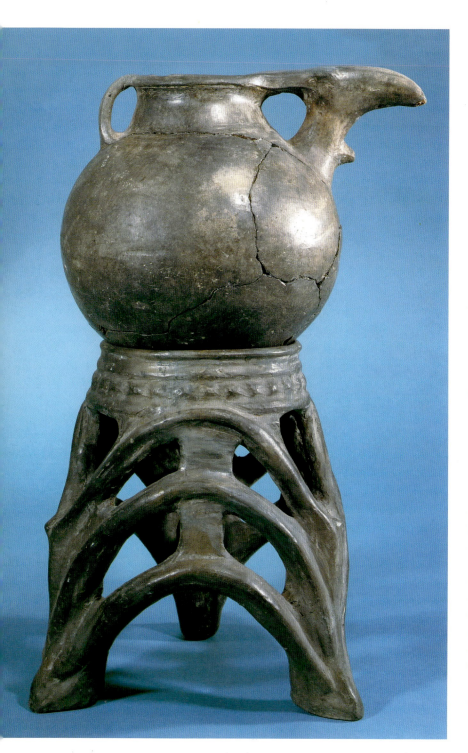

Burnished greyware bridge-spouted jug on tripod stand. North-west Iran. Height *c.* 30 cm (12 in).

vessels include conical bowls, solid-footed goblets, stemmed dish 'fruit-stands' (similar forms of which were also produced by silversmiths), and jars with upright handles decorated with incision and occasionally pellets imitating eyes. Spouted jars served as beer measures; beer and wine were popular drinks, but because of their coarse sediment, spouted pouring jars or filter-tipped straws were required to dispense the liquid.

In parts of northern Mesopotamia cylinder seals were used to impress designs into the rims and upper walls of jars, and red- and black-painted Scarlet ware was decorated with hematite or vermilion (cinnabar) and soot. During the Akkadian period new forms were developed, including basin-shaped pot-stands with three or four strap handles on the interior and jars with perforated double lug handles. Some of the most intriguing forms are troughs decorated in relief on the outside with snakes and scorpions, possibly to ward off evil spirits. Decoration included wavy-combed, comb-stabbed, incised hatched triangle and relief herringbone designs.

Second millennium

Shifting alliances and trade systems between various royal dynasties across the Near East brought a wider range of forms and techniques. Pottery production remained essentially an urban activity, but despite increased mass-produced plain and utilitarian wares, distinctive regional styles were developed. From Syro-Palestine a more sophisticated wheel was introduced that included a pair of close-fitting polished basalt or limestone axle-bearings. Modern replication experiments suggest that this bearing supported a wider, probably wooden, wheelhead that was turned by an assistant, leaving the potter free to make pots on this slow wheel, often working from a hump of clay – a method well suited to the rapid throwing of small to medium-sized vessels. Larger pots were coiled or assembled from prefabricated cylindrical sections joined together. Local, iron-rich clays could be used after careful preparation that included a brief pre-soaking before tempering with such materials as chopped straw, chaff or possibly dung.

In addition to plain utilitarian vessels, specialist pieces were made, including 'strainers', decorated and fish-shaped pastry moulds, 'pie-crust' and bevelled-rim pot-stands, as well as rodent traps,

painted. The earliest textual sources for ceramic production date from the Ur III period and describe workshops with between two and ten people working part-time under a supervisor. Pots were more likely to be produced in quantity in the summer and autumn months when drying was easier and fuel more abundant. Early Dynastic

animal-shaped wheeled toys and rattles. During the nineteenth and eighteenth centuries BC new styles of painted decoration appeared in different regions. Striking geometric and naturalistic patterns were applied in bituminous paint, but incised greyware lugged jars decorated with birds, bulls, boats and other designs are equally distinctive. A third style, known as Khabur ware, was decorated with repetitive but striking designs of hatched triangles, horizontal stripes, chequers and concentric circles. Three hundred years later Nuzi ware was produced. This was decorated with floral, geometric and naturalistic motifs, including birds, fish and goats, painted in white over reddish brown or black bands. Forms included goblets, beakers and large jars, the floral designs showing similarities to contemporary Aegean work.

First millennium

Assyrian power grew during the ninth to eighth centuries BC, culminating in the unification of Mesopotamia, the Levant and Egypt. Later, political power moved to southern Mesopotamia before the new Achaemenid dynasty emerged from southern Iran. The presence of specialist pottery industries is indicated by an Assyrian reference to 'the village of the pots'. The majority of Late Assyrian wares were plain and utilitarian, but some fine wares were produced, including polychrome blue, yellow, and white glazed wares in Babylonia and Assyria, which used recipes similar to those employed by contemporary Assyrian brick manufacturers. For Palace ware, finely levigated clay was used to throw beakers and shallow flared drinking bowls imitating metalwork, which was also the model for animal-headed drinking cups. Monochrome blue-glazed ware was common throughout the Neo-Babylonian and Persian periods.

IRAN

The hugely varied physical geography of Iran includes rugged mountains cut by valleys, surrounding a high central plateau with inhospitable salt deserts forming natural barriers across the central and eastern regions. South-west Iran, in contrast, is a geographical extension of the alluvial plains of southern Mesopotamia, while along the south shores of the Caspian Sea, forming part of northern Iran, there is dense jungle. From the Neolithic period onwards, different cultures and

kingdoms developed in Iran. Indo-European tribes, including Medes and Persians, gradually settled there during the second millennium BC. The Assyrian empire later dominated north-west Iran until 612 BC, when the Assyrians were overthrown by combined Median and Babylonian

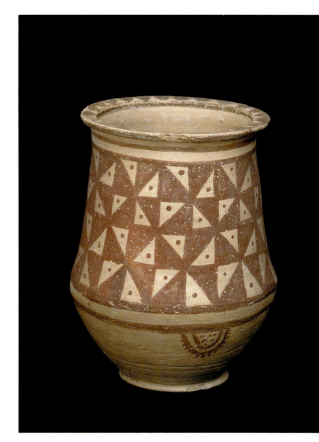

Painted pottery jar.
Khabur ware, 1900–1600 BC.
Height 18.75 cm (7.5 in).

armies. In 550 BC the kings of Persia conquered the Medes and established the Achaemenid empire, unifying Iran for the first time. The vast empire that was thus created extended from the Aegean to the Indus River and survived until the time of Alexander the Great.

As early as the eighth millennium BC people began to settle in agricultural villages and develop regional cultures. From about 6000 BC different styles of painted pottery, stamp seals and other objects appeared. The beginning of the Iron Age in the second millennium BC was marked by the appearance of new styles of architecture, burial customs, metalwork and the production of greyware ceramics. The so-called Amlash culture of north-west Iran was one of the most distinctive. The hilltop cemeteries have yielded spectacular

Three spouted earthenware flasks, one with bridge spout and painted decoration of a horse and geometrical designs, probably from Tepe Sialk in central Iran; a burnished jar with spout; a burnished wheel-thrown greyware jar with spout from northern Iran. Height (tallest) *c.* 12 cm (4.8 in).

discoveries of jewellery, gold and silver spouted vessels and Mesopotamian (Mitannian-style) cylinder seals, as well as a great variety of grey and red burnished wares. Over two hundred ceramic vessels found at the site of Marlik Tepe include a wide variety of ware such as trough-spouted bowls, basins or covers, globular flasks, and jars with long beak-shaped spouts.

The most spectacular group from Marlik consists of a series of eight burnished redware anthropomorphic vessels that includes squatting bear-like or standing nude female and male figures, often holding a spouted jar, ranging in height from twenty-five to fifty centimetres. Some of the figures closely resemble smaller cast-bronze statuettes also found at this site. The ceramic figures are heavily stylized, with exaggerated physical features such as prominent buttocks and swollen legs. Zoomorphic vessels were also found, most of them in the form of hump-backed bulls but also stags, rams, even a leopard.

During the Iron Age II (*c.* 1000–800 BC) a distinctive style of pottery developed in the Luristan area of western Iran. Typically the ceramics were built by hand and had medium to thick walls. Warm buff or light brownish in colour, some vessels were left plain, others decorated with a dark brown or reddish-brown paint after being lightly

burnished. Typical designs consist of concentric dotted circles, rosettes or wheels, horizontal ladder patterns, hatched and pendant triangles. A small number of globular hollow anthropomorphic figures holding spouted jars were made locally. The propensity of potters to decorate handles and spouts with small horn-headed animals is part of a wider local tradition also seen on Luristan bronzes. Beak-spouted vessels were often embellished with small pellets of flattened clay applied to the walls in imitation of contemporary local sheet-bronze vessels.

At Tepe Sialk, around 1000 BC, a series of long-spouted vessels were made. Ornate and ambitious in form, the shapes, perhaps inspired by birds or other creatures, were decorated with painted geometric forms as well as stylized designs of animals. These spouted vessels were probably made for ceremonial or ritual purposes and may have been used to pour water in formal (and practical) washing ceremonies. The representational designs on the pots owe a great deal to earlier traditions, as do the shape and decoration.

The final phase of the Iron Age came to a climax with the splendour and magnificence of the Achaemenid empire when, in the sixth century BC, the Medes were conquered by the Persians under Cyrus the Great (559–530 BC), who founded the

Achaemenid dynasty. A central administration was formed and efficient communications established, while ambitious building schemes included Susa and the magnificent city of Persepolis. Glazed tiles with imaginative designs and rich colours – turquoise, brown, yellow, green and white – were produced and used for wall decoration at the palace of Darius, in Susa. In the fourth century BC the empire was attacked by Alexander the Great, which brought its domination to an end. There was a revival under Parthian rule, followed in the third century AD by the vigorous Sasanian line, and a second powerful Persian empire was established that rivalled Byzantium in the splendour of its arts. The Sasanian period ended with the Arab invasions of about AD 641, with Islam replacing the established Zoroastrianism.

Ceramics in a wide variety of styles were produced in Mesopotamia, Iran and adjacent regions within the new Persian empire. The establishment of the imperial capital at Ctesiphon, at the heart of Mesopotamia, continued for seven centuries. The minor province of Parthia, located east of the Caspian Sea, was transformed in the reign of Mithradates I (*c.* 171–138 BC), becoming a powerful rival to Rome.

The political fragmentation of the Parthian state is to some extent reflected in the highly regionalized ceramic traditions of Mesopotamia and Iran, the majority of whose ceramics were thrown on the wheel and carefully wet-smoothed during the final throwing process. The range of ceramic objects includes lamps made by combining wheel-thrown reservoirs with handmade spouts, as well as storage jars, lids, cosmetic dishes and rat traps built by hand or from two-part moulds. The so-called pilgrim flasks, usually characterized by flattened sides, were used to hold liquid refreshment and were traditionally carried over the shoulder. They were thrown in two halves and later joined together. The inventiveness of potters is evident in the decorated amphorae, which were often embellished with

Four green- and blue-glazed jars with double handles. 2nd–3rd century AD, northern Syria. Height (tallest) 15.8 cm (6.3 in).

Glazed brick panel, extensively restored, from the east gate of the Achaemenid palace of Darius at Susa, *c.* 522–486 BC. This was part of a larger frieze depicting rows of guards in Persian costume converging from left and right. Each carried a long spear with a metal butt, quiver and strongbow. A variety of polychrome glazed and unglazed relief-decorated bricks were used in decorating the palace, including a monumental entrance staircase with rows of servants and crenellated battlements, and rosettes and palmettes. Height 200 cm (80 in).

'twisted-rope' handles and the bodies covered with incisions and applied pellets, studs and bosses, moulded female heads and horizontal 'pinched-ridge' rope patterns. Plaques added to the neck were press-moulded and carried a variety of motifs, including grasshoppers, Eros wrestling with a snake or playing a lyre, seated women and a figure holding a cornucopia. A typical product of the Seleucia area is eggshell ware, which consists of hemispherical bowls and two-handled vases, with walls thinned down after throwing.

Vessels glazed blue, green and occasionally brown are characteristic of Parthian ceramic production. Such glazes form part of a long tradition of alkaline glazing in Mesopotamia, dating from the Bronze Age (*c.* 1600 BC). The glazes were prepared by combining the ash produced by burning desert plants with crushed quartz pebbles or quartz sand to create a mixture rich in soda, lime potash and magnesia. The colours of green and blue are the result of the presence of small quantities of iron oxide with or without copper. Alkaline glazes are not well suited to earthenware bodies because of their high level of expansion, and they tend to craze badly or even flake off the surface, but nevertheless they were successfully applied. There is no evidence for the use of lead glazes in the Partho-Sasanian empire, although they were used in the West, by the Romans, and also in China.

One of the most famous examples of the use of glazed and coloured bricks is the Ishtar Gate built by Nebuchadnezzar (604–562 BC) in Babylon. Iron and copper were employed to colour the glaze, antimony to opacify it and render it white. The glazes provided a surface that was strong and weatherproof, with a range of brilliant colour effects achieved at the relatively low firing temperature of 1000°C. The first occurrence of tin oxide (prepared by calcining metallic tin) being added to a glaze to produce an opaque white came in the ninth century AD, when potters in Iraq used it to imitate the whiteness of Chinese porcelain.

Typical Parthian forms included wheel-thrown fish-plates, moulded lamps, one-handled flasks and ring-footed vessels. Two-handled pilgrim flasks were a Parthian innovation. Inspired by water bottles, some were decorated in imitation of embossed or stitched leatherwork. The confidence and skill of the Parthian potters is particularly well

demonstrated by a series of spectacular glazed 'slipper coffins', produced in sizes suitable for adults and children. These were covered with a blue or green glaze and decorated with either impressed or relief designs. At Uruk the most common stamped design depicted a trousered male figure with bunched-up hair, hands on hips, and a sword slung at his side.

Sasanian period

In AD 224 a Persian nobleman overthrew the last Parthian king and founded the Sasanian empire, naming it after an ancestor called Sasan. Eventually the empire extended from northern Mesopotamia to central Asia; its highly developed bureaucracy, army and agricultural infrastructure exerted a strong influence on early Islamic society following the Arab conquest in the seventh century. Large industrial sites dedicated to the production of ceramics and glass were developed alongside canals, and excavations have revealed square up-draught kilns measuring some four metres across. Written sources in the Babylonian Talmud refer to drawing water with 'a bucket of clay', religious prohibitions on the use of certain types of glazed ware for liquids, and the purchase of better-quality non-porous pots made by potters in an unidentified town called Be-Mikse. Glazed wares were produced mainly in and around the capital at Ctesiphon.

Throughout the sixth and seventh centuries potters across central and northern Mesopotamia produced large or medium-sized jars decorated with impressed designs, the dies of which were square or circular and carved from wood, the grain still visible within the pattern. Carved designs include geometrical patterns or figural motifs of rams, ibexes, hump-backed bulls, birds, scorpions, crosses and Catherine wheels – a reflection both of contemporary Sasanian styles and of the presence of an important Christian population in this part of the empire.

Large jars with rounded bases and three or four small handles constitute a distinctive Late Sasanian type that continued to be made in the early Islamic period. These were probably used to hold water, the crudely applied slip-decorated surfaces and finger patterns helping to ensure a stronger grip when the jars were transported. Torpedo-shaped jars with pointed bases were designed to be inserted into soft ground and may have been used to store and transport oil or wine. While the majority of vessels were of simple form derived from earlier local traditions, some new forms were based on Sasanian types of metalware. These included one-handled dipper juglets, larger flat-based pitchers with trefoil-mouth

pouring spouts, casseroles and jars with elaborate seatings for lids.

Also produced were animal-headed rhytons made in clay in imitation of metal vessels. The earliest of these date to the third century and are composite vessels with a portrait or bust, a prominent face and an animal-head spout with green, blue or brown glaze. Rhytons were later made in the form of a deer's head and decorated with a single green glaze. When the Arabs conquered Mesopotamia and Iran, many Sasanian ceramic traditions continued, often adapted to the new market.

EGYPT

The area of north-east Africa comprising the Nile and adjoining desert regions was the centre of one of the great early civilizations based on cereal production. Abundant wealth lay in the rich harvests from the fertile river silt, and the need for large-scale co-operative effort in drainage and irrigation promoted the growth of urban communities and central organization. In Predynastic Egypt from around 5000 BC the use of copper, the beginnings of writing and sea-going ships were known. The union of Upper and Lower Egypt, traditionally under King Narmer around 3100 BC, was the start of the Dynastic period. Pottery in Egypt was produced over another three millennia of dynastic civilization, the majority of it well made and overwhelmingly utilitarian in nature. Tradition was a significant aspect of Egyptian culture, and the early hand-building techniques of coiling or slow turning were never completely abandoned even after the introduction of the wheel around 2400 BC.

Much of the ceramic production in Egypt was for funerary purposes, and some vessels came to be used almost exclusively in tombs. In recent years the study of Egyptian pottery has advanced greatly, with greater attention given to methods of manufacture. The first potter's wheels used in Egypt were an improvement on the older system of turning the pot on a block of some sort. They consisted of a simple turntable that the potter had to rotate with one hand while shaping the vessel with the other – a process that is graphically shown in a Fifth Dynasty relief from the tomb of Ty at Saqqara. In the same relief other figures are shown making pots by hand and turning the wheel on blocks, indicating that both methods existed alongside each other.

Elaborate hand-built double bowl form in red-polished ware, *c.* 3600 BC, from Mostagedda, Predynastic Egypt. Height 22.8 cm (9.1 in).

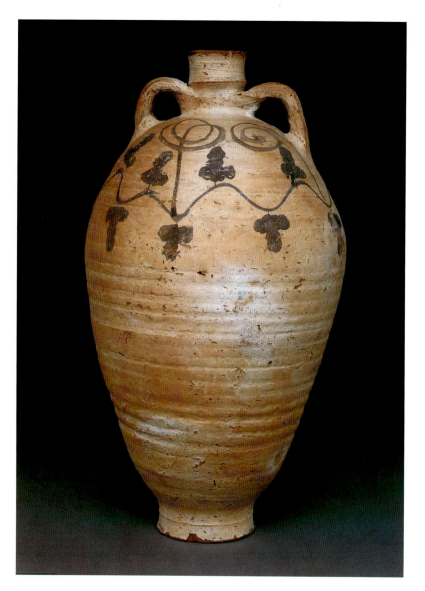

Pinkware earthenware amphora from Qasr Ibrim, 5th–6th century AD. Double-handled pottery bottle of the Ballana culture with painted decoration of tendrils. In Lower Nubia decorated wheel-made wares were produced at only a very few sites. Most Ballana pottery was made by hand for domestic use. The range of shapes was narrow and the decoration sparing and simple. Height 35.6 cm (14.25 in).

the earliest Nubian pottery, which was hand-built and thin-walled. After about 2500 BC the indigenous C-Group people of Nubia produced a distinctive range of handmade black-topped pottery vessels with incised decoration in repeat-pattern formation.

From around 2500 BC a rich and sophisticated culture developed in the fertile Kerma basin in Upper Nubia. During the Egyptian occupation of Lower Nubia, the Kerma state retained its independence. Kerma, which remained the capital for over a thousand years, had elaborate defences and large-scale religious structures. The Kerma peoples practised their own burial customs, such as the building of tumulus graves and the sacrificing of retainers to accompany their masters after death. A varied range of ceramics was produced, including thinly potted wares such as 'Kerma ware'; this black-top ware has thin walls and a rich red-coloured body. The Egyptians of the early New Kingdom took possession of many Nubian lands, establishing an Egyptian colonial government and introducing far-reaching cultural, social and artistic influence.

Predynastic Egypt

The first Predynastic farming communities in Egypt have been identified in northern Egypt and the Fayum area to the west of the Nile Valley and have been named the Fayum culture. It is likely that their pottery was a development of pre-existing wares; it was mainly monochrome and undecorated, although new shapes were introduced and making techniques became more refined. The main product was the distinctive black-topped redware. The tall storage jars with pointed bases, and beakers, all highly burnished, were probably fired upside down with their mouths buried in ash to achieve the black-coloured top – a firing technique that did not adapt easily to shallow bowls and dishes. Occasionally animals in low relief were modelled on the pots and, rarely, representations of animals were incised into the surface.

Red polished pottery was also made, and further technical improvements were achieved, resulting in more regular colour with a higher gloss. The range of forms was extended to include dishes and bowls, narrow-necked vases, bulbous flasks and long-necked vessels. Double-lobed and spouted vessels appear less frequently, as do vessels

The Middle Nile Valley

The land of Nubia in the Middle Nile Valley, which extended from south of Khartoum to the first cataract, encompassing the Nile Valley and adjacent desert regions, was a vital link between the ancient Egyptian world and the cultures of equatorial Africa. The cultures of prehistoric Nubia were part of a network of North African societies that stretched from the Eastern Sahara to the Red Sea. Nubian civilization – famed for its gold, copper, cornelian, jasper, diorite and amethyst – covered some six thousand years, during which the Kerma and Meroitic were great cultural and political periods. The first settled societies appeared in the central Sudan area between 7000 and 6000 BC and they produced

decorated with white-painted geometric patterns. Many of the pots were built by hand, although some appear to have been made or finished on a wheel.

Early red polished pottery made in the central Nile Valley constitutes one of the most aesthetically pleasing groups of wares produced in the country. Between 5000 and 4000 BC the flourishing Badarian culture of Upper Egypt produced a range of highly accomplished thin-walled vessels and the earliest representations of the human figure in the Nile Valley. Using carefully prepared red Nile clay, the pots were finely made with thin walls and lightly burnished to give them a dull shine. The firing fully matured the dense clay body, enabling it to be potted thinly without loss of strength. On the whole, forms were simple and combined well with the black, brown and red colours of the body and occasional combed decor-

The Old Kingdom

In about 3100 BC the separate peoples of Upper and Lower Egypt were united under King Narmer. The country was tightly governed, scientific knowledge and developments became carefully controlled, and art and architecture crystallized into a formal style exemplified by the great pyramids of Giza, built around 2600 BC. Rigid rules determined the production of paintings and sculpture, ensuring that in the following 3000 years little change took place.

During the Old Kingdom (*c.* 2700–2100 BC) the introduction of the efficient but slow potter's wheel from Mesopotamia necessitated the use of more carefully prepared clay, with grit and other material removed to facilitate the smooth handling of the clay body during throwing. Spouted ewers, lipped jugs, bowls with inward-curving rims, tall libation vessels, tall stands for ritual

Two red-polished pottery bowls. Hand-built earthenware, with finely made hard thin walls, 'chattered' decoration and 'smoked' rim, one from Mostagedda, the other from El Badari, Predynastic Egypt. Badarian, 5th millennium BC. Height (largest) 7 cm (2.8 in), diameter *c.* 23 cm (9 in).

ation. Beakers with flared rims were sometimes decorated with incised lines filled with white pigment. Badarian wares later became even finer. The entire production appears restrained and uncomplicated, consisting mainly of rounded cooking pots without rims or necks.

Around 4000 BC a new culture, known as the Naqada, emerged on the site north of modern-day Luxor and spread throughout Upper Egypt. It was the most influential of all Predynastic civilizations and was marked by the introduction of new styles of pottery, including highly accomplished red polished vessels, some decorated with white painted designs. The black-topped pottery of the Badarian culture continued to be made, although without the textured surface.

vessels and low stands for domestic pots were produced, their forms owing much to the contemporary interest in metalworking.

The most basic kilns were simple fires enclosed by a limited amount of brickwork to direct the flame. In the Old Kingdom kilns comprised more sophisticated circular or oval chimney-like structures of mud bricks, ranging in size from one to three metres across, with a stoke-hole at one side. The bricks on the floor were supported on a central wall or pillar in the middle of the firing chamber, and the pots were loaded from the top, with gaps left to allow the passage of hot gases. Similar up-draught kilns continued in use for much of the Dynastic period, and more substantial kilns did not appear until the Ptolemaic

Series of drawings showing the making and firing of pottery in ancient Egypt, from the tomb of Ty at Saqqara, 5th Dynasty, *c.* 2400 BC.

and Roman periods (after 332 BC), when the influx of foreign ideas enabled the production of ceramics in the Nile Valley on a much more industrial level.

One of the finest groups of ceramics is the red-slipped wares, used exclusively for funerary offerings. Jars, spouted ewers, pot-stands and a great variety of bowls with carinated rims were made. The earliest bowls of this type date from around 2600 BC and have been found at the site of Meydum, giving rise to the term 'Meidum bowl' – applied to the finely made bowls that reflect the respect for metalworking. These carinated bowls with thin walls, rounded bottoms and sharply angled sides were made from carefully prepared clay and are highly burnished. The simplicity of their form and decoration gives the bowls a refined, precise quality lacking in other contemporary wares. Variations of this general style continued to be made until the end of the First

Intermediate Period (*c.* 2000 BC) in areas from Middle Egypt northwards.

In the south different traditions arose. The pots produced here were most commonly made from Nile silt. Irrespective of the body used, all surfaces were covered with a polished red slip, a characteristic feature of these wares. During the Fourth and Fifth Dynasties (*c.* 2600–2350 BC), many of these bowls were made by shaping the lower part over a dome-shaped former and then adding a slow-turned rim. Later versions were thrown on the wheel. Sand and coarse chaff were often mixed into the Nile silt clay.

A limited number of pots found in desert valleys in Middle and Upper Egypt were made from cream-coloured clay. To this was added a variety of opening materials such as straw, the body becoming grey or buff in colour when fired. Decoration was sometimes painted on to the light-coloured pots with iron oxide, which gave a purplish-red when fired, and white slip. The natural stone markings of the grain of alabaster were also copied on to pots, although some had more elaborate designs of boats, men and women, birds, trees and other familiar objects. Since pottery was not considered one of the formal arts, few, if any, rules governed the decoration of pots and little regard was paid to the symmetry of the designs. This resulted in an unsophisticated and lively appearance that contrasts sharply with contemporary painting and sculpture. Some stylistic

Red-slipped bowl found at the Old Kingdom site of Meydum in Egypt. The type is still often referred to as the 'Meidum bowl'. This group also includes jars, spouted ewers and pot-stands and a great variety of bowls with carinated rims. The earliest bowls date from about 2600 BC. Diameter 28 cm (11 in).

Two hand-built vessels with painted decoration, one depicting spiral designs, the other showing boats with many oars and flamingos. Predynastic Naqada II culture, 3600–3250 BC. Height 22.9 cm (9.2 in).

developments were made; handles, for instance, fixed on to the side of the pots, appeared for the first time in Egypt. Forms became more cylindrical, imitating the sort of shapes produced by contemporary stoneworking.

Faience

An important development was the production of moulded glazed objects from a specially prepared quartz body which, when fixed, became vitreous, with a glaze developing on the surface. These wares are known as faience, or sometimes as Egyptian paste. Faience objects were manufactured in the ancient Mediterranean and Near East regions for five thousand years, faience beads found in both Egypt and Mesopotamia dating back to about 4000 BC. The skill with which gold, copper, precious stones, ivory, alabaster and wood were all worked prompted potters to make cheaper but equally attractive alternatives, and there were also efforts to devise a substitute for the much-prized soapstone. Faience was a development of these earlier techniques. It was produced by combining powdered quartz sand with an alkaline material that acted as a flux, causing the quartz sand to fuse at a temperature that could be achieved in a kiln and forming a hard and colourful stone-like material. The fluxes used were potash, which occurred in plant-ash, and natron, a naturally occurring sodium bicarbonate from deposits on dried-out salt lakes such as those in Wadi Natrum in the south-western Nile Delta. When fired, objects moulded from such a mixture acquired a shiny surface. If a small quantity of copper was present, rich turquoise colours resulted, while small quantities of manganese gave purplish shades.

The quartz-rich faience body lacked the plasticity of clay and was shaped more easily by moulding or modelling rather than being thrown on the wheel or used for hand-building, although thrown shapes were made in the Late Period (*c.* 650–332 BC), probably by adding a little clay to the mixture. Small pieces of jewellery, figurines, amulets, vessels for precious liquids such as

Faience Egyptian shabti with coffin inscribed for Amenmes. 19th–20th Dynasty, New Kingdom (*c.* 1307–1070 BC). Height 7 cm (2.8 in).

OPPOSITE
Ritual vase for 'Wine of Lower Egypt for the deceased lady Nodjmet'. 18th Dynasty. Height 79 cm (31.6 in).

Holy water jug with cover. Faience, from the tomb of Tutankhamun, Cairo.

perfumes or oil, inlays for coffins, furniture and temple walls came later. Small pots made in moulds were fashioned in quite complex shapes, the range of which includes baskets with lids and modelled pomegranates.

The Middle Kingdom

As trade increased, foreign influence became more pronounced; this particularly affected the manufacture of pottery in the Middle Kingdom (*c.* 2120–1795 BC). Imperial expansion overseas brought a variety of imported ware from countries such as Mycenae, Cyprus and Crete, all of which began to exert an influence on the forms of Egyptian pottery. Large numbers of small bottles with narrow necks and handles were imported; these probably contained precious perfumes or oils and were imitated by the Egyptian potters. The wheel became smoother and more efficient, and potters shown at work on the wall of the Egyptian tomb of Beni Hasan (*c.* 1900 BC) appear to be making the wheel revolve by pushing it with their hands. Throwing marks on the walls of pots suggest that by this time the wheel had sufficient momentum to continue spinning after being pushed – a momentum that required an efficient pivot, which may have been lubricated, possibly with wet clay, to reduce friction. Such pivots were made of paired stones, the upper having a smooth projection to engage in the socket of the lower stone. The wheelhead of fired clay or other suitable material would have been attached to the top of the upper stone, with the lower stone of the pivot set into the ground or fastened to the top of the vertical supporting stem. Early wheels had a short stem, and variations of this type continued to be used in the New Kingdom at the same time as the tall-stemmed wheel came into use.

During this period an assistant was employed to turn the wheel, which allowed the potter to work with both hands, but it is possible that this practice occurred earlier. It was not until the fifth century BC that the kickwheel was used in Egypt. The geometric patterns readily achieved with a spinning wheel began to be used by the Egyptians, and carefully thrown pots were joined together to produce quite complicated forms. Pots with pedestal feet were made for the first time, in imitation of those made in the Mediterranean region.

Numerous examples of finely made faience objects have been recovered from tombs of this period; these include figures of animals such as the small desert rodent known as a jerboa. Fine design details were often carried out in black, based on the use of manganese or iron oxides, and in many cases this created a striking contrast between the black decoration and the blue glaze.

The New Kingdom

Changes in burial customs during the New Kingdom (*c.* 1650–1070 BC) led to a reduction in the amount of pottery placed in tombs as well as altering its nature. It may be that pottery was no longer specially manufactured for burial purposes, since the New Kingdom pottery that has been found is, on the whole, more utilitarian and less adventurous. In the ruins of Akhetaten (Amarna) large quantities of painted pottery have been discovered that was made for the use of the court for religious purposes. These pots can be dated to the years 1380–1350 BC and are mostly large (some nearly a metre high) and complex, demonstrating the technical skill of the potters. Their ornate painted designs relate to the shape of the vessel, and after the pots had been fired motifs of garlands of flowers, geometrical patterns and tomb

scenes were painted on to them in red, blue, white and black pigment – decoration that seems to reflect the strongly naturalistic tendencies that inspired the art of the period.

Painted pottery continued to be made after 1350 BC, although by then its character had changed. Designs became more crowded and less carefully executed. Decorated pottery that had been made specifically for the use of the court was now produced for a wider group of people. Amphora-type storage pots were made in great quantities, one of the most characteristic forms being the drop-shaped vase, made in a variety of sizes. The extent of the decoration increased from banded lines to include painted designs, especially of floral motifs carried out in cobalt-based blue pigment.

Faience vessels were common, especially bowls with black decoration in manganese. The motifs often consist of plant forms, with the petals of the lotus-flower depicted on the outside and marsh scenes on the inside. Many of these vessels were made as votive offerings to the goddess Hathor. The bowls of chalice-shaped cups are often modelled in the form of a lotus, its stem made separately and joined later to the base of the cup. Numerous small objects were fashioned by pressing the faience body into a mould. Amulets, beads, small inlays and figurines were produced by this method, with the same moulds being used repeatedly. Large numbers of these small amuletic objects and sacred emblems such as the eye of Horus were produced in this period and later. The finest objects, such as the shabti figures (funeral servant statuettes), have generally been recovered from tombs.

Later periods

During the Third Intermediate Period (*c.* 1070–650 BC) regional differences became more pronounced, the pottery of southern Egypt differing from that produced in the Delta chiefly because of the relative absence of marl clay in the north. Well-produced wheel-made jars of marl fabric are common from Upper Egyptian sites and constitute some of the most recognizable of Egyptian ceramics. The greyish-green surface was often imitated by potters in the Delta, who made similar pieces from red silt clay but covered them with a layer of thin, cream-coloured clay slip.

Part of a large faience figure of the Egyptian god Bes, with the typical brilliant blue and green glaze of the Ptolemaic period (332–30 BC). Such figures were made in sections and then fused together. 26 x 18 cm (10.4 x 7.2 in).

During the Late Period (*c.* 650–332 BC) a renaissance of Egyptian culture influenced most arts and crafts but was less apparent in pottery. Shapes became more complex and the use of lead glaze, already employed in some regions, more general. The potter's wheel, too, continued to gain in efficiency, lessons having perhaps been learnt from the Greeks. A tomb painting of about 300 BC shows the god Khum sitting at a potter's wheel fashioning a human being; the heavy stone flywheel is being pushed round with the foot near the ground and the wheelhead is raised to a height of fifty centimetres.

The production of polished black wares in the Delta during the Ptolemaic period (332–30 BC) may have been intended to copy the fine black pottery of the Greek world. Faience continued to be produced extensively in Egypt until Ptolemaic and Roman times, when some large figures and vessels were made, many with a characteristic deep blue glaze.

In 30 BC Egypt became a Roman province and the Romans introduced their own methods of making pottery. Around AD 350 the Coptic branch of the Christian Church became a dominant factor and ancient Egyptian designs were fused with classical elements. At the Battle of Heliopolis in AD 640 the Islamic Arabs took control of Egypt, introducing further techniques and different styles.

INDIA

Early farming communities, identified in six regions of undivided India, produced terracotta figurines of both human and animal form in the far north-west until the middle of the sixth millennium BC. The production of clay vessels in the subcontinent has a varied regional history. At Mehrgarh, south-east of Quetta on the western banks of the Indus, vessels are seen at about the same time as figurines, in the middle of the sixth millennium BC. In other regions, such as the southern Deccan, pottery does not appear until about 3000 BC. The ware was handmade using the paddle and anvil beater technique. Later a slow wheel was used, but there is no evidence of the use of a foot-wheel. Three main groups have been identified: greyware, burnished redware and burnished blackware, most of which continued to be made in some form. Sothi ware, as it is called, is widely distributed over much of the Indo-Ganetic plains continuing into Pakistan. It is also found in the Harappa, Late Harappa and Post-Harappa periods.

The cities of the Indus Valley civilization (*c.* 2500–2000 BC) developed from the towns and villages of the river plains of Pakistan and north-west India. Three main cities are known – Harappa, Kalibangan and Mohenjo-Daro, situated on the Indus – as well as many smaller settlements. These sites, now gigantic mounds, provide evidence of the relatively advanced development of the cities, which must have been spectacular. The Indus Valley peoples evolved forms of town planning intended to accommodate large numbers of people; the layouts were complex, and the population was provided with running water and sanitation. They also developed writing and weights and measures. Buildings were constructed of mud and fired bricks, irrigation was practised, copper and bronze were smelted, Egyptian faience was made and stamped seals were used for

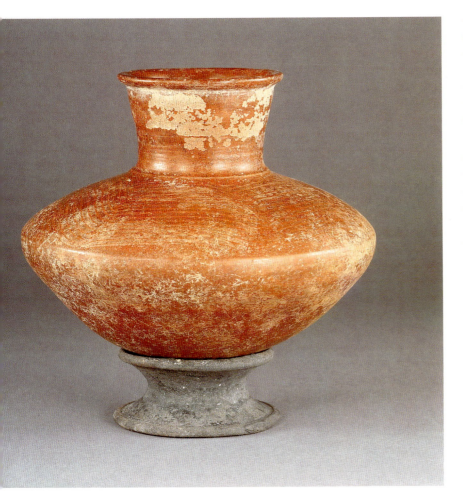

Jar on a stand. Russet coated earthenware, from tombs at Palambati, Coimbatore District, Tamil Nadu, India, late centuries BC. Height 18.3 cm (7.3 in).

with the Late Harappa period another culture, not yet fully defined, produced ochre-coloured ware, generally found in the Upper Ganga Valley.

The Vedic period (*c.* 1700–800 BC) coincides with the appearance of tribes who entered India through Afghanistan and gradually occupied the Punjab. Pottery known as grey painted ware appears about 1200 BC; this is made from finely prepared clay and thrown on the fast wheel in shapes that often achieve an eggshell thinness. The characteristic colour is the result of firing in a reduction or smoky kiln. The high quality of the vessels and the black-painted decoration suggest that it was made as luxury ware, while the coarser red and black wares were in everyday use. Vedic literature mentions a number of pots by specific name and function; the most common were for the preparation of *dahi* (yoghurt) and for the churning of this to make butter and buttermilk.

Around 400 BC India was a collection of self-governing kingdoms and tribal communities, identified by Chandragupta Maurya, who founded the unified Indian empire. In the north at this time a variety of wares was produced, including the well-fired northern black polished ware, which has a highly lustrous surface that ranges from jet black to steel blue and occasionally includes lustrous red, orange-gold and silver. In the group of pottery known collectively as Sunga-Kushan, moulded terracotta tiles were made with *mithuna* figures and animals such as elephants. There were also toys, sprinklers, bottle-shaped vessels (some with spouts), vases and ornaments. Red polished ware was also made. In Rajasthan Rang Mahal pottery was produced with a thick coating of slip with black-painted designs. At the same time bricks were fired and some glazed pottery produced.

Although faience was known in India as early as 4000 BC and the technology used to great effect on beads, bangles and other clay ornaments, few glazed pots were made. This is largely attributed to the Hindu religious belief that once a pot has been used for eating or drinking it should be thrown away – a hygienic practice but not one conducive to the production of glazed pottery for household use.

identification. In other areas developments took place independently of Mesopotamia. New crops such as cotton were cultivated, and animals such as the ox were domesticated. There is also evidence of long-distance trade.

Technically, the pottery is well developed. In terms of its accomplishment it can be compared with some of the highly refined but often unimaginative wares produced by the Roman empire, in that they were well potted but greatly standardized. Characteristic features are the skilfully painted designs of geometric and natural motifs. Rectangular kilns were in use, and vessels range from those measuring only a few centimetres high to cooking pots and vessels a metre in height for storing grain and water. Toys and figures were also made. The pottery is consistent across wide areas, suggesting efficient distribution. In parallel

The Ancient World

CYPRUS, THE CYCLADES, GREECE, ITALY

*Time's wheel runs back or stops:
potter and clay endure*

ROBERT BROWNING

Large 'bird bowl' with a water-bird between panels of geometric decoration, from Camirus, Rhodes. East Greek, 700–650 BC. Bird bowls, named after the birds that form a characteristic motif of their decoration, were made in many eastern Greek centres in the 7th century BC.

By 1500 BC the skills of the potter were well developed throughout the Mediterranean region. These skills included the refining of clays, the use of the smoothly running potter's wheel, and relatively sophisticated kilns that allowed a good red heat to be obtained and provided considerable control of the atmosphere. The rise of the Greek civilization brought a new emphasis on the arts, including pottery, which attained high technical and aesthetic levels. The Romans adapted and further refined the skills and techniques used by the Greeks, eventually taking them across much of Europe.

CYPRUS

Like other islands in the Mediterranean, Cyprus was subject to a wide variety of influences. In the Neolithic period (4600/4500–4000/3900 BC), handmade pottery was produced that was decorated with designs painted in red on a white ground or patterned by 'combing' the slip. In the Early Bronze Age (around 2000 BC) a variety of painted pottery was made, but at the start of the Middle Bronze Age (around 1900 BC) a new tradition of painted wares developed. The handmade vessels were carefully burnished and decorated with linear patterns in reddish or dark brown on a light ground. Two of the most common shapes were jugs (or juglets) and bowls with wishbone handles, and some of these were exported to Egypt, Syria and Palestine. During the fourteenth and most of the thirteenth century BC quantities of wheel-made pottery, usually of fine buff-coloured clay with designs painted in glossy brown, were imported from Mycenaean Greece. Large vessels such as amphorae (storage jars) and kraters (bowls for mixing wine and water) decorated with processions

Cluster vase, kernos, a type of elaborate multiple vessel with a series of small receptacles clustering round a larger central container. It may have had some ritual function, such as for the dedication of small quantities of different substances to a deity. Cyclades, 2200–1800 BC. Height 32 cm (12.8 in).

of chariots, bulls and birds were particularly popular. When the supply of the Mycenaean pottery dwindled, Cypriot potters started to make their own alternatives, adopting the fast wheel. Some vases, usually bell-shaped kraters, bore pictorial decoration, often of bulls or goats, carried out in a 'rude' or 'pastoral' style. Later, practical and simply decorated pots were made for domestic use.

More striking than the pots are the terracotta clay figures, often built larger than life size. These monumental forms, intended to be displayed in a public place, were built in sections and joined together after firing. Stylized in feeling, the figures with their flattened form giving them a front and back would have been influenced by contemporary sculpture. Other intriguing objects in clay include large bowls, some thirty-five centimetres in diameter, inside which are modelled figures and structures depicting some form of religious ceremony. One such piece shows a small shrine with highly formalized figures. In another the figures are involved in the worship of a snake and bull – both potent symbols of fertility.

THE CYCLADIC WORLD

The Aegean region, the area occupied by modern Greece, including Crete, and western Turkey, saw a number of far-reaching changes in the period known as the Greek Bronze Age, 3200–1000 BC, and by the end of the millennium the first major European civilization had developed in Crete. The separate but interconnecting cultures flourished in the islands of the central Aegean, Minoan Crete and Mycenaean Greece. There were relatively prosperous settlements, whose inhabitants depended for their livelihood on farming and fishing but also learned to utilize their metal resources. Sculptors crafted powerful works out of local marble. Across the area the skills of the potter were well developed. Vessels include collared vases, sauce-boats, bowls, beakers, cups and zoomorphic vases, the incised decoration of which, some of herringbone formation, is often filled with a white inlay. Elaborate multiple cluster vases were also produced for ritual purposes. Such pieces, typically incorporating a series of small receptacles arranged round a larger central container, are artistically and technically ambitious. From the Middle Bronze Age onwards the more dominant Minoan culture increasingly influenced the islanders and Mycenaean cultures,

although locally made pottery shows the continuation of independent artistic styles.

Crete

The Minoan culture on the island of Crete, named after King Minos who ruled between about 1350 and 1250 BC, is characterized by the dominance of the great palaces at Knossos, Phaistos, Mallia and Kato Zakro. Minoan civilization developed around 3000 BC and flourished for about eighteen hundred years, during which time particularly distinctive and technically accomplished vessels and terracotta figurines were produced. Pottery had been manufactured in Crete before the Minoan period and continued to be made long after the civilization had ended, but none had the same freshness of design and technical brilliance. Unlike other early civilizations, which tended to develop in river valleys, the Minoan culture was on an island where it was protected from invasion yet open to a wide variety of influences, largely through trade. While shielding the islanders from attack, the sea enabled their trading economy to flourish. Oil and wine were exported in pottery vessels in exchange for corn, the free trade helping to create a cosmopolitan and open atmosphere. Unlike the Egyptians, the Minoans had neither an oppressive priesthood nor a heavy and rigid artistic style, and the culture freely absorbed and reflected many different influences.

Chronologically the Minoan economy is linked to the civilization of the Near East and Egypt. Its pottery is distinctive, being technically and aesthetically varied. In contrast to Egyptian pottery, the carefully observed and drawn natural objects used in the decoration of Minoan pots give much of the work a freshness that seems almost modern. At various times immigrants from Egypt and Mesopotamia came to Crete and craftsmen such as potters and metalworkers were received as honoured members of society. Finely made earthenware appeared on the tables of the nobility, the specially made pots often being richly coloured with flowing designs. At their best, Minoan pots were thought good enough to bury in the tombs of Egyptian noblemen.

A wide variety of forms were made: tall-stemmed wine cups imitating chalices, handled vases, pitchers and large storage jars, as well as a range of delicate drinking cups and bowls with thin rims

Storage jar from Knossos, Crete, 1450–1400 BC. Height 114 cm (45.6 in).

Cycladic jug, 700–650 BC. Found on Aegina. Earthenware with spout modelled in the form of a griffin's head and painted decoration of a horse and a lion killing a stag. Height 41.5 cm (16.6 in).

and lively, exuberant handles. Painted decoration was, however, the chief characteristic of this ware. Between about 2000 and 1550 BC decorative themes were largely derived from nature. At first the designs were stylized, but during the middle Minoan period (1900–1700 BC) they became more flowing and naturalistic, echoing the smooth round forms of the unglazed pots. Colours used include white, red, blue and black, with designs often painted on to a dark ground. Vivid pictorial representations of plants and marine life are painted with great vigour, often over the whole surface of the pot. The detailed observation and naturalistic decoration of Minoan pots seem to indicate a prosperous and creative society.

Unlike the Greeks, the Minoans did not depict human figures in the designs on their pots. However, terracotta figurines were made in a great variety of forms. These may have represented worshippers or been votive offerings to be placed in sanctuaries and palace shrines. The forms were highly stylized depictions of male and female figures, often with their arms held across their chest, figures of the mother goddesses standing with arms raised above the head, and also small animals. Later figures were constructed using forms thrown on the wheel, and some have wheel-thrown heads.

Between 1700 and 1450 BC Minoan influence was widespread throughout the Aegean; many islands adopted aspects of the Minoan lifestyle and on the Greek mainland arts and crafts were extensively influenced by those of Crete. After the virtual destruction of many sites in Crete in about 1450 BC and the fall of Knossos, traditionally dated some seventy-five years later, the island continued to prosper, but as an outpost of the Mycenaean sphere of influence.

GREECE

On the Greek peninsula pottery, known from as early as the second half of the seventh millennium, was used for storage, eating, drinking and cooking. The vessels were built by hand from coils or slabs of clay and the surface was often slipped and burnished or polished, while decoration was incised or painted. The onset of the Bronze Age in the late fourth millennium BC and the introduction of the fast rotating wheel around 2000 BC brought a wider range of shapes. These included luxury vessels intended to hold precious trinkets, suggesting that they were made for trade as well as for domestic use.

Mycenaean culture flourished on the Greek mainland in the Late Bronze Age, from about 1600 to 1100 BC. The earliest phase is characterized by rich burial sites, their contents strongly influenced by Minoan culture. In the fourteenth cen-

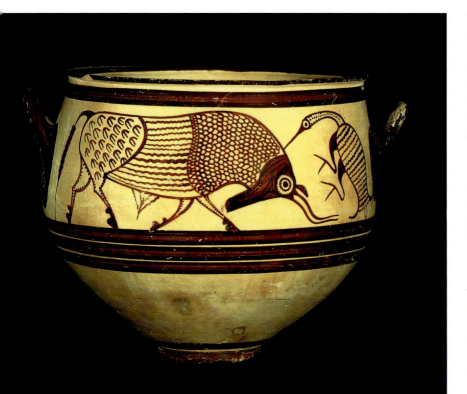

Pottery bowl, krater, decorated with a painted design of a bull and an egret. Mycenaean, 1300–1200 BC. Found at Enkomi, Cyprus. Height 26 cm (10.5 in).

tury BC the Mycenaeans built palaces similar to those of the Minoans but surrounded with fortifications. Clay tablets from the palaces, inscribed with script, indicate that the Mycenaeans spoke Greek. During the final phase the Mycenaeans grew greatly in power and prosperity, taking control of Crete around 1450 BC and trading widely with such lands as Egypt, the Near East and Italy.

Settlements were established abroad, islands such as Rhodes were colonized and trading posts were set up on the coast of Asia Minor and Egypt. Quantities of Mycenaean pottery have been found in Italy and Sicily to the west and along the trading routes to the east. Mycenaean vases, including many in the Pictorial style, flooded into Cyprus and even reached sites along the Syro-Palestinian coast and Egypt.

The Mycenaeans were a fierce and warlike race, a characteristic reflected in the pots they made. Gold was abundant and metalworking and ivory carving were highly developed. In contrast to this working of fine materials there was less concern with pottery, the shapes and decoration of which were hard and metal-like, although technically excellent. Early pottery consisted of grey Minyan ware, made around 1600 BC; the surface of the pots was soapy to the touch and the shapes closely reflected those made in metal. Around 1500 BC the influence of the warlike invading Achaeans from the north coast of the Peloponnese was combined with the Minoan influence from the south Aegean to produce distinctive, if unexciting, pots. The decorative motifs employed were still natural forms such as the cuttlefish, seaweed and shellfish used by the Minoans, but the designs no longer covered the entire surface and instead were positioned more formally. Chariot representations derived from Rhodes and Cyprus also appear. While Minoan potters filled all the available area on the surface of the pots with painted designs to produce fresh and effective results, Mycenaean decoration lacks this sense of spontaneity, although the quality of making is high. Decoration was applied as a fine lustrous slip, and both forms and decoration appear to be highly standardized, suggesting that the ware originated in major centres. Among the shapes the stirrup jar, the high-stemmed kylix, the deep two-handled bowl and the krater were popular. One series of kraters (mixing bowls) was decorated with figures in chariots.

Large and intimidating terracotta figures were also made. A group of such pieces, painted a dark brown and equipped with such attributes as hammers and swords, have been found in an area identified as the cult centre at Mycenae, and thus may represent deities. As befitting a warrior society, the Mycenaeans appear to have worshipped a warrior goddess, who is depicted in various ways.

Neither their strong citadels nor their prowess in battle could save the Mycenaeans from disaster and around 1200 BC a series of events contributed to the decline and eventual disappearance of the Mycenaean civilization. These changes were reflected in ceramics by a loss of technical quality, a reduction in the range of shapes made and, eventually, greater regional variety, although the culture survived on a more restricted scale until

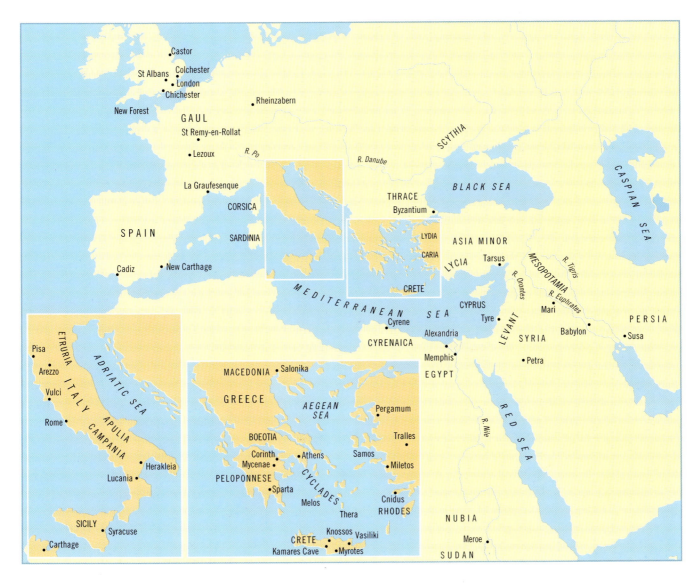

Map of the classical world.

around 1100 BC, the end of the Bronze Age in Greece. Many independent Greek city-states began slowly to develop, each producing its own wares. Potting skills flourished, reaching a high point in technical achievement in Athens around the sixth and fifth centuries. The Dorians, who had invaded from the north, influenced Greek architecture, sculpture and pottery. A fifth-century BC poet and politician claimed that Athens 'invented the potter's wheel and the offspring of clay and kiln, pottery so famous and useful about the house'. A further major development took place in Athens around 770 BC with the development of ambitious figurative scenes, marking the advent of one of the most significant aspects of Greek pottery – the use of the human form as a major decorative motif.

From around 1000 BC what is now known as classical Greek culture, based on the city-state, began to emerge. Art was an intrinsic element of this culture, closely linked with the ideas of community and religion. Patronage was channelled through assemblies, councils and magistrates, and was not the exclusive preserve of the privileged or wealthy. Carefully made and precisely decorated pottery was highly regarded, a status reflected in the use of pots at various times for grave monuments and as prizes for athletic success. Most pottery had a clearly defined function within the rituals and ceremonies of daily life, although it is the highly prized and special pieces that have survived rather than the ordinary objects of everyday life. Locally made undecorated pottery probably formed the largest part of the total production,

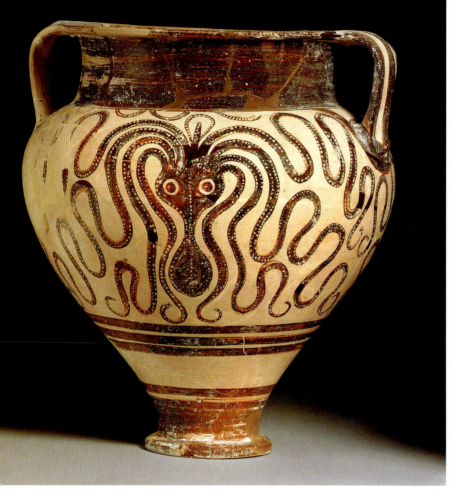

Double-handled jar with painted design of an octopus. Mycenaean, 1400–1300 BC. Found at Ialyos, Rhodes. Height *c.* 30 cm (12 in).

krateriskos (miniature mixing bowl) and *aryballos* (scent-bottle).

Greek artists brought a high degree of refinement and technical perfection to the pottery, producing designs that were both inventive and informative. The depictions of historical or mythological incidents employ a complicated system of references that would have been generally understood and include male and female deities. Some scenes needed no interpretation, such as those found on the base of wine cups, which were often lewd, depicting explicit sexual actions.

Making and decoration

From around 1000 BC the use of the wheel was widespread throughout Greece. Pots were made using the highly plastic, carefully prepared clays and thrown on a wheel propelled by an assistant – usually a young apprentice. The clay used for the decorated wares fired a yellow-red colour in a kiln with a clean oxidizing atmosphere. Athenian potters used Attic clay dug from the borders of the city, which fired rich red, while the yellower clays used by the Corinth potters were lighter in colour. Large pots were thrown in sections that were joined together when the clay had become sufficiently stiff to be handled yet soft enough to be moulded, at what is known as the leather-hard stage. At this point the pots were placed back on the wheel and the pieces scratched and moistened before being joined together. Surplus clay was shaved or skimmed off the surface with a metal or wooden tool. In this way any finger marks made while throwing could be removed and the profile, so important to the Greek pots, sharpened. By the time of the early Greek period the wheel had become much more efficient and smooth, an essential requirement for the throwing of the large forms and the turning of the leather-hard ware.

Decoration was achieved by using fairly simple techniques and the materials were employed in a sophisticated way. Glaze had been discovered earlier, probably in Mesopotamia, and may well have been known to the Greeks, although for some reason they chose not to use it. They preferred instead a fine clay slip which, when fired, lost its mattness and became slightly shiny and glass-like. The resulting surface, though sometimes described as a glaze, is not completely waterproof and cannot be regarded as a true glaze. The ingenious effect was

but, because this pottery was thought expendable, little of it has survived. Painted pottery was produced in two centres, Corinth and Athens, both of which had large beds of accessible fine red- or yellow-firing clays.

The majority of existing decorated Greek pots have been recovered from graves. Their decoration depicts mythical events and the compositions often have a narrative quality. Such paintings are a vital source from which to learn about the history and culture of the Greeks and for this reason they have been intensely studied.

Greek pots have two unique characteristics: one is their precise shapes and the other the detailed painted decoration. The forms are carefully designed and made, using crisp, clean outlines that owe much to metalworking. Each pot would be thrown, probably in sections, then carefully assembled and the surface skimmed to remove throwing marks, so making it smooth and suitable for painting. Skimming also further clarified the sharpness of the silhouette. Each particular shape was intended for a specific use and given a name that referred to this function, such as *stamnos* (wine jar),

achieved by preparing a slip from a fine clay contained a high percentage of iron oxide – ferric oxide (Fe_2O_3). In a kiln where there was plenty of oxygen the slip fired a glossy dense red colour. If the oxygen content was reduced (for example by burning damp wood or closing the air inlets into the kiln to create a smoky atmosphere) the flame, hungry for oxygen, would take it from the easiest available source – in this case the oxygen in the iron oxide contained in the clay. With a reduced amount of oxygen the iron converts to ferrous oxide, FeO, a form of iron that fires black rather than red. By using the carefully prepared slip, red and black colours could be produced on the same pot by the following method:

1. The pot was made in carefully prepared clay, which fired red in a clean, oxidizing kiln.
2. A slip was prepared from red clay to which an alkali, such as wood ash, was added; this caused the large clay particles to sink and the liquid containing the finer particles was then poured or syphoned off. This liquid was allowed to settle further and eventually a slip was made containing only the smallest clay particles. An acid, probably in the form of urine or wine, was added to make the mixture more fluid yet firm and more suitable for painting. The slip was then applied to the surface of the pot by painting or drawing, or, for the larger areas, pouring.
3. The pot was fired in the kiln with plenty of oxygen present (oxidized atmosphere) up to 900°C; at this stage all the undecorated surfaces as well as the decoration areas of the pot would be red.
4. Air inlets would now be partly closed and damp fuel burnt in the kiln to create a smoky flame, which would lower the oxygen content of the kiln; all the surface of the pot, including the decoration, at this stage would turn black.
5. Finally, in a brief oxidizing period with a clean bright flame, ample oxygen was reintroduced into the kiln to finish the firing. The body of the pot would quickly return to red. The decoration, painted in the denser slip with the finer clay particles and a greater percentage of iron oxide, would remain black longer and so the two colours would be achieved. Stopping the firing at the correct time was crucial to the success of the decoration: if the oxidizing fire continued too long, the slip would also turn red as

Large spouted and double-handled bowl, krater. Athenian Geometric, 735–720 BC. Earthenware with a painted scene showing a man grasping a woman by the wrist as he turns towards the ship, which holds two rows of oarsmen. This may be an early Greek representation of myth such as Theseus fleeing Crete with Ariadne or Paris abducting Helen, the ultimate cause of the Trojan War. From Thebes.

the oxygen began to penetrate its surface. Pots have been found that show evidence of this.

Form

The main pottery shapes evolved early in Greek culture and were a development of Minoan, Mycenaean and Dorian shapes. Most basic shapes were intended for holding liquid of some sort. Wine and water containers predominate, but smaller containers for oil and perfume were also

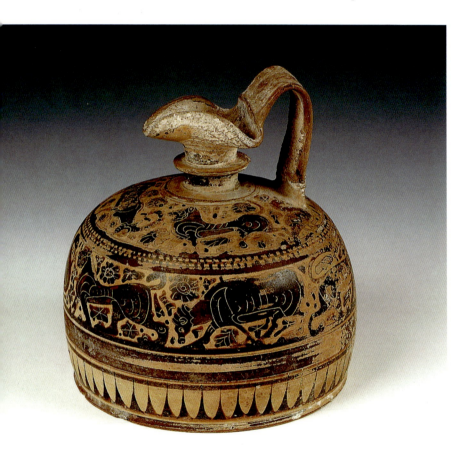

Jug, oinochoe, with trefoil lip and painted design of animals. Earthenware, Corinthian, *c.* 600 BC. Height 17.5 cm (7 in).

made. It was the Greek custom to drink wine mixed with water and the necessary vessels were the krater or large mixing bowl, the narrow-necked amphora for the wine and the three-handled water pitcher or hydria for the water. A tall-handled ladle or *kyathos* was used to pour the wine into jugs known as *oinochoai* or into flat two-handled cups known as *kylikes*. Sometimes the wine needed cooling and then a *psykter*, a vessel with a tall stemmed foot, was filled with wine and stood in cold water in a krater. Personal

toilet pots were also made. For the more precious liquids there were small bottles called *arybaloi*, *lekythoi* and *alabastra*.

Throughout the period of classical Greece, the forms of the pots remained essentially unchanged, probably because they proved to be practical and convenient in use. The majority were left plain or decorated with bands of black slip, or, later, covered entirely with black slip; decorated pots represent only a small proportion of Greek wares. Cooking pots of all kinds were produced very cheaply; metal was still an expensive luxury while clay products were not. Storage pots, saucepans, ovens, frying pans, stoves, cooking pots and braziers were all made. Water clocks, used to gauge periods of time in the law courts, consisted of a pot with a small hole that let out the water over a known period, the force of the stream indicating the length of time left before the water – and time – ran out. Plain and painted pots were exported in vast numbers as containers for olive oil or wine. Technically the ware was well fired and strong, but because it chipped easily the edges were often thickened to add strength. The pots are usually grouped into four main styles, based on the technique used and the style of the designs and corresponding roughly to four chronological periods.

Geometric style

The earliest recognizable Greek painted style, known as Proto-Geometric, began to emerge roughly around 1000 BC. Shapes developed at this time which, with some modifications, were to constitute the basis of forms used throughout most of the Greek period. Decoration was clearly defined, with light areas of clay and dark areas of slip forming simple balanced designs. Only black slip was used, although it occasionally fired dark brown. Bands of slip were confined to the shoulders and tops of pots; simple half-spiral designs and concentric circles were drawn in slip, a process that appears to have been carried out with mathematical precision. Completely abstract, the designs broke away altogether from the naturalistic style of the Cretans and the cramped convention of the Mycenaeans.

Around 900 BC the Geometric style (*c.* 1000–700 BC), so called because of its rectilinear geometric decoration, emerged more fully in Athens. This

Late Geometric pitcher from Athens, 730–720 BC. Earthenware with painted decoration of a figured frieze showing women mourning at funeral biers, with their hands to their heads in the ritual gesture of mourning common to many societies. Each of the deceased is laid out on a bier and covered with a shroud. Decorating the neck is an elaborate 'stepped' meander motif, so called after the slow winding River Maiandros in western Turkey, which is probably the most famous Greek Geometric pattern. Two clay nipples on the front of the vase, done in relief, may be intended to evoke the long-held idea of woman as vessel. Height 44.3 cm (17.5 in).

style is characterized by severely defined shapes with ornamental bands of patterns covering the entire pot. Decoration still included regular and mostly stylized abstract motifs, and gradually abstract human and animal figures appeared, but still confined to the borders. Following on from scenes of mourning around the bier and funerary processions, parades of warriors and chariots and battle scenes on land and sea were depicted. During the second half of the eighth century BC attempts at mythological narrative developed, shown in often complex, ambitious compositions. Very little is known about other art of this period and, since little has survived, it seems possible that these pots may have been one of the major art forms. They were often used as monuments on graves, their formality of shape and design giving them an austere beauty.

The still more balanced decoration of the mature geometric style usually incorporated the handle into the design. Decorative motifs included not only concentric circles, chequers, triangles, zigzags and the meander, but also the quatrefoil and swastika. As the style developed, plastic modelling began to be used on handles or rims.

Oriental or black-figure style

Around 700 BC the Greek city-states expanded, becoming artistically more accomplished and ambitious. The Greeks colonized much of the Mediterranean, and in the process came into much closer contact with the Near East and with oriental ideas of decoration. Pottery decoration of this period is known as the oriental or black-figure style (*c.* 700–550 BC), derived from the distinctive black figures painted on to the surface of the red pots, which combine black silhouettes with incisions for interior markings and areas of added purplish red and yellowish white.

A wider range of ornaments, different animals and foreign plants were introduced into the designs; the curve of the pots became less restrained and a great awareness of organic form seemed to develop. Pots decorated with animals, which had hitherto included only the goat and deer, were now incorporating the lion, bull, dog, hare, eagle, cock and goose, as well as the mythical sphinx and griffin. All these tended to be shown in peaceful, formal poses with little movement and no signs of aggression. In Corinth potters using the local

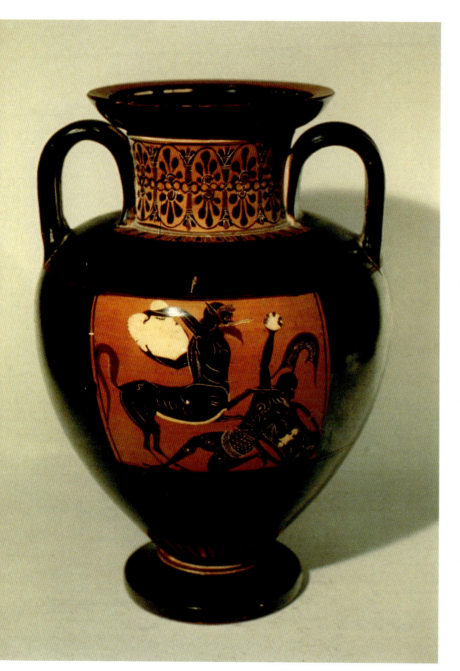

The potters of Athens found their greatest satisfaction in the study and drawing of the human figure, an aspect of their art indigenous to the Greeks and owing little to oriental influence. Battles, races and processions were favourite themes and later scenes from mythology were introduced. Little attempt was made to ensure that the drawing was anatomically correct or to place it in a background or indicate depth. On the figure a profile was used for the head but with a frontal view of the eye; limbs were also shown in profile, while the torso was shown either in profile or frontally.

Black figures were painted on to the red background and fine detail was scratched through the slip to reveal the red body. The finest designs are restrained and powerful in their execution, without any of the ponderousness that developed towards the end of the period. Early designs included a variety of border patterns, but gradually these were simplified and occasionally eliminated altogether. By convention, black was adopted for male flesh and white for female; purple-red was confined to drapery and accessories. Generally the colours are more sombre than those used earlier by the Athenian or Corinthian potters. The earliest potter's signature has been found on a fragment of krater dating to around 700 BC. The work of individual painters can be recognized and among the greatest are Lydos, Nearchos, Exekias and the Amasis Painter. While Corinthian potters developed a precise and elegant animal style, Athenian potters brought the black-figure style to its peak between 550 and 530 BC.

Red-figure style

Around 530–520 BC new decorative schemes were developed that eventually replaced the black-figure style. The red-figure style (*c.* 530–330 BC) is the last major Greek pottery painting style and may to some extent have been suggested by changes in contemporary art. Wall painting had become popular and painters were turning to this new and larger dimension in preference to the comparatively cramped and limited size and palette of vase painting. New techniques therefore had to be developed that allowed greater emphasis to be placed on accuracy rather than stylization if ceramic decoration was to continue as a medium attractive to the best painters. The red-figure technique gave painters scope to practise their newly acquired

Amphora, black-figure style, from Athens, *c.* 500 BC. Earthenware, with a red panel carrying a scene of warriors in a chariot and around the neck a double honeysuckle pattern. Height *c.* 40 cm (16 in).

yellow clays brought this animal style to perfection in the seventh century BC. Detailed friezes beautifully executed were shown in bands often no more than a few centimetres wide. Incised lines were used to convey detail and the success of the designs was unequalled elsewhere in Greece. Bands of figures in complex arrangements were also shown. Small areas of other colours such as purple, red, white and later yellow were subsequently introduced to heighten the designs, helping to break away from the austerity of the geometric style.

skills. Other competition came from overseas potteries that had been set up by emigrant potters who were producing work almost identical to black-figure pots, so an attractive alternative home-produced ware was required to help maintain export markets in the face of this competition.

The human figure, hitherto depicted stylistically and with minimum anatomical detailing, now became the object of serious study. The incised method of scratching through the black slip to show detail was no longer thought satisfactory and a finer, more precise method of drawing using brushed lines was devised. Instead of a black figure being shown on a red background, the process was reversed and the background was covered black, leaving the figure red in silhouette; detail was painted on to the figure with a thin, raised black line, or else a thinner brown line. The early red-figure style was founded on line drawing rather than shading.

As the style developed so figures were depicted more naturalistically, without such strict regard for the convention of abstraction. An element of reality developed with attempts to indicate depth by using three-quarter views and foreshortening;

draperies became more detailed and ornate dots were used to suggest hair and texture. Black-figure designs have a solemnity that became less austere in the red-figure work. In later designs figures are no longer planted firmly on the base line but, in a further attempt to create depth, move over the surface of the pot, often in uneasy arrangements.

White-ground and other wares

One other distinctive style of decoration that became popular at the end of the sixth century BC involved the use of a white slip background on which vase painters drew or painted in a manner more akin to the now lost free-painting of the period. The background of the pot was covered with a white slip and this was often supplemented by thin washes of colour, in red, purple or yellow ochre; this style, made in Athens, was known as Attic white-ground ware. As the white slip ground was fragile, the technique was reserved for pots of a more precious nature – for example small oil bottles or funeral pots. The scenes shown on them are peaceful and quiet, depicting such domestic activities as spinning; the effects are charming and delicate. Often a small container was concealed

Attic red-figured earthenware, cotyle, decorated with incised lines for ears and the finest period purple for inscriptions and details such as snakes' tongues. The scene depicts Triptolemos as a youth seated in a winged vehicle and holding corn. Persephone faces him, holding a jug and a flaming torch, and behind her stands Elensis, personification of locality. Demeter stands behind Triptolemos. Height 21.5 cm (8.6 in). Found near Capua.

White-ground oil flask, lekythos. Earthenware, Athens, *c.* 480–470 BC. The scene shows a woman carrying out domestic activities, holding a circlet. Behind her is a wool basket and an alabastron, and a cup is hung on the wall. Attributed to the Villa Giulia Painter. Height 35.7 cm (14.3 in).

overseas. One final black-slipped ware was developed in Athens around 220 BC – the so-called Megarian bowl. These bowls were produced by throwing clay inside a hemispherical mould with an impressed design, their form and decoration being stimulated by contemporary silver vessels of a similar shape. The future of such wares lay in the red-slipped Arretine ware made in Italy, developed into the late first century BC.

Figurines

Terracotta figurines of many kinds – some large, others much smaller in size – were produced in Greece, as they were in other Mediterranean countries. In the fourth century the craft of making small, high-quality figurines flourished, especially in Athens and the Boeotian city of Tanagra, which was endowed with ample supplies of suitable clay. Some of the hand-modelled animals look like toys, but the horsemen and horses reflect contemporary military activity, while the goddess figures with their elaborate dress and jewellery suggest the probable existence of larger-scale cult statues in bronze or marble that have not survived. Many figures were moulded and produced in great quantity. Subjects include religious figures such as Aphrodite and Eros as well as genre figures, for example comic characters. During the third century these figures were widely produced in many areas of the Mediterranean, and later Hellenistic types extended to an imaginative genre and new religious themes. However, with the establishment of Christianity in the fifth century AD the craft virtually disappeared.

THE ITALIAN PENINSULA

From the sixth century BC Rome expanded gradually from a small Latin city-state in central Italy into a vast empire that extended outwards from the Mediterranean basin. At its height in the second century AD it had provinces in northern and southern Europe, North Africa and the Near East. Its civilization dominated the classical world over the course of the millennium.

The Etruscans

Etruria, situated between Rome, Florence and the Apennine Mountains (roughly modern Tuscany), was the first major state in Italy. It was powerful, highly developed, and the people war-like. The

inside a larger outer pot, indicating the preciousness of the oil or perfume it held.

By the middle of the fifth century there was a marked decline in the quality of the drawing. The number of workshops in Athens began to diminish as many potters moved to work overseas, the 'craft drain' reaching a peak at the end of the fifth century BC following the defeat of Athens in the Peloponnesian War. An important red-figure school developed in south Italy, and by the fourth century these wares dominated the Italian markets. In the mid-fourth century BC Athenian potters produced the so-called Kertch wares in the red-figure style. These ornately decorated vases were much admired

Terracotta group of two seated women. Myrina, north-west Asia Minor, about 100 BC. The figures may depict Demeter and her daughter Persephone. Height 20 cm (8 in).

Bottle form, askos. Villanovan pot from Etruria, 900–700 BC. Earthenware with incised decoration.

Villanovans, who inhabited the region of Etruria before the Etruscans emerged around 700 BC, in the period roughly seen as the Italian Iron Age, were skilled metalworkers and potters; their dead were cremated and their ashes buried in urns. Pots were made by a combination of throwing and hand-building. Fairly coarse, iron-bearing clay was used and the surface was often burnished. Incised designs, often geometric in style, decorated some of the pots, although towards the end of the eighth century BC an oriental influence became evident withn the appearance of lotus flowers and mythical monsters.

The Etruscans absorbed many aspects of the Villanovan culture as well as influences from elsewhere, mainly the Near East. From Babylon they learned how to construct the vaulted arch, from Egypt how to make faience, and from Assyria and Phoenicia how to work gold and silver. Etruscan metalwork is one of their finest achievements and was prized throughout the Mediterranean area; their bronzework was widely exported both within the Mediterranean and to Celtic Europe.

Early Etruscan pottery was made from roughly mixed clay that fired a range of colours including black, brown and red. Around the middle of the seventh century BC grey-coloured pottery, often known as Bucchero Etruscan ware, appeared. Technically the pots are sound and their shapes reflect the contemporary concern within metalworking with finely worked-out and well-executed forms. Decoration usually consists of simple geometric designs, again boldly incised on a shiny black or grey surface.

In the early seventh and sixth centuries BC Etruscan pottery was influenced by immigrant Greek potters and by imported Greek pottery, at first by work decorated in the Greek geometric style and later by work in the red-figure style from Athens. However, the highly complex designs and symbols employed by the Greek potters meant little or nothing to the Etruscans, who simply copied the appearance of the ornate decoration they saw

LEFT: Large bowl, krater. Etruscan, *c.* 250 BC. Red and white design on black ground with yellow accessories above palmette, bordered by egg moulding. The scene includes young Heracles strangling the snakes. Height 49 cm (19.6 in).

without seeking to understand its meaning. As a result, despite the high technical standard of the work, the designs often appear crude in comparison with Greek wares. Although sculpture in stone was practised, the principal cultural medium was painted terracotta. Such objects were used widely for decorating the timber superstructure of temples and even, on occasions, for creating life-sized

size. In conquering neighbouring countries the state absorbed an extensive range of influences, far broader than had been available to the Greeks.

Throughout the Roman empire engineering and architecture were major concerns, with technical knowledge being introduced throughout the colonies along with ordered government. Industries able to produce the type and quality of goods

Etruscan earthenware vessel, pyxis, with incised design of birds and geometric patterns. Height 8.2 cm (3.25 in).

Stemmed bowl, krater. Roman, from Arezzo. Earthenware, red gloss ware, decorated in relief with rows of beads, wreaths, rosettes and figures which represent the seasons. It is signed by the potter, Cb. Ateius. Height 18.7 cm (7.5 in).

figured groups. Overall Etruria was a civilizing power and had a great influence on Rome during the earliest, formative stages of the development of the state.

THE ROMAN EMPIRE

According to legend Rome was founded in 753 BC, but it was not until the fifth century BC that the Romans freed themselves from the Etruscans. By 275 BC, however, Rome ruled the whole of the Italian peninsula, gradually growing in strength and

needed by a prosperous society were encouraged. A central tenet of Roman ideology was that conquered lands should, as far as was practicable, be as like the homeland as possible. As part of this policy the manufacture of a wide range of goods was encouraged and buildings were constructed. Production methods were efficient, effective in coping with the increasing needs of the developing state, and ingeniously devised so that the same methods of production could be adopted in different countries within the empire. In pottery, mass-production of high-quality wares led to uniform shapes, many of which imitated the form and decoration of contemporary silverware. Some shapes were left plain, some decorated. Other styles that were produced include a wide range of 'coarse' wares made for general use.

At different times pottery-making centres were established throughout the Roman empire, usually situated near the camps of the Legions or on a busy trade route; for example, at La Graufesenque in southern Gaul and later at Lezoux in central Gaul. At La Graufesenque twenty lists of pots stamped by Castus name thirty-eight workmen in his workshop and record the manufacture of half a million pots. As new pottery centres were set up, although many of the basic forms were standard, local styles did often influence the decoration. Gradually Roman making, decorating and firing techniques were taken over the whole of Europe, some surviving long after the Romans had left.

Red-slip ware

Arretium, modern-day Arezzo, gives its name to Arretine ware, which is the most famous, most technically sophisticated and finest of the Roman red-slip wares. The Romans had learnt from the Greeks how to prepare the fine clay slip by adding an alkali to fine particles of clay, but they chose to fire it a terracotta red rather than black. Roman ware of this kind is known by several names, including the Italian *terra sigillata* (sealed earth), used to describe pottery decorated with motifs or scenes. In addition to stamped wares, the term covers much undecorated work made in the same red clay. Examples found in Britain and Gaul are known as Samian ware. In general the pots can more accurately be included under the general heading red-slip ware. The beauty and accuracy of the making of the pots and the high-quality surface gloss indicate excellent craftsmanship. Initially it was probably Greek potters who were employed to produce these fine wares, although in time the majority of the potters were Italian.

Decoration on early Arretine ware is classical in origin and includes well-balanced and sensitive groupings of figures of Hellenistic origin, such as maenads, satyrs and fauns. Wreaths, masks, scrolls, swathes of fruit and flowers, birds, cupids and butterflies are among the motifs used. The raised decoration on contemporary metal objects, especially the fine work of the silversmith, was often copied directly by potters, who may even have taken moulds from original pieces. The delicacy of the incising technique used on the moulds allowed crisp detail that perhaps encouraged the notably naturalistic decoration.

Various methods of manufacture were employed. The most basic pieces were thrown on the wheel using carefully prepared red clay and then turned when leather-hard, to produce a ware that was thin-walled, delicate and stylish. Much of it was left plain, with little or no decoration. The more important pieces were made by pressing clay into intricately stamped moulds, a technique developed in late Hellenistic Greece and adapted by the Romans. Briefly, the method involved making a hollow mould with thick walls of clay (known as a pitcher mould). This was usually thrown on the wheel and while it was still soft a design, often based on contemporary metalwork, was impressed or incised into the interior. It was then biscuit-fired.

A common method for making the moulds was to produce an archetype of the finished pot in clay or plaster, with the decoration modelled in relief on the surface. When the archetype was dry a mould was made from it, which was then fired. To make a bowl, the mould was attached to a wheel-head and the inside smeared with clay, which was smoothed over as the wheel was rotated. As the clay dried it contracted, shrinking away from the walls of the mould and thus allowing it to be removed easily, leaving the decoration in relief on the surface. A foot, and sometimes a rim, was then thrown and added on to the moulded shape of the bowl. In addition to bowls and dishes, closed vessels such as jugs or bottles were made. The pots were finished by being covered in a slip of fine clay, which fired bright coral red in a clean oxidizing fire or black in a reduced kiln atmosphere.

Undecorated red-slip ware

Plain, undecorated wheel-thrown pots of red-slip ware were produced in great quantity. The shapes are simple and uncluttered, the crispness of the forms showing the influence of contemporary metalwork. At the time the most valued tableware was made from metal, and the undecorated pottery set out to imitate it in fineness and finish. The pots are characterized by a clean, precise quality

Two vases, Roman, the top one with incised decoration, the lower with trailed patterning. Height (top) 13 cm (5.25 in).

Askos, side-spouted jar, from Canosa, *c.* 270–200 BC. Earthenware, of native shape with painted and three-dimensional decoration on a pink ground, showing two winged marine horses flying over a brown sea. Terracotta figures are attached to the false spout and handles, and the foreparts of two horses to the walls. Reliefs of the head of Medusa and a dancing Maenad are also applied. Height 75 cm (30 in).

reflecting the mechanical production methods. Flat dishes apparently made in sets or services are common, as are cups, bowls and other domestic pottery. The place of manufacture is often stamped on the pot, sometimes falsely ('Arretine' has been found on pots made elsewhere). Potters also stamped their names on the pots; for example, Cerial, a potter working at Lezoux in central Gaul during the reigns of Trajan and Hadrian, stamped his on the floor of red-slip vessels.

As the Roman legions travelled farther west the main production centre of the pottery industry moved first to southern and later to central Gaul. During the second century AD the central Gaulish factories were the chief suppliers of red-slip ware to the British markets. Centres were also established in Britain in areas such as the Nene Valley near Peterborough, Aldgate and the New Forest (see chapter 6), but these were small in comparison with the potteries in Gaul. The Roman redwares were taken over hundreds of miles, essentially as a 'piggy-back' or parasitic trade. The principal cargo would be amphorae containing grain, oil and particularly wine, and the availability of this subsidized form of transport enabled fine red-slip wares to travel cheaply and in vast quantities.

Other wares

Only about one tenth of Roman pottery consisted of the fine quality red-slip wares or other fine wares. Red-slip wares were unsuitable for cooking as they were not able to withstand thermal shock. The vast majority of pottery was the so-called coarse pottery, used for storage, for the transport of foodstuffs and for the cooking and serving of food and liquids. Coarse pottery was made usually from local clay fired without a covering of slip. Most coarse pottery was thrown on the fast potter's wheel in a great variety of forms, many of which were required for particular local needs. Coarse wares were produced at a number of centres, although, like fine pottery, they could be transported hundreds of miles – especially in areas bordering on the Mediterranean. Even in coarse pottery there is a considerable measure of uniformity of form and function, reflecting the needs of Roman society across the empire. The forms are diverse and include cooking pots, storage jars, pestles and mortars, ink-wells and bowls for ceremonial rituals.

Potters working in centres away from Italy experimented with different decorative styles, which they often produced alongside the more standard wares. Many of the coarse wares fired a dark grey or black, but some were more lustrous, probably through being fired in a reducing atmosphere. A wide range of decorative techniques were used and the motifs and decoration were often more varied and freely interpreted as potters looked to materials other than metal for ideas. Glass and leather forms, for instance, were imitated. The cutting of cheese-hard pottery with a V-shaped instrument similar to a modern lino-cutting tool gave a design that closely imitates that of cut glass.

Some thrown pots decorated with applied ornament produced by painting or trailing thick liquid clay slip on to the surface of the damp pot were known as 'barbotine ware' (*barbotine* being the French word for slip). The Roman potters took this use of slip to a high technical and aesthetic standard, with early designs often imitating those made in relief from moulds but more soft in appearance. Hunting scenes are a common theme. In some areas white slip was used over a dark-firing clay to produce designs that were visually powerful and lively. In contrast to the more severe style of red-slip wares, the barbotine technique required speed and dexterity rather than exact precision, with results that were often freer in feel.

Increased prosperity, improved communications, greater efficiency, a more settled population and a boom in commerce of all types brought increased demand for high-quality pottery, encouraging even more rapid methods of production and mechanical methods of decoration. To meet the demand a number of new techniques were introduced, including rouletting patterns, made by a metal tool 'chattering' on the side of the pot as it turned on the wheel, and patterns created using a tool with a revolving toothed wheel.

Pottery oil-lamps – a cheap means of supplying illumination for domestic use, at shrines or in tombs – were used in classical lands throughout the Mediterranean and Near East from the Late Bronze Age. Fine quality lamps in ceramic were produced in great quantity by the Romans. Most were fabricated in moulds, although some were wheel-made. The most successful shape was devised in the mid-first century and remained in use for over five hundred years. This has a circular chamber for oil and a short rounded nozzle; most, though not all, have a handle. Most lamps were pressed from a two-piece mould made of an original lamp and many include relief decoration. If the lamp was moulded plain, a sprig design was sometimes added and the maker's name stamped on the piece. Lamps took many forms – one, for example, was modelled as a sandalled foot, with the hole for the wick made in the big toe. Decoration typically includes animals such as goats and elephants, as well as foliage and the human figure. Many examples are covered with a fine red slip.

Faience
Faience, which had been developed much earlier in Egypt and Mesopotamia, continued to be made in Egypt during the Roman occupation, but in more elaborate and ambitious shapes. Brilliant blue and turquoise colours were obtained by the addition of small percentages of copper in the alkaline-based mixture, and later other metal oxides were used to produce black, red, green, purple, yellow and white. Because the paste had to be carefully prepared and the raw material was difficult to work, faience wares were expensive to manufacture; as with the lead-glazed wares, the larger and more ambitious pieces were therefore regarded as luxury items. Fine vessels were produced in a wide variety of shapes, both plain and in highly decorative relief. In the city of Memphis six kilns of square construction, dating to the first and second centuries AD, have been excavated, indicating the extent of production of high-quality faience. Later Islamic potters developed the technique more fully, introducing a stronger and more workable body.

Lead-glazed ware
The last major group of wares made by the Romans is one with which many potters working today possibly have a direct connection: namely, lead-glazed ware. The technique of lead glazing had been discovered and employed during earlier periods in Egypt and Mesopotamia, although its use had never become widespread. Technically, glazed wares were more complicated to prepare and fire as the flame had to be kept well away from the pots. Because the glaze became runny, it often moved on to the kiln shelf, resulting in

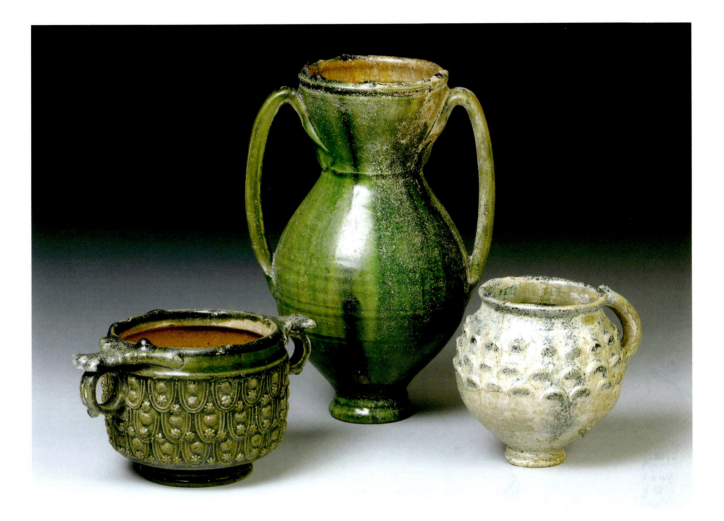

Three Roman vessels, all with vitreous glaze. Double-handled cup with applied scales, AD 20–70, said to be from Arles, southern France; double-handled vase, *c*. AD 70–100, said to be from Tharros; single-handled cup decorated with imbricated leaves, from Asia Minor, 1st century AD. Height (tallest) 17.5 cm (7 in).

failures in the kiln. This type of ware is therefore likely to have been regarded as a luxury item.

Red-slip wares were prepared by dipping the pot into a specially prepared clay slip and similar methods of application were used for the glazed wares. A green lead glaze was popular, and was applied to pots produced by a variety of methods. Some were made in moulds bearing impressed designs of applied figures or natural forms such as flowers, while others were thrown on the wheel and glazed. By 100 BC the technique of lead glazing was being practised in Asia Minor at Tarsus, Smyrna (Izmir) and other centres in the eastern Mediterranean. Glazing travelled through Italy, where it was very little used, to the Allier district of Gaul, notably Saint-Remy-en-Rollat, Vichy. Subsequently it spread into Germany and

was established at Cologne by about AD 100. The potters at Holt in Denbighshire, England, also made lead-glazed pots.

When the Roman empire collapsed, much of its ceramic knowledge was lost, although lead glazing continued to be used in Byzantium and may have formed the basis of later developments in Europe, such as Italian forum ware, which reintroduced lead glazing to much of Europe. Under the Romans pottery workshops were well organized, efficient and effective, introducing technical knowledge to virtually all parts of the empire. To produce pottery in the quantity required by expanding populations and large armies, production techniques were developed that foreshadowed many of the methods used by the industrial firms of today.

The Oriental World

CHINA, KOREA, JAPAN, SOUTH-EAST ASIA

With what skill did the potters work — it seemed as if they borrowed the secret from Heaven!

YI KYU-BO (1168–1241)

Lohan, large individually modelled figure. China, Liao dynasty (907–1125). Stoneware with sancai or three-colour glaze, from a cliff temple at Yixian, Hebei province. The pierced base may represent the famous stone of Lake Tai in Jiangsu province. The banding on the yellow robe represents patchwork, traditionally worn by monks as a sign of humility. Lohan, disciples of the Buddha, are traditionally found in groups of sixteen in ancient temples, eight pairs on either side of the main Buddha figure. Height 103 cm (41 in).

Potters working in the Far East made wares very different in style and purpose from those in the West. This was partly because of the high quality and wide distribution of an impressive range of raw materials, and partly the result of the widely held belief that art and religion were intimate aspects of daily life.

CHINA

China has one of the world's oldest continuous civilizations, despite invasions and occasional foreign rule. A country as vast as China with so long-lasting a civilization has a complex social and visual history, within which pottery and porcelain play a major role. Here, for the sake of simplicity, the development of Chinese pottery is dealt with chronologically, following dynastic changes; however, some dynasties were short and only the main ones are dealt with.

The function and status of ceramics in China varied from dynasty to dynasty, so they may be utilitarian, burial, trade, collectors' or even ritual objects, according to their quality and the era in which they were made. The ceramics fall into three broad types – earthenware, stoneware and porcelain – for both vessels, architectural items such as roof tiles and modelled objects and figures. In addition there was an important group of sculptures made for religious use, the majority of which were produced in earthenware.

The earliest ceramics were fired to earthenware temperatures, but as early as the fifteenth century BC high-temperature stonewares were being made with glazed surfaces. During the Six Dynasties period (AD 265–589) kilns in north China were producing high-fired ceramics of good quality. Whitewares produced in Hebei and Henan provinces from the seventh to the tenth centuries evolved into the highly prized porcelains of the Song dynasty (960–1279), long regarded as one of the high points in the history of China's ceramic industry. The tradition of religious sculpture extends over most historical periods but is less clearly delineated than that of stonewares or porcelains, for it embraces the old custom of earthenware burial ceramics together with later Buddhist images and architectural ornament. Ceramic products also include lead-glazed tomb models of the Han dynasty, three-colour lead-glazed vessels and figures of the Tang dynasty, and Ming three-colour and *fahua*-type temple ornaments, in which the motifs were outlined in a raised trail of slip, as well as the many burial ceramics produced in imitation of vessels made in materials of higher intrinsic value.

Trade between the West and the settled and prosperous Chinese dynasties introduced new forms and different technologies. One of the most far-reaching examples is the impact of the fine ninth-century AD Chinese porcelain wares imported into the Arab world. So admired were these

Rounded urn. Gansu Yangshao culture, China, *c.* 2500 BC. Earthenware, hand-built by coiling. The sweeping painted decoration in black and purple, applied with a soft brush, is typical of the Banshan phase. Height 34.3 cm (13.7 in).

Tripod vessel, li. China, Western Zhou dynasty, 10th century BC. Earthenware, hand-built with striated impressed decoration. Height 14.4 cm (5.75 in).

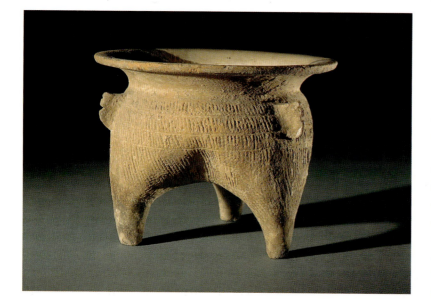

Chinese themselves adapted many specific vessel forms from the West, such as bottles with long spouts, as well as devising a range of decorative patterns especially for the European market.

Just as painted designs on Greek pots may seem today to be purely decorative, whereas in fact they were carefully and precisely worked out so that at the time their meaning was clear, so it is with Chinese pots. To twentieth-century eyes Chinese pottery may appear merely decorative, yet to the Chinese the form of each object and its adornment had meaning and significance. In a country where the written language had developed from pictorial symbols rather than hieroglyphics, this is perhaps less surprising. The dragon represented the emperor and the phoenix the empress; the pomegranate indicated fertility, a pair of fish happiness; mandarin ducks stood for wedded bliss; the pine tree, peach and crane are emblems of long life, and fish leaping from waves indicated success in the civil service examinations. Only when European decorative themes were introduced did these meanings become obscured or even lost.

From early times pots were used in both religious and secular contexts. The imperial court commissioned work and in the Yuan dynasty (1279–1368) an imperial ceramic factory was established at Jingdezhen. Pots played an important part in some Buddhist ceremonies. Long and often lyrical descriptions of the different types of ware exist that assist in classifying pots, although these sometimes confuse an already large and complicated picture.

Early period

The earliest pottery was made in the south-west almost ten or eleven thousand years ago, and was intended for utilitarian and ritual purposes. In addition to pots, small figurines in the form of pigs with triangular heads and large snouts have been found. One of the most distinctive groups was the earthenware produced on the plains near the Yellow River in the period 3000–1500 BC. These pots from Gansu province were coil-built in reddish clay fired and boldly painted with flowing geometric patterns in red, black or purplish-brown pigment. Stylistically they are related to those made in western Asia, southern Persia, Baluchistan and southern Russia, which suggests close communication at that time. Examples of these wares survive in good

pieces that they encouraged the development of earthenware made in imitation of porcelain as well as instigating research into its method of manufacture. From the Middle East the Chinese acquired a blue pigment, a purified form of cobalt oxide unobtainable at that time in China, which contained only a low level of manganese. Cobalt ores found in China have a high manganese content, which produces a more muted blue-grey colour. In the seventeenth century the trading activities of the Dutch East India Company resulted in vast quantities of decorated Chinese porcelain being brought to Europe, which stimulated and influenced the work of a wide variety of wares, notably Delft. The

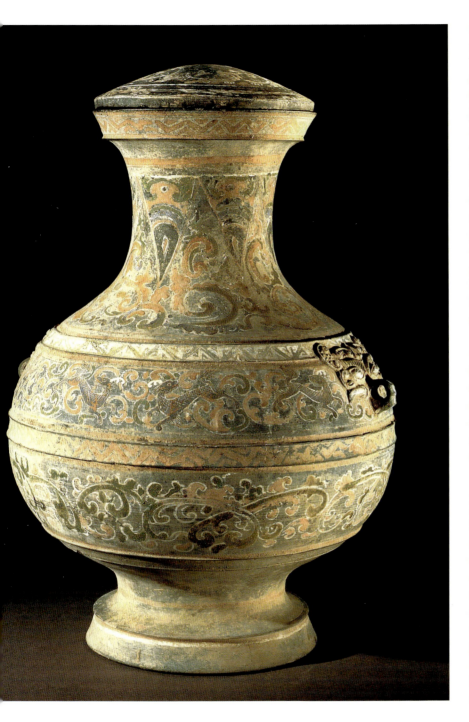

Double-handled burial vase. Earthenware wine jar and cover with painted decoration in imitation of inlaid lacquer vases (hu) of the same shape. The blue pigment derives from lapis lazuli. 1st century BC to 1st century AD, China. Height 48 cm (19.2 in).

the hollow legs provided the liquid contents with a greater surface area from which to absorb heat. The outside of these vessels is decorated with incised textured patterns. During the Chinese Bronze Age the casting of bronze and working of jade was brought to a high degree of refinement, and this greatly influenced the form of ceramic vessels. Bronze containers, many of which were intended for religious use, were highly valued and many potters imitated their forms. At this time a close relationship was established between bronze and clay. The metal was cast in three- or four-piece ceramic moulds and many bronze forms were based on pottery forms. In addition, many pots were fashioned in almost exact imitation of bronze and also jade vessels, and it was many years before pottery began once again to be made with real regard for the plastic qualities of clay.

During the fourth millennium the potter's wheel came into widespread use and had a profound influence on the forms of the vessel made. One group of wares made in the Longsham culture (*c.* 3000–1700 BC) is renowned for its well-made wheel-thrown thin-walled forms, fired almost to the point of vitrification with a surface that is black and lustrous.

Early dynasties (c. 1700–221 BC)
Major changes occurred during the Shang and Zhou dynasties, during which complex systems of government and religion were set up. Confucius (Kong Fuzi) about 550–480 BC proposed a philosophy or system of thought in which filial piety and reverence for tradition were emphasized. At much the same time Lao Zi developed Daoism, teaching that nature permeates everything, propounding a high and compassionate morality and stressing the virtue of withdrawal or non-intervention. Later cults developed the more mystical elements of Daoism.

Excavated graves, many discovered during the construction of the railways in the early twentieth century, proved to be a rich source of pottery as well as of other treasures of this period. At the time it was the custom to inter with the eminent dead items which they might need in the afterlife. Food in metal and bronze containers, as well as pots, was buried with the bodies of important rulers in specially constructed graves. Wives, servants and retainers were often immolated, a practice

condition because they were used as burial urns. The high quality of the painted decoration on the full swelling forms and the vigour and life of these pots give them a quality which to modern eyes appears pleasing, fresh and lively.

Of the range of cooking vessels, some of the most numerous were coiled out of grey clay and built with three hollow legs. This highly functional design could sit securely over the fire while

Map of the major ceramic centres of the Far East and South-East Asia.

second was the more sophisticated design of kilns, which provided greater heat retention together with control of the temperature to ensure more even heat distribution. These kilns also enabled clay to be fired to higher temperatures, which gave a harder and more fused body. This process, unique to China at the time, produced the earliest stoneware pots known. Around the same time it was discovered that a simple glazed surface could be made by dusting wood ash or a mineral such as feldspar on to the shoulder of the pot. At temperatures around 1200°C, such materials combined with the surface of the pot to form an attractive mottled glaze. The use of this method of glazing seems to have continued intermittently, becoming more widespread in the Han dynasty.

During the Warring States period (481–221 BC) the supremacy of bronze forms was challenged, mainly by the more fragile lacquer wares but also by the art of inlaying or coating bronze with more precious metals such as gold or silver. As a result there was renewed interest in making pots that were slightly freer and more clay-like in form. Glazing techniques were refined, with pale greenish-brown shades predominating at low stoneware temperatures. One fascinating group of wares was richly decorated with a pattern of coloured glass glaze, painted in spots, circles and dashes. These pots were jewel-like in appearance, contemporary glassmaking technology having been called upon to achieve a range of brilliant colours, although little of this intensity of colour has withstood the test of time.

IMPERIAL CHINA
Han dynasty (221 BC–AD 220)
In 221 BC China was unified under the 'First Emperor' Qin Shihuang, who ruled with great authority. Existing sections of the Great Wall were joined up and the script, currency, weights and measures were standardized. On Qin Shihuang's death the magnificent 'terracotta army', as it has become known, first excavated in 1974 and made up of more than seven thousand models of life-size warriors and horses, was buried with him. Apart from their size and vast quantity, the most arresting quality of these figures is the fine detail, whether in their hairstyles or their facial expressions, which vary greatly. The revival of Confucian philosophy had a profound effect on much

condemned by Confucius. Gradually the barbarian practice ceased and clay or wooden models were substituted for the human sacrifice.

The majority of the pottery that has been recovered was fired to earthenware temperatures and unglazed, but some was taken to higher stoneware temperatures. Shapes often seem to be derived from those made by bronze casting, though occasionally decorated with painted patterns. Two significant developments were made during this period which, although not widespread in their application until later dynasties, were of great importance to Chinese pottery. The first was the development of carefully prepared fine white clay fashioned into forms decorated in relief in the style of contemporary bronzes. These wares can be seen as the precursors of later porcelains. The

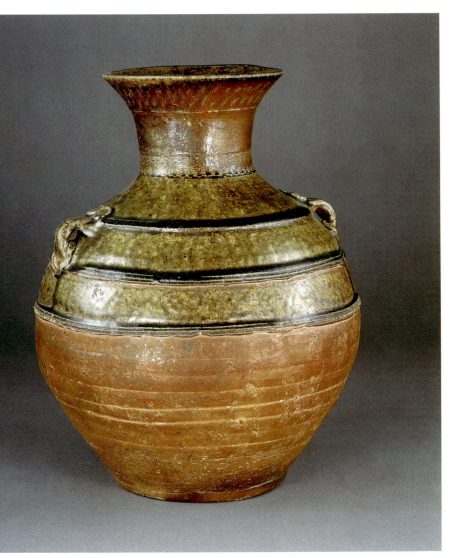

Glazed jar, China, Han dynasty, 1st century BC to 1st century AD. Stoneware, wheel-made and reduction-fired. The raised lines around the body of the jar prevent the glaze from running down the pot. The lower part of the body has re-oxidized red, after the initial reduction firing required to produce a green glaze. Height 33.8 cm (13.5 in).

available. The Han dynasty lead-barium-silica glass and glaze technology was highly developed and made use of earlier technology developed in China.

Few pots were now made entirely by hand-building techniques; instead, they were thrown on efficient potter's wheels. Others were made in complex ceramic moulds, again reflecting the influence of moulded bronze forms, although in ceramics this technique was more commonly used for figures and animal forms. Burial wares, many depicting people performing everyday activities such as playing board games, are typical of such moulded items. One of the influences of bronze objects on ceramics was to produce quite complex forms with decoration based closely on the metal wares. Ceramic vessels also copied the appearance of bronze, for example in the use of lead glazes coloured green. Over the years, as a result of contact with moisture in the soil during burial, this glaze has become iridescent and today it appears even more bronze-like than it did when originally made. Some ceramic vases even had ceramic rings modelled on the outside in imitation of their bronze equivalents.

Both stonewares and earthenwares were made at this time, but it is the low-fired wares that have survived in greater numbers, principally because many fine examples were interred with the dead. The so-called 'hill-censers' or 'hill-jars' form one of the most fascinating earthenwares groups. These jars, some twenty centimetres tall, were made for mortuary use and had a lid, on top of which was modelled a stylized mountain, hill or island representing the Daoist mythological Island or Mountain of the Blest. Reddish-grey clay was used and the lead-silicate glaze was tinted green, probably with copper oxide. Other ornament usually took the form of a frieze round the side depicting hunting scenes, which often included domestic and wild animals. Such designs were made in a mould and then applied to the pots. Miniature well-heads and cooking ranges were also produced. Braziers, cooking vessels, ladles, various bowls and dishes, tripod kettles, candlesticks and cups have all been found, as well as such pottery objects as miniature tables, all replicating objects found in everyday life.

Stoneware, which had first appeared during the Zhou dynasty, was now made in greater quantities and developed technically during this period.

of the art that was produced at this time, although Daoism with its mythical and mystical beliefs continued to attract many followers.

International trade brought stylistic and technical influences from other countries. Silk was exported by the overland route via Turkestan to the east Roman empire and by sea to India and Persia. The appearance of lead glazes in China is roughly contemporary with their emergence in Rome, although no connection has been established. The use of lead had several precedents in ancient China, the most important of which was in the production of a bronze alloy, where it served the same purpose as in a glaze, namely to lower the melting point of the base material. In the Warring States period lead carbonate was used as white face-powder for women, so the material was already known and

Lidded jar, China, first half of 8th century AD. Earthenware, wheel-thrown, with sancai three-colour resist decoration of stripes and florets that are typical of the ornament on polychrome woven silks of the period. The shape of the jar is known as *wannian* ('myriad year') because it was favoured for burials. Height 25.4 cm (10 in).

Pots made out of stoneware clay were placed in the hot areas of the kiln, while earthenwares with lead glazes were put into the cooler parts. Stoneware glazes were also developed, and consisted of combinations of finely ground feldspar or granite rock and wood ash which, when fired, produced thin olive-green glazes that enhanced and heightened the form. Although not strictly necessary from a practical point of view, since stoneware is impervious to liquid, the glaze added a further element of refinement. Many of the stoneware forms of this period are clearly based on bronze forms, with much of the decoration cut in low relief and similar in style to that seen on metal objects. It was usually limited to applied horizontal bands around the centre or shoulder of the pot. Incised combing was sometimes also used.

Tang dynasty (AD 618–906)

After a period of turbulence came a time of relative peace and prosperity, encouraging the production of art that was technically and aesthetically inventive. The widespread adoption of Buddhism, with its doctrine of personal denial and renunciation, was consolidated during the Tang dynasty. Overall this was a tolerant and creative period, which can be rated one of the richest and most artistically productive in China's history. Tea-drinking became popular, and some types of ceramic vessels were favoured over others for this purpose.

The northern capital, Ch'ang-an (present-day Xi'an), was the focus of international interest, attracting visitors and trade from a wide area. To the west the Roman empire had greatly diminished in size and strength, and Islam had not yet achieved its later success. Overland trade extended to Iran and Mesopotamia, and maritime trade to India, the Pacific islands and Japan. Religious tolerance encouraged the influx of a wide range of religious followers including Nestorian Christians, the Manichaeans from central Asia, the Zoroastrians from Persia and the Muslims from India. From AD 638 immigrants from western Asia brought Persian Sasanian material culture and the metalwork and glass vessels in particular had a strong influence on Tang pottery forms.

During the troubled times between the Han and Tang dynasties, the virtual cessation of trade deprived potters of the lead frit necessary for the earthenware glaze. When trade with the West was

Further improvements in kiln design enabled stonewares to be made more efficiently and effectively. Kilns were built into the side of a hill, enabling the heat to rise more easily within the kiln, with the result that higher temperatures were achieved overall, though pots nearer the fire-box tended to get hotter than those packed towards the rear of the kiln. The use of such kilns enabled temperature of around 1200°C to be achieved and this technology was to play a vital and creative part in the future development of Chinese pottery. The higher temperatures resulted in a greater integration of body and glaze, and the production of subdued natural colours of stone and rock. Such developments were particularly associated with the Yue district of south-east China, where fine pots were made.

The use of refractory clay able to withstand high stoneware temperatures without collapsing was a further major technological development.

resumed, lead glazing was reintroduced as lead frit of a much improved quality began to be imported. This enabled brighter, clearer colours to be obtained, which have retained their brilliance over the years. Hellenistic influences can be seen in some of the pots, for instance in the shape of flat pilgrim flasks as well as in ewers with handles and lips.

chevrons, dots and stripes, although the fluidity of the lead glaze as it melted and ran down the pot often softened the edges of the colours and dappled effects were common. Glaze was often applied to the top half of the pot, leaving a bare area at the bottom, which enabled the pot to be glazed quickly by dipping as well as acting as a

Tomb figures. China, Tang dynasty (618–906). Four painted terracotta equestrian figures of musicians, each made up of separate moulded parts luted together.

Many Tang forms are characterized by a full, swelling, almost bursting body contrasted with a delicate, fairly narrow neck. Each part of the pot relates to the other in a way suggesting movement and articulation, in contrast to the later Song wares that have smoother, more continuous curves. Decoration well suited the shape and size of the pot and was often bold and confident; it included moulded, incised, stamped and painted designs. The mouths of some vessels are lobed in a style derived from flowers. Bases were often tidily finished but had no turned foot.

Objects were made with a light buff-coloured body and covered with a clear lead-silicate glaze that could be tinted amber and brown with iron oxide, green with copper oxide, and sometimes, but rarely, rich blue with cobalt oxide; the coloured decoration was simple but effective. Geometric patterns were painted in contrasting colours on to the body employing such motifs as

buffer in preventing the glaze from running down the pot on to the kiln shelf.

On flat offering dishes, in an attempt to prevent the colours from running together, the design was impressed into the surface, leaving raised lines that acted as miniature walls to keep the colours separate. On these flat dishes the designs tended to be simple, based on foliage, flowers and birds, and were usually painted in three colours: amber, green and blue, often set against a white background. Much of this work recalls the characteristics of Sasanian chased metalwork.

Throughout the period stoneware and high-fired whitewares were made at various sites throughout China, and continual efforts seem to have been made to perfect a light-coloured body. White, the Chinese colour for mourning, was thought desirable at the elaborate ceremonial burials, influencing the search for a white body. A light-coloured body also enabled brighter and more vibrant colours to be achieved. Unlike in the West, where 'porcelain' signifies a white body that is even and translucent, at this time the term was used by the Chinese to describe virtually any ware emitting a clear, ringing note when struck; this did not have to be either white or translucent. For the sake of clarity it is simplest here to refer to white translucent ware as porcelain and other high-fired ware as stoneware. The term proto-porcelain is often used for a porcelain-like stoneware that is not translucent and, though whitish, is not porcelain.

The precise origins of porcelain are not yet known, but its greatest developments were probably made in the south in Jiangxi. Suitable materials were available for its manufacture and it was in this area, at Jingdezhen, that the famous imperial porcelain factory was established in the Yuan period. It was found that firing a mixture of white china clay (kaolin) and china stone (petuntse) to a temperature above 1250°C produced a strong, white translucent body. With the correct proportions of ingredients and a sufficiently high temperature, fusion of the particles with the body takes place, which results in a much glassier matrix than stoneware. This enabled vessels to be made with thin walls without loss of strength, properties that have come to characterize porcelain as we know it today. Although the Tang potters may have known this process, it was not fully developed by them; this was left to potters in the Song and Ming dynasties.

Various types of whiteware were developed in different parts of the country. In the north a fine

whiteware with a transparent glaze was made, and sometimes white slip was applied over the grey body to achieve a white appearance. In Henan fine grey-bodied stoneware pots were produced, finished with dark glazes sometimes splashed with a creamy-grey glaze. Such wares are thought to pre-date the Jun wares of the Song period with their characteristic glaze of a purple-red on a pale blue-green background. Yue ware is a general term covering the greenish-grey glazed wares made at the Yue kilns of Zhejiang province in east China, which were greatly admired for their jade-like appearance. Various sites producing greenwares have been found dating back to AD 250, though the finest wares were made during the Tang period. It was then that the use of a pale green glaze, sometimes opaque, sometimes transparent, was developed. Generically such pots are referred to as greenwares, but the glaze later came to be known as celadon and reached a peak of perfection during the Song dynasty. Some Yue wares were made from light grey clay and covered with a thin creamy-white glaze. Jars often have looped handles, vases have collar rims, and decorative chicken-head spouts often appear on ewers. Decoration consists of incised bands of diaper or star patterns.

During the Tang dynasty the range of pots was extensive and included lidded jars, vases, ewers, offering dishes, rhytons, spittoons and cosmetic boxes. In addition, potters made fine, simple and delicate tomb figures capturing all the grace and movement of the human figure, whether portrayed as a dancer, musician or actor. Horses and camels, too, were created, which combine an element of naturalism with stylization. These were usually made by press-moulding parts of the body and joining them together and then adding modelled detail. Coloured lead glazes were applied with great effect on some of the pieces, further helping to heighten their decorative qualities. Other pieces were decorated with coloured pigments, most of which over time have either worn or fallen off or lost their colour.

Song dynasty (960–1279)

In contrast to that of the preceding Tang period, the art of the Song potters was peaceful, poised, elegant and restrained, resulting in what some twentieth-century studio potters, notably Bernard Leach, regarded as some of the finest ceramics ever made.

Bowl and cover. China, Song dynasty, dated 1162. Stoneware, wheel-made, with carved fluted decoration. Height 12.5 cm (5 in).

With the court re-established in the south, potters were soon producing pots equal to those made by their predecessors in the north, and much of the work attained even greater delicacy as new techniques were deployed. Markets for these high-quality wares were established both across China and overseas. It is difficult to believe today that in those troubled times the arts of peace flourished so successfully. On the whole patronage tended to favour art which drew on established styles, such as that imitating the ever-popular bronze and jade, but this did not preclude the production of much more lively and inventive work that made sensitive use of the qualities of the clay.

Overall form was considered more important than decoration, thus shapes became more complex. Contours were more flowing than those preferred by the Tang potters and a wonderful stillness pervades the best work. Stoneware pots became as highly valued as objects made out of more precious materials and were collected by the court. Following the renewal of interest in Confucian philosophy, imperial patronage tended to encourage traditional qualities, with many potters believing that the imitation of jade was the ideal in a pottery glaze. Contemporary descriptions of glazes, such as 'mutton fat', 'congealed lard', 'rich and unctuous', equally describe the best qualities of jade. A crackle, or fine network of craze lines, on the glaze was greatly admired for its resemblance to jade.

Northern Song wares

For the sake of simplicity, Song pottery can be roughly divided into that produced in the north until 1127 and that subsequently manufactured in the south. Five major wares of fine white porcelain were made – Ding, Ru, Jun, Guan and Ge – and all were to some extent considered imperial. Ding ware, which was a further refinement of the earlier Xing ware, was particularly delicate; it was made from a body containing feldspar, which caused the mixture to vitrify at a relatively lower temperature, making it strong and glass-like, a quality particularly favoured by the Court. Ding ware, undoubtedly one of the greatest of the Song ceramic types, was made at Ding kilns in Jiancicun and in eastern and western Yanhanan in Hebei province in the north. The fine white porcelain has a coolness and simplicity that is technically excellent and visually enchanting. Items were often small and

Vase. China, Song dynasty, 11th–12th century. Porcelain, thrown and modelled, blue celadon glaze. Height 25.6 cm (10.25 in).

Even though some periods of the dynasty were troubled and uncertain, with invaders making frequent attempts to overrun the country, the arts in general developed highly sophisticated forms and the dynasty was enormously active artistically. Court patronage encouraged potters to develop new skills and produce fine and delicate work. Materials were carefully prepared and a wide variety of techniques practised. Highly sophisticated cross-draught kilns were used that allowed high temperatures to be obtained, facilitating the development of a range of rich glaze effects. Continual invasions by the Jin Tartars eventually caused the court to move, in 1127, from the northern capital of Kaifeng in Henan province to the southern capital of Hangzhou.

include bowls, plates, saucers, vases and lidded pots, all thinly coated with a dense ivory-coloured glaze, the ware reaching its peak in the eleventh century. Ding wares feature a variety of glazes, each of which had a different name. Ding itself was glazed brown-black or green, Baiting was brilliant and white, and Fending had the colour of ground rice. Tuding, which had a coarser body and a yellower glaze, was not necessarily made at the Ding kilns but may have been produced in Sichwan or Jiangxi. The ware had a high degree of finish, with foot rims finely turned on the wheel

Northern blackware bowl. China, Song dynasty (960–1279). Stoneware, wheel-thrown with oil-spot glaze. Diameter 9 cm (3.6 in).

adding elegance to the form, and some bowls were fired in the kiln on their rims, which as a consequence had to be left unglazed. The unglazed rim was subsequently covered with a fine metal, which indicates the high esteem in which the work was held. Decoration was delicate and restrained and included designs incised directly into the soft clay, such as foliage patterns interpreted with great freedom. Small moulded decoration was also used, though it lacked the clarity of incised work. Bowls eased after throwing and while still leather-hard into six lobes, known as foliate forms, and decorated with lotus sprays are particularly beautiful.

Jun wares, produced at Linru in Henan province, were a continuation of wares made before the Song period and were still being made long afterwards, but it was during this period that they reached their peak of perfection. Shapes were, for the most part, left plain, with great emphasis placed on rich glaze effects of a thick opalescent lavender-coloured mixture. During the firing the glaze flowed from the rim leaving a thinner layer white, which contrasts with the density of the rest of the glaze and often formed a thick roll of glaze near the base of the pot. Splashes of purple on some wares produced a startling and not altogether subtle effect, but acted as visual points of focus while also adding colour. Technically the work is greatly accomplished. Shapes that imitated the form of bronze objects, such as the rectangular bulb bowls that were covered with startling and rare purple glazes, were greatly admired, though less flamboyant forms such as globular jars and bottles, dishes and vases covered with rich and luminous pale blue glazes were also successful in their celebration of the art of the potter.

Celadon is the western name generally applied to wares with glazes in various shades of soft green obtained from mixtures bearing small amounts of iron, fired in a reduction kiln. The name derives from a character in a seventeenth-century French play who always appeared wearing green clothes. Various sites have been identified, each producing wares with different shades of green that range from a transparent dark olive to an opaque pale blue-green, although the basic firing technique was the same. The main group of celadons, made in the north and known as northern celadon, is characterized by a transparent dark shiny olive-green glaze, often used over finely carved floral designs that were picked out and heightened by the semi-transparent glaze. These pots have a depth of colour and vigour of design that distinguish them from the more refined celadons made for the sole use of the northern court. Conical bowls, spouted ewers, circular boxes and high-shouldered vases were typical northern celadon products.

Some of the finest pale celadons were the Ru ware from Henan province, made from about 1107 to 1127, which was the most highly prized and rarest group of celadons, produced primarily for the use of the court. Known specimens are few and when sold today command a price of many thousands of pounds. The forms are simple and well proportioned, though they tend to lack the vigour of other wares, their great beauty lying principally in the quality of glaze, which, often thickly applied, is smooth, opaque and pale bluish-green. An 1151 list of Ru wares presented to the Emperor includes a pair of wine bottles, a basin, an incense burner, a box, an incense sphere,

Meiping (plum blossom) vase, typically a tall form with wide shoulder and small mouth. Cizhou-type ware, north China, Northern Song dynasty, late 11th to early 12th century. Stoneware, with sgraffiato decoration incised in black and white slip. Height 29 cm (11.6 in).

lively painted designs. The decoration was usually carried out with dark brown or black clay pigment with freely painted designs of flowers and foliage applied in a direct and vigorous manner. The best designs have both the clarity of calligraphy and the spontaneity of a rapid sketch. Sometimes the white slip is scratched to reveal the darker grey or buff-coloured body. Peony designs combined with meanders and diaper patterns were popular. Colourless or cream-coloured glazes are the most common, and on some pieces red and green enamel decoration is used with great effect, as are rich-coloured transparent glazes that are a brilliant apple green, unlike the softer celadon green. Cizhou-type wares were produced for several hundred years, with typical forms including vases, wine jars, brush pots, pillows, bowls and boxes, all of which were produced for general as opposed to exclusively court use.

Southern Song wares

When the invasion of the north caused the Emperor to move to the south and establish a court at Hangzhou, northern potters also moved, taking their techniques with them. However, the southern potters were themselves quick to respond to the new demand for fine wares. Celadon wares were now produced at Longquan county in the southern part of Zhejiang. Characteristic of some ware is the use of a thick, dense, hazy, pale green glaze with a wide-meshed crackle. A light grey clay was used which, on unglazed areas, flashed a red colour during firing; this is often particularly noticeable on the foot ring where it contrasts well with the glaze.

On some of these celadons the decoration consists of dots of iron pigments, which in the firing turn a rich, dark, iridescent brown, contrasting well with the pale green glaze. Longquan celadons constitute the largest and most productive group of wares at this time and were exported to such distant places as Japan, central Asia, Persia, Iran, South-East Asia, Egypt and other parts of Africa. Conical bowls, flat dishes, incense burners, vases and dishes or basins with pairs of fish or dragons in unglazed relief were made. Modelling of dragons and other animals was often carried out on funeral vases. Much of the ware was mass-produced and classified according to quality, with low grades going to export, the better wares being kept for the home market.

four cups, two jars, incense holders and cylindrical censers, indicating the range produced.

By far the largest group of stonewares from different kilns in the north were those collectively known as Cizhou-type wares. These were made from light grey or buff-coloured clay and covered with white slip to give them a bright finish. These sturdy wares possess all the life and vigour that is lacking in some of the highly refined contemporary court wares and were often decorated with

Guan – meaning imperial – ware was produced in or near Jiaotanxia, primarily for the use of the court. The thick bluish-green or grey-green glaze was applied in many layers, giving it great depth and luminosity. A crackled effect was deliberately sought to give the ware the appearance of jade. The qingbai (blue-and-white) wares originated at different sites in Jiangxi, such as Jizhou, Nanfeng and Jingdezhen, and are in many ways the southern counterpart of the Ding wares. Shapes are fine and delicately potted, showing little or no influence of bronze forms, and were fired to a high temperature to achieve translucence. The pale blue or pale green glaze, sometimes called *yingqing* (shadow blue) was fired to a slightly lower temperature than the other wares. The thin fluid glaze tended to run and settle in hollows, enhancing any finely carved decoration.

Porcelain, however, constituted only a small part of the total ceramic output. Most pots were stoneware, the largest group being Jian ware, from Jianyang county in Fujian province in the south-eastern coastal area of China. Made from a dense stoneware body, the Jian wares are most famous for their thickly potted tea bowls covered in a rich, flowing dark brown glaze. Different types of glaze were given appropriate names, especially by the Japanese, who greatly admired the qualities of these wares and used them within the tea ceremony. Thick, lustrous dark brown glazes, which broke lighter brown on the rim or over relief decoration, were given the general name Tianmu (in Japanese pronounced *temmoku*), a glaze much admired and re-created by twentieth-century studio potters. 'Hare's fur' was a term used to describe a streaked glaze, while an 'oil-spot glaze' appeared to have spots of oil on the surface. Wares with dark or even black glazes were also made at a number of other sites including Henan and Jiangxi.

During the short-lived Yuan dynasty (1279–1368) the Mongol rulers involved themselves in and supported the pottery industry largely as a commercial venture. New wares produced at Jingdezhen included *shufu*, which continued the development of fine white porcelains glazed an opaque pale bluish-green colour and often decorated in low relief with motifs such as flowers and phoenix. Shufu wares were so called after the characters *shu* and *fu*, meaning privy council, indicating that they were intended for official use.

Other types of ware include *qingbai,* often made in the form of a *meiping* (plum blossom vase) with decoration confined to banded areas around the pot, and porcelain with underglaze blue- or red-painted decoration.

Ming dynasty (1368–1644)

The breakdown of the Mongol domination of the East brought the return of a new Chinese dynasty and, after an unsettled period, a time of prosperity encouraged a renewed flowering of the arts. The quiet and austere ideals of the Song period gave way to the predominance of colour and ornament. Enormous creative activity within architecture and the visual arts was reflected in the great variety of pots produced, in which the most formal contours were replaced by a looser handling of form. The range of shapes became more diverse and many took on more complex profiles. Wares produced for imperial use were highly finished, with little expense spared in their production. Imperial kilns, for example, were, if necessary, fired half empty and any pots considered imperfect were smashed in order to ensure that no inferior work left the workshop.

A number of major refinements took place in the manufacture of pottery during this period, including the production of a range of pure white porcelain of high standard and greater control of materials, the making process, enamel decoration and firing. The imperial ceramic factory established under government control at Jingdezhen, in the province of Jiangxi, became the main centre of production. Situated on a river that flowed into two major river systems, the 'ceramic city' of Jingdezhen had access to an efficient and cheap method of transport. It was also geographically well placed for the development of the industry; both china clay (kaolin) and china stone (petuntse) were available locally, as was kiln fuel. Various production sites were established in and around Jingdezhen, though not all have yet been identified. Whitewares in porcelain or fine stoneware were manufactured throughout the period; most pieces were decorated, by a variety of techniques that included incision, moulding and etching. *An hua* or 'hidden decoration' was a much admired method whereby the design was lightly carved into the body or painted in white slip. The pot was then covered with transparent glaze and the design

Stemmed bowl. China, Qing dynasty, reign mark and period of the emperor Yongzheng (1723–36). Porcelain with decoration of three copper-red fish reserved on a white ground. Height 15.7 cm (6.3 in).

Two Chinese porcelain vessels with underglaze blue and white decoration. Jar in guan form with decoration of phoenixes, peonies and qilin, Yuan dynasty, c. 1350. Height 48 cm (19.2 in). Lidded meiping vase with dragon decoration, Yuan dynasty, 14th century. Height 38.75 cm (15.5 in).

became apparent only under certain lighting conditions. During the reign of Yongle (1403–25) this decoration reached its peak in such forms as small delicate cups and bowls resembling lotus pods, made for holding in the hand.

It is, however, the classic and much admired blue-and-white ware of this period, achieved by painting a cobalt pigment on to a white glaze, that should claim first attention. Cobalt in various forms had been imported at different times from the Middle East, and with the re-establishment and expansion of trade during the Ming dynasty it was brought in the fourteenth century from Iran, where it had been used much earlier to decorate pots. The cobalt was probably imported in cake form; it was ground into a pigment then combined with a medium of some sort and painted directly on to the leather-hard porcelain body before the glazing and firing. The fresh and pleasing combination of a fine white glazed body and blue decoration had been much admired by the Chinese, who wanted to produce the style for themselves. The imported cobalt was rare and expensive and so added to the prestige value of the ware, but eventually a less pure supply was found from within China. The indigenous Chinese cobalt, an impure ore of cobalt and manganese, yielded a more subtle grey-blue colour rather than a pure blue. Mixed in the proportion of three parts imported ore to two parts Chinese ore, it produced a rich but soft blue, called at various times Sumatran blue or Muhammadan blue.

Blue-and-white wares made effective use of the traditional skills of Chinese calligraphers and artists. Decoration on early blue-and-white ware was outlined in dark blue with thin washes filling in the enclosed spaces. Much use was made of flower and plant designs arranged in geometric divisions of borders and panels. Perhaps the finest of these wares were made in the reign of Xuande (1426–35) early in the fifteenth century, when the designs became more orderly and the style as a whole less cramped. During the sixteenth century the human figure was more freely drawn and often set in landscapes, and Arabic or Persian inscriptions were incorporated into the designs. In

Jiajing's reign (1522–66) the blue became purplish and the designs broadened to include emblems and less formal subjects, for instance children at play.

A further technical refinement was the use of a thin wash of copper on the glaze, which when fired in a reducing atmosphere of the kiln produced various shades of reds. These ranged in tone from salmon pink to a dark pink-purple. The skill of obtaining these copper red colours was developed during the reign of Xuande, but as there was no easy method of controlling this technique to produce intricate designs, only relatively simple patterns were used. The copper gave a rich tomato-red colour that was often employed with great effect on such forms as delicate stem cups in the representation of flowers, fish or fruit.

Painting in coloured enamels (a type of low-temperature glaze applied to the fired glaze and refired in a muffle kiln), popular during the reign of Xuande, was further developed during that of Chenghua (1465–87). The range of colours available was extensive and decoration took a variety of forms. The so-called *doucai* style, meaning 'contrasting colours', employs washes of apple green, red, aubergine and lemon over a lightly drawn design in underglaze blue. Small items such as wine and stem cups are decorated with delicate designs of chickens and fruit. The so-called 'chicken-cups' possess the highly refined qualities associated with the reign and remain unsurpassed in skill or sensitivity.

One of the difficulties of using coloured glazes was keeping the different shades separate, and a particular technique developed at this time involved making a design on the pot separated by raised ribs of clay and applying different coloured glazes to the various areas. This produced richly coloured and decorated pots of jewel-like intensity. The directness of the technique encouraged simple bold patterns, which often seem to favour floral designs in turquoise, yellow, aubergine and dark blue against a dark-coloured background. The 'five-colour' or *wucai* style is a term applied to polychrome wares. Designs were outlined in dull red or black and the colours were thickly applied. The palette included tomato red, turquoise blue, yellow, green, aubergine and black. Yellow, the imperial colour, was developed especially successfully during the reigns of Hongzhi and Zhengde (1488–1521).

Jar, China, Ming dynasty, Wanli mark and period (1573–1620). Porcelain, decorated with two dragons set in an abstract landscape carried out in the wucai (five colour) process.

Towards the end of the sixteenth century the china clay deposits that existed near Jingdezhen were almost exhausted and other sources had to be found, while other fine materials necessary for the production of porcelain were equally difficult to obtain. With the overthrow of the Ming dynasty, production at the factory was severely disrupted, the wares falling in quality and quantity. There

During the two following reigns competent supervisors at the factory re-established and maintained a high standard of manufacture and the quality and finish of pots were carefully sustained. A wide range of brightly coloured monochrome glazes of the finest quality was introduced for use on ceremonial wares. In addition to red glazes, copper oxide was used to make the so-called 'peachbloom'

Ewer and bowl. China, Ming dynasty, 14th century. Porcelain with painted floral design in underglaze red.

were also new influences on the ceramics that arose from the impact of foreign trade, which affected both form and decoration. Some wares made for export were often of a generally inferior quality.

Qing dynasty (1644–1911)

During the Qing dynasty great emphasis was put on technical ingenuity and perfection, with the result that some of the work appears cold and unfeeling, however well it is made. From 1680 the Emperor Kangxi took a personal interest in the arts and sponsored the development of twenty-seven different handicrafts in the palace at Beijing. At Jingdezhen the imperial pottery factory was rebuilt in 1677, working conditions improved and the porcelain body became even more refined.

glaze, which varies in colour from red to peach-pink.

The Dutch East India Company, established in 1602, quickly became engaged in a substantial and thriving export trade with China. Later England, France, Denmark and Sweden were represented at Canton. The Europeans favoured some shapes and designs more than others and eventually the Chinese adapted their production accordingly. This had little noticeable effect on pots made for internal use in China, but around the early part of the eighteenth century such items as salt-cellars, cruets, and tea and coffee cups with saucers were produced for export. European motifs were incorporated into the Chinese designs, which as a result often became crowded and their original meaning either obscured or lost.

Decorated porcelain ware, produced in relatively large quantities during the reign of Kangxi (1662–1772), made use of the traditional Chinese floral designs of prunus, peony, lotus and chrysanthemum in addition to historical scenes. The main style of decoration was that employing related groups of enamel colours such as *famille verte*, in which large areas were painted in a range of different greens. Yellow, red, aubergine and black were also used in this way. Clear, fresh colours offered a wide variety of ornamental possibilities, enabling much of the porcelain to be decorated in the manner of silk-scroll painting with great detail. Designs were usually representations of nature and included flowers, fruit and rocky landscapes. The colours were often painted directly on to the pot, by a technique known as on-biscuit, and covered with glaze to produce a design with a soft and subdued quality, or alternatively they were painted on top of the fired glaze.

The reign of Qianlong (1736–95) heralded the last great period of Chinese ceramic activity. Clay and glaze were successfully used to imitate other materials that include birds' eggs, sand and bamboo as well as bronze and jade. Trade with the West flourished and much of the ware was taken to Canton to be decorated ready for export. Lacework decoration, in which pressed or deeply incised holes were filled with glaze (sometimes known as 'rice-bowls' after the rice-shaped translucent holes), was very popular. Although Jingdezhen remained a major production centre of fine wares, a variety of peasant wares were produced in many other areas, with potters making use of local materials for wares intended primarily for regional markets. In one area low-fired stonewares were developed that could be used directly on the naked flame. In addition to their technical excellence and beauty, the three major groups of ware – 'Swatow', Yixing and Dehua – were highly regarded and influential in the West.

'Swatow' ware, named after the port now called Zhantou, comprises a broad group of wares produced along the southern coastal region. Although made from porcelain stone, the body was not well prepared, giving the ware a rough, unsophisticated quality. Forms include large open dishes often decorated with great verve in green, turquoise, black and red enamel. Much of this ware was exported to Japan, where it was greatly admired, as well as to Europe, where it influenced many of the designs used on porcelain. Boats, mariners' compasses, crabs and crayfish were often incorporated into the decoration, as well as the more conventional floral designs. The wares were intended for everyday rather than special use, and the designs have a freshness and vivacity deriving partly from the rapid method of production.

Yixing and Dehua wares were exported to Europe in large quantities. The unglazed Yixing wares from Jiangsu province constitute the largest group and were made from finely prepared clays that fired a dense red-brown, the body acquiring a slight gloss at high temperature. The pots were either thrown and turned or, more usually, made by pressing thin layers of clay into clay moulds. Teapots in a wide range of shapes were a principal product, some smooth and round, others square or hexagonal in form. Later wares imitated materials such as bamboo or metal. Yixing ware stimulated European potters such as Böttger in Germany and the Elers brothers and Dwight in England in their research into the making of porcelain. These pots, sometimes known as buccaro ware, have a pleasing simplicity of form and colour; they continue to be made in China and are widely exported.

Dehua ware, produced at Dehua in Fujian province, has become known in the West as 'blanc de Chine'. Both technically and aesthetically it is a very different product from Yixing redwares, being a low-temperature porcelain that is highly vitrified and translucent and milky white in colour. Some vessels were produced with elaborate modelling of dragons on the necks of bottles, but the chief products were statuettes of the Buddhist goddess of mercy, Guanyin.

The nineteenth and twentieth centuries

The extensive patronage of the arts that had boosted creativity under Qianlong was not continued by his son, the Emperor Jiaqing (1796–1820). Many of the fine porcelains continued to be produced, but there was a general decline in artistic invention. Jiaqing's successors, too, failed to promote the arts, and although technical quality was maintained, designs became repetitive and often more ornate and intricate.

Teapot. China, Yixing ware, Jiangsu province, *c.* 1700. High-fired red earthenware or stoneware modelled in the form of bamboo. Height 10 cm (4 in).

Meiping vase (literally, plum blossom). China, fahua ware, probably from Shanxi province, 15th century, with decoration of lotus flowers and insects above waves and gadroons round the shoulder, all outlined in raised trails of white slip. Height 41.5 cm (16.6 in).

Korean vessels with openwork stands. Three Kingdom period, Kaya or Silla, 5th–6th century. Height (tallest) 29.8 cm (12 in).

In 1912 the Chinese Republic was established and China was again transformed into an empire, by its president Yuan Shikai. To demonstrate his authority he immediately ordered forty thousand pieces of porcelain to testify to both his own power and the skill of the ceramic industry, but his overthrow shortly afterwards brought the vast production to an end. Much of the finest work made at this time was paper thin, rather like eggshells. It was decorated in a similar way to silk and painted with traditional scenes or flower designs. The result, while technically accomplished, appears lifeless and dull in comparison with earlier wares. In 1921 the Jiangxi Ceramic Bureau was established to oversee production; it remained in operation until 1940 and the factory continues to produce vast quantities of ware. Under the People's Republic, established in 1949, imitation and reproduction has continued to dog ceramic production except in country districts, where some strong traditional wares have continued to be made.

An awareness of the need to increase production and export wares led to the British studio potters Janice Tchalenko and Stephen Coarse spending time in China in the 1980s, seeking to combine the best of traditional production with fresh ideas in the search for international markets.

KOREA

Korea is situated north-east of China, forming a natural link with the southernmost island of Japan. It was therefore inevitable that Korean ceramics would both reflect Chinese culture and be one of the means of conveying Chinese influence to Japan. Yet despite the fact that many Korean wares were closely related to those made in China, potters in Korea developed techniques and styles that became distinctively Korean, reflecting the country's strong indigenous culture. Divided into states or kingdoms from early times, Korea suffered invasion and occupation from China, Manchuria, Mongolia and Japan but remained a unified country from the seventh century to the twentieth. Early Neolithic wares were hand-built earthenware and had a variety of shaped bases including rounded and pointed, to enable them to sit more easily either on the ground or in the fire. 'Comb pattern' ware known as *Chulum* was produced from around 3000 BC to 2000 BC. During the Bronze Age (*c.* 900–300 BC) potters became more accomplished. The potter's wheel was introduced to Korea from Han dynasty China, and this, together with the use of closed kilns, enabled much-improved ceramics to be produced in both earthenware and stoneware. These included cups, spherical jars and steamers as well as a range of pedestalled vessels and bowls mounted, rather elegantly, on hollow stems, which were often split and carved. Most were probably intended to have covers, though few of these survive.

Lidded spouted ewer. Korea, Koryo dynasty, 12th century. Stoneware, in shape of melon with *sanggam* inlay decoration under a celadon glaze. Vegetable- and fruit-shaped celadons are typically Korean, as are the naturalistically modelled details such as the stalk forming the knob on the lid. Height 21 cm (8.4 in).

Silla period (c.50 BC–AD 935)

During the period known as Old Silla high-fired wares with a hard vitrified body were made, many of them decorated with mottled ash glazes. When the kingdom became united under one ruler in the period known as United Silla (AD 668–935), the Buddhist doctrine of cremation was adopted. The many surviving burial urns from this period were made in the form of ovoid covered jars, cylindrical boxes and long-necked bottles often decorated with floral and geometric designs. Stoneware at this time was often glazed an olive-brown colour and some whitewares were produced. During this period green lead-glazed earthenware was also made, probably using lead imported from China.

Koryo dynasty (935–1392)

The most notable ceramics to develop during the Koryo dynasty were refined stonewares with seductive grey-green glazes. It was in this period that Korean potters began to develop their own styles subtly different from those of China. Although the Korean potters were influenced to a large extent by the techniques and styles of the Song dynasty, after a transitional period lasting about 100 years they developed a range of fine pots covered with subtle glazes. Forms include bowls, vases, cups, bottles and sprinklers. Although still stylistically related to the northern celadons of China, the Korean celadon glaze often has a distinctive bluish tint. Decoration is incised, carved or moulded and is often carried out with great vigour. Floral scrolls, boys holding branches and the Buddhist motifs of ducks, water and lotus petals are all used. The official scholar Yi Kyu-bo (1168–1241) captured the quality of celadons in a poem, describing them as having 'the bluish-green lustre of jade. It was clear and bright as crystal, it was hard as rock. With what skill did the potters work – it seemed as if they borrowed the secret from Heaven!' Porcelain similar to the highly refined thin-walled, white-glazed Ting wares of China was also made.

One of the most distinctive methods of decoration at this time was a form of inlay known as *sanggam*, which may have been inspired by bronzes inlaid with gold and silver or lacquer with mother-of-pearl. The technique involved incising patterns into the leather-hard surface of the pots, which were then filled with an inlay material and the surplus wiped off. White inlay was made up principally of crushed quartz, and black of an iron-rich material mixed with glaze. Lace-like in effect, the technique is sometimes fine and delicate, at other times fussy and over-ornate. Other decorative features of Korean celadons are open-work designs and carving, for example lotus flowers in high relief. Korean potters used the technique of painting in iron brown or copper red under the celadon glaze with great skill.

Kilns were usually of the Chinese sloping 'dragon kiln' type, built like tunnels into the side

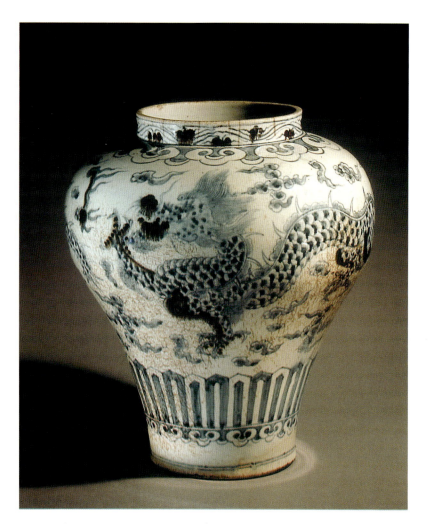

Large storage jar. Korea, Choson dynasty, 18th century. Porcelain, with underglaze cobalt blue and iron brown decoration of dragons and an inscription: 'To be passed down to the sons and grandsons of the Kin family'. Height 35 cm (14 in).

precise. The pottery is regarded principally as household ware, although there is evidence for its use in ritual and aristocratic settings.

White porcelains were the mainstay of ceramic production of the Chosôn dynasty, their manufacture surviving the upheavals of the sixteenth and seventeenth centuries. Imported refined Chinese whitewares inspired Korean potters to make both high-fired plain white ritual vessels and underglaze cobalt blue-decorated wares, and connoisseurs praised the snow-white colour and soft tones of the blue pigment of early wares. Plain white porcelain jars exemplify the seventeenth-century Korean taste for undecorated form. Despite irregular profiles and an often obvious visible seam, they embody aesthetic and contemplative perfection. On decorated vessels, patterns include floral designs painted in underglaze copper and flowing designs of dragons.

The Japanese invasion during the sixteenth century weakened the country, and wares made in the following years are generally of a rougher and less refined quality, though often still possessing great charm. Containers for daily use, such as bean pots, jars, wine flasks and bowls, are decorated with remarkably direct brushwork carried out in iron pigment, giving them a strength and vigour rarely found in the more sophisticated Korean wares. Production was established at the royal kiln at Punwon-ni, where it continued until 1883. Here decorative and functional objects were made, such as wine or tea pots and water droppers. The production of black- and brown-glazed stonewares continued throughout the Koryo and Chosôn dynasties. In the eighteenth and nineteenth centuries black- and brown-glazed wares known as *onggi* jars were produced to store pickles and condiments.

of a hill and fired with wood. They had been used in Korea for high-fired stoneware since the Three Kingdom period (57 BC–AD 668).

Chosôn (Yi) dynasty (1392–1910)

The Chosôn dynasty established their capital at Hanyang – modern-day Seoul – and continued to rule until 1910, when Japan annexed the country. During the five-hundred-year dynasty, Buddhist worship and funerary practices were outlawed in favour of creating an ideal Confucian society. Ceramic production falls broadly into two types of ware: punch'ông, made in the first two centuries of the dynasty, and white porcelain, produced throughout the whole period. Punch'ông can be interpreted as meaning 'green, powder-like dressing on a grey vessel'. Made at over two hundred kilns throughout central and southern Korea, punch'ông wares were a continuation of earlier celadon wares, but their forms, colour and decoration were generally less

The twentieth century

Visitors to Korea following Japan's annexation of the country were greatly impressed by both the richness of the ceramics they saw and the continuing vigour of country wares. The Japanese critic and writer Yanagi Soetsu helped set up a museum of Korean folk art in the 1920s that included ceramics, and when he and Bernard Leach visited the country in 1918 and 1935 they found many traditional country potteries still active. In the late twentieth century Korea's strong ceramic tradition enjoyed a revival after the difficult period of war and division, with many individual or studio potters calling on traditional techniques and forms. Contemporary studio ceramics reflect the rich history of indigenous styles and techniques in vessel-based objects, as well as the international concern with more provocative and ideas-based work.

JAPAN

While the Korean potters developed their own subtle styles closely akin to those of China, the Japanese pots, though still influenced by China and Korea, were much softer and more 'naturalistic' in feel. Whereas Chinese pots suggest precision, even severity, and are often intellectually conceived, and Korean ceramics are renowned for their natural, unsophisticated character, Japanese forms appear gentler and more intimate, reflecting perhaps the influence of the lower temperatures and moister climate of the country.

Trumpet-necked storage jar. Japan, Yayoi period, *c.* 400 BC to *c.* 3rd century AD. Cord-pattern relief moulding at the join of the neck and combed wave patterns on the raised band at the neck illustrate the persistence of Jomon forms into the Yayoi period. Height 44 cm (17.6 in).

Neolithic Japanese pottery, made within the period 10,000–400 BC, was fashioned entirely by hand-built methods and fired to low temperatures in bonfire or pit kilns. Collectively it is known as Jomon ware, a term coined in the nineteenth century, meaning 'cord pattern'. Unlike many other early civilizations, the Jomon people were not farmers but hunter-gatherers, living on abundant plants, nuts, birds and mammals of the forest along with shellfish and fish from the sea. During a further cultural division called the Yayoi period (400 BC–AD 300), Korean and Chinese cultural influences brought about changes in pottery styles, although many pieces retain vestiges of Jomon decoration.

Over the 10,000 years during which it was produced, Jomon pottery went through a number of distinct changes, but characteristic forms are the urns, often built up from thick cords of clay, the surface impressed with rope-like patterns. Open-topped bowls tapering towards the base seem also to have been a popular form. Immigrants from the Chinese mainland brought more sophisticated making and firing techniques and in the late Jomon phase (2000–1000 BC) a greater variety of pots were made, including spouted vessels. Later, shallow bowls and pedestalled vessels were produced. During the Tomb Mound Age (AD *c.* 300–600) near life-size figures were constructed from slabs and coils of clay to mark burial spots; these were greatly simplified to create effective sculptures of commanding power and strength. Animal and human figurines were also made, ranging from simple cruciform anthropomorphic representations to roundly sculpted figures.

Profound changes occurred in Japan between the fourth and seventh centuries AD. Buddhism reached the country around the seventh century and was adopted as the official religion, while at the same time extensive links were established with mainland Korea. In 794 Kyoto became the imperial residence and capital, a position it was to hold more or less continuously until the nineteenth century. Technological developments introduced from Korea included the production of pottery that had what may be described as a 'natural' glaze – that is, one achieved from the firing process rather than consciously applied to the surface of the pot. This came about largely through the introduction from Korea of the *anagama* or cellular kiln around the fifth century AD. This kiln was built over a channel cut into the slope of a hill. With its effective insulation and increased flow of air, it was able to attain temperatures in excess of 1100°C and eventually 1200°C. During what was probably a long, slow firing, hot ash from the wood employed to stoke the kiln settled on the surface of the pot, where it reacted with the clay to form an uneven glaze characterized by streaks down the side of the pot; this effect is known as an ash glaze. The *O-gama* (large kiln) was a version of the simpler *anagama* but bigger in size, and in the early seventeenth century the *nobori-gama* or climbing kiln, comprising a series of chambers rising up a hillside, was introduced. It was immigrant Korean potters who made virtually all the improvements to kiln design.

Even after the introduction of the *anagama* kiln and the potter's wheel, low-fired wares continued to be produced for everyday use. However, the new technology resulted in harder, stronger wares with some natural ash glaze. Such ceramics are known as Sue (offering) ware and have been found among the ritual grave-goods of stone-chambered burial mounds of the early Kofun period (third to seventh centuries). The vessels are thin-walled and the form uniform. Shapes include bottles and dishes, lidded vessels on pedestals

Rounded storage jar, Shigaraki ware. Japan, Muromachi period, 16th century. Stoneware, wheel-thrown with felspathic particles on the surface and within the natural ash glaze. Height 34.5 cm (13.8 in).

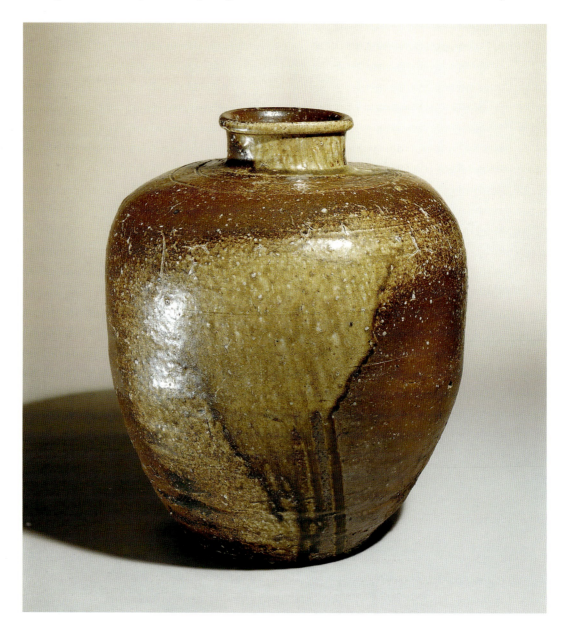

Storage jar. Japan, Tachikui, Tamba, Hyogo Prefecture, 18th century. Stoneware, wheel-thrown, poured or splashed iron glaze with ash deposits. Height 42 cm (16.8 in).

with pierced decoration, and geometric and combed wave patterns.

Elegant globular and long-necked vessels, some with spouts and handles and with moulded decoration, were made in the Sanage mountain area in the eighth and ninth centuries. Towards the end of the Heian period (794–1185) the Sanage potters migrated west to nearby Seto, where deposits of white-firing clay had been discovered in abundance. There is a story that a Japanese potter named Toshiro returned in AD 1227 from a visit to China bringing back more sophisticated stoneware production methods; on finding suitable clay, he established a pottery at Seto in the province of Owari. True or not, during the thirteenth century the Japanese began to make stoneware on a significant scale. At Seto potters experimented with ash glazes proper; that is, by applying a mixture of wood ash and clay or ground stone to the surface of the pot – a technique known in China for 1000 years and Korea for several centuries. Seto remained the only centre in Japan using this technique until the sixteenth century. Potters also began to make ash-glazed quasi-celadons in the Chinese manner. Eventually they developed black, amber and mottled glazes based on the Chinese *temmoku*-type wares to provide tea containers and other utensils for the tea ceremony.

By the thirteenth and fourteenth centuries other pottery centres had been established for the production of unglazed or naturally glazed stonewares. Each had its own characteristics and often the wares were made with the assistance of Korean potters or under their influence. In addition to Seto, major sites included Tokoname, Shigaraki, Tamba, Bizen and Echizen, and there were many other smaller potteries. The industry became more productive at the end of the sixteenth century when Hideyoshi's conquest of Korea prompted the immigration of Korean potters into Japan, bringing with them their skills, techniques and detailed knowledge of potting. Major social changes at that time resulted in the priests and aristocracy being supplanted as patrons by the more numerous groups of feudal lords and wealthy commoners.

A further significant development was the introduction into Japan from Song China of the ritual practice of the *wabi*-style tea ceremony, associated with the Zen sect of Buddhism. *Wabi* is a literary term related to the concept of material deprivation, which in the context of the tea ceremony has come to mean the rejection of luxury and a taste for the simple, the understated and the incomplete. At first conceived as an aid to meditation, the tea ceremony developed as a major aspect of Buddhism, with the tea masters increasingly acting as arbiters of taste in general. As the tea ceremony spread from the Zen Buddhist monasteries to the wealthier classes, demand grew for suitable utensils. Tea masters took a personal interest in the vessels required, often collaborating with the potter, who as a result gained an elevated position in society.

The ceremony required a number of specific ceramic items, each of distinctive form. These included a small jar for the powdered tea, a drinking bowl, a washing bowl, a cake dish and occasionally a water-holder, incense box, incense burner, fire-holder and a vase to hold a single spray of flowers. So highly regarded were the finest tea-ceremony vessels that Samurai would often select a valuable one as a reward for service. Each pottery centre produced characteristic ware. Black Seto largely consists of tea bowls, which, through their simple strong shapes and deep black colour, achieve a powerful, if austere, effect. The Seto black glaze had a lustrous and lacquer-like quality

Hanging flower vase. Japan, Iga ware, from Iga province, Momoyama period, 16th century. Stoneware made in 'natural' form for tea ceremony use. Such vases combine rustic and fashionable effects.

these wares continued to be made long afterwards. Tea utensils including water jars, flower vases and incense containers were produced under the direction of various tea masters, the best known being Furuta Oribe (*c.* AD 1580–1615). Characteristic Oribe ware is covered with a thick opaque glaze containing large amounts of feldspar and decorated with painted designs of houses, flowers and geometric patterns in green and blue. The most remarkable aspect of Oribe wares is their free and inspired decorative imagery, which includes patterns taken from the natural world – flowers, grasses, fruits and landscapes – as well as textile patterns and geometric figures. One group of Oribe wares features areas of rich green glaze.

The pottery produced in Bizen province, known from at least the thirteenth century, is a part of the Sue firing tradition, the earlier pots having grey or red-coloured bodies. Made from fine reddish clay, these pots have little or no ash glaze but show *hidasuki* (scorch marks) resulting from the burning of bundles of straw that were packed between the pots when the kiln was charged. The incidental marking on the surface, together with other irregularities, was greatly prized as a crucial aspect of the pots' aesthetic qualities, suggesting both accident and naturalism, but in recent centuries potters have deliberately contrived the burn marks and irregularities of shape, thereby distorting understanding of the origins of the ware.

The swelling-shouldered, narrow-mouthed jars of Shiga Prefecture, known as Shigaraki ware, are quite different in feel and appearance. Coarse white particles of feldspar can often be seen in the dramatic surface of the ash glaze, producing a distinctive effect. Tokoname wares are characterized by strong, powerful shapes that appear to celebrate the qualities of the clay, the throwing process and the firing technique. Large water jars continue to be produced there.

Kyu-shu, the Japanese island nearest to Korea, was the most receptive to Asian and Korean influence. This was reflected in such wares as jugs, large water jars, lipped pouring vessels, bowls and plates made in fine, dark-coloured clay and covered with a thick buff glaze with a coarse crackle. During the seventeenth century they were decorated in iron-brown pigment designs as well as black and white slip inlays.

which, despite being referred to as Seto ware, was actually made at the nearby Mino kilns in present-day Gifu Prefecture.

The most significant contribution of the Mino kilns, and regarded as some of the finest tea-ceremony wares, are the Shino and Oribe wares. Although the finest examples were produced during the Momoyama and early Edo periods,

Raku

Among the best known of all Japanese tea-ceremony ceramics are the raku wares, which were made originally by a family of Kyoyo potters. Raku is a method of producing a particular type of earthenware pottery by firing it quickly to a comparatively low temperature by placing the dry pot directly into a glowing kiln and removing it while still hot. To withstand such extreme thermal shock special refractory clay bodies are required that will not crack, split or explode during firing or cooling. In Japan the pots were often hand-made from a coarse-grained rough clay that could withstand the dramatic firing process. Forms tend to be slightly irregular and carefully considered for their 'natural' qualities. Glazes are often austere and simple. Raku tea bowls were greatly liked by the tea masters for their rough, natural qualities, as part of the ritual involved quietly studying and appreciating the qualities of the pot.

The late seventeenth century was a period of great sophistication in tea-ceremony wares, when their 'natural' qualities such as studied roughness and asymmetrical effects were much admired, eventually leading to a debasement of the forms. In addition the functional qualities of the pots diminished as the exaggerated aesthetic and sensual qualities became the chief consideration. As a result the bases of pots were often left un-trimmed, while the surface became rough and the glaze thick and treacle-like. Japanese tea-ceremony wares continued to have a great effect on many twentieth-century studio potters, both in Japan and across the world.

Porcelain

Like many other developments in the history of Japanese ceramics, the origins of porcelain are largely attributable to Korean influence. The Korean potter Li Sanpei, better known by his Japanese name of Kanae Sampei, is credited with the discovery of kaolin, white porcelain clay, in Japan when he was brought to the country after a Japanese expedition to Korea. The suitable white clay was found in 1616 at Izumiyama, near Arita in what is today Saga Prefecture on the western island of Kyu-shu. Early wares were heavily potted, mainly in the form of blue-and-white pieces produced for the domestic market. Under early Korean guidance the style matured rapidly and by the mid-seventeenth century the Arita potters were making a more refined and wider range of objects, some enhanced with bold enamel designs in red, yellow, green and blue. Japanese painted decoration tended to change the colours of nature – water was liable to flow red, flowers to bear green blossoms and trees indigo fruit. Porcelain was also produced at Arita for export to Europe, often in typical European forms such as the narrow-necked jug and bulbous or pear-shaped tankards with blue and white decoration.

Imari wares (after the port through which the porcelain was shipped) was the European name given to Japanese wares made at Arita and in the neighbouring villages for export to Europe. They were normally elaborately decorated in a palette that includes underglaze blue, iron red and some-times gilding. Production of the ware was greatly stimulated by the activities of the Dutch East India Company's trading post at nearby Deshima.

Typically Imari ware has rich, ornate enamel patterning over a milky white body. The under-glaze blue porcelain has a soft, restrained quality and the technique of decorating with overglaze enamels was sensitively used, with soft reds, yellows and blues employed in symmetrical designs on blue-and-white porcelain. During the

Tankard with European silver mounts. Japan, Arita export ware, Edo period, late 17th century. Porcelain, painted in underglaze blue. Tankards appear from around 1663. As the shape is purely European, wooden models were probably sent out to Japan to be copied.

eighteenth century exquisite porcelains were produced and a transfer technique was developed to enable the duplication of designs for place settings. Porcelain factories in Britain producing fine wares, such as Derby and Worcester, based many of their designs on Imari patterns.

Another type of Arita porcelain was the Kakiemon ware, this name deriving from a family of potters and enamellers who worked in Arita and who are traditionally credited with introducing overglaze enamelling on porcelain. Dishes and bottles, many of geometrical form, were produced and these were expertly decorated in a palette of iron red, blue, green, yellow and aubergine as well as gold. In comparison with the Imari wares, Kakiemon pieces appear lighter and more delicate.

Ewer. Kakiemon, Japan, *c.* AD 1660. Porcelain, the form inspired by the Middle East. The ovoid body is moulded and painted with iron red and blue and green enamel decoration, with two panels showing sprays of peonies within shaped cartouches reserved on foliate scrolls. Height 30 cm (12 in).

Kakiemon porcelain, after it began to be exported to Europe at the end of the seventeenth century, was copied by such major porcelain factories as Meissen, Saint Cloud and Chelsea.

Nabeshima porcelain, produced at Okawachi, north of Arita, was destined for the use of the ruling shogun and feudal lords. The range of production includes bottles, vases and dishes meticulously decorated with motifs of seasonal flowers or wintry trees. The designs are sometimes outlined in underglaze blue.

Fine porcelain was also made at Kutani in central Honshu in the nineteenth century, often featuring enamel designs painted in yellow, purple, blue and deep red. Patterns included birds and plants, figures in a landscape and patterns derived from textiles.

In the late seventeenth century the capital city of Kyoto expanded rapidly and the so-called Kyoto wares became important, especially the production of earthenware. The potter Nonomura Ninsei is particularly associated with Kyoto. He developed painted enamel decoration on simple forms and influenced, among others, the great decorator Kenzan Ogata (1663–1743). Trained originally as a calligrapher, Kenzan developed an economical, near-abstract style of spontaneous and powerful brushwork, with soft browns, blacks and blues his preferred colours. Other notable individual potters, Mokubei and Dohachi, followed him. In the twentieth century, influenced by the ideas of Bernard Leach and the Japanese arts and crafts movement, Japanese potters such as Hamada Shoji, Tomimoti Kenkichi and Kawai Kanjiro, while acknowledging the history of Japanese ceramics, added a modern sensibility (see chapter 13). In the mid-1930s they travelled round the islands visiting the many country potteries then still in operation, and were impressed by the technical quality of the work and the unselfconscious aesthetic understanding of the potters.

The long tradition of local potteries and great master-potters continues today, as does the feeling for the use of 'natural' qualities of the clay in the pots. Studied 'accidental' decoration on asymmetrical forms was often highly valued. Japanese pottery, though owing much to Chinese and Korean influence, developed a controlled freedom that is completely indigenous to Japan, and even today Japanese ceramics continue to exert a strong influence on studio potters in many different parts of the world.

SOUTH-EAST ASIA

Much research is being carried out into ceramics produced in countries including Thailand, Vietnam and Cambodia. The earliest known ceramics come from the excavations of prehistoric sites, the most famous of which is at Ban Chiang in the north-east of Thailand. Shapes found include rounded bowls mounted on a pedestal and footed beakers with engraved patterns, which date to the second to first millennia.

During the Medieval period glazed stonewares were produced, the technologies of glazing and firing owing much to processes used in China, though the shapes and designs were of local inspiration and developed their own distinctive style. Some of the most important groups of ceramics are those made at Sawankhalok and Si Satchanalai, both associated with the Thai capital at Sukhothai. Such ware is generally made from relatively coarse-grained high-fired clay, often covered with soft grey-green celadons. Shapes included boxes, bowls and jars of various shapes as well as roof tiles and antefixes, figurines and miniature animals. The vessels, which included green-glazed celadons and painted wares, were widely exported to other parts of South-East Asia via ports on the Gulf of Thailand. After the abandonment of Sawankhalok around 1450, similar wares continued to be made at other kiln sites.

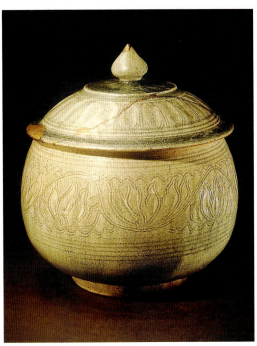

Covered jar. Si Satchanalai, northern central Thailand, 14th–16th century. Stoneware with incised decoration and green glaze. Height 24.5 cm (9.75 in).

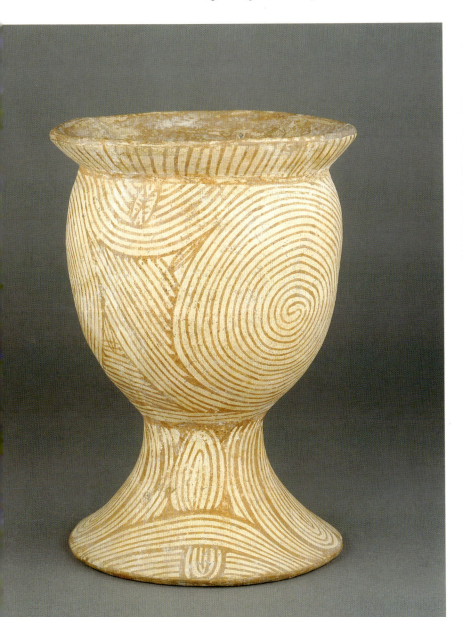

Jar with red-fired decoration. Ban Chang, northern Thailand, second to first millennium BC. Height 25.4 cm (10.2 in).

The Islamic World

That which has been evenly fired
reflects like red gold and shines
like the light of the sun

ABU'L QASIM

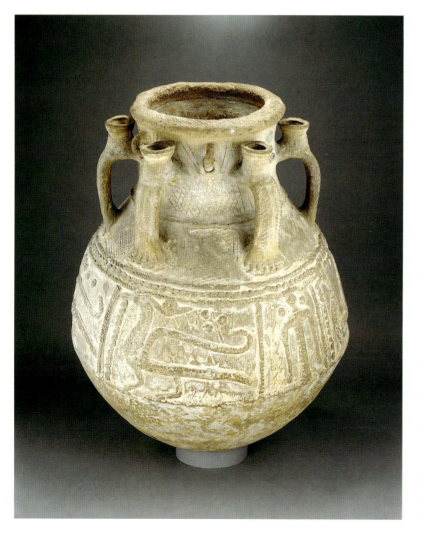

The advent of Islam in the seventh century and the subsequent Arab conquests led to the formation of a huge empire that extended from the borders of India in the east, through Iran, Mesopotamia and north Africa into Spain. In 622 the inhabitants of Medina, a prosperous trading city, welcomed the Arab prophet Muhammad (570–632), born in western Arabia, who came to be seen as a successor to Abraham and Jesus. His religious teachings – that there is no God but Allah and Muhammad is his Prophet – quickly built up a strong following and in due course the new faith spread throughout the empire, providing the framework within which a cohesive religious, political and social culture became established.

Muslims believe that the revelation of God is twofold, coming first from the writings of the Prophet, known as the Qur'an (or Koran), the Holy Book of Islam, and secondly from the relation of the manner of life of the Prophet. Traditionally accounts of what the Prophet said or did were passed on by word of mouth, but by the ninth century a complete record of them had been made, known as the Hadith or Traditions of the Prophet. Muhammad declared that the Qur'an, written in Arabic, was the word of God, and because he forbade its use in translation it came to be read in a single language throughout Islam, which had the effect of unifying diverse peoples.

Tile frieze from Kashan, Iran, late 13th century. Muslims believe that God revealed the verses of the Qur'an to the Prophet Muhammad at Mecca and Medina in the early years of the 7th century. On this tile is the beginning of the Arabic phrase 'In the name of God, the Merciful, the Compassionate', which begins all but one sura (chapter) of the Qur'an and is spoken by devout Muslims before the start of any action. Here it is moulded in Kufic, a style of squared script, and decorated with lustre overglaze. Height 55 cm (22 in).

Water cistern, habb, from Mesopotamia, 8th century or earlier. Earthenware, with relief decoration. Containers similar to these were made in the area for many hundreds of years. Height c. 94 cm (37.6 in).

The establishment of ordered government that covered such a vast geographical area, coupled with the growth of towns and industries, favoured the development of extensive trade both internally and internationally. The exchange of goods with China by both land and sea brought potters into contact with Chinese ceramics, which had a significant influence on Islamic pottery over three successive periods. The whitewares of the Tang dynasty (618–906) inspired Islamic potters in Iran and Egypt in the ninth century to create a stone-paste body that would emulate the whiteness and translucency of the Chinese material. In the eleventh and twelfth centuries the fine Song porcelains were a second influence, and finally the blue-and-white wares of Ming China stimulated yet another wave of change and development. Lacking the technical experience or suitable raw materials to create true porcelain, Islamic potters skilfully adapted the Chinese work to their own taste, materials and knowledge.

The Islamic faith not only directed the way of life of its followers, it also shaped the art that embodied Islamic teaching. Largely brought about by strictures against figural representation within Islam, in the field of pottery there was a fashion for geometric designs and arabesque patterns, typically consisting of a continuous stem with split palmette leaves or variations of this motif. However, it is a common mistake to assume that there are few representations of the human figure or of living creatures within Islamic art; many such depictions were made on the walls of palaces and even more modest homes, and also on ceramics. Just as images of national leaders are displayed throughout the Islamic world in both public and private buildings today, so they were in art of the past. In religious settings, however, such imagery was discouraged on the basis that man should not to attempt to usurp God's role as the creator of living things.

The creation of illuminations and lettering for copies of the Qur'an and the decoration of religious buildings constituted major sources of employment for artists in the Islamic world. For this reason non-figurative representation was inevitably developed at the expense of figurative work, with geometric and floral designs flourishing to a much greater extent than in the more icon-oriented Christian world.

The technique of lustre painting, a process that had originally been developed on glass, was adapted in Iraq in the ninth century for use on previously fired glazed pottery, probably because it could successfully imitate the appearance of precious metals like gold and silver. Much attention was given to the manufacture of such fine decorated pottery and there is at least one record of verses being dedicated to the beautiful ceramic bowls adorning the table of a wealthy man. The prohibition of wine meant the absence of wine jars, whereas in Greece, for example, many types of such containers had fuelled export trade throughout the Mediterranean area. In their place water containers were made, often with long tapering spouts. In the thirteenth century the production of lustre-decorated tiles to enhance mosques became widespread. Many bore wording in the Arabic language, in either the more angular Kufic or the cursive Arabic letters, but gradually such inscriptions evolved into mere patterns. Over time the colour range was extended and decoration in which coloured oxides were painted directly on to the pot or on to the unfired glaze was developed.

The Islamic potters had neither the technical knowledge nor suitable materials to fire to high temperatures. In an attempt to imitate the whiteness and brilliance of Chinese porcelain at the lower earthenware temperatures to which all their ceramics therefore had to be fired, the Abbasid potters carried out innovative experiments that resulted in the development of a white opacified glaze on to which coloured decoration could be painted. The use of this opacified glaze eventually spread across Europe – into Italy (where it became known as maiolica), Spain (where it formed the basis of the so-called Hispano-Moresque wares), and to the rest of western Europe. The technique of applying lead glaze over coloured slips also passed into Europe through Byzantium and Italy.

Although Islamic pottery is now admired mainly for its variety of decorative styles, the range of vessels produced was extensive, encompassing well-designed functional objects such as water containers, water pots with long tapering spouts for ablution rituals, cups, beakers, braziers and spittoons as well as the richly decorated bowls that tend to receive most attention today.

Islamic art is an amalgam of many powerful cultures including the Byzantine, Persian and Chinese, but no matter how strong the foreign influence, the Islamic potters were adept at adapting the forms and designs they encountered for their own purposes. The two great characteristics of Islamic pottery are its practical forms and its inventive and assured decoration, which reflects and celebrates its diverse cultural and religious influences.

EARLY ISLAMIC WARES, 632–*c*.1150

Muhammad's successors, the first caliphs or rulers of Islam, were preoccupied with military expansion. By 710 the Islamic empire stretched from Spain to central Asia, absorbing the lands of the Roman empire in the west and the Sasanian empire in the east. Pottery, like all the arts, developed slowly within the expansion of Islam, and objects produced for the Umayyads (661–750), who established their caliphate in Damascus in 661, are often indistinguishable from those made for their predecessors. Some types of glazed pottery, such as Egyptian lamps with relief decoration, perpetuated a form that had originated in the Roman period and continued under the Byzantines, while to the east Iranian potters went on making turquoise-glazed storage jars from the Sasanian into the Islamic period.

In 750 the Umayyads were overthrown by the Persian house of the Abbasids (750–1258), who established Baghdad on the Tigris as their capital, moving the centre of artistic influence from Syria, with its strongly Western background, to Mesopotamia. At Baghdad a beautiful and exotic city was built that rivalled Constantinople, the capital of the Byzantine empire, in both splendour and

Two bowls. Iraq, 9th century. Earthenware, with white glaze.
ABOVE: Bowl with star motif painted in blue with splashes of green.
RIGHT: Bowl painted in blue with a design of half-palmettes. Diameter (both) *c*. 20 cm (8 in).

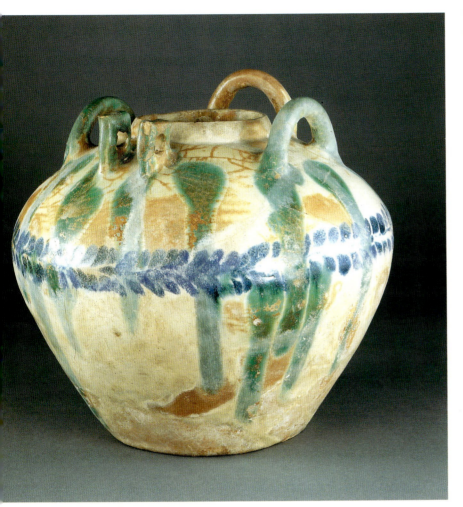

Large jar. Iraq, 9th century. Earthenware, the shape based on Chinese Tang export ware, painted with blue garland and green drips on a white glaze. Height 26 cm (10.4 in).

but powerless. The transfer of power to the east opened Islamic art to the artistic traditions of Sasanian Iran and it was during this period that the major distinctive features of Islamic art became established, such as the use of calligraphic script, arabesque lustre decoration, and an enduring admiration for and imitation of Chinese pottery.

In addition to the large group of unglazed wares that were made across the region a wide range of glazed pottery was produced, which can be divided into three major types – lead-glazed ware imitating Chinese Tang splashed ware, white tin-glazed ware with painted decoration, and lustreware. Unglazed water pots had been produced in buff clay for centuries throughout the whole area of the Near East and even today these continue to be made. Much of their success lies in the slightly porous quality of the unglazed clay, through which water seeps, causing loss of heat as it evaporates and thus helping to keep the water inside the vessel cool and fresh. Such pots were often made up in quite complex forms and decorated with applied, stamped and incised ornament.

Lead-glazed splashed wares

Tang polychrome splashed wares from China were imported in the ninth century and at first Islamic potters were sufficiently impressed by them to produce almost exact copies. Red clay was used for the body, which was then covered with a white slip over which a transparent lead glaze was poured. On to this various colouring oxides were splashed. The fluidity of the glaze caused the iron-yellow and brown colours to run down the pot, yielding an attractive mottled effect.

Later, copper green, manganese purple, aubergine and black were introduced to extend the colour range and Islamic potters began to improvise their own methods of decoration. Patterns were scratched through the white slip to the underlying clay body before the glaze was applied, using the technique known as sgraffito. These scratched patterns tend to be traditional in design, often taking the form of palmettes and rosettes, with added areas or splashes of colour that may bear little relationship to the patterns beneath. Although at first glance the appearance of such wares resembles that of Chinese pots, inspection of the clay body makes clear the distinction between them.

commercial success. Architects planned the circular city and constructed its palaces and mosques, poets extolled its luxury, and arts and scholarship were pursued in the expanding and prosperous environment. At this time the majority of pots were destined for the use of the local inhabitants and so were produced in and around the new capital. New techniques of ceramic glazing and decoration were developed which included blue-and-white and splash wares, inspired by Chinese pots, as well as lustrewares, a purely Islamic invention.

In Iran a succession of local dynasties sprang up which, from their capital at Damascus (now in Syria), were engaged principally in physical and spiritual conquest, largely outside Abbasid control. The most important of these dynasties were the Samanids (819–1005) and the Ghaznavids (977–1186) in eastern Iran and Afghanistan, and the Buyids or Buwayhids (977–1062), who invaded Iraq in 945, leaving the Abbasid caliphate in place

Coloured lead glazes were also applied over vessels decorated with patterns moulded in relief, rich green and yellow runny lead glazes having already been in limited use during the Roman occupation of Egypt. Green, brown and purple coloured glazes were applied over relief decoration influenced by the Graeco-Roman naturalistic style.

White tin-glazed wares

Greatly impressed by the highly refined white-wares imported from China, Islamic potters sought to reproduce such pots themselves. A clear lead glaze applied over a white slip created a superficial similarity but failed to achieve the brilliance and beauty of the Chinese wares, so the potters adapted a technique employed by the Egyptians: that of adding tin oxide to the clear glaze. Discovery of the opacifying effect of tin oxide on a clear glaze had been made some thousand years earlier by the Babylonians, who had used it with great success on bricks and tiles but not, as far as is known, on pots. The technique was now rediscovered in Mesopotamia. The opacified white glaze proved smooth and reliable; it was relatively simple to apply and did not need to go over a white slip. The suspended particles of tin rendered the glaze opaque and snowy white, and at the same time it became more stable than a transparent lead glaze over white slip, moving or flowing very little in the kiln. When applied to a well-purified yellow or pinkish clay, the glaze achieved a whiteness comparable to that of the white Tang wares.

It is unlikely that the potters developing the process realized what far-reaching effects the use of tin glaze was to have. Not only was the white surface quite easy to achieve but it was functional too, proving an excellent base for painted decoration. Islamic potters were quick to respond to the possibilities presented by the pure white surface, and although some were content to leave dishes and bowls plain, others almost immediately set about decorating the unfired glaze with painted designs. Colouring pigments such as copper green, manganese purple and sometimes antimony yellow were applied to the unfired surface of the glaze, but the most popular was cobalt blue, of which deposits of suitable ore were readily available.

Cobalt is one of the most reliable of the ceramic pigments, giving shades of blue when used on or in a glaze. Later, cobalt ore was exported to China, where it encouraged the blue-and-white porcelain of the Ming period. Early Islamic dishes decorated with cobalt blue have simple, often naive designs and can be recognized by the soft, blurred quality of the decoration, caused by the fact that the pigment, when applied to the raw tin glaze, was inclined to spread and lose definition. Local varieties of this ware were made in Egypt and Syria, but these lack the blue colour and instead are painted in green and purple or black on a coarser 'candle-grease' glaze. In the Samarkand area green alone was used for the dominant half-palmette.

Lustrewares

Although the origins of lustre, a technique in which fired pots are decorated with a lustrous metallic coating, have not been fully resolved, it is thought to have evolved in Egypt for use on glass around 700–800 and eventually been brought by craft workers to Mesopotamia. To achieve the effect of metallic lustre, potters required detailed knowledge of the materials and great skill in firing the kilns. Too much heat and the lustre burnt away, too little and it remained matt and did not shine. The discovery of lustre, which came into widespread use towards the end of the ninth century, may have been prompted by the famous gold dishes fashioned by Sasanian goldsmiths.

Lustre is one of the few techniques used in Islamic pottery that can be said to be entirely indigenous to the Near East rather than to China. Briefly, the process involves the preparation of a special pigment made by mixing the sulphates of gold, silver or copper with red or yellow ochre to serve as a carrying medium. This pigment is then painted on to the fired glaze and the pot fired a third time in a smoky (reducing) atmosphere to a low temperature. During this firing the metal oxide is reduced to metal and suspends itself on the glaze to form a dull metallic film. Burnishing removes the ochre, revealing the lustre in all its brilliance. Unfortunately, lustre rarely retains its brilliance and over the years often changes colour. At its best, however, as described by the fourteenth-century chronicler Abu'I Qasim, it 'reflects like red gold and shines like the light of the sun'.

Bowl from Nishapur, Iran, 10th–11th century. Earthenware, with painted decoration in black and red slip depicting a long-necked ewer and foliage motifs under a colourless glaze. Diameter 27 cm (10.8 in).

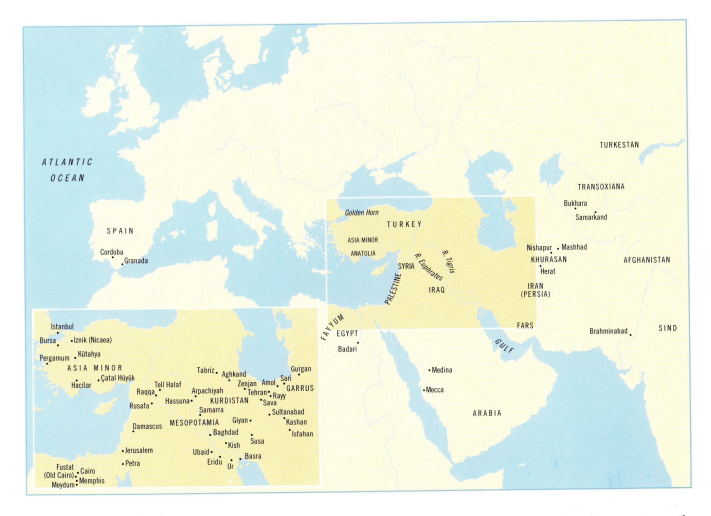

Map showing major pottery centres across the Islamic world, *c.* AD 1000.

In Mesopotamia during the Samarra period (836–92), a uniform coat of lustrous pigment was successfully applied to lead-glazed pottery. The same workshops, probably located in or near Baghdad, that produced pieces with lustre decoration also made the blue, green and purple-painted wares. Early lustrework included many shades of brown and yellow and was often used in combination with other types of colouring pigment. On some pots plain gold lustre was used on a white tin glaze, on others ruby lustre was painted on the white background either alone or together with other colours. Gold and silver lustrework was also produced. When the lustre was very thinly applied it appeared as yellow-brown or olive. Because the technique was so complex, some centres, for example Nishapur in Persia, failed to produce lustreware successfully and turned instead to other decorating techniques such as underglaze painting, sometimes devising designs that imitated lustre. Lustre decoration consists mainly of floral and geometric motifs, with the human figure shown only occasionally.

Because of the skill required, lustrewares were produced at a limited number of centres, such as Basra in Iraq, Kashan in Iran and Raqqa in Syria. Pots were made for local markets, but because the centres were situated on trade routes there was good access to other regions of the Islamic world. In the tenth century Iraqi lustrewares were exported to Iran, Egypt, North Africa and Spain. As the Abbasid caliphate declined in power in the tenth century, a new centre of lustreware production developed in Cairo under the Fatimid dynasty (969–1171). Although the lustreware potters of Cairo were rarely adventurous with the ceramic shapes, their painted designs and depictions of human and animal figures are among the finest to be found in Islamic ceramics.

Lustreware produced at Raqqa in Mesopotamia was similar to that made earlier in Egypt. In Persia, however, following the style used in the contemporary production of finely decorated or *minai* wares, the designs on lustrewares became generally smaller and more complex. Figures were often set in formal foliage designs, sometimes on horseback; animals and birds were common and, later, panels were used to separate the designs.

Lustrewares made at Kashan, the main centre of production in Persia, are particularly distinctive, principally because of the density of their decorative detail, most of which was scratched through the painted lustre before it was fired, and the delicacy of their execution. The spread of the Mongol empire, which at one time linked China, Russia, India and Persia, brought with it much Chinese influence. This is evident in the dress and ornament subsequently depicted on pots and the adoption of flower designs such as the lotus. Kashan was one of the few cities to survive the Mogul invasion, although one report suggests that the craftworkers were spared so that they could continue working. Production of lustreware continued well into the fourteenth century. Designs included faces with long eyes and flowing patterned backgrounds often incorporating flying cranes. In addition to pots, lustre-decorated wall tiles were also made in Kashan. These were often used to decorate *mihrabs* (prayer niches) in

mosques as well as the interiors and exteriors of buildings.

THE SAMARKAND REGION AND PERSIA

In 820 Tahir ibn-al-Husayn was appointed governor of the lands of Baghdad, eastern Persia and the territory beyond the River Oxus, which were largely independent of the central government in Baghdad. The most distinguished dynasty was that of the Persian Samaniids (875–999), who had Bukhara as their capital and Samarkand as their chief city. Trade routes to the East passing through Samarkand introduced diverse influences that had a broadening effect on the pottery produced in the province, encouraging experiment and innovation. The court sponsored a revival of literature in the Persian rather than the Arabic language, and there arose a vigorous school of potters who devised wares quite distinctive in quality and appearance from those made elsewhere. Painted pottery produced in eastern Persia, sometimes known as Samarkand ware and probably potted at such centres as Samarkand, Nishapur and Sari, demonstrated a unique quality long before pottery of any great interest was made in other regions.

The ninth and tenth centuries saw what, in many ways, was one of the highest and purest interpretations of Islamic ideas in pottery. While unglazed vessels continued to emulate long-established traditional ware, significant developments took place in the production of glazed and decorated pottery. Potters in Samarkand made the discovery that painted decoration, usually so apt to run and lose definition under the fluid lead glaze, remained much more stable when the metallic colouring pigment was combined with a paste of fine slip. To provide a ground for painting, finely potted wares in red or pink clay were usually covered with a coating of white slip. In addition to white, a vivid tomato red and a purplish black were employed. The clay content made the pigments stiffer and so more difficult to apply, which encouraged the use of simple formal designs rather than intricate patterns.

Decoration was carried out on the white or coloured slip with black or purplish brown as well as dark brown, dark red and aubergine underglaze pigments. Confident of the quality and attractiveness of the surface, potters left large areas of the

Bowl from Iraq, Abbasid dynasty, 9th century. Earthenware with opaque white glaze. Painted with polychrome lustre decoration of 'peacock's eye' design, thought to derive from millefiori glass, with stylized Kufic inscription. Diameter 18.3 cm (7.3 in).

bowls white, thus giving them their most striking characteristic. This contrasts sharply with the decorative techniques developed later in Persia, whereby most of the surface was patterned. Using the skills of the calligrapher, quite complex bands of designs in Kufic script were painted on to the pots, often around the rim of bowls. Such phrases as 'Generosity is [one] of the qualities of the blessed', 'Peace and blessing', 'Good fortune', 'Blessing' or 'Good fortune and perpetuity' appear. Stylized patterns were developed from the Kufic script, decorative dots were added and occasionally animals and birds in abstract form are seen in the patterns. Human figures never appear on Samarkand work, and recognizable animals or birds seldom. The startling and dramatic brilliance of the colours remains one of the ware's most admirable features.

In the absence of precise archaeological evidence, attribution to specific centres remains a problem, although notable differences between potteries can be observed. The so-called Sari wares are thought to have been made at a pottery centre south of the Caspian Sea that produced decorative wares by the standard method but introduced a wider range of colours, adding a particularly beautiful green to the palette. Lively designs include birds moving across bowls, while radiating stalks and flowers are typical of this ware. The pigments used have retained their brightness over the centuries and the seemingly modern conception of the designs gives these bowls an enduringly fresh feel. In the area of Nishapur, buff or grey clay was used for the body and the designs were painted with thick slip colours of brown-black, green, carnelian red and a bright mustard yellow.

Throughout Byzantium, eastern Anatolia and Cyprus, as well as along the Syrian coast, a tradition of producing lead-glazed, sgraffito-decorated pottery existed for several centuries. The earthenware body with a covering of white slip was decorated with incised designs and smudgily painted with colour, most often amber or green, on the lead glaze. Pottery of this kind had a wide distribution, extending from Constantinople as far as Antioch, and was no doubt produced at numerous centres.

Bowl from Egypt, Fustat (Old Cairo), 9th century. Earthenware, decorated with palmettes painted in lustre on white ground. Diameter *c.* 30 cm (12 in).

Mesopotamian potters had used the technique on their lead-glazed bowls under splashed colour decoration, but in the tenth century it was further refined by Persian potters. In the Garrus district, lying south-east of the Caspian Sea, the so-called 'champlevé' or carved style was developed, characterized by designs cut rather than scratched into the white slip. The successful combination of slip and body was covered sometimes with a clear transparent glaze, sometimes with one tinted green. Fine lines scratched through the slip in simple geometric designs produced an effect very like that of chased metalwork. In the Amol and Aghkand district, green, brown and purple colouring oxides were painted on to the carved slip in designs that incorporated animals and birds. The technique was brought to perfection around the late twelfth and thirteenth centuries.

EGYPT AND SYRIA, 950–1250

The Fatimids (909–1171) first gained power in North Africa, but in 969 they entered Egypt and founded a new capital, Cairo, to the north of the original Muslim capital of Fustat. From Egypt the Fatimids extended eastwards into Syria and the Hijaz, taking control of the holy places of Islam. It was a prosperous period, during which trade was undertaken with India and the Christian Mediterranean and access gained to the gold mines of Africa. Fatimid court artists produced a wide range of fine objects including magnificent textiles, finely carved ivories, and gold and silver vessels as well as delicately lustred pottery ones. Although failing to surpass the potters of Mesopotamia in terms of the shape of the pots, they produced technically excellent and beautiful lustreware with colours ranging from rich, deep copper red to pale lemon yellow. The designs combined diverse elements: a degree of naturalism, the order and formality of oriental patterning, and some Christian influence. Fantastic birds, animals and human figures are depicted, as are priests and incense-burners. Nasiri-Khusrau, who visited Egypt from 1046 to 1050, wrote: 'At Misr [the Arabic name for Egypt] pottery of all kinds is made … They make colours for them like those of the stuff called bugalimun. The colours change according to the ways in which the vessel is held.' This reference to bugalimun, a shot silk, conveys exactly the changing reflective colour of lustreware.

Bowl from Iraq, 9th century. Earthenware with tin glaze decorated with painted lustre design. Diameter *c.* 19 cm (7.5 in).

The decline of the Fatimid dynasty in the twelfth century and the destruction of the Cairo potters' quarter in 1169 coincided with the appearance of lustrewares in Syria at Raqqa and in Iran at Kashan. The earliest Syrian and Iranian lustrewares display a reliance on the pictorial conventions of Fatimid wares, suggesting that Egyptian lustreware potters may have emigrated to those countries.

The Zengids (1127–1223) were among the most important of a number of small dynasties ruling in the Jazira and northern Syria after the Seljuk Turks ousted the Fatimids from the area. They were based at Mosulk, a prosperous city that had strong trade links with Iran and the Far East. The Ayyubids (1169–1260) began in the service of the Zengids, but in 1171 Salah al-Din (Saladin) conquered the Fatimids and re-established Sunni Islam in Egypt. The skills of the craftsmen attracted the patronage of the courts of Cairo and Damascus, ensuring the spread of the new styles and techniques throughout the Ayyubid kingdom. Ceramic production was established in potteries along the Euphrates in northern Syria, particularly at Raqqa, where, as in Iran, potters were using a new frit body to produce finely potted wares with underglaze and lustre decoration.

IRAN, 1100–1250

In 1083 the invasion of the Seljuk Turks from Central Asia marked the beginning of a long period of Turkish rule in Iran. The twelfth century was one of the most innovative periods of Islamic art, but it was also one during which Seljuk power declined and the empire was divided. The Khwarazm Shads dominated western Iran while the Ghurids ruled in the eastern part of the country. Potters based in Kashan developed a new ceramic body that fired hard and white and was glazed in monochrome blue, turquoise, black or white. This was used to great effect as tile mosaic in a number of buildings at Konya and elsewhere in Seljuk territory. The potters also introduced lustreware to Iran, improving the quality of underglaze painting and devising a method of painting over the glaze known as the *minai* technique.

Fine white porcelain wares were imported from Song China around the end of the tenth and beginning of the eleventh century, and writers in the first half of the eleventh century refer with

admiration to the translucency and refinement of the Chinese wares, with their thin walls, white porcelain body and ivory-white or bluish-white glaze. These wares stimulated Islamic potters to experiment with the production of a similarly strong white body, which they did by using a combination of ground glass, quartz and white clay that became hard, vitrified and bright at earthenware temperature and is known as stone paste or frit ware. A similar mixture had been used much earlier by the Mesopotamians and Egyptians for the production of a hard white paste covered with a transparent alkaline glaze, although whether or not there is any direct connection between this and the fritware body is uncertain. Whereas potters of the Early Period had imitated only the surface colour and to some extent the shape of the Chinese wares, Islamic potters in Egypt, Syria and Iran were more ambitious.

Fritware

The new ceramic body that came into use in the eleventh century is akin to the soft paste porcelain of eighteenth-century Europe, being a combination of white-firing clay and a flux that induces a glassy body. It is described in the fourteenth-century treatise of Abu'l Quasim as consisting of ten parts ground quartz, one part ground glass and one part fine white clay. At earthenware temperatures this produced a harder, thinner fabric than the reddish or buff earthenware bodies of earlier Egyptian and Iranian pottery. The thinness and whiteness of the fritware body may have been the original source of its appeal, since these were qualities much admired in Chinese ceramics. The white paste was exceedingly hard, compact and fine, and when potted thinly enough the walls of the vessel became translucent after firing.

One disadvantage of the fritware body was that its low clay content reduced its plasticity and made it difficult to throw on the wheel, although medieval potters nevertheless succeeded in doing this. On the other hand, the body was well suited to the production of moulded forms as well as being compatible with the alkaline glaze. This contributed to the greatly expanded range of colours and shapes of Iranian ceramics from the eleventh century. The body also had the advantage of eliminating the need for an opacified white glaze as the transparent clear glaze gave the desired white ground. However, the coarser body used for ceramic tiles continued to require an opaque white glaze as a ground for lustre painting.

Many of the fritware bowls were left quite plain, with lobes and nicks in their rims similar to those of Chinese wares. Sometimes Chinese cloud-scroll ornament appears on the interior of bowls, faintly incised under the glaze like the hua or 'secret decoration'. Further translucent effects were achieved by patterning the walls of the vessel with pinholes that were subsequently filled in by the colourless glaze, giving an effect of great delicacy. Many of these bowls were decorated with carved designs picked out by the transparent fluid glaze.

When mixed with water, the powdered quartz and alkaline frit served as an excellent glaze that fused well with the body. The glazes could be coloured by the addition of metal oxides including copper turquoise, cobalt blue and manganese purple, which, in the alkaline-based glaze, produced rich, deep shades.

Whitewares dating from the middle of the twelfth century are rare because of the difficulties at that time in making and handling the clay body, but as skills slowly improved greater quantities were successfully produced. The refined nature of such pots made in the thirteenth century can hardly be over-praised and their delicate quality has rarely been matched. Later, a range of faceted bowls were made by pressing the white clay into moulds in forms closely based on contemporary metalwork. Although the definition of the moulded ornament seldom has the precision of carved decoration, the use of the richly coloured glazes makes these bowls very attractive.

Decoration on the Seljuk wares was often carved in bands round the bowls or, on faceted bowls, in panels. Subject matter was dealt with in a rhythmic style and calligraphic inscriptions were often interwoven with foliage. Kashan, 125 miles south of Teheran, was one of the most renowned production centres in Persia, where work of a high technical and artistic standard was made until well into the fourteenth century. Complete genealogies of potter families, some dating from the tenth century and continuing for four hundred years, have been drawn up. Kashan, never a seat of government, developed as a peaceful industrial centre and vases made there were given special mention in lists prepared after the capture of Baghdad by Hulagu Khan in 1258. In addition to being used for bowls, moulds were also in common use for the production of tiles, which were manufactured in large quantities to decorate the walls of mosques and tombs. Tiles bearing finely painted designs were made in shapes such as crosses or stars that would interlock to form complex but flowing patterns.

Other important pottery centres include Rayy (the Rages of the Book Tobit), which stood on the main route across north Persia. Among its ruins, five miles south-east of present-day Teheran, large quantities of pottery have been found. Outside Persia, Raqqa, an ancient caravan city on the

Octagonal bowl. Western Iran, 12th–13th century. Earthenware, fritware with moulded and carved decoration under a monochrome turquoise glaze. Height 13 cm (5.2 in).

Bowl. Iran, 12th–13th century. Earthenware, with green rim and incised decoration through white slip, reflecting the influence of Sasanian engraved metalwork.

Euphrates in Syria, was an equally significant production centre whose style was associated with that of pots made at Cairo. To the south-east of the Caspian Sea lay Gurgan, where high-quality lustreware as well as other types of pottery have been found. In 1942 treasure of extraordinary beauty was discovered that had been buried when the Mongols invaded and destroyed the town in 1221. The inhabitants had hidden their possessions, packing precious vessels inside earthenware jars then carefully burying them in sand. Many of the ceramics are attributed to the Kashan and Rayy potteries, but archaeological evidence suggests that some pots were also made at Gurgan. All the pots can be dated between 1200 and 1220.

Painted and decorated wares

One of the continuing technical problems confronting Persian potters was that of producing pots with colourful decoration that would retain its richness and definition in the firing. Earlier potters had found that colouring oxides painted under a lead glaze ran and lost their crisp patterning because the glaze was too fluid and absorbed the pigment, causing it to flow and run. Eastern Persian potters succeeded in making the pigments more stable by combining them with small amounts of white clay, but although this helped to stabilize the colour, the pigments lost their fluidity and this restricted the range of designs.

Various bold experiments were devised. In one technique, known as lakabi (carved), developed in the twelfth century, the white clay body was carved or incised so as to leave thin raised lines, or a design was outlined by them, to prevent the pigments from running together. Visually the result was highly effective, producing an almost jewel-like quality with the coloured carved design set against a white background. Although the technique lent itself particularly well to flat dishes, which were decorated with formal designs of animals, birds and figures coloured in rich blue, yellow, purple and green, jars with concave sides and scrollwork decor-

ation were also made. Syria appears to have been the main production centre.

Potters also found that coloured pigments were less likely to run under an alkaline glaze containing potash or soda than under one fluxed with lead, and pots so decorated form a major group of wares. The so-called silhouette-painted wares, made in Persia in the twelfth century, have solid areas of colour painted or otherwise applied on to the surface of the pot and covered with an ivory-tinted or deep turquoise glaze. The thick black pigment was applied direct to the pot and designs were sometimes carved through the sombre ground. Foliage and figures, frequently in combination, were favourite themes, as was calligraphic script, often laid out with pleasing symmetry. The dramatic intensity of the design is inherent in the technique itself. Some dishes have a high pedestal foot, which is also occasionally seen in lustreware from Rayy. The most characteristic form is the bowl with a high, cylindrical foot and gently opening straight sides.

Gradually the colour range was extended and a method of decoration devised whereby colouring oxides were painted on to the pot or the unfired glaze. At Raqqa in northern Syria hunting scenes as well as geometric or flowing designs and vegetal motifs were depicted in black, blue and red-brown painted under clear or turquoise-coloured glaze. Production at Raqqa was brought to a halt in 1259 when the Mongols invaded the city, although the technique continued to be practised and further developed in other parts of Syria until the fifteenth century.

Two other methods of polychrome painting on ceramics were devised in order to extend the range of possibilities of the palette beyond the few colours that could withstand the level of heat necessary in the glaze firing. Potters realized that a pot could first be glazed and fired before applying coloured pigments, which could then be 'fixed' in a subsequent low-temperature firing that would not destroy the colours. Since the ninth century the process of double firing had been well known to the producers of lustre-decorated ceramics, and the Persian potters may have evolved their technique from this. *Minai* (enamel) decoration combined underglaze cobalt blue supplemented with enamel colours. The decorative process was quite complicated and required several firings to achieve the

Raqqa ware dish from northern Syria, late 12th century. Earthenware, fritware *laqabi* dish, decorated with harpy birds. Diameter *c.* 50 cm (20 in).

final piece: the pot was biscuit fired then covered with an opaque white or sometimes turquoise or pale blue glaze and fired again; a third, much lower-temperature enamel firing followed. Enamels are a type of low-temperature glaze, today prepared in frit form by heating the ingredients in a crucible until they melt and then grinding them to a powder. Mixed with a suitable, usually oil-based, medium, enamels can be painted on to the fired glaze surface that do not lose definition during the firing. A varied range of strong colours could be obtained at the low temperature and the enamel technique allowed designs to be painted with great clarity and precision. On the *minai* bowls, blue, black, green, chestnut brown, dull red, white and leaf gilding were used, with many of the designs outlined in black.

One process involved painting parts of the design in clear pale blue, purple and green on or under the raw glaze before the pot's first firing. Black outlines and other supplementary colours mixed with vitreous flux were then added and fixed in one or more further, low-temperature firings. Notable among the supplementary colours are a shiny black, chestnut, Pompeian red, white and leaf gilding. Sparing no effort in the cause of enrichment, the potters, perhaps inspired by metal wares, often built up in relief those parts intended ultimately for gilding, foliage or pierced bosses being applied to the surface of the pot at the leather-hard stage. Where layer over layer of colour was built up, the pot had to withstand several firings.

Much early *minai* decoration reflects the influence of lustrewares and includes the depiction of large figures, formally arranged. Later the figures became smaller, a move that may have been related to the production of illuminated manuscripts and an interest in miniature painting generally. Court scenes, enthroned rulers surrounded by attendants, scenes from Persian legends and narrative scenes are all fairly common, as are ornamental arrangements of horsemen and hunters, while other vessels feature arabesques or geometric designs. Many designs show contemporary scenes in great detail, serving as a valuable social record of the time.

Bowl from Kashan, Iran, late 12th century. Earthenware, fritware with *minai* decoration in a design depicting a ruler and his attendants, sphinxes and griffins over a cream glaze. Diameter *c.* 19 cm (7.5 in).

Because *minai* wares have been the subject of much forgery, it is still difficult to identify accurately the centres of production, although the finest pieces are believed to have been made at Koshai. The term *minai* is now often used inaccurately by dealers and collectors to describe a number of different enamel techniques.

IRAN AND AFGHANISTAN, 1250–1500

The Mogul invasions under Genghis Khan and his successors from 1219 onwards left widespread destruction, but they also introduced Far Eastern culture through the family connection of the Il-Khanids (1256–1353) with the Great Khan of China. By the 1330s the Il-Khanid empire was disintegrating, and a number of successor states took power, some of which provided small but important centres of patronage such as those at Tabriz, Shiraz and Baghdad. At this time Chinese motifs such as lotus and peony flowers, phoenixes and flying cranes became established elements of decoration and architectural tilework increased in popularity, becoming widely used in mosques and palaces.

The lustre technique was by now limited almost exclusively to the production of tiles, especially monumental friezes. Both tiles and vessels were also decorated by means of an overglaze technique known as *lajvardina* whereby gilding and coloured enamels were applied over a coloured glaze, the process deriving its name from the cobalt blue or rich turquoise glaze used as the background. On this ware the colours are limited, usually to black, red and white, sometimes with gold leaf, which makes it less immediately attractive than the *minai*

Two bowls, probably from Iran, 14th century. Earthenware, moulded with fish motif in the base and covered with a turquoise glaze in imitation of imported Chinese celadons. Diameter (larger) 23.7 cm (9.5 in).

Sultanabad region to the west. Forms include narrow footed bowls and stocky jars, and decorative motifs were largely based on natural subjects such as birds and foliage. The range was extended to include pierced ware, with painting under a turquoise glaze, and later more naturalistically painted decoration appeared. It is probable that skilled potters travelled widely and settled wherever their skills and abilities were most valued.

The invasion of Timur (Tamberlain) at the end of the fourteenth century reunited Iran under Timurid rule. Timur's successors, however, were unable to maintain control over much of the empire. In the east there was a rapid turnover of contenders for the throne, while the west was lost altogether to two Turcoman tribes. Timurid art was influenced by a further period of contact with China, which is reflected, for example, in the widespread use of dragon handles on pottery. Ming porcelains flooded the court and were imitated by local potters, and ceramics made during Timurid times reflect the Chinese influence both in their design and in their blue-and-white colour scheme. Coloured and gilded floral or geometric tiles were popular, many of them being decorated in the *cuerda seca* (literally 'dry cord') technique, which allowed a wide range of colours to be used without their running or merging.

EGYPT AND SYRIA, 1250–1500

The Mamluks, a hierarchical military regime of Turkish origin, ruled Egypt and Syria. Cairo, capital of the Mamluk state, was the main centre of artistic patronage and production, although it was closely rivalled by the markets of Damascus. The Mamluk amirs (officers) were lavish patrons and their titles became a prominent element in the decoration of the many objects they commissioned, heraldic blazons being used as symbols of rank and office. Popular decorative motifs, many inspired directly by contemporary Chinese silks and porcelains or derived from Mongol Iran, included lotus and peony flowers, dragons and phoenixes.

Chinese porcelain, both blue-and-white and celadon, was admired and imitated by local potters. The Mamluks checked and defeated the Mongols and gave refuge to artists fleeing from Mesopotamia and Persia. Centres of pottery production were re-established at Damascus, Cairo and Syria. The main products in Syria and Egypt were painted in

pieces. The decorative designs, combined with Chinese elements, are often restricted to scroll-work, geometrical patterns and leaves; human figures and animals rarely appear. The manufacture of *lajvardina* wares is attributed to the Sultanabad region around the end of the thirteenth century or the beginning of the fourteenth, although literary sources attribute their production to Kashan.

One group of ceramics, known as Sultanabad wares, are characterized by a sombre colour scheme and slip decoration, indicating a change in taste. In Persia the painting technique of using coloured pigments combined with a stabilizing agent such as a small amount of clay had been in use under the glaze from the beginning of the thirteenth century at Kashan, and from about fifty years later in the

Large dish. Iznik, Ottoman Turkey, 16th century. Earthenware, white glaze painted with design of a pheasant, conventional flowers and foliage. Diameter 37.5 cm (15 in).

north-west Anatolia with their capital at Bursa. Despite a shattering defeat by Timur at the Battle of Ankara in 1402, in 1453 Sultan Mehmed II captured Constantinople, finally bringing to an end the Byzantine empire. Known to the Turks as Istanbul, the city became the capital of the new Ottoman empire, which was to last for over six hundred years until its collapse in 1919 when Mustafa Ataturk created the modern Republic of Turkey. For the following century and a half the Ottoman empire was at its height, both politically, culturally and economically. During this time Selim I (1512–20) conquered Mamluk Egypt and Syria, so appropriating Mamluk claims to be the protectors of the Muslim holy places and up-holders of the Muslim orthodoxy, and began a bitter war with the nationalistic Safavids in Iran.

The Ottoman empire was enriched by tribute, booty and the services of conscripted craftsmen from Europe and the East. This brought the Ottoman arts closer in some respects to contemporary Europe than to Islam. The potteries of Iznik reached a peak of luxury production, and grand architecture was built on an unprecedented scale.

Iznik ware

The principal manufacturing centre of Turkish Ottoman pottery was Iznik (Byzantine Nicaea) in western Anatolia, which supplied the court with luxurious vessels and tiles to decorate newly founded mosques, palaces and other buildings. The flowing designs combine purely Turkish motifs with elements ingeniously interpreted from imported Chinese blue-and-white porcelain. In the late fifteenth century, when Mehmed the Conqueror set up his palace at Topkapi Saray in Istanbul, Iznik ceramics were decorated in monochrome cobalt blue. Gradually, over the following century, the designs became looser and more colourful, with a subtle but rich palette. The brilliant colour combination of blue, turquoise, green and relief red was introduced after the reign of Sultan Süleyman the Magnificent came to an end in 1566. By the late seventeenth century, Iznik ceramics had passed their peak, although wares continued to be made. Their influence, however, was still evident in the nineteenth century, when potters such as William de Morgan in England and Cantagalli in Italy studied the early wares and sought to re-create their technical and aesthetic effects.

underglaze blue and black. Large and heavy bowls, albarelli and jars, often containing strong oriental spices and medicine, were exported to Europe. Designs in relief were painted in blue and black; following Mamluk convention, they often featured heraldic devices set within circular medallions. In addition, a modified version of the sgraffito technique was employed in Egypt, decoration on the wares having an incised outline and often appearing in low relief. Blue-and-white tiles were also produced.

TURKEY, EGYPT AND SYRIA, 1500–1700

By the fourteenth century the Ottomans were established as a small Turcoman principality in

Iznik wares were first isolated as a separate group in the 1860s, and identified as work characterized by vigorous drawing and a rich range of underglaze colours in which manganese purple and greyish green are particularly striking. At the time they were attributed to Damascus and therefore became known as Damascus ware – a name that is still occasionally used. Excavations have since revealed that the ware was made at Iznik and that Damascus did not become a production centre for Ottoman pottery until the seventeenth century, although tiles had been made there in the second half of the sixteenth century. Principal sources for Iznik decoration are Chinese Yuan and early Ming blue-and-white porcelains, Ottoman chinoiserie (particularly as shown in the designs of silks of about 1550 onwards) and naturalistic flowers of both botanical and horticultural interest, which may in part be drawn from European herbals and botanical works of the period. Overall, Iznik wares are diverse and represent some of the finest pottery made within the Islamic culture.

In addition to white slip-covered red-bodied earthenwares bearing sgraffito or slip-trailed decoration and lead glazed, two main types of ware have been identified: the painted polychrome wares, still sometimes known collectively as the 'Damascus' group, and the blue-and-white wares. The Damascus ware is characterized by a bright and rich decorative style painted on to a fine white clay slip and finished with a clear, shiny transparent glaze. Large dishes, standing-bowls, jars, ewers, lamps, pen-boxes and wall tiles were made in a sandy, whitish clay body. Decoration, usually painted or stencilled, includes a wide range of colours such as deep cobalt blue, turquoise, green and purple. Underglaze red had always been a difficult colour, but in the mid-sixteenth century it was discovered that Armenian bole, an iron-rich earth generally

Dish. Ottoman Turkey, Iznik, *c.* 1580. Earthenware, white glaze painted with an arrangement of florist's flowers. Diameter 31.8 cm (12.75 in).

Crouching cat. Kashan, Iran, 13th century. Earthenware, hollow, semi-opaque white glaze with painted lustre decoration.
Height *c.* 12.75 cm (5 in).

used as a base for gilding (and, according to contemporary palace records, as a remedy for indigestion) could give a vivid tomato red when used as an enamel pigment. This greatly extended the range of colours available with its deep, rich, jewel-like quality. The pigment needed to be applied thickly and is consequently raised above the other decoration, adding to its precious qualities. Patterns and designs are generally derived from naturalistic renderings of such flowers as carnations, roses, tulips and hyacinths, while borders are often filled with arabesques and scrolls.

The reign of Sultan Süleyman (1520–66) represented a period of great innovation within the Iznik ceramic industry, during which craftsmen drew on a wide variety of sources. Some Iznik dishes are decorated with three bunches of grapes as their central motif, a reinterpretation of the Chinese blue-and-white (and celadon) design formation. Later potters drew more freely on the natural world, showing tulips, hyacinths and carnations alongside cloud scrolls and tadpole-like leaves, as well as sailing ships, snakes, lions, trees and even figures shown in profile.

Iznik tiles ordered for the Süleymaniye mosque in Istanbul (1550–57) were used to spectacular effect, and for the next twenty years or so vast quantities of such tiles were ordered for the imperial Ottoman palace and religious foundations. In the eyes of the authorities Iznik was a tileworks, the making of pottery being seen as little more than an inconvenient distraction. From the late fifteenth century Iznik ware deteriorated in style, and towards the end of the seventeenth century it ceased to be produced. It had, however, been widely exported to the Levant, the Crimea, Venice, Moscow and even northern Europe and was imitated in the later seventeenth-century 'Candiana' wares associated with Padua.

Even when the Iznik potteries were at their height, other sites in Turkey were producing similar work, the most significant being Kütahya. Production at Kütahya flourished in the eighteenth century, although pottery and tiles had been made there very much earlier, and the workshops still continue to produce ceramics. Other centres include Diyarbekir, where a separate tile manufactory was set up in the sixteenth century, and

Damascus, which became active in the second half of the sixteenth century. Unglazed vessels are also believed to have been produced on the island of Lemnos and in the suburbs of Istanbul. By the eighteenth century production seems largely to have been restricted to Kütahya, where attractive polychrome pottery and tiles with decoration that incorporates aspects of folk art were produced.

Blue-and-white wares

The blue-and-white wares, sometimes known as Miletus ware after their excavation on the site of that name, were produced in large quantities at Iznik from the fifteenth century. By around 1489 there are mentions of Iznik pottery in Ottoman palace inventories. These seem to refer to fine blue-and-white wares catering for a demand for Chinese porcelains, which at the time were in short supply in Turkey because of a breakdown in trade. The record of a cruet ordered by an Armenian deacon, Abraham, dated 1510, indicates that these wares were also made in Kütahya. The reddish earthenware body with a white slip was painted under the alkali-lead glaze in dark cobalt blue and sometimes purple, turquoise or green. Most bowls and dishes were decorated in dark blue on the white ground, often with a central rosette, a cluster of fleshy spiralled leaves or a stylized diaper pattern. Some are painted with flying birds, six-pointed stars or interlocking arabesque panels filled with tiny spirals. A characteristic feature is the use of rings of narrow radiating petals. While the ware is greatly indebted to Chinese celadon of the Yuan and early Ming dynasties, the lavish decoration is also in the tradition of Timurid and Ottoman chinoiserie of the early fifteenth century.

Towards the end of the fifteenth century a new white fritware was produced. The quartz-frit body was of the general type used earlier in Persia but also contained lead and was covered with a fine slip. The glaze is also of the lead-soda type and contains four to eight per cent tin to make it opaque, which indicates technical innovation rather than the mere transference of an existing technology. The Iznik fritwares are technologically

Flask. Iznik, Ottoman Turkey, c. 1530. Earthenware, white glaze, painted in cobalt blue and turquoise, with a spiral design probably derived from manuscript illumination. Height 43 cm (17.2 in).

superior to those produced earlier in Egypt, Syria and Persia in imitation of Chinese porcelain. Forms are often adventurous and include large dishes and bowls, hanging lamps, candlesticks, flasks and even a pen-case. Decoration includes tight, interlacing arabesques and highly stylized floral motifs, often incorporating inscriptions. Although clearly influenced by Chinese porcelain, this ware is more in the spirit of adaptation than imitation, with designs of Buddhist origin such as the peony and breaking wave pattern often placed alongside European motifs.

After the vigorous Ottoman campaigns of the early sixteenth century in Iran and the eastern Mediterranean, the availability of Chinese porcelains was restored. Iznik blue-and-white wares then probably ceased to be made for the court, although imitations of early Ming dishes decorated with vine clusters may have been ordered to replace breakages or to make up services. Other types of blue-and-white wares were made until the end of the sixteenth century. At Kütahya and Iznik a second group of blue-and-white wares was produced, probably from the 1520s onwards, which has been known generally as 'Golden Horn' since the discovery of a large quantity of shards at Sirkeci on the south shore of Golden Horn in 1905–9. Flasks, dishes, tankards, tiles and great basins on pedestal feet were produced. In addition to cobalt blue, some designs are outlined in olive green, with touches of turquoise. Delicately painted spiral designs are characteristic, and the ware is remarkable for its wide range of Italianate-style shapes and flowing decoration.

The rundown of production at Iznik in the seventeenth century is closely linked to the slow decline of the Ottoman empire itself, although attractive ware continued to be made. In the

seventeenth century gold leaf was often used to enliven dull colours, and tiles were painted with stylized views of the Holy Places, including Mecca and Medina. A number of dishes were made with Greek inscriptions on the rim, incorporating such mottoes as 'O Lord, Lord, avert not thy countenance from us, May 25 year 1666', and 'O Lord, protect our Lord and Archpriest, June 19 1667'.

IRAN, 1500–1900

The first Safavid Shah, Ismacil I (1501–24), established his capital at Tabriz and rapidly brought all Iran under his control, despite the damaging

inroads made by the Ottomans in Iraq and the Uzbeks in Khurasan. Under two hundred years of stable government the arts flourished. Safavid power and culture reached a peak under Shah Abbas I (1588–1629), who beautified the city of Isfahan with palaces, bridges, markets and mosques, bringing about a renaissance in architecture and the applied arts, particularly ceramics. He was himself a collector of fine pottery and his collection still exists in the shrine of the Safavid family at Ardabil in Azerbaijan. Interest in all types of pottery engendered a major revival of the craft.

Kashan again flourished as a pottery centre and the technique of producing fine wares in a soft-paste type of porcelain was reintroduced. The range of wares manufactured was wide, but the imported, and renowned, Chinese green-glazed celadons were particularly admired and these were emulated using a smooth grey-green glaze. The fine-walled Gombroon ware, so called because it was shipped through the port of Gombroon (modern-day Bandar Abbas) on the Persian Gulf, was exported to India and Europe where in the seventeenth century it became very fashionable, especially in England. The pots, which included jars, bowls, plates and ewers with tapering spouts, were characterized by a fine, white, slightly translucent body, sometimes with pierced or incised decoration covered with a shiny glaze. Lustre-wares, having ceased to be made during the four-teenth century, were reintroduced in the late

seventeenth century, designs of stylized flowers being painted in red or yellow-brown on a white or deep blue glaze, showing little or no evidence of foreign influence. Equally important are the so-called 'Kubachi' wares – attributed to northern Persia as this is where they have been found – which made inventive use of the technique of underglaze painting. Large plates and dishes are painted in brown, green, yellow, dull red, black and white under a clear, colourless crackled glaze. Typical early designs are animals, figures and even portraits, but later plant and foliage designs predominate. Shapes include ewers with elegant long tapering spouts.

In 1732 the declining Safavid dynasty was overthrown, and an unsettled period ensued during which a series of military states existed. In western and southern Iran the principal ruler was Muhammad Karim Zand (1750–79), who set up his capital at Shiraz. On his death the Zands were ousted by a rival Turcoman tribe, the Qajars, who by 1794 controlled the whole of Iran from their new capital at Tehran. Under the Qajars architecture and the arts in general became increasingly indebted to European models, particularly in terms of decoration. Late Safavid blue-and-white

pottery demonstrates the way in which different styles and traditions were synthesized, with designs including a flowering prunus tree, a landscape with birds, cloud scrolls and a single lotus blossom, all taken straight from Chinese porcelains. Carnations also appear, and these may have come from Iznik ceramics. On Kirman polychrome wares the flower was often combined with decoration in strong sealing-wax red. Interest in tilework continued, but in this period it was strongly influenced by a wave of Iranian revivalism, begun under the Safavids and inspired by Achaemenid rock-reliefs and the sculptures of Persepolis.

During the nineteenth century the general standard of most crafts declined. Traditional pottery of high quality continued to be made, however, and until quite recently it was possible to replace old tilework on mosques and tombs with modern work made to a standard on a par with that of five or six hundred years ago.

BELOW: Pair of vases in the shape of bath clogs. South-eastern Iran, 17th century. Earthenware with painted decoration, modelled in the form of clogs after Dutch (Delft) prototype. The soles are dotted to imitate nails. Height *c.* 10 cm (4 in).

OPPOSITE: Bottle from Iran, Safavid dynasty, late 17th century. Earthenware with opaque white and cobalt blue glazed ground and painted lustre decoration of vegetal and animal designs, closely resembling the gold and silver decoration of manuscript margins. Probably produced for patrons in Isfahan, the Safavid capital. Height 26 cm (10.4 in).

LEFT: Shallow bowl from Iran, early 18th century. Earthenware, so-called Gombroon ware, soft-paste porcelain with pierced decoration filled with glaze and painted decoration in blue and black. Diameter *c.* 18 cm (7.2 in).

Continental European Earthenwares and Stonewares

BYZANTIUM, ITALY, SPAIN AND PORTUGAL, GERMANY, FRANCE, THE LOW COUNTRIES, SCANDINAVIA

Who is the potter, pray, and who the pot?

THE RUBÂYÂT OF OMAR KHAYYÁM

The technology involved in the production of prehistoric pottery in Europe was relatively simple and little archaeological evidence of it has survived. Pots were built by hand by joining together coils or rings of clay and smoothing off the surface, often with some sort of temper being added to the clay body to make it more workable. The vessels would have been fired in well-prepared bonfires rather than true kilns. To achieve a more even firing, the stacked pots were sometimes covered with turves in a process known as clamping. This allowed a more controlled and longer firing and resulted in pots that were grey in colour and more vitrified.

The period of the Iron Age in western and central Europe (*c.* 750 BC–AD *c.* 50) is divided by archaeologists into the Hallstatt period (up to *c.* 500 BC) and the La Tène, or Celtic, period (*c.* 500 BC until the Roman conquest). In the earlier of these periods potters fully understood how firing and after-firing conditions affected pots, and consequently were able to decorate them with combined patterns of red, black and white. These highly regarded vessels were used as offerings in burials, with containers made from sheet bronze influencing the form of many of the ceramic pieces. During the La Tène period, in the area extending from Britain to Romania decorative styles made use of existing Hallstatt motifs and incorporated Greek and Etruscan influences. Pottery making and firing

techniques continued to develop, shapes becoming more refined, surfaces smoother and the firing more controlled. The decoration of this period is often typically Celtic in feel, featuring patterns of flowing interlocked lines.

Despite most of the ceramic technology introduced by the Romans being lost following the

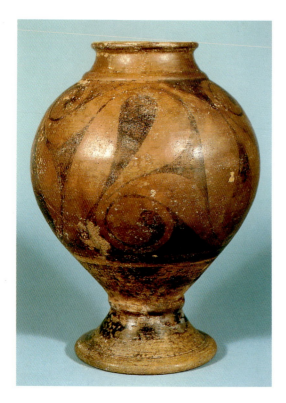

Pedestal jar, 400–350 BC, found in Prunay, Marne, France. Earthenware, wheel-thrown with scroll decoration of three upright and three inverted repeats of the same motif, which would have required careful measurement of distance and angle. The pattern is produced by a reserved red coating, with secondary black areas as the background. Height 31.5 cm (12.6 in).

cultures, and each technique was perfected to meet a growing demand for more sophisticated wares as societies became more settled. Lead-glazed earthenwares constitute the largest group of such wares. Although the Romans had further developed the technique of using lead as a flux in the glaze, successfully taking it across much of Europe, whether this technology remained in continuous use or was reintroduced is not clear. The lead-glazed surface was hard-wearing and lent itself to a variety of decorative processes. In Byzantium potters explored the possibilities of the clear glaze over designs often scratched through white slip, while in other parts of Europe more complex decorative techniques were developed. Tin-glazed wares make up the second major group, with potters taking up and developing the use of white opaque glaze from the Islamic world. So successful was this process in Spain and Italy that from the fourteenth century it extended into northern Europe, initially for the production of tiles. Stonewares and salt-glaze constitute the third group of wares. High-temperature wares were developed in Germany around the late thirteenth or early fourteenth century, the technique of salt-glazing being introduced some three hundred years later.

BYZANTIUM

In AD 330 Constantine declared the ancient Greek city of Byzantium the new capital of the Roman empire. The city was regarded as the 'new Rome' and its name changed to Constantinople in honour of the emperor. The Byzantine empire endured for 1000 years, gradually developing its own distinctive characteristics but retaining many of those of the old Roman empire. Only in 1453, when the Turkish armies overran Constantinople, did the last vestiges of the Roman empire disappear. Geographically the city had a powerful and commanding position; it was well fortified and had a good harbour, while its location served as the meeting point of Europe and the Orient on the strategically powerful waterway connecting the Mediterranean with the Black Sea. It is little wonder that Constantinople has been described as the crossroads of the world. At different times it defended itself against Christians, Muslims and pagans, absorbing many aspects of the various cultures.

Large pottery dish from the 'Dergerfield' Barrow Cemetery. Hallstatt period, *c.* 700–600 BC. Earthenware, hand-built, decorated with complex patterns combining excised and stamped techniques with polychrome coatings. Diameter 39 cm (15.6 in).

collapse of their empire, certain skills may have remained in modified form. In Germany coarse pottery continued to be made, some indicating a knowledge of Roman forms. Little progress took place within the pottery industry until technical advancements were stimulated by economic prosperity and social change. Around the seventh century AD an industry developed in the Rhine Valley in which pots produced largely for domestic use were elaborated with simple painted decoration in red clay. Forms, too, were simple, sometimes bearing incised decoration. During the ninth century improved firing methods enabled higher temperatures to be achieved in the kiln, which produced a harder, tougher, more vitrified ware. Pots made in the Rhine Valley at centres such as Pingsdorf and Badorf were imported into England from the tenth to the twelfth centuries.

In due course three major making, glazing and firing techniques came to dominate the ceramics of continental Europe. Regional variations emerged that reflected the development of individual

Dish from Cyprus, 13th–14th century. Earthenware, incised decoration through white slip revealing a red body, with painted decoration of green and brown. Diameter 20.2 cm (8 in).

Early influences may have come chiefly from the West, but the demise of Rome as the centre of the empire brought significant changes. An oriental influence in art soon manifested itself in the form of an emphasis on formal style, vivid colouring and rich ornament.

Unlike Islam, Byzantium placed no ban on the use of gold and silver vessels for domestic purposes. Pottery was less highly valued, therefore the craft tended to cater for everyday needs rather than the luxury market; there is no evidence, for instance, of lustreware being made. The red-slip wares that had been produced widely throughout the Roman empire continued to be made in various parts of the eastern empire for some time after AD 300, but the pots lack the precision or high quality of those produced under the Romans. The art of lead glazing was retained and during the eighth and ninth centuries was employed on a wide range of thrown forms. Green and pale amber lead glazes were used. During the Isaurian period (717–876) green glazes were applied on some of the most pleasing Byzantine ware.

Only during the period of the Palaeologans (1261–1391), when the country became impoverished by constant wars and religious and social upheaval, causing the gold and silver vessels on the royal table to be replaced by ones made of clay, did the craft begin to gain status. Much excavation has still to be carried out to identify the major production centres, but chief among them were probably Constantinople, Salonika, the Caucasus in southern Russia, Corinth and Cyprus.

Around the eighth and ninth centuries Byzantine pottery began to develop its own distinctive qualities. Though primarily incorporating aspects of Christian belief, the style itself derived from two major sources: the formality and symmetry of the classical Graeco-Roman wares and the freer, more rhythmic style of the Orient. Unlike the naturalism and humanism of Greek art, Byzantine art was more ritualistic and stylized, often drawing on typical Graeco-Roman themes but rendering them in a more formal manner. The broad origins of many of the designs used on Byzantine pottery are indicated by the animals they depict. The dove, a common Christian symbol, appears, as do ducks, which were commonly used in Egypt; fish, shown with open mouths, also recall those used by the Egyptians. Lions and leopards of a heraldic type, with long, waving tails, reflect western influences, while hares and the human-headed lion are more Persian in character. The griffin and centaur are mythological rather than representational in nature, but there are also depictions of animals such as deer, dogs and gazelles. The favourite creature, however, appears to have been the eagle, indicating goodness, alertness and power. The human figure tended to be shown in either stylized or formal poses, reflecting perhaps the fact that the Byzantine Church regarded the representation of humans as idolatrous. Broadly, Byzantine pottery falls into two main types: that made in a whitish body, glazed and often decorated with underglaze painted designs, and that fabricated from red clay covered with a white slip, often with incised or sgraffito decoration.

White-bodied wares

Whitewares, forming the most impressive group of Byzantine pottery, were developed around the ninth century AD under the Macedonian dynasty. Plates, dishes, cups, goblets and bowls with long hollow stems were produced; colour, in the form of an underglaze, was painted directly on to the whitish biscuit pot and the whole covered with a

Map of major European pottery production centres.

transparent glaze. Various shades of brown appear, as do amber, green, blue and occasionally bright red in the form of small dots and outlines. Designs incorporate crosses and rosettes as well as animals, figures and birds. Tiles destined for architectural use, made from white clay and decorated with underglaze colours, also formed a part of regular production.

Undecorated ware covered with a yellowish glaze probably constituted the majority of pieces produced and was intended mainly for domestic purposes, being both cheap and quick to make. Containers for liquids, in the shape of jugs and beakers, are the most common forms, together with dishes, plates, strainers, cups and cooking vessels. One group of white-bodied ware, known as petal ware, is decorated with flattened balls of clay that were applied to the pot while it was still soft and one side of the pellet smoothed into the side, the result having something of the appearance of fish scales or petals. Impressions of stamps made from clay or wood were often used to decorate the insides of bowls, and real or imaginary animals were popular decorative subjects.

Red-bodied slipware
The commonest forms of Byzantine ceramics are the lead-glazed, slip-decorated incised wares dating from the twelfth to the fourteenth century. The use of fine white slip over red clay to produce a

Dish, Byzantine, 12th century. Earthenware, with incised decoration through white slip of a stork and splashes of brown glaze.

Large dish. Italian, probably Ferrara, *c.* 1480–1510. Reddish earthenware, wheel-thrown, with a covering of white slip and incised decoration which reveals the dark red clay body in the design of a young man and woman standing back to back. The overall effect is heightened with green, brown, yellow, purple-grey and transparent glazes. Diameter 40 cm (16 in).

light-coloured body evolved around the tenth century and the technique was used to great effect on the inside of bowls. Many are decorated with incised (sgraffito) patterns and covered with either a clear or coloured transparent glaze. Early incised ware has a linear decoration in which the design was made with a fine point. Geometric patterns of scrolls, dots and zigzags are common. Spatial decoration was achieved by using a flat chisel-like tool to remove large areas of the slip, so allowing the darker body to show up the white design in slight relief. The wide range of motifs included circles and wavy lines, stylized trees, chequered patterns, crosses, rosettes and five-pointed stars as well as animals, fish and birds, some apparently inspired by textiles or metalwork; the human figure appears only occasionally. Some slipwares are painted with green and brown underglaze colours. Marbled ware, produced by using different coloured slips that were swirled round the inside of bowls, was made around the middle of the fourteenth century. Recent archaeological finds at a workshop at Serres in northern Greece have uncovered many examples of such ware.

On the evidence of present excavations, Byzantine pottery appears to lack the magnificence and mystery of Byzantine architecture, mosaics or ivory carving – the imperial or sacred arts. Byzantine ceramics, in comparison, are muted and humdrum rather than exotic, although archaeological records indicate that there was a flourishing industry. The use of a clear or tinted lead glaze spread throughout Europe, extending in the ninth century to Germany, the Low Countries and Britain.

ITALY

In Italy the Roman pottery tradition was continued in various forms, but because of the breakdown of central government and a consequent decline in the arts, little artistic or technological development took place. Contact with the Byzantine empire, through Venice and Ravenna in the north, was probably responsible for the wider use of lead glazes. Recent excavations have brought to light a range of domestic pottery produced around the seventh and eighth centuries, which is glazed in a dark green or yellow lead glaze. At Ostia, the port of Rome, and also in Rome itself vessels dating to the ninth century have also been found. On these, decoration for the most part is limited to combed lines or applied pellets of clay in the shape of rosettes.

Lead-glazed incised wares

During the Renaissance a large part of northern Italy produced lead-glazed, incised, slip-decorated earthenware. The technique was widely used in the Byzantine and Islamic world and had been introduced into northern Italy before 1300. In Italy the reddish-bodied earthenware was covered with a pale cream-coloured liquid slip and decorated by scratching away part of the slip to reveal the darker body underneath. The ware was then covered with a clear or tinted lead glaze. In the north, Venice and Ravenna were subject to intensive influence from Byzantium, as were Sicily, Apulia and Calabria in the south. In these areas the lead-glazing tradition continued to develop, and around 1300, in imitation of and

Four jugs. Italian, Orvieto district, 14th century. Earthenware, wheel-thrown with painted decoration. Height (tallest) 30 cm (12 in).

competition with the white opaque glaze being used in other parts of Italy, white slip was used to give a light-coloured ground.

The incised or scratched designs were often heightened with coloured oxides of brown and green that tended to run into the glaze, producing a washy effect. Although the decorative technique of scratching or cutting a design through slip was little used in his native town of Castel Durante, the contemporary potter Piccolpasso describes this type of decoration as *sgraffio*, and from this the word *sgraffiato* was coined, although the term 'incised slipware' is often preferred. From about 1450 larger and more ambitiously decorative pieces began to be made in north-east Italy, competing with maiolica for the luxury market. Uncertainty still exists about where they were produced, but this may have been in or near Venice, Padua, Florence, Ferrara and Bologna. Some fine plates with modelled border patterns of leaves were made, the designs on which often reflected Gothic rather than Renaissance

influences. The incised decoration frequently displays a caricature-like directness of drawing which, in many ways, is just as vivid an expression of the culture of fifteenth- and sixteenth-century Italy as that of maiolica.

Tin-glazed wares

Italy's long tradition of painting may have influenced the move towards decorated pottery and its development as a branch of the arts of the Renaissance. By 1500 two developments within the visual arts had significantly influenced the production of painted ceramics: renewed interest in the ornament and subject matter of ancient Rome, and the technologies of printing, woodcuts and engraving, which made the work of artists readily available as a design source for decorators. Maiolica potters depicted allegorical, classical and religious themes, producing work of such skill and accomplishment that their pots were accepted as a form of pictorial art. The creation by 1510 of a fully narrative style – *istoriato* (storytelling) – was unique to Italy and had no earlier precedent. The finest pieces were produced as collectors' items rather than for practical use.

The technique of painting such complex designs on the powdery surface of the glaze before it was fixed presented technical as well as artistic problems. The limited number of pigments available restricted the colour range and the direct painting method did not allow rubbing out or overpainting. This imposed a tight structure on the designs that could be executed but at the same time encouraged the development of a superbly bold and fresh style of decoration.

At some time during the fifteenth century the term maiolica came to be used for tin-glazed earthenware made in Italy, the word having previously been used exclusively to describe lustred pottery imported from southern Spain. Commercial competition with the Spanish spurred Italian potters first to imitation and then to rivalry. The Italians successfully ousted the Spanish imports from their local markets and eventually captured the entire European market, exporting both wares and potters.

Medieval pottery, c. 1200–c. 1500

The use of white tin glaze on pale red-bodied pots was widely known in northern Italy by 1250. The glaze was prepared by combining ground tin (imported mainly from Devon and Cornwall in England), lead oxide and silica in water to make a liquid suspension.

The bodies and glazes of maiolica were in the same tradition as those of Islamic lustrewares and their predecessors. Calcareous clay bodies were available that fired pale colours and were readily covered with the opaque white glaze. Plenty of dried wood was required for the firing and to reduce the risk of fire an edict of 1465 prohibited bringing brushwood and broom into Deruta, a maiolica town, except on the day preceding kiln firings. After the first or biscuit firing, the pots were dipped in the tin glaze, which, when dry, provided a powdery white absorbent surface for painting. Sometimes the glaze was tinted by the addition of cobalt or manganese. Inside the kiln ware was packed in saggars (ceramic boxes), to protect it from the flames and flying ash, and fired to about 1000°C.

In early maiolica colouring metal oxides were limited to copper green, usually painted in broad areas, with the designs often outlined in manganese brown or purple; blue was not introduced until later. Designs of this time reflect the Romanesque style of decoration in which natural forms are freely translated into linear patterns that at their best are ordered and stylized. Birds or beasts supporting a coat of arms were common, as were decorative themes similar to those of the Islamic potters. In addition to such natural forms as vegetables, foliage and animals, abstract and geometric patterns are found, but the human figure is rare. Little or no attempt was made to create an illusion of depth, volume or movement and the designs inclined to the static and orderly. Occasionally modelled details in low relief enrich the design. Trailing vines, bunches of grapes and coats of arms, for example, were modelled on pots made in Orvieto.

Unlike later maiolica wares, early pottery of this kind was made to be used rather than collected. The only medieval pottery items intended solely as decoration were dishes or basins known as *bacini* that were set into the brickwork of churches and other buildings. Until about 1500 Florence and Faenza dominated tin-glaze manufacture in Italy. The finest, whitest and most durable smooth and semi-matt tin glazes ever known, as well as a rich and reliable palette of subtle ceramic colours, originated in Faenza. During the fifteenth century Italian tin-glazed ware developed more ordered designs, mainly because of two major foreign influences: from northern Europe the Gothic style and from Spain the Oriental. Shapes – such as bowls, dishes and storage jars – tended to be those that had been made during the early Archaic period. Both the insides and undersides of bowls were glazed white and often decorated. Different regions produced distinctive ware, much of which reflected local influences. As the technique developed, so the palette was extended to include a range of primary colours as well as green, purple and brown.

Extensive trade in the fifteenth century between Italian towns such as Florence, Pisa and Lucca and the Spanish cities of Barcelona and Valencia brought into Italy the richly coloured and decorated lustrewares of Valencia. Their splendour and fine quality acted as a spur to Italian potters, and from around 1450 the maiolica workshops of

Three pharmacy storage jars. Italian, Florence district, *c.* 1420–50. Earthenware with relief blue decoration that incorporates designs of a man in contemporary costume, the 'oak-leaf' spray and the lion rampant. Height (tallest) 36 cm (14.4 in).

north-central Italy began to devise a brilliant new decorative language. The 'Florentine green family', which was painted with foliage, developed into a decorative style of great distinction. One of the patterns consisted of a symmetrical repeating design recalling the markings on peacock feathers and was painted mainly in green on a white background. In Tuscany a series of two-handled globular jugs was made using a rich ultramarine blue, or less commonly a green pigment applied in slight relief. Oak leaves, derived from a Valencian design, formed a popular decorative motif. Italian potters also took up the Valencian flower design and leaf pattern, while centres such as Faenza and Pesaro developed their own versions of both the 'peacock-feather' design and the so-called 'Persian palmettes'. Other design elements included pointed leaves, interlaced strapwork, profile drawing and, to ornament empty spaces, groups of dots, hatching or tight curls.

Initially, Italian maiolica potters imitated the appearance of Spanish lustrewares by using yellow and purple designs, from which developed several inventive styles of decoration incorporating figure painting. Whilst Italian in feel, such designs are often placed within the original Spanish ground motifs. Gothic influence is reflected in the more formal designs, although the motifs appear not as pictorial images but as types or symbols, for example foliage, radiating beams of light, initials, sacred monograms and heraldic emblems; religious figures and animals were also used. A period of settled government and increased prosperity in the second half of the century saw the beginning of new styles of decoration that reflected the adventurous spirit and expansive ambition of the Renaissance. The palette was extended to include orange, which was often used instead of lime yellow.

Particularly notable in this period is the work of the potter-sculptor Luca della Robbia (1399–1482), who produced figures and reliefs using polychrome tin glaze. He and his nephew Andrea were the first artists to apply the tin-glaze technique to sculptural forms, successfully combining modelled detail – usually on works with a religious theme, such as a Madonna and Child – with sensitive use of the white glaze and a limited range of colour. Under Andrea's sons the workshop also made a number of apothecaries' vessels as well as statues and reliefs.

Renaissance style (c. 1500–1600)

The Renaissance (rebirth), a re-evaluation of the classical cultural inheritance that originated in Italy in the fourteenth century, engendered a transformation not just of the Italian but of the whole European way of life. In pottery the technical quality and artistic strength of maiolica lifted its social status, thus shaping European ceramic taste for over a century. By 1500 the technique of maiolica was well established throughout much of northern Italy and individual production centres had developed their own recognizable characteristics. The whole nature of pottery decoration had departed from that based primarily on Spanish and Gothic influences towards a completely indigenous style reflecting the themes and aspirations of the Renaissance.

Favourite local meeting spots at this time were the pharmacies, lavishly decorated with ornately painted maiolica drug vases. Both this fashion

and the contemporary habit of displaying large decorative dishes on sideboards and tables reached a peak during this period, encouraging potters to produce richly decorated ware. Largely thanks to the patronage of the wealthy nobility, the work of individual ceramic artists began to be more clearly identified and their skills more highly valued. Ceramics has an advantage over painting in that it is an imperishable medium, and local schools of painting influenced pottery decoration, many designs being based directly on prints, or more rarely drawings, by famous artists.

By about 1500 improved technical control of colour and greater skills in drawing had facilitated a new kind of ware in which the surface was treated like a canvas for painting, and by about 1515 *istoriato* pottery was being made in various centres. From 1500 to 1520 the most dynamic production centre was Faenza, where designs were often painted on a bluish glaze, many also having blue as their keynote colour. Although forms generally had become more sophisticated, their complexity was often overshadowed by the ornateness and skill of the decoration. Favourite forms were plates and bowls, which provided a suitable background for detailed pictorial compositions. Some wares were fashioned into quite intricate and ornate shapes that reflected the influence of metalwork and this added to their precious quality. Because of the restricted range of colours and the limitations of working on glaze, the quality of the decoration, however complex, was related as much to that achieved in maiolica as to painting in oil, but the new *istoriato* style incorporated elaborate narrative scenes. Mythological, allegorical and religious subjects were depicted and cupids, satyrs and dolphins were introduced. However, in Umbria, the home of Saint Francis, religious subjects continued to predominate.

The major production centres include Sienna, Florence, Cafaggiolo, Faenza, Padua, Deruta, Gubbio, Castel Durante and Urbino, Venice, Palmero, Castelli and Montelupo, each of which developed its own distinctive style and technique.

Dish, Italian, probably Deruta, *c*. 1450–90. Earthenware, wheel-thrown, painted in blue, orange and green showing a young man holding a spear and shield in a central panel surrounded by flowers and tendrils. Diameter 38 cm (15.2 in).

The two adjacent towns of Castel Durante and Urbino became renowned in the sixteenth century for the work of the pottery painters Giovanni Maria, Orazio Fontana, Francesco Avelli and Cipriano Piccolpasso. These centres were particularly famed for grotesques and elaborate classical *istoriato* dishes. Around 1556–7 Piccolpasso wrote a three-volume treatise entitled *The Three Books of the Potter's Art*, a highly informative text describing the art and craft of the potter. He described and illustrated in detail the techniques used by the maiolica and lustreware potters, providing clear practical information on the making, decorating and firing of pots. Shapes, colours, glaze recipes and decoration are all detailed and the books give a fascinating account of contemporary workshop practice. The

drawings and descriptions of potters' equipment, including wheels and kilns, continue to intrigue potters and historians today.

At Urbino around the middle of the century a highly elaborate ware was developed that featured moulded decoration and intricate polychrome painting. The history of maiolica in Urbino and the nearby town of Castel Durante has been confused by the supposition that the painter who signed himself 'Nicola', dubbed 'the Raphael of maiolica painting', was a certain Nicolo Pellipario. Documentary research into the Urbino archives reveals that the potter Nicola is more likely to have been Nicola di Gabriele Sbraghe, sometimes known as Nicola da Urbino, who had an important workshop in Urbino until his death in 1537/8. There is

Dish on a low foot by Nicola da Urbino, Italian, Urbino, *c.* 1525. Earthenware, wheel-thrown, painted in blue, yellow, green, grey, brown, orange, black and white, showing Trajan stopping outside Rome to hear a petition for justice, with a wreathed shield of arms on the tower. Diameter 26.5 cm (10.6 in).

no evidence that he ever worked outside Urbino.

Lustreware was made in Italy for the first time at Deruta, near Perugia in the mid- to late fifteenth century, when use was made of skills learnt from Moorish potters who had fled from the Christian conquest of Spain. Because lustre decoration allows no tonal changes but relies for its interest on surface reflections, designs tend to be simple and bold. Early pieces successfully made use of a combination of lustre and one other colour on a white background. On later work surfaces were made in relief, with scales, bosses and gadroons enhancing the effect of the lustre and further imitating the appearance of precious metals as they caught and reflected the light. Early Deruta lustreware made effective use of the shape of dishes by employing the rim as a border framing the central area, which would feature a design such as a bust or heraldic arms. Leandro Alberti, in his *Description of the Whole of Italy* published in 1550, wrote 'The earthenwares made here are renowned for being made to look as if they were gilt. It is such an ingenious technique that up to now no other workman in Italy has been found to equal them, though attempts and experiments have been made.' There is good reason to suppose that in addition to Deruta and Gubbio, lustrewares were also known in Faenza and at Cafaggiolo.

Potteries at Cafaggiolo enjoyed the patronage of the Medici family and produced fine, richly coloured and designed pictorial wares with historical, allegorical and religious themes, and also grotesques. A famous Cafaggiolo plate of about 1510, now in the Victoria and Albert Museum, shows a maiolica painter at work on a dish watched by two admiring aristocratic clients, his dress no less elegant than theirs; this indicates the high

status of the decorator. The Urbino artist Francesco Xanto Avelli wrote poetry, put literary tags on his dishes, painted elaborate moral and political allegories of his own invention, and described himself grandly as 'painter'. At Gubbio in Umbria, Giorgio Andreoli (known also as Maestro Giorgio) brought lustre decoration to perfection, developing particularly successful iridescent golds, ruby reds and pearly silver. Designs were often painted by Nicola da Urbino and lustred by Giorgio Andreoli. From about 1530 onwards moulded and gadrooned forms were developed specifically for use with lustre, and from about the middle of the century tinted backgrounds were used, grey and pale blue being the most common shades, with white often added to provide highlights.

Lustre production required great skill in the firing and had a high failure rate, therefore the wares were an expensive luxury. Piccolpasso estimated that only six in every hundred pieces met the requisite standard. Given the expertise required, it is not surprising that only in Gubbio and Deruta did lustreware come to be made, by specialist workers, on anything approaching an industrial scale.

Later wares

Around the middle of the sixteenth century there was a movement against the *istoriato* style of pictorial representation, which may have come to be thought too literal. The development at Faenza of a fine, smoother white glaze encouraged the restriction of decoration to small, intense areas on

Large plate from northern Italy, late 16th century. Earthenware, with relief modelling of the Virgin adoring the Child in the centre, glazed brown and white.

Pharmacy jar. Italian, Castel Durante, 1519. Earthenware, wheel-thrown, painted in blue, green, orange, yellow and purple, depicting two pairs of monsters flanking a garland encircling a shield of arms. On the neck are masks, shields and owner's mark incorporating FF and a double cross. Inscribed on tablets: *A di xi de Octobre fece 1519/ Ne la Botega d Sebastians d Marforio/ In Castel durâ.* Height 36.5 cm (14.6 in).

colourful detail of the *istoriato* style was avoided. Skilled potters travelled from Italy throughout Europe to teach the technique.

In the seventeenth century there was a renewal of interest in religious subjects and a marked dislike of unpainted areas. New colours were introduced, for example pea green, but the palette was generally restricted. At Castelli thinly potted wares were decorated with designs that made use of perspective, a convention that had previously been little used by maiolica painters. Shapes generally became more complex and were often based on gold, silver, copper and bronze objects. Applied ornament in the form of monsters, sphinxes and mermaids added a further decorative element, and internal divisions were introduced within vessels, which demonstrates the move towards greater imitation of objects fashioned in metal. Plaques were made for purely ornamental purposes.

Although by the eighteenth century Italy had lost its leading role in the development of European tin-glazed wares, the initiative having passed to the Low Countries, lively and varied production continued at several centres, with potters upholding the tradition of Renaissance maiolica as well as responding to imported Chinese blue-and-white porcelain and the faience of France and Germany. Many forms emulated those of silverware. Talented maiolica painters were rare, however, and many travelled widely.

Nineteenth-century Italian potters continued to produce wares based closely on Renaissance pieces – most notably Ulysses Cantagalli (1839–1901) of Florence, whose imitations of classical pieces were so well carried out that they have confused many connoisseurs.

SPAIN AND PORTUGAL

The most distinguished pottery made on the Iberian peninsula before the Roman armies invaded it in 218 BC, conquering the remainder of the region over the following two hundred years, was that produced in the east, where Celtic invaders had settled by the sixth century BC. Trade with Mediterranean countries brought, among other goods, Greek decorated pottery, which the Iberians attempted to copy. This eventually led to the development around 500 BC of a painted style indigenous to the Iberian region. Light-coloured clays firing yellow or pink were used to produce

which designs were often painted entirely in blues or yellows. In this work the roots of the style of decoration now known as baroque, which developed at the beginning of the seventeenth century, can be identified. Shapes were not limited to those traditionally made but were based more directly on the forms of objects produced in precious metals, including table services made up of many pieces. Among the individual items made were plates, dishes, ewers, wine-coolers, candelabra, drug pots, flasks, ink-stands, busts and obelisks, often in complex forms. At its best, decoration was delicate and limited to a palette of dark and light blue, yellow and orange. The drawing was often lively, having the freshness of a sketch, and the elaborate and

thin-walled, wheel-made pots. Goblets, flat-based jugs, low-footed bowls and urns were produced, their most distinctive feature being the decoration painted on to smooth, slip-covered vessels. Iron and manganese oxides were used that fired a wine-red colour. Designs were rich and varied, incorporating geometric shapes as well as stylized birds, fish, plants and the human figure.

The region remained under Roman rule until the fifth century AD, acquiring from Rome many cultural characteristics, including language, that have since evolved and survived into modern times. In the fifth century the country was invaded and conquered by various Barbarian tribes, of which one – the Visigoths – became its ruler, making Toledo in the centre the capital. Various groups of pottery have been identified from this time. These include Palencia ware, found in and around Palencia and characterized by its decoration of red or brown strips recalling red-painted Pingsdorf ware; low-fired wares include red earthenwares decorated with impressed and moulded designs, generally left unglazed. Pottery decorated with simple yellowish or greenish glazes was also made. Trade and contact with the Byzantine empire during the seventh and eighth centuries may have been the means by which the glaze was introduced into Spain; alternatively, it may be that Roman techniques of painting and glazing survived in some form.

In 711 Muslim armies invaded from the south, conquering most of the region during the course of the following decade. The establishment in 756 of the Caliphate of Cordova, under the Ummayads (756–1031), introduced a completely different religious and cultural life. The Islamic religion and Arabic language, literature and arts became dominant throughout the peninsula. The advent of Muslim culture eventually led to the development of a distinctive pottery style whose influence was to spread throughout Europe. In this period Cordova became the intellectual centre of the Western world, with Christian scholars from France and Italy travelling there to study Arabic and exchange ideas. However, many Christians within the country resisted the Muslim influence, continuing to uphold the religious and legal traditions of the Visigothic period.

In northern Spain in the period from the eighth to the tenth centuries Islamic techniques were little known and Visigothic traditions persisted. The best known ware, 'grey ceramics', consists of roughly made vessels produced on the slow wheel, usually in rounded forms, and includes storage jars decorated with simple incisions. Some groups of red-painted ceramics were also made. In the following two hundred years the faster wheel was introduced, as were more efficient kilns and a greater diversity of form and decoration. Grey-wares, greatly improved, continued to be made. They included in Catalonia *ollitas* or cooking pots together with small jugs, and at Campoo red-painted wares produced in a great variety of forms; in Leon and Galicia some were white-painted. In the thirteenth and fourteenth centuries the *mudéjares* products from Valladolid were produced. Characterized by the use of Islamic motifs on their distinctive shape and metallic decoration, these were of a quality far lower than that of wares made in the south. During the tenth century Murcia was an active production centre whose output encompassed a variety of forms, techniques and decorative motifs and included glazed vessels in green and manganese. There is also evidence to indicate that lustreware production began in Murcia between the twelfth century and the first half of the thirteenth.

By the second quarter of the thirteenth century a wide range of techniques were in use, including sgraffito on manganese and applied decoration combined with incision and stamping. Not only lustrewares but also coarse wares were of a high quality, including heat-resistant cooking pots in many sizes, miniature ovens, glazed open forms for the table, large bowls and jars, and lamps. Production declined during the fourteenth century, despite the introduction of incentives for potters to settle in the city.

Lustreware

The greater part of Spain remained under Muslim control until 1212, when the Christians won their greatest victory at Las Navas de Tolosa; by 1248, with the capture of Seville, they had taken over most of the peninsula. In general Muslims were allowed to remain both in Spain and in the central and southern parts of Portugal, which did not become independent until 1514. By 1300 only the Nasrid rulers of Granada maintained a Muslim enclave in the west, which flourished until 1492,

Urn from Spain, province of Valencia, *c.* 500 BC. Earthenware, red clay with stylized floral patterns and decorated handles. From the cemetery of Oliva. Height 55 cm (22 in).

Ewer, Spanish, from Valencia, early 16th century. Earthenware, wheel-thrown, tin-glazed, painted in cobalt blue with overglaze lustre decoration. Below the spout is a European blazon.

cobalt blue, the use of which had previously been unknown in Spain. The Arabic scholar Ibn Said (1214–86), writing around the middle of the thirteenth century, referred to the 'golden' pottery glazed and gilded that was made at Murcia, Almeria and Malaga in southern Spain, while in the fourteenth century several Arab writers, including Ibn Batuta (1307–77), spoke in praise of lustred ware from Malaga. As the power of the Christian kingdoms made it increasingly difficult for Muslim potters to trade, many migrated to nearby Manises, where they continued to make similar shapes and patterns, their knowledge and skill forming the basis of an industry that was to flourish for nearly three hundred years.

After the Christian reconquest of Spain, the potters, still largely Muslim, continued to produce wares for their new masters. Muslims living under Christian rule were known as Mudéjares, while Christians living under Muslim rule were known as Mozarabs. As was the case in architecture, Christian pottery was strongly influenced by the international Gothic styles. The decoration on lustre tin-glazed pottery – sometimes known as 'Hispano-Moresque wares' although this term is used to encompass all tin-glazed wares, including those without lustre decoration – reflects the eclectic nature of the contemporary culture. Traditional Muslim motifs are varied, many following older themes from the eastern Mediterranean such as animals and birds, and vegetal decoration including the 'Tree of Life' design as well as human and geometric motifs. With Valencia no longer in Arab hands but home to an Islamicized population, Arab potters first conserved their practices then passed them on to the Christians, combining in their work a repertoire of Gothic motifs with stylized Arabic inscriptions, palm trees, heraldic animals and, exceptionally, grotesque figural scenes.

Fine examples of Spanish lustreware were exported throughout Europe, and the coats of arms painted on some pieces indicate that they were special commissions from royal, noble or mercantile families. Florentine merchants ordered sets of lustred tableware direct from Valencia, to which the Tuscan banks and trading companies were linked through a common involvement in western Mediterranean trade. Spanish imports of lustred pottery into Italy were a major factor in raising the status of pottery from the utilitarian to an art

when it was captured by Ferdinand of Aragon and Isabella of Castile. Nasrid pottery, made at a number of centres, provided coarse wares and fine tablewares and embraced a variety of techniques and forms. The major categories were vessels for the preparation, serving and consumption of food, as well as portable stoves, lamps, water bottles, urinals and trays, albarelli and funnels.

Production of lustrewares and tiles (*azulejos*), by far the best known and finest of the wares made in Spain, was started by potters from Fatimid Egypt, probably in the late twelfth century. Immigrant potters settled in fairly large numbers in Murcia and Malaga, bringing with them their detailed knowledge of lustreware and underglaze techniques. They also introduced

form in Renaissance Italy. Lustred pottery, long accepted as a luxury commodity in the Islamic world, and Valencian wares were more highly valued than native pottery and were imitated by Italian potters.

Spanish lustrewares can be divided into three main types, which roughly follow each other chronologically. The first, employing predominantly Moorish designs, was made at Malaga in Andalucia, southern Spain. The second was produced at Manises, a suburb of Valencia, around the end of the fourteenth century and included some of the finest lustrewares ever produced. This ware incorporated some Gothic motifs into what were primarily Muslim designs and is often described as being of the *mudéjares* style. A third group of wares, made from about 1600, was produced in and around Talavera and Seville and up the eastern side of Spain in a region extending from Catalonia to Granada. Much of this work was inspired more by Italian tin-glazed wares than Hispano-Moresque styles. From the fifteenth century at least eight different lustreware formulae are known. All have similar ingredients, which include copper, silver, iron oxide and vinegar.

Early lustrewares (c. 1200–c. 1400)

Bowls, dishes and pitchers as well as storage jars were produced in the early years, many of their forms and designs being Islamic in character, influenced particularly by wares made at Rayy, Kashan and Raqqa. Designs were usually carried out in two shades of blue on a white ground painted on to the raw glaze, and finished with copper-golden lustre. Kufic script was used as decoration, as were foliage designs of great complexity, while geometric motifs were also popular. Large decorative vessels made in sections, probably in a mould, are perhaps the most famous products to have been made in Malaga, the so-called Alhambra vases, associated with the Alhambra Palace, being a prime example.

Standing over a metre high, these magnificent vessels represent a remarkable technical achievement. So highly prized were they that special niches were built into the Alhambra to accommodate them. The high, flat, winged handles mark the vases as decorative objects with no obvious functional use, their purpose having been simply to celebrate the skills of the potter. Their ornate painted decoration often consists of bands of Kufic script, while some bear panels depicting animals. These impressive vessels are an indication of the prosperity and wealth of the country at that time and of the generally high status of lustreware, which was exported to Sicily and Egypt as well as to England.

Lustre-decorated ware also sometimes exhibits the technique known as *cuerda seca* ('dry cord'), whereby areas of dry pigment, usually black, separated the different coloured glazes and prevented them from running into each other. The cuerda seca technique was developed in Valencia, mainly for use on flat dishes, during the eleventh and twelfth centuries, probably because of the failure at the time to produce lustre. It became popular again in the fifteenth century, when formal designs decorated vases as well as dishes.

Other areas, notably Aragon, Valencia and Catalonia, continued to produce pots very much in the *mudéjares* style, although there were variations from region to region. Following the Catholic reconquest of Andalusia in 1487 much of the vitality of the pottery industry seemed to be lost and almost no lustreware was produced there after the beginning of the sixteenth century. Muslim potters fled from Murcia and Granada to reconquered Valencia, and it was here that lustreware of a different style and brilliance thrived in the fifteenth century.

Middle period (1400–1700)

At the end of the thirteenth and beginning of the fourteenth century, Manises, near Valencia, became the main centre of production. Early wares combined cobalt blue underglaze painting with lustre, many of them featuring elaborate but refined decoration. References to Manises potters travelling to France at the request of local officials indicate the high regard in which the Spanish pottery industry was held. Following the capture of Valencia by the Christians, potters came under the

influence not only of Islam but also of the Catholic Church, with its strong emphasis on Gothic style. As a result Valencian pottery decoration became distinguished by the merging of the Gothic religious and secular emblems with the Islamic, giving rise to the *mudéjares* style. Previously, Valencian potters had made pots in imitation of their Andalusian predecessors, but gradually they developed a distinctive style of their own in which the blue-and-white and lustred wares exhibited a more European character. Brilliant gold as well as iridescent blues, reds and yellows were combined with deep cobalt blue underglaze painting.

European Gothic influence was apparent in the more naturalistically rendered ornament, the use of heraldic devices and shields, and inscriptions of a Christian nature rendered in Gothic script. Muslim influence was particularly evident in the treatment of ornament, and intricate designs continued to be made that incorporated stylized Kufic script, often in combination with Gothic emblems. Typical plant and foliage motifs include berries, flowers and bryony leaves as well as golden and blue vine leaves; birds and animals were also popular, but the human figure was rare. Heraldic devices such as the eagle, lion and dragon were employed, and armorial motifs designed for the royal families of Spain and other parts of Europe. Gothic inscriptions include text such as *senta catalina guarda nos* (Saint Catherine protect us) placed around the rim, encircling a central design featuring a deer and foliage.

The lustre designs remained stylized but took on greater naturalism. The combination of arabesque ornament and animal motifs encouraged free decorative treatment, often producing exquisite results. In one example a naturalistically painted deer sits happily under a beautiful arabic Tree of Life design. Around the middle of the fifteenth century Manises ware became very popular in Italy, ware for this market often being decorated with the coats of arms of prominent Italian families.

In the late fifteenth and early sixteenth centuries, Renaissance-style decoration from Italy spread further afield. Shapes began more closely to imitate those of precious metalwork and designs those of paintings, although classical motifs of leafy garlands and swathes of fruit and flowers, grotesques, masks and acanthus scrolls failed to

gain wide popularity. Dishes became more elaborate in form, with petals, scallops and raised repoussé work incorporated into the designs; woven brocade velvets seem to have influenced some of the more ornate work. While the tops of the magnificent painted dishes can be admired for their technical skill and richly patterned decoration, the undersides are equally engaging, often bearing simpler but no less attractive designs. With its shiny surface, metallic gleam and ornate patterning, lustreware was well regarded and highly valued, most of the magnificently decorated dishes being made for special occasions. Dining tables were not laid with individual place settings but guests served themselves to portions of food from central dishes – a tradition that encouraged potters to make these as ornate as possible.

Shapes other than dishes are generally few and simple. Following the Arabic tradition, cylindrical jars with concave sides, known as *albarellos*, were widely made for the use of the apothecary. Pots for storing dry foodstuffs, bowls, drinking mugs and round platters were also produced. However, with the unification of Spain under the Catholic monarchs, the growth of strong trade and the absence of the Muslim law forbidding the use of precious metals for dishes, lustre lost its attraction and was replaced by other materials.

Other lustrewares

Given the great success of lustrewares, it is hardly surprising that many potteries were keen to produce them, albeit often in a less sophisticated form and with considerable verve and simplicity. Centres included Calatayud, Aragon and Muel, where designs included stylized lions and Christian inscriptions around the border. In Catalonia grey ceramics in the form of small cooking pots and jugs had been produced from the eleventh century, and following the introduction of the fast wheel in the twelfth century the industry developed rapidly. Recent discoveries of waste material from pottery kilns that had been incorporated into the structure of churches in Barcelona built in the fourteenth and fifteenth centuries reveal the extent of the plain and decorated wares produced at that time. Tin-glazed and lustrewares were initially imported from Aragon and Valencia and later from Italy, but after the middle of the fifteenth century potters from Italy and Valencia settled in Barcelona and produced such wares there. In addition to lustrewares, green and brown polychrome wares and blue decorated pottery were made. The decorative motifs largely imitated

Albarello, apothecary storage jar. Spanish, from Catalonia, 14th century. Earthenware, wheel-thrown and decorated. Height 25.5 cm (10.2 in).

those of other production centres, perhaps in order to secure local custom in the face of outside competition.

Later tin-glazed wares

Other centres produced distinctive pottery without lustre decoration. At Talavera de la Reina and Puente del Arzobispo (Toledo) in central Spain tin-glazed wares were produced of which the earliest record dates to 1484. These early wares

were decorated mainly in a style influenced by Italian or Flemish work, but in the late sixteenth century a more distinctive regional style began to emerge. Dishes, basins, jugs and other domestic wares were produced in increasing quantities and to a high quality, largely replacing silverware when its use became heavily restricted after the introduction of sumptuary laws in 1601. A great variety of shapes were produced, which were covered with a milky-white glaze and painted with designs in blue, emerald green, yellow and orange. The most popular subjects were soldiers, bust portraits, animals and birds, and coats of arms surrounded by a framework of partially hatched foliage. Talavera pottery was said to stimulate the appetite, its shining purity enhancing the savour of food. Towards the end of the sixteenth century, this production centre had displaced Italian imports, successfully bringing together Castilian decorative motifs with more delicate forms in imitation of Italian vessels. As a mark of its success, in 1575 the pottery received royal patronage, allowing it to be successfully traded throughout Spain. A group of potters from Talavera de la Reina were sent to establish a pottery at Puebla de los Angeles in the then newly acquired colony of Mexico.

The individual character of Talavera pottery is evident in large white dishes, often made from coarse clay and vigorously painted with dark blue figures of songbirds, deer, rabbits and heron enclosed in borders of rough foliage and tendrils, or portrayals of equestrian figures, hunting scenes and animals. Colours such as manganese purple and reddish-orange were added later. Many of the pots are large, the range including dishes, two-handled jars, basins for lemonade, jugs, barrels and cisterns. Also made were candlesticks and inkstands, often in fanciful human or animal shapes. During the seventeenth century the palette was extended to include intense copper greens, yellows and purples. A monochrome blue-and-white style was developed that was strongly influenced by contemporary engravings depicting, for example, landscapes, wild beasts or children at play. A writer in the seventeenth century favourably compared Talavera plates with those from China, and the pottery was generally highly regarded. During the eighteenth century, however, the quality of the work deteriorated, although pottery with vivid green decoration is still made in the area to this day.

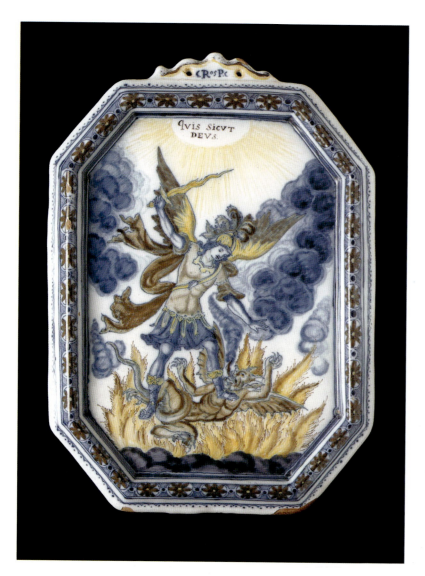

Plaque, Spanish, from Alcora. Earthenware, white tin glaze, painted decoration. Height 23.75 cm (9.5 in).

objects. The most distinctive aspect of Alcora tin-glazed ware is its significant development of pictorial painting. Forms include panels painted with saints and biblical or mythological scenes, often including many figures painted in a wide range of colours. Production declined around 1800 in the face of competition from English cream-coloured ware and European soft-paste porcelain.

Portuguese maiolica

The origins of Portuguese maiolica are obscure, but there was a great flowering of the craft in the sixteenth century. In 1552 there were ten potteries in Lisbon alone. While some European-style wares were made, including Italian-style albarelli, the most characteristic wares were those decorated in the manner of Chinese export porcelain of the Ming dynasty. In the seventeenth century trade between Portugal and China soon brought the influence of blue-and-white porcelain, and designs from late Ming wares were adopted on some of the finest Portuguese ceramics. Among the most distinguished pottery produced in Portugal are the maiolica tiles and vessels. While much of the work shows similarities with that made in Spain, and later Italy and the Netherlands, the painted polychrome tiles in particular, featuring flowing foliations and cornucopias, developed a distinctive style of their own. Polychrome as well as blue-and-white tiles were produced in great quantity, some panels being used in preference to tapestries and altar cloths.

During the eighteenth century Portuguese maiolica was strongly influenced by French pottery, in particular that produced at Rouen, although it was never as meticulously drawn. The most important pottery centres were given a great incentive in 1770 when a ban imposed on all imported porcelain except that from East Asia served to boost the domestic market. Wares made at the royal factory of Rato in Lisbon, first directed by the Italian potter Tomás Brunetto (d. 1771), were usually in the high rococo style and included tureens in the shape of heads, hens and geese. In the nineteenth century porcelain was made at Lisbon and at Vista Alegre near Oporto, from 1824, and ceramics for everyday use as well as more decorative wares continued to be manufactured, many with a white tin glaze and colourful painted decoration.

At Alcora in Valencia a long-established industry making coarse earthenware was transformed in 1727 by the establishment of a factory to produce tin-glazed and other wares, artists being brought from France to teach the new styles of form and decoration. The resultant beautifully modelled ware has painted decoration in blue or in a combination of blue, yellow, green and brown on a bright white background. Arabesque designs of great delicacy were popular, as were subjects copied from engravings and rococo floral motifs. Output included animal-shaped spice pots and tureens similar to those made in Strasbourg and *trompe l'œil* dishes decorated with false comestibles. The work was remarkable chiefly for its extravagant and grandiose forms – busts, elaborate chandeliers, large wall-cisterns, basins and similar

Ewer, Portuguese, early 17th century. Earthenware, tin-glazed with painted figurative cobalt-blue decoration, probably copied from an imported Chinese porcelain ewer, *c.* 1700, from the Jingdezhen kilns in Jiangxi province, China. Height 28 cm (11.2 in).

Embossed dish, German, 1694. Earthenware, lead-glazed, with the design of a man and woman, inscribed ANNO 1694. Diameter 31.8 cm (12.75 in).

Dish from a workshop in the Werra River region, central Germany, *c.* 1590–1624. Earthenware, wheel-thrown, with decoration incised through white slip to reveal the red body with green overpainting and decoration of Eve holding the apple, and yellowish lead glaze. Diameter 23 cm (9.2 in).

GERMANY

In the late ninth century a flourishing pottery industry was operating in the Rhineland, in the Badorf and Pingsdorf areas, producing red-painted and lead-glazed wares. Lead-glazed pottery, first brought to northwest Europe during the Roman period, was made in England and France as well as the Rhineland. It has not been ascertained whether, following the collapse of the Roman empire, production techniques were lost and later reintroduced or whether they were used continuously in some form. Pots with glazed exteriors are known to have been made in Hamburg around 900, more or less at the same time as in England, and in the Low Countries by the eleventh century.

The vast majority of pottery was simple utility ware, its form determined primarily by its function but with individual regions developing their own styles. Simple burnish and slip decoration was used, along with lead glaze, iron wash and ash glaze. Late medieval pottery in northern Germany included grey earthenware, and in southern and parts of central Germany oxidized yellow or red earthenware was made as well. Although the technology of lead glazing was known, it had little significance until the mid-fifteenth century other than for use on stove tiles in central and southern parts of the country.

Highly decorated earthenware has a long tradition in southern Germany, the Alpine region, Bohemia, Saxony, Silesia and Hesse. From the twelfth century glaze was employed for artistic effect on wall and floor tiles. A hundred years later coloured lead glazes were used for ornamental brickwork on the façades of buildings in northern Germany and for stove tiles. In the Lower Rhineland the production of unglazed reduced-grey earthenwares includes such forms as cooking pots and ladles, many of which were exported in large quantities. By the mid-fifteenth century the range of forms had broadened to include large storage vessels, tripod cooking pots, deep bowls with pulled spouts and small jugs. At much the same time red earthenware pottery with an interior coloured lead glaze appears, some of it with white slip decoration. In the Lower Rhine glazed wares replaced the unglazed greywares. Glazed wares include large comb-decorated dishes, tripod cooking pots and cauldrons, and frying pans, the colour of the glaze ranging from reddish-orange to bright yellow.

The main production of earthenware pottery in south Tyrol started around 1520–30, although stove tiles, decorated with lead glazes coloured black, copper green, iron yellow or brown, had been made since the fourteenth century. The pots themselves, usually thrown on the fast wheel, could be produced relatively quickly, but applying decoration to the more ornate pieces was time-consuming. Most were made from local clays that fired shades of pink or red; they were often covered with a white or cream-coloured slip and a

clear lead glaze, and frequently decorated with colouring oxides. The glaze, being costly, was applied only on the top surfaces of such vessels as bowls rather than underneath, where it would rarely be seen. The disadvantage of lead glaze is that, unless it is well formulated, on contact with acid foodstuffs such as curdled milk or vinegar poisonous lead compounds are formed, making the vessels unsuitable for storing substances of this kind. The use of acid-soluble lead-oxide glazes for domestic pottery was eventually forbidden in Germany by the Reich's law of 25 June 1885.

Shapes were designed to be sound and practical since the vessels were destined for use in or around the home or farm. Forms include cooking pots of many sizes, jugs, dishes, plates, bowls and a wealth of smaller items such as toys, teapot-warmers and warming pans. A variety of influences were absorbed. Decoration, incised through a white slip and picked out in runny coloured oxides, was often a local adaptation. Designs were either incised through a layer of slip or modelled or moulded on to the surface. Slip-trailed decoration involved a clay slip (or *Schlicker*) of thick consistency being trailed on to the leather-hard surface of the pot by means of a tool such as a cowhorn or a small earthenware pot fitted with a goose-feather quill cut into a fine nozzle. Slip-trailed motifs include anthropomorphic, zoomorphic, botanical and geometric designs, many outlined in sgraffito. Bordering these central designs are geometric or botanical patterns that sometimes have a dark brown background defined by spirals or concentric circles. A common motif was that of full-length male and female figures, shown either separately or together.

Some of the finest and most ornate German slipwares with coloured decoration were made in the Werra and Weser regions in the second half of the sixteenth century. Werra ware (sometimes referred to as Wanfried ware) was produced at a number of sites along the River Werra and exported in quantity through the port of Bremen to the Low Countries, England, Scandinavia and North America. The main colours are white with green, dark brown and yellow, and designs include abstract geometric patterns, plants, leaping stags, hares, lions and birds as well as representations of people, particularly finely-dressed women and men, many shown holding a drinking glass.

Portrait busts, biblical scenes, saints and allegorical motifs also appear. In addition to dishes, typical forms are pipkins, jugs and wall tiles. Weser slipware was produced at a number of centres in the *Pottland* between the Weser and the Leine. On the areas that were to be decorated the hard-fired pinkish-white clay would be coated with a white or cream slip on to which a design of alternate wavy green and red-brown lines was applied. Also employed on Weser-ware dishes were designs of birds or of bearded faces (sometimes known as Bartmann face masks). The decorative patterns of geometric, botanical and zoomorphic motifs found on slipware produced in the Lower Rhineland are more akin to contemporary Netherlandish maiolica and north Holland slipware than to the more anthropomorphic decoration of the Werra and Weser regions. The demand for maiolica in the first half of the seventeenth century brought the production of first Werra and later Weser ware to an end, but other workshops continued to make more basic wares.

From the sixteenth to the twentieth centuries lead-glazed slip-decorated wares produced in the north German plains, the Lower Rhine, the Altes Land and the Probstei were well made, featuring a variety of trailed, incised and modelled decoration. More ornate decorative pieces such as dishes were produced in addition to the everyday cooking pots, platters, baking moulds (some with a design of an embracing mermaid and merman), colanders and storage vessels. The range of pieces extended from ceramic toys and ink-stands to teapot-warmers, with decoration typically depicting fashionably attired ladies and gentlemen, animals such as deer and floral designs. Inscriptions were usually uplifting or had moral overtones, for example: 'This dish was made by hands and preserved by good sense.' When German potters, especially those from rural districts, emigrated to America, they took with them all their native customs and practices; the American earthenware known as Pennsylvania Dutch derives largely from the slipware produced in southern Germany during the eighteenth century.

Tin-glazed wares
The appearance of Italian tin-glazed ware in Germany in the sixteenth century may have provided the stimulus for German potters to devise

Plate, German, from Bavaria, c. 1750. Earthenware, tin-glazed, with enamel decoration, made at the Ansbach factory.

a colourful alternative product. It is also possible that this coincided with the arrival of immigrant Anabaptist Italian potters fleeing from cities such as Faenza, which had come under the control of the Pope in 1510. Some of the earliest German maiolica wares were produced at Nuremberg in the sixteenth century, although maiolica tiles, mainly for stoves, had been made earlier in Bavaria and the Tyrol. Widespread production began around the late seventeenth century, when dishes and drug jars were produced whose design and shape showed a strong Italian influence. Other early centres include Hanau, Frankfurt and Berlin, where much of the production was designed in the style of Dutch delftware. The decoration is principally blue on a white ground, reflecting the influence of the landscapes and figure subjects found on Chinese export porcelain. Although Chinese-inspired themes were prevalent throughout the golden age of German maiolica in the eighteenth century, local motifs do appear, one of the most popular depicting songbirds among scattered foliage.

Stove tile. German, from Cologne, dated 1561. Earthenware, lead glazed, and moulded with figure of Rhetoric beneath a Renaissance arch. This is one of the tiles in the Seven Liberal Arts series, after an engraving of 1539 by Hans Sebald Behan. Height 33.4 cm (13.4 in), width 23.5 cm (9.4 in).

During the early eighteenth century tin-glaze factories continued to be established in increasing numbers in Germany, where special services were made in response to the growing popularity of beverages such as tea, coffee and chocolate. Combined with the development by Johann Friedrich Böttger in 1709 (see chapter 7) and subsequent commercial production of hard-paste porcelain, this new demand affected the design and decoration of tin-glazed wares in general. For example, the fine naturalistic painting referred to as 'German flowers', first employed on Meissen porcelain, was adapted for use by tin-glaze potters at Strasbourg in France, where this style of decoration became known as 'Strasbourg flowers'. This in turn affected German tin-glazed wares. They were further influenced by the Du Paquier porcelain factory at Vienna, which was flourishing at the time.

Throughout Europe maiolica factories adapted themselves to, and even expanded under, the changing conditions of the eighteenth century. In addition to Hanover, in Germany these factories were situated principally in the southern and central regions, including Bayreuth, Brunswick, Fulda, Höchst and Crailsheim. As the century progressed, the Chinese-inspired decoration was superseded by a more native style, with birds and foliage, figures, land- and riverscapes, the double-headed eagle, coats of arms and naively rendered buildings among the more popular motifs. Tin-glazed earthenware became an acceptable cheaper alternative to the fine porcelain wares that served the expanding market for luxury goods. It was, however, the large-scale introduction of English cream-coloured wares, with their high quality and extraordinarily low prices, that finally brought about the collapse of the European industry around 1800.

FRANCE

In France a tradition of highly decorated pottery with slip, polychrome and relief decoration arose from the twelfth and thirteenth centuries onward. The most common forms are jugs and related vessels. One group of wares comprises both jugs and other hollow vessels with flowing green, yellow, brown or blue glaze, or, not uncommonly, splashed yellow and green glaze, sometimes decorated with medallions in the form of coats of arms, flowers

A flourishing maiolica factory established in 1666 at Frankfurt-am-Main produced highly decorative ornamental wares that contrasted favourably with the more mundane pieces made in nearby Hanau. On these wares the decoration, usually painted in blue, was covered in the clear glaze known as *kwaart* to add depth and shine. Plates and dishes were made, some left smooth, others ribbed, on which the rims were sometimes lobed. Vases, jugs and basins were also produced. At Frankfurt typical designs reflected a strong Chinese influence, for example a scene in which 'Chinamen' were set in a stylized landscape with rocks, shrubs, birds, butterflies and insects. Also painted were naturalistic designs that were more European in character, such as those on wares made at Hanau.

Dish from the workshop of Bernard Palissy, The Tuileries, Paris, *c.* 1575–1600. Earthenware, *pièce rustique* with relief modelled and moulded decoration and coloured glazes of marine animals, shells and plants. Palissy often moulded shells and animals from life and was famous for his experimental coloured glazes. His patrons included Anne de Montmorency and Catherine de Médici. Length 52.3 cm (21 in).

and faces. From the thirteenth century Saintonge became one of the primary production centres, supplying pottery to Britain and northern Europe as well as serving more local markets, its success linked to the English acquisition of Gascony and the development of the wine trade. The fired off-white or buff body of ware from this centre was often covered with areas of green glaze. Forms include large cooking pots with lids, small jugs, and large globular *pégaux* with parrot-beak or tubular spouts and strap or bucket handles. During the sixteenth century, although the jugs remained largely plain, dishes and bowls were often decorated in green and brown glaze; designs comprising painted green and brown botanical and geometric patterns were typified by finely drawn brown lines and fine 'feathery' leaves.

In the sixteenth century polychrome ware was also produced in the style of Bernard Palissy (whose work is described later in this section), the range including dishes and oval and round bowls sometimes pierced with scalloped flanges. Among the different types of object made were chafing dishes, costrels (a type of pilgrim's flask, usually of an elongated pear shape), oval incense vessels and objects in the shape of boots. Polychrome moulded and modelled decoration was common, incorporating motifs such as heraldic medallions, animals and birds as well as scenes depicting a variety of biblical, mythological and allegorical subjects.

Other main production centres in France include Rouen and the Beauvais and Loire regions. Jugs from the Loire, made from around 1500 to 1700, were mostly globular in form with a strap

Ewer, French, attributed to Saint Porchaire in Bordeaux, *c.* 1550. Earthenware, lead glazed, with inlaid slip and applied decoration. Height 29.4 cm (11.75 in).

handle. In the Beauvais district a variety of fine wares were produced that were superior in quality to those made elsewhere in north-west Europe, the items being referred to in an inventory of 1399 as *godet de terre de Beauvais garny d'Argent*, 'godet' signifying a cup with a spreading rim. In the early part of the sixteenth century a distinctive style of lead-glazed pottery with sgraffito decoration was perfected. Designs were varied and range from busts to stylized flowers, borders of wavy lines and interlaced heart-shaped motifs, sometimes accompanied by inscriptions in Gothic lettering.

Tin-glazed earthenware

The technique of tin glazing, usually known in France as *faïence*, appeared in southern France at Avignon, for use on tiles, as early as the twelfth or thirteenth century. However, its use did not become widespread until the sixteenth century, when Italian artisans settled in Lyons, Montpellier and Nîmes. The pots produced at these centres are almost identical in their shape, decoration and general style to contemporary Italian wares. Some of the earliest of them were decorated with painted geometric designs in copper green and manganese. Large decorative dishes with ornate borders and vases of elaborate form were made. Other major factories were set up at Nevers, Moustiers, Marseilles and Strasbourg.

At Nevers in central France the pottery industry that developed towards the end of the sixteenth century adopted a naturalistic style of decoration in which designs of birds and sprays of flowers were carried out in blue and white on a white or a pale yellow ground; painted designs on imported Chinese blue-and-white porcelain wares were also imitated. Around the middle of the century, in the north at Rouen, the work of Masséot Abaquesne (active 1526–59) is more sombre. In addition to tiles, early products from Rouen include albarelli and flat-rimmed dishes. Situated quite close to Paris and the French court, Rouen developed as a major production centre at the end of the seventeenth century. A highly ornate style evolved there, which utilized intricate motifs resembling ironwork or lacework that probably owed much to contemporary Chinese ceramic ornament. The finely moulded shapes were based largely on the work of ornamental engravers and silversmiths, and the designs, incorporating drapery, foliage and other Renaissance motifs, were usually carried out in blue on a white ground.

One of the earliest markets for tin-glazed earthenware was the medical profession. Between 1520 and 1640 vessels made for the storage of medicines and herbs included albarelli for drugs and *chevrettes* (round spouted jars) for syrups and liquids. In a contract of 1545 an apothecary in Rouen ordered 4,152 drug jars – a strong indication of the popularity of the ware. Sometimes albarelli were used to display flowers, thus elevating their aesthetic status. From 1640 to 1715 the market expanded to take in the minor nobility, the clergy and the upper bourgeoisie, who ordered luxury items such as chargers and giant jardinières.

Bernard Palissy (1510–90) had been the first major European potter to establish an individual style, and even today his work influences industrial and studio potters worldwide. Although trained as a painter of stained glass, Palissy was so inspired by Italian maiolica that he chose instead to become a potter, setting himself the task of developing a range of enamel colours that would outshine those of Italy. Perfecting these took him sixteen years, during which time he came close to bankruptcy, even having on one occasion to stoke the kiln with his own furniture. Finally, however, he did succeed in inventing fine glazes and brilliant colours that adhered well to the body.

Dish, French, from Lyons, dated 1582. Earthenware with tin glaze painted in yellow, brown, orange, purple, green, black, grey and white, depicting Pharaoh and the serpents (Exodus 7). Diameter 41.5 cm (16.5 in).

Palissy is best known for his *rustique* wares, which consist of dishes on which are modelled natural forms such as reptiles, fish, insects, shells, mosses and plants. Usually oval in shape, the dishes are decorated with carefully arranged landscape settings that might, for example, include a stream flowing round the dish, with reptiles posed on the banks and in the water. In later pieces classical figures are included in such compositions. Palissy also devised large-scale ceramic grottoes, constructing one in the Tuileries garden in Paris. Although his reputation is based to a large extent on his own often fantastical writings, in which he describes his adventures as a potter, alchemist, artist and land-surveyor, his ceramic style influenced many later potters. Copies of Palissy ware were made at many tin-glaze potteries, including those at Delft and Lambeth, and some studio potters today take a great interest in his work.

During the eighteenth century the French tin-glaze industry underwent further expansion as the influence of imported Chinese porcelains largely superseded that of Italian and Dutch delftware. In 1689 and 1709, in order to meet the cost of the ruinous wars of the Spanish Succession, Louis XIV decreed that all gold and silver vessels should be melted down, thus providing the stimulus for the French faience industry to devise acceptable alternative wares. Shapes for the table were borrowed from the more expensive but ill-fated metalwares, the potters often using the actual moulds used by the gold- and silversmiths. The range of forms was extended to included pitchers, sugar-casters and mustard pots. Produced at such factories as Sèvres, special table services, some of them bearing armorial crests, were also commissioned, while ceramic house furnishings included wall sconces and washbasins.

Around 1750 the demand for ware resembling porcelain in appearance but manufactured more cheaply encouraged faience producers to add further refinement to their products in the form of enamel decoration. At Rouen many pieces were decorated with a repeating triangular motif directed towards the centre (*style rayonnant*), their outlines enriched by the use of such colours as red and yellow. The range of vessels was also extended to include many more accessories for the table, including fashionable ice pails, dredgers for powdered sugar, boxes for precious spices, salt cellars and basins. The middle of the century saw the adoption of a rococo style of decoration that reflected the influence of contemporary artists such as Watteau and Boucher. Garlands of naturalistically painted flowers and shells framed finely drawn pictures with amorous or pastoral subjects.

A number of technical changes took place at Strasbourg, near the German border, in the second half of the century. Hitherto colours had been painted directly on to the unfired tin glaze, this process sometimes being referred to as in-glaze decoration because the colour was absorbed into the glaze during the firing. The new technique, copied from the porcelain factories, involved using specially prepared coloured enamel glazes that were painted on to the surface of the fired glaze then fixed in a third, low-temperature firing. The main advantages of enamels were the extensive range of bright colours that could be obtained and the high degree of definition achievable by skilled painters.

In the late sixteenth century production became centred in northern Holland, although slipware of the same general type was made widely throughout the Low Countries and across to northern France. By this time the range of forms embraced dishes, bowls (produced in three sizes), cooking pots and pipkins, small jugs and impressive hand-built fire-covers. The decoration on these wares consists of trailed pale yellow slip, sometimes overpainted in green on such detail as leaves. Fluent brushwork adds to the attraction of the ware, and design motifs include animals and birds as well as the male and female figure. Among the botanical designs are pomegranates, tulips and thistles, while geometric patterns include rosettes and chequers as well as heraldic and religious designs. Some designs were picked out in sgraffito.

In the late fifteenth century to the early sixteenth a flourishing ceramics industry developed in the coastal provinces of the Netherlands, from southern Flanders to northern Friesland, where there were ample supplies of suitable clay and fuel to the fire the kilns. In the north, decrees banning the construction of houses in wood gave potteries the incentive to manufacture tiles and bricks, while domestic utensils with lead glazes, some with slip decoration, were also produced.

Tin-glazed earthenware

By the end of the fifteenth century large-scale production of tin-glazed pottery had begun in north-western Europe. By 1550 a number of potters in Holland were producing tin-glazed ware in addition to their other work, a flourishing maiolica

Fire cover, Netherlands, dated 1598. Earthenware with white slip-trailed decoration and green painted decoration depicting double-headed eagle in the centre, derived from the arms of the empire but here used in a purely decorative manner.

Porcelain painters from Germany brought with them the requisite knowledge and skill for a fresh style featuring naturalistically painted flowers and finely modelled figures, akin to that of maiolica, to be developed for the tin-glazed ware. Tureens modelled in the shape of vegetables or animals – a particularly popular shape being a boar's head – were also made as showpieces for sideboards or banqueting tables.

THE LOW COUNTRIES

Early coarse earthenwares produced in the Low Countries were made using a grey-firing clay, but in the thirteenth century a fundamental change took place (some two hundred years before it did elsewhere in Europe) when redwares were introduced for the finer products – the highly decorated Flemish wares in particular. The body fired red or orange and the lead glaze ranged from yellow to greenish-brown in colour. Typical forms were kitchenwares such as cooking pots, pipkins and skillets, to which sgraffito decoration was sometimes applied.

Dish, Low Countries, perhaps Delft or Haarlem, c. 1640–70. Earthenware, thrown, tin glaze, painted in polychrome with a scene of a woman in a wooded landscape along with two hunters and horses. Diameter c. 45 cm (18 in).

industry, started by Italian immigrants, having arisen alongside the production of lead-glazed wares. It was during the early sixteenth century that names of immigrant Italian potters first appeared in the Antwerp records, including those of Janne Maria de Capua, Jan Francesco de Brescia, Pieter (or Petrus) Frans van Venedigen, and most notably Guido da Savino from Castel Durante. Guido da Savino and his successors belonged to the Guild of St Luke, the corporation of painters, glassworkers and engravers, and as such held the status of artists rather than artisans. Perhaps not surprisingly, the style of the earliest maiolica made in the Low Countries was based heavily on contemporary Italian work. In addition to floor tiles, pots used by pharmacists, such as the albarelli and large and small gallipots (ointment pots), were made. Fruits, flowers and ornaments were popular decorative motifs. Gradually a number of Flemish families, mostly members of the middle classes, became involved in the tin-glaze industry, while the artisan-potters continued to make lead-glazed wares.

From the middle of the sixteenth century specialist maiolica potters began moving out of Antwerp. Some emigrated to England, Germany or Spain and even more to the northern Netherlands, where, setting a high technical standard, they created what was in effect a new industry but one greatly aided by the specialist skills already existing in the region. Prior to 1600 the most important centre of the industry in Holland was Haarlem, where at least three major factories were established before 1570. Potters from Antwerp were also working in Amsterdam in 1584 and 1587; they were the first to be called *geleybakker* (*geley* meaning maiolica). The industry in Delft became established slightly later, eight new factories being set up there between 1584 and 1620.

The activities of the Dutch East India Company, founded in 1602 under the protection of the Dutch government, resulted in large amounts of blue-and-white Chinese porcelain (described as 'more costly than crystal') being imported into Europe. The strength and fineness of the Chinese wares posed a real threat to the tin-glaze potters, many of whom turned to the production of tiles or ceramic objects that were quite different in style and form from oriental wares, while others sought to imitate the Chinese wares as closely as possible. A number of technical advances were made in order to achieve this, including the use of a transparent lead glaze applied over the decoration (known to the Dutch as *kwaart*, thought to be a corruption of the Italian word *coperta*, meaning 'cover'), which gave the pots an even, lustrous gloss and added greater depth to the colours. The use of enclosed ceramic boxes, or saggars, to protect the pots from the flame, the elimination of spur marks from the face of the pieces and the use of finer, chalk-based clay all further improved the quality of the product. The resulting wares, virtually identical in appearance to the blue-and-white wares of China when decorated in the same colours, became known as *Hollants porceleyn*.

The Netherlands potters benefited from the disruption in trade caused by the fall of China's Ming dynasty in 1644, which caused a drastic reduction in the volume of Chinese wares arriving in Europe. Tin-glaze potters seized this opportunity by filling the gap with objects of high quality expertly painted in the Chinese style. Many forms were borrowed from earlier styles, or even German stonewares, and the lobed form was derived directly from Dutch silverware. The polychrome decoration on plates, dishes and other shapes included finely painted scenes and biblical subjects, some based on engravings or paintings. One image of the creation of Eve was taken from a woodcut by Lucas Cranach

Pair of William and Mary pagoda hyacinth vases, with a vase and double cover. Dutch, Delft. Earthenware, tin-glazed with blue painted decoration.

Cabbage-shaped tureen, cover and stand. Philippe Mombaers factory, Brussels, *c.* 1750. Earthenware, naturalistically modelled overlapping leaves and moulded applied insects. Height 34 cm (13.5 in).

Table top. Scandinavian, probably Rörstraad, *c.* 1740. Earthenware, tin glazed with painted decoration in blue depicting the Virgin Mary kneeling in prayer at an altar and facing the Angel of the Annunciation, holding a beribboned staff inscribed AVE MARIA GRATIA PLENA, the edge with a broad border of seeded latticework, shells and foliage. Length 57.5 cm (23 in).

(1472–1553). Portraits, genre paintings, still-lifes, emblematic images, heraldic motifs and proverbs were all used as models for ceramic decoration.

In addition to the blue-and-white and polychrome wares produced in the Chinese and Dutch styles, a range of other ceramics were made at Delft. Many were adapted from Chinese and Meissen originals and include figures and modelled wares as well as milk jugs in the shapes of cows, parrots on rocks and shoes. One of the most noteworthy forms is the pyramidal multi-tiered hyacinth vase, probably suggested by a Chinese pagoda. Tiles were produced in quantity, with the favourite motif of baskets and flowers rendered in orange, yellow, red, green, purple and occasionally black to brilliant effect. Using carefully prepared clays, red earthenware teapots based on imported Chinese wares were also made. In the eighteenth century green, red and yellow were added to the earlier palette of blue and purple. Polychrome wares, imitating Chinese enamelled porcelain made during the reign of K'ang Hsi (1662–1772) and the rival Arita Japanese porcelain known in Europe as Imari ware, were also produced.

SCANDINAVIA

Finely made and carefully decorated lead-glazed slipwares were produced in Scandinavia in the sixteenth and seventeenth centuries. In Denmark the production of glazed earthenware with some simple slip decoration dates back to the thirteenth and fourteenth centuries. As in the rest of the northern countries, some of the potters who settled in Denmark came from northern Germany and this led to the production of high-quality slipwares in the late sixteenth and seventeenth centuries. Pottery made in Sweden during the seventeenth century includes dishes with slip-trailed design of birds and drinking bowls with a floral-shaped handle, all of good quality. In Norway, the majority of the first potters were German immigrants.

Scandinavian tin-glazed wares are distinguished especially by their use of the rococo style of decoration that developed in the late eighteenth century, which is characterized by a mixture of rock- and shell-like motifs set within a framework of scrolls. The clean, fresh enamel decoration and inventive forms of Marieberg in Sweden recall work produced at Strasbourg, while the blue and manganese purple-painted decoration of Rörstraad

in Sweden and Herrebøe in Norway are these potteries' own invention. At the Danish Store Kongensgade factory, and later at nearby Kastrup in Copenhagen, a general move towards rococo around the middle of the eighteenth century is largely attributable to the activities of two men: Johann Buchwald, who worked at several factories, and J.E.L. Ehrenreich, the founder of Marieberg.

Vessel from Pingsdorf, near Cologne, 9th century. Earthenware, wheel-turned with frilled foot, hard buff clay with red painted decoration, in a form that reflects Roman influence.

Ehrenreich later moved to Stralsund in Pomerania and then to Königsberg in East Prussia, where a range of beautiful colours was developed that included a rich blue.

GERMAN STONEWARES

By the fourteenth century, fully fused stoneware, hard and impervious to liquids, had been developed in the Rhineland. This was ideal for domestic purposes, whether for drinking, decanting, transport or general storage. Pottery workshops were generally situated in areas where there were deposits of clay suitable for high-temperature firing as well as a plentiful supply of wood for the firings (which could last as long as several days). The widespread introduction of salt glazing in the sixteenth century led to a requirement for large and regular quantities of salt, which was usually brought by boat from the North Sea and the Baltic. Later, cobalt and manganese were required for colouring. In response to rising demand both locally and from rural and urban communities across the European continent, workshops throughout Germany, from the Rhine to the Oder, increased production, adapting their wares to the growing and changing market.

A number of sites have been identified in relation to the early development of the stoneware body. At Siegburg in the Rhineland proto-stoneware of the mid-twelfth to late thirteenth centuries was fired to temperatures around 1000–1100°C, while near-stonewares fired to around 1100–1200°C were produced in the late thirteenth century. By the second quarter of the fourteenth century true stoneware was being produced, fired to 1300–1400°C; it was to continue to be made for the following three hundred years. The higher temperatures were achieved by improvements in kiln technology, with kiln builders lowering the level of the stoke-hole and introducing a new type of horizontal kiln.

Early high-fired ware (c. 1000–1200)

The development of high-fired ware in Germany, where it was produced for the first time in the West, was the continuation of a long pottery tradition in the Rhine Valley as well as being greatly aided by the presence of abundant supplies of refractory clay. Unlike red earthenware, the grey clay with its high sand content was able to

withstand higher temperatures without collapsing. Ample wood and, later, good quality coal was available as fuel to fire the kilns. Proximity to the Rhine also enabled the wares to be transported easily and at low cost, so ensuring access to extended markets.

Stoneware has a hard, dense, impervious body that emits a clear ringing sound when struck. In some ways it is similar to porcelain in that both are highly vitrified and have a low level of porosity, but stoneware is not usually either white, translucent or thinly potted. The fact that glazes capable of being fired to high temperatures were unknown to the early German stoneware potters was, at this stage, relatively unimportant since the high-fired body was more or less impervious to liquids and the purpose of the wares was primarily functional rather than aesthetic.

By the late Middle Ages and early modern period the fast wheel was in general use. The characteristic 'frilled' base of some pots was formed by leaving a residue of clay that was then thumbed to produce the distinctive foot-ring. Over the course of the sixteenth and seventeenth centuries the crisp profiles became increasingly complex and were achieved with the use of wooden templates. String marks on the base of pots indicate that they were cut off and removed while the wheel was still

in motion, which suggests a measure of mass-production. As potter's wheels became ever more efficient, the size and height of forms increased and the early squat stoneware forms evolved into taller, more slender shapes. The objects most commonly made seem to be jugs, cooking pots and cooking utensils, on which washes of fusible red clay were used both as decoration and to enhance the surface texture of the pot by making it smoother.

A major defining characteristic of Renaissance and later German stoneware is the use of mould technology to produce delicate relief ornament, often using designs based on contemporary woodblocks. This process had the great advantage that, unlike painted designs, the patterns, once created, could be produced in quantity and with great accuracy. The emergence of the Cologne stoneware industry during the early sixteenth century coincided with the introduction of woodblock

printing and the increasing accessibility of single-sheet designs, which provided a ready source of material for the pattern. Designs include figurative and botanical friezes, portrait roundels, and oak-leaf and rose-plant ornament applied naturalistically over the entire surface. The Rhenish stoneware industries of Siegburg and Raeren used engravings by such artists as Heinrich Aldegrever, Sebald Beham and Virgil Solis. In the seventeenth century armorials and pattern books replaced individual sheet engraving.

The process of making the relief involved cutting the original negative design in stone then pressing it with clay to produce one or a series of die impressions, which would be lightly fired. These were then pressed into soft clay, which was fired to produce the final negative mould. In order to apply the relief decoration to the pot, the mould was filled with clay, the surplus smoothed off and the back pressed on to the moistened or slip-painted surface of the vessel, causing the clay relief to adhere to the surface.

Salt-glazed stoneware

The first true glazes on stoneware appear in the Rhineland during the fifteenth century and are thought to have developed from the observation

Large flagon from Siegburg, Rhineland, *c.* 1560–85. Stoneware, wheel-thrown, with areas of cobalt blue on a streaky ash glaze. Moulded decoration of three applied shields of arms are supported by full-length figures in contemporary dress. The arms are those of Spain, the Holy Roman Empire and the Duchy of Jülich-Kleve-Berg. Height 38 cm (15.2 in).

that the potassium-rich vapour from the wood used for the firing reacted with the surface of the pots to form a glaze. Alongside the invention of hard-paste porcelain, salt-glaze is probably Germany's most important contribution to the art of pottery. The practice first developed in the Rhineland during the fifteenth century, when it was found that salt thrown into a kiln at high temperatures produces vapours that react with the surface of the clay to form a thin layer of glaze. The theory that the discovery of salt glazing arose from the use of discarded salted-herring barrels for the firing has not been proven.

Several factors contributed to the development of salt glaze. The local stoneware clay reacted well with salt (sodium chloride) which, when thrown into the kiln towards the culmination of the firing, volatilized into sodium and chlorine, the sodium combining with the surface of the clay to produce a chemically simple but extremely tough

and resistant glaze. According to the amount of iron present in the clay body, the glaze so formed would be either smooth and brown or at other times may have had a surface texture resembling orange peel. Sometimes it would have been mottled brown and cream, the colour and texture depending to a large extent on the clay body. The use of different types of clay slip also led to variations in colour, but invariably the glaze coating was thin, which heightened rather than concealing the surface of the pots and was well suited to the fine relief decoration.

Stoneware manufacture was stimulated by the increased consumption of ales and wines throughout Europe and the need for suitable vessels for both storing and serving them. Around 1500 the relatively coarse malt liquor was greatly improved by the addition of hops, a new ingredient that made it far more palatable and resulted in a widespread increase in the consumption of ale. Inns and taverns became popular social centres and stoneware drinking vessels were in great demand. England, along with many other countries, also enjoyed this new brew and a thriving trade developed there to provide the country with the necessary vessels. Wine was transported throughout Europe in stoneware wine bottles.

Like other types of ceramics, German stonewares provide a rich source of information on material life at the time. By virtue of its robust, highly durable, non-porous body and stain- and odour-resistant surface, stoneware was particularly suitable for the transport, storage, drinking and decanting of liquids and for preservation, pharmaceutical and sanitary uses. The high level of vitrification of the body made it unsuitable for cooking purposes but excellent for the storage of food. A list of wares and prices drawn up in 1552 by the Siegburg potters' guild includes forty-four individual terms that relate directly to functional items intended for specific markets. These include *Bierpot* and, for kitchen and dairy use, *Milchduppen*. Other wares were intended specifically for export to Saxony in southern Germany.

In addition to a range of pots, devotional figurines, toys and spindle-whorls for the spinning of thread were made, but drinking vessels constituted the majority of the ware. The tall, narrow-necked *Jacobakanne* jug and funnel-necked jug and beaker are depicted in dining scenes of the

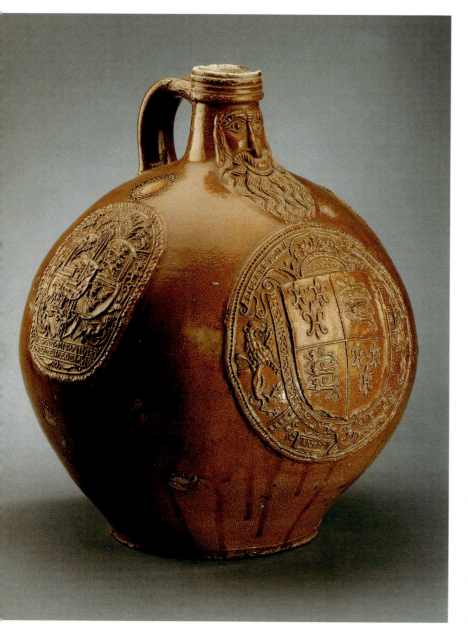

'Bartmann' pitcher. Frechen, Rhineland, 1594. Salt-glazed stoneware, with applied medallions moulded with a reversed version of the arms of Denmark, in the centre a medallion with the Tudor arms and the inscription ELISABET DIE GRACIA REGINA, ANNO 1594. Height 36.5 cm (14.6 in).

Raeren, near Aachen, lying in present-day Belgium, was the main centre for the production of red-brown salt-glazed stoneware. Here the art of salt glazing was fully developed, an iron wash being used to achieve a rich, bronze-like surface. Between 1475 and 1525 a new range of vessel forms was introduced, including specialized drinking vessels such as globular mugs, funnel-necked drinking jugs, bottles with tapering necks and a wide variety of other jugs and tankards as well as ointment pots and other household utensils. The finest vessels, of which the drinking mug was the most common, were made in the second half of the sixteenth century. Round-bellied mugs of fine clay with little or no decoration other than a band of pattern in relief round the neck were produced with a rich, brown glaze. Large jugs thrown on the wheel were turned to remove throwing marks and perfect the profile. Other popular forms ranged from handled jugs, some standing nearly a foot high, pilgrim flasks for holding spring water, puzzle jugs and jugs in the shape of cannon to pocket flagons fashioned in the form of prayer books.

Friezes of fine relief decoration were popular both for the scenes depicted and for their ornamental value, the detail being heightened by the salt glaze. They were designed with great originality by, among others, Jan Emens (Jan Emens Mennicken), the leading potter at Raeren from about 1566 to 1594, whose work tended to depict classical scenes that often included naked figures of male and female gods. Some of the designs, based on engravings specially produced by German artists, featured religious themes and scenes documenting social events such as parties or festivities. Later Emens created an impressive series of huge jugs with double friezes of classical subjects.

Certain wares were specially manufactured for particular markets and exported widely across Europe, some of the pieces being decorated with appropriate coats of arms. The application of royal arms may have been speculative, with an eye to a specific destination. Portraits of prominent figures such as kings and queens were also featured, again so that the wares would be attractive to particular foreign clients. These trade connections are underlined by the recovery of a Siegburg pot with applied relief decoration depicting a version of the imperial double-eagle, the badge of the Hanse station at the steelyard on the London waterfront. The

fifteenth century. Beer – the 'liquid bread' of medieval and early modern European society – is more likely to have been drunk from vessels with a wider opening, more stable base and larger capacity. The specialist production of mugs, tankards and drinking jugs for the export market began at Siegburg and Langerwehe during the fourteenth century, followed by Raeren in the fifteenth, Cologne and Frechen in the sixteenth, and the Westerwald in the seventeenth century. Subsequently, large jugs and pitchers specifically for drinking, decanting and serving purposes were developed in increasing variety.

dominance of Raeren stoneware in Britain suggests a monopoly of the cross-Channel trade.

In the sixteenth and seventeenth centuries one of the major products at Frechen and Cologne was the full, round-bodied pitcher with a narrow neck and small handle, often capable of holding a large volume, decorated with a bearded face mask or *Bartmaske*. It is possible that these masks originated from the popular tradition of the Wild Man, a mythical creature who features prominently in northern European folklore. The image appeared in illuminated manuscripts and graphic arts as well as on textiles, tapestries, metalwork, glass and architectural ornament. In Britain such bottles gained the name Bellarmine, thought by popular tradition to emanate from Cardinal Roberto Bellarmino (1542–1621), a zealous opponent of Protestantism in the Low Countries and northern Germany, and to have been applied to the bottle forms in jest.

Pots made in Cologne were similar to those produced at Raeren in that they had a comparable brown colour, achieved by the use of an iron wash over the pot that yielded various shades from chestnut to a dull yellow. The decorative motifs tended to imitate precious stones in metal settings and the influence of the Italian Renaissance can be seen in designs of portrait heads set within ornamental arcades. Texts such as 'Drink and eat, do not forget God' in Gothic script were often combined with classical motifs of acanthus leaves and medallions.

Early in the sixteenth century potters were banished from the centre of the city of Cologne, because the poisonous chlorine fumes emitted by the kilns during the salting process were thought to be excessive, and moved to the nearby city of Frechen. Here, good plastic clay and a warm welcome from the city led to the growth of a prosperous industry, which by 1650 was equivalent to that of Raeren a hundred years earlier. At Frechen decoration took the form of applied scrolls of foliage and stamped leaves and rosettes placed symmetrically over the full-bodied pots.

White salt-glazed stoneware (c. 1300–1800)

In the abbey town of Siegburg, on the River Sieg in Germany, white-firing stonewares were developed that contrasted with the brown wares made at other centres. Accounts referring to potters are first found in 1427, suggesting a well-established industry probably dating back to the twelfth century. Production reached its height in the fifteenth century, although over the following two hundred years, which brought the influence of Renaissance motifs and subject matter, wares of high technical and artistic quality continued to be produced. Unlike other Rhineland clays, the local clays fired a clean white, which gave them a distinctive character. The importance of the industry is confirmed by the fact that well-established guilds protected both it and the potters, and long family traditions spanning hundreds of years are recorded.

Hard and vitrified pottery in light-firing clays was produced in this area before about 1400. *Jacobakannen* dating to the fourteenth century, thrown on the wheel, bear the throwing rings and typical 'pie-crust' decoration at the base. Later, jugs of a similar style were produced, but with the surfaces embellished with relief decoration of applied rosettes and grotesque faces.

It was around the middle of the sixteenth century that the finest whitewares were produced at Siegburg, although getting the white clay to react well with the salt remained a problem. While the white clay was refractory, in comparison with the brown salt wares the glaze tended to be thinner, less shiny and drier in feel, but despite its more 'dry' appearance the colour proved successful. New forms and a technically and artistically advanced range of applied relief ornament were introduced, largely influenced by developments in Cologne. The tall, cylindrical *Schnelle* tankard became standard at all workshops, as did the use of engravings by artists working in the print medium. In addition to figures and narrative scenes derived from engraved bible illustrations by artists such as Sebald Beham, Virgil Solis and others, printed mythological, allegorical, historical and heraldic subjects provided the source for relief designs at this time. Towards the last quarter of the sixteenth century cobalt blue-painted decoration was introduced that was intended to highlight the applied relief designs.

Forms included tall, slender tapering drinking mugs and ewers with long spouts that imitated metal forms and were reserved for dispensing the best wine, in addition to puzzle jugs, large candlesticks and baluster jugs. Fine detailed relief decoration included religious subjects such as the

Garden of Eden, the Temptation, the Annunciation, the Last Supper and the Flagellation. There were also, in stark contrast, anti-Catholic scenes showing clergy and monks indulging in wild debauchery, as well as mythological scenes and heraldic devices. The larger or more complicated objects, such as candelabra, were made in moulds, but the majority were thrown on the wheel and often left with the throwing marks, which gives them a pleasant and lively appearance. Specialist and ornate vessel shapes were produced, including covered goblets, spouted jugs and standing costrels.

Coloured wares

The district of Westerwald – sometimes known as *Kannenbäckerland* ('pot-maker country') and containing one of the richest sources of pottery clay in north-west Europe – was home to several pottery-producing towns, of which the most important were Grenzhausen, Grenzau and Höhr. After many potters had fled to this region from the ravages of the Thirty Years War (1618–48), and following the decline of the potteries at Cologne, Siegburg and Raeren, the industry suddenly acquired a new vitality with the introduction of colour. Stonewares made in the area had hitherto been brown, white or cream, depending on the body used, but the introduction of cobalt blue and manganese purple, the only two colours capable of withstanding the high-temperature firing, allowed a new range of ware to be produced that was both coloured and ornate, potters moving into the area often bringing with them their own applied relief moulds. A prosperous industry developed that was to flourish for some two hundred years, with the ware traded heavily not only within the Rhineland but across Europe and eventually even to North America, Africa and the Far East.

Salt-glazed stoneware tends not to favour the development of bright colours, but ultramarine, navy blue and aubergine purple combined with the grey-white background to produce a startling, if sombre, effect that was much admired in the nineteenth century. The pots, made from clay that fired a light bluish-grey, were decorated with bold, if not perfectly executed, designs that comprised notches, plain circles and rosettes relying for their effect on the added colour. The ware owed its popularity mainly to the vogue for colour, stimulated perhaps by the colourful maiolica wares, while drinkers no longer, it appears, sought either amusement from the friezes of relief decoration or instruction from the texts. Dishes, plates, tableware, figures and, later, modelled objects such as ink-stands were produced. In the eighteenth century monochrome wares were influenced by contemporary tin-glazed earthenware and porcelain finewares, and in particular the growing fashion for the drinking of tea and coffee.

Enamel-decorated ware

Creussen, near Bayreuth in Bavaria, was the production centre for the fourth and most costly German stoneware style, featuring decoration with coloured enamels. Although the first dated examples were made in the second decade of the seventeenth century, it is evident that the region has a far longer tradition of lead-glazed earthenware production, with one family of potters specializing in the manufacture of lead-glazed stove tiles. The Creussen stoneware industry began at some time in the sixteenth century and was possibly initiated by immigrant potters. The stoneware is a light reddish-brown in colour, covered with a thick lustrous salt glaze in varying shades of dark brown. One of the most common forms that was made is the wide-bodied *Bienenkorb* tankard with a spayed base, which was usually left monochrome and decorated with reliefs. More spectacular are the painted wares decorated in the style of colourful German and Bohemian enamelled glass. Usually these wares have a dark glaze against which the painted enamels are in greater contrast. The long-established glass-painting industry in Creussen, much of whose output was used in churches and cathedrals, made use of opaque low-temperature lead glazes known as enamels. This technique was adapted for use on the stoneware pots, the enamels being successfully fused in a second, low-temperature firing on the pots. The technique came into use around 1620 and continued to be employed for some 130 years.

Greyish-brown clay was used and shapes were kept quite simple, the two most popular being the broad, shallow *canette* or drinking mug and the plain oviform jug. The brightly coloured opaque enamels had a palette of blue, yellow, red, white, green and occasionally gold, with borders and fillings of chainwork or ropework and foliage added

Bouffioux stonewares are typically brown-bodied or blue-grey imitations of contemporary stonewares made at Raeren, Frechen and the Westerwald. Large pieces such as barrels, bottles with face masks, chemists' jars and boxes for holding medicines, pills or powders were made, as well as canisters, pocket flasks, cruets, ink-stands and teapots. Ornament was kept to a minimum and consisted of medallions and simple raised lines and popular grotesque masks, imitating those made at Frechen.

It was through the German Frechen potters that stoneware production was introduced into England, albeit on an experimental scale, around 1660–80 at the old Woolwich ferry approach to the Thames, at about the time when John Dwight was experimenting with the manufacture of high-temperature wares in Wigan. By the late seventeenth century at least some of the essential elements of producing stoneware were understood in Britain. Suitable clays from the West Country were already in use by London delftware potters as an admixture, and it was found that stoneware temperatures could be achieved with the square wood-fired updraught delftware kilns, although earlier, in 1636, David Ramsay had already devised a sea-coal-fired kiln designed to achieve high temperatures.

Salt-glazed stoneware had a profound effect on seventeenth- and eighteenth-century pottery in England. German stonewares were highly regarded, special pieces having been presented to Elizabeth I, for example. It took great technical skill to achieve the clean, sharp relief decoration and careful kiln control was required to obtain a good glaze. The artists who designed the relief decoration became well known and their work recognized for its distinctive qualities. The finest salt-glaze pots were often mounted on stands and their rims covered with finely engraved metal; in the case of jugs, ornate metal lids were also fitted.

Two pewter-mounted stoneware tankards. Germany, Creussen. LEFT: Possibly from the workshop of Hans Schwarz, *c.* 1600–20, with applied band of baroque portrait medallions and the inscription 'Wolff Albrecht Bömer Capitan'. Height 30 cm (12 in). RIGHT: *Apostelkrug*, late 17th century, cover dated 1699, with a central band modelled and coloured in enamels with twelve apostles, named on a banner, flanking a blue-ground medallion of the Agnus Dei. Height 19 cm (7.5 in).

in the same colours. The formal designs were carefully worked out to suit the scale of the piece as a whole. Glass-painters may have been employed to decorate the pots, and simple bands of figures, representing for example planets, apostles and electors, were successfully used on tankards and similar objects. In later work the whole body was covered with enamel decoration, the effect becoming complex and over-elaborate.

Other styles

An equally crisp, if simpler, style similar to that employed at Raeren was developed at Bouffioux and the neighbouring villages of Châtelet and Pont-de-Loup in what is now southern Belgium and at other places in the Walloon country from the early sixteenth to late eighteenth centuries.

Britain

*c.*2000 BC − *c.*AD 1800

No handycraft can with our art compare
For pots are made of what we potters are

TEXT ON 18TH-CENTURY ENGLISH POT

THE NEOLITHIC, BRONZE AND IRON AGES

Early pottery in Britain is associated with the advent of farming about six thousand years ago, although no concrete evidence has been found of workshops, sites of manufacture, kilns or claypits from that period. The development of larger living sites and defended hilltop settlements testifies to the social, demographic and economic progress that took place during the later Bronze Age, and burial practices changed over time. However, the location of pottery production sites remains undiscovered, or unrecognized, and whatever spiritual or symbolic significance may have been attached to surviving vessels is still obscure, or at best open to learned speculation.

Pots were built by hand, usually by coiling and smoothing, and are typically brown and buff through to dull pink and red in colour. The open firings that were used are well attested ethnographically and have been replicated by archaeologists, who found them to produce a temperature as high as 800°C in thirty minutes. Such firings make heavy demands on the clay body as it has to be able to withstand the thermal shock of the flame without cracking. Although some clays inherently possess good firing properties, most bodies, in order to fire successfully, required the addition of what is known as an opener, filler or temper, in the form of a non-plastic material such as grit, chaff or shell. In Wessex crushed flint and shell were commonly added to pottery throughout the Neolithic period, while many Beaker wares of the Early Bronze Age are made from a body containing ground-up fired clay known as grog.

The introduction into Britain of a new burial rite in the Early Bronze Age was the starting point for the creation of a wide range of pottery styles. Around the first part of the second millennium BC drinking vessels in the form of beakers were made, copied from wares brought by migrations of the so-called Beaker people, who probably originated in southern Spain. Beakers were the first vessels to be placed with the dead and various styles of them evolved over a period of several centuries, between about 2230 and 1600 BC. Simple incised chevron designs on the sides of the beakers helped to provide a better holding surface as well as adding a decorative element, the pattern sometimes being inlaid with white clay or pigment of some kind. The pots were probably used as containers to hold food and drink intended as nourishment for the dead and may also have had other ritual significance. The finer Beaker wares are normally made from a body to which a finely crushed temper has been added, and the surface would have been rubbed smooth with a pebble or other tool before being decorated with an impressed or incised pattern. It was not long before vessels with a distinct shoulder began to be made, and these served as models for later cinerary urns.

Group of Bronze Age vessels, urns and beakers, from Britain. Earthenware, hand-built with incised and impressed decoration. The wide range of surface colours is due to firing conditions and varies from red-orange in oxidized firings to black-brown in reduction. Height (tallest) 20 cm (8 in).

During the period of around 1500–1000 BC vessels with a prominent shoulder and sides tapering to a narrow base were produced to hold the bones of an incinerated body for ceremonial burial, and as burial practices diversified so new styles developed. In the north of Britain not only containers for the cremated remains of the dead but also food vessels have been found. Shapes of cinerary urns vary across the country: in the south-west the so-called Trevisker urns, in Wessex biconical urns, and in the highland areas enlarged food vessels as well as encrusted and collared urns. By the late Bronze Age a range of larger urns was being produced.

During the Iron Age (750 BC–AD 43) in Britain there was a move away from scattered homesteads towards more defined settlements or villages, reflecting population growth and the increased agricultural activity. From the second century BC until the Roman conquest extensive contact with continental Europe led to marked changes taking place in ceramic technology and production methods. The walls of pots became thinner and the surface was smoothed in order to imitate metal. Indigenous production of wheel-thrown pottery did not occur on any significant scale until the first century BC, and even then hand-building methods continued alongside. The shapes that emerged include a pedestalled urn, of a style that had been introduced into northern France some three to four centuries earlier, and forms generally became more symmetrical and sinuous.

THE ROMAN OCCUPATION

The Roman invasion and conquest of Britain in AD 43 brought into the country a sophisticated ceramic technology that involved the use of more carefully prepared clay, a more efficient potter's wheel and an improved design of kiln. Pottery was produced at many sites across the country using locally available clay and in forms intended mainly to meet local needs. Surviving shards have provided abundant material for archaeological analysis, enabling the evolution of the craft to be plotted, the range of clays to be identified and a detailed picture to be built up of manufacture, supply, use and chronology. While commonplace household earthenware was largely of local production, certain types of the most sophisticated wares were traded over wide areas and often across provincial boundaries.

The majority of pots were multi-purpose containers used principally for the storage, preparation and cooking of food, although some of the finer and more decorative wares were intended for serving food at the table. The existence of specialized types

quest until the end of the second century AD, after which its enormous popularity in the north-west provinces waned. Excavations at sites such as Chichester and Upchurch indicate that, for a brief period, some red-slip wares were made in Britain. Coarse unglazed pottery was produced in fairly substantial quantities at a number of sites, and the vessels and utensils made at different places often displayed individual characteristics. A few centres

Two pedestalled bowls (tazze). Roman Britain, Colchester, Essex, 2nd century. Earthenware, thrown with decorative edgings, possibly used as part of religious ritual. Height (shorter) 9.5 cm (3.8 in).

of pottery indicates the adoption of certain aspects of the Roman lifestyle. For example, the large amphorae used for wine, oil and other luxuries, such as the prepared sauces and dried fruit that began to be imported, served as models for potters in Britain. So too did *mortaria*, bowls designed specifically for pounding and puréeing ingredients to produce the complex blends of flavours that were typical of Roman cooking. Other forms include face-urns, used as containers for cremated bones, and pedestalled bowls or tazze, which are likely to have been used in religious rituals.

The large quantities of Roman red-slip wares that came into Britain form part of a long tradition of fine tableware dating back to the Hellenistic prototypes. Fine red-slip ware was produced in standard forms, some with moulded decoration, at well-established manufacturing sites, principally in Gaul. It was imported from the time of the con-

covered their pots with a thin, pale-yellow lead glaze, one such example being Holt in Denbighshire, where this glaze was applied to thrown bowls with white slip decoration.

Regional sites of production

One of the largest and most important sites for the production of everyday pottery was Castor in Northamptonshire. The development of Castor can be attributed partly to the proximity of Ermine Street, the major London-to-York road, and partly to the availability of excellent local plastic clays. A wide variety of wheel-thrown pots, basins, jugs, mixing bowls and beakers for domestic use were made from the local clay, which fired a pinkish-buff colour, and dark grey or black-coated wares were also produced. Different-coloured clay slips were employed to decorate some of these pots, the beakers in particular. Scrolls and leaping animal

that often fired to a deep red or purple. Many of the forms consist of broad copies of those made at Castor, but the New Forest potteries also developed their own distinctive wares, such as shapes with impressed sides recalling the form of leather bottles. Wares with white decoration were also made, some having patterns in the form of rosettes, stars or crescents impressed into the surface, others painted in slip and decorated with abstract designs built up exclusively of straight lines and circles.

Stonea

Close to the modern town of March, in the heart of the flat Cambridgeshire fenland, a small raised 'island' of firm ground at Stonea was an important settlement, which had streets, thatched timber houses and a central stone building. Wares found at Stonea Grange include relief-decorated jars made at the Nene Valley near Peterborough. These have a pattern in relief that was produced by the barbotine process of trailing thick slip on to the surface. The designs are mainly hunting scenes with deer and hounds or stylized phallic motifs, most spectacularly a winged phallus, while one colour-coated pottery jar is decorated with the schematized depiction of a chariot race.

SAXON AND NORMAN BRITAIN

After the withdrawal of the Roman legions in the fifth century, England was settled by the Anglo-Saxons, a mix of Germanic peoples whose burials, in which the remains were frequently accompanied by grave-goods, were either inhumations (the corpse itself being buried in a grave) or cremations (whereby the body was first burned and the ashes placed in a pottery urn for interment). From about 400–650 an essentially rural society developed in which pottery was produced locally by hand-building methods in a limited range of forms and styles, many based on wares made prior to the arrival of the Romans.

This pottery falls into two main categories: vessels recovered from settlements, most of which survive as little more than fragments, and those found in cemeteries, which are often intact, having been used either as containers for cremated ashes or as vessels to accompany an interred body. The bulk of known material comes from the large burial grounds of eastern England; southern England,

Map showing major centres of pottery production in Britain.

designs were trailed in thick slip on to the pot using a technique known as barbotine decoration. Designs were freely applied, resulting in a pleasant liveliness, and the decoration often resembled the work of contemporary silversmiths. The decorated pots were sometimes dipped in dark brown or black pigment to colour the surface, and occasionally purple or red tones were achieved.

New Forest ware

Potteries in the New Forest area, dating from the third or fourth centuries, produced various types of vessel, including a dark-coloured plain ware

where inhumation was preferred to cremation, has yielded fewer examples. The finest wares are cinerary urns with high shoulders, decorated with incised designs, applied clay and impressed patterns, all of which were made by coiling and smoothing or pinching the clay. To achieve the relatively low temperatures needed, firings took place in little more than bonfires over stacks of pots. Some wares destined for domestic use were slab-built while on others burnishing was carried out, probably to make them stronger and more waterproof. Decoration generally falls into three main types – linear, plastic and stamped – these elements being employed either separately or in combination. Geometric motifs are found, as well as horseshoes and swastikas. Pottery for use in or around the home was probably intended mainly for storage, cooking and food consumption, and some vessels have lugs on the side to enable them to be suspended by a cord or thong.

Around the seventh and eighth centuries major technical advances were made as trade with the Continent increased and immigrant potters

Biconical cremation urn, Anglo-Saxon. Earthenware, from Castor by Norwich, with round bosses, stamped swastikas and other decorative motifs.

settled at sites along the east coast, bringing with them new skills and forms. In due course the fast wheel came to England and the use of a low-temperature glaze made from the lead ore known as galena was introduced. In the Low Countries and the Rhineland both the fast wheel and the lead glaze had been in use since their introduction by the Romans or reintroduction by the Byzantine empire. It is significant that the east coast of England, particularly the area near the Wash where immigrant potters first arrived, was quick to respond to and make use of these technological improvements. In the remainder of the country hand-building production methods and either open firing or very simple kiln arrangements continued to be employed.

Saxo-Norman wares (c. 700–1066)

Three distinct groups make up what are known as the Saxo-Norman wares. The first – St Neots – is soft, grey and soapy to the touch, usually with substantial amounts of powdered shell added to the body, which opened it out and thus improved its working qualities. The body is often fired a bright red, purple, brown or dark purple, which suggests that firing took place in a kiln in which there was little separation between flame and ware. Deep bowls, shallow dishes, cooking pots (fifteen to twenty centimetres high) and jugs with rouletted decoration were made.

Ipswich ware, the second group, was produced from the tenth to the twelfth centuries but may have been made as early as the eighth century. It can be seen as the forerunner of Thetford ware and shows a distinct Continental influence. The body is hard, sandy and grey, and the forms closely resemble those that were produced in the Rhineland. Cooking pots, bowls and storage vessels, some decorated with applied and impressed bands of clay, were made, as well as spouted pitchers. No glaze was used.

The last and most technically advanced of the three groups is Stamford ware, so named because it

Ewer from East Anglia, 11th–12th century. Earthenware, wheel-made, with tubular spout, handles, wide mouth and a convex base, and a thin layer of clear yellow glaze. Based on imported Rhineland ware. Height 17.5 cm (7in).

Four medieval jugs, all found in south-eastern England. Earthenware, thrown and decorated with coloured slips. LEFT TO RIGHT: early 13th-century jug made and found in London; mid 13th-century zoomorphic decorated jug made in Kingston; 13th-century jug made in Rouen, found at Sutton Courtenay Abbey in Oxfordshire; late 12th-century incised tripod pitcher made in London. Height (tallest) 20 cm (8 in).

was first found at Stamford on the borders of Northamptonshire and Lincolnshire. Made from the local estuarine clay, which has a low iron content, it is both finer and whiter than the other two types. What makes Stamford ware so exceptional is that parts of the cream-coloured pots are covered with a transparent glaze, usually tinted pale yellow but sometimes dark green or darker red-yellow. This may have been the first glazed pottery to be produced in England since Roman times, the glaze probably being applied by dusting the powdered galena (a natural form of lead sulphide) on to the shoulders of the damp pot. The spouted pitcher, by far the most common form of Stamford ware found, usually has three strap handles, a tubular spout and a rounded base trimmed with a knife round the edge. Stamford ware was widely distributed and sold throughout the east Midlands.

Medieval pottery, 1066–c.1450

The Norman conquest of 1066 is generally accepted as the beginning of the Medieval period in Britain. Medieval pottery became bigger, technically better and artistically more inventive and in some ways can be seen as reflecting the architectural developments of this period, which heralded the construction of fine ecclesiastical buildings and substantial houses. Pottery has a limited number of uses, and since most people ate off wooden platters and drank from horn or leather containers (pewter, silver or gold vessels being available only to the rich), pots were employed mainly for preparing and cooking food and for storing and serving drinks. Within British society as a whole pottery held no great status at this time. Most potters struggled to eke out a living and potting was little more than a small-scale seasonal activity alongside agricultural work, the absence of potters' guilds confirming the low status of the craft during this period. However, at some point the scale of pottery production increased and by the thirteenth century most towns had at least one pottery-making centre, usually located within or immediately outside the walls.

During the thirteenth and fourteenth centuries potters in Britain produced some of the most elaborate ceramics in Europe, which are of great interest from both a technical and an aesthetic point of view. Well-thrown and thinly potted jugs and pitchers were decorated with coloured slips and glazes and sometimes embellished with figures of humans and animals, the frequently ornate patterning influenced by contemporary metalwares and pottery imported from the Continent. Considerable technical advances were made, including the more careful preparation of clay, the mixing of a range of coloured slips and glazes, improvements to the potter's wheel and more sophisticated kiln construction. The precise design of the wheel is not known, although two types are represented in manuscripts of the time. One is the cartwheel type, consisting of a wheel fixed to a central shaft, which the potter rotated by hand; the other is a type of kickwheel made up of a central shaft with a wheelhead at the top and a solid flywheel at the bottom that was kicked by the potter. The cartwheel type is generally associated with the European mainland, the solid flywheel and later crankshaft types with Britain.

According to the medieval writer Eraclius, the glazing was carried out by sprinkling lead filings or lead oxide on to the surface of an unfired pot that had previously been coated with a layer of flour and water to bind the powder to the surface. Depending on the type of local clay used, the body varied in colour from red to buff and usually had an addition or filler, such as ground shell or sand, to improve its throwing and firing qualities. Firing was to 900–1000°C, a clean or oxidized firing producing a clear, colourless or pale yellow gloss, a smoky or reduction firing an olive colour. Adding copper to the glaze resulted in a bright apple green. By this time kilns had evolved to become semi-permanent updraught structures in which the burning fuel was kept separate from the ware. Prior to the development of such kilns, pottery had been fired in clamp or bonfire kilns in which pots, fuel and flame were in close contact. Wood was the fuel used to fire the kiln, although coal may have been employed if readily available in the vicinity.

Pottery imported from the Continent, and from France in particular, had an important influence on both form and decoration at this time. During the twelfth and thirteenth centuries polychrome slip-decorated pottery with applied rosette designs and relief patterning was produced in northern France, notably at Rouen. A Rouen jug found at Sutton Courtenay Abbey, at Abingdon in Oxfordshire, features painted red slip on a white ground, applied white pellets of clay and rouletted patterning. Inspired by forms and decorative techniques of this kind, English potters improvised their own patterns and designs as well as developing new shapes. Many of the more highly decorated vessels were probably intended as tableware pieces.

Aquamaniles, elaborately fashioned in the form of animals or knights on horseback, were also made at this time for the purpose of containing water and dispensing it at table. Forms were based on contemporary vessels made in silver, the most common shape that was made – or at least that has survived – being the jug or pitcher. Some of the finest jugs, produced during the thirteenth century, are tall and slender. Their handles, functional and sturdy in form, were placed on the jug in such a way as to be both practical and aesthetically pleasing and reduced in size to make them less liable to break. The handles are invariably joined firmly to the pot, some literally poked through the clay wall and smoothed over to give added strength, with the tail end occasionally splayed out to add a decorative pattern. Both flat strap-like and round handles were made.

Aquamanile, 13th century. Earthenware with glaze, modelled in the form of an animal. Such objects were often based on metal shapes. Height *c.* 20 cm (8 in).

Jug with spout from Nottingham, 14th century. Earthenware, modelled with animals and facial details, and a green glaze. Height 42 cm (16.5 in).

The decoration on these jugs is simple but effective and their form dominant and uncluttered, although designs vary across the country. Human and animal figure decoration was popular. A bearded man was often modelled on either the rim or the spout of the jug, while animals depicted include lions, dragons, stags, birds and even apes. At Rye in East Sussex vessels were decorated with such unusual motifs as jousting scenes, a figure of Christ, ships, fish, and an elephant with a howdah. More abstract patterns, covering the entire surface of the jug, were sometimes created using thin rolls or pellets of clay, often of a contrasting colour to that of the body. Patterns include leaves and flowers as well as geometrical motifs such as triangles or circles added to the surface, loosely based on organic forms and with added rudimentary leaf shapes. At Cheam simple designs were boldly painted in slip of a contrasting colour. A notable characteristic of many of the earlier jugs is their convex or sagging base, which may represent a continuation of the tradition of rounded bases that would sit firmly on uneven earth floors, or more probably in the embers of a fire, or may simply be a product of the making process. The introduction of wooden tables and flat surfaces necessitated the thumbing of the bottom edge of the pot and this feature is often found on many later jugs. Occasionally small tripod feet were added.

During the fourteenth century the highly decorated pottery with its repertoire of applied, slipped, modelled, stamped and polychrome ornament gave way to a less varied and plainer range of kitchenware comprising large pitchers or jugs, cisterns, cooking pots, cauldrons, drinking jugs, and large bowls or dishes. Pots include pipkins, saucepans and flat frying pans. Flasks and pilgrim bottles in many sizes and forms, some flattened, that have been found at Old Sarum in Wiltshire may have been made locally and indicate the wide range of shapes prevalent at this time.

Floor tiles

The extent of tile production in medieval times reflected the need for smooth, flat, hardwearing floor surfaces that were easy to keep clean. Most floor tiles were probably made by pressing red terracotta clay into wooden moulds that contained a simple relief design. At the leather-hard stage the concave design would have been filled with clay of

Four floor tiles, late 13th century. Earthenware, white slip on red clay, with incised decoration depicting an archbishop. From a Benedictine abbey at Chertsey, in Surrey. Dimensions (top tile) 22.5 cm (9 in) square.

Two lobed cups, 'Tudor Green' ware. British, 15th century. Earthenware, thrown and modelled, with green glaze. Height (left) 8.75 cm (3.5 in); diameter (right) 10 cm (4 in).

a contrasting colour, usually buff or white, and the surface smoothed over. Simple heraldic motifs, armorial shields and stylized flowers and animals were popular designs. Tiles of this type were often used for the floors of cathedrals and abbeys, where the soft earth colours added a further element of warmth and richness to the interiors of these magnificent buildings. An early example from Halesowen Abbey is dated 1290, and tiles still in their original position can be seen in the chapter houses of York Minister and Westminster Abbey. Other tiles were covered with a layer of white slip through which the design was scratched or carved.

In the fourteenth century decorated floor tiles were made predominantly by commercial tileries, the large scale of their production resulting from the widespread popularity of decorated pavements, which were to be found in locations ranging from royal palaces, monasteries and churches to merchants' houses and urban sites. In the first half of the sixteenth century maiolica floor tiles bearing Renaissance designs were imported from the Continent, and a small number of tiles decorated with similar motifs and lettering were subsequently produced in Britain.

POST-MEDIEVAL EARTHENWARE (1450–1650)

On both sides of the Channel drastic changes in ceramic technology and design took place from the mid-fifteenth century onwards in the wake of broader economic and social trends.

Closer commercial and cultural links were forged across national boundaries, the urban mercantile and artisan classes gained greater purchasing power, and alterations were made to housing design whereby working and living spaces were formally separated to provide privacy and comfort. These factors, together with refinements in dining habits and a consequent move towards individual rather than communal utensils, contributed to a considerable expansion of the role played by ceramics. As prosperity rose, so too did the level of interest in household goods, spurring potters to devise new ranges of ware that included many items for use at table. Such ware was finely potted, sensitively decorated and evenly glazed. In Britain during this period a dramatic increase was seen in both the variety and number of ceramic forms as a result of efforts to expand the domestic market.

Wares imported from continental Europe had a profound impact on the pottery manufactured in Britain. From the mid-fourteenth century stonewares from the Rhineland came into the country in increasing quantity, stimulating potters in Britain to imitate their form and decoration. Technically superior to British wares by virtue of their robust, impervious body and lustrous ash and salt glaze, and produced in a diversity of shapes in response to changing needs, for four hundred years they were to remain the largest single category of ceramics to be traded to Britain. During the reign of Elizabeth I (1558–1603) it is estimated that around three thousand such vessels were landed in Exeter every year. In the early sixteenth century the introduction of applied surface ornament based on contemporary printed sources marked a further shift in the social value of Rhenish stoneware in north-western European dining culture. The relief decoration enabled it to compete, in terms of appearance as well as function, with more ornate metal- and glassware and with the polychrome-painted tin-glazed ceramics of Italy, Spain and the Low Countries.

During the last decade of the fifteenth century, imports of continental painted tin-glazed earthenwares, which entered Britain alongside the Rhenish stonewares, grew in both quantity and range. Spanish lustrewares, Italian polychrome-painted maiolicas and their imitative Netherlandish counterparts form the three main groups of these 'luxury' wares. One popular form, the 'flower' or 'altar' vases, carried designs of the sacred monogram (IHS), which, in combination with the religious character of the painting, suggests that these vases were intended for display or even for devotional use. Moreover, such pieces indicate that ceramics had by this time attained a greatly elevated status. The demand for maiolica and lustreware, like that for relief-decorated stoneware, extended to mercantile and artisanal consumers.

The radical diversification in the output of English lead-glazed earthenwares during the sixteenth century was a response partly to the impact of imported wares and partly to expansion within the domestic market. The new forms that proliferated in the potteries based along the Thames Valley in London and Surrey as well as in Essex indicate the increased sophistication of urban lifestyles. The shapes that were made at these centres include large pitchers, cauldrons, pipkins, frying pans and dripping dishes, chafing dishes, condiment dishes, goblets, culinary stamps, water-sprinklers, distilling apparatus, bird pots and fuming pots. The so-called 'Tudor Green' wares – green- and yellow-glazed smooth whitewares produced on the Surrey–Hampshire border – were based directly on imported wares, particularly Rhenish stonewares.

By Tudor times (1485–1603) the range of objects produced had been further extended to encompass cisterns, stove tiles and candle brackets, usually finished with a smooth glaze. Many items were decorated with stamped or applied relief designs, some incorporating the initials of the reigning monarch, others with decorative motifs typical of Renaissance decoration, such as flowers and leaves in neatly ordered arrangements. Jugs became much more squat in form and were often covered with a rich moss or speckled cucumber-coloured glaze that was applied in liquid form to facilitate smoother, more even application. Designs of Tudor roses and armorial shields, inspired by the finely moulded relief decoration seen on imported German salt-glazed ware, were used on many tiles and pots. Both the form and the colour of ceramic jugs tended to emulate contemporary metal flagons.

From the late fifteenth century local industries in Yorkshire and the north Midlands developed a range of fine-bodied drinking-cups with a dark brown-black lead glaze and applied pads or strips of white clay over a red body. This 'Cistercian ware', so named following its discovery in the course of excavations of Cistercian monasteries,

Wall candle bracket. English, 16th century. Earthenware, with moulded and modelled decoration and lead glaze.

Group of tablewares. English, 17th century. Earthenware, thrown and decorated with slip-trailed decoration, redware produced by potters of the Metropolitan slipware industry in the Harlow area of Essex. LEFT TO RIGHT: two-handled sucking cup; single-handled cup bearing the inscription 'Obeay the King'; plate with a four-pointed star design.

was at one time distributed widely throughout England. However, its production seems to have been disrupted by the dissolution of the monasteries between 1536 and 1540 and ceased altogether in the seventeenth century. The hardness of the ware indicates the use of a relatively high firing temperature. The ware is characterized by a dark red body with a dark brown glaze stained with manganese, which was applied both inside and out. Occasionally trailed white slip and applied pads of white clay were used in the decoration. Drinking cups with several handles were made, preceding the similar but much more common drinking vessel known as a tyg. This tradition of hard-fired, slip-decorated earthenware was continued at Tickenhall in Derbyshire throughout most of the seventeenth century.

The introduction of smokeless ceramic-tile stoves into the domestic interior around 1600 radically changed heating technology and at the same time provided an additional market for potters. Initially most stove tiles were imported, but later they were produced in Britain by earthenware potters on the Surrey–Hampshire border. Some of these tiles are moulded with relief decoration, the designs incorporating arms and monograms of

Tudor and Stuart monarchs from Henry VII to James I (d. 1625). Often the same moulds were employed in the production of cisterns and candle sconces.

ENGLISH EARTHENWARES (*c.* 1650–1800)

A major characteristic of a new class of wares that began to be produced at sites throughout the country was the use of applied white slip on a red-firing body. The fast, effective and versatile decorative techniques of slip-trailing and incising designs on to a slipped surface enabled potters to develop a range of attractive and marketable items. Many of the new pieces were inspired by the wares brought over by immigrant communities of merchants and craftsmen from the Low Countries, northern France and Germany who had settled in south-east England during the fifteenth and sixteenth centuries. Continuing the spread of slipware production across Europe and motivated by the growing interest in decorative earthenware for use at the table, England developed its own slipware industry around 1600.

Slip-decorated wares were embellished and glazed when leather-hard and fired only once.

Although slip had been applied decoratively to the surface of pottery for some four hundred years, it was not until the beginning of the seventeenth century that slip-trailing with the aid of a cow-horn and quill became a standard feature of much of Britain's earthenware production. It is significant that the formative stages of this development coincided with the permanent establishment of the tin-glazed earthenware industry, which made use of new technology and design, transforming the nature of the English pottery market. London

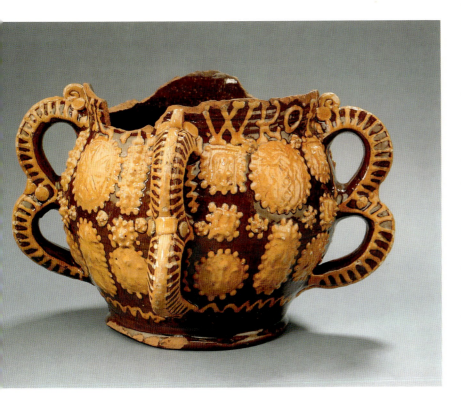

Large cup made in Wrotham, Kent, mid-17th century. Earthenware, with four double- looped handles and white slip-trailed decoration on a red ground of badges and medallions, moulded from reliefs on contemporary Rhenish stoneware, with trailed inscription 'N...M...Wroth...'. Height *c.* 14 cm (5.5 in).

tin-glazed wares set the fashion in decorative ceramic tableware for much of the seventeenth century, although imported wares from the Netherlands, Beauvais and around the Werra and Weser rivers of central Germany were also widely distributed. During the early to mid-seventeenth century a number of distinctive regional slipware styles emerged across the south-east and south-west and in the Midlands.

Metropolitan slipware
The output of the Harlow redware industry that developed in Essex was destined largely for the London market, hence the term Metropolitan slipware. These wares featured trailed designs in cream-coloured slip on an orange-red body, the designs incorporating a wide range of geometric, botanical and figurative motifs as well as religious or secular inscriptions. Many of the trailed motifs that were used derived from contemporary Dutch and Werra slipwares, but the use of trailed slip for texts was unique. Usually in block capitals, the messages were typically popular aphorisms advocating humility before God, the importance of charity, or loyalty to the crown. Expressions such as 'Feare God', 'Fast and Pray' and 'Be not hy minded but feare God' convey the strong Puritan ethos of the period and the extent to which Protestant values affected everyday life. Following the restoration of the monarchy in 1660, the use of pious inscriptions declined in favour of geometric motifs and secular messages such as the royalist slogan 'Obeay the King'.

Wrotham slipware
Inspired perhaps by the Metropolitan wares, potters in Wrotham, Kent, also produced a range of red earthenware with white slip decoration, although they developed their own ornate style. Production of these wares continued until the early eighteenth century. Among the forms made were posset pots, two-handled mugs, candlesticks, and notably a straight-sided mug (tyg) with four triple- and double-looped handles, suggesting that it was intended for some special use and hence valued and preserved. The vessels' handles often have entwined coils of red and white clay, but the most significant characteristic of Wrotham slipware is the combination of slip-trailed decoration with circular, oval or rectangular applied pads of white clay impressed or stamped with designs. In addition to carrying the potters' initials and dates, most of these relief-moulded designs have a heraldic bias; they include armorial shields, fleurs-de-lis, rosettes and bearded facemasks. The technique employed was based on that used on German stonewares, and Wrotham potters often produced moulds directly from contemporary imported German stoneware Bartmann bottles of the mid- to late seventeenth century, making the rather crude reliefs in white clay.

Sgraffito wares
By the beginning of the seventeenth century a distinctive local slipware tradition using red clay, white slip and clear glaze had developed around

Barnstaple and Bideford in north Devon and at Donyatt in Somerset. Production of this style of pottery flourished as these ports became the focus of trade across the Irish Sea and Atlantic Ocean during the seventeenth and eighteenth centuries. A distinctive feature of the ware is the use of the sgraffito technique, which involves incising or scratching through a layer of slip when almost dry to reveal the body beneath. The fact that Beauvais sgraffito slipware has been excavated in the region confirms the influence of continental imports. Both the French and the local products were twice fired, a practice still rare at the time. Production of sgraffito-decorated slipwares later extended to neighbouring centres such as Bristol and Wales.

The incised decoration incorporated a variety of symbolic and popular motifs such as tulips, trefoil-shaped flowers, hearts, sunbursts, facemasks and stylized birds. Designs on the 'harvest jugs' (so called because they were originally intended for carrying beer to harvesters working in the fields) were particularly complex, often including drinking rhymes, dates and the names of the makers in addition to intricate all-over patterns and pictorial images. A jug in the British Museum, dated 1780, is decorated with a double-headed eagle, flowers and a crowned heart with an incised rhyme detailing the potter's skill in transforming a lump of clay into a carrier for ale.

Among the items made at Fremington in north Devon were seven sizes of pans (the largest fifty centimetres in diameter), cooking pots including pipkins, owls-heads, butter pots, gallipots and oval and round baking dishes. The pottery also produced *steins* for pickling pilchards (which were sent to Cornwall), colanders, large oval dishes for hams, drainpipes, tiles and even chimneypots.

Harvest jug. North Devon, late 18th century. Earthenware, red clay covered with white slip and incised decoration of coat of arms, figures, flowers and plants, inscribed 'Drane by me Thomas Amman, made by me Edward Reed'. Height 32.5 cm (13 in).

Staffordshire slipware

In his *Natural History of Staffordshire* of 1686 Robert Plot identifies Burslem as the centre of a regional slipware industry spread out among the villages of Stoke-on-Trent, Hanley, Fenton, Longton and Tunstall. Archaeological evidence suggests that pottery production in this region dates back to the thirteenth century, and by the late seventeenth century the availability of coal to fire the kilns and extensive outcrops of workable clay had led to north Staffordshire having the greatest concentration of pottery workshops in the country. By 1650 the art of slip-trailing was firmly established in the area and slips of different colours were often used. The earliest excavated slip-decorated earthenware, from Eccleshall Castle, can be dated to 1646–50 and includes porringers and cups. Production of lead-glazed earthenwares generally seems to have been well established some time earlier, serving markets beyond the local area; for example, Staffordshire butter pots, used by farmers for storage and distribution, were well known throughout the Midlands. In general the wares were functional, being destined for agricultural and household use. Staffordshire slipwares, which reached their peak around the end of the seventeenth century, fall into three groups: flatware, such as plates and dishes; hollowware, comprising drinking vessels, jugs and lidded pots; and miscellaneous wares such as candlesticks, cradles, moneyboxes and chimney ornaments.

The elaborately decorated trailed-slip dishes produced from 1670 to 1730 represent some of the finest slipwares in the country. Dishes and shallow bowls ranging in diameter from thirty to fifty-five centimetres were either thrown and turned on the wheel or made by pressing flat sheets of clay into hollow clay or wooden moulds. The slip decoration on these wares is particularly well developed, having been executed with great vigour and assurance. The larger dishes were 'specials', made for particular occasions such as weddings or christenings and proudly displayed on dressers as family heirlooms. Reddish-buff clay was used for the body of the dishes, which would be covered with a layer of white or cream slip to form the background for the trailing of red, dark brown and tan slips. Designs were outlined with trailed slip and filled in with a wide variety of patterns. Human figures were drawn with little or

Two large slipware dishes made in Burslem, Stoke-on-Trent, by members of the Toft family, late 17th century. Earthenware, with decoration trailed in light and dark brown slip on white. LEFT: Portrait of a cavalier with head of King Charles, dated 1677, signed by Ralph Toft. RIGHT: Portrait bust of King Charles, signed by Thomas Toft. Diameter *c.* 40 cm (16 in).

no regard for anatomical detail and, like those painted on the tin-glazed blue-dash chargers, have the naive quality typical of the work of talented but untrained artists. Compositions tend to fill the entire area and are characterized by a successful combination of figurative and abstract design that lends them a unique charm. Favourite subject matter included popular historical, mythological or religious scenes, with typical designs depicting Charles II hiding in the oak tree, portraits of well-known figures and cavaliers, coats of arms, mermaids or Adam and Eve. One of the most admired was the Pelican in her Piety, symbolizing the Eucharistic sacrifice of Christ's death on the cross. Posset pots and cylindrical handled cups were also made, decorated with complex trailed and 'jewelled' slip ornament, rosettes and tulip designs as well as lengthy inscriptions.

Among the finest wares is a series of dishes bearing the names of local manufacturers such as Toft, Taylor, Simpson and Wright. Magnificent dated dishes made by the Burslem potter Thomas Toft between 1671 and 1689 include portraits of Charles II both as monarch and as prince in the oak tree, and of his queen, Catherine of Braganza, as well as cavaliers, pelicans, eagles, unicorns, the royal arms and fleurs-de-lis. Toft's designs are

beautifully balanced and set within a rich trellis border pattern on the rim of the dish, the name of the potter often being incorporated into the pattern. The extent to which these wares were influenced by contemporary tin-glaze and wriggle-worked images on pewter chargers has yet to be clearly established.

From the end of the seventeenth century the quality of slip decoration declined as 'combed' or 'feathered' decoration gained in popularity. This involved trailing one or more lines of coloured slips side by side and drawing across them with a fine point to produce a feathering effect. The technique was used on a range of hollow- and flat-wares including owl jugs, on which it was employed to represent feathers. Another type of decoration was marbling or 'joggling', whereby the different trailed lines of slip were swirled to produce a marbled effect. Press-moulded relief dishes would be made by pressing a flat slab of clay over a hump mould bearing one of many incised designs, which included stylized figures, animals and flowers. The potter Samuel Malkin of Burslem (?1668–1741) created a series of dishes depicting Saint George and the dragon, the sun tree, Lot's wife and the 'wee three Loggerheads'. The often quite complicated designs, left in relief,

Three-handled posset pot. English, probably Barnstaple, Devon. Earthenware, with zoomorphic spout, applied modelled figures on the sides and clear glaze, inscribed with the date 1682. The inscription suggests that this was a marriage or betrothal gift. Height 15 cm (6 in).

could easily be repeated and subsequently decorated with slips of different colours.

Other centres

In the seventeenth and eighteenth centuries a number of local pottery centres throughout Britain produced red earthenware with a lead glaze, individual workshops developing their own forms, according to local needs, as well as their own styles of decoration. However, no other centre achieved the technical skill or artistic assurance of the Staffordshire potters, although some employed similar slip techniques. Various different methods of decoration were adopted. White clay was often applied in relief and slips were occasionally coloured dark brown or black. The use of green slip or glaze did not become widespread until the late eighteenth and early nineteenth centuries.

Potters were often quick to respond to innovative design possibilities and on late eighteenth-century Sussex pottery printer's type was pressed into the surface as part of the decorative motif. The impression was inlaid with clay of a different colour, usually white, and bore either inscriptions or ornamental patterns. At Rye and Brede large full-bodied jars and pipkins were decorated with impressed patterns, sprigs of leaves and printer's type. Other major centres included Ewenny and Buckley in Wales, and Halifax.

Wedding plate. English, Rye Pottery, Kent, 19th century. Earthenware, thrown with modelled and moulded decoration with spray of corn, oak leaves and flowers and fruit around the rim. Diameter 35 cm (14 in).

Country potteries, many of which had been set up during the eighteenth century, operated throughout much of the nineteenth century. They produced a wide range of thrown pots, usually made from red earthenware clay and finished with a clear lead glaze, that were largely destined for local markets. Llewellyn Jewitt's *Ceramic Art of Great Britain* of 1877 lists numerous small potteries, many of which remained in operation for only a short time. The main products seem to have been pitchers, mugs, bottles, bowls, vinegar kegs and settling pans, with simple but strong forms well suited to their use. Candlesticks and tans, or carpet bowls used for playing the game indoors, were also in common production.

Many of the local styles of decoration developed in the eighteenth century were maintained during the nineteenth, and a number of potteries in Kent, some using the dark red-firing Wealden clays, continued the slipware tradition begun in the seventeenth century. In Sussex, Burgess Hill was noted for its agate ware, which included goblets, posset pots and basins. Fuddling cups with intertwined handles and basins and salt pots with incised decoration were made near Ilminster in Somerset, while spice chests, moneyboxes, puzzle jugs and cradles were produced in Yorkshire.

Two tin-glazed dishes. English, late 17th century. Earthenware, thrown with painted decoration. LEFT: Fluted circular bowl painted in blue, manganese and yellow, with in the centre an oriental figure seated on rockwork, in the border a figure seated before a fence and another by rockwork with schematic trees beneath a blue line rim. Brislington, *c.* 1685. Diameter 29.5 cm (11.8 in). RIGHT: Blue-dash royal equestrian portrait charger painted with King William III in ermine-edged blue robes and holding a sceptre, riding a prancing stallion, with the initials W R above his head and flanked by schematic trees, on a striped green and ochre ground and within a blue-dash rim. London, *c.* 1690. Diameter 35.5 cm (14.2 in).

White tin-glazed earthenware

From the thirteenth century onwards, tin-glazed earthenware was imported into Britain from the Mediterranean region. White tin-glazed earthenware (sometimes known as 'whiteware', or 'delftware' after the Dutch town of Delft, noted for its production) was imported from the Low Countries, where it was made in great variety, from the sixteenth century. In Britain the production of white tin-glazed earthenware was concentrated in three main centres – London, Bristol and Liverpool – but because potters are known to have moved around between centres, accurate identification of it is difficult. From its inception in the sixteenth century until the early seventeenth century, the delftware industry was based almost exclusively in London and workshops expanded rapidly from 1630 to meet increasing demand. The first two Bristol potteries, at Brislington and Temple Back, opened in the second half of the seventeenth century and were followed by further potteries in Bristol as well as others in Liverpool, Wincanton and Lancaster and in Ireland and Scotland. All these factories supplied local markets, with some also exporting pieces to America.

The earliest tin-glazed ware, however, was made in Norwich by Jacob Jansen and Jasper Andries, two potters from Antwerp who arrived in Britain in about 1567 and began producing tiles and a limited range of pots. In 1570 they petitioned Queen Elizabeth for a patent to make tin-glazed earthenware in London, specifically stating that they made tiles and 'Vessels for potycaries'. In 1571 Jansen moved to Duke's Place, Aldgate in London and Andries to Colchester in Essex. Production at Norwich continued until the end of the seventeenth century.

Tin-glazed ware requires a special calcareous body that enables it to take the glaze well. This was produced by combining a number of different clays, which London potters obtained by importing specific types from areas such as East Anglia (via the port of Yarmouth), Suffolk and Aylesford in Kent. So perfect were these mixtures for the manufacture of tin-glazed ware that as well as being supplied to production centres in England some clays were exported to Holland in the seventeenth century for use by the potters of Delft. White clay came almost exclusively from Poole in Dorset, from where shipments were sent out more or less daily. Cornish tin mines were the source of tin for potters in both England and the Netherlands. Aside from the fact that tin-glaze was relatively easy for potters to produce once the technology was known, the greatest attraction of earthenware was its smooth white surface, which was pleasant to handle and provided an excellent base for painted decoration. Moreover, it resembled the highly prized Chinese porcelain that was beginning to reach England in considerable volume.

Unfortunately the ware had the considerable disadvantage that the body was not strong and so chipped easily, and when the porous red body was revealed the ware became not only unattractive to look at but also unhygienic. Production therefore tended to be reserved for pieces designed as much for display as for practical use. The limited range of forms that were made include tankards, pill and ointment pots, wig stands, wine bottles and, most notably, flat dishes or chargers. The latter offered a suitable surface for painted decoration and, like the slipware plates made by Toft, became an art form in their own right. Many of the dishes were finished with a decoration of blue strokes around the rim and hence became known as blue-dash chargers. Blue, green, yellow and brown were the chief colours used in the painted decoration. Early designs emulated those of Renaissance Italy, but an English style slowly developed, characterized by bold, freely drawn designs that often possessed a naive simplicity. Informal portraits of kings and queens and other well-known personalities, imbued with a delightful caricature quality, decorated the dishes, as did biblical subjects, especially Adam and Eve in the Garden of Eden, and formal floral designs of tulips and carnations.

During the Commonwealth of the mid-seventeenth century new drinking habits arose. Tea, coffee and chocolate were often preferred to alcohol, and special cups or mugs were made in which to serve such beverages. Production of the full, round-bodied wine bottles with narrow necks that imitated the form of contemporary German stoneware bottles, which had hitherto been very popular, all but ceased.

Continuing the oriental tradition, vessels were produced for the use of apothecaries in a wide range that included spouted pots for syrups and oils, globular drug jars, cylindrical and squat jars for powders, pills, ointments and confections, and pill slabs. The decoration often featured a description of the contents together with a floral design. Barbers' bowls were frequently adorned with motifs of scissors, combs and other tools of the trade, painted in blue on the white glaze.

Towards the end of the seventeenth century the palette brightened and was extended to include shades of red. Shapes, too, became more diverse, some being modelled and moulded after the work of the French potter Bernard Palissy, who supplied rustic pottery to the French court. Constant contact between Dutch and English potters brought further foreign influence into Britain, but the English potters never achieved the sophistication of the Dutch work, which in some cases succeeded in imitating Chinese porcelain almost exactly. Nevertheless, the naive combination of Chinese and English design motifs has a unique charm, amply illustrated in one example depicting English soldiers set in an English landscape, which has a band of Chinese mythological heads as a border.

Potters working in small units were able to respond quickly to changes in taste and style, developing an ever-expanding range of objects for use in and around the home. In addition to producing plain and moulded flatwares, potters made various sizes of bowls, jugs, mugs, cups and goblets as well as ornaments, containers in the form of cats, fuddling cups (in which three or four miniature vase-like containers are joined together), puzzle cups, posset pots, flasks and flagons for wine, candlesticks (often in the shape of figures), trays, baskets, sauce-boats, teapots and decorated plaques. Production also extended to a wide variety of tiles, made for use either singly or to make up larger panels, bearing pictorial designs including religious and mythological subjects, landscapes, animals, birds, baskets and flowers.

The importance of maritime trade prompted many potters, particularly those based in Bristol and Liverpool, to make use of nautical themes. Ship-bowls commissioned by the captains of English trading vessels were often inscribed with both the name of the captain and that of the ship

Candlestick in the form of a cat. Earthenware, tin-glaze with sponge decoration and painted detail with initials B R E, dated 1674.

he commanded. Bristol potters also made bowls of this kind for visiting ships' captains.

Towards the end of the eighteenth century the colours used developed a softer look, some taking on a pleasant watercolour quality. The number of forms had been extended to include a variety of objects for the home such as rectangular flower-holders, pen-and-ink stands, puzzle jugs, and a full complement of tea-drinking items comprising cups and saucers, sugar bowls, milk jugs, teapots and tea caddies. However, the introduction and success of industrially manufactured cream-coloured wares in the second half of the eighteenth century led to a decline in the popularity of tin-glazed ware, and by around 1800 production of it had virtually ceased.

STONEWARE

The term stoneware is used to describe clay that has been fired to a high temperature, usually above 1200°C, which is hard, vitrified and virtually impervious to liquids. Salt-glazed stoneware (more commonly referred to simply as salt-glaze) is fired to similar temperatures but is glazed by introducing common salt into the kiln at maximum temperature. Because stoneware is vitrified, unlike tin-glazed earthenware it can be potted thinly without loss of strength, although the high temperature required in its manufacture precludes the use of both lead glaze and colours painted in the tin-glaze style. The technique of firing pottery to a high

Delftware tea caddy. English, made in Liverpool. Tin-glazed, octagonal in form with grey-blue decoration. Height 10.5 cm (4.2 in).

temperature was introduced into England from the Continent, and the finest of the pots so made were highly prized, often being enhanced with finely crafted silver mounts. Increasing demand for Rhineland stoneware in England during the sixteenth century prompted several attempts to manufacture it in Britain, as well as efforts to control its importation. In 1671 war broke out between England and Holland and the importing of large quantities of Rhenish stoneware bottles and drinking mugs was curtailed, which further encouraged English potters to produce their own ware of this kind.

In 1641 Thomas Browne, Tobie Steward and Nicholas Burghley had been granted a twenty-one-year patent to make 'all manner of stonepott[es]', although no such wares have as yet come to light. Other entrepreneurs brought over potters from Frechen to make stoneware in England. Excavations at the old Woolwich ferry approach on the Thames have revealed that a limited range of well-potted mugs and Bartmann bottles was made by immigrant potters using clays and moulds from Frechen. The search for a home-made alternative to the robust Frechen stoneware tavern mugs and bottles continued fruitlessly until the middle of the seventeenth century; only the forms were successfully imitated, in tin-glazed and red lead-glazed earthenware, by potters in London, Essex and southern England. A Captain William Killigrew secured the services of the Rhineland potter Symon Wooltus and his son of the same name in order to establish a pottery at Southampton in around 1666. The pottery successfully produced stoneware bottles and around 1672 was being operated by Wooltus's son on Killigrew's behalf.

John Dwight

By far the best known of England's early stoneware potters is John Dwight (*c.* 1633–1703), the 'son of a yeoman farmer from North Hinksey near Oxford'. Dwight attended Christ Church college,

Two mugs, Fulham, early 18th century. Thrown salt-glazed stoneware. LEFT: 'Pint' mug stamped with an impression of Britannia and with A R excise mark (Queen Anne) beneath the handle. Height 12 cm (4.8 in). RIGHT: Globular mug with a W R excise mark (William III) beneath the handle. Height 9.5 cm (3.75 in).

Bottle from Fulham, *c.* 1685. Salt-glazed grey stoneware, with two bands of spirally twisted inlaid marbled clay, white and purplish-black in colour, with white sprig decoration, probably 'marbled porcellane' of John Dwight's patent of 1684, ornament cast in brass stamp. Height 18.8 cm (7.5 in).

they emulated. Bartmann bottles were also made at Fulham, the applied mask decoration again being of higher quality than contemporary Frechen products. The fine relief decoration of such motifs as busts, animals and foliage was picked out and heightened by the salt glaze. Other forms made include large jugs with throwing ridges and thumbed bases.

Dwight's ignorance of the essential ingredient china stone was to prevent his ever discovering the secret of true porcelain. Nevertheless, in the course of the experiments he conducted in an attempt to produce a light-coloured body he added calcined flint to the clay and achieved a hard whitish-grey body that was closely akin to true porcelain. One body was made up of white clay from Dorset combined with sand imported from the Isle of Wight. From the white body Dwight produced small mugs and modelled figures that ranged from mythological subjects to near life-sized portrait busts, one of his most successful pieces being a model of his dead child, Lydia. In 1684 he obtained a second patent covering not only the same products as before but also 'Marbled Porcellane Vessels' and 'the opacous redd and dark coloured Porcellane or China' copied from imported Chinese Yixing red stonewares, which he produced making use of the iron-bearing clays from Staffordshire.

The Elers brothers

Despite holding patents, Dwight was not alone in seeking to produce stoneware in England, and during the years 1693–8 he sued those he believed had infringed his manufacturing rights. It is likely that in Staffordshire the Wedgwood brothers had carried out experiments to replace their mottled earthenwares with salt-glazed stonewares, but with little success. By agreement with Dwight, the Dutch brothers David and John Philip Elers made unglazed fine red stoneware, in far greater quantities than did Dwight himself. Of high Saxon-Dutch descent and formerly silversmiths, the Elers brothers were highly inventive and produced ware of fine quality. After the accession of William of Orange to the British throne they left their own country to settle in England, moving in the 1690s to Bradwell, near Newcastle-under-Lyme in Staffordshire, a remote area at the time. Here, by methods they attempted to keep secret, they produced unglazed red stonewares in the Chinese

Oxford, where he read 'civil Law and Physick a little, but mostly Chymistry', his interests spanning both the legal and the scientific. In 1672 he obtained a patent for the sole right of producing 'The mistery of transparent Earthen ware commonly knowne by the names of Porcelaine or China and Persian Ware, as also the misterie of the stone ware vulgarly called Cologne Ware'. Dwight was the first potter to be granted a patent for the manufacture of stoneware in Britain. He had developed his own bottle kiln in the early 1670s in Fulham, where he concentrated on producing reproductions of imported Rhenish wares and Westerwald blue-grey stoneware mugs for the tavern trade. Either left plain, with a wash of cobalt blue or manganese purple, or decorated with an applied vertical strip medallion decoration, these wares were in many cases both aesthetically and technically superior to the imports

style. Although David Elers had lived in Cologne and was familiar with salt-glaze production, he chose not to introduce this process into Staffordshire. The Elers brothers subsequently moved to London, where they made slip-cast stoneware teapots at Vauxhall until their business fell into bankruptcy in 1700. By that time their other potteries, most notably the Pickleherring factory at Southwark, were also producing stonewares.

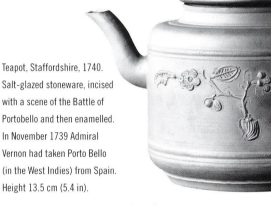

Teapot. Elers, red stoneware. Height 11.25 cm (4.5 in).

Teapot, Staffordshire, 1740. Salt-glazed stoneware, incised with a scene of the Battle of Portobello and then enamelled. In November 1739 Admiral Vernon had taken Porto Bello (in the West Indies) from Spain. Height 13.5 cm (5.4 in).

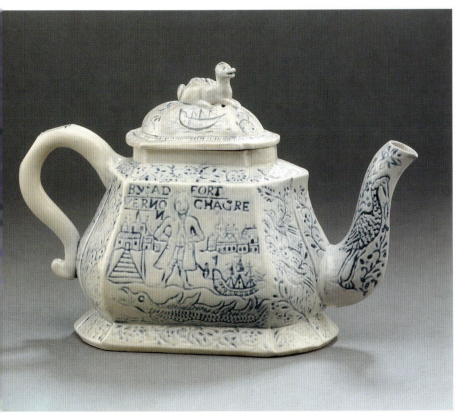

Although the brothers tried hard to protect the production processes of these fine, attractive and unusual wares, rival potters succeeded in infiltrating their workshops and thus discovered the techniques used. Successful manufacture involved careful preparation of the local clay and the use of fine relief decoration of moulded flowers, leaves and other motifs made in sprig moulds. The Elers' wares, which were slip-cast and lathe-turned to a fineness unprecedented in English pottery, are characterized by crisp, clean forms based on the Chinese Yixing wares. Small teapots, coffee pots, tea canisters, teacups and jugs made from fine red clay were first thrown on the wheel and when leather-hard turned on the wheel or lathe to give them a smooth, sharp contour, free from throwing marks. Some were left plain while on others sprigs of relief decoration were added, often featuring Chinese motifs. Plum blossom in the Chinese style also appears, as do birds and figures. The sharpness of the Elers brothers' pots reflects their earlier training as silversmiths, an impression reinforced by the fact that some pieces were adorned with silver rims.

Staffordshire salt-glazed stonewares

Few Staffordshire clays are capable of withstanding the high temperatures required for stoneware without warping, distorting and collapsing, and it was not until the discovery that calcined flint added to a clay body made it more refractory and able to tolerate greater heat that stoneware could be produced. This breakthrough has been attributed to several different potters, and it is indeed possible that it may have been made by more than one. The addition of flint also helped whiten the body, which later aided the development of creamware (see chapter 11).

Following the Elers brothers' success in achieving high firing temperatures, by about 1720 a range of well-potted domestic white salt-glazed stoneware was being produced widely in Staffordshire. Contemporary accounts record that when salt was being thrown into the kilns the whole of the surrounding area became covered in a thick grey fog, which indicates the prevalence of the technique. At its best, Staffordshire white salt-glaze could rival porcelain in its thinness, delicacy and refinement of decoration, although not in the richness and depth of the glaze or the whiteness of the body. A surface wash of white 'Pipe Clay from Bideford' (in north Devon) did help to lighten the body but did not always take the salt well. White clay soon began to be added to the body along with the ground flint, which produced a whiter-firing clay generally known as white stoneware or 'common white'.

Around 1720 scratched blue salt-glazed ware was developed, inspired perhaps by the Ming dynasty blue-and-white wares. Designs were first incised into the surface of the white clay while it was still leather- or cheese-hard, then filled with a cobalt blue stain. The limited blue-and-white palette and unsophisticated designs prevented the somewhat crude decorative technique from appearing harsh or gaudy, and the precisely thrown and turned pots were further enhanced by their decoration. From the 1720s white salt-glazed stonewares were produced, both moulded and thrown and lathe-turned, which were commercially successful for some fifty years until superseded by the cream-coloured lead-glazed earthenwares.

The introduction into Staffordshire of plaster of Paris moulds around 1740–50 significantly extended the range of forms that could be made quickly and repetitively. In addition it enabled them to be made in asymmetrical and angular shapes that could not be achieved by throwing. The moulds were filled either by pressing in thin sheets of clay or by slip-casting, which involved pouring in a thick mixture of clay slip to form a 'skin' on the wall of the mould then pouring off the surplus. Many forms had ornate carved designs that included humorous and fantasy figures, for which these methods of making were ideal. Teapots were fashioned in exotic forms such as a kneeling camel or a house, sometimes with a 'Chinese' design. Imported Chinese fine white porcelain continued to challenge the ingenuity of the industry and the high-temperature white clay body was widely adapted by potters as an alternative to porcelain. The rounded drinking mug, at one stage replaced by the more practical straight tankard, was soon reprieved and used to symbolize the extravagant thirst of the fat-bellied drinker in the popular print of 'Toby Philpot'

published in 1761, which became the inspiration for many thousands of Staffordshire Toby jugs. When the fashion for three-dimensional Toby jugs waned, the print was reproduced as an applied sprig on English 'hunting' mugs and jugs from about 1800 until well into the twentieth century, although Toby jugs continued to be made in a huge number of guises.

Other salt-glazed stoneware centres

From the end of the seventeenth century brown salt-glaze ware was manufactured in the Midlands at three main centres: Nottingham, Chesterfield and Derby. Nottingham had been a major production centre for earthenware since medieval times, and in 1693 James Morley and family began production of brown salt-glaze in the town. Using local clays that responded well to the salt, they produced wares of great refinement on which the use of an iron wash resulted in a rich brown surface with a silvery quality that brought out the crisp preciseness of the forms. Products made included loving cups, mugs, teapots and jugs, some in the form of bears with removable heads, which were used as cups. The excellent properties of the Midland clays together with the potters' mastery of the salt-glaze technique gave these wares a rich, smooth, brown, lustrous quality. Delicately potted, thin-walled and lightly made, the pots were decorated by incising and carving rather than having relief patterns. Design motifs consisted of bold, freely drawn scrolls, foliage and flowers scratched into the soft clay, as well as neatly incised patterns and inscriptions, and openwork cut with a knife or punch.

Salt-glazed stoneware continued to be produced by many small potteries. In the London area it was made at Mortlake, Lambeth and Vauxhall, while outside London production continued well into the nineteenth and early twentieth centuries at Nottingham, Bristol, Waverley Pottery, Portobello, Glasgow and at Crich and Denby in Derbyshire.

Unfortunately the hard, slightly rough surface of salt-glazed ware tended to abrade silver cutlery. This drawback became a factor in the cessation of production, towards the end of the eighteenth century, of most stoneware intended for practical use at the table, in the face of the growing popularity of the cream-coloured ware produced by the larger pottery industries that developed in

Toby jug, 'Admiral Lord Howe'. Staffordshire, *c.* 1770–80. Earthenware, depicting the figure seated on a barrel and holding a jug of foaming ale, with a spaniel asleep at his feet. The handle is modelled in the form of a sheaf of leaves. Height 24.5 cm. (9.8 in).

Modelled figures, Staffordshire. Stoneware, salt-glazed, in the form of a seated row of stylized figures known as a pew group.

pottery made by the Martin brothers from 1877 to 1914. The use of salt glaze on sanitary products such as pipes continued until the 1950s, when the Clean Air Acts made their firing impracticable.

FIGURE MODELLING

The production of modelled figures has been a hugely popular element of the ceramic industry. Made in a range of different clays and glazes including unglazed redware, salt-glazed stoneware, red-and-white earthenware and tin-glaze, these items represent some of the liveliest and most inventive work ever produced. Many of the earlier modelled pieces are naive rather than naturalistic in style and, like the Toft dishes, constitute some of the great highlights of English folk art. Typical themes are subjects such as Adam and Eve, musicians and stylized seated figures known as pew groups, sometimes enhanced by scratch-blue decoration. Many of the finest English pieces were fashioned in salt-glazed stoneware and are probably the work of Aaron Wood. One of the best-known modellers, Obadiah Sherratt (*c.* 1775–1846), worked in Burslem, Staffordshire. His figures were often given titles and in addition to classical subjects such as Neptune he modelled a wide variety of genre scenes ranging from fanciful circuses to brutal animal killings.

Staffordshire. The production of sanitaryware, such as pipes and sinks, agricultural forms, water filters, fountains, stewpots and hot-water bottles for the home, as well as that of more decorative pieces, continued throughout the nineteenth century, culminating in the salt-glaze vases produced at Doulton's London factory and the studio

The figures were intended as ornaments for the home and their subjects are often portrayed in a humorous or satirical manner. Since few modelled figures bear a signature, virtually none can be attributed to any particular maker, but various styles can nevertheless be identified. Other notable pieces of the same type include agate-ware cats, often in the form of candlesticks, jugs in the form of bears, and horsemen, musicians, the crucifixion, birds, and figures such as vicars and Moses, shepherds and shepherdesses. Toby jugs in the form of a seated stout man holding a pot constitute a large group of such wares, this form having become immensely popular and its manufacture widespread.

'Bull-baiting' group, Burslem, *c.* 1835, modelled by Obadiah Sherratt. Earthenware, with a tethered bull tossing a terrier into the air while another dog snaps at his head, with the figure of a showman standing nearby. Inscribed 'Bull Beating' and 'Now Captin Lad'. Height 33.5 cm (13.25 in).

European Porcelain

GERMANY, FRANCE, ITALY AND SPAIN, SCANDINAVIA, THE LOW COUNTRIES AND RUSSIA, BRITAIN AND IRELAND

This is the porcelain clay of humankind

And therefore cast into these noble moulds

JOHN DRYDEN, DON SEBASTIAN, I. I.

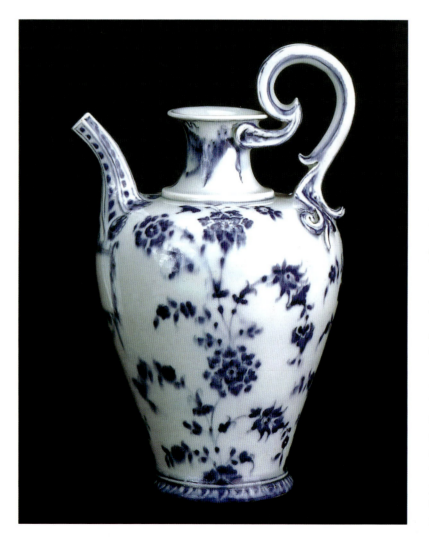

Porcelain is the English name given to the hard, white, translucent, high-fired wares that have been produced in China for over a thousand years. Porcelain was made in China as early as the Tang dynasty (AD 618–907) from a mixture of petuntse (china stone) and kaolin (china clay), the quality of both the body and the design reaching a high degree of refinement over succeeding dynasties. The fine, thinly made shapes, subtle deep glazes and later the richly painted decoration of Chinese porcelain were greatly admired in Europe, where it was widely collected by members of the aristocracy. The word porcelain is an anglicization of French *porcelaine*, which itself stems from the Italian word *porcellana* (cowrie shell), adopted to describe porcelain because of the ware's resemblance to the glossy surface of the shell; there may also be a link with the Italian word *porcella*, a diminutive of *porca* (sow), in connection with the whiteness and smooth, compact texture of this animal's skin.

When porcelain began to be shipped to Europe in large quantities, brought over from China by various East India companies throughout the seventeenth century, it became known as 'white gold' and precipitated the 'rage for porcelain' among the aristocracy. The fine wares were highly valued and greatly prized, soon becoming a prestigious commodity that was sold by silversmiths and jewellers alongside objects fashioned from precious metals.

MUSSELBURGH

SCOTLAND

Glasgow • Edinburgh

IRELAND

Belleek

Liverpool
Pinxton
• Derby
Swinton • Longton Hall
• New Hall
• Coalport
Swansea • Worcester
Nantgarw • Bristol
Lowestoft

Plymouth

Chelsea
Bow
London

DENMARK

Copenhagen

Nieuwer Amstel • Oude Amstel
Amsterdam • • Weesp
The Hague • NETHERLANDS
Oude Loosdrecht

Berlin

GERMANY

Meissen
Dresden

Lille
Tournai
Rouen
St Cloud Chantilly
Sèvres Paris
Sceaux Vincennes
Mennecy

Kassel

Höchst
Kelsterbach

Niderviller

Strasbourg

FRANCE

Augsburg
Zurich

Munich
Nymphenburg

Vienna

AUSTRIA

Limoges
St Yrieix

Nyon

SWITZERLAND

Vinovo

Le Nove Venice
Este

Pisa
Florence
Doccia

SPAIN

Madrid
Buen Retiro

Alcora

Naples

Map of major 18th-century European porcelain factories.

Ewer. Italy, Medici workshop, Florence, 1575–8. Porcelain, painted in underglaze blue in a floral design. Height 25.5 cm (10 in).

The porcelain made in Europe falls broadly into three main categories: hard-paste, soft-paste and bone china (which may be regarded as medium-paste). Many factories, including those at Sèvres in France and Worcester in England, either manufactured two or all three of these types at the same time or progressed from one to another as new technical discoveries were made. The hard-paste variety, fired to temperatures of 1260–1300°C or above, is considered to be 'true' porcelain – that is, the closest equivalent to that made by the Chinese. Soft-paste porcelain, fired to around 1000–1100°C, is a European invention produced by adding a flux such as a glassy frit to the body to make it vitrify at low temperature. The bone china body was developed in England and contains about fifty per cent bone ash, comprised of the calcined and ground bones of animals, usually cows or horses. Today's bone china vitrifies at a temperature in between those of soft- and hard-paste porcelain, typically around 1180–1200°C.

The great prestige attached to Chinese porcelain, and indeed its high commercial value, gave many the impetus to attempt to discover the secret of its manufacture. The first European porcelain was produced under the patronage of Francesco I de' Medici, Grand Duke of Tuscany, in Florence in the late sixteenth century, but the Medici porcelain, as it has become known, bore little technical resemblance to the Chinese material it was intended to imitate. It contained no china clay, for example, and because of the difficulties involved in its manufacture it was produced in only limited quantities. A further attempt to manufacture porcelain was made a century later at Rouen in France by Louis Poterat (1641–96), but there are few pieces that can be safely attributed to his enterprise. An added incentive to the production of fine porcelain wares arose when tea, coffee and chocolate gained popularity among the wealthy and demand rapidly developed for high-quality containers from which to drink such beverages.

THE EUROPEAN CONTINENT

Porcelain was a luxury item from the outset and great resources were required in order to develop and manufacture it. Whereas the survival of tin-glazed earthenware workshops tended to be wholly reliant on their profitability, porcelain factories on the Continent often enjoyed the patronage of princes or wealthy members of the aristocracy. The motivation of such patrons was often as much self-aggrandizement as the desire to succeed in commerce, since sponsoring the manufacturer provided them with a ready means of obtaining the finest wares for their own use as a mark of their wealth and power. But at the same time their backing gave the factories concerned the opportunity of producing a highly priced and much sought-after commodity. Many patrons amassed vast collections of oriental porcelain that served as an inspiration for continental potters in the design of their own pieces. Because porcelain was so costly to manufacture it was initially treated as purely decorative, but soon practical items such as cups and saucers, sugar boxes, milk pitchers and teapots were also made.

Experiments carried out across Europe in the attempt to discover the formula for producing 'true' porcelain frequently involved adding materials such as soapstone, alabaster and glass to a white-firing clay body in the hope that this would cause it to become glassy and translucent at low temperature. However, such bodies, often dry and granular in appearance, were likely to be quite brittle, and some were prone to crack when they came into contact with hot water. Furthermore, they had a critical firing point beyond which they would distort, which resulted in heavy losses in the kiln that added to production costs. Although such problems did little to deter numerous efforts to set up porcelain works, only a relatively small number remained in operation for any great length of time.

GERMANY

The secret of producing true porcelain was finally unravelled in about 1709 in Meissen by the German chemist Johann Friedrich Böttger (1682–1719), alchemist to Augustus the Strong, Elector of Saxony, in collaboration with the scientist Ehrenfried Walter von Tschirnhausen (1651–1708). Böttger approached the task in a scientific manner, systematically testing raw materials he thought might be suitable, in various combinations. Despite working in primitive and unhealthy conditions, the adverse effects of dust and smoke and the great heat of the kilns often leaving him exhausted and ill, around 1706–7 Böttger managed to achieve fine brownish-red stoneware hard enough to be polished on the lapidary's wheel. Not long afterwards, using a white clay brought specially from Colditz in Saxony, he succeeded in producing a white porcelain body that proved to be reasonably workable and, when glaze-fired, could be decorated with enamel designs.

On the basis of this discovery, the Meissen factory near Dresden was established in 1710 under Böttger's technical direction, its initial aim being to produce pots and ornaments for the use of the royal family. If technically successful, the enterprise

Stoneware coffee pot and cover. Germany, Saxony, Meissen (Böttger), *c.*1710. Red porcelain. Height 15.8 cm (6.25 in).

intended also to make items for general sale, and the first wares aimed at a commercial market appeared around 1713. Following stoneware forms, the products included statuettes of dwarves and saints, copies of Chinese blanc-de-Chine wares and 'pagoda' figures, in which the porcelain was often left white to display the qualities of the highly prized material. Rapid technical and artistic advances made during the 1720s owed much to the contribution of Böttger's successor, the colour-chemist and painter Johann Gregorius Höroldt (1696–1775). A more refined body was developed and this was used in the manufacture of an expanding variety of wares that included vases, bottles copied from Japanese originals, small covered vessels, and tea and coffee services. Höroldt further improved the enamelling process and increased the range of colours, as well as devising his own designs for vignettes and chinoiserie scenes.

The finely modelled and painted figures and table services produced at Meissen from the early 1730s established the factory's reputation as the foremost producer of porcelain in Europe. The dining tables of the wealthy had traditionally been decorated with small figures modelled in either wax, sugar or gum by cooks and confectioners, but demand for objects of a more permanent nature encouraged production of the first porcelain figures at Meissen in 1727, when Johann Gottlieb Kirchner (b. 1701) was appointed as the factory's first chief modeller. Initially Kirchner made figures of saints and animals in baroque style as well as life-sized animals and birds to adorn the Elector of Saxony's Japanese palace in Dresden, built specifically to house his vast collection of oriental porcelain. The size of the pieces posed daunting technical problems even for such a skilled artist as Johann Joachim Kaendler (1706–75), who took over as chief modeller in 1733 and was to become Meissen's most famous sculptor. This highly talented and inventive artist fashioned some of the finest individual figures and groups ever produced at the factory. Although Kaendler's work pre-dates the highly distinctive European style of porcelain modelling in which elements of naturalism were combined with a sophisticated and colourful decorative treatment, it possesses a sense of liveliness unmatched by any imitator.

Kaendler's figures are vigorously modelled, typically in dramatic sculptural poses wherein the

Broth bowl, cover and stand. Germany, Saxony, Meissen, *c.*1735. Hard-paste porcelain, thrown, enamelled and gilt decoration. Diameter (basin) 16.9 cm (6.75 in).

Meissen figure of Punchinello. Height 15.5 cm (6.2 in).

and some of his best known figures are those of *commedia dell'arte* characters such as Harlequin, Columbine and Scaramouche. Kaendler's creations were an instant success, setting the style in terms of both form and concept for virtually all other porcelain factories' figurative work. The bright glaze and strong colours of the pieces provide ample evidence of the artistic and technical skill that went into their production, the wide range of coloured enamels with which they were painted adding to their appeal. Later, assemblages of figures were produced that were even more artistically ambitious and technically challenging. In addition to his well-known figures, Kaendler modelled substantial pieces in the form of fountains and pyramids, large-scale creatures such as cocks, goats and dogs, and life-sized busts including a laughing Chinese man and woman.

It was around the middle of the eighteenth century, when the popularity of baroque became tempered by a growing taste for the lighter and more delicate rococo style, that the mood of the porcelain figures shifted from the sombre to the light-hearted and colourful and fragile-looking decoration began to be applied. Pieces were made on a smaller scale and new subjects were introduced such as lovers in idyllic pastoral settings and allegorical or mythological figures. Since the rococo style favoured asymmetry, rock- and shell-like forms were often incorporated.

Towards the end of the century Meissen designs were to combine reaction to the excesses of rococo and late baroque with renewed emphasis on the antique. The more austere approach to both form and decoration that developed at that time represents the style now known as neoclassicism.

In addition to figures, Kaendler and his team of modellers designed an extensive range of dinner services, tea and coffee sets, centrepieces, candlesticks, toilet sets and other decorative but useful items that became highly fashionable throughout Europe. Count Heinrich von Brühl, the factory's director, personally commissioned the largest and most ambitious service, known as the Swan. Each plate was painted with the count's coat of arms and all were finely modelled in low relief in designs of swans and other birds. The tureens in particular were created in sumptuous curving forms and featured elaborately modelled mermaids, dolphins and other marine creatures.

characters are often portrayed making flamboyant or theatrical gestures. Typical subjects of his pieces, which range in height from a few inches to several feet, include exotic birds, figures from distant nations and couples in romantic or chivalric poses. He also made humorous depictions of court jesters,

The 'porcelain rage' among the wealthy aristocracy was nowhere more clearly expressed than in the fashion for decorating entire rooms with the precious material. Walls would be covered with ornate porcelain panels, porcelain cornices built, plaques inlaid into furniture and rooms generously furnished with porcelain vases, figures and mirror-frames in the popular rococo style. Porcelain rooms were usually commissioned for royal palaces. Many, especially those in Germany, reflected a taste for the Chinese style; Johann Friedrich Eosander von Goethe designed a particularly

Vase. Austria, Vienna, Du Paquier's factory, 1721. Hard-paste porcelain, moulded, enamelled and gilt decoration. Height 24.4 cm (9.75 in).

notable example for the Charlottenburg Palace, near Berlin. Other examples of entire rooms decorated with porcelain were to be found at the Neustadt at Dresden and the Residenz in Munich, at Arnstadt and Andbach, and in the Dubsky Palace, Vienna. The craze reached its height when Augustus the Strong decided to furnish the whole of his Japanese palace with oriental and Meissen porcelain. In due course the advent of the more restrained neoclassical style brought the vogue for porcelain rooms to an end.

When the Meissen factory first opened great efforts were made to guard the secrets of porcelain manufacture. Nevertheless, Böttger's kiln-master, Samuel Kempe, succeeded in acquiring and absconding with them and was employed by the Prussian minister Friedrich von Gorne to set up a factory at Plaue-an-der-Havel, where fine red stoneware was produced until 1730. The formula for white porcelain otherwise remained primarily in the possession of Meissen for some forty years, with the two notable exceptions of Vienna and Venice.

In 1719 two Meissen craftsmen revealed the factory's technical secrets to Du Paquier, who established a rival enterprise in Vienna which, in its early years of operation, produced some of the finest examples of baroque porcelain. The forms, in general distinctive, are largely interpretations of silverware and show a fondness for symmetrical scrollwork. Around the late 1720s a decorative style developed that involved interlacing scrolls and foliations derived from ornamental prints. When the Empress Maria Theresa purchased the factory in 1744 the existing range of products continued for a while to be produced, but subsequently the business went over to manufacturing tableware in the rococo style. In the final period of the factory's operation (1784–1864) a range of tableware was made of which some was in miniature, typical forms being cylindrical coffee cups with angular handles and plain urn-shaped vases. The painted decoration, applied in fine detail, was often richly gilded and the distinctive ware came to epitomize Viennese taste.

When Saxony was defeated in the Seven Years War of 1756–63 control over the secrets of porcelain production was lost and its manufacture became more widespread. In the latter part of the eighteenth century there were twenty-three factories in the German states producing porcelain to the Meissen formula. One of the most successful was Nymphenberg, set up in 1747, which became one of the seven great porcelain manufactories of the eighteenth century. For a short period – around 1755–67, under the patronage of Maximilian III Joseph, Elector of Bavaria – Nymphenberg porcelain surpassed all others in the delicacy of its modelling and the fine decoration of its figures. The factory is still in production. The royal porcelain factory in Berlin, established in 1752, became renowned mainly for the work it produced in the neoclassical style in the late eighteenth and early nineteenth centuries.

Tableware. France, Saint-Cloud factory, c. 1700–20. Soft-paste porcelain painted in underglaze colours, inspired by Chinese porcelain. The set includes an inkstand, sugar bowl, toilet pots and a cup and saucer. Height (tallest) 12.8 cm (5 in).

FRANCE

In France the four main factories producing soft-paste porcelain were Saint-Cloud, Chantilly, Villeroy-Mennecy and Vincennes-Sèvres, while hard-paste was made at Strasbourg.

At Saint-Cloud on the River Seine soft-paste production began as far back the early 1690s, after the painter Pierre Chicaneau discovered the secrets of its manufacture, and a fine glassy body was made there until 1766. The factory had been founded in 1664 with royal privilege for the manufacture by Claude Révérend of tin-glazed earthenware, which continued to be produced until the end of the eighteenth century. The manufacture of soft-paste may originally have involved patronage by Philippe, duc d'Orléans, brother of Louis XIV, of the potter Henri Trou (c. 1650–1700). The duc d'Orléans was a collector not only of rock crystals and precious metals but also of Chinese porcelain vases, his pieces often serving as models for the factory. One of the most characteristic aspects of Saint-Cloud porcelain is its inventive and evocative decoration. The painters were encouraged to be daring and expressive and devised a great variety of innovative ornamental designs, which appear on wares that include finely painted blue-and-white porcelains in the Chinese style. Also developed at Saint Cloud was a series of ornamental motifs known as 'grotesques'. These were based on earlier Renaissance designs by the French architect and engraver Jacques Androuet Ducerceau (1510/20–85), who left more than 1600 prints and among them two pattern books of grotesque ornaments. Some of the factory's shapes were derived from silver forms and featured, for example, bold reeding and gadrooning. The earliest Saint Cloud porcelain was intended almost exclusively for decoration or commemoration, but the repertoire was expanded to include a wide range of fine tableware, such as teacups and saucers, small dishes for sweets and vegetables, spice dishes, ice pails and containers for salt, as well as decorative pot-pourri pots and vases. Larger forms included chandeliers, covered bowls and stands, wine- and liqueur-coolers and candlesticks. Plates and platters were not produced, because of complex technical problems.

In common with other soft-paste factories, Saint-Cloud produced wares in pure white in imitation of the blanc-de-Chine imported from Fukien province in China. Prunus blossom designs were applied in relief, frequently combined with European designs, and modelled motifs such as the overlapping leaves of artichokes and pineapples were popular, as were stylized flowering plants.

Around 1730 a factory was established through the influence, and possibly partly with the capital, of Louis-Henri, duc de Bourbon, prince de Condé on his estate at Petit Chantilly. Condé secured the services of Ciquaire Cirou (1700–55), formerly a craftsman at Saint-Cloud, who directed the factory until 1751. The prince owned an extensive collection of Chinese porcelain and Japanese Arita wares and this served as an inspiration for the factory's designs. Many Chantilly pieces were decorated with Kakiemon designs, or with European motifs in a rococo style using the Kakiemon colour palette of flat, unshaded iron red, usually with a matt surface, as well as pale yellow, clear blue and turquoise green. Asymmetrical designs were composed with a pleasing balance between pattern and white space. The body was covered with a white tin glaze, which greatly enhanced the intensity of the painted colours. Chantilly is known for the diversity of its production. At the outset oriental forms and decorative motifs were used; later, wine-coolers with rudimentary grotesque handles, bowls, jugs, salt cellars and spice boxes came into production, together with large decorative bowls and extravagantly decorated rococo pot-pourri and spice dishes.

As was also the case at Saint-Cloud, many forms were moulded rather than thrown. The Chantilly factory ended the century under the ownership of an Englishman, Christophe Potter, who made hard-paste porcelain. The factory continued to produce hard-paste and creamware throughout the nineteenth and into the twentieth centuries.

The early history of the factory at Villeroy-Mennecy is unclear, but, like Chantilly, it is likely to have been set up with the aid of an influential patron, in this case the duc de Villeroy. For about twelve years both faience and porcelain had been made in the hamlet of Villeroy by François Barbin (1689–1765), until the closure of his factory in about 1748. In 1749 Barbin and his wife, together with their son Jean-Baptiste Barbin (1720–65), established a porcelain factory in Mennecy, which soon prospered. Many of the wares they first produced were strongly influenced by those made at Chantilly, even in the use of the tin glaze, but slowly the factory's own characteristics developed. Its varied products included snuff and patch boxes, often with moulded basketwork decoration or covers fashioned as figures of shepherdesses or animals, especially dogs. The factory also produced knife- and fork-handles with coloured decoration over the glaze featuring figures in the Chinese style, cane-handles with commedia dell'arte characters, a range of tableware including jugs and basins, glass-coolers and vases, and also a wall fountain. Plant designs were applied in a free manner using shades of pink and bright blue. Various small figures such as orientals, musicians, 'cris de Paris' and animals were made, while impressive sculptural works and large biscuit portrait medallions were another element of the factory's substantial output. In 1773 production was transferred to Bourg-la-Reine.

Vincennes-Sèvres was destined to become the national porcelain factory of France, and the most famous in Europe during the second half of the eighteenth century. The enterprise was founded at Vincennes in 1740 by Claude-Humbert Gérin (1705–50) in association with the brothers Robert (1709–59) and Gilles (1713–after 1752) Dubois, whose porcelain formula Gérin had learnt while working at Chantilly – although the formula finally used differed considerably from theirs. Early production was inspired largely by Meissen porcelain but in time the wares took on a distinctive character of their own. The factory captured the imagination of Madame de Pompadour (1721–64), mistress of Louis XV, and it may have been she who engineered the granting in 1745 of a royal licence to manufacture 'porcelain in the Saxon manner'. In 1751 the Crown in effect assumed control of the factory.

Although it produced many different products, Vincennes-Sèvres became particularly well known for its finely modelled artificial flowers mounted on slender metallic stems, which were used to embellish lamps, clocks, chandeliers and candelabra. These were decorated in a range of bright colours that had been developed by means of considerable experimental work,

Plate. France, Chantilly factory, c. 1760. Soft-paste porcelain with lead glaze, moulded with six large lobes alternating with six smaller lobes, and painted decoration. Diameter 24.5 cm (9.8 in).

Pair of vases with covers. France, Sèvres factory. Soft-paste porcelain with designs showing Venus and Adonis, after Charles Eisen from Montesquieu's *Temple de Gnide* (1872), and Apollo and Leucothoe, after an engraving by C. Monnet. Height 31.6 cm (12.5 in).

Figure of Europe. Hard-paste porcelain, moulded, part of a series of the Four Parts of the World, attributed to Johann Wilhelm Lanz at Paul-Antoine Hannong's Strasbourg porcelain factory, *c.* 1752–4. Height 26.2 cm (10.5 in).

and special vases were produced for displaying them. Madame de Pompadour created a famous winter flower garden of the colourful ceramic blooms at Bellevue. Less exotic products included plates, bowls, goblets, trays and ice pails, many of the items painted with naturalistically rendered flowers. Under the influence of the artist François Boucher (1703–70) an individual style, no longer in imitation of Meissen, was created at Vincennes, in which a wide range was produced of domestic and ornamental wares as well as figures and groups.

In 1756 the factory moved into new premises at Sèvres, between Paris and Versailles, which had been designed by Lindel on the orders of Madame de Pompadour and included a warehouse for the display of the porcelain products. While some relatively simple objects were produced, the majority of the wares were sufficiently ornate and richly decorated to be in demand for the adornment of palaces throughout Europe. These elaborate pieces were almost as costly as silver or gold, and items of Sèvres porcelain were often bought by the French royal family as gifts for visiting dignitaries.

In 1769 the discovery of deposits of china clay at Saint-Yrieix, near Limoges, enabled a hard-paste body to be produced at Sèvres that was claimed to contain 'no frit, alkali, or lead or other metallic substance'. Gradually the original curving and sinuous forms gave way to more strictly ordered geometric shapes and forms based on the antique vases and urns later described as neoclassical. The factory continued to make hard porcelain as well as soft-paste with its waxen, milky-white glaze until the turn of the century, when production costs became prohibitive. In the aftermath of the Revolution the Sèvres factory was taken over by the State in 1793, and in 1800 Napoléon Bonaparte appointed as its director Alexandre Brongniart (1770–1847), who held the position until 1847. Almost at once Brongniart stopped the costly manufacture of soft-paste to focus on making hard-paste, standardizing it to an exceptionally hard and refractory variety that was to remain in production throughout most of the century. In addition he developed a wide range of decorative painted designs, at the same time extending the range of shapes by introducing techniques for casting products such as chemical ware in moulds and manufacturing large plaques. An artist in his own right, Brongniart also created designs for vases, many inspired by Etruscan wares.

Under the direction of Victor Regnauld during the period 1852–70 further improvements were implemented and the production of an eggshell porcelain with light, lacy openwork decoration was introduced. In the last three decades of the century major artists were invited to participate in the creative activities at Sèvres, among them Félix Bracquemond (1833–1914) in the early 1870s and the sculptor Auguste Rodin (1840–1917) from 1879 to 1882. In 1887 the artist-potter Théodore Deck (1823–91), while continuing with his own individual work, accepted the post of art director, a position he held until his death. Deck made a number of radical changes at the factory that included the development of a new siliceous soft-paste body. This enabled larger pieces to be made without cracking or splitting, which could be richly coloured in subsequent low-temperature firings.

Another of his innovations was the development of a porcellanous stoneware; this could be used to make architectural items and its high level of plasticity rendered it equally suitable for modelled pieces. Taxile Doat (1877–1909), another of the artists employed at the factory, gained success as a studio potter in his own right, as a specialist in pâte-sur-pâte, following his association with Sèvres.

Twentieth-century production at Sèvres continued to build on earlier success and included monumental wares such as decorative panels, fountains, richly enamelled sculpture and items for interior decoration in a variety of ceramic bodies. Buttons, flagons and chess sets were also made. After the Second World War the studio potter Émile Decœur (1876–1953) was appointed stylistic consultant and helped bring about a revival of artistic creativity at Sèvres, introducing new designs for cups and vases in order to exploit the full potential of coloured glazes. In the 1960s the factory initiated a policy of collaboration with well-known artists and designers with a view to creating a new range of ornamental and functional forms. Unlike most other factories, Sèvres continues to employ a wide variety of making processes, including hand-throwing and turning, moulding and slip-casting, which is used in the production of both standard and special items.

Other French factories also manufactured soft-paste porcelain, in their own individual styles. Orléans, from around 1753 to 1782, produced a range of tablewares including tureens, salt cellars, water jugs, sugar bowls and sauce-boats, together with figures modelled both singly and in groups. Porcelain production was also carried out at Crépy (about which little is known), at Lunéville, known primarily for its modelled figures, and at Bourg-la-Reine, a factory under the protection of Louis Charles de Bourbon, comte d'Eu that is generally considered as a continuation of the Villeroy-Mennecy enterprise.

The first French hard-paste porcelain was produced at Strasbourg. In common with several others, this porcelain factory developed from an existing pottery making tin-glazed earthenware. Around the mid-1740s Paul-Antoine Hannong (1700–60) began experimental work on porcelain, assisted by workers from both Meissen and the Höchst porcelain and faience factory (established near Mainz in Germany in 1746). The earliest porcelain production at Strasbourg dates from 1751–4, at which time a variety of tablewares were made, together with modelled figures of subjects such as Flora, the Four Parts of the World, seated Chinese figures and hunters. A further period of porcelain manufacture began in 1768 when Joseph-Adam Hannong (1734–c.1800) took control of the business and, despite substantial debts, conducted extensive experiments as well as increasing production. However, the Strasbourg factory ceased operation in late 1781, by which time it was in vast financial deficit. Hannong produced a range of new shapes, initially in a traditional style, which gradually gave way to a strongly neoclassical mood characterized by fluted legs on tureens and vegetable dishes, and handles in the form of goats', lions' or rams' heads with acanthus-leaf ornament. Decoration included monochrome blue flowers, iron-red landscapes, naturalistic flowers, chinoiserie, genre scenes in the Tenniers style, gallant, pastoral and mythological subjects, fables, and ribbon, garland and flower motifs. Groups and individual figures, both with enamelled decoration and left plain, depicted subjects from mythology as well as characters involved in such pursuits as hunting and gardening.

The first person in France to make hard-paste porcelain from French raw materials, in the form of china clay from Alençon, was Louis-Léon-Félicité, duc de Brancas, comte de Lauraguais (1733–1824), who worked at the Château de Lassay around 1763 to 1768. Hard-paste was also produced at Niderviller, Lorraine, at a factory established in 1749 by Jean-Louis Beyerlé, director and treasurer of the Strasbourg Mint. Although this factory became renowned for its modelled figures in both earthenware and porcelain, it also manufactured a considerable quantity of tableware, most of which was painted with flowers. François Leperre established a factory at Lille, which was producing hard-paste porcelain in the 1780s. Some of Leperre's most skilfully made pieces are covered vases with dolphin handles. One of these is painted with scenes of a kiln firing and has a lid pierced for pot-pourri, while others are painted with flower garlands, scrolls and birds. In the late eighteenth century Limoges became the centre of the French porcelain industry, a great number of factories having based themselves there in order to make use of the local supplies of china clay.

Ewer and basin. Italy, Naples, Capodimonte factory, *c.* 1745. Soft-paste porcelain, moulded with sea creatures, seaweed and coral naturalistically painted in enamel colours. Modelled by Giuseppe Gricci (*c.* 1700–70), who was appointed sculptor to Charles of Bourbon in Naples. Height (ewer) 28 cm (11.2 in).

Figure of a dancing faun. Hard-paste porcelain, modelled by M. Soldani-Benzi after a late Hellenistic statue in the Uffizi, Florence, *c.* 1750.

flowers, and battle scenes. Many of the modelled figures were left undecorated while others were painted in muted pastel shades. One of the factory's first major projects was a porcelain room at the palace at Portici (1757–9), the walls of which were covered with porcelain panels decorated in the rococo style. Although wares were produced mainly for the royal court, public sales were held annually on Saint Charles's Day.

In 1759, when the king succeeded to the throne of Spain, the entire porcelain factory was moved to the palace of Buen Retiro outside Madrid. The early pieces manufactured in Spain are almost identical to those produced in Naples and this has resulted in much confusion with relation to

ITALY AND SPAIN

As already stated in the first section of this chapter, it is Italy that can lay claim to having carried out the first successful experiments to produce a form of porcelain in Europe. In Florence, at the instigation of the Grand Duke Francesco I de' Medici between about 1575 and his death in 1587, objects more ornamental than practical were produced in the newly developed material, including dishes, basins, jugs, vases and bottles. Many were decorated in blue in designs of grotesques, arms, and flower and leaf patterns.

Italian porcelain manufacture was not resumed until the eighteenth century, when workmen from the Meissen factory assisted in the establishment in 1719 of a factory in Venice, which was to remain in production for some twenty years. Among the products made there are rectangular sugar boxes and teapots of octagonal form, probably moulded after silver models. Other notable Italian porcelain factories include that set up by Geminiano Cozzi in Venice in the second half of the eighteenth century and the still extant Doccia factory near Florence, where regular production began in 1737 and other types of pottery were also made in addition to porcelain.

The most famous of Italy's porcelain factories was founded in 1743 by Charles IV, King of Naples and Sicily (later Charles III of Spain) in the royal palace of Capodimonte at Naples. At first, inspired largely by a wish to rival Meissen and Vienna, soft-paste porcelain was made. The ware was of a creamy-white colour and subjects included chinoiserie, landscapes with small figures, fruit and

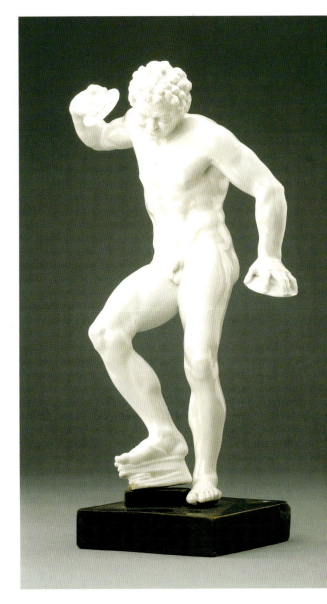

attribution. Production at Buen Retiro was strictly for the court until 1788, when attempts were made to put the factory on a more commercial footing. It then concentrated on the manufacture of figures rather than vessels, but without the use of imported Italian materials the quality of the body deteriorated.

Dish for a custard cup, with apple thorn decoration, from the Flora Danica dinner service. Royal Danish Porcelain Factory, *c.* 1790–1802. Part of a magnificent porcelain dinner service, all the pieces of which were painted with named botanical specimens.

In 1771 Charles's son Ferdinand revived the production of Capodimonte porcelain in Naples, where it continued until 1806. Decoration during this period ranged from the usual sprig and flower patterns to carefully painted scenes in colour of views of Naples, figure painting of peasant characters, depictions of Mount Vesuvius, and fishes copied from contemporary engravings. Motifs in the classical style included festoons, cornflower sprigs, key-feet and Pompeiian scrolls, and many of the vessels were based closely on historical pieces. Modelled figures ranged from the grandiose and spectacular to modest and unpretentious portrayals of small figures; groups of middle-class citizens

dressed in the fashions of the day were also produced. The factory finally closed in 1806.

SCANDINAVIA, THE LOW COUNTRIES AND RUSSIA

In Denmark the manufacture of soft-paste porcelain was begun, after several false starts, by two Frenchmen who produced it on a limited scale in Copenhagen from 1759 to 1765. Charles Buteux had formerly been employed at Sèvres and Louis Fournier at Vincennes, and both had also worked at Chantilly. Their work included tablewares strongly influenced by the French style, painted in soft enamel colours with decoration of small sprays of flowers, cupids and blue or pink scale patterns. China clay was found on the island of Bornholm in 1755 but was not used in the porcelain body until 1771/2, when Franz Heinrich Müller, an able chemist, conducted experiments that were to lead to the formation in 1774 of a porcelain manufacturing company of which Queen Juliane Marie was a principal shareholder. A licence was granted the following year and in 1779/80 the concern was taken over by the crown, thus becoming the Royal Danish Porcelain Factory. The factory's hard-paste porcelain production included large and elaborate vases and complete tea and coffee sets. Its most important project, however, was the magnificent dinner service known as the Flora Danica – this being the title of the huge botanical catalogue from which its painted plant and flower designs were comprehensively and faithfully reproduced. Made up of nearly two thousand pieces, the service was in production between about 1790 and 1802. It was originally intended for Catherine II of Russia, who died in 1796, but ultimately, though never quite completed, went to the Danish king. Flora Danica porcelain continues to be made. From 1835 the distinguished Danish sculptor Bertel Thorvaldsen (1770–1844) designed extremely successful figures for the royal factory.

In Sweden porcelain production began in 1766, again after a number of unsuccessful attempts, at the factory at Marieberg near Stockholm, best known for its faience. At this time management of the concern was taken over by the Frenchman Pierre Bertheven, who succeeded in developing a workable soft-paste porcelain. Of particular note among the items produced at Marieberg are the reeded lidded cups intended for cream, jelly or custard and painted with flowers, and the small vases, pot-pourri jars with applied flowers, and figures in the Mennecy style. The factory's figure-modelling included images of Swedish peasants.

In the Low Countries porcelain was produced at various centres. François-Joseph Peterinck, with the help of Robert Dubois, produced soft-paste porcelain in Tournai in 1750. The tablewares were strongly influenced by Meissen but the factory did evolve a highly individual style of decoration that included exotic birds and scenes from Æsop's fables painted in underglaze blue. Tournai also produced a wide range of pastoral figure groups, designed in line with contemporary French taste by artists who had worked at Mennecy. In Holland the first successful porcelain factory was established at Weesp near Amsterdam, where hard-paste was made from 1757. Here the designs reflected current European styles, but with the use of openwork and moulded decoration giving the porcelain an identity of its own. The factory moved twice, first to Oude Loosdrecht then to Amstel near Amsterdam, where it remained until closed down in 1820. At these two sites production was focused almost entirely on tea

and coffee sets and table services similar in form and decoration to Meissen and other German wares.

In Russia the St Petersburg porcelain factory first made hard-paste in 1748, although regular production did not begin until 1758. By 1800 there were at least twenty privately owned factories in Russia, and by 1861 seventy. The imperial factory enjoyed its greatest period under Catherine the Great, a collector of French and German porcelain. Notable wares in the neoclassical style were produced, a favourite design making use of dark ground colourings and elaborate gilding combined with Italian-style scrollwork. Cameo-painting in the antique style was another feature of the production. Painted decoration included depictions of Russian peasants taken from contemporary engravings. In 1803 Alexander I reorganized the factory, initiating the manufacture of new products such as huge, profusely gilded classical vases with elaborate enamelling, often closely emulating oil painting. The peasant figures, idealized and romanticized, were popular throughout the nineteenth century.

After the 1917 revolution the St Petersburg works became the State Porcelain Factory, its traditional mark of a crown over the emperor's initials being replaced by hammer and sickle designs, sometimes incorporating in Russian the inscription 'for the sake of the starving'. The factory's output was quickly brought into line with the 'agitprop' campaign. New designs created for the stock of blank hard-paste plates held by the factory incorporated vibrant colours and motifs conveying revolutionary ideals. Liberal use was made of images of peasants and soldiers and a typical legend was 'Knowledge in your head means food in your belly'. In 1922 members of the constructivist and futurist art movements designed pieces in a style characterized by abstract and geometrical forms. Production of high-quality wares continued, with many shapes reflecting the new styles.

BRITAIN

The circumstances surrounding the production of porcelain in Britain were quite different from those on the European mainland. In comparison with their continental equivalents, early British factories were small in size and their operations often quite modest in scale. Very few were set up with aristocratic or royal patronage, and although some had substantial financial backing the majority operated

Plate. Russian, dated 1922. Porcelain, painted overglaze with the slogans 'Petrograd' and 'Uritsky Square', decorated at the State Porcelain Factory, Petrograd, by Ekaterina Yakimovskaya, after a design by Alexander Shchekotikhina-Pototskaya (1892–1967), showing a Commissar crossing Uritsky Square, which was named after the Jewish revolutionary Mosei Uritsky, who was assassinated in 1918. Diameter 23 cm (9.5 in).

Teapot with two spouts with internal division for two types of tea. England, Bow factory, c. 1760–65. Soft-paste porcelain, enamelled, gilt, with silver mounts. Height 21.4 cm (8.5 in).

Tea caddy. England, Lowestoft, mid-1760s. Soft-paste porcelain with oriental-style decoration, intended to hold green tea. Height 12 cm (5 in).

for only quite short periods of time before being forced to close. Nevertheless, factories in Britain produced porcelain of great technical sophistication and feeling, much of it having a naive quality of great charm and character.

A variety of soft-paste bodies were devised, some more successful than others. A number of factories produced a type of soft-paste body known as bone china, which was peculiar to Britain. This contained bone ash made up of the calcined bones of animals – an ingredient that had first been proposed for porcelain composition in Germany in 1689. The bone china body was comprised of a mixture of china clay, Cornish stone and bone ash that not only yielded a satisfactory workable alternative to true porcelain but was also cheaper both to make and to fire. This medium-temperature body was a strong rival to true porcelain in terms of its whiteness, strength and translucency. Unlike soft-paste bodies made with the addition of a glassy frit, bone china is fired to temperatures up to 1200°C, which results in a far superior body. It also largely overcomes the earlier problem of loss of shape, since bone ash is not in itself a glass but reacts with the other ingredients to produce a hard

translucent body that is suitable for many types of richly coloured decoration. Although early experiments had taken place elsewhere, the development of the bone china body was ultimately achieved in England. The artist Thomas Frye (1710–62) and the potter Edward Heylyn (1695–c. 1758) of Bow first took out a patent for its use in 1744, acquiring a second patent in 1749 for the manufacture of china using calcareous earth.

A workable soft-paste porcelain was first produced in Britain in about 1745. The earliest factories were in London, at Stratford-le-Bow, Chelsea and Limehouse, but these were soon followed by others in Newcastle-under-Lyme and Longton Hall in Staffordshire, in Derby, at Vauxhall in London and in Liverpool. Frye, a painter and mezzotintist, set up the factory at Bow in east London, where he produced some of the finest English porcelain, much of it with a soft ivory colour. A range of useful wares, made in a bone-ash type of porcelain, frequently combined incongruous elements in their decoration with a result that was both naive and charming. Figure pieces were initially copied from Meissen, but shortly after 1750 a series of originals began to be modelled of subjects such as Muses, Varity, Lovers with a Birdcage and Lady with a Negro Page. In 1750 the factory was styled 'New Canton' and the influence of China and Japan came to dominate its functional wares. So successful was the Bow factory that it exported large quantities of tableware and figures to the North American colonies. Production continued at Bow until 1776.

In Lowestoft in Suffolk, as in Bow, a type of bone-ash porcelain was made. The factory was in operation from 1757 to 1802, its output including mainly tablewares, unpretentiously decorated, and miscellaneous small objects such as pounce pots, eye-baths and vases as well as commemorative wares. The earliest blue-and-white Lowestoft porcelain bore naive painted decoration and its shapes tended to follow the forms of salt-glazed porcelain. Small figures were produced of putti and of animals such as cats and sheep. In the early period underglaze blue decoration predominated, but later other colours were employed, many in imitation of late Chinese 'export porcelain' with figures in pink, red and blue. The rococo and Chinese styles remained in favour, although armorial shields became a further element of the Lowestoft wares.

Other factories developed their own variations of soft-paste porcelain, some by adding a glassy frit to the white-firing clay. The fritware body presented considerable production difficulties, chiefly because it had to be fired to a very precise temperature; exceeding this, even only slightly, caused the pieces to distort and lose shape in the firing. The composition did, however, produce a translucent body that could be thinly potted to resemble hard-paste porcelain. The first soft-paste porcelain factory in England to use a frit of this kind was founded around 1745 at Chelsea, which was then a village on the outskirts of London. Items produced there include small, delicate teapots and other teawares, salt cellars in the form of crayfish, and modelled figures. Both the shape and decoration of many of the forms derived from silver vessels, and relief decoration often consisted of moulded leaves and flowers, festoons and overlapping leaves. Around 1760 a silversmith, Nicholas Sprimont, became director at Chelsea in partnership with Thomas Briand, a French chemist, and the factory subsequently became the foremost manufacturer of English porcelain. Briand, a skilled inventor, had addressed the Royal Society on the subject of porcelain a few years earlier, claiming to hold the secret of its manufacture.

Under Sprimont's direction the factory produced work of exceptional quality, the cool white, slightly opaque glaze enhancing the inventive shapes. Although Sprimont had little knowledge of ceramics he had a sound understanding of form and decoration. Like that at Bow, the Chelsea factory had a strong tendency to take Meissen shapes and decoration as its inspiration, not only because the German work was so superbly modelled and made but also because it was the most successful commercially. At Chelsea the shapes of many of the tureens, sugar boxes and other vessels followed the fashion for imitating natural forms such as animals and fruit and vegetables. Some pieces were decorated with finely modelled and applied leaves and flowers, all of which were naturalistically coloured.

The figure ornaments produced at Chelsea were some of the finest made in England. Despite the influence of contemporary Meissen work, the Chelsea factory developed its own distinctive style that featured boldly and simply worked pieces sensitively coloured with discreet washes of soft-toned colours. The factory was one of the few that succeeded in attracting custom from the aristocracy, the royal family even sending a magnificent service of Chelsea china to the Duke of Mecklenburg. Busts were produced of George II, both as Prince of Wales and later as king, and of the Duke of Cumberland, probably in about 1750. In 1770 William Duesbury, the owner of the Derby factory, purchased Chelsea and operated the two businesses in tandem until 1784, when the London works was closed down.

Porcelain was first made in Derby around 1748 by a French chemist, Andrew Planché. Early production was aimed at the London market, much

The Roman Chanly. England, Chelsea, *c.* 1763. Soft-paste porcelain, enamelled and gilt. Modelled by Joseph Willems after an engraving by W. Panneels of a painting by Rubens. Height *c.* 60 cm (24 in).

Chocolate cups and saucers. Derby and Bristol, late 18th century. Soft-paste porcelain, made for the 'Ladies of Llangollen', Lady Eleanor Butler and Miss Sarah Ponsonby, who set up an idyllic 'Gothic' home together at Plas Newydd.

of it imitating the wares produced at Chelsea. In 1756 Duesbury and his partner John Heath purchased the factory and began manufacturing items strongly influenced by Meissen, but by 1770 much of the tableware had acquired a markedly individual character. Tureens and leaf-shaped dishes were made, as well as teaware and baskets. In particular, distinctive styles of bird- and flower-painting were developed at Derby. In the 1770s Sèvres became a major influence, and the figure pieces were often based on contemporary prints. During the 'Crown-Derby' period (1784–1811) wares were decorated with painted Derbyshire landscapes and a naturalistic style of flower-painting was introduced.

In Staffordshire the earliest porcelain factory was set up around 1751 at Longton Hall, one of the few porcelain manufactories with a potter – in this case William Littler (1724–84) – as one of its founders. This enterprise was to operate for less than ten years, but distinctive pieces were produced during its short existence. In addition to porcelain Littler made salt-glazed stonewares. The porcelain tends to be rustic and unsophisticated in character but possesses great charm and verve. Wares that were made include dishes in the form of folded leaves, often with yellowish green enamel, as well as plates, sauce boats, tureens and teapots. The factory also made figures that were skilfully modelled and painted. However, in 1760 it went bankrupt,

whereupon Littler moved to Scotland, where he later opened a new porcelain factory at West Pans, near Musselburgh.

The factory established at Worcester was to become one of the most enduring and influential of all the British porcelain manufacturers. Set up at Warmstry House in 1751 by Dr John Wall and William Davis, over time it established an impressive tradition of finely made and decorated wares second only to those of Chelsea in artistic importance. In the early years soapstone or steatite from Cornwall was used as a flux in the body, a composition thought to have been introduced by Wall, who was a physician and painter as well as a businessman. Unlike that of other contemporary porcelains, this body could be thrown and turned very thinly and was capable of withstanding contact with boiling water without cracking. The factory developed a substantial trade in technically well-finished tablewares of sound practical shape, specializing in teawares, sauce boats, pickle dishes and pots for meat paste.

In the late 1750s Worcester adopted the quicker and less expensive process of transfer-printing on its porcelain wares. Early images were printed in black, later ones in shades of blue. Designs reflected the vogue for prints and were also influenced by wares imported from China. Many were adaptations of the Chinese-inspired 'willow pattern' created in

England later in the eighteenth century, which was so successful that it became widely used as a standard design. Painting in underglaze blue remained popular throughout much of the nineteenth century, considerable use continuing to be made of Chinese motifs, often freely copied and adapted.

In the early nineteenth century a more restrained, neoclassical style was adopted, although in due course this gave way to more elaborate colouring. The so-called Worcester-Japan designs, free adaptations of Kakiemon and Imari patterns displaying a combination of ornateness and exoticism, reflected the widespread public interest in the 'Japanesque' during the last decades of the nineteenth century. Later the factory developed a high-temperature porcelain body that possessed great resistance to thermal shock coupled with good mechanical strength. This was used for a wide range of practical and decorative tablewares as well as a variety of laboratory equipment. The factory is still in production, but now as Royal Worcester.

In 1813, William Billingsley (1758–1828) set up a porcelain factory in the Welsh town of Nantgarw in Glamorgan, making the boast that his soft-paste was equal in quality to that of Sèvres. The principal items the factory produced were a range of decorative plates, many with borders of raised flowers, and other well-made tablewares of excellent quality. Billingsley moved production to Swansea a year later, and back to Nantgarw in 1817, but in 1820 he left to join Coalport.

John Rose had established a porcelain manufactory at Coalport towards the end of the eighteenth century and in 1799 bought the nearby Caughley factory, where he continued to produce blue-printed teawares. An astute businessman, Rose developed a ware that was technically sound and made ingenious use of shapes that tended to imitate those of continental and earlier English manufacturers. Around 1820 he devised a lead-free glaze to eliminate the risk of lead poisoning, many of his glaze workers having been badly affected by the materials they handled.

Perfection of the standard English composition of bone china is attributed to Josiah Spode (1755–1827), who around 1796 was marketing what he described as 'English china'. Spode's father, also named Josiah, had been apprenticed to the distinguished potter Thomas Whieldon in 1749 and established the Spode factory in Staffordshire in

1761 to make cream-coloured and blue-painted earthenware. After his father's death in 1797 Spode took over management of the factory and began to develop new lines, including a highly refined and workable bone china.

Aided by the fact that Spode's perfection of the bone china body coincided with a sharp fall in imports from China, the factory prospered. Its pieces were of high technical merit and included elaborately gilded vases with coloured grounds. Having perfected the body to the extent that the factory was able to produce it in reliable quantities, Spode became the first Staffordshire potter to manufacture porcelain dinnerware. A tour of the Stoke manufactory and showroom by the Prince of Wales in 1806 led to Spode being appointed to supply fine bone china and other ceramic products to the British royal family. In 1833 William Taylor Copeland took over the business, producing a wide variety of fine and practical wares including such objects as footbaths with blue-and-white decoration. The factory continues to this day, although it now forms part of a large industrial group.

High-temperature porcelain

In comparison with soft-paste, little hard-paste, or 'true', porcelain was produced in Britain, largely because the essential raw materials of china stone (petuntse) and china clay (kaolin) were either not known or not available. However, in the mid-eighteenth century William Cookworthy (1705–80), a Quaker apothecary living in Devon, did find suitable raw materials in vast outcrops in Cornwall. It was he who, in 1754, initiated high-temperature porcelain production in England after reading accounts of experiments carried out in France on the basis of a detailed description of porcelain manufacture sent home from China by the French Jesuit missionary Père d'Entrecolles. A great deal of mystery surrounds Cookworthy's mineral discoveries, but it is possible that they were connected with a visit he received in about 1745 from an unidentified American who showed him samples of china clay. It is thought that this gentleman, who claimed to have discovered the material 'at the back of Virginia', may have been Andrew Duché, a potter from Savannah, Georgia (see chapter 10).

Although not himself a potter, Cookworthy had considerable knowledge of the physical and chemical changes that take place when materials are

Vase and cover. England, Worceste (first period). Soft-paste porcelain, painted with two panels of chinoiserie figures on a blue scale background. Height 35.5 cm (14 in).

Mug. Plymouth, *c.* 1768–70. Hard-paste porcelain. Height 27.8 cm (11 in).

OPPOSITE:

Large serving dish. Derby factory, *c.* 1810. Soft-paste porcelain with Imari-style decoration copied from Japanese Imari porcelain.

taken to high temperature, and after many years of research he succeeded in producing true porcelain. In 1768, armed with a patent entitling him to manufacture hard-paste porcelain, he acquired the financial backing to help set up a factory in Plymouth. Production at Plymouth was destined to be short-lived, but in the two years during which it did take place there the factory's porcelain was occasionally of a very high quality. Most of it, however, turned out technically imperfect, disfigured by fire-cracks and misshapen in form. Decoration included painted designs in a darkish underglaze blue, although some ambitious pieces such as large teapots and coffee pots were painted in colours in the Worcester style. The deep, clear red and leaf-green colourings that were later to characterize Bristol porcelain were introduced at Plymouth, while a brownish-crimson was used on the rococo scroll-work bases of the often excellent early figures.

The economics of production rapidly rendered the Plymouth operation unviable and in 1770 its activities were transferred to Bristol, under Cookworthy's technical direction but with Richard Champion as his manager and partner. In Plymouth the market for the more expensive porcelain pieces had been far from buoyant and it was hoped that Bristol, with its larger population and well-to-do merchant class, would provide an advantage in this respect. Champion was able to fund the new factory's operations with capital raised from his Quaker colleagues and this allowed a number of technical developments to be made, such as improvements to the body and the construction of more efficient kilns. Unfortunately these measures failed to resolve the financial problems of the enterprise, and with production still proving unduly costly the capital quickly dwindled.

Nevertheless, Champion's output at Bristol, predominantly in the Sèvres style, was ambitious. A new set of figures – probably modelled by Pierre Stephan, who had also worked variously at Derby, Etruria (Stoke-on-Trent) and Coalport – was created, which depicted such subjects as the Seasons, the Elements and Venus and Adonis. Other notable Bristol wares include large vases, usually of hexagonal form and with grandiose decoration of applied flowers. In addition to fine wares Champion produced what is known as 'cottage china', simply decorated with festoons and sprigs, with no gilding. Like the items made at Ply-

mouth, Bristol porcelain is recognizable by its clear, almost translucent quality.

The insurmountable financial difficulties at Bristol having finally led Champion into bankruptcy, in 1781 the factory was closed and its production moved to New Hall in Staffordshire, where a consortium of potters – friends of Josiah Wedgwood – hoped to turn the operation into a commercial success. Alongside Bristol 'cottage'-style ware, hard-paste porcelain continued to be produced at New Hall, albeit in diminishing quantity, with tea and coffee services in a limited range of patterns comprising the bulk of the factory's output. Later, similarly decorated wares were made in a glossy bone china. The New Hall works was shut down in the 1830s.

Expertise in the handling and firing of both hard- and soft-paste bodies improved markedly during the nineteenth century, enabling larger and ever more ambitious items to be produced. Much of the ware lost its naive quality at this time, its early simplicity giving way to greater sophistication as the technology advanced. So skilled did manufacturers become that in addition to large decorative vases and full-scale dinner services they were able to produce huge panels, many of which were incorporated into architectural interiors. Other impressive objects included fireplaces made by the Copeland factory, vast vases of ornate design, many with enamelled and gilded decoration, and even fountains. The popularity of bone china soon overtook that of frit-based bodies, the ware's high translucency and soft white glaze easily outshining the rival products.

Of the many factories that switched to the production of bone china in the nineteenth century, one of the most notable is Rockingham in Yorkshire, which was unusual in that it operated under an aristocratic patron, Earl Fitzwilliam. Wares produced by this pottery in the 1820s include its well-known black-brown glazed and brown salt-glazed stoneware and earthenware. Rockingham porcelain is distinguished by its somewhat florid 'revived-rococo' style and often lavishly gilding, a famous example being the 'rhinoceros vase' made for Wentworth House. Equally characteristic are green-glazed vases in the form of folded leaves and painting in the botanical style. Rockingham ware became very fashionable, the factory's elevation to the status of royal patronage adding to its success.

Circular basket and cover. Ireland, Belleek factory, 1891–1926. Porcelain, woven base supporting lattice sides and domed cover, applied with intricately modelled flowers. Height 20.3 cm (8 in).

As the efficiency and technical sophistication of production methods improved, so costs began to fall, the manufacture of bone china becoming little more expensive than that of good quality cream earthenware, despite the fact that it was considerably stronger and more delicate. The consequent reduction in bone china prices diminished the appeal of porcelain, to the extent that by the second half of the nineteenth century most of the specialist porcelain factories had closed down. Production of porcelain thus moved largely into the hands of companies working with several different bodies and became centred in Stoke-on-Trent, where such factories as Copeland and Minton dominated the field.

IRELAND

In 1857 the Belleek Pottery was founded in Belleek, County Fermanagh. Three men were responsible for the venture: John Caldwell Bloomfield, who had discovered deposits of feldspar, china clay and other materials on his land; David McBirney, a wealthy businessman; and William Armstrong, an architect with a passion for porcelain and a knowledge of pottery manufacturing techniques. Initially producing a diverse range of wares from floor tiles to hospital wares, the pottery channelled some of the profits from these into developing a method of making fine porcelain. In 1863 a number of workmen were recruited from Stoke-on-Trent and a reliable porcelain body was at last perfected. Typical Belleek products include highly intricate open-weave baskets with applied modelled flower decoration, which had to be built by hand. The most extensively made products, however, were teawares, some of which were fashioned in the form of shells and covered with a soft green or nacreous glaze.

American-Indian Pottery

Every sort of pottery, made in a thousand forms
from great water jars to little jugs

BERNARD DIAZ, ON THE GREAT MARKET
AT TIATELOCO, NEAR TENOCHTITLÁN

Water bottle. North America, eastern woodlands, Temple Mound period. Earthenware, hand-built 'orangeware', with painted spiral decoration in dark pigment. From Tennessee. Height 25 cm (10 in).

It is believed that the first native Americans were people who migrated from the Asian continent more than 25,000 years ago by way of a northern land bridge over what is now the Bering Strait of north-west Alaska, later moving southwards through the continents. In Mesoamerica and Andean South America the origins of agriculture, involving the cultivation of such crops as maize, beans, squash and in South America the potato, date back several thousand years; the first pottery is thought to have been made in the region shortly afterwards. European presence in the Americas begins with the expedition led by Columbus in 1492 and the subsequent Portuguese and Spanish conquests – of the Aztecs by Cortez and of the Incas by Pizarro. Spanish settlers won control over most of the area from Texas to Argentina, while the Portuguese colonized the Brazilian coast. By this time there were already many culturally and geographically distinct groups occupying virtually the whole of North, Central and South America.

American-Indian pottery is unique in several ways. Early wares were made by cultures within which the wheel was either unknown or its use not developed (mules and sleds would have been used for transporting heavy goods while litters carried the rich or important). In several areas basket-making developed before pottery-making, and often a technique similar to the coiling method of building baskets was used for making pots. Glaze as it is generally understood in the West was rarely used, although glaze-like surfaces were achieved by burnishing. Coloured clay slips and pigments were used for decorative rather than functional purposes, as, for example, on pottery made in the south-west of North America. In addition, pots were decorated in a variety of ways with either incised or relief designs. Firings were carried out in pits or in bonfires, although in some areas the firings were sufficiently sophisticated to allow the atmosphere to be controlled in such a way that the black colouring associated with reduction firing could be obtained.

In general, pottery was modest in size and squat in form. Various different kinds of pot were made for storing the staple foodstuffs of seeds and maize. Cooking pots, one of the largest of the functional types of ware, display the characteristics of vessels used by societies living at ground level. Many of the vessels have rounded rather than flat bases, which enabled them to sit more easily in a fire or on an uneven surface, while some bowls have tripod legs that would have kept them steady on uneven floors. Also, faces modelled on pots tend to be directed upwards in such a way that they can be clearly seen when the pots are placed on the ground.

Not only the methods used for constructing pots but also their forms were greatly influenced by basket-making. Although the three main techniques

on pots made by the Mayans. Geometric motifs, in endless combinations, make up the most common designs and are found throughout much of the Americas. In some cases quite basic shapes are used, arranged in satisfying divisions of space, while in work from certain areas the abstract repeating patterns seem to have been influenced by local textile designs.

The widely practised custom of burying pots with the dead has resulted in the survival of large quantities of pottery, much of it preserved in good condition. Within some cultural groups, such as the Moche culture of Peru, pots were painted with, or had modelled on to them, a great variety of scenes, many of which reflected the needs and activities of everyday life: eating and hunting, lovemaking and punishment.

American-Indian pottery not only serves as unique evidence of social history, preserving in detail events that might otherwise have remained unrecorded, but is also a distinctive art form in its own right. The territories in which it was first made are diverse both geographically and geologically, ranging from hot swampy lowlands and arid desert to highlands and cultivated valleys. In North America early pottery was made in areas from the east to the Pacific Slope, taking in what is now North Carolina and the Ohio and Illinois region. The craft reached its highest level of development in Mexico, Central America and Peru, the influence of wares from these regions extending to the inhabitants of territories that correspond to modern-day Arizona and New Mexico.

SOUTH-WESTERN NORTH AMERICA: THE PUEBLO INDIANS

In North America some of the most important American-Indian pottery was produced within small communities – in what is known as the 'pueblo' tradition (after the Spanish for village or town) – in the south-western area roughly covering the modern states of southern Colorado, Utah and

Bowl. North America, Hopi, early 20th century. Earthenware, hand-built, with painted decoration that reflects the interest of the potter, Nampeyo, in 15th- and 16th-century American pottery. Diameter 26 cm (10.25 in).

used for building pottery – coiling, moulding and modelling, employed either separately or in combination – allow almost any shape to be made, the majority of pots are rounded, often closely resembling basketry forms. Decorative motifs, adapted to the medium of clay, appear on the pots in a variety of styles. Many are based on the animal and insect world, some creatures being portrayed with acute naturalism, others in a greatly simplified and abstracted manner. Mimbres black-on-white ware, for example, features insect images depicted both naturalistically and in the form of patterns. Also highly stylized are the complex scenes that appear

Water jar. North America, New Mexico, Zuni, 19th century. Earthenware, hand-built, painted with traditional designs depicting animal with 'spirit line' to stomach or heart. Height 26 cm (10.25 in).

OPPOSITE:

Map of major pre-Hispanic pottery centres in south-western North America, Mesoamerica and western areas of South America.

Nevada, all of Arizona and most of western and central New Mexico. Across this vast territory for twelve thousand years people dwelt in small nomadic bands and were dependent on hunting and gathering for their subsistence. It was to this region, encompassing mountains, deserts and plateau, that pottery as a technology extended from Mexico some time after 500 BC. Thin-walled bowls, cylindrical jars, ollas (jars with rounded sides and necks), handled pitchers, ladles and mugs were all built out of carefully prepared pink or red clay. Decoration and shapes evolved radically both before and after European settlement in the south-west at the end of the sixteenth century.

Three major cultures that flourished during the two millennia up to AD 1500 have been identified. The first is the Mogollon culture, centred in the eastern Arizona mountains and west-central New Mexico from around 200 BC, which had fallen into decline by about AD 1200. Towards the end of this period the Mogollon began constructing large apartment-like dwellings, and within the same

culture the Mimbres people produced highly sophisticated black-on-white pottery, notably between about AD 1000 and 1150.

The Hohokam culture (*c.* 300 BC–AD *c.* 1400) was based in southern and central Arizona, this region serving as the first filter through which Mesoamerican influence reached North America. As a result of their connections with the south, Hohokam communities displayed many Meso-american traits. They devised complex irrigation systems as well as engaging in jewellery and pottery manufacture and copper casting. At the beginning of the fifteenth century the Hohokam ceased to exist as a cultural entity.

The third important culture is that of the Anasazi – generally considered to be the ancestors of America's present-day pueblo people – who lived in the plateau region making up the 'Four Corners' of Utah, Colorado, Arizona and New Mexico. Only in the case of the Anasazi (although the same may be true of the Hohokam) can a continuous cultural tradition be traced that survived from prehistoric into historic times. In the first century AD the Anasazi already had a well developed basketry technique and a hunting and gathering economy that showed signs of incipient agriculture.

American-Indian peoples settled in villages or pueblos scattered throughout the south-west of North America. The widespread trade that was conducted between pueblos extended into the great civilizations of central Mexico, some of the most commonly traded and highly valued objects being beautifully decorated ceramic jars and bowls. The earliest appearance of pueblo pottery, in the form of bowls and jars in a polished red or brown ware, is found within the Mogollon culture between 300 and 200 BC and plain wares continued in use alongside later painted pottery throughout the existence of this culture. The majority of Mogollon painted pottery was decorated with geometric patterns believed to have been adapted from earlier basket-ware designs.

The best-known group of wares associated with the Mogollon culture is that made by the Mimbres people, who inhabited the Mimbres River Valley in west-central New Mexico. During its nine-hundred-year history Mimbres pottery evolved from a plain brown undecorated ware to bowls adorned with spectacular figurative black-on-white

NEVADA

UTAH

COLORADO

• Mesa Verde

CALIFORNIA

ANASAZI

San Juan R. N A V A J O • Taos

MOGOLLON

SINAGUA

Little Colorado R.

Chaco

San Ildefonso • Santa Clara

Zia

Santa Fe

• Flagstaff

ARIZONA

Santa Ana

Santo Domingo

Laguna • Albuquerque

Colorado R.

HOHOKAM

Acoma

Phoenix

Salt R.

Gila R.

Gila R.

SALADO

NEW
MEXICO

Rio Grande

• Tucson

APACHE

MIMBRES

MEXICO

TEXAS

NICARAGUA

CARIBBEAN SEA

ATLANTIC
OCEAN

COSTA
RICA

PANAMA

VENEZUELA

COLOMBIA

ECUADOR

Amazon R.

BRAZIL

MOCHE

Chanchan

CHIMU

Recuay

PERU

Chancay

Machu Picchu

Cusco • INCA

Nasca

NASCA

L. Titicaca

• Tiahuanaco

Tacna

BOLIVIA

CHILE

ARGENTINA

Copiapó •

Colorado R.

NORTH AMERICA

Mississippi Valley

CHIHUAHUA

GULF OF
MEXICO

WEST
INDIES

MEXICO

Teotihuacán

El Artollilo, Zacatenco, Tlateloco

NAYARIT

HUASTECA

Cholula

Yucatan Peninsula

Mexico City

JALISCO

Isla de
Sacrificios

Maya Lowlands

COLIMA

Tula

BRITISH HONDURAS

Matlatzinca

CARIBBEAN SEA

GUERRERO

TABASCO

Puebla

GUATEMALA

Monte Albán

Maya
Highlands

HONDURAS

OAXACA

NICARAGUA

Vera Cruz

SALVADOR

COSTA RICA

Chiapa de Corzo

COCLÉ

Nicoya Peninsula

CHIRIQUI

PANAMA

Isthmus of Panama

PACIFIC
OCEAN

Two vessels with handles. North America, Arizona, Upper Gila area and Salt River Valley. Earthenware, with painted decoration. Height (left) 8.5 cm (3.4 in); (right) 12.5 cm (5 in).

Oval bowl. North America, New Mexico, Mimbres, *c.* 1000–1130. Earthenware, hand-built, painted with design of figure giving birth, and with a 'kill' hole in the centre. Diameter 17.5 cm (7 in), height 6.25 cm (2.5 in).

designs. The earliest vessels (*c.* AD 200) were made of a brown-firing clay in shapes similar to gourds and include jars intended for cooking and storage. After AD 550 techniques were developed for producing red pottery using a coating of red slip, and decorated pottery was first made around AD 650. The geometric patterns that appear on Mimbres pots are varied and inventive, incorporating scrolls, circles, triangles, squares and rectangles. In stylized figurative designs the subjects depicted include animals, reptiles, fish and insects as well as both single and composite figures.

Almost all the decorated bowls that have survived intact were recovered from funerary contexts.

It was standard practice during most of Mimbrian history to place a single bowl in the grave of a deceased person, and the unblemished condition of many surviving pieces suggests that they may have been made specifically for this purpose. Occasionally several bowls were buried, together with utility wares. In the case of many Mimbres grave goods a hole, commonly referred to as the 'kill' hole, was deliberately punched into pots before they were interred; various reasons for this practice have been proposed, but the ritual of which it is likely to have formed a part has never been positively identified. The imagery on many of the pieces is equally ambiguous, relating to death and life after death, but also to life in this world.

Some Mimbres pottery reveals a knowledge of wares made in other parts of the south-west. The early black-on-white pieces bear a close similarity to vessels made by the Hohokam, whose pottery designs may have inspired the first Mimbres figurative decoration. Mogollon pottery continued to be made after the European conquest, but form and designs evolved only slowly and accurate dating remains difficult.

Towards the end of the nineteenth century Nampeyo of Hopi decorated her pots with yellow and red feather designs. Although this was seen as innovative at the time, it was in fact the reinvention of a prehistoric style. More recently, potters such as Lucy Lewis (1897–1992) and Maria Chino of Acoma pueblo have made effective use of both traditional Acoma patterns and realistic Mimbres figure designs, similar techniques being adopted by Joseph Lane Wolf and his sister Grace Medicine Flower of Santa Clara pueblo.

Distinctive styles of decoration emerged within different American-Indian cultures. Developments in Zuni pottery (made in the western part of New Mexico, around the Zuni River, a region occupied continuously from approximately AD 700) were influenced significantly by ideas brought into the area by people arriving first from the north and later from the west and south. Zuni pottery is characterized by the use of painted decoration that often covers the top section of the outside of the pot. Black and dark red pigments were used on a pale grey background. Designs often depict animals such as deer, enclosed within a structure of some kind and placed near to a plant thought to represent the animal's food. The deer is usually shown with a lifeline to the heart – a means, perhaps, of indicating a spiritual dimension. In the late nineteenth century Zuni potters were still producing skilfully made effigy vessels and figurines, but their ceramics proved to have only limited appeal for the growing tourist market which, in the case of some groups, had become the main incentive to continue making such items. Over the past hundred years the production of Zuni cooking pots and water jars has gradually

pots made at Santo Domingo a white slip background is decorated with pure geometric and more openly spaced black designs. Hopi pottery, made in north-eastern Arizona, is decorated with black designs on a yellow slip.

The Anasazi culture endured for almost twelve centuries before its growth was brought to an end. In the sixteenth century the Spaniards came across some sixty Anasazi pueblos, whereas only two dozen exist today. Like Mogollon wares, Anasazi

Rounded pot. North America, New Mexico, Acoma, made by Lucy Lewis, *c.* 1970. Earthenware, hand-built with painted decoration. Diameter 29 cm (11.5 in).

declined, although vessels continue to be made for religious and other purposes.

Like the Mimbres ware, Acoma pottery is decorated with a band of pattern covering the upper two-thirds of the pots, the designs, often floral, painted in black and yellowish-red pigments. On

vessels were originally plain grey or red in colour. The earliest painted pottery, dating to around AD 600, is decorated in black on grey, but the use of black on white soon came to predominate throughout the Anasazi regions. Black-on-red, red-on-orange and polychrome wares appeared later.

OPPOSITE:
Mary Histia (1881–1973),
an Acoma potter known for her
large water vessels delicately
painted with polychrome
designs, photographed in 1900.

Bear effigy pot. North America,
Navajo Indian Reservation,
Tuba City, Arizona, 1983.
Earthenware, hand-built,
painted decoration. Height
18 cm (7.2 in). Lolita Begay,
'sister' (niece) of Hopi-Navajo
potter Nathan Begay, was
twelve years old when she
made this white-slipped bear.

Bowl. Arizona, San Ildefonso
pueblo. Maria Martinez (potter),
Julian Martinez (decorator),
1934–43. Height 12 cm (5 in).
Earthenware, polished
blackware decorated with a
twisting serpentine *avanyu*
figure with an arrow and
interspersed geometric shapes.
The avanyu is a horned serpent
and symbol of thanksgiving
for water and rain.

Other Anasazi pottery includes surface-textured pieces such as the corrugated ware that first appeared around AD 800–1000 and was made by leaving the coils unsmoothed. Anasazi pottery shows considerable differences from period to period, subculture to subculture and even village to village, and variations are evident in the pottery styles of the historic (1540–1880) and modern periods (from 1880). This ware is still made today in such pueblos as Picuris and Taos and, with painted surfaces, in San Juan, Santa Clara and San Ildefonso.

Within the Anasazi culture pueblo potters continued to fashion prehistoric-style pottery even in the historic and modern periods. Acoma pots made between 1600 and 1900 tended to be mainly functional in form and lavishly embellished, often with busy, lyrical polychrome designs. Today pottery-making is carried out predominantly by pueblos in four specific regions: the Hopi pueblos in Arizona, the Plateau pueblos of Acoma, the northern Rio Grande pueblos of Santa Clara, San Ildefonso and San Juan, and the southern Rio Grande pueblos of Santo Domingo and Zia in New Mexico. Among the most widely known modern work is that of Maria Martinez (1884–1980) of the San Ildefonso pueblo.

The Hohokam culture, based on irrigation agriculture, developed primarily in the desert areas of the Gila and Salt River Valleys of Arizona. Hohokam pottery first appeared around 300 BC as a plain ware, either grey or brown in colour, and this was later followed by a slipped redware. Pots were built with coils, but whereas the Mogollon and Anasazi scraped down the walls of their pots to smooth them off, the Hohokam flattened the coils and then smoothed them by means of a version of the paddle-and-anvil technique whereby the clay wall was supported by an inner anvil and beaten on the outside with a paddle to smooth and strengthen it. The Hohokam also produced clay figures, usually in human forms. Their pots often have a sharply defined shoulder created by the junction of the rounded base with the straight walls, a feature that is likely to have developed out of the particular building method used. Red-on-grey decorated ware began to be made around the beginning of the first century AD and by 700 the dominant colouring was red on buff. Gradually the geometric designs found on

early decorated work gave way to a more realistic portrayal of natural forms. Much of the ware reflects a Mexican influence, which is particularly evident in the clay figures and vessels with legs.

By the end of the fourteenth century the Hohokam culture had all but disappeared, probably as a result of a combination of adverse factors that may have been brought about by climatic changes, social disarray and possibly foreign invasion.

Roughly in the region of the Mississippi valley, in the south-west and central areas of the northern continent, the complex culture of the Mississippians developed, in which people lived in towns or villages and intensively cultivated the land. This culture continued from about AD 800 until the arrival of the Europeans.

In common with other Mississippian peoples, the Caddoans in Arkansas created vessels that were often left unpainted but had incised or modelled decoration, some figural, some more abstract. On many bowls the head and tail of a bird or animal would be modelled into the rim, the body of the pot representing that of the animal, and special pieces of this kind were often covered with finely incised decorative motifs. Incising was a common form of decoration on Caddoan vessels and refined patterning was frequently used on ceremonial pieces. The Caddoans built clay sculptural figures as well as pots.

When the Atchison, Topeka and Santa Fe Railroad reached Santa Fe in 1880 the event heralded a new era for the pueblo people. As far as pottery-making was concerned the effects were both bad and good: although the new rail link meant that there was now a plentiful supply of commercial

Cylindrical tripod vessel. Central America, Teotihuacán, 150 BC – AD 750. Earthenware, hand-built, incised with 'reptile eye' glyph in dark slip. Height 12.5 cm (5 in).

MESOAMERICA

The central region of America known as Mesoamerica, covering much of modern Mexico and Central America, encompasses highlands and lowlands, tropical forests and deserts. Although each culture within the area developed its own customs and distinctive style of pottery decoration, all appear to have displayed aspects of a common cultural heritage that embraced astronomy, hieroglyphic writing, bark-paper or deerskin books, maps and calendars, and *tlachtli*, a curious ballgame played with a rubber ball in a carefully prepared and defined court. Small hand-modelled figurines associated with crop fertility rites are found throughout much of Mexico, the best known being those from the lakeside villages in the high central plateau known as the Valley of Mexico. In early settlements of about 1500– 1000 BC finely made dishes and storage jars were produced, indicating the existence of a well-established ceramic tradition.

During what is referred to as the formative or pre-classic period (*c.* 2000 BC–AD 250), communities settled in permanent lakeside villages and started to cultivate the fertile uplands of the Valley of Mexico, this region becoming the centre of Mexican unity. The final centuries of the first millennium BC saw the development of the vast city-state of Teotihuacán, which began to dominate the political, economic and religious life of the area. By AD 600 it was to have become the largest urban centre in the Americas, housing more than 100,000 inhabitants.

It was in the hot forest lowlands of Tabasco and southern Vera Cruz on the Gulf Coast of Mexico that the first important Mexican culture arose – that of the Olmecs (*c.* 1200–400 BC), a name applied to this ancient civilization in the sixteenth century after the people occupying the region at the time of the Spanish conquest. Olmec settlements featured public plazas, impressive earthen platform architecture and colossal stone sculptures of Olmec rulers. Long-distance trade brought jade into the area and this was worked by skilled artisans. Some Olmec pottery figures, freely modelled either as groups depicted in everyday scenes or as individual studies and often painted with white clay and red pigment, reveal a preoccupation with the human life cycle. Other items made by the Olmecs were bowls, neckless jars, long-necked bottles, spouted

alternatives to the vessels traditionally made and sold in the area, at the same time it brought in a steady stream of tourists eager to purchase mementoes of their travels. These new developments were to affect both the quality and quantity of work produced by pueblo potters. In some pueblos pottery production declined drastically and never fully recovered, while in others the potters began to cater specially for the tourist trade, often by turning to the manufacture of smaller, easily transportable objects. At Hopi a Tewa Indian potter called Nampeyo revived the ancient Sikyatki pottery forms and designs, interpreting them in her own style. This encouraged a renaissance of pottery production at Hopi as well as winning fame for Nampeyo herself.

In the twentieth century Maria Martinez, a potter in San Ildefonso pueblo in New Mexico, discovered a new technique for firing her pots, which transformed the ware into a lustrous black and gained her work international recognition.

designs were normally incised, sometimes before the pot was fired and sometimes afterwards – the latter option resulting in a finer, drier line. Another mode of decoration was 'negative' painting, a resist technique whereby a design was painted on to the pot in hot wax or some similarly resistant substance. The pot would then be dipped or coated in a different-coloured pigment that would stick to, and colour, the body of the pot except where the design had been applied. Thus the design would ultimately be picked out in the colour of the body itself, the resist material having been burnt off during firing.

The eventual fall of Teotihuacán marked the end of the classic period. The era that ensued was to be one of violence and aggression, a time of sporadic wars and large-scale human sacrifice to the gods. In the post-classic period the Aztecs gained a dominance they would retain until overthrown by the Spanish under Cortez in 1519–21.

As the classic Vera Cruz civilization waned, the Huaxtec peoples of the northern Gulf Coast continued to prosper. In this area many pottery vessels were made and modelled then painted with bold black designs on a contrasting ground of white slip. Some of the most elaborate of them depicted half-animal, half-human composite beings derived from Mexican folklore, while vessels modelled in the form of turtles served as a suitable metaphor for the emergence of the earth from the primordial sea.

In the independent cities that grew up during the classic period, much effort was devoted both to intellectual and scientific activities and to the worship of numerous deities. Impressive temples and pyramids were built, and sculpture, painting and pottery was produced for ritual purposes (although pots were also made for everyday use).

It was the classic period that saw the rise of the Maya (250 BC–AD 1000), the most accomplished of all Amerindian civilizations, whose beginnings lie in Mexico, Guatemala, Belize and Honduras. High on the list of the Maya's achievements is the invention of hieroglyphic writing, which allowed names and the dates of events such as births and marriage alliances to be recorded. Developing more or less independently in an area largely secure from invasion, the Mayan culture was distinguished by unrivalled achievement in the fields of astronomy, mathematics, writing, art and architecture. Little

Woman holding a child. Mexico, Classic Veracruz, AD 300–1200. Earthenware. Height 15.7 cm (6.3 in).

trays, bowls and jars with three tall feet, and jars with stirrup spouts. Flat dishes were often fitted with hollow 'mammiform' legs in the shape of female breasts.

During much of the classic period (AD 250–c. 1000) Teotihuacán, controlled by the priesthood, enjoyed all the advantages of peace, order and flourishing trade – including that in pottery. For use in the rites and ceremonies that took place throughout the year, marking the phases of an agricultural calendar based on the changing of the seasons, models of figures in ritual attire were made, representing natural deities or characters from Mesoamerican mythology. A range of fine orangeware was traded widely. Decorative techniques involved covering vessels in a fine slip of black, brown, red or white, which was often burnished by rubbing with a smooth pebble to develop a shine (sometimes described as polishing). Some pots were left plain while others were decorated with simple geometrical patterning. The

interest in military expansion was evident until the post-classic period.

Early Mayan ceramics indicate a strong influence from Teotihuacán, but after the city's destruction and abandonment in the second half of the first century AD a more distinctive style came into being, partly through pots being fired to a lower temperature. This allowed new techniques of decoration to be devised that made use of coloured pigments of great brilliance, although a certain measure of durability was relinquished in the interests of greater aesthetic effect. Hieroglyphics and animals were often incorporated into the decoration, but the most impressive designs are the scenes of Mayan ceremonial life. Sacrificial cups in the shape of animals were also made, and other important wares include effigy incense-burners, plates, open bowls, and tripod vessels with slab feet of Teotihuacán derivation.

An air of militarism pervaded the Mayan culture during the post-classic period, from around AD 950. For a variety of reasons the Maya's ceremonial sites in the central region had been abandoned, and Mexican invasions led to a glorification of war that spawned a more aggressive ethos in general. Many other aspects of Mexican culture were adopted,

Vessel with head emerging from serpent jaws. Central America, Isla de Sacrificios, *c.* 900–1521. Height 12.7 cm (5 in).

Incense burner. Central America, Mixteca (1200–1521). Earthenware, hand-built with painted decoration, used for burning small balls of copal gum and rubber in ceremonial rituals. Height 20 cm (8 in); length 57 cm (23 in).

Vase. Casas Grandes, Chihuahua, Mexico. Earthenware, hand-built, geometric ornament in black. Height 24 cm (9.6 in).

such as elements of the religion, the worship of Quetzalcoatl and the practice of human sacrifice.

The range of pottery that was made expanded from vessels and figurines built by hand to include elaborate pieces produced in great quantity by moulding. The pottery was technically accomplished, if, in its early stages, relatively dull and uniform. One of the most common vessels is the tripod vase with slab or cylindrical feet supporting a cylindrical body, typically with gently flaring sides. Decorative techniques employed included incising and *champlevé*, but the most notable is the polychrome style in which pots were covered in a dark brown or black slip scraped away to show the dark body, which was sometimes painted in with cinnabar. A stucco technique was also developed, whereby the surface of the pot, usually a cylinder with three feet, was covered with plaster and this was then carved and the design filled with coloured clays. The result was fragile and decorative rather than practical, but the pieces seem to have been appreciated as much for their technical virtuosity as their artistic qualities.

The stabilizing influence of Teotihuacán in Mexico was felt all over Mesoamerica until the civilization that had built up around it fell victim to invasion from the north. A number of new states

were set up, under the rule of a belligerent military class whose religious beliefs demanded human sacrifice. The principal invaders were the Toltecs (meaning artificers), who established their powerful city-state of Tula near Teotihuacán. Their king, Topiltzin, claimed the title of Quetzalcoatl, or Feathered Serpent, the hero of Mexican mythology.

Several types of pottery were produced by the Toltecs, including a red-on-cream ware known as Matlatzinca and, the most characteristic, an orange-on-buff ware painted with wavy lines (forerunner of the Mazapan style of pottery).

Other city-states also developed distinctive pottery styles before eventually succumbing to Aztec rule. In the mountain region of Oaxaca in southern Mexico, where the Mixtec and Zapotec peoples resisted out-and-out Aztec domination, chamber-tombs were furnished with increasingly elaborate funerary urns made up of cylinders bearing dignified representations of deities and human and animal figures. In due course pottery decoration in general became more severe and abstract, but a number of regional styles endured – two in particular. The first of these is Mazapan, named after the site where this ware was found. It is characterized by decoration in the form of painted parallel wavy lines in red or white slip on plates,

Jug. Mexico, Aztec, Mixteca pueblo. Earthenware, hand-built, with painted decoration of butterflies. Height *c.* 10 cm (4 in).

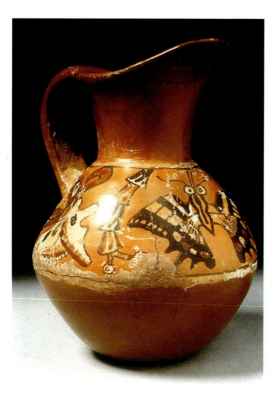

jars, cylindrical vases, bowls and biconical cups made in a fine orange clay with a hard, lustrous surface. The second main group is known as plumbate ware because its lustrous black appearance was originally thought to come from lead, although in fact it was the result of careful control over the firing. The forms of plumbate ware were varied but all were black, hard and shiny.

In western Mexico a distinctive pottery tradition and tomb form developed around 1600 BC and over the course of the following thousand years a range of lively figural sculpture was produced, some of which came to be buried in deep shafts and chamber-tombs similar to those found in Ecuador and Colombia. The animal designs that often feature on these ceramics include dogs, snakes, birds, turtles and marine creatures such as fish and crabs. Western Mexican cultures continued to stand apart from the great classic centres such as Teotihuacán until about AD 800–900, when Toltec and Mixtec influences began to intrude.

In the post-classic period, after the fall of the Toltecs, another people from the north, the Aztecs, settled around Lake Texcoco in the Valley of Mexico. Around AD 1325 they established their capital, Tenochtitlán (modern-day Mexico City), on an island in the lake. Over the following century the Aztecs gained absolute supremacy in the region, assimilating in the process many of the elements and icons of existing cultures, the most powerful of these being the Mexica, from whom modern Mexico takes its name. By the late fifteenth century the Aztecs had established firm rule, their splendid capital of Tenochtitlán forming the heart of an empire that would go on to encompass much of Mayan Mesoamerica. The society that developed was based primarily on ecclesiastical rather that secular power and within it often gruesome rituals were performed in which priests carried out mass human sacrifice; that of children was believed to be the most effective in securing the favour of the gods.

Early Aztec pottery continued indigenous local traditions, much of it bearing stylized or abstract designs painted in black. Later, many designs took on a more naturalistic style and featured sensitive representations in black on red or orange of butterflies, birds and other forms of wildlife as well as floral patterns. Thinly made and well-fired orange-coloured ware was produced, and bi-conical and chalice-shaped cups were made for the drinking of *pulque*, a potent alcoholic drink made from the fermented juice of *maguey*.

Mixteca polychrome pottery made at Cholula, decorated using different-coloured slips, was one of the finest and most highly regarded of the Aztec wares, and reputedly the only pottery that King Montezuma would deign to use. Polychrome ware was primarily a luxury commodity, decorated in a wide palette of colours including cream, yellow, red ochre, burnt sienna, grey and black. Human figures, religious and secular symbols, plumes and scrolls were among the decorative devices used, the designs having a full, busy quality. A great deal of pottery was traded and the Spanish soldier Bernard Diaz reported seeing at the great market at Tiateloco, near Tenochtitlán 'every sort of pottery, made in a thousand forms from great water jars to little jugs'.

SOUTH AMERICA

Pre-Hispanic ceramics that have been found in burial sites across the Americas emphasize the extent to which the pre-Columbian potters imbued their work with religious or magical symbolism. In Peru the word *huaco*, meaning sacred, has come to denote any ceramic artefact that has a votive or spiritual significance. In common with North and Central America, the west coast and western Andean mountain region of South America (in present-day Argentina, Bolivia and Peru) produced distinctive pottery made without the use of the wheel and fired without glaze. There seems to have been little trading of goods between the peoples of Central and South America, although raw materials were certainly exchanged. Some of the most spectacular archaeological finds of recent times have been made in Peru.

The basic techniques for making pots were established in the earliest Peruvian pottery traditions of the first millennium BC. Firing pots in a clean or oxidizing flame would yield a red or buff colour, while those fired in a smoky or reduction flame turned grey or grey-black. Early designs were made by incising or texturing the surface of the pot before it was fired. Later, resin-based paints began to be applied after firing, which produced colourful polychrome ceramics, and around 100 BC these were replaced by polychrome slip paints, developed particularly by the Nasca.

During the Cuprisnique culture (*c.* 1200–200 BC) the people inhabiting the north coastal region of Peru were producing fine pottery around 800 BC, one of the chief forms made being single-spouted bottles used for maize beer and other drinks. By the late period more elaborate, gourd-shaped pots were

made in a white or buff body, topped by a stirrup handle and sometimes decorated with a red inlay. Some stirrup-spout bottles were modelled with low relief decoration of animals and of human and animal heads. A type of resinous paint was sometimes applied to the pottery to render it waterproof, and decorative techniques included negative painting as well as the incising of designs.

In the north coastal valleys on the Chicama River variety in ceramic shapes constituted a major art form within the Moche culture (AD 500–800). The most distinctive shape made was the stirrup-spout bottle, an ancient Cuprisnique form that had first appeared in the highlands. Other bottles take a variety of shapes: some round and globular and decorated with scenes and designs, some more box-like and some modelled in the form of effigies. The use of the stirrup handle became a significant feature of Moche ceramics, the device proving comfortable for carrying while the spout was efficient for drinking or pouring and the form protected the bottle's contents from contamination.

The Moche were a settled agrarian society dependent primarily on a combination of maize cultivation and maritime resources for their subsistence. They were also ingenious engineers who built complex irrigation systems involving aqueducts and canals, although their use of adobe brick rather than stone as their principal building

Three vases showing facial deformities. South America, Peru, Chimu, Mochica, 100–700. Earthenware with painted decoration. Height (left) 33 cm (13.2 in).

Double-spouted globular vase with convex base. Peru, Nasca. Earthenware, with painted polychrome decoration. Height 27.5 cm (11 in).

material precluded the construction of large masonry structures. Artistic production was linked primarily to ritual activities carried out during seasonal agricultural festivals, many pots being made in the shape of fruits such as the pineapple or squash. Moche pottery was produced mainly by pressing clay into formers or moulds made out of fired clay. Although well made technically, it thus displays a characteristically mechanical quality even with the addition of modelled detail. Many Moche pots were stylized representations of human or animal figures, adapted to the form of the vessel.

Moche art developed strong stylistic conventions that are similar in some ways to those of the Egyptians. The human figure, for example, is portrayed in three standard views, each emphasizing a different part of the body. Legs are shown from the side, usually in a striding stance suggesting movement, and the torso is depicted frontally with the shoulders square, while heads are shown in profile but with the eye depicted in full, as though facing to the front. However, representations of royal figures sometimes depart from these rules, as do relief figures on pottery, and the decoration on pots in general tends to reflect greater freedom of expression than was granted to other art forms. Most Moche art revolves around cultural traditions and is rich with religious symbolism and portrayals of secular ceremonial scenes involving pageantry and warfare. This contrasts strongly with the direct depictions of animals and birds that were modelled on to pots with refreshing vigour. These exhibit a depth of detail that could only have come from close observation, although little attempt was made to suggest perspective or volume.

Moche pottery, of which much has been preserved through its interment in tombs, has been closely studied for the light it sheds on this people's way of life. The contemporary scenes modelled and painted on to their pots suggest that in warfare the Moche were energetic and probably largely triumphant; their warriors are depicted using weapons such as axes, clubs and spears, wearing helmets and carrying shields and drums. The architecture shown on pottery includes religious and military structures in addition to simple thatched dwellings. The Moche's polytheistic religion is indicated by the representation on their pottery of numerous gods, such as those of maize and other agricultural products; a feline

deity is also very much in evidence. Music was played at both religious and secular ceremonies using wind and percussion instruments made from clay, for example the flute, trumpet, bugle and rattle.

Although their roads appear to have been well made, there is no evidence that the Moche had wheeled vehicles. Instead, long trains of llamas were their primary means of transport, while for the coastal islands there were boats and rafts. Fish provided a valuable source of nutrition and were caught by several methods, using harpoons, hooks and nets supported by gourds that acted as floats. Moche dress, shown in considerable detail on the pottery, was more elaborate and ornate for men than for women, especially the intricate headdresses. On portrait jars depicting specific individuals the faces were shown looking upward, and while these were basically mould-made, they would be embellished to show individual characteristics such as scars.

Whistling vessels are common, nearly all of those found having been funerary offerings. The first to be recorded in Peru were made towards the end of the first millennium BC, seemingly inspired either directly or indirectly by the innovative artistry of the Chorrera culture (1000–300 BC) of the neighbouring coastal region to the north (now Ecuador). As well as flutes, pan-pipes, whistles, rattles, bells and trumpets, whistling vessels assume many other guises. There is a wealth of bird and animal imagery and vessels were often so constructed that when water was poured from the spout it caused air to be sucked in through a whistle. Whistling vessels continued to be produced by native artisans in the centuries following European contact, and simple ceramic whistles and whistle figurines are still made today.

The majority of Moche pottery was produced in a two-piece mould and the halves subsequently joined together. Coils of clay were added to finish the top and the stirrup spout was modelled using three tapered wooden rods as forms, with any detail added at this stage. Decorative patterning may include single figures or scenes, sometimes shown almost identically on each side of the vessel. Some scenes that wrap around a globular bottle have a focal area on either side; in some cases each side may define the realm of a particular deity, while others show, for example, the presentation of

captives on one side and a sacrifice on the other. While Moche ceramics reveal a great deal about this people, interpreting the corpus of information is not straightforward, given the absence of written texts.

The heartland of the Nasca culture of the south coastal region (AD 100–700) lay in the Ica Valley

Whistling vessel in the form of an owl. South America, Peru, south coast, 650–750. Earthenware, hand-built, double-chambered. The duct whistle is contained within the hollow head of the owl. Height 13 cm (5.2 in).

and the drainage of the Nasca River. For the Nasca, as for the Moche, the sea was a rich source of both food and mythology. Marine themes were commonly represented on Nasca ceramics, but whereas the Moche favoured the use of moulds, Nasca potters preferred coiling and smoothing. Some of their vessels were made of slabs of clay joined along the edges. After the initial forming, the vessel would be paddled or scraped to form thin walls and further refine the shape. Relief features were modelled, or occasionally appliquéd.

In contrast to Moche ceramics, which emphasized modelled form with painting carried out in a limited palette of white, red and black, Nasca wares display a wider and more vivid range of

colours and a flatter representation of form, even in the more sculptural pieces. Eight colours – black, red, white, yellow, green, brown, violet and cream – are known, although it was usual to use no more than five on any one pot. Designs were often outlined in black, early patterns being based on animals and fruit, often placed on a plain red background. Motifs included supernatural beings, some with a strong feline identity, as well as birds, fish and animals, sometimes outlined in black as well as being coloured. Gradually the range of themes extended to embrace religious and mythological subjects. Many Nasca decorative motifs are similar to those found in the textiles of this people's predecessors, the Paracas, who were highly skilled weavers. Among the typical Nasca shapes are vessels with a bridged double spout.

The Lima culture (200–600) that grew up in the central Rimac Valley brought substantial settlement within the area and monumental structures were built, which now underlie the modern city of Lima. The ceramic traditions that developed here

Vase. Peru, Chancay. Red earthenware, hand-built, modelled in the form of a man holding a cup, coated with white slip on which details of head, hands, etc are rendered in dark brown, with loop handle at the back of the head. Height 35 cm (14 in).

were based on adaptations of earlier white-on-red techniques and feature primarily black painting on red slip. Typical Lima stirrup bottles are decorated with painted and modelled scenes, which are often depicted in great detail.

The late Moche period heralded the rise of the Huari culture (650–800), whose capital lay to the south of Moche territory in the central and southern highlands of Peru. Over a three-hundred-year period, from the beginning of the decline of the Moche culture but before the Chimú gained hold of the north coast, the Huari became established as a dominant power. They engaged in vigorous interaction with their rivals in far distant areas of the Andes, such as the powerful Tiahuanaco in what is now Bolivia and the Nasca and Pachacamac on the south and central coastline of Peru.

No distinctive Huari style of pottery emerged, the vessels made by this culture incorporating elements of a diversity of other wares that show certain similarities in terms of imagery. Decoration was often carried out in polychrome slip painting and much of it is traceable to Nasca ceramic techniques. Double-chambered vessels are represented in several styles, with the two parts connected by means of a strap-like bridge and hollow tube.

Following the gradual collapse of the Moche culture and the absorption of influences from the south, a new state – that of the Chimú (*c.* 1100–1550) – emerged in the north, with its capital at Chanchan. In many ways the Chimú can be regarded as artistic successors to the Moche. They used moulds to produce similar forms to those of their predecessors, although their pottery never attained the same high quality. Chimú pots are mainly monochrome, in grey, black or red, many having been burnished and reduction-fired. The Moche modelling tradition was reintroduced by Chimú potters, perhaps operating in small independent groups, but their wares lacked the spirit of the earlier work. Stirrup spouts and double whistling vases continued to be made, but the designs used on Chimú wares were rarely narrative. Patterns of repeated geometric, zoomorphic and anthropomorphic forms render Chimú work ambiguous in comparison with Moche ceramics, on which the scenes portrayed contain great detail and often convey valuable information. In the late period Chimú potters produced ceramic vessels in large quantities by the use of press moulds, the surface frequently being burnished to achieve a smooth, polished effect.

OTHER SOUTHERN CULTURES

The Tiahuanaco culture, centred on or near Lake Titicaca in Bolivia, was highly organized both politically and architecturally; archaeological evidence has survived of huge gateways and walled cities. In general the pottery is severe in style, lacking the richness of colouring achieved in the work produced by other communities. Tall, concave cylindrical forms are typical of the city-building stage of the Tiahuanacos' development. In the Chancay Valley around AD 1000–1200 a distinctive, if somewhat unambitious, pottery style arose. Thin, porous jars were made in egg-like shapes, with the base more rounded than the top. Humanoid features, often diminutive, were applied in relief, sometimes combined with black-and-white painted decoration.

Vase. South America, Peru, from the Ucayali River region of the Upper Amazon. Clay, with painted decoration. Height 108 cm (43.2 in).

Modelled figure, thought to be Inca, with painted decoration.

figures dressed in elaborate fabrics; animal motifs also appear. The Inca conquest led to the introduction of distinctive polychrome pottery, which in some areas was adapted to the local style.

THE INCAS

In the fifteenth century the Incas (1450–1550), whose capital was at Cuzco in the southern Andes, rapidly expanded their territory. Over time they seized power over the entire inhabited Andean region of South America, building a vast empire that embraced all of modern-day Peru, Ecuador and Bolivia as well as large areas of Chile and Argentina. Under their highly organized, despotic and paternalistic regime control was maintained by means of a network of roads, on which those they conquered were forbidden to travel. The Incas established an elaborate but efficient administrative system and exercised rigid bureaucratic discipline over all the peoples they ruled. Their own society assimilated many of the skills of these indigenous cultures, including those of weaving, metalwork, architecture, crop cultivation and pottery.

Pottery produced in and around Cuzco was endowed with particular prestige, fine craftsmanship being closely associated with the status of the capital. The thin-walled vessels were made, fired and decorated with considerable technical skill and the wares have a distinctive character. Pots were made by hand and often patterned with coloured slips, notably red and black on a buff-coloured ground. Ornamentation was typically based on the repetition of a limited number of geometric forms set within well-defined bands. There is scant evidence of experiment or improvization, both shapes and designs appearing to have been carefully worked out and controlled.

Pottery forms show little change over the Inca period. Among the most distinctive of the wares are narrow-necked water bottles with a pointed base, ranging in height from eight to a hundred centimetres and sometimes called aryballos in view of their resemblance to the Greek form. The well-ordered bands of skilfully applied painted decoration usually feature such designs as hatched diamonds and triangles or stylized plants, butterflies and bees. Bottles were made with lug handles that allowed them to be carried on the back with a rope. Also produced were plates fitted with small

ARGENTINA

In the highland region of north-west Argentina and a large part of northern Chile several different pottery styles developed. Among the most notable is that associated with the Diagnite culture, a people who were occupying a substantial area at the time of the Spanish landings in the sixteenth century. Various types of ware have been identified, one of which is thickly potted and bears red, white and grey-black geometrical decoration that often incorporates zigzag motifs and conventionalized faces. Other forms of vessel found include oval-bodied jars and head or spout jars. One of the best-known shapes, produced in north-west Argentina and sometimes referred to as the Santa Maria urn, is a large vessel with a small base and an ovoid body with strap handles. Its distinctive decoration, executed in black on a yellow or white ground, appears to represent highly abstracted human

bird-head handles as well as jars and flat-based bowls with broad strap handles, many of which were intended for cooking purposes.

Invasion by the Spanish in the sixteenth century irrevocably transformed life in the Inca territory of the Americas. Some indigenous cultures were completely annihilated, although certain of the more isolated communities remained relatively untouched while others adapted to a combination of Hispanic and indigenous traditions and technologies. The Spanish brought with them not only Catholic iconography such as scenes of the crucifixion and representations of saints and penitents, which soon began to appear on ceramics, but also the potter's wheel, knowledge of enclosed kilns and the technique of lead-glazing.

Although some present-day communities have adopted modern pottery-making processes, there are many that continue to employ pre-Hispanic methods, some of which have remained virtually unchanged over the centuries. In Ráquira, in Colombia, ancient and modern technologies are used side by side. Following the tradition of the pre-Hispanic Chibcha people, potters in the surrounding villages make largely utilitarian pieces such as hand-modelled or moulded pots, while in the town itself mobiles, animals and Nativity scenes are produced. Before the Spanish conquest potters in many areas produced blackware by controlling the firing of pots and the manufacture of this type of ware continues today in such places as Quinchamalí, near Chillán in Chile, where two-thirds of the population work with clay in a tradition dating back to the pre-Hispanic era. Blackwares are also produced in La Chamba in Colombia, where pale brown and terracotta pots are also made. The rich terracotta colour is achieved by painting the surface with a slip made up of an iron-rich clay from the Magdalena River and burnishing it with a river stone prior to firing.

In communities across Latin America there remain large numbers of artisans who work using traditional techniques, often to supply the local market with pots needed for the preparation of particular dishes such as *humintas* (in Bolivia and Peru), fried bananas, rice, and especially the toasted corn dish known as *chicharrón*, which, it is considered, has to be cooked in a traditional vessel in order to achieve an authentic flavour. Other potters cater for the tourist trade, fulfilling the demand for highly decorated wares. Most of the styles have changed substantially over the years but still include important characteristics of the traditional indigenous wares.

Seated figure,
Tumaco. Earthenware.
Height 38.75 cm (15.5 in).

Living Traditions

MODERN TRIBAL AND INDIGENOUS SOCIETIES

*I went down to the potter's house
and found him working at the wheel*

JEREMIAH XVIII: 3

Kerere of Shani, a potter in Shani, north-eastern Nigeria, holding one of her ceremonial earthenware hand-built pots, 1986. Kerere was the wife of a former chief of the Shani and she made all the ceremonial pots for the community.

Throughout the world there exist small communities of people who have retained their cultural identity more or less independently of the advanced civilizations that have grown up around them. Within these long-established cultures local customs and crafts continue to play a prominent role in everyday life and it is therefore not uncommon to find age-old methods of pottery-making in use to this day, preserved as a living tradition. In some communities the way in which ceramics are made has changed hardly at all over the years, while in others traditional skills and techniques now go hand-in-hand with modern manufacturing processes. The vessels produced are rarely made for their own sake but typically serve a specific purpose connected with rituals, ceremonies or domestic practices, and even the most basic of them are likely to incorporate some decorative element that is not merely aesthetic but conveys a particular meaning within the culture.

Over the past twenty years or so magazines dealing with the subject of studio pottery, such as *Ceramic Review* in the United Kingdom and *Studio Potter* in the United States, have published a wide-ranging series of illustrated features on traditional potteries around the world, most of them written not by ethnographers but by working potters, who were frequently astonished and delighted by the skills and work they encountered in the course of their research. Covering pottery-making practices

in countries as far apart as India, Central America, Nigeria, Thailand, the Sudan, Japan, Egypt, Yemen, Cyprus, the Philippines, Algeria, Jamaica, Nepal, Indonesia and Burma, these articles testify to a diverse and flourishing craft worldwide.

In many communities pottery-making is traditionally carried out on a seasonal basis, sometimes because potters need to supplement their income with agricultural work at certain times of the year, sometimes, as in India, simply because during the monsoon season nothing will dry. In West Africa potting is exclusively a seasonal activity, permitted only after the start of the dry season has been marked by a public ceremony performed by the rain-chief, who fires the grass on the top of his mountain, so drying the pots and stones that are believed to govern rainfall. Throughout the world men and women alike work as potters. Although there was often a convention in the past whereby women carried out the hand-building while men worked on the wheel, this is no longer invariably the case. Nevertheless, the more specialized skills such as throwing continue, in general, to be the preserve of male potters. In some parts of Africa the making of pots is still carried out according to a long-standing tradition by which highly skilled women make use of only the simplest of tools to produce the vast majority of pots. In the North Cameroonian village of Dowayo the women of a single family produce all the pottery, not only

making and firing it but selling it as well. In many areas of North Africa it is the responsibility of men to throw pots on the wheel. Until the 1960s potters in the Japanese village of Onta, on the southern island of Kyushu, used to farm in addition to making pots, but rising demand for their work has motivated them to concentrate exclusively on their potting activities. In Darn Kwen in Thailand potters supplement their income from farming by making large jars for the storage of rainwater. On the island of Cyprus huge pots about a metre across, known as *pytharia* (giants) and used for wine-making or as containers for olive oil, are produced by skilled itinerant potters travelling from village to village.

Potter throwing small cups from a hump of clay on a wheel in India.

CLAY

Clay, the potter's basic raw material, is usually gathered locally, the majority of potters winning and preparing it themselves. In major pottery-making centres in North Africa, such as Nabeul in Tunisia, Fez in Morocco and Al-Fustat (Old Cairo) in Egypt, clay is quarried on the outskirts of the towns. Casual workers dig out the clay, which is then carried to its destination by cart or donkey. In Egypt, although the plastic yellow clay from Aswan is much the preferred material, the cost of ferrying it down the River Nile precludes its regular use. Instead, local potters make use of a less expensive mixture of *tabbiny*, a highly calcareous buff-coloured field-clay from El Tabbin forty kilometres up the river, and the black alluvial Nile clay known as *tina nili*. Stones and other impurities are removed and the clay lumps left to dry before

being crushed, soaked and kneaded into a workable consistency. Large quantities of clay are prepared by systematically treading the mixture by foot and then storing it to allow it to sour and age, so increasing its plasticity. In West Africa, women – the traditional rural potters – dig and transport local clay then crush it and mix it with a grog of ground potsherds.

One of the most spectacular methods of clay preparation is that used at Onta on the Japanese island of Kyushu, where the industry has changed little in nearly three hundred years. When first dug from the surrounding mountains the clay is rock hard and it therefore has to be powdered before it can be made into a plastic body. This is achieved by the use of water-powered crushers which, over a period of ten days, pound the clay to powder, from which the body is then prepared by slaking, sieving and settling. In San Miguel Aguasuelos in Mexico twenty-eight women who make up an informal co-operative of potters produce their work in their own kitchens-cum-dining/living rooms. Here the clay is very unusual in that it becomes quite hard, emitting a ring if tapped, when fired to a temperature of only 600–700°C. The clay is dug as dry pieces, beaten with a wooden mallet and watered, then, after any stones have been removed, it is finally wedged before use.

MAKING

There are two principal ways in which traditional pottery is made: by the use of hand-building methods, which include various types of coiling and/or variations of the paddle and anvil technique, and by throwing on the wheel. However, there is great diversity in the manner in which these processes are carried out.

In Indonesian villages the women produce practical wares by coiling and pinching the clay on a wooden turntable, which is often set on the ground. Most such potters make only simple items for everyday use, for example plates, bowls, braziers and round casseroles, but some of the more adventurous of them build large urns with moulded faces and animal forms related to native and religious symbols, including horses, oxen and dragons. The female potters in Kornos, Cyprus, make pots on a small square tournette or hand-wheel while sitting on a low seat, using a variant of the coil-and-smooth technique.

Throwing on a potter's wheel operated by kicking a flywheel with the foot. Photographed in 1990 in a pottery village near Luxor in Egypt.

on to the pot with a feather in traditional flower and leaf patterns.

Throwing is generally carried out using one of a variety of simple foot-driven wheels. At Al-Fustat in Egypt the wheel is a solid structure incorporating an axle and flywheel, which is either set in a pit or raised to the level of the workbench, and curiously tilted at an angle of five to ten degrees so that the potter has to lean backwards only slightly to see the line of the pot. Pots are produced rapidly, their shape refined by turning off surplus clay when the piece is leather-hard. Some of the smaller forms are thrown from the top of a large semi-centred lump and cut off from the still rotating hump with a string. Using this type of wheel, a team of potters can each handle a lump of clay at least ten kilos in weight, keeping a boy permanently busy preparing clay for them and carrying away their thrown pots.

The wheels used by potters in many parts of rural India consist of a large, heavy wheelhead set into a pivot bedded in the ground. In the Darjeeling region, in Jalpaiguri District, a large concrete wheel some 75 centimetres in diameter is balanced on a stone pivot, and once the wheel is in motion its weight alone is sufficient to keep it revolving long enough to produce a pot. The thrust needed to set the wheel turning is produced either by pushing it round by hand or, more usually, by fitting a stick into a socket in the outer edge of the wheel and propelling it round before releasing the stick. This method of making requires soft clay that can be thrown at high speed, although for larger pieces the throwing may have to be halted from time to time so that the motion of the wheel can be reactivated. Pots are cut off the wheel with a string and either left as they are or tidied using a wooden tool; alternatively, when leather-hard they may be formed further by being beaten on the outside with a paddle while supported on the inside. All the pots serve a functional purpose, the larger ones being used for storing either water or grain such as corn, wheat, rice or millet. Many of the smaller pots are made for use as incense-burners, oil-lamps and piggy-banks, while the small conical vessels are for drinking tea. Each piece is fired once, some pots subsequently receiving a coating of a 'glaze' made from the bark of the mango tree and kyhre, a plant extract mixed with soda and red slip that gives the surface a darker hue and a soft sheen.

In San Miguel Aguasuelos in Mexico the larger pots are coiled, the smaller ones pressed and moulded with the fingers. A number of different types of vessel are made, including large narrow-mouthed pitchers designed to be held in the hand for carrying water, wide-mouthed vessels with three lugs for hanging, and several other forms of water-carrier. Decorative ware consists mainly of bell-shaped large and small figures of women, the very small ones fitted with a tiny clapper so that they ring, as well as moneyboxes and little dolls and animal toys. Red iron oxide earth is dug locally and formed into a red pigment, which is then painted

Ayanaar horses. Tamil Nadu, India. Terracotta, life size.

the annual festival of Ganeshchaturthi. In Tamil Nadu in southern India magnificent horse sculptures, fired in situ and sometimes over four metres high, are presented each year to the god Aiyanar. The task of faithfully reproducing these traditional models is undertaken with great intensity, the spiritual fervour that goes into their production being as evident in the completed work as the power of the form itself. In the relative isolation of this region, tradition is still very much alive and experiment is minimal. The clay figures of guardian horses that protect each village are also constructed with genuine reverence and thus charged with spirituality. In eastern Gujarat figures of elephants, tigers and buffalo are also made, although the animal by far the most commonly represented is the horse. If modelled by hand these sculptures are solid, if made in separate wheel-thrown sections they are hollow, the sections being joined together at the leather-hard stage and decoration added. Finger impressions are a popular form of decoration but little attempt is made at realism. The more prestigious pieces are further enhanced with red slip made from either levigated clay or ochre or a white chalky material, which is wiped or splashed on to the figures to attain a smoother surface and add depth of colour before the pieces are fired in a bonfire.

One of the few traditional potters in Jamaica is Ma Lou, who makes practical forms ranging from cups and saucers to cooking stoves, building the pots by coiling and burnishing them when leather-hard. Her most successful product is the *yabba*, a rounded-based vessel traditionally considered the most important pot for cooking Jamaican dishes. Because the clay from which it is made is rendered quite porous by the addition of large quantities of sand, the *yabba* can be placed directly on to an open flame without this causing the vessel to crack on sudden contact with the intense heat.

Potters in north Khartoum in the Sudan make their pots by coiling, using one of two different methods that each consist of two separate stages, depending on the type of vessel concerned. On pots known as *black zeer* first the neck and shoulders are coiled up, then when leather-hard the pot is stood on its rim to complete the belly and base, after which it is further smoothed and shaped with the aid of water and a gourd. The other method is performed in reverse, with the base of the vessel

Like those in India, potters in Darn Kwen in Thailand also work on wheels that sit close to the ground. The Thai wheels consist of a disc sawn from a teak-wood log, which spins freely on a pivot of hardwood stuck into the ground. An assistant pushes the wheelhead so that the craftsman has his hands free to throw the pot.

In India not only vessels but also modelled pieces are produced, notably terracotta figures of animals and deities. In areas such as eastern Gujarat models of animals are assembled from sections thrown individually on the wheel. In Bengal in the east large sculptures of the goddess Durga are made at Durga-puja, while in Maharashtra (central India) processional images of Ganesha are produced for

Potter beating out a pot using a paddle supported on the inside with an anvil. Photographed in Egypt in 1990.

The *zeers* after firing, showing the effects of reduction. Photographed in the Sudan.

constructed first. The pot is built in a shallow hollow in the ground, coils of clay being joined together to form the bottom part. This section is then allowed to stiffen before further coils are added to create the top section. The form known as *dawagin zeer*, used for housing hens during egg-laying, is very similar to the *black zeer* used for water storage. The fine clay, obtained locally, is made more workable by being tempered with donkey dung at a ratio of one to one. This not only

renders the clay more plastic but during the firing the dung burns away, so increasing the porosity of the pot.

On the small Cycladic island of Sifnos a 300-year-old pottery-making tradition still continues, although only in remote areas. In the tiny village of Heronisos the male potter throws, among other forms, three-foot-high beehives that are sold for local use. The hives are thrown in two sections, each weighing around 10–12 kilogrammes, which are then joined together. The lids are pierced with holes of exactly the right size to admit bees while excluding their predators. All the clay used on Sifnos is fine red earthenware, which each potter digs for himself and hauls to his workshop on donkeys or mules. The throwing is carried out using home-made stand-up kickwheels, the fly-wheel being kicked round with the right foot.

In Thailand ancient making techniques are combined with quite sophisticated firing methods. Coil-thrown and paddle-and-anvil making pro-cesses are employed in a diversity of ways and in various combinations in different parts of the

A Zambian potter with her Bemba water jars. The black glaze effect is achieved by burnishing with a carbon pebble. Two of the pots were later spoilt in the firing as a result of small stones that had not been removed from the clay.

sits on a low stool at the wheel, the pivot of which is slanted about fifteen degrees from upright away from the thrower. Thus far the method is not unlike that practised in Al-Fustat in Egypt, but here the similarity ends. The wheel itself consists of a pointed hardwood stake set in the ground, on the top of which is a removable wooden wheelhead; surrounding the potter is a further series of wheelheads on upright stakes. Throwing is carried out by the potter flattening a ball on to the wheelhead with a piece of wood then adding a clay coil that is thinned and thrown with one hand while turning the wheel with the other until the pot is complete.

In Kebkebiya, Sudan, it is women who are the potters. Building each piece by hand using the coiling technique, they produce thirty different types of vessel in a range encompassing not only domestic items for the storage and carrying of food but also ablution vessels, drums, ink-pots and incense-burners. The pottery-making in Grande Kabylie in northern Algeria, again carried out by women, is still largely a seasonal activity. The main period of production runs from about May to September, when there is little work to be done on the land and the dry weather is reliable for firings. One characteristic shape made here is a branched candlestick or oil-lamp; other popular items include traditional water- or oil-storage jars (still used in most households, although some of the older forms are now largely preserved as decorative pieces), made in such a way that they lean against a wall for stability.

The making method used at Grande Kabylie involves the pot being burnished with a pebble when leather-hard to achieve a slightly shiny finish and a more resistant surface. After this process, which can take several hours, the pot is decorated using creamy white, brick-red and black slips and pigments, all made from materials the women have gathered from the surrounding area. The black, a manganese oxide compound found as pebbles in the river bed, is produced by grinding the pebbles with water in a larger hollowed-out stone. The mostly geometric designs used on the pots date back to the Mediterranean Bronze Age. It is traditional for many pots to bear the raised motif known as 'the hand of Fatima' (daughter of the Prophet), a device believed to ensure protection against envy and witchcraft, but in modern work this motif is often incorporated into the design in

country. In the village of Phon Bok large storage pots are made by the smear–coil–throw method. Each potter has an assistant who prepares the clay and turns the wheels by hand, as required. Potters work on a series of eight or nine pots at a time, moving along the row of turntables and building up each pot in stages until it is about 30 centimetres in height, at which point a wooden profile is used to fashion it into its final shape. At Ratchburi in southern Thailand water-storage vessels known as golden dragon jars are the principal product made. Here clay is dug from nearby paddy fields and mixed well before use, and the jars are either coiled or thrown on the wheel, the three individual parts of the jars being made by three different potters (all male). Young women apply the decoration in thin coils of soft white clay, using a stencil of the dragon design as a guide.

One of the most unusual hand-building techniques in use in Thailand is a hand-turned wheel throwing system whereby the male or female potter

highly stylized form. Patterns are painted on to the pots, with black used to outline the blocks of colour. On the water- and oil-storage pots the designs traditionally stress symmetry and balance within the basic shape, which recalls the female form and includes representation of the breasts and pubic triangle. Used on rugs and shawls as well as

Making a round-bottomed cooking pot, photographed in Guatemala. Some of these pots will be pierced to provide utensils for processing the traditional food of corn.

pots, the designs may derive from the tattoos of which these people are inordinately proud.

In Guatemala pottery-making takes place in a number of different locations, with processes and finished products varying from place to place. The women make functional pots by hand as a year-round activity, whereas the tile- and brick-making carried out by the men is a seasonal occupation. At San Marcos women dig the clay locally and add white sand for water jars and strainers, calcium carbonate for pots to be used in cooking. The pots are built by first squeezing then adding on coils; the rim is then smoothed with a wet piece of leather. The corn-strainer is one of the most popular forms made, as corn has been at the centre of Mayan cookery for thousands of years and clay pots, strainers and cooking discs have traditionally been used for processing it. The strainers, which have two lug handles, are punched with numerous holes at the leather-hard stage then burnished with a smooth stone when dry.

Nicaragua has been described by one observer as a 'production potter's paradise'. Two main types of traditional pottery are made: heavily decorated pre-Columbian-style pots and functional rustic wares. Employing imported techniques and designs a new style of pottery is also now produced, but this fails to compare with the authentic look and feel of the traditional work. In the village of San Juan de Oriente almost every home seems to have a small pottery workshop with a kiln outside. A mixture of local coarse grey clay and a more plastic red clay from the north of the country is used, and most of the pots are thrown on the wheel, including the bodies for pre-Columbian-style figures, to which press-moulded heads and feet are added. Dipped in a creamy white slip and then burnished, these ornate pieces contrast strongly with the hand-built work made at Tolapa. Here items such as water jars, some two to three feet tall, cooking pots and flat dishes for making tortilla (a thin maize bread) are produced by coiling, with the surface smoothed using a piece of gourd.

FORM AND DECORATION

In many areas potting practices continue to be governed by a combination of tradition and economics, in that local requirements determine what is produced while the range of wares is limited by traditional making and firing methods and available materials. In Greater Cairo, where the majority of the fourteen million population is made up of poor people with rural or peasant roots, there continues to be a steady demand for earthenware as opposed to plastic or aluminium vessels. Flower-pots, storage barrels, jars and spouted jugs are made in large quantity, but the most important commodity is the array of different water pots. Three of the main shapes are the *zir*, the *ballaas* and the *qulla* water bottle. The *zir*, which may be anything from twenty-five centimetres to nearly a metre in height, is a modified version of the ancient amphora. Although it is designed to stand in a frame so that the water filters through the porous body and drips clean into a drinking vessel beneath, few now use this slow process. The *ballaas* has a more rounded base and is thrown in two sections, as is the taller, more slender *qulla*. The water pots are usually left plain or given minimal decoration. As E. W. Lane wrote in 1860, *qulla* 'are made of greyish, porous earth, which cools the

A potter sits to decorate the surface of a pot with laterite, photographed in Thailand.

rains are due, at which time the land has to be prepared for planting.

One of the most industrious rural potteries in the same region is to be found at Tatiko. Satisfying all the fundamental criteria of tradition, practicality and attractiveness, the items made by the women of this village range from small moneyboxes to huge forty-litre water-coolers, beautifully bellied and decorated in a characteristic style. The women dig their own clay from a source well over a kilometre away and carry the loads back on their heads. They then remove the larger stones and organic material from the clay, after which it is thoroughly pounded and wedged to render it workable. The round pots are coiled and smoothed, and patterning added to the surface is rubbed with a fine powder, also obtained locally, to achieve a bright red colour. The finished pots are allowed to dry slowly inside the mud huts to prevent them from cracking.

In South Africa many traditional potters whose work straddles the boundary between functionality and artistic expression have been recruited into the studio pottery movement. One such example is Ma Thomas (her name meaning 'the Mother of Thomas'), a prolific potter working in the popular genre of Venda pots who learned the secrets of the craft from her mother and grandmother. (This tradition seems unlikely to be carried on, however, since Ma Thomas's own daughter has chosen not to become a potter.) The rounded hand-built forms that Ma Thomas makes are inscribed with borders and simple geometric patterns and coloured with graphite and ochre. Her pots are not only popular within her own community but also find a ready market in the nearby cities. While local customers buy her pots for practical and ritual use, those from the city acquire them for their aesthetic value.

In different parts of the world a variety of vegetable-based pigments are used by potters to finish their biscuit-fired household vessels. In Fez in Morocco the resin of the thuya tree is boiled down to form a viscous black liquid called *qutran* and this is used to great effect in the decoration of white-bodied vessels, the potter using his finger to create often quite intricate geometric patterns. The tar in the pigment imparts a distinctive flavour to the water stored in the vessel, and once this is lost the pot is discarded and replaced by one that has been freshly decorated.

water deliciously, by evaporation; and are, therefore generally placed in a current of air. The interior is often blackened with the smoke of resinous wood, and then perfumed with the smoke of *qafel*-wood and mastic.' Today it is more likely to be orange-flower water that is used to scent the contents.

In rural West Africa pots are formed by pulling out the clay from a lump or by coiling, or a mixture of both. The most commonly made container is a small, semi-spherical bowl standing on five ball-shaped feet, used at mealtimes to hold a sauce to complement the millet paste that is served in a calabash. Other forms include two different sizes of a round-bellied cooking pot that can be placed directly on to the three-stone hearth. More elaborate pieces include the classic West African water jar, which is a spherical, long-necked vessel with incised and roulette decoration.

Ceremonial pots made in the Shani area of South Borno in northern Nigeria are hand-built by coiling and then burnished. Decoration is painted on to the pit-fired pots using a mixture of ground bonemeal and gum arabic. Another of the forms made is a double pot used for filtering water. Ashes from the fire are placed in the top pot, which has holes in the base, then water is poured in, which seeps slowly through the ashes into the lower pot. The filtered water is a valuable source of mineral salts for use in cooking. As in many other areas, potting here is a seasonal activity. Clay is gathered during the dry season from dried-up waterholes and river beds, and making continues until the

In parts of Tunisia and Morocco pots are sometimes fired in a second, glaze firing. It is customary for glazed decoration to be applied in a single colour, usually a green derived from copper oxide, but on some pieces both yellow and green are used and around Fez one of the most widely recognized types of ware is decorated in cobalt blue on a white tin glaze. Pottery made in urban North Africa, which is exported abroad as well as being marketed throughout the region, is distinguished by its elaborately decorated polychrome glazed surface. Alongside traditional forms, innovations such as plant pots and eggcups have been introduced in order to meet the demands of the expanding tourist industry.

The rounded hand-built cooking pots taken from the open firing of the Igbara Odo Pottery Commune in Nigeria are painted with a coating of 'glaze' made up of locust-bean juice. This turns the pots a gleaming mahogany brown as well as helping to strengthen them.

Burnishing is another technique used in various parts of the world. This involves rubbing or smoothing the surface of the leather-hard pot with a pebble or simple tool, which compresses the clay particles, making the surface smooth and shiny and increasing water resistance. The Hausa people in northern Nigeria decorate many of their water pots by this method, burnishing the covering of red slip to make it waterproof but leaving an unburnished area around the neck to allow for evaporation through the clay, which cools the contents of the vessel. In Omdurman in the Sudan red burnished pottery is decorated with incised designs that mimic the stamping and contrast stitching found on leatherwear.

FIRING

Traditional firing methods can be divided into two basic types: those that form part of a complex 'bonfire' technique and those taking place in a more permanent kiln structure of some kind. Firing to the low temperatures needed for earthenware, without using a kiln, is carried out in a variety of ways. In Indonesia the bone-dry pots are covered with dried leaves, bamboo and coconut husk with an insulating layer of discarded broken pottery on the top. Once lit, this material takes about two hours to burn through, so the fired pots are often dotted with red and black marks produced by the

smoke and flame. In rural West Africa the Dowayos people achieve their low-temperature firings by a quick and simple bonfire system that results in serviceable ware. They believe that firing, like cooking, must be carried out in the open air. The pots usually fire red but are sometimes rolled in leaves while still hot, which creates a smoke that turns them black.

In Kebkebiya, Sudan, pottery is fired in a shallow open pit on the sandy river bed. The bottom of the pit is covered with cow dung and straw before the largest vessels are placed in it, mouth to mouth on their sides, with the others piled on top, and the whole pile is then covered with cow dung and set alight. The firing may take up to two hours to burn through and is allowed to die down before the first pots are poked out.

In Jamaica Ma Lou fires her pots by stacking them in an orderly fashion with all the openings facing upwards. The bottom row is placed on a single row of sticks, which allows the heat to travel under the mound as well as over the top and round the sides. A stack of about six dozen pieces of varying sizes is built and wood piled all around until it is completely covered both at the sides and on the top. Dried palm leaves are spaced out on the top of the mound and finally golfball-sized chunks of donkey dung are placed round the base to help set the wood alight. After two hours of burning the fire is left to die down uncovered, the result being bright terracotta-coloured pots.

In parts of Malaysia where the humidity is very high, low-temperature firings are carried out by placing the pots on top of wooden structures about a metre tall. The wood is ignited from the bottom, allowing the pots to dry thoroughly before full temperature is reached. The firings last approximately one hour.

In the Nigerian village of Tatiko firing is an exciting spectacle. First of all, sticks, bark, threshed guinea-corn heads and wet and dry grass are gathered. If the ground is wet, a two-and-a-half centimetre layer of dry sand is put down first, then a layer four times as thick of grass and guinea-corn heads, followed by a top layer of sticks and bark. All this material is laid in the form of a circle some three or four metres across. To help prevent cracking, before being carried to the firing site the pots are preheated by inverting them over hot ashes. Large pots are placed in the centre of the circle,

Pottery kiln stacked full of pots. Photographed in 1990 in an Egyptian potters village in Cairo.

over the sticks and bark, with smaller ones around them and the very smallest stacked on top. Finally the whole thing is covered with a protective layer of broken pots to retain the heat. The clamp is lit from glowing embers and when the fire is well under way more grass and guinea-corn heads are thrown on to raise the temperature. The firing takes about forty minutes in all and the pots are left to cool overnight.

Outdoor kiln structures can, of course, only be used in suitable weather conditions. They are usually round, standing approximately a metre high and about two metres across and tapering slightly at the top. Within the kiln structure the ware is carefully stacked in such a way as to allow movement but avoid breakages. Often a layer of broken shards is placed over the dome of pots, and sometimes a layer of ashy soil, while the debris from previous firings provides further insulation round the edge of the mound. The long, thin strips of wood that are used as fuel are introduced

through a series of vents at the base, which also serve to encourage a draught, and straw is thrown on the top to intensify the heat. A typical firing takes about forty-five minutes to an hour.

In rural North Africa there is still a strong local market for single-fired pots, which are used exclusively for domestic purposes, principally the storage and transportation of water. These vessels are fired in updraught kilns, the simplest of which are domed cylindrical structures consisting of a firing chamber built at ground level and a packing chamber above, the roof of which is pierced with holes. The pots are loaded into the kiln through a central doorway. The firing is long and slow, mainly to allow the pots to dry out completely but also because this achieves a more even heat distribution; it may go on for as long as several days, depending on the size of the pots. The fuel used is likely to be maize stalks, sugar-cane or wood, although sometimes hardboard and even old tyres and shoes may be used.

In San Miguel Aguasuelos in Mexico the kilns are made up of roughly constructed stone and clay walls, a metre or so high and about a metre and a half in diameter. The dried pots are heaped over a mound opposite the arched stone entrance then covered with old flat crocks and tiles. On top are placed two layers of leaves from the castor oil plants that grow in abundance in the area. Dried maize-cob leaves and first thin then thick slivers of wood are used for igniting the kiln and firing continues over a period of eight or nine hours, the temperature rising to between 600°C and 700°C.

In the Far East firing to stoneware temperatures takes place in specially built permanent structures such as through- or down-draught kilns. At Onta in Japan a large co-operative climbing kiln known as a *noborigama* is used and firings take from twenty-four to forty hours, reaching temperatures of 1220–1260°C. At Darn Kwen in Thailand the circular kilns, four or five metres in diameter and up to two metres high, have a chimney and firebox placed opposite to each other. The firing is fuelled by large pieces of wood and takes about five days. At Ratchburi a snake kiln sixty metres in length fires to mid-temperature and holds some three thousand pots, raw-glazed with a mixture of soda ash and clay, which are ready in the relatively short time of twenty-four hours. In Bangkok a twenty-four-metre wood-firing snake kiln is used to produce smaller blue-and-white glazed porcelain such as traditional Chinese-style teapots and bowls, as well as more modern speckled tea sets that are popular with Westerners and fashion-conscious Thais.

POTTERY IN LOCAL RITUALS

In North Africa, as in many other regions world-wide, ceramic vessels continue to play a prominent role in traditional ceremonies that mark such life-cycle events as births, marriages and deaths. In Egypt the ritual performed to celebrate *al-sebu*, the seventh day following the birth of a child, involves the use of either a water pot (for a girl) or a pitcher (for a boy), both of which are made with seven spouts for holding candles. In the Maghreb the *methred*, a footed plate or dish, is used in rural and urban communities alike for serving couscous or pastries; during Tunisian wedding celebrations the bride is traditionally presented with a whole series of these vessels. The first *methred*, which is filled with food after the marriage ceremony has taken place, is greeted with cries of good luck from the bride's friends and, later, family. In parts of Tunisia and Egypt, when a death occurs in a family specially made pottery vessels are placed on the grave in the belief that the soul of the departed

Pots photographed in Grande Kabylie, Djurdjura Mountains, northern Algeria. Earthenware in traditional handled forms, with painted decoration.

Storage jars photographed in China, *c.* 1975. Stoneware, thrown and glazed.

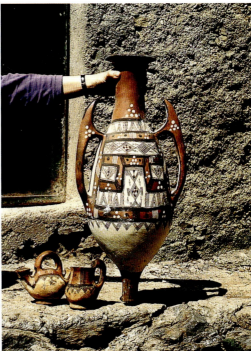

Tree of Life made for the Day of the Dead, with skeletons in Mexican regional costumes, by potters Alfonso and Marta Castillo, Izúcar de Matamoros, State of Pueblo, Mexico, 1989. Height 105 cm (42 in).

relative may revisit the tomb in the form of a bird and need to satisfy its thirst.

In rural West Africa special pots are made to order for use in the enactment of ancient ancestral rites, in which they serve as substitutes for the skulls of dead rain-chiefs. Both here and in many other parts of Africa the female potter is traditionally a mistress of childbirth who uses potting as a practical model to explain the mysteries of life. All infants are portrayed as red, wet and fragile and boys as prone to fevers until circumcized, a procedure that is compared to being 'fired' like pottery. When there is a death in the community a pot is broken over the corpse; a woman's spirit is thought to take up residence in her water jar. The association between childbirth and the female potter is a powerful pan-African theme that takes on a variety of often highly complex social meanings. For example, it is believed that making human or animal images endangers fertility, therefore young women potters are barred from doing so while older women (and men) are not. Broken pottery may relate to someone of either gender and any age, since the whole human life cycle is equated with that of a pot.

In east, central and southern Africa widespread ritual use is made of pottery when imparting moral teachings to the young. Representational terracotta figurines play a major part in ceremonies connected with puberty, birth, ancestry and initiation into special groups. One such rite, performed on females between the onset of puberty and marriage, marks among other things the assumption by the girl concerned of full responsibility for her own procreative powers and the dangers that go with them.

FUTURE PROSPECTS FOR TRADITIONAL POTTERIES

It is impossible to be sure what the future is likely to be for traditional hand- and wheel-produced pottery. Even in Al-Fustat in Egypt, where much of the population lives in considerable poverty, locally produced plastic and metal vessels are gradually taking over from traditional ceramic ones; despite their low cost and ecologically-friendly water-cooling properties, traditional ceramic containers are rapidly being ousted by modern refrigerators. Unable to compete with such sophisticated products, potters are either going out of business or focusing on the production of decorative items for the tourist market. In Kornos in Cyprus forty-three potters formed a co-operative in 1953, but by 1981 only twelve of them remained. Although the demand for their pots remained buoyant, the hard work involved in preparing the clay and making and firing the pots for limited reward failed to attract young artisans to the craft.

Until twenty or so years ago the women potters of Grande Kabylie, on the crests of the lower hills of northern Algeria's Djurdjura mountains, made all the domestic wares for their community, including roof tiles for the local houses. However, plastic and metal products have now almost totally replaced their once widely used functional household pots, while plastic jerry-cans stand side by side with ceramic water jars. The local wares are still made, but only by a few older women, the preservation of traditional pottery skills now being dependent largely on sales made to tourists.

In Mexico, too, the survival of traditional pottery-making is in constant doubt. The introduction of modern technology and increased oil production have led to the widespread use of plastic products, not least because they are often cheaper, harder-wearing and longer-lasting than their ceramic

height, are still considered a necessity and remain in daily use in many rural communities, whether for storing grain after harvest or for storing the water needed during the five-month dry season, and this situation is unlikely to change in the foreseeable future.

In his 1994 book *Smashing Pots* Nigel Barley argues that in Africa pottery remains an essential element of everyday life despite the advent of modern aluminium vessels, enamelware and plastic products, and even more informal containers improvised from Western-style industrial packaging. And indeed, this is borne out by the modern urban markets where mugs, kettles and yam-steamers imported from China and Japan are sold alongside indigenous earthenware pots. In particular it is Barley's contention that pottery is an integral part of the lifestyle of African communities because it provides models for local thinking – about the human body, the seasons of the year, processes of procreation and the concept of reincarnation. 'Over the whole continent,' he writes, 'indigenous production is enormous and probably increasing.'

Ceramic vessels often have an advantage over their plastic or metal rivals in that they are cheaper to make, but this is equally often counteracted by their being heavier and less durable. It is, perhaps, much more likely that traditional pottery's prospects of salvation lie in its intrinsic qualities. Taking Guatemala as an example, tortillas, a major constituent of the staple diet, neither burn on nor stick so readily to pottery discs. In addition, people believe that water stored in a clay rather than a plastic jar stays cooler and retains a better flavour. Most important of all, the average rural Guatemalan believes that food quite simply tastes better when cooked in a pottery vessel – a notion with which it is difficult to disagree.

TOP:
A pottery-seller in a village in the Punjab, India.

ABOVE:
A range of mostly unglazed pots for sale at the Potters' Market in Safi, Morocco.

RIGHT:
Locally made pots for sale in Nabeul, Tunisia.

counterparts. This decline in popularity of traditional pottery has prompted a search for alternative markets, principally within the expanding tourism sector, but the new bias towards commercial considerations has affected not only potters' motives but also the aesthetic quality of their output. Nevertheless, the overall nature of Mexico's rural economy is such that some degree of demand for pottery is very likely to be sustained, the abundance of clay in the area and entrenched resistance to change particularly favouring its continuation. The large hand-made storage jars, a metre and a half in

Modern America

... designed by an American artist, made from American clay at an American pottery, burned at American kilns and decorated by American workmen.

OFFICIAL COMMENT ON A STATE DINING SERVICE
ACQUIRED BY THE WHITE HOUSE, 1918

Vase. Mexico, *c.* 1800.
Earthenware with white tin
glaze. Height 21 cm (8.4 in),
diameter 11.5 cm (4.6 in).

Large plate. Pennsylvania
Dutch style, attributed to
Henry Roudebuth, dated 1776.
Earthenware with painted and
incised decoration.

The traditions of American, as distinct from American-Indian, pottery stem from the designs, shapes and techniques introduced by early settlers from Britain and continental Europe, who arrived on the east coast in great numbers during the sixteenth and seventeenth centuries. As late as 1875 there was still a high proportion of immigrants among the potters working in the United States, as is revealed by a statistical analysis of the New York State census for that year: of the state's three hundred and sixty-seven potters, thirty per cent were German-born and twenty-three per cent English, with Americans making up only forty-one per cent of the total. It is little wonder, then, that American pottery styles show a strong European influence.

In common with other artisans who settled in North America, potters were quick to adapt to their new environment, willingly tailoring their working methods to the often unfamiliar indigenous raw materials and their products to the needs of the growing immigrant communities. Through their skill and inventiveness, distinctive styles and shapes of American-made ceramics gradually emerged. But relations between the European newcomers and the native Americans were not always amicable – as evidenced by the palisade built in 1756 around the vulnerable Moravian settlement of Bethabara, just outside modern-day Winston-Salem in North Carolina. Nevertheless, within this community the Moravian potters Gottfried Aust and Rudolf Christ,

no longer constrained by the rigorous guild system that operated in their home country, were able to produce not only essential utilitarian vessels but also high-quality slipware with decoration ranging from the fastidiously ornate to the free and vibrant.

A clear progression can be traced from the early forms, techniques and organization of American pottery-making to the large-scale industry that ultimately developed. At first, operating either alone (though usually with the help of family members) or in small teams, many potters were obliged to combine their potting activities with seasonal agricultural work, but it was not long before a steady market built up for their wares, boosted by an initial paucity of low-priced European imports. Not only did the fragility of ceramic goods make them difficult to ship in bulk, but they tended to generate a lower return than other cargo. The extent of the demand for locally produced pottery is indicated by an American newspaper report of June 1761, in which it is stated: 'People gathered from fifty and sixty miles away to buy pottery, but many came in vain, as the supply was exhausted by noon.' It seems that little had changed more than fifty years later; in 1814 Norman L. Judd, of Rome, New York, remarked that 'ware here is ready cash'.

In the period up to 1800 two main types of pottery were made: red earthenwares (commonly known as redwares) and stonewares. Redwares can be seen as the quintessential pioneer pottery and could be made with clean clay from virtually any local deposits, which was found to be perfect for firing to the low temperatures required. The pots were either thrown on the wheel or made by draping clay over a hump mould, the finished products normally being sold locally, within a fifteen- to thirty-kilometre radius. Precisely when redwares were first made in America is not known, but it is thought to have been at some time early in the seventeenth century, chiefly in the New England colonies, particularly Massachusetts and Connecticut, and in the eastern part of what later became Pennsylvania. Production of stoneware began around 1700 and continued well into the twentieth century.

In New Mexico Spanish colonists made use of a variety of pottery. Most of it was unglazed ware made by the American Indians, although a record of 1694 states: 'Some Pecos Indians arrived with glazed pottery to sell, probably imported.' While the privileged ate off handsome majolica tableware from Puebla de los Angeles in New Spain, most Hispanic settlers in New Mexico made do with the local pueblo Indian pottery. Whether the majolica wares were imported or manufactured in Los Angeles is not clear. From around 1790 for about a hundred years functional pottery was made by New Mexican Hispanics using techniques such as coil-and-smooth borrowed from the native Americans. The vessels were intended either for the storage, transportation, preparation and serving of food and drink or for personal hygiene uses. Beanpots and cooking pots were common forms. In the latter part of the nineteenth century production of this ware came to an end, the railroad having brought cheap glazed products to take its place.

RED EARTHENWARES

Pottery imported into North America for sale to pioneer communities was expensive and by the early part of the seventeenth century immigrant potters had set up their own workshops, providing wares to meet the needs of a diverse and rapidly expanding population. Pots produced at Jamestown, Virginia between 1625 and 1650 included a variety of vessels for home and farm use, such as storage jars, pitchers, bowls, mugs, porringers and milk pans, all made on the wheel using local red earthenware clay. Decoration, often applied direct to the surface of the pot, was usually minimal: simple designs of straight or wavy lines incised with pointed sticks.

Dish. Red earthenware, press-moulded with yellow slip trailed on red ground with the word 'Concord', and lead-glazed. Length 39.5 cm (15.8 in).

Among the first named potters whose work is recorded are Philip Drinker, who arrived at Charlestown, Massachusetts in 1635, and Dirck Claesen, mentioned in records of 1657 as making pots in what is now New York (although it was originally named New Amsterdam when founded by the Dutch). The potter Joshua Tittery, from Newcastle-upon-Tyne in the north of England, is known to have settled in Pennsylvania in 1683, while another British settler, Gabriel Thomas, wrote in 1698 that 'great encouragements are given to tradesmen and others ... *Potters* have Sixteen Pence for an Earthen Pot which may be bought in *England* for Four pence.'

The first potworks of any great size to appear in the records is the Burlington Pottery, set up as an investment by the Englishman Dr Daniell Coxe, a court physician to Charles II and later Queen Anne. Although he never visited America himself, Coxe owned a vast tract of land in western New Jersey. Some time between 1683 and 1688 he sent out to America a team of skilled craftsmen charged with the task of building a pottery works on a site in or near the present-day city of Burlington and operating it on his behalf. John Dewilde, described as a 'Citizen & Potter of London', was appointed to manage the project, with 'potter servant' William Gill, from Lambeth in London, employed as a workman. Initially the new enterprise used clay brought over from England, even though the local clays were excellent. So too was the potential market, but nevertheless the venture was to prove a financial failure.

Two types of potter's wheel were in general use in America: the English 'kick' or treadle wheel, turned by pushing or kicking a treadle connected by an arm to the flywheel, and the simpler-to-construct continental wheel, which, because it was operated by the potter pushing a large flywheel round with his foot, was sometimes known as a 'paw' wheel. Glazing involved dusting lead powder, usually imported from England, on to the surface of the pots when they were leather-hard; on firing this would produce a thin but serviceable coating of glaze. With the introduction of biscuit firing, pots could be finished with a more substantial coating of liquid glaze. Lead was occasionally obtained by oxidizing the linings of tea chests, but the more expensive imported product was preferred since it yielded superior results. Other useful glaze materials, such as iron oxide, could be gleaned from the blacksmith's anvil while yellow ochre and umber were dug from local deposits. Also readily available was manganese, which produced shades of brownish pink in the glaze, and although copper (used to colour the glaze green) was costly, it was found that an adequate substitute could be obtained by burning old copper utensils in the kiln.

In the early years pots were fired in 'groundhog' kilns, wood-burning brick kilns some three to four metres in length that were built with an arched roof and had a packing door at one end and a chimney at the other. The firing temperature was judged chiefly by the length of the escaping flames and the colour achieved inside the kiln, bright red indicating a temperature of around 900–1000°C. Although these kilns remained in use in the South well into the twentieth century, the type that came to be

Dish. American, initialled E W, dated 1796. Red earthenware, press-moulded with slip-trailed decoration depicting a cockerel. Diameter 33 cm (13.25 in).

Map of major pottery centres of North America, 1700–1900.

more commonly used was the upright 'bottle', 'beehive' or updraught kiln. This had the advantage that it could be incorporated into the structure of the pottery workshop, although this did pose the risk of a serious fire breaking out. Sophisticated control methods were developed that made use of glazed 'draw trials' – sample batches that could be hooked out of the kiln and examined to check the state of the melted glaze.

Records survive that reveal the conditions on which early American potters took on young apprentices. Boys were indentured from the age of about fourteen for a period of seven years, during which time they were given food and lodging, supplied with clothing and taught to read and write; in return they were expected to work long hours and to master all the various pottery processes. Though long and possibly arduous, such an apprenticeship would no doubt have proved worthwhile in the end. Demand for pottery rose steadily as the new communities grew, giving the trained potter ample opportunity to make a reasonable living.

It is likely that clay stewpots and roofing tiles were produced in New Jersey, probably by Dutch settlers, as early as the seventeenth century; this is indicated by the remains of a firehole, thoroughly vitrified, that was found near South Amboy in 1893. By the mid-eighteenth century America's pottery industry was well established. Most pots were glazed inside and out and some were decorated with colouring oxides or slips poured down the outer surface, a technique especially popular in Connecticut. German potters who settled in Pennsylvania after 1730 gradually adapted their shapes and decorative styles to local requirements, bringing new forms such as pie dishes and beanpots into regular production. All the basic raw materials they needed – red earthenware clay, white slip for decoration and lead for the glaze – were available in abundance.

The white slip, which contrasted well with the red body, was trailed on to the surface of the pots in lively semi-abstract patterns; on dishes and plates it provided a bright, clean-looking lining on to which designs could be painted or scratched. Decoration on these wares ranges from basic manganese slashes to elaborate slip-trailed lettering in white clay. Abstract geometric patterns make up most of the designs, but sometimes wording – for example, 'Clams and Oysters' or 'New York City' – appears, while certain items bear personalized inscriptions such as 'Mary's Dish', suggesting that they were the work of a local potter. In other areas, such as Galen and the Shenandoah Valley of Virginia, the pieces produced were splashed with several colours, reflecting the influence of European tortoiseshell wares.

Basic pottery items included jugs and pear-shaped flasks, used for vinegar and drinks such as whiskey and cider as well as water, and jars for the storage of oysters, tomatoes, sweetmeats and other foods. More robust wares ranged from water-coolers and milk churns to chamber pots, washboards, poultry-waterers and spittoons. Large quantities of bricks, flowerpots and drainage pipes were also produced, together with novelty items such as moneyboxes in the shape of fruits and doorstops or mantel ornaments modelled as dogs and lions.

The use of inscriptions on plates and platters intended as display pieces is a distinguishing feature of Pennsylvania Dutch slipware (the 'Dutch' in this term being a corruption of *deutsch*, meaning German). The wide-ranging mottoes and sayings on these pieces serve as an enlightening guide to the beliefs and customs of the diverse communities that set down roots in Pennsylvania. Swedish, Dutch and English settlements along the Delaware River were already well established when the English Quaker William Penn (1644–1718) founded the city of Philadelphia in 1681 and Penn's reformational zeal encouraged a further wave of European immigrants, notably the anabaptist Mennonites from Germany, whose descendants form today's 'Pennsylvania Dutch' communities. Lutherans and Reformed Church groups from Bavaria and Aus-

Jar made by Jonathan Fenton, 1793–6. Stoneware, thrown, salt-glazed, stamped with 'BOSTON' and the initials J F. Height 32.5 cm (13 in).

tria also arrived, followed in 1727 by the Swiss and later by Scots-Irish Presbyterians.

Pennsylvania Dutch slipware is often known as tulipware, from the flower designs with which it is most frequently decorated. However, various other floral motifs appear, as do ferns, the pomegranate, birds and hearts. Some redwares were decorated with trailed slip, usually applied to the red body, while other wares were covered with a white or creamy yellow slip through which the design was carved or scratched to reveal the dark body underneath; both types were then covered with a transparent lead glaze.

Improvements in making methods and more sophisticated firing and decorating techniques were introduced by the itinerant potters who travelled from one pottery to another, helping to produce wares for use within the local community before moving on. Although redware thrived in areas where it faced no competition, people became increasingly aware of the drawbacks of earthenware, and in particular the health hazard posed by the lead glazes. In 1785 an article in the *Pennsylvania Mercury* described lead glazes as 'unwholesome' and proposed that their use be banned, observing that not only did lead tend to scale off the pot but was 'imperceptibly eaten away by every acid matter; and mixing with the drinks and meats of the people becomes a slow but sure poison'.

By the 1860s ranges of redware products were being made only in isolated areas, such as sections of the South and the Mormon settlements of Utah, and by 1900 few but the flowerpot manufacturers were still in business. Earthenware cooking pots remained popular, however.

STONEWARE AND SALT-GLAZE

The beginnings of stoneware production in America can be dated to around 1700. The French Huguenot immigrant Anthony Duché and his elder sons are recorded as having made stoneware in Philadelphia in the 1720s, and twenty years later one of the sons, James, went to New England to help Isaac Parker set up stoneware production, although this venture was not a success. The American stoneware was almost steel-hard; impermeable and durable when properly fired, it was much tougher and harder-wearing than redware. What is more, because it did not need glazing the risk of lead poisoning was avoided. A variety of different glazes and softly coloured slips were, in fact, introduced at various times to add splashes of colour and enhance the appearance of the pots, but none contained lead.

One difference between redware and stoneware is that on redware there is rarely any mark identifying the manufacturer, whereas stoneware is often stamped, incised or inscribed with not only the name but also the location of the pottery at which it was made. Some pieces even give the name of the merchant who sold the ware – a sure indication that pottery was gaining in status.

While many local clay deposits were suitable for the manufacture of red earthenware, it was less easy to find sources of workable stoneware clay that was heat-resistant. Beds of such clay were, however, found in and around New York City, which became one of the earliest centres of production along with New Jersey, the Carolinas and Pennsylvania. Around 1730 William Crolius, a German immigrant from Koblenz, set up a stoneware pottery in New York that was to continue in operation until 1887. A second German potter, John Remmey from Neuweid (who married into the Crolius family), established another workshop nearby which remained in business until 1820. The pottery produced by Remmey and Crolius falls into the general category of utilitarian ware, vessels such as jugs, jars, crocks, butter churns and teapots making up the bulk of the production. The pots were generally thrown on the wheel and the majority, with the exception of a few special presentation pieces, were unsigned. Most of their stoneware was decorated with incised, stamped or cobalt-brushed designs and salt-glazed to produce its characteristic mottled appearance, in shades of cream and brown.

From the mid-nineteenth century New Jersey grew to become America's foremost pottery-producing region, aided by its strategic position along the Atlantic seaboard between two densely populated major seaports, New York and Philadelphia. The region also benefited from an abundance of clays that were eminently suited not only to earthenware, stoneware and porcelain production but equally to the manufacture of bricks and tiles. Some hundred years earlier James Morgan had discovered near South Amboy a substantial vein of high-grade stoneware clay, which by 1800 was being transported by boat or barge as far as Boston and along the southern coast. With the completion of the Erie Canal in 1825, clay from New Jersey and nearby Staten and Long Islands could be transported up the Hudson River and along the canal to central and western New York State and even into Canada. By the middle of the nineteenth century the rapid expansion of the railroads had provided an alternative means of long-distance transport that allowed stoneware clays to be delivered more easily to inland potteries. This further encouraged the making of stoneware and hastened the demise of redware production.

When potteries producing high-fired wares were established in Massachusetts (where the clay used was shipped from New Jersey) and Connecticut, it was not long before their products were competing strongly against the earthenwares. Potters in some of the German workshops of Pennsylvania, among others, responded by learning the new firing techniques and using them in combination with their normal production methods. By this time most high-temperature wares were glazed by introducing salt into the kiln, a technique that had originally been brought over from Germany.

Philadelphia was another of the pioneering centres for stoneware production. Like New York, it had the advantages of ample local deposits of suitable clay, a prosperous and expanding population and proximity to flourishing seaports – all factors that encouraged high-volume production, much of it to a very high standard. Pots of fine quality were also made at Yorktown in Virginia. On most of these stonewares a salt glaze was used, which yielded subdued mottled brown and grey surface colours. Other types of glaze were developed for use at high temperatures, most notably a handsome and practical shiny black and brown obtained by the use of a naturally occurring dark iron-bearing clay formed into a slip glaze.

Ever-expanding production led to a certain measure of division of labour being introduced into

Jar. American, mid-19th century. Salt-glazed, thrown, with elaborate incised decoration, rubbed with cobalt, depicting a man with an arrow in his mouth standing in an oak tree. The design may illustrate Longfellow's poem 'The Arrow and the Song'. Height 27.5 cm (11 in).

potteries. By the nineteenth century many crafts-men were able to concentrate on the making of pots by employing others to decorate them. The decoration tended to be simple and direct and was usually scratched on to the surface of the pots. Incised straight and wavy lines as well as stylized floral patterns were used to great effect by potteries in New York. Some designs were coloured in with cobalt blue, one of the few oxides able to withstand high-temperature firing. Potters working in the Shenandoah Valley favoured a lively woodpecker design, well placed and swiftly drawn on the side of the pot. A variety of fish, bird and flower motifs were also used – some scratched, some painted, but invariably with a crisp, impressionistic feel. Many of these designs have a naive, untrained freshness that enhances the form. Jugs, pitchers and other containers were often stamped with the name of the factory at which they were made, together with a number probably indicating the capacity of the vessel. Like the earthenwares, most of the stonewares were highly functional in form.

Following the establishment of Federal Government in 1789 a tariff was introduced whereby a duty was imposed on all imported goods. This had the effect of stimulating demand for American-made stonewares since it rendered even the most basic wares from England prohibi-tively expensive to ship.

YELLOWWARE

One of the clays found in New Jersey, Pennsylvania and Ohio produced a yellow-firing body that lent itself well to the production of moulded wares, principally in the form of kitchen items such as mixing bowls and baking pans. By the 1830s sizeable factories making what has become known as yellowware had been established. The first well documented factory, the American Pottery Manufacturing Company, was set up by David Henderson of Jersey City. The functional products manufactured at his workshops pro-vide an indication of the local diet: they range from mixing bowls (some with pouring lips), milk pans, pitchers,

pie plates, beanpots and ovoid or oblong baking and serving dishes to pudding moulds and custard pots. Decoration was minimal and typically con-sisted of embossing or bands of coloured slip, while a covering of transparent alkaline glaze gave a smooth, bright, practical finish.

Yellowware manufacture was at its height between the 1860s and the 1930s, a period that saw the establishment of more than a dozen large factories concentrated in East Liverpool, Ohio alone. Other major centres of production were Cincinnati, Philadelphia, Baltimore and Trenton, New Jersey. Although yellowware is still made in the United States, the demand for it has been drastically reduced by the introduction of industrial white earthenware and modern heat-resistant kitchenwares.

INDUSTRIAL PRODUCTION

The development of the American ceramic industry in the eighteenth and nineteenth centuries was peppered with instances of commercial failure. In general pottery factories were strong on talent, as they were able to draw on a ready pool of skilled craftsmen from Europe, but their management was often inefficient and their production unprofit-able. Although by 1800 US potteries had begun producing a varied selection of wares, the better-off consumers continued to favour products imported from Britain and the Netherlands.

During the nineteenth century industrial manu-facture developed in scope and quality and all manner of pots began to be produced – from red- and black-glazed teapots and coffee pots to lustre-decorated pitchers. There was a huge rise in the production of utilitarian stonewares, with small potteries in many areas of the United States and Canada making impermeable stoneware vessels that were easy to clean and suitable for storing foodstuffs of every kind, even highly acid vinegars and pickles. As farming methods in the agrarian culture of North America improved, higher levels of food production during the warm season increased the importance of safe and efficient food storage. Stoneware vessels were more hygienic than earthenware or staved wooden containers and con-siderably less expensive than those made of metal. As well as the standard flowerpots and chamber pots, special stoneware forms were made for con-serving milk and for protecting laying hens. Few

Water-cooler. Made in New York, 1825. Stoneware, salt-glazed, thrown and inscribed 'Mr. Oliver Gridley/Newburgh July 1 1825'. Mr Gridley is thought to have been the ironmaster of the Queensborough furnace below Newburgh, New York. Height 37.5 cm (15 in).

Pitcher. USA, *c.* 1880.
Buff-coloured stoneware
with relief of decoration
of leaves and hazelnuts.
Height 21.5 cm (8.6 in).

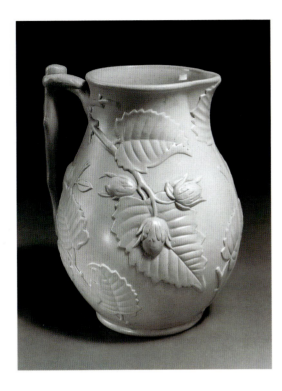

tablewares were produced in stoneware at this time, and stoneware cooking pots were equally rare until special bodies were devised at the end of the century.

It was not until the 1830s that pottery factories of any great scale in the European style were set up, and many did not prosper until after the Civil War of 1861–5. Industrial production methods were based on the use of patterns and moulds, with the clay obtained from local deposits, particularly around Bennington in Vermont. In the second half of the nineteenth century a number of ceramic factories were established at East Liverpool, Ohio and Trenton, New Jersey.

At Bennington Captain John Norton, a veteran of the American War of Independence, first made earthenware around 1793 and twenty years later was producing stoneware. Many of his pieces show evidence of the Germanic tradition, for example his long-necked, full-bellied jugs and ovoid jars decorated with cobalt-painted incised designs. Around 1845 Christopher Webber Fenton, sometimes dubbed the 'American Josiah Wedgwood', went into partnership with his brother-in-law Julius Norton in the Norton pottery, where he helped to devise new ranges and generally expand production. The lines he added include what is known as Rockingham ware, characterized by a

mottled brown glaze. This was later enhanced by sprinkling different-coloured oxides on the pots to produce a mottled effect in blue, yellow, orange and green.

The partnership was short-lived, however, and in 1847 Fenton launched his own business, Lyman, Fenton and Company. Here he made a wide variety of well-designed products including virtually every kind of domestic vessel together with decorative and ornamental wares. By 1853 Fenton was sufficiently boosted by his success to give the firm the grandiose title of the United States Pottery Company. By this time his ambitious and impressive production programme ran to plain white in addition to yellow earthenware. As well as the more common domestic tablewares it covered just about everything that could be made in clay, from water and coffee urns to footbaths and spittoons. A number of fine ranges were also introduced, including Parian porcelain and semi-porcelain as well as speciality products decorated with mottled glazes, known as 'lava' or 'scoddled' ware.

Fenton's Parian ware is similar in appearance to Wedgwood's famous and much admired jasperware in that it has relief decoration in white contrasting with a coloured body and is left 'dry' or unglazed. This similarity owes much to the fact that Fenton

Pitcher. Probably made at
William Farrar's Geddes
Rockingham Pottery, *c.* 1858.
Stoneware, slip-cast, with
relief moulded grapes, vine
and plants, spatter decoration.
Height 26.25 cm (10.5 in).

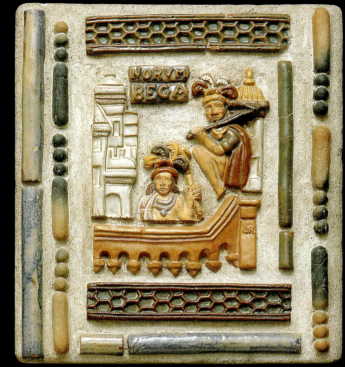

Tiles from the Moravian Pottery and Tile Works, Salem, North Carolina, 1913. Earthenware with relief decoration. FROM TOP LEFT: Montezuma; Norum Bega; The Fountain of Youth. Height (tallest) 40 cm (16 in).

employed the services of John Harrison, a potter who had worked as a modeller at the Wedgwood factory in England. The strength and durability of the Parian ware made it extremely popular. It had a light-coloured vitrified body as a result of the discovery close to the site of the pottery of a large bed of china clay, an important element of the ware's composition. Within the Parian range utilitarian vessels including pitchers and jugs were produced as well as more decorative items such as vases and urns in the jasper style, with applied relief decoration. Another of Fenton's employees who had worked for Wedgwood as a modeller and designer was the talented potter Daniel Greatbach, who created a variety of practical and novelty wares for the company, including cow-shaped milk jugs, flasks in the form of books, candle-holders and small models of reclining animals.

Despite apparent commercial success, the United States Pottery Company was constantly dogged by financial difficulties, and in 1858 these brought about the collapse of the operation. Fenton then moved on to Peoria, Illinois, where he set up a new factory, again producing a range of whitewares.

Numerous other potteries that sprang up during the early and mid-nineteenth century also survived for only a few years. One such enterprise was the Jersey Porcelain and Earthenware Company, which again benefited from the modelling skills of Greatbach. Among the forms produced by this factory were hound-handled pitchers, and many of its wares were inscribed with patriotic slogans and decorated with such noble motifs as portraits of national heroes and the famous American eagle and flag design. With the aim of developing finer and whiter wares the firm experimented with the use of china clay. Evidently impressed by the quality and tone of the company's products, the Franklin Institute awarded it a silver medal for 'the best china from American materials'.

It was frequently the less ambitious potteries that were the most successful commercially. The well-established Moravian Pottery at Salem, North Carolina already had a history of making red earthenware pots, many with slip-trailed decoration of simple lines and formalized flowers, when the itinerant potter William Ellis initiated the production of both stoneware and fine Queen's ware at the factory in 1774. He also introduced industrial

Pitcher. Factory not known, made *c.* 1880. Earthenware, modelled leaf decoration and maiolica glaze, with a trio of vertical leaves and graceful curling leaves entwining the base. Height 12.5 cm (5 in).

manufacturing methods, such as the making of pots from moulds. The Moravian Pottery produced a wide variety of animal forms as well as its more refined pots based on European creamwares.

One of the most popular types of pottery made in America in the late nineteenth century was majolica ware, which consisted for the most part of an elaborately modelled cream-coloured body covered with a variety of brightly-coloured glazes. In addition to tableware and vases, a number of potteries made more unusual forms such as leaf-shaped serving dishes and pitchers modelled in the shape of cabbages or owls. Griffin, Smith and Hill of Phoenixville, Pennsylvania, who manufactured Etruscan majolica, are among the best-known American producers of this ware.

PORCELAIN

In America, as in Europe, the ultimate aim of most pottery manufacturers was the production of porcelain, which carried a high prestige value and was therefore able to command high prices. When the ladies of Plympton, Massachusetts met in each other's houses for tea in the 1760s it was customary for each to take along her own teacup, saucer and spoon, the quality of these items being seen as a clear indicator of social status.

Several attempts were made to produce fine white wares of sufficient quality to compete with European imports, but these met with little success. As early as about 1738 Andrew Duché, one of the sons of the Huguenot stoneware potter Anthony Duché, claimed to have successfully produced true porcelain in Savannah, Georgia by making use of the large deposits of china clay found on nearby Cherokee Indian territory. Having settled in Savannah and established a successful earthenware factory there, Duché believed he had 'found out the true manner of making porcelain or Chinaware' and so applied to the trustees of the colony for funding in support of his work on the new body. However, there is scant evidence that his plans ever came to fruition. Some time around 1743/5 he travelled to England in the hope of selling or exploiting his porcelain formula, but on his return he failed to progress his trials beyond the experimental stage. At about the same time the discovery of deposits of fine white clay near Philadelphia prompted several other potters to make similar attempts, but these, too, were unsuccessful.

It is likely that Duché made some useful contacts while in England. He is believed to have met Edward Heylyn and Thomas Frye of Bow, who in 1745 applied for a patent for the manufacture of porcelain specifying the use of 'an earth, the product of the Chirokee nation in America'. Duché had taken with him samples of the American china clay, which he may have shown or given to the English porcelain pioneer William Cookworthy in Plymouth, Devon. Although Duché is not mentioned by name, in a letter of the time Cookworthy refers to a visitor bringing samples of such a clay

Pitcher. Union Porcelain Works, c. 1876. Probably designed by Karl Müller. Porcelain with relief decoration of a bearded Uncle Sam, a figure of Gambrinus (a mythical Flemish king, said to be the first to brew beer) and a ram atop a barrel impressed with the pottery's initials. Height 24.5 cm (9.75 in).

from 'the back of Virginia'. Whoever it was that introduced the material to Cookworthy, he was justly convinced that china clay was an essential raw material for the production of hard porcelain. Josiah Wedgwood had china clay imported into England from America prior to vast deposits of it being discovered in Cornwall.

By far the most important, if short-lived, commercial attempt to produce soft-paste porcelain in America was made by the factory established by Goussin Bonnin and George Anthony Morris at Southwark in Philadelphia. From 1770 to 1772 the Bonnin and Morris factory succeeded in manufacturing fine white American china on a substantial scale. Using clay from the banks of the Delaware River combined with calcined animal bones, a bone china body was made that was used to produce a range of pots based mainly on contemporary styles of English wares, which included bowls,

jugs, fruit baskets, and plates with cut decoration. Some of the pieces were decorated with painted designs while others were transfer-printed in underglaze blue. Skilled potters were brought over from England to work in the factory, some of whom may previously have been involved with the Bow works in Stratford, London.

Despite high manufacturing costs and the special skills needed to make use of indigenous materials – not to mention intense competition in the form of the 'dumping' of low-priced vases from England – the production of porcelain in America did get under way in the early nineteenth century, although still on a fairly modest scale. A Dr Mead made a range of porcelain in New York City, and in 1825 William Ellis Tucker and Thomas Hulme opened the Philadelphia China Factory to specialize in the production of well-fired hard bone china. Unable to recruit local people with the requisite skills, they brought over craftsmen from France, England and Germany. Between 1830 and 1850 wares in imitation of Sèvres pieces with floral border patterns were produced. A number of designs incorporated elaborate monograms and coats of arms, and often the portrait of an eminent person formed the centrepiece of the decoration. Famous works by American artists were copied, including a Gilbert Stuart 'Vaughan' portrait of George Washington and Charles Willson Peale's painting of 'Mad' Anthony Wayne. The factory was later renamed the Tucker and Hemphill Works.

The first documented attempt at porcelain production in New York State is that of Joel Farnam of 'Stillwater' (Mechanicville), who on 25 October 1845 was granted Letters Patent no. 4,242 for a 'new useful improvement in combinations of matter which may be concerted or manufactured into… potteryware'. One of the earliest porcelain manufacturers in Brooklyn was the firm of Cartlidge and Co. (1848–56), established by Staffordshire-born potter Charles Cartlidge shortly after his arrival from England. This factory made fancy teawares such as slip-cast pitchers moulded with designs of maize stalks, and a range of smaller items including buttons, umbrella handles, doorknobs and drawer-pulls. It also issued a range of portrait busts of well-known American figures such as Daniel Webster, Zachary Taylor and Chief Justice Marshall, as well as making a range of finer customized products:

cameos, brooch medallions and miniature family portraits. Also in Brooklyn, the Union Porcelain Works (1861–1922) set up by Thomas Carl Smith manufactured hard-paste porcelain with ornamental modelling. Under the skilful art direction of German sculptor Karl Müller the factory produced figural relief panels in the Dresden style together

Covered pitcher. Buffalo Pottery, New York, 1910. Stoneware, decorated with a transfer design in 'Blue Willow', a pattern based on the traditional design and introduced into America by this pottery. The Larkin Soap Company set up Buffalo Pottery as an adjunct to its main commercial activity, giving customers coupons that could be redeemed for premiums, including pottery items. The operation continued until 1956. Height 14.6 cm (5.75 in).

with mandarin-head finials, polar bear handles and rabbit-form feet. Other products were ornamental vases and fancy tableware as well as ivory biscuit porcelain with gilded and painted decoration in the style of English Royal Worcester wares.

John Hancock, who had served his apprenticeship at the Wedgwood factory, and James Bennett from Derbyshire were among a number of English potters who set up factories in the Ohio Valley, an area that became one of the principal centres of the American ceramics industry. By 1880 there were twenty-three potteries in East Liverpool, firing a total of sixty-seven kilns. The factory run by German immigrant William Boch and his brother produced wares with decorative motifs depicting patriotic events such as the Boston Tea Party and images of revolutionary soldiers and American Indians, similar in both technique and decoration to the output of the Tucker and Hemphill Works.

The Boch brothers' work was shown at the Crystal Palace Exposition in New York in 1853.

At the time of the American Civil War in the 1860s the distribution of goods was well established and many small potteries were successfully manufacturing wares on an industrial scale. Some earthenware forms continued to be made in country potteries, particularly during and immediately after the conflict when communications were difficult, and a few stoneware workshops survived for some years, although these declined in number as industrial production increased. In due course advances in technology and the advent of a more industrially based society caused the production of country pots to draw to an end. By the 1880s the majority of small potteries in the northern and central eastern states had closed down, leaving only those in the southern highlands. These continued to operate for a number of years, but as the network of roads and railways expanded, enabling industrially produced wares to be transported cheaply and efficiently even to remote areas, they too were finally forced into closure.

By the turn of the century the American ceramic industry was beginning to refine its production techniques. Nevertheless, when President Theodore Roosevelt was renovating the White House in 1902 and sought to purchase top-quality china tableware that had been manufactured in America, no wares could be found that reached a sufficiently high standard. Walter Scott Lenox of Trenton, New Jersey was determined to meet this challenge. By about 1906 he had perfected a translucent, ivory-tinted product (described as 'fine china' to distinguish it from porcelain) equal in body and durability to the finest European wares, and before long Lenox china was on display in leading stores such as Dulin & Martin Co. of Washington, DC.

It is a testament to the success of Lenox china that the situation at the White House was very different in 1918, when President Woodrow Wilson had no difficulty in ordering a state dining service of superior quality that could proudly and justly be claimed to have been 'designed by an American artist, made from American clay at an American pottery, burned at American kilns and decorated by American workmen'.

The Lenox company has continued to supply the state dinner services for the White House ever since, most recently for the Clintons in 1994.

Craft into Industry

BRITAIN 1750–1950

Hath not the potter over the clay, of the same lump

to make one vessel unto honour and another unto dishonour?

ROMANS IX: 21

Coffee pot and cover. English, Staffordshire, 1760–70. Cream-coloured marbled earthenware, moulded and glazed. Height 22.8 cm (9 in).

The industrialization of Great Britain that started to gather pace in the mid-eighteenth century was to have vast and far-reaching effects on pottery-making – throughout the land and beyond. As heightened commercial activity began to bring greater prosperity to various sections of society, living standards rose and with them the demand for practical household pottery and tableware that was more refined, durable and aesthetically pleasing. Manufacturers responded by taking steps to improve their wares, with the result that major technological advances were made in both production methods and design. By the middle of the nineteenth century social reforms and rapid progress in the fields of science and engineering had led to the development of entirely new series of products, including many types of sanitaryware and specialized ceramics for industrial applications.

Britain's potteries gradually set about equipping themselves for the large-scale manufacture of ever more refined products, but until the end of the eighteenth and first part of the nineteenth centuries established production techniques were often used alongside the new mechanized methods. Tin-glazed earthenwares, for example, continued to be made (mainly around Bristol and Liverpool), but a faster decorating process was adopted whereby designs could be transfer-printed on to the glaze.

Although traditional brown stonewares were still in demand for use in taverns and for food storage

purposes in kitchens, there was also a growing market for more decorative fine stonewares and these soon began to be made in unusual and intricate shapes. In addition to the various conventional production techniques employed, many pieces were cast in moulds using slip or liquid clay and were similar technically to the cream-coloured earthenwares that were now being manufactured, largely in Stoke-on-Trent. The new stonewares were not only inexpensive to produce but ideal for use in the home.

North Staffordshire was a particularly suitable location for enterprising potters wishing to take advantage of the expanding market for ceramic products. The area not only offered an abundance of workable clays and easily accessible outcrops of bituminous coal but also had a highly skilled local workforce, albeit organized mainly in family-run workshops. Ever since the late seventeenth century there had been more small potteries in this area than anywhere else in Britain, producing a diverse range of wares that included coarse storage vessels, milk pans and butter pots, black-glazed, mottled and domestic salt-glazed stonewares, elaborately decorated slipwares and unglazed red stonewares. On the verge of industrialization, with the craft of the potter firmly established in the region, north Staffordshire was poised to become by far the largest ceramic manufacturing centre in the country and one of the most influential in the world.

The area of Staffordshire around Stoke-on-Trent, still popularly known as the Potteries, has no navigable rivers and thus owes much of its success to the piecemeal construction during the second half of the eighteenth century of a network of inland canals that became the arteries of early industrial Britain. Especially important was the Trent and Mersey canal, begun in 1766 and opened in 1777, which enabled the safe, efficient and low-cost transportation of goods to the ports of Liverpool and Hull, and on to London and abroad. Conversely, raw materials such as white-firing plastic clay from Devon and Dorset, flints from the south of England and the newly discovered china clay from Cornwall could be carried easily by sea and canal to the Potteries.

Until the second half of the eighteenth century Staffordshire potters typically worked in small units, the family home often doubling as a workshop manned by no more than about eight people. The spread of this 'cottage industry' soon resulted in the area becoming unhealthily crowded. Soot and smoke pollution from the kilns made for poor living as well as working conditions, and because clay tended to be dug from as near to the potteries as possible, some local pits grew to dangerous proportions. In addition to the workshops that grew up in or alongside domestic dwellings, purpose-built factories began to be established, such as Roger Wood's Ash Pottery at Lane, which was opened in 1756, and Josiah Wedgwood's first pottery, set up in 1759. By the turn of the century the industry had expanded to over three hundred potworks in Burslem alone, from a total of only sixty-seven some fifty years earlier.

In north Staffordshire as a whole there were about 130 working potteries in the mid-eighteenth century, mostly making the standard products of the day – salt-glazed stonewares and red and black lead-glazed earthenwares, far more refined in style and quality than earlier types. These were made in large quantities for domestic use but soon gave way to the new creamwares. Around 1750 production was reintroduced of the fine red stonewares that had been made in the area between about 1693 and 1698 by David and John Philip Elers (see chapter 6), but whereas the Elers brothers' pots had been slip-cast from carefully prepared and refined clay, some were now thrown on the wheel and decorated with applied relief decoration.

The development of appropriate clay bodies was an essential element of the numerous technological advances made during the industrialization of the pottery industry. When calcined flint and later white Devonshire clay were added to the clay mixture, resulting in a stronger light-firing body, this proved suitable for making a near-white salt-glazed stoneware. Its production, by moulding, throwing and lathe-turning, began in the early 1720s and continued for some fifty years. Gradually a cream-coloured earthenware body with good plasticity was devised, which could be finished with a near-colourless lead glaze. This was used to make a variety of thrown and turned shapes that in due course replaced both tin- and lead-glazed red earthenwares throughout Europe. It was these new 'creamwares' that were to make the fortunes of Josiah Wedgwood and other notable potters.

The many advances made in ceramics during the 1750s and '60s resulted in an unprecedented diversity of new forms, glazes and multi-coloured bodies. Among them were marbled bodies or glazes formulated to resemble hardstones and applied on forms derived from classical marble vases, and

teawares fashioned in the form of fruit and vegetables. Listed in the first potters' price-fixing agreement, dated 1770, are twelve different sizes of dish and five sizes each of sauce-boat and stool-pan (chamber pot) along with such items as butter tubs and stands, cups and saucers, plates and tureens.

Until the eighteenth century domestic pots made in Britain, and indeed most other countries, were intended mainly for practical use by working-class communities, but with the rise of a prosperous new middle class a wider market was created. In order to exploit this commercial opportunity, sophisticated making processes were developed and more refined wares introduced that were capable of competing with imported oriental and European porcelain. By the later decades of the century the efficiency of industrial production methods was such that pottery for use at table and in and around the home could be manufactured in bulk rapidly and reliably, at a relatively low unit cost, employing a less highly skilled labour force. However, the livelihood of independent artisan potters inevitably suffered as the ceramic industry grew steadily in size.

A number of eighteenth-century innovations have come to be identified with individual potters, principally through the writings of Simeon Shaw in the early nineteenth century. But however attractive it may seem to rely on Shaw for information, his statements cannot always be taken as definitive, largely because many processes evolved over time. For example, he credits Enoch Booth, a potter operating in Tunstall, with the introduction into Staffordshire in about 1750 of the practice of biscuit-firing earthenware, whereas others attribute this to Samuel Bell at his Pomona workshop at Newcastle-under-Lyme some years earlier. Biscuit-firing involved giving the ware an initial firing that rendered it easier to handle by making it stronger while still yielding a body very suitable for taking the liquid glaze, made up of a mixture of lead, flint and clay suspended in water. Potters producing tin-glazed earthenwares had been practising biscuit-firing long before this time, as the white opaque tin glaze had to be applied evenly and to a sufficient thickness to cover the red body.

JOHN ASTBURY

John Astbury (1686–1743) is believed to have learnt many of his manufacturing secrets while employed by the Elers brothers, and certain of his

Tea-kettle. Staffordshire, *c.* 1760. Earthenware, moulded with applied relief decoration, glazed. Height 12 cm (4.8 in).

Teapot, covered jug and lidded bowl. Staffordshire, late 18th century. Thomas Whieldon and Josiah Wedgwood developed a range of vessels modelled in the natural forms of fruit and vegetables such as pineapple and cauliflower, using a transparent green glaze. Height (tallest) 13.4 cm (5.4 in).

work, in particular some unglazed red stonewares with engine-turned decoration, is certainly reminiscent of the Elers brothers' in terms of its thinness and the use of applied and stamped relief decoration. Astbury is best known, however, for his fine, light-coloured earthenware in the form of teapots and other tablewares decorated with relief patterning, usually of white pipe clay. Finished in a lead glaze with a yellowish tone, these are made in clay that varies in colour from red to buff but appears much darker under the transparent glaze. The stamped reliefs, often quite crudely applied, include motifs of stags, lions, birds, harps and shields.

In 1725 Astbury and his son Thomas established a pottery at Shelton, where they are believed to have made the first use of white Devonshire clay (sometimes known as ball clay from the shape produced when it was dug with pointed shovels) in order to produce a body with a lighter colour. The Astburys are also credited with introducing calcined and ground flint as an ingredient, which

resulted in an even lighter-coloured body. The early pieces made from this may be seen as an early version of creamwares, albeit with a brown or yellow tinge to the glaze.

RALPH DANIEL

Although the Elers brothers had probably made use of plaster of Paris in Staffordshire as far back as the 1690s, Ralph Daniel, a member of a large family of Cobridge potters, was the first to employ plaster moulds in the mid-eighteenth century, following a visit to the Continent in 1740. Moulds had previously been made of such materials as alabaster, fired earthenware or similarly hard-wearing substances, and the introduction of plaster of Paris was a vital step in speeding up the production of identical pieces, which could be either symmetrical or non-symmetrical in form. Plaster of Paris moulds were relatively easy to make and were suitable both for slip-casting and for the technique of pressing, whereby thin slabs of clay were eased into the mould. Plaster moulds had many advantages: they were highly absorbent and therefore cast the pieces quickly, and the moulds themselves could be reproduced in quantity not only for the production of plates and cups but also for more complex objects such as teapots and embossed tureens.

The plaster of Paris moulds were cast from an original model commonly known as a 'block', the making of which demanded great skill and precision. One of the most renowned block-cutters in Stoke-on-Trent was Aaron Wood (see 'Other Notable Creamware Manufacturers' below), whose work was finely carved and beautifully precise. However, because Wood worked for various potters, including Thomas Whieldon, and was responsible for a number of contemporary designs, accurate attribution of his wares is difficult. Either Ralph Daniel or his son Thomas is also believed to have been the first potter to practise enamel painting in the Staffordshire area.

THOMAS WHIELDON

Thomas Whieldon (1719–95) was one of the foremost potters of his day and became a successful manufacturer, elevating himself from the status of tradesman to become a member of the landed gentry. It is probable that his first pottery was set up in 1740 at Fenton Vivian, where he not only made use of but often enhanced the latest technical developments, producing a wide variety of wares including red and black earthenwares, red stonewares, agates, salt-glazed stoneware and cream-coloured earthenware. His stonewares ranged from simple tavern wares to elegant table services and he also modelled earthenware figures.

Whieldon is known chiefly for his tortoiseshell wares (although a number of north Staffordshire potteries made similar pieces from the mid-eighteenth century onwards). In the case of both these and his agate wares either the body or the glaze of an item such as a knife-handle would be formulated to imitate the natural material. Agate ware was produced by partially mixing together clays of different colours in such a way that the finished piece took on a marbled appearance similar to that of the stone from which the ware takes its name. In the case of tortoiseshell ware colouring oxides were dusted on to the transparent glaze. Initially only manganese was used, which gave a brown-pink finish, but soon a whole range of different oxides was introduced that produced greens, yellows, dark browns, purples and greys, the degree of irregularity varying according to the colour absorbed into the thickly applied glaze. Whieldon also made black-glazed wares as well as a range of pottery with coloured glazes that were sometimes given marbled effects. Since these pieces are unsigned, accurate identification is difficult – hence the frequent use of the term 'Whieldon-type'.

In 1754 Whieldon took into partnership the young Josiah Wedgwood, an arrangement that was to work exceptionally well on both sides. Wedgwood was industrious and ambitious, and Whieldon, not only a master potter but an astute businessman, was content to allow the younger man the freedom to develop his own range of wares. One of the projects on which Wedgwood was engaged at Fenton was the development of

Dessert plate. Staffordshire, Wedgwood, *c.* 1774. Creamware, decorated with a view of Castle Acre Castle in Norfolk, based on an engraving by William Ellis dated 18 December 1772, after a drawing by Thomas Herne. The piece was inadvertently decorated with the oak-leaf border of the dinner service rather than the ivy-leaf of the dessert service and was therefore not forwarded with the rest of the set to Russia as part of the 'Frog' service made for Catherine the Great. Diameter 25 cm (10 in).

Tureen with lid and stand, and cream bowl with lid and stand. Staffordshire, Wedgwood, *c.* 1775–85. Earthenware with painted decoration. Height (tureen) 30 cm (12 in); cream bowl 15 cm (6 in).

improved colours and glazes for the agates and creamwares. Together he and Whieldon perfected a transparent green glaze and this was used successfully on teapots and other vessels modelled in a variety of shapes, many of them derived from natural forms. These included pineapples and melons (reflecting the widespread popularity of the exotic fruits that had recently begun to be imported into Britain) as well as more familiar foodstuffs such as cabbages and cauliflowers. As a result of the fine workmanship and skilful interpretation that went into the making of these wares, and their richness of colour, their appearance is not at all crude but possesses a free quality that was widely emulated.

JOSIAH WEDGWOOD

Along with potters such as Whieldon, Josiah Wedgwood (1730–95) played a significant role in transforming the diverse scattering of small, independent pottery workshops that were operating in the area now known as Stoke-on-Trent into what was to become arguably the world's leading centre of ceramic production. Wedgwood, whose family had a long history of pottery-making, was quick to embrace the latest business methods and responded energetically to developing markets, showing a particular interest in the growing demand for more refined pots that could compete in quality with imported oriental and Continental porcelain. His sound artistic judgement, dogged pursuit of the highest standards of technical excellence and extraordinary talent for organization (aided by a marked flair for publicity) laid much of the groundwork for the continuing industrialization of the British pottery industry over the following century.

Born the thirteenth child of Thomas Wedgwood (1685–1739), proprietor of the Churchyard Pottery at Burslem in the heart of 'The Potteries', Josiah Wedgwood helped in the family business after the death of his father and was apprenticed at the age of fourteen to his brother Thomas for a period of five years. In 1754 the still young Josiah went into partnership with Thomas Whieldon, for whom he carried out many projects, including the development of a range of coloured glazes. Five years later he set up a factory on his own account at the Ivy House in Burslem, where he made all the contemporary varieties of Staffordshire pottery, much of the work engine-turned to achieve crisp, clean forms. His output included blackware, salt-glazed stoneware, red stoneware, Whieldon-type wares and distinctive earthenwares in the new cream-coloured body.

Quick to recognize the value of other potters' technical improvements, Wedgwood wasted no time in incorporating these into his own work, especially in pursuit of his ambition to develop a truly fine, pale, hard-fired range of earthenware pieces for use in the home. By the early 1760s he was producing a ware described as 'a species of earthenware for the table, quite new in appearance, covered with a rich and brilliant glaze, bearing sudden alterations of heat and cold, manufactured with ease and expedition and consequently cheap, having every requisite for the purpose intended'.

Wedgwood's cream-coloured earthenware, based on strong, simple, elegant shapes, was markedly different in appearance from the hand-made red earthenware produced by many local potters. His forms often emulated the work of the silversmith both in style and in the restraint of their decoration, while his skilful use of the clay produced crisp, uncluttered lines. Wedgwood produced tablewares of virtually every kind, taking great care over the design of spouts, handles and lids to ensure that they were not only aesthetically pleasing but made to exactly the right proportions to perform their function efficiently. Decoration on these wares tended to be limited to simple feather-edged mouldings and beading and some pierced designs, with painted decoration confined to edges and borders. Wedgwood's creamwares, vastly superior in style and quality, were to provide a firm foundation for his future financial and artistic success. Cream-coloured earthenwares were also being produced on an increasing scale in other Staffordshire potteries and soon creamwares had virtually replaced white tin-glazed wares, although salt-glazed vessels continued to be made for food storage, for use in inns and for industrial purposes.

However, beyond question it was Wedgwood who perfected creamware. So high was the quality of his work that it won him royal patronage, and in 1756 Queen Charlotte, consort to George III, ordered a tea service to be made with 'a gold ground and raised flowers upon it in green'. This commission led to the range being renamed Queen's ware, and Wedgwood's success enabled him to take over larger premises nearby, which became known as the Bell Works. By this time the close-ground dense creamware body, made up of

Devonshire ball clay combined with flint and covered with a thin coating of lead glaze, was fast becoming accepted as the standard product of the ceramics industry. It was used in various forms not only by British potteries but also by manufacturers throughout much of Europe and America. The fine white body could be moulded, took detail well and was suitable for decoration with pierced open-work designs, while its pale surface made it ideal for the application of colours, in particular under-glaze blue. For a time Wedgwood sent his cream-wares to Liverpool to be decorated with transfer prints by the engraver John Sadler, often selecting suitable engravings himself from those available in books or from print shops. So popular did Wedgwood's work become that he frequently had difficulty in meeting demand and had to commission other Staffordshire potteries to supply him with blanks, which were then finished at his own factory.

It was in Liverpool in 1762 that Wedgwood met the merchant Thomas Bentley (1730–90), with whom he entered into a fruitful partnership a few years later, under an agreement restricted to the manufacture of vases and other ornamental pieces. Bentley's interest in neoclassicism, a style fast becoming fashionable in mainland Europe, engendered in Wedgwood a similar taste for the antique and together they planned the construction of an 'ideal' factory in which to produce the ornamental wares. This was to be built on a 350-acre estate two miles from Burslem, acquired in 1766. Wedgwood officially opened his new factory in 1769, calling it Etruria – a name inspired by the Greek vases that archaeologists had recently discovered in ancient Etruscan tombs. His wonder at the richness of ancient culture revealed by these finds, and by excavations at Pompeii and Herculaneum begun in 1738 and 1748, inspired him to apply the neoclassical style to many of his decorative and architectural pieces.

One of Wedgwood's greatest commercial, and indeed organizational, achievements was the fulfilment of an order from Catherine II of Russia for an extensive dinner and dessert service for fifty people, destined for use in the imperial palace near St Petersburg. Completed in 1774, this became known as the 'Frog' service from the emblem of this creature that appeared on all nine hundred and fifty-two of its individual pieces, each of which was

Blackware. Staffordshire, Wedgwood, *c.* 1790. First edition of the Portland vase. The original is a cameo-glass vase of the first century AD in the British Museum. Wedgwood made between thirty and forty copies of the 'first edition' and further editions followed. Height 25 cm (10 in).

enamelled in sepia and depicted its own unique view of an English country house and landscape scene. The creamware used for the Frog service was enhanced technically by the addition of china stone and china clay, which not only achieved an even lighter-coloured body, covered with a pale cream glaze, but enabled the pieces to be made even more thinly with no loss of strength. This new whiteware, often known as pearlware, easily rivalled porcelain in its delicacy and colour.

In about 1775 dry unglazed pots began to be made in the most famous of Wedgwood's ranges, his blue-and-white jasperware. The body was a fine-grained vitrified stoneware containing carbonate or sulphate of baryta, known as cawl, which was obtained from Derbyshire. Although the body was most commonly coloured blue, a number of different stains were devised, including sea-green and yellow. The forms of the ware, derived from the shapes of classical Greek vases, were decorated with fine semi-translucent applied reliefs of classical motifs such as draped figures, portrait heads and garlands of flowers. In addition to a variety of vessel forms, the process was used to make fine jasper cameos, which were sent in large quantities to the Birmingham firm of Boulton and Watt to be mounted in cut steel jewellery. The form and decoration of many jasperware pieces were based on French or Italian prints of classical subjects. To work on the forms and the detailed relief modelling on the unglazed stonewares Wedgwood employed several leading sculptors, notably John Flaxman (1726–95) and his son, also called John (1755–1826). The most notable technical achievement within the jasperware range was to be the production in 1789 of the black Portland vase, of which a series of copies were produced. This piece was based on the Roman original that had been made in dark blue glass with white figures in relief and was owned by the Duke of Portland. Jasperware remains the range most closely associated with the Wedgwood name and continues to be produced at the Wedgwood factory, now located in Barlaston near Stoke-on-Trent.

Even as the high-quality jasperware was consolidating Wedgwood's position at the forefront of the ceramics market, he was devising yet more new ranges, including the redware known as rosso antico, ornamented with applied decoration in clay of a contrasting colour.

Impressive technical and aesthetic developments were also taking place on the architectural side of the business. In the late 1770s the ranges of ware that Wedgwood created at Etruria became increasingly ambitious, both artistically and technically, his neoclassical forms having become heavily influenced by the architectural and decorative work of the Adams brothers. He made imaginative use of the creamware body, producing vases in antique form and decorating them with a variety of glazes that imitated naturally occurring semi-precious stones such as agate as well as porphyry, marble and fine-grained granite.

The first body used by the Wedgwood–Bentley partnership for ornamental purposes had been the fine-grained black composition known as basalt ware, which may well have been developed from a mixture devised originally by the Elers brothers, although this has not been proven. The unglazed black basalt body, which was sometimes decorated with red figures in a style inspired by ancient Greek pottery, was used in the production of pieces that

included intaglio and relief plaques as well as vases and ewers.

Wedgwood's business acumen made him well aware of the need to market his ceramics in an active manner by presenting them to potential purchasers at every opportunity. Having opened a London showroom in Newport Street in 1768, to which pots were sent by canal and sea, six years later he set up another in Greek Street, where he famously exhibited the Frog service that had just

Chestnut bowl with cover and stand. English, Leeds factory, 18th–19th century. Cream-coloured earthenware with pierced decoration. Height 25 cm (10 in).

The Wedgwood 'Pegasus' vase. England, Staffordshire, Etruria (Stoke-on-Trent), 1786. Pale blue-and-white jasperware with white reliefs, designed by John Flaxman (the younger). Height 46 cm (18.4 in).

been completed for Catherine the Great and later (1790) a Portland vase from the first edition of this piece. In 1783 Wedgwood published his first ever pottery catalogue, of the Queen's ware, an innovation that reflected a new-found confidence in the extent to which industrial mass-production was sufficiently advanced to allow wares to be produced in reliable quantities to a uniform standard. These Wedgwood creamwares were made in large volumes and exported extensively to the Continent, where they were soon copied by European factories, including those at Meissen and Vienna.

In addition to being a successful manufacturer and retailer of ceramics, Josiah Wedgwood was a committed supporter of liberal and humanitarian causes such as the anti-slavery movement and the American struggle for independence, even becoming involved in the early stages of the French revolution. He was also active in encouraging the construction of roads and canals, which he considered essential to the expansion of British industry. On his death in 1795 he left a fortune of some £250,000 and a business that had gained an international reputation both for the exceptional quality of the work it produced and for the low price of its tablewares in comparison with products made in other materials, including silver. He also left a legacy of meticulous design and sound business practice to the Wedgwood company, which continues to produce high-quality ceramics, many of them still in the style of the original wares.

OTHER NOTABLE CREAMWARE MANUFACTURERS

Wedgwood's immense success proved a strong incentive for his competitors to produce creamwares of an equally high standard. Other notable Staffordshire potters working independently included Humphrey Palmer of Hanley and John Turner (d. 1786) of Lane End. Turner, who had served his apprenticeship with Whieldon, produced creamwares and stonewares of a quality easily matching that of Wedgwood's work, while much of his jasperware has a slight gloss, making it more akin to porcelain than to stoneware. Like Wedgwood, Turner prospered from his endeavours, exporting much of his work to Holland. The operation of his factory was later continued by his sons John and William, the former subsequently becoming manager of Minton and Co.

Bone china teapot, designed by James Hadley and described as 'Square kettle, with dragon handle, decorated with bronze and gold in Japanese style' by the Worcester Royal Porcelain Company, the manufacturer. English, design registered 1872. Height 19.5 cm (7.8 in).

Of particular note is the work of the Wood family of Burslem, known principally for their modelled figures. Aaron Wood (1717–85) was apprenticed to Thomas Wedgwood in 1731 and later became one of the most famous mould-cutters of his time, working for many of the Staffordshire potters, including Thomas Whieldon. His elder brother Ralph (1715–72) produced well-modelled figures and other wares with colourful glazes. Some of the most effective freely modelled figures of the time are attributed to the Woods, including some of the famous 'pew groups' (possibly originated by John Astbury), which normally depict two or three figures in stylized costumes, one of them often playing the bagpipes, sitting on a wooden pew. Ralph Wood is often credited with modelling the first of those quintessentially English ceramic pieces the Toby jugs, which typically take the form of a stout seated male figure holding a jug of beer and a pipe and wearing a three-cornered hat. Among other notable potters in the Wood family are Ralph's son, also named Ralph (1748–95), and Aaron's son Enoch (1759–1840).

Another important centre of creamware production was Leeds in Yorkshire, where the local industry revolved around the Green family's workshops at the Old Pottery, set up around 1760. The chief characteristic of Leeds ware is a smooth, glassy glaze with a faintly greenish tone said to be produced by its arsenic content. The distinctive decoration on the ware often consists of pierced or punched designs and twisted handles made of woven strands of clay with leaf and flower terminals, while some pieces are pierced with heart- and diamond-shaped motifs. The Leeds potters were evidently confident of the effectiveness of the pierced decoration as they left the remainder of the ware plain, relying on the strength of the form and the depth of the glaze to provide appeal. Other wares were transfer-printed, and some early enamelled decoration includes charming designs, mainly in red and black. Because much of the Leeds work is similar stylistically to that made in Staffordshire, in the absence of identifying marks it is not always easy to make accurate attributions.

In the late eighteenth century creamwares were also made at Temple Back, Bristol and Swansea in the west of Britain, in Liverpool, at Swinton and Castleford in Yorkshire, at Sunderland in County Durham and in Newcastle, Northumberland. On the Continent, similar wares were produced in France and Germany.

NINETEENTH-CENTURY POTTERY PRODUCTION

Throughout the nineteenth century British pottery companies were pre-eminent in the field of functional, hard-wearing and decorative tableware. The adoption of streamlined manufacturing methods and fine-quality transfer printing enabled them to produce wares in large quantities to a consistent standard. Major factories such as Wedgwood continued to dominate the making of tablewares in Stoke-on-Trent, but many others, of varying size, were in close rivalry for the new and expanding markets. Wedgwood's main competitors were large firms such as Spode and Minton, both of which had been established in the late eighteenth century but made their reputations during the nineteenth, initially through their success in the production of porcelain.

Josiah Spode (1733–97) served his apprenticeship, from 1749, with Thomas Whieldon, at that time Staffordshire's leading potter. Spode began producing his own work in 1761 and entered into various partnership arrangements before acquiring premises for himself. By 1776 he was running his own factory in Stoke. Here he employed as managers his two sons, Josiah and Samuel, who

China plate. England, Hull, Belle Vue Pottery, 1826–41. Ironstone, printed with the famous 'willow pattern' design. Among other products, Belle Vue Pottery produced a range of wares for domestic use, printed with a variety of landscapes or painted with floral designs, as well as 'novelty' wares decorated with mocha patterns.

became active on both the production and marketing sides of the enterprise. The younger Josiah Spode (1754–1827) had a particular awareness of fashionable taste and was soon to open the business's first London showroom in order to promote its wares to the discerning clientèle of the capital.

The Spode enterprise was progressive in outlook and initiated a series of innovative measures; it was the first Staffordshire factory to install a steam engine in order to grind materials such as flints and colours more efficiently. Early Spode products include blue-painted 'pearlware' (cream-coloured earthenware with a faint blue stain rendering it pale grey-blue), creamware, green-glazed earthenware and 'dry' stoneware such as black basalt and red stoneware. In 1784 Spode perfected a technique for printing patterns from hand-engraved copper plates on to unglazed biscuit, adapting this to produce the blue-and-white designs that were to prove by far the most popular of the factory's wares. The

Plate. Mason's 19th-century Ironstoneware, with oriental-inspired decoration and the original paper design.

Spode factory became one of the primary producers of blue-and-white printed pottery and, in common with Minton, did much to popularize the now universally familiar 'willow pattern'. Widely believed to have been introduced by Thomas Turner of Caughley in about 1780, the English willow pattern was based on a popular scene depicting a Chinese fable. To motifs of a willow tree and a pair of doves were added several features taken from other designs, including a pavilion and a lake with three Chinese people standing on a bridge.

On the sudden death of Josiah Spode the elder in 1797 his son Josiah Spode took control of the Stoke factory, leaving the London operation in the hands of his father's long-standing employee William Copeland and his own son William. It is Josiah Spode the younger who is credited with devising the first successful commercial formula, in 1800, for the English version of porcelain that became known as bone china – a strong, translucent, pure white body that gives a clear sound when tapped. By 1805 the Spode range of bone china wares was well established and generating a healthy profit. Following a visit by the Prince of Wales to the company's premises in 1806, Spode was appointed 'Potter and English Porcelain Manufacturer to His Royal Highness', which greatly added to the factory's prestige.

The history of Minton and Co. – which over the years has operated under a number of different company names – begins in 1793, when the highly successful transfer-print engraver Thomas Minton (1765–1836) moved into the production of pottery. Having already carried out engraving work for his future rivals Josiah Spode and Josiah Wedgwood, at first Minton concentrated on the production of blue-printed cream-coloured earthenwares with the aim of taking low-cost, high-quality tablewares to a wider market. From 1796, on completion of the construction of his Stoke factory, he sold large quantities of ware through his brother's retail outlet in Swallow Street, London, and also began exporting products to America. Pattern books of 1799 illustrate the diversity of form and decoration of Minton's hand-painted tea wares. In the nineteenth century the decoration became more lavishly ornate, and a varied range of functional wares was developed. Dissatisfaction with the general standard of design in ceramics led Minton to experiment with new, simpler tableware shapes. One notable set was designed under the supervision of Sir Henry Cole in 1846 and issued under the name of Felix Summerly, the declared intention being 'to obtain as much beauty and ornament as is commensurate with cheapness'. This tea service with its strong, clean lines continued in production until the end of the century.

Minton's sons Herbert and Thomas entered the firm in 1817 (though the latter was to leave in 1821) and as Thomas Minton and Sons the factory expanded into the production of more decorative and ornamental wares, some of them made on an impressively large scale. Tablewares in stoneware or Parian with relief-moulded decoration were also manufactured in large quantities. The Minton factory is also renowned for what came to be known as majolica ware. This white earthenware with brightly coloured glazes on technically accomplished and often highly elaborate forms was perfected by Joseph François Léon Arnoux and officially introduced at the Great Exhibition of 1851. The term 'maiolica', meaning the technique of painting coloured oxides on to an opaque white tin glaze, was modified to 'majolica' to describe tablewares and later also figures, ornaments, tiles and conservatory furniture that were coated with coloured glazes painted on to moulded forms with raised decoration. The best-known of Minton's majolica designs are those based on vegetable and floral forms, including green-glazed plates with moulded leaf designs. So successful was the new range that in 1852 the Sèvres factory in France set up an experimental majolica workshop with a view to entering into competition. The Minton factory was among those that imitated the work of the French Renaissance potter Bernard Palissy (see chapter 5), producing dishes modelled in relief with realistic representations of plants and animals and coloured with deep rich glazes. Also copied were the coloured earthenwares of the Italian Lucca della Robbia (1400–82), while another popular Minton range was a group of eccentric teapots in the shape of Chinese figures, monkeys, boats, fish and cats. Other producers of high-quality majolica include Josiah Wedgwood and George Jones (d. 1893), who established the Trent works in Stoke, where he manufactured serving dishes, vases and candelabra.

Minton and Co. was heavily influenced by the Gothic revival that gained momentum in England in the first half of the nineteenth century. In the 1840s Herbert Minton (1793–1858) collaborated with the architect Augustus Pugin (1812–52) to manufacture such wares as encaustic and printed tiles based on medieval designs for domestic, ecclesiastical and public buildings. Minton floor tiles were used extensively at the Palace of Westminster.

In common with firms such as F. & R. Pratt and Copeland, Minton also developed large-scale terracottas, although at the forefront of the market for architectural ceramics was Henry Doulton (discussed in later sections of this chapter and in chapter 12), whose company became well known for its monumental sculptures and water fountains as well as its many other ranges of products. One of Doulton's most impressive architectural pieces was to be the large public fountain, designed by John Sparkes and modelled by George Tinworth, erected in London's Kennington Park. The fashion for terracotta extended to the production of decorative plaques for architectural use and led a number of small potteries to specialize in the medium, for example the Watcombe Art Pottery, which concentrated on small-scale terracotta manufacture.

Among the other innovative nineteenth-century manufacturers was Mason's, founded in 1813 when Charles James Mason (1791–1856), of Lane Delph in Staffordshire, took out a patent for 'Mason's Patent Ironstone China', which he had developed from an opaque earthenware originated by John Turner of Lane End. Mason devised a series of bodies: one was strong and white while another incorporated powdered slag of ironstone as one of its ingredients. Much of Mason's ware is printed in blue and painted with 'Japan patterns'. The white-firing body proved very popular and this encouraged a number of other potteries to venture into the production of similar wares. In addition to tablewares, the range of items manufactured included moulded fireplaces, bedposts, punch bowls and footbaths, all of which were heavily decorated in the oriental style.

Lustre ware jug. Sunderland, Garrison Pottery, probably from the partnership of Dixon and Co., *c.* 1815–20. Earthenware, cream body with transfer and coloured decoration depicting the Wear Bridge with sailing ships, the reverse with the 'Northumberland 74', the verse 'Have communion with few' and, beneath the lip, 'Mr George Wilds, Norwich'. Height 21 cm (8.25 in).

SMALLER POTTERY FACTORIES

In addition to the diverse and large-scale activities of the leading factories such as Wedgwood, Spode and Minton, lower-volume production, often of specialist ranges, was carried out at numerous smaller factories, not only in the Staffordshire area but throughout Great Britain. 'Cottage' earthenware could be produced at low cost by small potteries, whose output often catered for particular aspects of contemporary taste. It was the desire for novelty pieces among the rapidly expanding populations of urban centres that prompted the production of ranges such as mocha and lustrewares. Mocha, which first became popular around 1830 and is characterized by branching decoration resembling the markings of the ornamental quartz known as mocha stone, was used on pieces including measuring jugs, ale mugs, chamber pots, jugs, pitchers, and shrimp and nut measures. Careful preparation of the slips was necessary to give a natural look to the branch, feather and moss patterns, which were usually executed in brown or black on a background of brown, cream, orange or green.

On the more ornate lustrewares patterns tended to be painted quickly on to the pots, with eye-catching effect. Lustrewares were produced in large quantities during the nineteenth century, not only in Staffordshire but also in Newcastle and particularly Sunderland in the north-east of England, in Leeds in Yorkshire and in Swansea, Wales. A principal difference from the lustre used around a thousand years earlier in the Middle East (see chapter 4) was that this version was prepared by combining metal salts in an oil base. During firing a layer of metal would be deposited on the surface of the pot with great reliability and without the need for a complicated reduction process. Applied thickly and evenly, the lustre gave the appearance of genuine metal; this method was often used on forms copied directly from silverware, although it was later replaced by electroplating on metal. Applied thinly, the lustre took on an iridescent quality producing bluish, reddish, purple or mother-of-pearl reflections. This technique was frequently used in combination with others, primarily transfer printing or 'resist', whereby designs were created by leaving parts of the pot plain. Verses and quotations are commonly found on lustreware jugs and plates and the printed

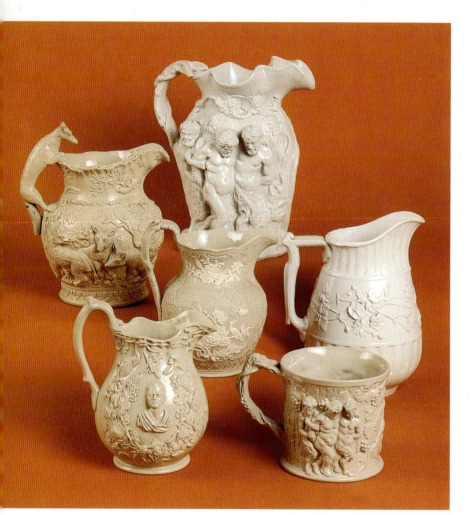

Six jugs. Staffordshire, Minton, *c.* 1830–92. Stoneware with relief-moulded decoration, including 'Sir Walter Scott' jug, grey jug with foxes and dogs, pale blue 'Bacchus' jug, grey 'Bacchus' mug, grey jug with white relief-applied birds and flowers, and grey jug with relief-moulded strawberry plant border. Height (tallest) 22 cm (8.75 in).

the piece. Occasionally jugs were cast in the shape of the natural object represented in the design, for example a log or a lily-of-the-valley plant. An advertisement of 1855 illustrates a wide selection of these jugs, bearing such titles as Stag, Apostles, Oak, Grape Gatherer and Babes in the Wood. Each is in the appropriate Gothic, rococo or Renaissance style, with the jug and modelling formed as one.

Parian porcelain was made by combining feldspar with china clay to produce a low-temperature vitrified white body, which was first used for the production of figures and portrait heads that were left unglazed, although a glaze was used on the tablewares and vases for which the technique was later adapted. The Belleek factory, established in 1857 on the River Ferne in County Fermanagh in Ireland, produced a range of porcelain vases in which a thinly made ivory-white body was ornamented with natural forms and covered with a white iridescent glaze. Parian porcelain allowed pots to be made extremely thinly, often in quite complex shapes. In Stoke-on-Trent W. H. Goss used a similar type of body for a range of wares that included portrait busts, and from around 1880 until the outbreak of the Great War in 1914 the firm produced small pieces bearing heraldic motifs such as the shields of schools and universities and the arms of English towns and coastal resorts. Much of this 'heraldic china', as it became known, was produced for sale as souvenirs to the growing numbers of seaside holidaymakers and families enjoying the day trips to the coast that were becoming increasingly popular in Britain. The Goss range of small vessel forms was subsequently extended to include accurate copies, in full architectural detail, of buildings such as lighthouses, chapels and the homes of famous people.

Large and small factories alike made extensive use of the process of transfer-printing designs on to their pottery, especially the popular English blue-and-white willow pattern. Printed wares were the cheapest to produce and were originally monochromatic, although further colours were later introduced. One of the principal firms to experiment with multi-colour printing was the Staffordshire company of F. & R. Pratt (established in 1774), which operated at the Fenton Potteries. The transfers used were mainly pictorial and the pots were consciously made in such a way as to show the decoration to its best advantage. At different

designs are not only decorative but act as documentary evidence of events, personalities, pious mottoes and even licentious verses of the time.

Equally popular were the ornately moulded and decorated jugs and other decorated containers that were produced in white or cream-coloured stoneware, usually unglazed, by many English factories. These pieces were usually made in a body of unglazed white clay, or occasionally terracotta, which, as the body vitrified during the firing, acquired a soft sheen. During the 1840s Gothic designs were fashionable, but these later gave way to classical or Renaissance motifs, for example amorini disporting themselves among garlands of flowers. Some objects were decorated with contemporary genre scenes such as a group of gypsies or a boy bird-nesting, but among the most successful designs were the simpler motifs of a plant that appeared to grow from a rusticated handle and extended in a carefully arranged pattern over the entire surface of

Six vases. Doulton, various decorative techniques for designs entitled 'Silicon', 'Natural Foliage', 'Chiné', 'Carara', 'Impasto' and 'Marqueterie'. Height (tallest) 28 cm (11 in).

times the company used local and exotic scenes with Chinese details, a rural cottage with crows and rustic figures, intricate baroque borders and Gothic designs.

Small ornamental pieces known as 'flatbacks' became popular in the second half of the nineteenth century. Made as single or grouped earthenware figures and animals, these were intended for display on a mantel shelf or in a similar position where they could stand flat against a vertical surface. Flatbacks were typically pressed, moulded or slip-cast in simple shapes, occasionally with finer detail added, then painted in a range of bright underglaze colours or enamels and gilded. These ornaments were offered as fairground prizes as well as being sold cheaply around the county. Modelled with a naive charm and always vividly coloured, the figures reflected topical, religious, heroic or mythological themes and were attractive, lively and frequently humorous. From 1851 onwards, Sampson

Smith (1813–78) of Longton in Staffordshire was one of the many potters who produced flatbacks.

THE GREAT EXHIBITION

The official aim of the Great Exhibition of 1851, staged in Joseph Paxton's purpose-built Crystal Palace in Hyde Park, London (later re-erected in Sydenham), was to celebrate the magnificent technical achievements of 'the industries of all nations'. In practice, however, the majority of its many thousands of exhibits showcased Britain's own manufacturing prowess, extolling the country's perceived status as the 'workshop of the world'. On display were not only huge items of machinery and all manner of manufactured goods but also a variety of sculptures and ceramics. Among the items shown by Minton were a series of Parian figures (several of which were purchased by Queen Victoria), a Parian fireplace in Renaissance style, and scaled-down models of public statues.

Cream tureen. Minton, *c.* 1851. Bone china and Parian with painted fruit, flowers and exotic birds. Height 26 cm (10.25 in). The tureen was purchased by Queen Victoria at the Great Exhibition of 1851.

Water filter. Staffordshire, Doulton, *c.* 1870. Stoneware, decoration by Eliza Simmance. Height 35 cm (14 in).

The range of tablewares and ornamental and sculptural ceramics exhibited by British manufacturers amply demonstrated the scope for ingenuity presented by the latest production techniques. However, the standard of design evident in the displays did little to support Britain's claim of world leadership. On the contrary, the inferiority of much of the British design in comparison with that of the foreign wares on show was all too apparent, despite the care taken by manufacturers to select only their best work or even to produce pieces specifically for the event. Britain's ceramic design showed itself to be for the most part either unduly derivative of continental work, such as the French Sèvres porcelain, or generally overelaborate and fanciful.

Typical of the ceramics guilty of such failings were two vases, each about a metre high, that had been specially made by Charles Meigh and Sons. Modelled in relief with foliage and birds and decorated with painted scenes, they were described in the catalogue as: 'Large vases, with portraits of the Queen, and view of the Exhibition Buildings; and of Prince Albert.' The vases were awarded a prize medal, perhaps as much for their sheer size and complexity as for their elegance; they are now in the Victoria and Albert Museum. The main Wedgwood exhibit took the form of an artificial cave filled with terracotta pots, intended to simulate an Etruscan tomb. Represented in the 'tomb' were aspects of the Gothic, neoclassical, neo-Renaissance, neo-rococo and Celtic revival styles.

Overall, the Great Exhibition was a huge success for Britain. Not only did its innovative approach to the presentation and marketing of goods and equipment attract more than six million visitors and generate worthwhile business for many of the participating companies, but it set the standard for a whole series of similar international exhibitions promoting art and industry across the world – notably in Paris, New York and Philadelphia. The second London exhibition took place in 1862. Britain's ceramic manufacturers were well represented at most of the international fairs and exhibitions held in the remainder of nineteenth century, with leading pottery companies such as Minton and Copeland frequently winning medals.

Despite its favourable outcome in other ways, the 1851 exhibition raised widespread misgivings about the standard of industrial design in Britain, prompting much reappraisal of the interrelationship between the styling and function of manufactured goods. This contributed to a proportion of the substantial proceeds from the event being invested in a plan to construct a comprehensive centre for the arts and sciences in the capital. It was this scheme that led to the foundation of the large complex of museums and institutions now at South Kensington, including – most significantly for the future of ceramic design – the Royal College of Art (so named by Queen Victoria in 1896). Closely linked with the origins of the college are those of the Victoria and Albert Museum, established at the same time to house collections demonstrating 'the application of fine art to objects of utility', thus increasing the public's appreciation of good design. However, the ceramic forms first displayed by the museum tended to be informed as much by fashion as by the strength and durability of the design.

Catalogue, page advertising the sale of decorated pedestal water closets, 19th century. Published by Doulton & Co., of Lambeth, London, Paisley and Paris.

CERAMIC PIPES AND SANITARYWARE

In the mid-eighteenth century the son of John Philip Elers approached Josiah Wedgwood with a proposition for making ceramic pipes for drainage purposes, but for once Wedgwood's vision and entrepreneurial spirit deserted him and he rejected the idea. In the event, it was to be another hundred years before a substantial nationwide market for these products began to emerge. By the early nineteenth century the population of Britain's cities and towns was rising at an alarming rate, with the lack of adequate sanitation in urban areas giving rise to serious hygiene problems and repeated outbreaks of disease; 1831 saw the first in a series of cholera epidemics that affected all levels of society. As the need for efficient sewage treatment and supplies of clean water grew increasingly urgent, social reformers campaigned vigorously for the creation of a workable system of public sanitation. In 1842 the barrister Sir Edwin Chadwick (1801–90) published a paper in which he put forward the idea of using glazed pipes for a network of sewers and drains to serve entire communities. The ceramic manufacturer Henry Doulton later joined Chadwick in pressing for sanitary reform, stressing the need for improvements to piping and more effective methods of joining the pipes together.

A number of pottery manufacturers in Stoke-on-Trent and elsewhere set up production to meet the anticipated demand for sewage and water pipes, but Doulton was probably the first to realize the extent of the potential market. His company was ideally placed to serve the urgent need for piping in the capital, where the public health risk posed by overcrowding and insufficient sewerage was acute. Doulton persuaded his father and brother to form a separate company to specialize in the production of sanitarywares, and in 1846 Henry Doulton and Co. was established in Lambeth High Street, initially to manufacture sewer and water pipes in vitrified salt-glazed stoneware, largely by mechanical methods. The factory remained in operation at this site until the early 1950s.

The passing of the 1848 Public Health Act prompted other firms to enter into competition by producing cheaper alternatives in earthenware, but their pipes failed to rival the strength of those made by Doulton, which became widely used for domestic and public drainage in Britain and overseas.

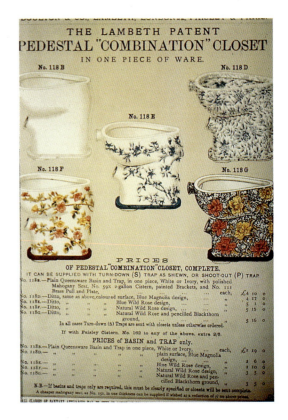

Doulton later produced other sanitary furniture, including a stoneware water closet and the world's first stoneware sink to replace the unhygienic traditional type made of stone.

The call for proper sanitation and clean water supplies intensified after Prince Albert's death in 1861 from what was thought to be typhoid and a near-fatal fever later suffered by the Prince of Wales. For the first time running water began to be pumped under pressure, making it available both up- and downstairs in the homes of the wealthy and enabling bathrooms and lavatories to be installed. Further developments in domestic plumbing included the invention of a system of isolating or 'disconnecting' living spaces from sewers by means of a water trap that sealed out gas emissions and unpleasant odours. In addition a more efficient water closet, using flushing water, was perfected by sanitary engineer Thomas Crapper, who invented a syphonic system and 'Crapper's Valveless Waste Preventer'. The pottery industry's practice of decorating ceramics was extended to the new lavatory basins, usually finished with a white opaque glaze, and many were transfer-printed with blue designs.

Hundreds of miles of stoneware piping were laid and as the efficiency of domestic and industrial plumbing improved through the use of the trap and syphon a new industrial sector gradually built up around the production of sanitary fittings. Vitrified earthenware products such as pedestal water closets, washbasins and urinals were produced by pottery factories specially equipped to handle and fire these large and often complex forms. Many of the original sanitaryware manufacturers, such as Shanks, Johnson Brothers, Ideal Standard, Armitage and Twyfords, are in operation to this day.

Within the ceramics industry as a whole, by the late nineteenth century more efficient production methods had been developed. Almost all earthenware products (with the exception of closed forms such as teapots and coffee pots) were made by jollying and jiggering, whereby clay is pressed by an armature into or over a rotating plaster of Paris mould, although a small of number of shapes were still thrown on the potter's wheel. Until the mid-twentieth century these processes were carried out largely by hand, even in the making of sanitary items such as washbasins and lavatory bowls, for which often quite intricate moulds were needed.

Another technical development that helped transform the production of many types of ware involved the creation of shapes by slip-casting – that is, pouring a specially prepared clay slip into a plaster of Paris mould. Casting slip, a form of liquid clay, is prepared by adding a deflocculant such as a strong alkali to any ordinary clay slip, which increases the proportion of clay to liquid, so reducing the water content. The slip is poured into the mould and left until a thick skin or wall has formed against the mould's inner surface, at which stage the surplus slip is drained away. When the casting of sanitarywares began, the various pieces were often made in separate moulds and when leather-hard joined (or luted) together manually. For some shapes an efficient production method was that of extruding clay from a giant mill, which proved especially suitable for making sewage and water pipes. The production of sanitaryware, and other ceramics, has continued to evolve. One of the more recent developments is that of dust-pressing dry clay into moulds under high pressure, the great advantage of which is that it requires virtually no water, so the pieces dry quickly with minimal shrinkage or distortion. Even in today's advanced manufacturing environment, however, the ceramic industry continues to require skilled labour.

Doulton and Co.

The business of Doulton and Co. was built up by its diligent and ambitious founder, John Doulton (1793–1873), who served his apprenticeship in London at the Fulham Pottery, a workshop run by descendants of John Dwight. In 1815 Doulton invested all the funds he had in a small potworks in Vauxhall Walk, Lambeth, entering into partnership with Martha Jones, who had inherited the business from her late husband. The foreman, John Watts, was also taken into partnership and by 1826 (by then operating as Doulton Watts) the factory was manufacturing in quantity a range of utilitarian salt-glazed stoneware vessels, notably bottles for ink, black-leading and beer. Also produced were a variety of decorative items ranging from inkwells, dog and bird whistles, moneyboxes in the form of cottages and miniature replicas of police truncheons to spirit flasks both in novelty shapes such as fish and pistols and as figurative representations of prominent people. Around 1830 the building of two new kilns enabled the factory to extend its production to architectural terracotta wares for gardens, chimneypots, roof tiles and large ornamental pieces. Working with a moulder, Doulton threw much of the larger ware on the potter's wheel, often supplying huge jars to special order. Other products made by the company included acid-resistant chemical vessels in stoneware.

Of the five of John Doulton's eight children who went into the business, by far the most go-ahead and visionary was his second son, Henry (1820–97), who joined the firm in 1835 after attending University College School. A few years later Henry was to celebrate his twenty-first birthday by making a 300-gallon chemical transport jar, which his father proudly boasted was 'the largest stoneware vessel in the world'. During the 1840s the firm became a major producer of drainpipes, gullies and basins as well as decorative architectural ceramics for the construction industry, and the increasing need for, and profitability of, its utilitarian ceramics led to the opening of further stoneware pipe factories in Lancashire and the West Midlands.

In addition to its industrial products the firm manufactured large quantities of high-quality tableware, as well as a range of pieces such as hunting jugs and teapots, often decorated with relief patterning. Many of these vessels were inscribed with the company names and slogans of distillers and brewers, for whom they were a convenient mode of advertising in the many public houses being built at the time. Other small items produced included ashtrays, tankards, bottles, pump-handles and ornamental ware. In common with many other pottery manufacturers, Doulton and Co. also made water filters, in plain brown or cream, packed with a special charcoal that purified the water. The great danger of cholera during this period heightened public awareness of the need to drink clean water and greatly stimulated the demand for such filters, while Doulton's design of an improved version incorporating blocks of carbon within the stoneware container gave him an edge over his competitors.

Henry Doulton was adventurous both as a potter and as a businessman. His contributions to the company's product range included such inno-

vations as a water-tight ceramic screw for hot-water bottles, an air-tight storage jar and a steam-driven potter's wheel. He even turned his hand to reproducing historical pieces, exhibiting a copy of a sixteenth-century Rhenish salt cellar at the International Exhibition of 1862.

Prosperous and deeply interested in art, in the 1860s Doulton embraced the concept of 'art pottery' (see chapter 12) and as an initial departure in this direction formed a creative partnership with the nearby Lambeth School of Art through its art master John Sparkes. The Doulton factory fired

Stockyard at Royal Doulton's pipe factory in Erith, Kent, *c.* 1954.

ABOVE RIGHT:
Insulator manufacturing at Doulton's factory in Tamworth, Staffordshire, 1950s.

many pieces for the School, including large terracotta portrait plaques.

In 1877 Doulton purchased a major share in the Nile Street Pottery at Burslem in Staffordshire and in due course the business's entire manufacturing operation was transferred to Stoke-on-Trent. When Henry Doulton was knighted by Queen Victoria he became the first potter ever to receive this honour. In 1901 Edward VII conferred on the company the royal warrant, giving it specific leave to use the name Royal Doulton.

CERAMICS FOR INDUSTRY

From the late eighteenth century throughout the nineteenth demand built up for ceramic products for use within industry. Clay proved an ideal medium for the vessels used in many industrial processes. Not only was it versatile and relatively inexpensive, but high-temperature firing rendered it strong and non-porous; factories handling chemicals found ceramic containers suitable for the safe storage of often highly corrosive materials. Even such illustrious pottery manufacturers as Wedgwood responded to this growing market by

developing special bodies and producing ceramic vessels for laboratory and industrial purposes.

Such was the demand from developing industries for ever more precise shapes that some ceramic manufacturers began to focus their production on industrial products. Recognizing the large potential market for components connected with new technologies such as telephony and telegraphy, in 1862 Bullers Ltd moved from Devon to Staffordshire and began specializing in porcelain for use in electrical equipment. The company produced mainly insulators, sometimes of huge dimensions. Both porcelain and high-fired earthenware proved ideal materials in which to make electrical insulators, not least because they possessed the essential attribute of not conducting electricity. The vitrified body was not only relatively cheap to make but strong, clean, durable and capable of being shaped into complex forms ranging in size from tiny washers to the vast electrical insulators themselves. The insulator body did not require a high level of plasticity but it did need great mechanical strength when fired. Usually made up of half clay, a quarter quartz and a quarter feldspar, this strong body, appropriately adapted, proved equally suitable for the manufacture of industrial components such as spark plugs for use in internal combustion engines.

Bullers also made small ceramic items such as door furniture, and porcelain chemical containers in various sizes. Unlike tablewares, which had to be fashionably designed with a view to attracting new markets, porcelain vessels destined for industrial use were strictly utilitarian in form and devoid of decoration. The result was a range of ware often seen as epitomizing the worthy concept of 'fitness for purpose', such products being held up as examples of good design even before the 'modernist' trend for simplicity and functionality. Bullers Ltd is also noted for setting up a small art studio at its factory in the 1930s, in collaboration with Gordon Forsyth (see below) and under the direction of Anne Potts (b. 1918). Producing figures and ornamental wares as well as a range of tablewares, the studio continued in operation until 1952.

THE TWENTIETH CENTURY

The Design and Industries Board was set up in 1915, but not until after the First World War did it begin to make headway in supporting initiatives deemed likely to further its main purpose – namely, to raise the general awareness of good commercial design. Actively pursuing a similar mission was the Scottish-born ceramic designer Gordon Forsyth (1879–1952). After working for ceramic manufacturers including Minton, Hollins and Co. and Pilkington Tile and Pottery Co., and in wartime serving as a designer with the Royal Air Force, Forsyth became a highly influential teacher at the Stoke-on-Trent School of Art. An enthusiastic modernist and strong advocate of simplicity in both form and decoration, he encouraged creativity and self-expression in his students and encouraged them to sign and date their work.

Despite spells of acute economic depression, during the inter-war years British society overall prospered, which boosted the campaign for design-consciousness. A new cult of interior decoration prompted manufacturers to introduce products in keeping with popular taste, and in the late 1920s and early 1930s pottery factories eagerly embraced

BELOW: 'Sung Vase' by Charles John Noke (1858–1941). Royal Doulton & Co., *c.* 1930. Bone china, painted in brilliant hues of red, purple, yellow and blue with dragon design. Height 45 cm (18 in).

BELOW RIGHT: Earthenware plate, designed by Alfred Powell for Josiah Wedgwood & Co., *c.* 1920. Diameter 27.5 cm (11 in).

the vogue for art deco, the fashionable style that had arisen (and derived its name) from the 1925 Exposition des Arts Décoratifs et Industriels Modernes in Paris. The predominant design trend from about 1890 until the outbreak of war in 1914 had been art nouveau, and while this still showed a certain measure of influence, in general art deco rejected its twisting, flowing lines and sinuous plant-like forms in favour of symmetrical geometric patterns and stylized rather than organic motifs.

Fierce competition among the four hundred or so potteries in Stoke-on-Trent made them keen to gain a commercial edge. Many new products were created and aggressive marketing strategies, often revolving around work commissioned from named designers, were implemented throughout the 1920s and '30s. It was a period that marked a number of innovations, for example the 'cube teapot', in

OPPOSITE: Tea set decorated with the famous Crocus design. Clarice Cliff, *c.* 1930.

RIGHT: Pesaro shell dish. Bone china by Mirko Bravi, Italian winner of Josiah Wedgwood Bicentennial Award. This form, inspired by Wedgwood's love of shells and designed with the aid of computer technology, went into limited production in 1995. Height 17.5 cm (7 in).

BELOW: Tea or coffee service. Pot, jug, sugar bowl, cups and saucers. Susie Cooper, *c.* 1930. Height (pot) 20 cm (8 in).

which function gave way to style, and in 1929 the first 'oven-to-table' wares, marketed by Wiltshaw & Robinson. Many manufacturers raised their public profile by exhibiting at promotional events such as the annual British Industries Fair and inviting contemporary artists – among them Frank Brangwyn, Laura Knight and Graham Sutherland – to create new 'modern' designs for existing shapes.

One of the best-known early twentieth-century ceramic designers is Clarice Cliff (1899–1972), who studied under Gordon Forsyth. Her bold work carried out in the art deco style between 1928 and 1939 is striking in both form and decoration. Cliff made dramatic use of strong, vibrant colour, stylized patterns and geometric motifs. Her well-known designs include the futuristic Sliced Circle, Melon and Crocus designs and the fantasy landscapes Summerhouse and Tree and House. The pieces were virtually all hand-painted, their forms based on cubes, cylinders, spheres and cones. In 1930 Cliff was appointed art director of the A. J. Wilkinson company's Newport works, and over the following decade nearly eight and a half million pieces were sold of the wares she designed for the Bizarre range. Very much capturing the spirit of the age and sold at affordable prices, Clarice Cliff's inventive ceramics successfully combined functionality with design and the influence of her style soon became evident in many other factories' wares.

At the Wedgwood factory original art deco work was produced under the art direction of skilled designers and decorators such as Alfred (d. 1960) and Louise Powell, who created painted decoration,

Daisy Makeig-Jones (1881–1945), responsible for the exotically ornate Fairyland Lustre range, and Victor Skellern (1909–66), another of Forsyth's protégés. More modern and crisp in style were the special ranges designed for Wedgwood during the 1930s by freelance artists: John Skeaping (1901–80) modelled stylized animal designs, while the New Zealand-born Keith Murray (1892–1981) created minimal 'modern' shapes with semi-matt coloured glazes on austere forms. Also employed by Wedgwood on a freelance basis, the artist and illustrator Eric Ravilious (1903–42) adapted many of his elegant engraved images to the restrictions of ceramics to design a series of successful printed patterns, including an alphabet set.

Other twentieth-century ceramic designers of note include Susie Cooper (1902–95), yet another former student of Gordon Forsyth. Among other ranges, she created lustrewares for A. E. Gray and Co., also designing tea- and tableware for various manufacturers, again including Wedgwood (of which her business became a part). Charlotte Rhead (1885–1947), born into a famous pottery family, created ceramic designs embracing many of the ideas of the Arts and Crafts movement (see chapter 12) and later produced art deco designs.

Ranges of matt-glazed wares were produced by Carter, Stabler & Adams and by Pilkington's Tile and Pottery Co., while much of the fine bone-china teaware manufactured by Shelley Potteries was designed by Eric Slater (b. 1902), who designed virtually all the ceramics for Shelley's display at the 1946 'Britain Can Make It' exhibition.

The Arts and Crafts Movement

GREAT BRITAIN, THE UNITED STATES, GERMANY AND AUSTRIA, SCANDINAVIA, THE NETHERLANDS, HUNGARY, ITALY

Art made by the people, and for the people,
as happiness to the maker and the user

WILLIAM MORRIS

Large vase, *c.* 1882–8, by William de Morgan, Merton Abbey period. Earthenware with painted design of mythical sea serpents and dragons in 'Persian' colours under a clear glaze. Height 100 cm (40 in).

As Britain entered the Victorian era the impact of the 'industrial revolution' was beginning to be felt throughout the land and concern was growing as to its social implications. Meanwhile a contest was brewing in the art world between the classicists and those in favour of a revival of Gothic styles in architecture and the decorative arts. Fervent advocacy of the Gothic on the part of such luminaries as Pugin, Ruskin and Morris, informed to a great extent by religious and moral considerations, was to give rise to a wider public debate on the perceived decline in overall aesthetic standards brought about by the mass-production of manufactured goods.

It was within this complex scenario that the Arts and Crafts movement emerged in England during the second half of the nineteenth century. Like so many others, this 'movement' gained its title in retrospect. At the time it centred largely around the far-reaching influence of William Morris's teachings and their manifestation in the form of attempts to revive or retain handicraft traditions in the face of increasing mechanization. The arts and crafts philosophy quickly found favour in Europe and by the turn of the century was being taken up with enthusiasm in the United States. In combination with rapid technological progress, it was to have a profound effect on the pottery industry worldwide.

As the efficiency of manufacturing processes increased, so too did the speed and technical reliability with which ever larger batches of wares

could be produced, while economies of scale helped keep costs low and prices competitive. At the same time continual refinements were being made to decorating techniques, greatly expanding the scope for innovation and providing every opportunity for manufacturers to design ceramic products for the mass market that were both visually appealing and functional. Instead, some of the larger factories became preoccupied with creating excessively intricate pieces to show off their new capabilities. Reaction to such work was to contribute to an increasing focus on the concept of 'applied art' and the establishment of specialized art and craft schools intended to ensure that high artistic standards were applied to the design of manufactured goods.

In England one of the first men in public life to express concern over the perceived ill effects of industrialization on artistic and social values was the influential art critic and social reformer John Ruskin (1819–1900), who declared that mechanization was dehumanizing, debasing both the quality of life of the workman and craftsmanship itself. His championship of a craft rather than a machine aesthetic was eloquently expressed in the second volume of *The Stones of Venice*, published in 1853, in which he argued that the Gothic style was superior to all others since it was the least mechanistic. A great many leading artists, architects, designers and writers of the Victorian era

came to espouse Ruskin's views, notably William Morris. While still an undergraduate at Oxford, Morris was deeply affected by Ruskin's chapter 'On the Nature of the Gothic' and his commitment to the ideal of a just society in which hand-crafted work was valued for the creative effort invested in its making and the craftsman spiritually uplifted by his labours. Building on Ruskin's theories, he

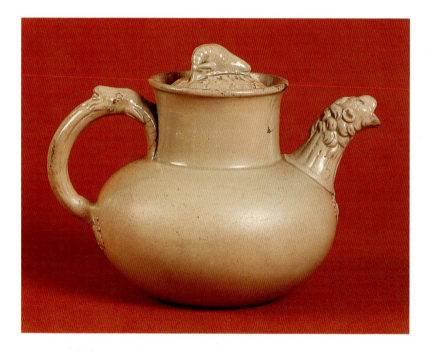

Teapot, *c.*1846, 'Felix Summerly', designed by Sir Henry Cole. Tinted earthenware with goats' heads on vine leaves modelled on the spout and handle, produced by Minton and awarded a silver medal by the Royal Society of Arts in 1846. Sir Henry Cole (1808–82), a civil servant, was keen to raise the standard of design in industry. His aim in the design of the teaset was 'to obtain as much beauty and ornament as is commensurate with cheapness'. Height 15.8 cm (6.3 in).

formulated strong views of his own which soon attracted a substantial following.

It was Morris's writings and example that formed the cornerstone of the Arts and Crafts movement, motivating a number of those working in architecture, handicrafts and both the fine and applied arts to join forces in order to promote simplified functional design, the natural use of local materials and the reinstatement of individual craftsmanship. The Arts and Crafts movement held much in common with the closely related Aesthetic movement, both factions being equally antagonistic towards the mechanical and unfeeling aspects of art in the industrial age. It did not, however, subscribe to the elitist and much-parodied doctrine of aestheticism that enshrined artists in an 'ivory tower' and advocated 'art for art's sake', a phrase coined to sum up the contention that art should be purely aesthetic and need serve no moral, religious or political purpose. One important belief that lay at the heart of both schools of thought was that art

should encompass not only painting and sculpture but also everyday objects such as factory-produced flower vases, umbrella stands and tableware. This contributed to the development of a large market for 'aesthetic' objects, which prompted a number of ceramic manufacturers to set up special departments to design and produce art pottery.

As the Arts and Crafts movement spread further afield, a new mode of design and decoration began to emerge. Impressed by the detailed flora in paintings by the Pre-Raphaelites and their followers, and even more so by the distinctive plant and flower motifs that became the hallmark of William Morris's work, European artists and designers turned to nature for their own inspiration. In France this led to the appearance towards the end of the nineteenth century of art nouveau, an extravagantly flowing asymmetrical art style typically featuring sinuous trailing and climbing plants portrayed in an exotic manner. The style was also characterized by the use of coiled or meandering curvilinear ornament, either in abstract arrangements or in more representational plant form, as well as details such as billowing hair, rippling water and draped fabric. In pottery, as in other fields, the art nouveau style was eagerly adopted as a means of breaking away from the relentlessness of historical revivals and moving towards an entirely fresh outlook on product design. Shapes from nature became incorporated into stylized decorative patterns and a new feeling for colour arose – features that would continue to be evident in the designs of pottery manufactured during the twentieth century.

Quickly taken up on an international scale, art nouveau retained its French title in Britain and America while other countries adopted alternative terms in their own language. The London store of Liberty and Co. (originally an Anglo-Japanese warehouse, founded in 1875 as A&C) embraced the new style wholeheartedly. It was soon commissioning ranges of specially designed products and became so closely associated with art nouveau that in Italy the style came to be referred to as the *stile Liberty*. The term 'art nouveau' is taken from the Maison de l'Art Nouveau opened in Paris in 1895 by the collector, publisher, designer and art dealer Siegfried Bing. French art potters whose work was displayed and sold in Bing's showroom include Alexandre Bigot, Pierre-Adrien Dalpayrat,

Edouard-Alexandre Dammouse, Auguste Delaherche, Clément Massier and Emile Müller.

Perhaps the major single influence on the European ceramics produced over the last few decades

Tiles made by Morris & Co. Earthenware, with decoration of floral motifs and ships in sail.

of the nineteenth century was that of Japanese stonewares and porcelains, particularly those associated with the tea ceremony. Following the re-establishment of trade with Japan in 1859 large quantities of Japanese artefacts were imported into Europe and many European artists and designers made visits to the East. The appearance of Japanese arts and crafts at the second of London's great international exhibitions in 1862 created an instant stir, and it was not long before fashionable ceramic pieces designed in the studios of British pottery factories began to follow a vogue for modified oriental styles. The equal impact made in France when Japanese wares were shown at the Paris exhibition of 1878 is reflected in certain aspects of the art nouveau style.

Artistic responses to the social and economic changes of the nineteenth and early twentieth centuries took many forms and varied from country to country. The following section looks at the work of notable ceramic designers, such as

William de Morgan and the Martin brothers in Great Britain, George E. Ohr in the United States and the artist-potters in France. It also discusses the work of the art studios that were established by manufacturers to meet growing demand for affordable but well designed and made decorative pottery, and also the art potteries set up specifically to produce art wares.

GREAT BRITAIN

In the nineteenth century rapid urban expansion, a substantial rise in population and the development of huge overseas markets greatly aided the growth of the British pottery industry, by then firmly centred around Stoke-on-Trent in Staffordshire. Not only did this area lead the world in both the quality and quantity of its ceramic products, but a series of significant technical improvements were made there. Keen to demonstrate the capabilities of its new techniques, the pottery industry deployed considerable ingenuity in creating complex and ostentatiously ornate objects that were frequently more spectacular than tasteful. Companies such as Minton and Worcester took great pride in displaying specially designed pieces at the 1851 Great Exhibition in London, but both the materialistic tone of this event and the poor design of many of the British exhibits drew severe criticism. The overall outcome was the dawning of an era in which good design began to be seen as essential to the success of mass-production.

WILLIAM MORRIS (1834–96)

In addition to being a prolific poet and writer and an articulate social idealist, William Morris was a gifted designer and a versatile craftsman. He lectured and wrote extensively on art and craft, arguing that the two should not be separated, and both his writings and his output as a designer and artist-craftsman had far-reaching influence. In the ceramics field they provided the impetus for considerable innovation, by pottery manufacturers such as Doulton and Co. and the Martin brothers as well as by individuals such as Morris's good friend William de Morgan.

As the leading light of the Arts and Crafts movement, Morris was a strong supporter of manual as opposed to machine manufacture and frequently expressed concern over the division between maker and designer. Believing that hand-crafted items enriched the life of both those who created them and those who used them, he was in favour of a craft-based system akin to that of the medieval guilds and argued for the artisan again to be involved in all aspects of production. Morris was also a committed socialist whose ideals centred around an egalitarian desire for art for the common man, although this, like so many of his views, was perhaps informed as much by a deep personal abhorrence of the soul-destroying effects of industrialization and what he perceived as the ugliness of the modern world as by socialism as such.

He did, however, practise what he preached by personally mastering a range of different crafts (even turning his hand to clay modelling) and creating a craft co-operative to build and decorate his new home, the Red House. In 1861 this developed into the manufacturing and interior decorating business of Morris, Marshall, Faulkner & Co. (later Morris & Co.). Founding the enterprise as a company of 'fine art workmen', Morris enlisted the collaboration of several members of his immediate circle, notably the architect Philip Webb as well as the painters Edward Burne-Jones, Dante Gabriel Rossetti and Ford Madox Brown. The Firm, as everyone involved referred to it, was to exert a fundamental and lasting influence on English interior design. It produced all manner of skilfully crafted hand-built furniture and furnishings for grand houses and churches, including metalwork, stained glass, tiles, fabrics, tapestries and wallpaper. Inevitably, hand-made work of such high quality proved expensive to produce and the enterprise did little to realize Morris's dream of art for the masses.

Inspired by Morris's theories on the vital link between art and craft, in 1884 a group of architects joined forces with decorators and craftsmen to form the Art Workers' Guild, making Morris an honorary member. This led, a few years later, to the formation of the Arts and Crafts Exhibition Society, the aim of which was to increase public awareness and appreciation of hand-making skills. Whilst initially sceptical about the scheme, over time Morris became so enthusiastic that he participated actively in the first exhibition in 1888 (by giving a demonstration of weaving) and took on the presidency of the society in 1891. The following year he was elected Master of the Art Workers' Guild, by then the nucleus of the Arts and Crafts movement.

WILLIAM DE MORGAN (1839–1917)

Although William Morris's own work in the ceramics field was largely restricted to creating painted designs for earthenware tiles, his opinions on arts and crafts stimulated numerous potters to experiment and to hone their skills by making objects using traditional hand-making techniques. The potter most closely associated with the Arts and Crafts movement is William de Morgan, a friend of Burne-Jones and Rossetti and a practising devotee of the Pre-Raphaelite style. De Morgan met Morris in 1863 and was persuaded to give up his fine art training to design stained glass for 'the Firm'. He also designed tiles and painted furniture panels, but his personal interest drifted increasingly towards the finishing aspects of ceramics. In 1872, wishing to develop his own work and in particular to try out new glazes, he set up a kiln at his parents' house in Fitzroy Square, London. It was not long, however, before his experiments caused a fire that destroyed the roof of the property.

From then on de Morgan concentrated all his efforts on ceramics, making painted wares based on Turkish and Persian forms and working on ways of accurately reproducing traditional lustre decoration effects. Now living in Chelsea, he set up a showroom nearby and employed several decorators to carry out his designs. His early tile patterns include flowers, birds and animals, often painted in Persian colours on a cream or white ground.

The reputation of William de Morgan grew, and in the late 1870s the distinguished artist Frederic Leighton commissioned him to produce, and advise on the installation of, special patterned wall tiles for a grand Arab Hall he was adding to the Kensington house he had designed and built in 1866. De Morgan's task was to produce tiles that would match as closely as possible genuine Islamic ones that Leighton and his friends had found in Cairo, Damascus and Rhodes. The installation at Leighton House, now an art gallery and museum, reveals no obvious difference between the authentic tiles and those made by de Morgan.

In 1882 de Morgan transferred his business to Merton Abbey in Surrey, close to the new riverside works of Morris and Co., where he established a pottery and employed a thrower to make vase forms. In 1888 (now married to the artist Evelyn Pickering) de Morgan formed a partnership with the architect Halsey Ricardo (1854–1928) with a

view to building a factory near his house in The Vale, Chelsea. In due course the business moved into the new Sands End Pottery in Fulham and together the two men began undertaking ambitious projects such as the innovative tiling that characterized Ricardo's buildings. In view of the complexity involved in translating de Morgan's often ornate designs from paper to ceramic, the pottery workshop had to be highly organized, with members of the skilled workforce allocated specific tasks and expected to carry out precise instructions.

Inspired to rediscover 'the lost Art of Moorish or Gubbio lustres' of the fourteenth and fifteenth centuries, de Morgan developed a range of rich lustre colours by employing traditional techniques, for example the use of thick clay pigment and a reduction, or smoky, firing. Much of his work was based on the use of copper and silver, the colours so produced including pink, yellow and grey. The lustre decoration was used to great effect on a limited range of shapes such as tile blanks and vessels, supplied by Wedgwood and other firms but mostly by Davis of Hanley in Staffordshire. Some of the larger shapes were specially thrown to de Morgan's design. His complex lustre effects were often achieved by the use of two or more lustres

and the designs, mostly of excellent quality, include animals, fantastic beasts, ornate swirling foliage and ships. So successful were the lustre pieces that in the mid-1890s de Morgan was commissioned by the P&O shipping line to make tile panels for its luxury liners. He also created relief designs for moulded tiles and plates by Ricardo. On the so-called Persian wares he attained a palette of brilliant blues, turquoise, green and clear red, which he used to create flowing designs painted on to a white slip underneath a clear glaze. Much of his colourful decoration has a strong affinity with William Morris's wallpaper and fabric designs.

De Morgan's work was costly to produce, however, and despite its wide artistic acclaim his business was never profitable. Production at the Sands End Pottery continued under his direction until 1907, the pottery itself remaining in operation for four more years, but thereafter de Morgan abandoned ceramics altogether, devoting the last years of his life to the writing of novels.

THE MARTIN BROTHERS
The brothers Robert Wallace, Charles, Walter and Edwin Martin were the first group of English potters to develop a method of working similar to

that used by most twentieth-century studio potters,
encompassing all aspects of small-scale production.
Their business was founded by Robert Wallace
Martin (1843–1923), the eldest of the four
brothers, who trained initially as a sculptor,
principally under one of Pugin's chief assistants,
and at that stage would have been influenced by
the Gothic revival. In 1860, the year in which his
brother Edwin was born, Wallace Martin became a
student at the Lambeth School of Art. For a while,
attending classes in the evening, by day he assisted
the sculptor Alexander Munro, at whose studio he
made his first terracottas. One of Wallace's fellow-
students at Lambeth was George Tinworth, who
was later to be recruited into Henry Doulton's
pioneering art pottery venture. From 1864 Wallace
studied at the Royal Academy Schools and by the
late 1860s he had set up his own terracotta workshop, the firing of his modelled sculptures being
carried out at Doulton's salt-glaze factory. His
production experience was gained by working at
potteries in Devon and, for a brief period around
1871, Staffordshire; he also decorated pots fired at

the famous Fulham Pottery originally established
by John Dwight.

Together with three of his five brothers, Wallace
Martin opened a studio at Pomona House, Fulham
in 1873, the work they produced there being fired
at local potteries. On the strength of the success of
this enterprise, in 1877 the Martin brothers moved
into a fully equipped workshop (which until then
had been a derelict soap factory) at Southall in
Middlesex, where they both made and fired salt-
glazed stoneware. Wallace was responsible for
modelling the Martin brothers' strange and innovative 'Wally' birds, grotesque-featured face jugs
and other sculpted items. The pottery produced
owl-like vessels throughout the many years it was in
production. The Martins' eccentric, medieval-style
creatures conjure up a mysterious world combining
aspects of both the real and the imaginary. The
heads are removable from the body, and although
not airtight the pieces may have been used as
tobacco jars. Many of the face jugs are modelled in
much the same spirit, with faces leering out of the
side of the jugs.

The pots made at Southall were salt-glazed in subdued colours and the use of painted oxides gave dark blues and purplish and dark browns. As well as decorative vases and jugs with relief, incised or painted decoration, the objects produced include larger architectural pieces such as fireplace surrounds and fountains, as well as chess sets and some tableware. Firings took place twice a year until 1899, when this was reduced to a single annual firing. Within the enterprise Charles Martin (1846–1910) served as business manager and also handled sales at the pottery's showroom in Brownlow Street, Holborn. On the recommendation of George Tinworth, the two youngest brothers, Walter (1857–1912) and Edwin (1860–1915), had both studied at the Lambeth School of Art as well as working for a while at Doulton and Co. before they joined the family business, where both of them contributed to the throwing and decorating of the pots. Walter tended to look after technical aspects of the work such as the coloured glazes, also becoming the most expert at the wheel, while Edwin was responsible for many of the pottery's fish and flower designs.

Thrown ware, especially vases and jugs, made up the majority of the workshop's output, although also made were punch bowls, lamp bases, puzzle jugs, double-walled vases, and miniature tea and coffee services. Stylistically the wares fall into three more or less chronological phases. The first is characterized by classical influences, with decoration carved in deep relief together with incised patterns; this style continued until the early 1880s. In the middle period the predominance of Renaissance and Japanese styles is evident in the softer, more subtly conceived shapes. Although colours and decoration remained subdued, cobalt blue was painted on the grey stoneware body and a rich deep-brown glaze was often applied. The shapes subsequently became simpler and more rounded. Incised patterns were used sparingly and Renaissance designs featuring formally arranged foliage appeared. In the final period, from around 1895, flowing art nouveau lines are introduced, this later work demonstrating an effective integration of form and decoration. A wider range of colours and textured surfaces derived from plant forms and fish were used with considerable success.

When the youngest Martin brother, Edwin, died at the beginning of the First World War, only Robert Wallace Martin, now over seventy, remained. Production at Southall dwindled and finally ceased altogether after Wallace's death in 1923. Over the years a number of assistants had been employed at the Martin brothers' pottery works, but none became well known in their own right. Wallace's son Clement Wallace Martin, who had worked in the studio, continued to make similar wares until the 1930s. The workshop building was struck by lightning and destroyed in 1943.

CHRISTOPHER DRESSER

Although not himself a potter, Christopher Dresser (1834–1904) exerted a powerful influence on ceramics. Widely regarded as the father of industrial design, he worked in a vast range of materials and mediums, among them glass and metal as well

Coffee pot, cup and saucer, 1879–80. Earthenware, white body, with design of blossom branches painted in underglaze black under a yellow ochre glaze. Designed by Christopher Dresser, Linthorpe Art Pottery, Middlesbrough. Height (tallest) 26.3 cm (10.5 in).

as ceramics. He also wrote extensively and influentially on decorative design, notably in his books published in 1862 and 1873. In the 1860s and '70s Dresser worked as a freelance designer, undertaking varied work for a number of different manufacturers, including Minton and Wedgwood. His use of stylized plant motifs reflected his early study of botany, and a government-sponsored visit to Japan in 1876/7 led him to incorporate elements of Japanese design into his work.

In 1879 he set up the Linthorpe Art Pottery near Middlesbrough in association with the businessman John Harrison, and on Dresser's recommendation Henry Tooth, an artist with little knowledge of pottery, was appointed manager. During his three years as art director at Linthorpe, Dresser produced distinctive shapes that combined simplicity with grace. His work there can be divided roughly into two groups. The first consists of vessels carrying stylized animal and plant motifs while the second is made up of often extraordinary shapes derived from a variety of exotic sources, some contemporary, some ancient. A good example of the latter is his 'Peruvian pottery', based on the Pre-Columbian Peruvian bridge-spouted vessel. Most of Dresser's pots were highly glazed, the 'Linthorpe glaze' being characterized by speckled, richly flowing colours.

In 1882 Tooth left Linthorpe to establish the Bretby Art Pottery at Woodville in Derbyshire, in partnership with William Ault. Here umbrella stands, jardinières, vases and hanging pots were produced, as well as pieces resembling hammered copper, bronze and steel and carved bamboo. In 1887 Ault in turn moved on to set up his own enterprise in competition with Linthorpe, the Ault Pottery at Swadlincote, Derbyshire. On the closure of the Linthorpe Art Pottery in 1889, Ault acquired its moulds and continued to produce Dresser's designs – which has caused problems with the attribution of this work ever since.

HENRY DOULTON

Prominent among the ceramic manufacturers who put art and craft theories into practice is Henry Doulton, who pioneered art pottery by setting up a studio at his factory specifically for ceramic design and decoration. When he first joined the firm built up by his father, John Doulton, it was producing a range of stoneware vessels for domestic and industrial use, but by the mid-nineteenth century, largely as a result of Henry Doulton's own foresight and entrepreneurial flair, the business had greatly extended its product range and had become a major manufacturer of drainpipes and sanitarywares.

The Lambeth-based pottery of Doulton and Co. was thus already on a sound commercial footing when in 1854 the Lambeth School of Art opened nearby. Over the next few years Henry Doulton forged close links with the school, becoming increasingly enthusiastic about the new concept of applying art to industry. This encouraged the school's enterprising art master, John Sparkes, to propose the setting up of a scheme whereby his students could make use of Doulton's factory facilities and decorate pots made in its workshop. The plan proved so successful that in due course Doulton recruited many of the students who had taken part in the scheme and in 1866 his factory began producing art pottery on a commercial basis.

The young decorators employed in Doulton's art pottery studio in Lambeth worked on shapes specially made in the factory and their pots would be dotted among the sewage pipes to be fired in the large salt-glaze kilns. One of his most successful appointments was that of George Tinworth, who specialized in figural and sculptural pieces. Notable among the many women who were employed for their 'finger dexterity and deftness' was Hannah B. Barlow, who became known for her sensitive incised animal designs; her sister Florence and brother Arthur also worked as Doulton decorators. Towards the end of the century over 300 people were employed in Doulton's art studio. Some of the signed work by his protégés was shown in 1871 and 1872 at exhibitions in South Kensington, where it was greatly admired by Queen Victoria, among others. A Professor Archer of Edinburgh, in a review in the *Art Journal*, was generous in his praise and pointed out that Doulton 'played no tricks with the clay by trying to make it do more than it was capable of doing well'.

In 1872 earthenware was introduced into the studio and experiments led to the making of 'faience' (this term covering any earthenware with relief modelling decorated with coloured glazes). Other products that began to be made include white Doulton stoneware resembling marble in

appearance, sold around 1887–96 as Carrara. This
was usually covered with a transparent matt glaze
then painted with coloured enamels or given lustre
decoration and gilded. The material could also be
modelled in relief or pierced and was often decorated with foliage designs or strapwork in dull red
or sage green.

Production of art wares continued in a separate
studio until the First World War. The experimentation with high-temperature glazes begun by
Charles Noke and John Slater in the late 1890s was
stepped up on the arrival of the ceramic chemist
Cuthbert Bailey, who collaborated with Bernard
Moore, an expert in the production of Chinese red
glazes such as flambé and sang-de-bœuf.

OTHER BRITISH FACTORIES PRODUCING ART POTTERY

Doulton's example soon prompted other manufacturers to open art studios. In 1872/3 Minton Ltd

established its Art Pottery Studio in London at
Kensington Gore, fitting it with an unusual kiln
claimed to have been designed to consume its own
smoke. Pots made at Minton's factory in Staffordshire were brought to London to be decorated so
that the artists, in their search for design inspiration, could make use of the South Kensington
Museum and the horticultural gardens. Among a
number of other experiments that also sought to
relate the industrial production of pottery to the
work of the artist, both Wedgwood and Worcester
set up small art departments for the design and
decoration of 'art pottery' that could be produced
in their factories.

In 1891 the four Pilkington brothers set up a
factory for the production of tiles at Clifton Junction, near Manchester, after suitable clay had been
discovered there in the course of a search for coal
seams. William Burton, formerly a chemist
at Wedgwood, took technical and artistic control;

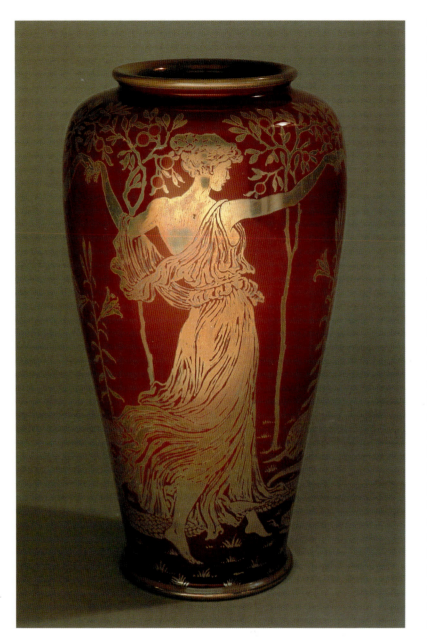

Vase, earthenware, painted in gold lustre on a scarlet red ground, with the daughters of Hesperus guarding the golden apples, protected by a serpent. Decoration designed by Walter Crane, painted by Richard Joyce on a shape probably designed by Lewis F. Day. Made at Pilkington's Tile and Pottery Company, Clifton Junction, Manchester, 1906. Height 34 cm (13.5 in).

developed: one had an opalescent effect, another resembled the skin of fruit, a number of pink and red flambé glazes produced a lustrous sheen, and the development of an iridescent lustre resulted in the production of lustre-painted ware. The company's art pottery studio, set up in 1903, employed the services of many gifted artists and designers of the time, including Gordon M. Forsyth (see chapter 11), Walter Crane (the first president of the Arts and Crafts Exhibition Society), Lewis F. Day and Charles F. A. Voysey. The production of ornamental wares ceased in 1937, although tile manufacture continued until after the Second World War.

The Della Robbia Pottery in Birkenhead – which took its name from the Florentine family of sculptors famous for their terracottas of the Renaissance period – produced painted lead-glazed wares from 1894 to 1906. Much of the ware consisted of tiles for architectural use, but in addition relief-moulded hollowwares with bright green glazes were made, and the work was signed by the individual makers. The robustness of Della Robbia earthenware is in great contrast to the delicacy of the vessels produced by the Ruskin Pottery established by William Howson Taylor (1876–1935) at Smethwick, near Birmingham, where commercial production began in 1901. Specializing in decorative wares inspired by Chinese ceramics of the Song and Ming dynasties, Taylor developed a range of original coloured glazes with mottled, flambé, sang-de-bœuf and lustre effects, mainly on a porcelain body. His special interest in glazes led to the creation of often spectacular tones. He created multi-layered surfaces of great depth and richness, also devising a range of lustre colours including yellow, orange and pearl. He tended to use simple shapes that reflected those of wares from the Far East. Like many of his contemporaries, Taylor jealously guarded his production methods and glaze ingredients. Shortly before his death he destroyed all his notebooks, with the result that his secrets were lost forever.

Also worthy of mention in connection with rich oriental glazes is the work of Bernard and Samuel

later joined by his brother Joseph, he remained with the enterprise until his retirement in 1915. In addition to wall, floor and fireplace tiles, the factory manufactured a variety of small ceramic items and some decorated pieces; rich, ornate glazes played an important part in their production. In 1900 the Pilkington display at the Exposition Universelle in Paris included architectural earthenware tiles, pots, and a pair of lion figures, made from moulds by the sculptor and painter Alfred Stevens, that were covered with a brown crystalline glaze called Sunstone. Influenced considerably by oriental wares, other dramatic glazes were later

'Victoria Wine Cooler', shape number 631, *c.* 1851, produced at Minton. Earthenware, modelled and majolica glazed. Height 64 cm (25.5 in).

Vase, 1910, by William Howson Taylor, Ruskin Pottery, West Smethwick, near Birmingham. Stoneware with flambé glaze in blue, red and purple, with green marking. Height 27.5 cm (11 in).

Moore. Located at Longton, Stoke-on-Trent, the Moore brothers made a range of high-quality table-wares and ornamental pieces, as well as imitations of heavily gilded Chinese cloisonné enamel and reproductions of Japanese pottery. Burmantoft's, established in 1858 in Leeds and a branch of the Leeds Fireclay Company from 1889, produced wares ranging from umbrella holders and pedestals for plant pots to decorative panels for architectural purposes. The company's faience was made from a hard, buff-coloured earthenware body that took colour well. Production of Burmantoft's art pottery ceased in 1904 but the firm continued to manufacture glazed bricks and terracotta.

The West Country was home to a number of very different workshops. Watcombe TerraCotta Co., established in 1869 near Torquay, made use of a local deposit of red clay to produce fine art pottery characterized by decoration with enamel or turquoise glazes and intricate modelling. Much of the ware was produced by slip-casting into moulds and the range included tea services, plaques, figures and architectural ornament. In 1901 the pottery became part of the combined Royal Aller Vale and Watcombe Potteries and produced a variety of functional as well as ornamental wares. Production finally ceased in 1962. The Aller Vale Pottery, near Newton Abbot, had been set up in 1865 to manufacture a range of domestic earthenware products but later introduced architectural pieces, terracotta and slip-painted ware. After receiving the patronage of Queen Victoria's daughter

Princess Louise, the firm traded as the Royal Aller Vale Pottery, selling its products through Liberty and Co. Thrown, moulded and slip-cast wares were made, some heavily decorated (by students from the local art school) with such motifs as sea-weed, shells and flowers under glossy glazes. The Liberty catalogue for 1892 lists an extensive range of domestic and ornamental ware with decoration derived from Iznik pottery.

At Barnstaple in north Devon, an area renowned for high-quality traditional pottery, Charles H. Brannam introduced Barum wares in his father's old country pottery workshop. Combining fashionable design elements with the characteristics of traditional Devon slipware, the thrown shapes were decorated with sgraffito or painted slips. However, the onset of the First World War forced the firm to abandon many of its earlier styles in favour of simpler wares with monochrome glazes.

In Somerset Sir Edmund Elton opened the Sun-flower Pottery at his home at Clevedon in 1881, at first employing a flowerpot-maker to throw pots under his supervision before learning to carry out the work himself. Elton aimed for highly decorative effects. On forms that were modelled and irregular in form he created asym-metrical relief patterns of flowers and foliage, built up of coloured slips with sgraffito outline, which stood on a background of mottled shades of blue and green. In addition he produced pots with raised floral motifs in coloured slip set against streaky grounds, usually in blue, and most notable of all was his development of a range of metallic, crackled glaze effects. The Sunflower Pottery con-tinued in operation until 1930.

UNITED STATES OF AMERICA

In the United States the term 'art pottery' is generally used to describe ceramics that were made with a consciously artistic intent during the period roughly from the time of the Philadelphia

Two vases and a jug. Earthenware, with thick metallic crackle glaze of gold and platinum, by Sir Edmund Elton (1846–1920). Sunflower Pottery, Somerset, after 1902. Height (tallest) 20 cm (8 in).

Centennial Exposition of 1876 until the beginning of the First World War. The making of pottery of this kind was one aspect of a more generalized artistic movement that arose around that time, partially in an attempt to establish a genuinely indigenous American style over a wide range of artistic mediums. Art pottery in the United States encompasses both ceramics made by artist-potters operating independently – for example, George E. Ohr and Adelaide Alsop Robineau – and the work of potters and decorators employed in highly organized factories, who typically worked on shapes specified by the factory and manufactured ranges of art wares for distinct markets.

An extraordinary variety of objects came to be produced in art potteries, some with meticulously painted decoration that was often naturalistic in style, others in which the effect relied largely on form and the quality of the glaze. Pots were made by throwing, by hand-building and by slip-casting and moulding. Although some enterprises, such as the Grueby Pottery, were male-dominated, it was by no means unusual in American art potteries for the decorators to be mostly female, and several women founded successful businesses of their own – notably Maria Longworth Nichols and Mary Chase Perry Stratton.

The American Art Workers' Guild, established around 1885 in Providence, Rhode Island, influenced work in the United States for some thirty years. Also important was the establishment of arts and crafts exhibition societies and the publication of design periodicals such as *The House Beautiful, International Studio* and *Keramic Studio.*

The creation of art pottery in America started out principally as a leisure pursuit for upper-class ladies, among whom the activity soon became immensely popular – so much so that in many states the lady potters set up societies through which to exhibit and sell their work. When a china-painting class was begun by the Cincinnati School of Design, one of the first students, Mary Louise McLaughlin, grandly proclaimed that 'tidings of the veritable renaissance in England under the leadership of William Morris and his associates' had reached America. Another of the early students at the school was Maria Longworth Nichols, whose father was a patron of the Cincinnati Art Museum. Both women were later to be recognized as pioneers of American art pottery.

Vase, decorated by Maria Longworth Nichols, either at her own studio or at the Rookwood Pottery, *c.* 1880. Earthenware, moulded body with applied decoration in high relief of a dragon painted in white and dark blue with black outlines. Height 26 cm (10.4 in).

MARIA LONGWORTH NICHOLS AND THE ROOKWOOD POTTERY

Maria Longworth Nichols (1849–1932), the granddaughter of a real-estate millionaire, rented a small studio space at the Hamilton Road Pottery owned by Frederick Dallas, where, inspired by books of Japanese prints and by the French and Japanese pots she had seen at the 1876 exhibition in Philadelphia, she began researching into clay, bodies and glazes. Her early work included the development of high-fired 'granite ware' and the making of relief-decorated vases, often with designs featuring aquatic motifs.

Her fellow-potter McLaughlin, meanwhile, had formed an eleven-strong Pottery Club, which she had not actively encouraged Nichols to join. Feeling snubbed by this omission, Nichols decided to set up her own rival establishment where she and her circle could pursue their fashionable hobby of pottery decoration. For this purpose her father bought her a disused schoolhouse, which she named 'Rookwood' after the family estate.

Nichols soon became more ambitious, however, and in 1880 she put the Rookwood Pottery on to a commercial footing, expanding her repertoire of grotesque animals in the Japanese style and continuing to develop her own art pottery alongside the commercial production of items such as tableware, cooking pots and vases. She immediately took on Henry Farny, a well-known artist specializing in American-Indian themes, as a full-time decorator. For a brief period she also employed Karl Langenbeck (1861–1938), a neighbour with whom she had collaborated early on when he received a set of china-painting colours from Germany and who was now a fully trained ceramic chemist. Another short-lived venture in the 1880s was the Rookwood School for Pottery Decoration, which had Clara C. Newton (1848–1936), a studio potter in her own right, as its secretary and instructor.

The workshop's products quickly won huge popularity and became widely imitated, and it was not long before the Rookwood Pottery was acknowledged as the leader of America's craft industry. As the Rookwood style gradually developed, the colours used in the work became more refined and the forms simpler, decorated with naturalistically rendered plants and animals. In 1883 the innovative use of an atomizer allowed the fine spraying of colours to be introduced, resulting in the development of Rookwood Standard ware whose subtle gradations of colour from dark brown to orange to yellow and green prompt the description 'Rembrandtesque' tones. Crystalline glazes were later used: Tiger Eye was noted for its 'strange luminosity' and its 'striations and sparkling particles of gold', while Goldstone gave the effect of 'glistening particles in adventurine, but rather more limpid'. (William Burton at Pilkington's Tile and Pottery Co. in England achieved similar effects.) Rookwood's matt glazes also became very popular, setting a trend that was followed by many other potteries.

Espousing a philosophy closely akin to that of William Morris in England, Nichols attempted initially to divorce herself from the 'factory system' by holding artistic integrity paramount and running her workshop along philanthropic lines. However, after the appointment in 1883 of a shrewd businessman, William Watts Taylor, as manager, the factory became highly organized, and despite its image as a paragon of arts and crafts ideals, the large demand for Rookwood wares led to the adoption of numerous labour-saving technical processes in the interest of low-cost mass-production. Nichols' aims had been to provide secure employment for talented artists and decorators while fostering originality, shunning duplication and encouraging individuality. In practice, the degree of artistic licence afforded to Rookwood decorators was considerably less than the pottery's prolific publicity would suggest; they are even said to have been fined for misnumbering vases, which were produced according to strict 'division of labour' principles.

After the death of her husband in 1885 and her subsequent marriage to lawyer and diplomat Bellamy Storer, Nichols became less and less involved with the pottery on a day-to-day basis. After travelling in Europe, in 1889 she settled in Washington, leaving the pottery under the total control of Taylor. In due course she transferred her interest in the business to him, but she retained a studio at Rookwood for her own use and there achieved lustrous copper-red glazes. Eventually she moved with her husband to Europe, where she lived for the remainder of her life.

Taylor ran the firm until his death in 1913. Under his management the company flourished and received many prestigious prizes, the first being the gold medal at the Exhibition of American Art Industry in Philadelphia in 1899. The following year its commercial future was assured when the Standard and Tiger Eye wares, displayed by an agent, were awarded the gold medal at the Exposition Universelle in Paris. So impressed were the judges by the artistic quality of the pieces that doubt was expressed as to whether they could in fact be reproduced; when further samples had to be brought over from America as proof, the favourable publicity that ensued was enough to seal Rookwood's high reputation. The Rookwood Pottery continued in production until 1967 and its ware are now much sought-after.

MARY LOUISE McLAUGHLIN

Mary Louise McLaughlin (1847–1939) was strongly influenced by the display of Charles Haviland's work at the 1876 exposition in Philadelphia. She experimented with painting in slip onto the unfired clay, describing her work as Limoges faience. In 1879 she organized the Cincinnati Pottery Club 'to uphold the standard of good craftsmanship of the best workers in the different branches of pottery'.

Ever inventive, McLaughlin not only devised a method of inlay decoration but also discovered the secrets of making high-fired porcelain. This was eventually used for pots, on which she carried out highly skilled decoration very much in the art nouveau style, successfully exhibiting her work at the World's Columbian Exposition in Chicago in 1893.

THE NEWCOMB POTTERY

The revolutionary notion that women could be trained in a skill that would enable them to make an honourable living was one of the essential tenets of the Arts and Crafts movement. It was also a primary motivation for the establishment in 1894 of the Newcomb Pottery in the American South, where men made the forms using local clay, while women carried out the decoration using mostly naturalistic designs based on local plants and vegetation.

The pottery was set up at the Sophie Newcomb Memorial College, the women's division of Tulane University, Louisiana, at the instigation of Ellsworth Woodward, a teacher of the decorative

Vase made at Newcomb College Pottery, Louisiana, USA, late 19th century. Earthenware, painted with design of trees, with clear glaze. Height 20 cm (8 in).

college pottery and production was increased. Despite substantial demand for its output, the Newcomb Pottery, unlike Rookwood, never wavered in its pursuit of the arts and crafts ideal. It continued to receive financial support from the university and at no time operated on a commercial basis.

ZANESVILLE, OHIO: 'CLAY CITY'
Samuel A. Weller

Samuel A. Weller (1851–1925) established his first pottery in Fultonham, Ohio, producing red earthenware umbrella stands, jardinières and flowerpots there before moving to Zanesville. His factory achieved success by manufacturing wares based on Rookwood's while also developing highly individual pieces of its own, often in collaboration with well-known designers. In 1894 Weller acquired the Lonhuda Pottery, where he collaborated with W. A. Long to create the 'Louwelsa' range of slip-decorated vases; these featured patterns of fruit and flowers as well as portraits, often of American-Indians. This production continued until 1948.

arts who was dedicated to the cause of vocational training for women, and his brother William. After a year of experimentation a formal programme of practical training was implemented, leading to an advanced qualification in art and design. One of the main aims of the pottery venture was to provide an outlet for work created by the college's art graduates.

The Newcomb Pottery adhered strictly to the principle of allowing total creative freedom in every aspect of production, even specifically forbidding duplication to ensure that each piece made was a unique and original hand-crafted item. Professional potters were brought in to work on hand-throwing, glazing and firing, as these were considered unsuitable tasks for the female students. Mary G. Sheerer taught underglaze slip decoration and china-painting as well as contributing to the development of a range of products including bowls, coffee sets, vases and table-lamp bases.

Gradually an identifiable Newcomb style developed that made sensitive use of painted decoration and matt glazes. In 1901 a new building – its architecture again true to the ideals of the Arts and Crafts movement – was constructed to house the

Vase, Weller Pottery, 1901–10. Earthenware, decorated by Jacques Sicard with gold floral decoration on blue, green, purple and red metallic background. Height 55 cm (22 in).

John B. Owen

The potter and tile manufacturer John B. Owen (1859–1934) moved to Zanesville in 1892, having formerly run his business from Roseville, Ohio since 1885. Employing Maria Longworth Nichols' former colleague Karl Langenbeck as chief chemist, Owen produced wares including teapots and jardinières. W. A. Long became associated with Owen's pottery from 1896, developing the 'Utopian' range, which was painted with flower and animal designs as well as American-Indian portraits in slip against a dark background.

Roseville Pottery Co.

When Owen moved out of Roseville his premises were taken over by a new enterprise calling itself the Roseville Pottery Co. and making stoneware items for the home under the management of George F. Young; over time the business would be run by four generations of his family. The company later bought out another local pottery and a further two in Zanesville, which became its principal base in 1901 and its exclusive one from 1910. It was at this stage that Roseville began producing a range of art pottery known as Rozane, moulded from local clays, in an attempt to compete with Rookwood's Standard ware. Gradually the firm developed a more original style of its own that featured crystalline glazes. In 1904 Frederick Hurten Rhead (1880–1942) became art director, introducing the Della Robbia range. Under the direction of F. H. Rhead and later his brother H. G. Rhead, further Roseville lines were added, each being given a name indicating its artistic influence: Aztec, Donatello, Mostique, Pauleo. The Roseville Pottery was closed in 1954.

The English-born potter F. H. Rhead had moved to America in 1902, bringing with him a strong feel for modern design, and art nouveau in particular, that was to inspire designers in several factories. He worked for Samuel Weller before joining Roseville. Rhead wrote articles for *Keramic Studio* and in 1910 became an instructor at the University City School of Ceramics in Missouri, later setting up his own pottery in Santa Barbara. Much of his work was based on oriental wares and incorporated conventional modelled or applied decoration.

Plate, Hugh Robertson, Chelsea Pottery US, Massachusetts, 1891–5. White earthenware, with grey crackle glaze and border design of ten dolphins and stylized waves, moulded and painted in blue. Diameter 22 cm (8.75 in).

Vase, Grueby Pottery, Boston, after 1899. Earthenware, yellow body, hand-thrown form with applied leaves and deep green matt glaze. Height 30 cm (12 in).

OTHER AMERICAN ART POTTERIES

Almost as important as the work of the Rookwood Pottery was that of the brothers Alexander, Hugh Cornwall and George W. Robertson and their father, James. Based in Chelsea, outside Boston, the Robertsons produced undistinguished brown wares until 1872 but from then on began to focus on making art pottery, calling their new enterprise the Chelsea Keramic Art Works. Much of their early work, made in fine red earthenware with minutely detailed decoration, was inspired by ancient Greek terracottas. Later, impressed like so many others by the French and oriental pots shown at the 1876 exhibition in Philadelphia, they went on to devise a range of slip-decorated wares and carried out experiments that led to the development of rich red glazes. However, the business was beset by failures and the family came near to bankruptcy.

In 1891 a new business was established on a more commercial basis under the control of Hugh Robertson. Known as the Chelsea Pottery US, its main product became an attractive 'Cracqule' ware, which was characterized by a grey crackle finish used to great effect on both ornamental and functional pieces. In 1895 the pottery moved to Dedham, where the Robertsons traded under the name of the Dedham Pottery; the workshops were closed down in 1943.

Closely associated with the Robertsons' work is that of John Low and the J. & J.G. Low Art Tile Works. The Lows, father and son, worked at the Chelsea Keramic Art Works before setting up their own tile factory in 1878, with George W. Robertson acting as their glaze technician. By 1882 the firm was also producing art pottery jugs and vases with modelled decoration. The potter William H. Grueby (1867–1925) was employed by the Lows for a time prior to setting up his own pottery, where he produced tiles and other architectural earthenware, basing some of his work on historical styles. On visiting the Chicago World's Fair in 1893, Grueby was greatly taken by the work of the French

Vase, designed by Louis Comfort Tiffany for Tiffany Furnaces Favrille Pottery, Corona, New York, *c.* 1905–14. Porcellaneous stoneware with relief decoration. Height 13 cm (5.2 in).

styles of decoration but also to the oriental wares on display in the city's museums. Back in America he worked on developing matt glazes (attempting in particular to re-create those of the Chinese Ming dynasty) and modelled pots in which design and decoration merged, borrowing heavily from the fluidity of art nouveau. In 1899, suffering from tuberculosis, Briggle left Rookwood and moved to the healthier climate of Colorado Springs. Soon afterwards he set up his own art pottery there, where he designed and modelled vases and plates with relief decoration of plant forms and occasionally animals, achieving a close relationship between decoration and form that was enhanced by the use of monochrome matt glaze. Van Briggle's ceramics were made to a high technical standard and soon became highly acclaimed, but sadly he did not live to enjoy his success. His wife Anne carried on the business, however, and in 1908 she opened a new factory, which she named the Van Briggle Memorial Pottery.

Louis Comfort Tiffany (the son of Charles Lewis Tiffany, founder of the famous Tiffany & Co. jewellery concern) was a distinguished artist and designer in a number of different mediums. A committed devotee of the Arts and Crafts movement, he put the ideas of William Morris into practice in much of his work, as well as in the co-operative ethos of the interior decoration business he set up before developing a greater interest in art glassware. Unlike Morris, however, Tiffany did succeed in producing hand-crafted objects at a low enough price for them to become widely accessible. In Paris Tiffany had particularly admired the lustre pottery of Clément Massier as well as the more avant-garde work of Dalpayrat, Delaherche and Bigot. After buying lamp-bases from Grueby Faience, he began making his own ceramics and showed his first pieces in 1904. Using the same trade name as his glass, he marked his wares Favrille Pottery and offered them for sale in limited quantities at the new Tiffany & Co. building in New York. Some pieces were made on the wheel but most were slip-cast; the decoration consisted of abstracted designs of plants and flowers. To achieve a more natural appearance, for some items he cast moulds from natural plant specimens and hardened them with lacquer. Tiffany's rich and ornate glazes included matt, crystalline and iridescent types; the colours included a splodged green created to

potters Auguste Delaherche and Ernest Chaplet. Their combination of strong form, innovative plant-like decoration and matt glazes prompted him to experiment with developing similar glazes himself. In addition to its existing wares, the Grueby Faience Company began producing ornamental vases, many decorated with vegetal forms in low relief; these were thrown by hand and the designs executed by women decorators following exact patterns. Conceived as a 'happy merger of mercantile principles and the high ideals of art', Grueby Faience came close to realizing many of the ideals of the Arts and Crafts movement.

The influence of art nouveau is much in evidence in the work of Artus Van Briggle (1869–1904) and Louis Comfort Tiffany (1848–1933). Briggle trained as a painter before acquiring pottery skills at Rookwood. His two years' study in Paris had introduced him not only to the latest European

Dish, Roycroft Workshops, made by Buffalo Pottery, *c.* 1909–10. Earthenware with transfer-printed geometric ornament in deep green and rust red on cream ground. Length 17.5 cm (7 in). Roycroft Workshops were founded as an Arts and Crafts printing community in 1900, but later expanded to include other household goods. This dish was designed by Dard Hunter (1883–1966) who visited Vienna in 1908, the Viennese influence evident in the geometric border decoration.

resemble moss and others ranging from light yellow to black, suggesting old ivory.

Art nouveau designs continued to influence numerous potters, although some workshops – for example the Clifton Art Pottery, established at Newark, New Jersey in 1905 – tried to evolve a style based on traditional American-Indian pots. Clifton Indian Ware included vases, jugs, mugs and ornamental and souvenir items. The Fuller Pottery, which operated from 1814 at Flemington, New Jersey, produced a range of art stoneware made from the local clay. The art products, including flower-holders in the form of animals, candle-holders and clock cases, were fired alongside more commercial domestic wares.

One of the few individual potters to emerge at this time was George E. Ohr (1857–1918). Ohr

first learned the craft from Joseph F. Meyer, a friend who later worked at the Newcomb Pottery. After a two-year tour of potteries all around America, Ohr settled in Biloxi, Mississippi, where he opened his own studio. He had an ability to throw extraordinarily thin forms, which he then glazed with unusual mottled, tortoiseshell and metallic glazes. In stark contrast to that of his contemporaries, Ohr's handling of clay was expressionist and gestural (his twisted shapes have often been described as 'tortured'), and as a result his work was little understood or appreciated at the time. He made thousands of pieces, of which no two were precisely the same, ranging from very small items to huge pots as tall as a man. Both Ohr's appearance and his almost surreal art could be said to have anticipated the later Salvador Dalí.

Tea pot and coffee pot, made by George E. Ohr, Biloxi Art Pottery, Biloxi, Mississippi, after 1900. Earthenware, built in two parts, and glazed. Height 19.5 cm (7.75 in).

His unconventional hairstyle, outrageous whiskers and eccentric behaviour – including a tendency to proclaim himself 'the greatest art potter on Earth' – may have been calculated to draw attention to his work; not surprisingly, they earned him the title 'The Mad Potter of Biloxi'. In 1909 Ohr closed his pottery down after hiding away his stock of pieces, aware, perhaps, that they were ahead of their time. For this reason his work remained largely unknown until 1972, when the cache was sold by his family through a dealer, so bringing a new audience to these exceptional and original ceramics.

ADELAIDE ALSOP ROBINEAU

The painter, potter and porcelain-maker Adelaide Alsop Robineau (1865–1929), a major pioneer of the American ceramic movement, began her career in china-painting before tackling the more exacting medium of porcelain. Although she operated on only a small scale, from a studio at her home in Syracuse, New York, Robineau became an influential potter, producing often highly ornate and superbly executed work. She was also instrumental in disseminating information on ceramic developments and techniques to the growing ranks of American art or studio potters. In 1899 Robineau ventured into publishing with *Keramic Studio*, a magazine aimed primarily at the amateur potter and china-painter, which she continued to edit until her death.

One of many articles Robineau published by the French potter Taxile Doat (who, like her, taught pottery at University City, Missouri) dealt with the making of porcelain and acted as a stimulus for her to extend her own skills. She began learning porcelain-making with Charles Binns, one of the leading teachers of the time, at Alfred University, where classes had been held since 1901. Robineau's pots were mostly decorated with incised and carved decoration enhanced by the jewel-like quality of the matt and crystalline glazes. Her greatest success was the award of the Grand Prize for fifty-five pieces shown at the International Exposition of Decorative Art in Turin, Italy in 1911.

MARY CHASE PERRY STRATTON

Mary Chase Perry Stratton (1867–1961) was the founder of, and motivating force behind, the Pewabic Pottery in Detroit. Like so many of America's female art potters, Stratton first became involved in ceramics through the women's china-painting movement. Keen to work with clay, she established a studio and workshop in which to experiment with clay bodies and glazes, and in due course this evolved into a full-scale pottery works. The early production of her Pewabic Pottery included vases, teapots, mugs, candlesticks, tiles and lamp bases. Many of the shapes were based on oriental forms and all were hand-thrown then

'Scarab Vase'. Porcelain, intricately carved and pierced with an overall scarab pattern, glazed pale turquoise and white,and incised on the base THE APOTHEOSIS OF THE TOILER. Made for the Women's League by Adelaide Robineau, 1910. The vase is reputed to have taken over a thousand hours of work. Height 41.5 cm (16.6 in).

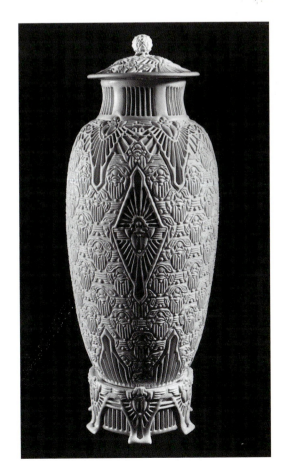

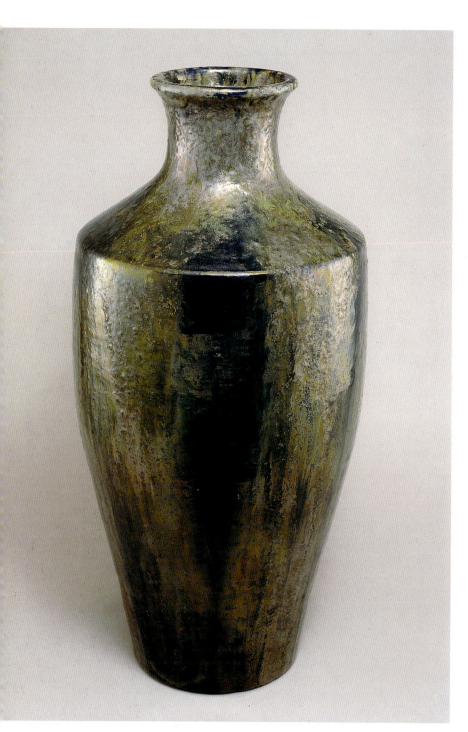

Vase, probably created by Mary Chase Perry Stratton, Pewabic Pottery, Detroit, Michigan. Earthenware with iridescent lustre glaze in gold, deep blue and pinkish-grey. Height 62.5 cm (25 in).

covered with a gloss, matt, lustre, iridescent or flow glaze. Pewabic tiles became the pottery's main product line and numerous commissions for these were received from architects, principally for use in churches and public buildings. In 1966 the pottery was gifted to Michigan State University and in 1981 its long-term preservation was assured when it was taken over by the Pewabic Society.

FRANCE

Forming part of wider revival in the visual arts, the studio pottery movement that arose in France in the second half of the nineteenth century was inspired to a large extent by oriental high-fired wares and Middle Eastern earthenwares. Many ceramic artists worked in or in conjunction with factories, while others set up their own individual studios.

Joseph-Théodore Deck (1823–91) was one of the first French potters to create objects in clay that were intended as individual works of art in their own right. Trained as a chemist and sculptor, Deck worked initially in pottery stove factories before settling in Paris and opening his own atelier there in 1856. His early products include Renaissance-style historicist wares. In common with de Morgan in Britain, Deck was inspired by Iznik and Persian pots and lustrewares and based much of his work on them, producing ceramics with floral decoration in turquoise and blue with touches of red and green. Not only is his work of a high technical standard, it is also artistically inventive, the pigments smooth and rich.

Deck's later output was influenced by the imported Japanese stonewares shown at the Paris exhibition of 1878, which stimulated him to make pots fired in the reduction kiln. He achieved some of the first flambé glazes of the period, as well as celadons, which he used over incised decoration; these pieces were first exhibited in 1884. Chinese bronzes constituted a further source of inspiration. In 1887 Deck's book *La Faience* was published and in 1888 he was appointed art director of the Sèvres factory, where he made improvements to the soft-paste porcelain and developed a stoneware body for the manufacture of vases, sculpture and garden ornaments.

Originally a lithographer and etcher and subsequently a painter (but outshone in this medium by his wife Marie), Félix Bracquemond (1833–1914) not only became involved in ceramic decoration himself (designing large plates that were produced in earthenware by Joseph-Théodore Deck), but actively encouraged other artists to work in the medium. In 1871 he accepted the position of art director at Sèvres, but he stayed there for only a short time before leaving to take up a similar post with the Haviland company. Here he employed the services of such artists as E.-A. and

Bowl and pear-shaped vase, 1925, by Emile Decœur. Stoneware, thrown. Height (tallest) 10 cm (4 in).

Vase by Taxile Doat, Sèvres factory, Paris, 1895–7. Hard-paste porcelain, slip-cast, with pâte-sur-pâte decoration of four circular medallions of Nôtre Dame, the Hôtel de Ville, the Louvre and Arc de Triomphe. Height 90 cm (36 in).

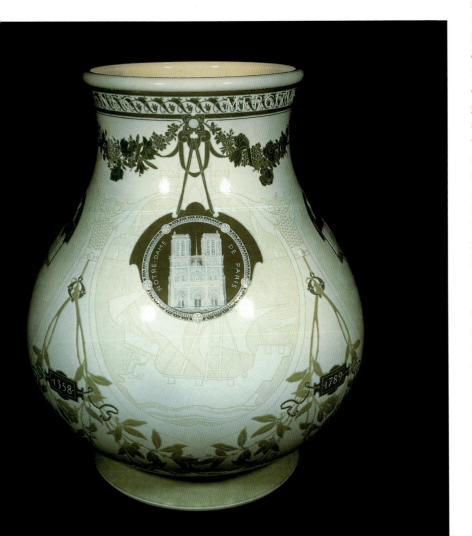

A.-L. Dammouse and Ernest Chaplet. Bracquemond's own designs in earthenware and porcelain were influenced by both Japanese and French Impressionist works.

The New York-born porcelain manufacturer Charles Haviland (1839–1921) established the family business of Haviland & Cie in Limoges in 1864 in collaboration with his father, David, and his brother Théodore. The company produced wares decorated with lines and dabs and featuring small bouquets of lilies-of-the-valley and moss roses. Haviland subsequently settled in Paris, in 1873 opening an experimental studio in Auteuil which Bracquemond directed. In 1881 Haviland himself took over as director, at the same time setting up a further studio in Paris; here Ernest Chaplet worked on developing brown stoneware and later porcelain, too, was produced. The company was dissolved in 1891 and Charles Haviland and his eldest son, Georges, set up a new firm called Haviland and Co.

Some potters responded more freely than others to oriental influences and to the artistic revival of the 1870s by indulging in experimentation and improvisation. Ernest Chaplet (1835–1909) was one of the important early pioneers. For a time he worked at factories such as Sèvres (his home town) and the Laurin firm, making painted earthenwares. In 1875 Chaplet joined the Haviland studio at Auteuil, benefiting from Bracquemond's policy of engaging designers who were already working in impressionist and Japanese-inspired styles. In 1881, influenced in equal measure by the traditional brown stoneware of Normandy and by oriental wares, Chaplet began to produce stoneware in simple forms ornamented with Japanese-derived designs in low relief and coated with rich deep glazes. He later reproduced the classic Chinese sang-de-bœuf glaze. In 1887 he set up his own workshop at Choisy-le-Roi, where he produced more austere forms and developed further decorative glazes. Chaplet was a major influence on numerous contemporary potters, including Albert Dammouse, Adrien Dalpayat and his son-in-law Emile Lenoble, all of whom contributed to the remarkable blossoming of studio ceramics in France.

The French artist-potter Taxile Doat (1851–1939) specialized in the pâte-sur-pâte technique, which consists of building up a raised surface by successive applications of liquid slip, and also produced gourd-shaped vessels, often covered with a crystalline glaze. In 1877 he joined the Sèvres factory, remaining there until 1909, when he travelled to America and helped to establish the University City Pottery at St Louis, Missouri. During the 1890s Doat had installed a kiln at his own home, where he developed flambé, crystalline and metallic glazes. His study *Grand Feu*

Three bottles and a lidded pot, c. 1925, by Martin St Honoré, Henri Simmen, Georges Serré and August Delaherche. Stoneware, reduction fired. Height (tallest) 23 cm (9.5 in).

Ceramics: A Practical Treatise on the Making of Fine Porcelain and Grès was published in the United States by Samuel Robineau. Doat's ceramics exerted a great influence on American ceramists such as Adelaide Alsop Robineau, who published fourteen of his articles in *Keramic Studio*; his articles were also published in other art and craft magazines, including *Art et Décoration*. Doat returned to Sèvres in 1915.

Over the period from 1891 to 1916 radical changes were made to production at Sèvres under the direction of Emile Baumgart and Alexandre Sandler. Experiments with crystalline glazes had been made from as early as 1885, but they did not go into regular production until the mid-1890s, at which time they became greatly admired. Crystalline glazes, with their reflective surface and hint of the exotic, were used by a number of European factories at this time, including the porcelain works in Copenhagen and Berlin, as well being used by many smaller art potteries.

In addition to being a painter, an engraver and a skilled and inventive ceramist, Jean-Charles Cazin (1841–1901) was also an influential teacher, serving as director of the Ecole des Beaux-Arts and curator of the museum at Tours, where he carried out experiments on earthenware. Cazin's work in France was brought to an end when he fled from the troubles of 1871 to settle in London, working there as a teacher both in Kensington and at the Lambeth School of Art; among his pupils were R.W. and W.F. Martin. At the Fulham Pottery he made stoneware jugs and mugs, often with Japanese-style decoration.

Artists such as Auguste Delaherche (1857–1940) productively absorbed the influence of art nouveau. Delaherche's early career was in architectural ceramics, but in 1887 he took over from Chaplet at the Haviland studio and there produced stoneware goblets, tobacco jars and pitchers with the aim of making work that was inexpensive and thus available to all. In 1894 Delaherche left Paris and built a workshop and kiln at Armentières near Beauvais; here he concentrated increasingly on high-temperature glaze effects, later producing porcelain. French artist-potters were among the first to experiment with copper-red glazes inspired by Chinese ceramics and Delaherche's copper-red glazed stonewares were shown to great acclaim at the Exposition Universelle in Paris.

The ceramist Pierre Adrien Dalpayrat (1844–1910) was equally concerned with oriental glazes and achieved spectacular sang-de-bœuf effects in a deep red speckled with green. The sculptor and potter Jean Carriès (1855–94) used wood ashes and feldspar in the production of his glazes, which featured a trickled effect. The influence of art nouveau was particularly evident in vases made in the form of gourds and other natural forms, such as those of Georges Hoentschel (1855–1915), who collaborated with Carriès. Hoentschel was strongly affected by Japanese ceramics and much of his work derived from floral forms. The art nouveau style is also reflected in the thrown forms with matt glazes in yellow, green and buff produced by Alexandre Bigot (1862–1927). Bigot opened a workshop in Paris for the production of vases, figures, tiles and other decorative stoneware with flambé glazes.

Emile Decœur (1876–1953) studied with the sculptor and ceramist Edmond Lachenal (1855–c.1930), from whom he learnt faience techniques, glazing and firing; the two subsequently collaborated. Among Lachenal's work was furniture made in stoneware, which was displayed at the 1900 Exposition Universelle. Decœur also developed an interest in stoneware, experimenting with flambé glazes and ornamental techniques; some of his finest pieces were vases in vegetable forms, with minimal decoration. In 1907 Decœur established his own studio at Fontenay-aux-Roses, where he made both porcelain and stoneware, abandoning ornament altogether in favour of refined shapes and sophisticated glazes. From 1939 to 1942 he served as artistic consultant at Sèvres.

Several showrooms in Paris specialized in promoting innovative decorative art, among them Meier-Graefe's La Maison Moderne and the Maison de l'Art Nouveau opened in 1895 by Siegfried Bing (1838–1905). It was Bing's policy of handling new and experimental work that contributed most to the initial spread of art nouveau in France.

In contrast to their counterparts in Britain, French artist-potters regarded their ceramics as fine art and showed them in art galleries alongside works by painters and sculptors. This fluidity between art and craft allowed fruitful links to be forged between potters, painters and sculptors and industry. The painter Paul Gauguin (1848–1903) worked successfully with clay, collaborating with

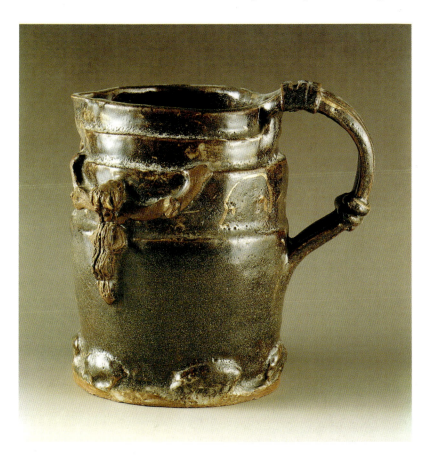

Bowl, *c.* 1931, Emile Lenoble, France. Stoneware with carved decoration. Diameter 17.5 cm (7 in).

Handled earthenware tankard form, modelled by Paul Gauguin and glazed by Ernest Chaplet, Paris, 1880s.

Chaplet to produce cylindrical vases and mugs in reduction-fired stoneware decorated with Breton scenes featuring figures, sheep or geese, and trees. Gauguin also made vessels and portrait vases, dishes with modelled figure decoration, and later figures such as Eve and Black Venus. His connection with potters prefigured later partnerships entered into by artists such as Joan Miró and Georges Braque, both of whom collaborated with the Spanish-born potter and ceramic chemist Llorens Artigas, and Picasso, who made ceramics at Vallauris in the 1940s and '50s in association with Georges and Suzanne Ramié. Unlike Gauguin, Picasso drew on the traditional brightly coloured tin-glazed earthenware of Spain and southern France and on terracotta wares.

In southern France the Massier family pottery at Vallauris produced a range of lead-glazed decorative ware. In the 1880s Clément Massier (1845–1917) set up his own pottery at Golfe-Juan, where he devised a method of reproducing the traditional lustre technique. His workshop manufactured pots and plaques with richly iridescent nacreous glazes in peacock blue or emerald green, decorated with stylized plant designs including rose, cactus and foliage, which again reflected the art nouveau style. Jacques Sicard, who worked closely with Massier, later introduced the technique at Samuel Weller's pottery in the United States.

GERMANY AND AUSTRIA

It was not until the beginning of the twentieth century that the influence of the Arts and Crafts movement and art nouveau – in German *Jugendstil* ('youth style') – gained any great hold in Germany and Austria. The origins of art pottery in Germany owe much to the example set by the Belgian architect and interior designer Henry Clemens van de Velde (1863–1957). Drawing his inspiration in large part from the arts and crafts ideals of William Morris, van de Velde became a pioneering practitioner of the art nouveau style. He designed interiors for Bing's new gallery in Paris, and when these were shown in Dresden in 1897 they received a much warmer reception in Germany than they had in France. This prompted van de Velde to settle in Berlin in 1900 and later that year the Westerwald district council obtained permission from the Ministry of Trade in Berlin to invite him to contribute to an initiative to reverse the moribund trend of the

local salt-glaze pottery industry. Despite his lack of experience in the medium of ceramics, van de Velde succeeded in making full use of the potential of glaze effects. Breaking with tradition in terms of both shape and decoration, in his first designs he introduced fluid art nouveau forms on which he used sang-de-bœuf glazes fired in salt-glaze kilns.

In 1901 Henry van de Velde was called to Weimar, where he conducted seminars at the art school; one of his students was Otto Lindig (1895–1966), later to become associated with the Bauhaus (see chapter 13). Another influential teacher was Max Laeuger (1864–1952), potter, painter, sculptor, architect and designer, who contributed to the spread of new ideas by encouraging innovation and employing art nouveau shapes and decoration in his own experimental work in lead-glazed earthenware and majolica. Van de Velde also carried out architectural and design work in Weimar, including the rebuilding of the art school in 1904 and the creation in 1906 of a new school of arts and crafts (*Kunstgewerbeschule*), of which he was appointed director.

In 1903 the Meissen factory commissioned van de Velde to design a tea and dinner service that would be 'modern' in feel but nevertheless appeal to the popular market. After some manufacturing difficulties, the service was finally produced two years later, its elegant forms carrying a linear whip-lash decoration in blue or matt burnished gold. Innovative designs were also used for the salt-glazed stonewares produced at Höhr-Grenzhausen, one notable contributor there being the modeller Peter Dümler (1860–1907), who later set up in business on his own.

Peter Behrens (1868–1940) shared much in common with van de Velde. Both had trained as artists before turning to architecture and interior decoration. In 1895 van de Velde had designed and furnished his own house at Ukkel, near Brussels, which became something of an art nouveau landmark and brought him commissions for other houses, mainly in Germany. Five years later Behrens followed suit by designing his own house in Darmstadt together with all the fixtures and fittings, including ceramics; his pottery designs were later used by the company Porzellanfabrik Gebrüder Bauscher, established in 1881 by August Bauscher to specialize in hotel porcelain. One of Germany's more forward-looking ceramic manufacturers, Bauscher was keen to apply the *Jugendstil* to his company's ranges and commissioned artists to design forms as well as decoration. Among others to espouse the new style was the Nymphenberg porcelain manufactory, which in 1906 set up a studio specially for the designer Adelbert Niemeyer (1867–1932) to create decorative pieces.

Work influenced by art nouveau and oriental styles was also produced at the pottery in Altona founded by the German ceramist Hermann Mutz (1845–1913) to manufacture tiled stoves. Mutz and his son Richard (1872–1931) developed a distinctive range of pieces including stoneware vases and bowls based on Japanese pots, on which richly coloured glazes were used. Richard Mutz later produced wall fountains in collaboration with the sculptor Ernst Barloch (1870–1938). After moving to Berlin in 1904 he again collaborated with Barloch to make pots with brightly coloured 'runny' glazes. In 1906 he formed the Keramische Werkstätten Mutz und Rother in Liegnitz for the production of architectural ware.

After working for the large firm of Villeroy & Boch in Mettlach, Jacob Julius Scharvogel (1854–1938) set up a workshop in Munich in which to produce art nouveau-style stoneware. He was later appointed director of the Grand Ducal Ceramic Factory in Darmstadt, where he focused on producing stoneware with rich glaze effects. In 1897 Scharvogel became co-founder of the Vereinigte Werkstätten für Kunst und Handwerk in Munich. Here, in collaboration with Theodor Schmuz-Baudiss (1859–1942) and other designers, he made more complex forms with relief decoration. Wilhelm Kagel (1867–1935) studied at the Kunstgewerbeschule at Munich and worked at Garmisch-Partenkirchen before building his own kiln in 1905. He established a workshop for the large-scale but low-cost production by hand of wares that would combine artistic and technical excellence. Working initially in high-fired earthenware and later in stoneware, he often used patterns of garlands and stylized blooms inspired by southern German folk art.

The Rosenthal porcelain concern, founded in 1879 as a decorating workshop by Philip Rosenthal

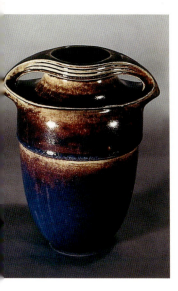

Vase, designed by Henry van de Velde and made by Reinhold Hanke, Höhe-Grenzhausen, Rhineland, *c.* 1902. Salt-glazed stoneware, buff body, cast, with deep, purplish red sang-de-bœuf-type glaze turning to brilliant blue. Height 23 cm (9.2 in).

(1855–1937), soon began producing whitewares and opened a branch in Asch, Bohemia. In 1891 production was started at the newly built Porzellanfabrik Philip Rosenthal & Co. in Selb, Bavaria, with a workforce of 225; by 1905 the enterprise employed a total of 1,200 workers. Some of the Rosenthal tablewares were left plain to emphasize the elegance and modernity of the shapes, while others had painted decoration. The Botticelli and Darmstadt services were decorated with slender stems and heart-shaped leaves, the Donatello range with a cherry design. As well as tableware the company manufactured industrial porcelain, along with stoneware and other ceramic bodies. In addition it continued to produce tableware and ornamental pieces in the traditional Westerwald style, using designs that featured relief decoration in blue and grey.

SCANDINAVIA

In Denmark some of the first studio pottery was that made in the 1880s by the designer and ceramist Thorvald Bindesbøll (1846–1908), who worked in earthenware creating vases and other decorative forms that he enamelled in blues, greens, browns, yellows, black and cream, often working from his own watercolour sketches. Between 1883 and 1890 Bindesbøll designs were produced by the factory of J. Wallman (established in 1867 at Utterslev) and other manufacturers in the Copenhagen area.

Another pioneering Danish factory was Kæhler Ceramics, established in 1839 at Næstved, Seeland by Joachim Christian Herman Kæhler for the production of earthenware, initially in the form of stoves (which were manufactured until 1888). In 1872 Herman August Kæhler (1846–1917), who had worked in Berlin, inherited the business from his father and introduced a number of changes, including the introduction of red metallic glazes on well-designed vases bearing motifs of flowers, stylized leaves and other natural forms painted in lustre. When his son Herman J. Kæhler (b.1904) in turn took over the company, he initiated the manufacture of glazed stoneware. Decorated with similar design motifs, the range of items produced included bowls and jars with brushed decoration designed by Herman's brother Nils A. Kæhler (b.1906). The pottery later began production of architectural stoneware.

Two lidded containers, designed and made by P. Ipsens Enke, Kongelig Hof Terracotta factory, Copenhagen, *c.* 1875. Earthenware with classical-style ornament and scenes after Thorvaldsen. Height 24 cm (9.5 in).

Dish and mug made by Alfred W. Finch, Iris Workshop, Finland, *c.* 1900. Red earthenware, thrown, with incised decoration through coloured slip. Height 6 cm (2.4 in).

In addition to manufacturing its high-quality tableware ranges, the Royal Copenhagen Porcelain Factory (see chapter 7) also commissioned artists working in various mediums to design individual pieces, for example the Danish sculptor Bertel Thorvaldsen. Also based in Copenhagen, Kongelig Hof Terracotta, the factory of P. Ipsens Enke, established in 1843, became widely known for its Greek-style vases and other classically inspired ceramics. Finely made and often highly detailed, these were exhibited throughout Europe during the 1870s. On some pieces both the shape and the decoration were taken directly from ancient vases, although more freely interpreted styles were also used. Some scenes were copied, with extreme precision, from Thorvaldsen's marble reliefs of mythical and allegorical subjects.

It is the founding of the Central School of Arts and Crafts in Helsinki in 1871 that marks the introduction of the Arts and Crafts movement into Finland, where the influence of the potter Alfred William Finch (1854–1930) and his work

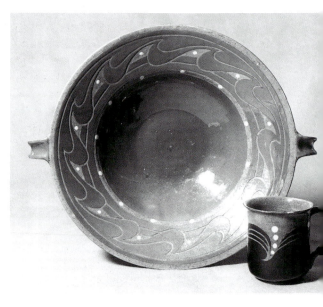

at the Iris workshop is significant. Finch, born of British parents, studied in Belgium at the Brussels academy and there learned to make earthenware pottery. On a visit to England in the 1880s he

Vase made at Fayencefabriek Amstelhoek, near Amsterdam, designed by C. J. van der Hoef, before 1910. Earthenware, glazed yellow and brown, with inlay decoration. Height 29.4 cm (11.6 in).

Double-handled vase made at Königlich-bayerische Porzellan-Manufaktur, Nymphenberg, c. 1905. Hard-paste porcelain, decorated with a pattern of intertwining tendrils and stylized flowers and leaves. Height 17.5 cm (7 in).

Tall vase made at Tegel-en Fayencefabriek Amphora, near Leiden, designed by C. J. van der Hoef. Earthenware, buff body, decoration in underglaze colours of blue and ochre, with a central motif of stylized addorsed deer. Height 38.8 cm (15.5 in).

Wide-mouthed vase made at Plateelbakkerij De Distel, Amsterdam, designed by Bert Nienhuis, 1904–11. Earthenware, moulded, matt glaze and in-glaze decoration of stylized butterflies. Height 15.4 cm (6.2 in).

Tall vase made at Gustavsberg porcelain factory, Stockholm, designed by Josef Ekberg, 1908. Porcellanous stoneware with underglaze relief decoration. Height 30 cm (12 in).

became aquainted with the theories and work of the Arts and Crafts movement. Later, he accepted an invitation from the potter and painter Anna Boch to work at Boch Frères at La Louvière (Saint-Vaast) in Belgium, where he made vases, goblets, jugs, dishes and plates in red earthenware with simple, almost rustic, slip decoration featuring elements of the art nouveau style. His ceramics were later sold at van de Velde's gallery in Paris.

In the late 1890s the designer Louis Sparre invited Finch to Finland to help set up a pottery at the Iris workshop in Borgå, Porvoo, east of Helsinki that he had established for the production of furniture and glass as well as other art works. Here Finch made a range of mainly functional wares featuring swirling slip decoration in floral patterns, with linear designs often cut through the slip. When the Iris workshop closed down in 1902, Finch was appointed Head of Ceramics at the Faculty of Industrial Arts in Helsinki, where he experimented with complex high-temperature glaze effects on stoneware.

Important among Finch's pupils at the Helsinki art school are E. Elenius and Toini Muona, who later joined Arabia, Finland's major ceramic manufacturer. For this company they designed stoneware dishes and vases in strong angular forms with monochrome glazes. Around 1900, seeking to put into practice the philosophy of the English Arts and Crafts movement, under the artistic direction of Thure Öberg Arabia commissioned designs from the Finnish industrial artist Axel Gallen-Kallela (1863–1931).

In the early years of the twentieth century many Scandinavian ceramic manufacturers, in common with those in Germany, adopted the technique of high-temperature firing and set up small design studios specifically for the use of artist-potters. Pottery designers thus benefited from having factory facilities and technical expertise close at hand, while in exchange the manufacturer gained an on-the-spot source of original design ideas. In Sweden this arrangement allowed Josef Ekberg, chief designer at the Gustavsberg factory, to produce some notable work, while in Norway it helped the Porsgrund porcelain factory in particular to develop distinctive lines. In Denmark Bing & Grøndahl of Copenhagen, under the art direction of J.F. Willumsen, encouraged individual artists to give free rein to their imagination in the creation of unique pieces.

THE NETHERLANDS

A particularly rich flowering of ceramics took place in Holland in the last decades of the nineteenth century. The contemporary emphasis on arts and crafts had prompted the opening of a number of new pottery factories, and four designers – Theodorus Colenbrander, C.J. van der Hoef, Bert Nienhuis and W.C. Brower – came to dominate the industry.

The Rozenburg Plateelfabriek was founded in 1883 in The Hague by the German ceramist Wilhelm Von Gudenberg and soon became noted for its creative earthenwares. Experimentation was carried out with the production of high-quality wafer-thin porcelain in eccentric shapes and a new range of colours was used in the decoration, characterized by stylized motifs of flowers and insects. These bone china pieces made a considerable impact when exhibited in 1899 and 1900 and many other factories began to imitate the work.

The designs featured elements of European stylistic trends such as naturalism and symbolism as well as being influenced by art nouveau.

The textile and ceramic designer Theodorus Colenbrander (1841–1930) worked as art director at Rozenburg between 1884 and 1889, creating vases, plates and display pieces decorated with painted floral motifs in bright shades of blue, green, red, brown, yellow, purple and white. In addition to being informed by the current European styles, his work showed the influence of batik patterns from the Dutch colony of Java. In 1912 Colenbrander was appointed a decorator at the Zuid-Holland factory, which had been established in 1898 in Gouda. Here he decorated large plates and other ceramic pieces both with patterns based on Iznik wares and with hand-painted floral designs, making ample use of brown and matt blue.

In common with many other designers, Christian Johannes van der Hoef (1875–1933) had trained as a sculptor. He designed ceramics for various factories and served for some years as director of the Amstelhoek factory, near Amsterdam. The ideas of the English Arts and Crafts movement were influential in the small workshops at Amstelhoek, which had been set up by W. Hoeker for the production of ceramics, metalwork and furniture. The pottery workshop made functional earthenware in red clay, with red or green glazes. Van der Hoef's distinctive designs for Amstelhoek featured two-colour inlaid decoration derived from traditional peasant pottery and incorporated the flowing lines of art nouveau. From about 1908 to 1910 van der Hoef worked for the newly founded firm of Amphora, where he designed both shapes and decoration. In 1910 the Amstelhoek business merged with De Distel, a factory that had been operating since 1895 in the production of painted earthenware and tile panels.

The potter Willem Coenraad Brouwer (1877–1933) worked for a time at the Goedewaagen factory in Gouda, where he had his own kiln. He showed his first individual ceramics in 1899 and six years later moved to Leiderdorp. Using coarse clay, glazed either green or yellow, Brouwer produced chunky vases in simple, rounded shapes with incised decoration, and among his decorative designs were regular, abstract or floral patterns as well as others based on animal forms. His later work

Teapot made at Koninklijke Porselein-en Aardewerk Fabriek Rozenburg, The Hague, Holland, 1899. 'Eggshell' porcelain, cast in a revolving mould to enable the handle and spout to be formed in one piece with a four-sided body, with a design of exotic fish among water-weeds on a white ground. Height 14.2 cm (5.6 in).

includes heavy pots covered in white or grey crackle glazes, his use of slip decoration and contrasting glazes emphasizing the patterns and suggesting the influence of both Dutch peasant pottery and the work of A.W. Finch. Brouwer's powerful designs were also strongly influenced by the play of lines and forms in Maori decoration, which he had studied at the Ethnographical Museum in Leiden.

Bert Nienhuis (1873–1960), who had trained originally as a painter, worked for De Distel from its foundation in 1895 until 1911, becoming head of the decorating department in 1901. Nienhuis developed a distinctive linear style of decoration in light colours on a matt-glazed ground. An influential figure in Dutch applied arts, Nienhuis taught at several art schools, in 1917 taking charge of a pottery department set up at the Quellinus school in Amsterdam. Some of his designs were produced at Goedewaagen in 1935.

Long-established Dutch firms also responded to the growing interest in new trends in ceramic design. From 1877 to 1919 the Delft factory of De Porceleyne Fles, which had been in operation since about 1650, was under the art direction of Adolf Le Comte (1850–1921). Inspired by Japanese styles and techniques, Le Comte inaugurated production of a range of wares with abstract decoration and metallic glazes, later introducing decorative tiles, matt-glazed or painted with enamels and shaped to follow the design.

The sculptor and ceramist Joseph Mendes da Costa (1863–1939) trained in his father's stone-masonry workshop in Amsterdam and studied at the Rijksschool voor Kunstnijverheid before designing production earthenware. Together with the sculptor L. Zijl he became a member of the Labor et Ars group, formed in 1885 as a reaction against sterile academic attitudes to the applied arts. In 1898 Mendes da Costa set up his own pottery, where he made coarsely textured domestic brown earthenware, making use of medieval design elements that endow his work with a curiously mystical quality. In addition he modelled stoneware animals, figures and groups, on which he employed a grey glaze flecked with blue and brown. From the turn of the century Mendes da Costa worked with the architect H.P. Berlage and other members of 't Binnenhuis, an influential association of architects, artists and designers; he also taught at the Industriesschool in Amsterdam.

OTHER NOTABLE EUROPEAN CERAMICS

In Hungary the Zsolnay factory, established in 1862 to produce earthenwares, extended its output to include decorative pieces patterned with Turkish and Persian motifs, often using shapes derived from pre-Columbian American and Chinese ceramics. Developed in an experimental workshop under the direction of Vinsce Wartha (1844–1914), the factory's best-known products have a rich red iridescent glaze on which the etched decoration is highlighted with gold lustre.

In Italy the old-established Cantagalli factory was transformed in the late nineteenth century by the two brothers Ulisse (1839–1902) and Romeo Cantagalli. The company is best known for its production of Renaissance-style ceramics, which include direct copies of celebrated Renaissance maiolica pieces. From about 1880 Cantagalli revived Iznik pottery techniques and wares of this type continued to be made well into the twentieth century.

Artist-Potters

Pots, like all other forms of art, are human expressions:
pleasure, pain or indifference before them depends upon
their natures, and their natures are inevitably projections
of the minds of their creators

BERNARD LEACH, *A POTTER'S BOOK*

Coffee service by Otto Lindig (Germany), 1923. Earthenware, thrown and turned. Height (tallest) 18.8 cm (7.5 in).

The air of change and experiment following the ending of the First World War involved ceramists as well as artists, designers and architects. In 1919 in Germany the Bauhaus school of design was established at Weimar under the direction of Walter Gropius and introduced radical new ways of integrating art and technology. Gerhard Marcks was head of the ceramics department at Dornburg and he and other practising potters taught the theory of design and its practical application on industrial wares and individual pieces to students who included Otto Lindig (1895–1966), Theodor Bogler (1896–1968), Marguerite Wildenhain (née Friedländer), and Richard Bampi (1899–1965). The ideas of the Bauhaus, with its emphasis on functionalism, fitness for purpose and truth to materials, not only had a profound influence on the ideas of potters in Germany and other European countries but on many artists in America.

In Britain and on the Continent the number of potters experimenting with studio ceramics continued to increase. Some were inspired by traditional artisan pottery but more by oriental wares, in particular the large quantities of Song dynasty ceramics found in burial chambers revealed during the building of railways in the early years of the century. Following on from the work of artist-potters such as Théodore Deck, Auguste Delaherche, Ernest Chaplet and others in France, the Martin brothers in Britain and George Ohr in

the United States, later artists such as Roger Fry, William Staite Murray, Charles Vyse and Bernard Leach in England and Charles Binns in America further developed the identity of the artist-potter, producing work that was both expressive and creative. For Murray, being an artist-potter meant making objects of art that had no other purpose than to be beautiful, while for Leach it signified an involvement in all the processes of making, firing and production across a range of functional tableware as well as individual pieces.

BRITAIN
Well before the First World War, a number of art schools in Great Britain set up small pottery departments, often employing throwers from the

Vase by Roger Fry (UK), Omega Workshops, London, 1914–15. Earthenware, white tin glaze with painted cobalt blue decoration. Height 25 cm (10 in).

went on to set up the Coldrum Pottery near Wrotham, Kent, where he made red earthenwares decorated with white slip very much in the manner of traditional wares of the area. From 1909 he worked in Chelsea, there devising a range of high-fired wares in the Chinese style. After the First World War he established a pottery in Sussex making figures and high-fired decorative wares again inspired by Chinese pots, employing matt glazes often in blue and grey-white that he called Soon ware. This production continued until the late 1940s.

THE OMEGA WORKSHOPS

In 1913 the art historian and painter Roger Fry (1866–1934) set up the Omega Workshops in London to produce well-designed works of domestic utility. Inspired by the new awareness of Post-Impressionism, the Workshops sought to produce decorative and useful articles for use in and around the home, including furniture and carpets as well as a range of hand-thrown and cast ceramics, much of it decorated by fine artists. Pots were specially thrown by Fry or designed by him and made by the firm of Carter and Co. in Poole, Dorset, with artists including Vanessa Bell and Duncan Grant carrying out the decoration. In contrast to the sombre colours of high-fired stoneware pots, Fry's own shapes were simple and sometimes futuristic in feel, the decoration often colourful and fresh.

For a time the Workshops flourished, offering a wide variety of artefacts for the modern stylish home. The pots, inspired largely by English delftwares, are usually covered with opaque glazes coloured grey-white, deep blue or turquoise, some with minimal decoration, others more ornate with flowing designs of flowers and geometrical motifs. Although the ceramics often lack the technical skill of industrially made work or the sense of individuality of oriental-inspired pots, from a design point of view the dishes, bowls, vases, inkstands, paperweights, jampots, cruet sets and tiles are fresh and forward-looking. Although the Workshops continued throughout the First World War, they were closed in 1919, mainly because the artists associated with decorating the objects had decided to pursue their own careers in fine art. Individual artists associated with the Omega Workshops, such as Duncan Grant, Vanessa Bell

industry in Stoke-on-Trent to teach basic skills. Richard Lunn taught pottery at the Royal College of Art in London from 1903 and wrote one of the first how-to-do-it pottery books, simply entitled *Pottery*, in 1903. Among his students was Dora Billington (1890–1968), who went on to teach and inspire many students first at the Royal College and from 1926 at the ceramics department at the Central School of Arts and Crafts in London. A pottery course was established at Camberwell College of Arts and Crafts under its Principal, W.B. Dalton, who was passionately interested in ceramics and experimented with stoneware made in the Chinese tradition. Former Camberwell students include Roger Fry, William Staite Murray and Reginald Wells. Reginald Wells (1877–1951) and Phyllis Keyes, continued to make and decorate pots, vases and plates in the Omega style, with floral or figurative designs.

EARLY INDIVIDUAL POTTERS

The Martin brothers' Southall pottery (discussed in chapter 12) had only a limited influence in stimulating others to follow its style, or indeed on the work of studio potters generally in the twentieth century. When the pottery finally closed, it disappeared with little trace. The potter whose work comes nearest to the Martin brothers' style and methods (although she is unlikely to have been familiar with their output) is the Australian-born Denise Wren, née Tuckfield (1891–1979). In England Wren studied design at Kingston-upon-Thames School of Art under the designer Archibold Knox, learning to make coil pots. She and her husband Henry D. Wren set up the Oxshott pottery in Surrey, where Denise Wren taught herself to throw and build a number of small high-temperature coke-firing kilns making reduction-fired stonewares and later salt-glazed stonewares. During the 1920s and '30s the Wrens helped engage the interest of the public in hand-made pots, exhibiting widely, demonstrating at exhibitions and writing such books as *Handcraft Pottery* (1928) and *Finger-built Pottery* (1932).

Bowl and vase by Charles and Nell Vyse (UK), *c.* 1927. Stoneware, thrown, reduction fired. Height (tallest) 30 cm (12 in).

Their daughter Rosemary D. Wren assisted her parents and eventually took over the pottery.

Charles Vyse

Charles Vyse (1882–1971) was a sculptor who turned to ceramics, producing with his wife Nell individual pots and figurines. Vyse trained as a modeller and designer at Doulton and Co. and attended Hanley Art School, from where he won a scholarship to the Royal College of Art in London. In 1919 he set up a studio in Chelsea working with his wife, a skilled ceramic chemist, making single figures and groups as well as developing a range of fine stonewares strongly influenced by classical Chinese wares. Technically competent and also visually attractive with brush-decorated designs, the pieces are explorations of the strong shapes and decoration of Chinese wares rather than particularly innovative. The Vyses's series of lively colourful earthenware figures of 'local characters' included trades such as The Balloon Woman, The Tulip Girl, and fantasy creations such as a nymph riding a seahorse. These were made by a small team of women, with many of the figures based on popular and mythical subjects, which today are admired as much as a social record as for their skill in modelling.

William Staite Murray

Although William Staite Murray (1881–1962), Charles Vyse and Bernard Leach shared a similar admiration for oriental ceramics, each had different concepts of the role of the artist-potter. Murray saw himself as an artist involved with ideas and concepts, producing ceramics that had no purpose other than to be beautiful and was not concerned with the functional aspects of pots. As an associate of radical, avant-garde painters such as Cuthbert Hamilton and Wyndham Lewis, Murray sought to incorporate such ideas in to the decoration of his ceramic forms. An early champion of studio pots as objects of art, Murray regarded them as a type of abstract art and sought to promote them as such.

After living in the Netherlands for a short time, where he collected Delft and Chinese export ware, Murray studied painting in France before experimenting with potting in London around 1912. At Camberwell School of Art he learnt to make earthenware with painted decoration. Inspired by the strength and refinement of Song dynasty wares, in

Tall vase by William Staite Murray (UK), *c.* 1930. Stoneware with incised and painted decoration of bird. Height *c.* 50 cm (20 in).

where his ideas made a profound impression on many of his students. Some of the most notable include Thomas Samuel Haile (1909–48) whose lively slip-decorated earthenware jugs and plates reflect the freedom and spontaneity of Surrealist ideas, Heber Mathews (1905–59) who later became pottery advisor to the Rural Industries Bureau, Henry Hammond (1914–89) who became head of ceramics at Farnham School of Art, and made pots in the oriental style with strong and vigorous brush decoration depicting such natural forms as flowers or fish, and Robert W. Washington (1913–97), who became involved in education but also made pots and later sculptures.

Bernard Leach

The figure of Bernard Leach (1887–1979) towers over studio pottery in Britain, his work and ideas inspiring potters throughout the world. Leach saw himself as a courier between East and West, bringing together the oriental aesthetic of quiet contemplative forms in high-fired stonewares and porcelains with traditional English slip-decorated earthenwares and the ideas of William Morris and the Arts and Crafts movement. Leach was born in Hong Kong and at the age of ten was sent to England, attending school until he was sixteen when he enrolled at the Slade School of Art in London. This was eventually followed by a period at the London School of Art where he was introduced to etching and a wider range of contemporary art. In 1909 he went to Japan intending to teach etching but was so inspired by the process known as raku, in which pots are placed directly into a glowing hot kiln and removed when the glaze has melted while still red hot, that he decided to become a potter. Leach studied traditional court pottery under the sixth Kenzan, becoming familiar with the ideas and methods of oriental ceramics such as raku and high-temperature reduction-fired stoneware and porcelain. Through books he became aware of the liveliness and simplicity of seventeenth- and eighteenth-century English slipware and made pieces inspired by it. Leach introduced the ideas of Morris and the Arts and Crafts movement to Japan, helping fuel a Japanese revival of interest in the folk craft tradition and skills that were being lost in the rush to industrialize.

1919 Murray built a high-temperature kiln in Rotherhithe where he fired to stoneware temperatures. Typical forms include tall, slender vases that recall the shape of medieval jugs, and bowls. Fascinated by Far Eastern high-temperature glazes, Murray was particularly stimulated by his contact in the early 1920s in Britain with the Japanese potter Hamada Shoji, who was helping Bernard Leach set up a pottery in St Ives, Cornwall. From then on Murray sought to perfect glazes based on classical Chinese types such as copper reds and the black-brown temmokus. Like painters and sculptors Murray gave his individual pieces titles and successfully exhibited them alongside paintings by artists such as Ben Nicholson and Christopher Wood in galleries usually showing only fine art. His large, often monumental, high-shouldered vases with their swirling brushwork of floral or abstract patterns have great strength and originality.

Murray's greatest influence was as professor of ceramics at the Royal College of Art from 1925

In 1920 Leach returned to Britain with the Japanese potter Hamada Shoji (1892–1978) to

set up a studio pottery in St Ives, Cornwall. They built a large oriental-style wood-firing reduction kiln and a small updraught kiln for earthenware and raku. Despite early technical difficulties local materials were found with which to make the wares. Leach produced individual pieces, mostly in stoneware but also some large decorated earthenware plates with slip-decorated designs. These earthenware dishes, some sixty centimetres in diameter, were decorated by Leach with great verve, bearing designs that make use of both occidental and oriental themes. A quantity of tableware was also made, and in the 1940s a range of standard shapes was developed in stoneware, largely by Leach's son David (b. 1911), with many of the items glazed only on the inside leaving the body to be toasted a rich orange-brown colour by the heat of the kiln. This was intended to 'provide sound, handmade pots sufficiently inexpensive for people of moderate means to take into daily use'.

In *A Potter's Outlook,* a pamphlet written in 1928, Leach set out his ideas about the work of the potter, writing that he was determined to 'counterbalance the exhibition of expensive personal pottery by a basic production of what we called domestic ware'. He also wrote about his disappointment with the low-key reception to his work in England especially after his huge success in Japan, a problem that brought recurring financial difficulties. These resulted in him setting up a small pottery on the Dartington Hall estate in Devon at the invitation of Dorothy and Leonard Elmhirst with a view to relocating the Leach Pottery. Although Leach lived at Dartington from 1936 until 1940 his Pottery remained at St Ives, continuing in production until his death. In the mid-1930s Leach returned to Japan, visiting many country potteries where he often designed and decorated pots and introducing him to wider aspects of Japanese traditional work. Further visits followed during the 1950s, '60s and '70s, and he and his work were greatly venerated there.

Virtually from the start Leach worked with a small team. Some were student potters who remained at the Pottery for a few months, others for a few years to study the craft. In addition a small number of workers were employed to mix clay, fire kilns and pack pots. In 1930 his son

Lidded pot and bottle by Norah Braden (UK) and two bottles by Katharine Pleydell-Bouverie (UK), *c.* 1930. Stoneware, thrown and reduction fired. Height (tallest) *c.* 25 cm (9.5 in).

Vase by Janet Leach (UK), *c.* 1990. Stoneware, thrown, matt black body with poured glaze decoration, reduction fired. Height 23.8 cm (9.5 in).

Bottle by Bernard Leach (UK), *c.* 1940. Stoneware, thrown and altered, with white slip and glaze, reduction fired. Height *c.* 22.5 cm (9 in).

empathy for the East combined with a softer more western quality, the strong eastern influence expressed through understanding rather than emulation. Individual stoneware and porcelain pots are often decorated with subtly incised, carved or painted designs in soft browns and grey-blues with motifs derived from the natural world, and included flowers, trees, plants and oriental landscapes. Glazes tended to be those associated with the Far East, notably soft celadon greens, black-brown temmokus and white-cream ash glazes. His earthenware dishes capture the best qualities of traditional English slipware. Although form rather than decoration was one of his principal concerns, his graphic skill is especially evident in his control and use of brushwork.

Leach advocated an holistic approach to art and life, believing like Morris that the objects of every-day life influence the quality of life of the maker and the user. He emphasized simplicity and qui-etude, the Bauhaus concept of 'less is more' res-onated sympathetically with the Anglo-Japanese ideal of the plain brown pot. To Leach form was determined as much by functional requirements as aesthetics, in which frivolity, self-expression and exploration of content had little place. He expounded his ideas though his pots, the many stu-dents who worked at his pottery, and his writing, most succinctly in *A Potter's Book*, published in 1940 and in print continuously since. The book is a combination of philosophical ideals and practical information, detailing methods and techniques as well as the ideas that inspired him. For many pot-ters *A Potter's Book* serves as both inspiration and practical guide, a sound and illuminating account of the work of one sort of studio potter. The book, perhaps more than any other single factor, has influenced studio potters throughout the world, ensuring that Leach's ideas are widely disseminated and taken up by generations of potters.

At St Ives Bernard Leach accepted pupils who took up his ideas. Notable in the 1920s and '30s were Michael Cardew (1901–83), Katharine Pleydell-Bouverie (1895–1985), Norah Braden (b. 1901) and Harry Davis (1910–86). Since 1945 many foreign students have spread Leach's ideas internationally such as the American Warren MacKenzie in Minnesota, the Canadian John Reeve, the Belgium potter Pierre Culot and the Australian potter Gwyn Hanssen Pigott. In the

David joined the Pottery, effectively managing the team until he left to set up his own workshop in 1955. Together with the other workers in the Pot-tery Leach was involved in the decorating and firing processes, successfully combining the tradi-tional work of the potter with that of an artist.

At their finest Leach's high-fired pots have great

Lidded jar by Michael Cardew (UK), c. 1975. Stoneware, thrown with painted decoration. Height c. 27.5 cm (11 in).

early 1950s he met the potter Janet Darnell (1918–97), who later became his third wife, and whose own understanding of Japanese pottery, particularly that made by the Bizen and Tamba potters, further influenced his ideas. At the Leach Pottery Janet Leach made powerful individual bottles by a combination of throwing on the slow wheel and hand-building with coiling and throwing. Although her vessels have great spontaneity and are informed by the processes of making and firing traditional Bizen pot of Japan, she introduced an individual quality that places them securely in the world of contemporary studio pottery. Bottles, seemingly freely thrown, are pushed or modelled to add an element of drama, disrupting and enlivening the form. Some of the smaller pieces were placed in or near the firebox of the kiln, which allowed them to take up the effect of the firing process, becoming encrusted with small lumps of ash or dramatically marked with orange flashing. Other bottles, dishes or vase forms, thrown from a black-firing clay, are decorated with a startling swish of glaze, accentuating movement and form.

Michael Cardew

Leach's most important pupil is Michael Cardew (1901–83). Unlike Leach, Cardew was initially drawn to traditional English slip-decorated red earthenware rather than high-fired stoneware, and he set up his workshop in the old country pottery

at Winchcombe in Gloucestershire in 1926. A retired traditional potter was employed and together they revived the production of thrown sgraffito slipware for use on the table and around the home. In 1939 he left the pottery in the hands of Raymond Finch, who had been one of his students, to establish the Wenford Bridge Pottery in Cornwall, where he built a high-temperature kiln and later made high-fired reduction wares. In 1942 he accepted the post of ceramist at the West African Institute of Arts, Industries and Social Sciences, Achimota in the then Gold Coast (now Ghana), where later he founded the Volta Pottery at Vumé-Dugamé, making stoneware with a dark-coloured body.

Much of the experience gained in this period formed the basis of his book *Pioneer Pottery*, published in 1969, which covers in detail the native Nigerian pottery and includes technical notes, which continue to be an invaluable guide for studio potters. The book also deals with Cardew's philosophical attitude and the nature and role of the studio potter in modern society. Many of Cardew's shapes and decorative motifs derive from his admiration for traditional African pots. Although Cardew admired oriental wares he did not want to emulate them, and unlike Leach favoured dark-coloured bodies and dense opaque glazes, many of which he devised from natural materials. Brushwork decoration also reflected African influences with simple divisions of the surface enlivened with animal motifs. His pottery at Wenford Bridge, Cornwall is continued by his son Seth.

Katharine Pleydell-Bouverie

After studying pottery at the Central School of Art and Craft in London, Katharine Pleydell-Bouverie (1895–1985) spent a year at the Leach Pottery in 1924/5 at the same time as Michael Cardew. The year was spent, as she put it, 'general stooging', but provided a useful basis for her later work as a potter. Intrigued by high-temperature firing and oriental form, Pleydell-Bouverie went on to set up her own studio at her family estate at Coleshill, first with Ada 'Peter' Mason (who had also worked at the Leach Pottery) and then with Norah Braden, another Leach student. Pleydell-Bouverie specialized in developing her own wood-ash glazes, using them on simple, strong forms fired in wood-burning kilns.

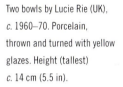

Two bowls by Lucie Rie (UK), c. 1960–70. Porcelain, thrown and turned with yellow glazes. Height (tallest) c. 14 cm (5.5 in).

Harry Davis

Harry Davis (1910–86), with his wife May, worked at the Leach pottery in the 1930s, helping to maintain the financial viability of the pottery at a difficult time. Following Leach's ideas, Davis continued the tradition of making well-designed, functional, high-fired tableware at the Crowan Pottery they set up in Cornwall. Local materials were found and the power of a water wheel was harnessed to work machinery. Davis combined great technical understanding with a profound commitment to function, producing a range of consistently strongly made, well-designed and hard-wearing stoneware and porcelain tableware thrown on the wheel. In 1962 Harry and May Davis and their family left England to start up a pottery in New Zealand, where they established a workshop similar to Crowan, prospecting for and making use of indigenous raw materials. Subsequently both Harry and May spent time in Peru, working with the Peruvians trying to introduce new potting techniques and processes that would help form the basis of new small industries.

POST SECOND WORLD WAR

The end of the Second World War in 1945 brought, for the studio potter, wider recognition. Three main strands are identifiable. One is a continuation of the ideas based on oriental forms, techniques and aesthetics put forward by potters such as Bernard Leach and William Staite Murray; the second is a broad interpretation based on ideas emanating from the Continent, and centred around concepts of modernism such as those put forward in the work of Lucie Rie; the third is a reaction against what was perceived as the Anglo-Japanese tradition of high-fired, softly coloured glazes and functional ware, in favour of brightly painted earthenware and the use of hand-building techniques rather than throwing.

Lucie Rie

The Austrian Lucie Rie (1902–95) is one of the most influential potters of the post-war period. Rie developed a range of work – mostly thrown on a continental kick wheel – that is innovative in both its use of flowing lines and bright glazes that owe little to the subtle tones or weighty-looking contemporary pots inspired by Far Eastern wares. Born in Vienna, Rie studied pottery at the Kunstgewerbeschule under Michael Powolny and later came under the influence of the ideas of the Bauhaus. Typical pots at this time were small earthenware bowls or beaker forms with textured glaze surfaces, often successfully shown at national and international exhibitions. With the advance of the German forces Rie moved to Britain in 1938, bringing with her the simplicity and directness of Bauhaus design and a more experimental use of colour and texture, often on austerely simple forms.

Although highly respected on the Continent Rie was virtually unknown in Britain, where she not only had to re-establish a studio but also her

Thistle pot, spade pot and round pot by Hans Coper (UK), c. 1970. Stoneware, thrown and assembled, electric kiln fired. Height (tallest) c. 25 cm (10 in).

surfaces achieved by applying several glaze and slip layers. In contrast to Leach's muted greys and browns Rie's glazes tend to be rich and vibrant and include dense yolk-yellows, glossy whites, soft matt pinks and delicate blues. Form predominates, and decoration, whether as simple incised lines scratched on to a matt dark-brown pigment or as volcanic textures, is always subservient to it. In working as a potter in the centre of a large city Lucie Rie both changed the popular perception and extended the range of studio pottery, moving it away from its association with the rural and rustic towards more sophisticated, urban qualities. Today Rie is acknowledged as one of the most significant studio potters of the twentieth century.

As a teacher at Camberwell School of Art Rie influenced many students, and her work has inspired many contemporary potters. Rie continued making pots in her late 80s, throwing bowls, vases and bottle forms, producing new volcanic glazes and surfaces. Widespread international acclaim and a major retrospective exhibition at the Sainsbury Centre, Norwich and at the Victoria and Albert Museum, London in 1982 brought renewed interest in her work. In their emphasis on form rather than decoration and on glaze and body colour, her work epitomizes many of the subtle possibilities that can be achieved at stoneware temperatures in an electric kiln.

Hans Coper

The most important potter associated with Lucie Rie is Hans Coper (1920–81), who became enthralled by clay and the work of the artist-potter while helping to fill button moulds and apply glaze in her studio. Coper was born in Germany and arrived in Britain in 1939 with no experience of potting. After the war he quickly learnt to throw and continued to share Rie's cramped London studio until 1958. Initially they collaborated on a range of tablewares that were Scandinavian in feel, with clean, simple lines, some bearing the seal of both potters, but Coper saw himself primarily as a sculptor and developed an individual style very different to that of Rie. His thrown and assembled vessel-based forms are often derived from ancient Egyptian or Cycladic pots or bronze forms, the colours limited to blacks and buff-white. Surface finishes are matt blacks and creams and subtly textured to bring out the form of the piece. Some early bowl and dish forms are

career. She set up in a mews house in Paddington, London, where she remained until her death. For a brief period she worked with earthenware, producing pots in terracotta, and after the war made a wide range of decorative buttons, mirror frames, umbrella handles, necklaces and other items for the fashion trade. Meetings with Bernard Leach, who impressed her with his concern for 'completeness' in a pot, and W.B. Honey, head of the ceramics department of the Victoria and Albert Museum, eventually led her to rethink her pots and acquire a high-temperature electric kiln for the production of stoneware and porcelain.

For some years after the war she worked in partnership with Hans Coper, a refugee who had arrived from Germany at the outbreak of hostilities. Coper originally came as an assistant helping to make fashion jewellery and accessories, but in the late 1940s he decided he wanted to become a potter and collaborated with Rie to produce a range of simply designed tablewares with a white inner glaze and a matt black on the outside. In addition each made individual pots and bowls. Typically, Rie's work is finely thrown, turned and delicately balanced. On individual bowls, bottles and dishes she developed a range of dry, gritty, textured

Bottle by David Leach (UK), 1994. Stoneware, thrown and turned with painted ilmenite decoration on temmoku glaze. Height *c*. 40 cm (16 in).

decorated with incised stylized birds, suggesting the influence of Picasso, though the sombre colour range softens the effect of the patterning and integrates the decoration with the pot.

By working in series and assembling sections thrown on the wheel, Coper explored a limited number of forms, each one building upon and illuminating others. Typical shapes include flattened, envelope-like forms known as spade pots, hourglass-shaped vases, rounded organic figurative shapes and, towards the end of his life, delicate, slender oval forms some ten centimetres in height. In one series the rounded, buttock and breast-like forms are reminiscent of the human figure interpreted in an abstract way. Coper's work combines the strongest traditions of the craft with a high degree of individual expression. For some years he taught at the Royal College of Art and helped renew interest in hand-built forms, influencing among others Alison Britton, Elizabeth Fritsch, Jacqueline Poncelet, Glenys Barton, Paul Astbury and Geoffrey Swindell (whose work is discussed in chapter 14). A joint exhibition of Rie and Coper held in 1997 at the Barbican Art Gallery, London, served further to highlight the shared ideas as well as the individual qualities of these two potters.

THE FIFTIES AND SIXTIES

The setting up of the Crafts Centre of Great Britain in London in 1948 (now Contemporary Applied Art), with the help of funding from the Board of Trade, and the Craftsmen Potters Association (now Craft Potters Association) ten years later did much to promote and foster the work of the growing number of studio potters. New small craft shops and galleries also sold pottery, most notably Primavera in London.

At the end of the 1950s and the beginning of the '60s studio pottery was developing along two identifiable though often overlapping lines. One focused on the tradition of the artisan potter, characterized by a range of hand-thrown useful pottery and individual pieces very much in the Leach tradition of high-fired stonewares. This approach was promoted in many ceramic departments in art schools by lecturers, several of whom had direct or indirect associations with the Leach tradition. The other approach, roughly centred around the Central School of Art and Design in London, was more experimental and inventive, with many ceramists inspired by Picasso's work and the energy it embodied. Most worked at earthenware temperatures and explored the use of painted and incised decoration, often in bright colours.

TABLEWARES

Throughout the 1950s and '60s followers of Leach's ideas established potteries making well-designed, hand-made domestic pottery produced in quantity and sold at reasonable prices. In its celebration of hand-making through the use of unglazed, tactile surfaces, thickly thrown walls and dark glazes, much of the work suggests a way of life as well as a particular approach; the best is understated, both in making and firing. Many of the pots are intended for use in the kitchen and living room, for cooking or serving food: the shapes well-considered and practical, throwing on the wheel being the preferred method of making. Glazes tend to be dark coloured or neutral with a minimum of decoration. These pots evoke a particular sort of wholesomeness, an awareness of environmental issues, a concern with organic, home-grown foods and a rejection of purely materialistic values. Raymond Finch (b. 1914) at Winchcombe Pottery, Gloucestershire, and David Leach (b. 1911), eldest son of Bernard, at Lowerdown Pottery, Devon, are distinguished potters in this tradition. David Leach, very much in the style of his father, made sensitive interpretations of oriental forms as well as a range of domestic pots first in slip-decorated earthenware and later in reduction-fired stoneware and porcelain. Also important is the work of Robin Welch, Richard Batterham, the Australian potter Gwyn Hanssen (now Gwyn Hanssen Pigott), Colin Pearson, Derek Emms and Geoffrey

Two teapots by Ray Finch (UK), Winchcombe Pottery, *c.* 1982. Stoneware, thrown and turned, with matt white cream and temmoku glaze, reduction fired. Height *c.* 22.5 cm (9 in).

Whiting, all of whom had either worked at the Leach Pottery or for a potter who had, and all of whom made high-fired stonewares. Others of note include John Leach (Bernard Leach's grandson), Andrew and Joanna Young, David Frith and potteries such as Dartington Pottery and Highland Stoneware, all making pieces to a high standard with skill and ingenuity.

Although Leach's pottery served as a model for many potters, not all fired to high temperature but preferred the wider colour range and red terracotta of earthenware. A good example of a potter exploring earthenware techniques to make func-

tional ware is Alan Caiger-Smith (b. 1930), who after studying at the Central School of Art in London set up the Aldermaston Pottery in the mid-1950s. Working with a small team of potters making wheel-thrown, tin-glazed tableware decorated with colourful painted underglaze designs, Aldermaston Pottery produced forms such as goblets, mugs, casseroles and plates. Caiger-Smith went on to experiment with traditional reduction-fired lustres devising a range of beautiful lustrous colours and textures. Briglin Pottery, set up in London in 1948 by Brigitta Appleby and Eileen Lewenstein, both of whom had studied at the Central School, also made tablewares in earthenware decorated with white tin-glaze but showing a strong Scandinavian influence. Kenneth Clark, who was born in New Zealand but studied in London at the Slade School of Art and the Central School, also set up a workshop in central London where he produced earthenware pots as well as a range of decorative tiles.

The establishment of the Studio Pottery Course at Harrow School of Art (now Westminster University) in the early 1960s was a recognition of the growing interest in studio pottery and the need for skill-based courses. At Harrow students learnt as much by working alongside experienced professional potters as from formal lectures – an affirmation of the power of Leach's ideas. Students were encouraged to follow Leach's model, firing to high temperature in a reduction kiln. Other art schools set up similar courses, often offering these as vocational training in workshop pottery techniques. The opening of the Dartington Training Workshop (now the Dartington Pottery), on the Dartington Hall estate in the workshop originally set up by Bernard Leach, was a further sign of the perceived interest in this sort of pottery teaching. As well as training apprentices the pottery also produced a range of reduction-fired stonewares for the retail market.

THE PICASSIETTES

Not all potters were concerned with making functional wares and several moved away from throwing on the wheel to the more contemplative process of hand-building using coiling, modelling or moulding, consciously producing individual objects which were conceived almost as sculpture. At the Central School of Art students such as

William Newland (1919–98), Margaret Hine and Nicholas Vergette (dubbed the 'Picassiettes' by Bernard Leach) were attracted to earthenware, hand-building and bright colours. Newland's work was typical of their eclecticism, moulding Staffordshire-type figures, hand-built terracotta, 'Indian' sculpture, 'Italian' majolica and other slip-decorated wares with energetic trailed decoration. Hine and Vergette made decorative objects such as stylized bulls, birds and goats that have a sculptural quality. All were responding to the jocular animal-drollery figurative formula in a new guise, largely inspired by Picasso's own experiments with popular Mediterranean zoomorphic ceramics.

Their work is part of a liberalizing force within studio ceramics in England and was taken up by artists such as James Tower (1919–88) who made pots reminiscent of fish-like shapes with dramatic black and white linear decoration. Potters such as Ian Auld (b. 1926) and Dan Arbeid (b. 1928) also employed hand-building methods, treating the vessel as sculptural form rather than functional object. All were in various ways reacting against the influence of Leach, deliberately avoiding utilitarian pots, brown glazes and the effects of reduction firing. Sculptors using clay also retained an important allegiance to the tradition of the material, exploiting its qualities and associations. Gordon Baldwin (b. 1932), Graham Burr and Eileen Nisbet (1929–90) used throwing or hand-building techniques, often in combination, to make objects that use the qualities of the material, firing to medium or high. Baldwin in particular has gone on to produce powerful sculptural pieces, which

Two bowls by Mary Rogers (UK), 1977. Porcelain, pinched and decorated, electric kiln fired. Height *c.* 10 cm (4 in).

Figure of a bull by William Newland (UK), 1954. Earthenware with incised decoration showing white through a purple-brown glaze. Height 35.9 cm (14.3 in).

while retaining references to the vessel, explore the qualities of clay and abstract form.

Many potters found inspiration in natural forms, seeking a focus for their work and reacting against the growing sophistication of glazes and skills that in themselves have little meaning. Mary Rogers (b. 1929), who trained as a graphic designer before taking up pottery, made small fine-walled bowls by pinching and squeezing

stoneware and porcelain clay, with the shapes derived from flower or organic forms. Decoration is reminiscent of patterns such as the dappling on an animal's back or the strata of rocks. Delicate and sensitive, her poised and precise pots combine simplicity of making with a sophisticated concept. Peter Simpson also used sensitive hand-building techniques to create forms derived from fungi, carefully building them up with layers of flat clay like fins that he enhanced with matt glazes, which highlights the delicacy and fragility of the forms.

As the international language of ceramics began to develop in the late 1960s the anarchistic work of American potters was shown in Britain. Tony Hepburn (b. 1942) was one of the first British ceramists to find inspiration in this work, making slipcast forms of everyday objects such as telephones and milk bottles as well as lustre-decorated non-functional cups and saucers. His ceramics are a successful blend of social comment and skilled making that explore the ability of clay to take on a whole variety of forms. In the centre of bowls and dishes he would melt pieces of brightly coloured glass, which were startling in their effect and indicative of the new directions of the 1970s.

UNITED STATES OF AMERICA

One of the first potters to address the training of studio potters in the US was Charles Fergus Binns (1857–1934), often known as the 'father of American studio pottery'. Binns served a traditional apprenticeship at the Royal Worcester Porcelain works in England before eventually moving to the US, where he became head of the new ceramics school at Alfred University in New York State. Here he devised a thorough and practical course that firmly embraced the ideas of the Arts and Crafts movement, but he extended it to include all types of pottery-making, industrial as well as hand-building methods. He continued to inspire and influence the ideas and work of numerous students for many years, establishing Alfred University as a highly regarded and serious course for students. In his own ceramics Binns combined a high degree of perfection, making neat, decorative classically inspired vases, with well-controlled glazes.

Binns published papers on various technical aspects of the craft and wrote three important books – *The Potter's Craft, The Story of the Potter* and *Ceramic Technology* – as well as contributing to various technical and educational magazines. Many of Binns's students became influential potters and teachers throughout the 1920s and 1930s. Notable are Myrtle French, who graduated in 1913, Arthur E. Baggs (1886–1947) and William G. Whitford. French went on to teach at Alfred and in Chicago, where she encouraged her students, including Glen Lukens, to experiment with unfamiliar techniques and materials. Baggs became technical and artistic director of Marblehead Pottery in Massachusetts, introducing a restrained way of using stylized natural forms that were then carried out in limited colours. Their work often reflects the precision and tight control advocated by Binns and is in great contrast to that of the artist and potter Henry Varnum Poor (1888–1971). Poor trained as an artist at Stanford University and in London and Paris before taking up ceramics, commenting that it was the only medium in which the artist retained complete control. Poor produced plates and dishes with figurative decoration, and carved tiles.

Different ideas were current on the West Coast of America, where Glen Lukens (1887–1967) was one of the early leaders. Moving to California in the mid-1920s, he became professor of ceramics at the University of California architectural school in Los Angeles some ten years later, remaining there until the 1960s. Lukens advised that a student should 'follow his own tastes in creation, building modern shapes with an emphasis on line, form and methods of surface enrichment'. Inspired by artefacts of ancient cultures from New Mexico to Egyptian faience, he used the alkaline deposits of the arid Death Valley Desert to produce bright glazes such as 'Mesa Blue' and 'Death Valley Yellow', which were trailed and dribbled on to his pots. Otto Heino (b. 1915), who was a student under Lukens, went into partnership with his wife Vivika (b. 1909) to make a range of decorative and functional wares that sought to achieve a direct simplicity in both form and decoration.

EUROPEAN INFLUENCES

During the period 1920–45 considerable numbers of immigrant potters arrived in America from Europe, many having studied at the Bauhaus, bringing a radically different approach to making and designing ceramics. A major educational centre for progressive ceramics in the USA in the

'L/S Teapot 1' by Anthony Hepburn (UK), *c.* 1972. Earthenware, cast and modelled, with printed decoration. Height *c.* 17 cm (6.8 in).

Egg-shaped vase by Charles F. Binns (USA), 1929. Stoneware, thrown, with runny glaze, reduction fired. Height 18.8 cm (7.5 in).

Footed bowl by Glen Lukens (USA), *c.* 1936. Red earthenware with thick, pitted yellow glaze. Diameter 29 cm (11.5 in).

'Jazz Bowl' by Victor Schreckengost (USA), 1931. Earthenware, with abstract city decoration, designed for Cowan Pottery Studio, Ohio. Diameter 40.5 cm (16.2 in).

studied under Gerhard Marcks at the Bauhaus Pottery Workshop at Dornburg from 1919 to 1925. Friedländer directed the pottery workshop at Burg Giebichenstein, Halle, together with Marcks until 1933, and designed for the Staatliche Porzellanmanufaktur in Berlin from 1929 to 1933 when she and her husband emigrated to Holland, setting up a workshop at Putten. With the outbreak of war Marguerite moved to America in 1940, Frans first to England and then America in 1947. His work, bold and simple in shape, often carries decoration featuring curved leaves, sea shells or the movement of water. As professor of pottery and sculpture at the School for American Craftsmen at the Rochester Institute for Technology in New York from 1950 until 1975, he inspired students with his belief in primacy of form and the importance of 'vision'.

In 1948 Marguerite set up her workshop at Pond Farm, California, ceasing to design shapes for industry and instead concentrating on hand-built forms. Her full, flowing, growing, 'organic' forms are decorated with wood-ash glazes or coloured slips to highlight the clay quality of the work, in sharp contrast to the academic precision of ceramists such as Charles Binns. In addition to

inter-war years was the Cleveland Institute of Arts where a Viennese designer and follower of the Wiener Werkstätte, Julius Mihalik, was professor. Several students and independent designers associated with the Cleveland Institute worked for the Cowan Pottery, Ohio, established in 1913 by Reginald Guy Cowan (1884–1957), who had studied under Binns at Alfred. The pottery produced inexpensive slip-cast earthenware figures and, after 1920, high-fired porcelain. A number of talented designers and decorators were employed, and their work was issued in limited editions. Notable is the work of Paul Manship, A. Drexel Jacobson, Thelma Frazier and Victor Schreckengost. One of Schreckengost's most successful pieces is a bowl he designed, entitled 'Jazz', that was initially intended for Eleanor Roosevelt. It depicts scenes of New York rendered in abstract style and covered with a rich blue glaze over dark-coloured decoration. It became a limited edition piece produced in two sizes and captures the adventurous spirit of the time.

Other immigrant potters from the Wiener Werkstätte include Susi Singer (1895–1949) and Vally Wieselthier (1895–1945), whose work embraced hand-modelled earthenware figures and decorative pieces. Equally important were the potters Frans (1905–80) and Marguerite Wildenhain (née Friedländer, 1898–1985), both of whom had

Tall vase by Marguerite Wildenhain (USA), 1954–6. Stoneware, thrown and turned, with plant design. Height 15 cm (6 in).

the more decorative pieces, functional pots such as teapots, covered jars, planters, bowls, cups and candlesticks were made which related much more to European studio pottery than to pots made in America at that time. Marguerite Wildenhain's philosophy – of truth to materials and the importance of form – had an important influence on contemporary studio ceramics.

Earth crater bowl by Gertrud and Otto Natzler (USA), 1956. Earthenware, with volcanic, crater-like glaze. Diameter 31.25 cm (12.5 in).

Bowl by Warren MacKenzie (USA), 1989. Stoneware, thrown and altered, reduction fired. Diameter 37.5 cm (15 in).

The two potters Gertrud (1908–71) and Otto (b. 1908) Natzler, born in Vienna, arrived in America in 1938, settling in Los Angeles. Their creative partnership began in 1933 when they met and opened a pottery producing simple, refined forms, such as bowls, which ranged from very shallow to deep and tall. In America they concentrated on individual pieces in earthenware. Gertrud threw and turned the shapes, usually bowls or full, rounded bottle-forms, and Otto developed and concentrated on devising textured and cratered glazes. The finish on the ware is highly accomplished and includes crystalline and lustre surfaces as well as rich colours such as yolk-yellow. After Gertrud's death Otto made slab-built forms. Maija Grotell (1899–1973), another European immigrant, was born and trained in Finland and studied with A.W. Finch before settling in America in 1927. Much of her work was thrown on the wheel and decorated with semi-abstract designs with a distinct 'modern' feel.

POST-WAR CERAMICS

After the Second World War the number of artists working with clay vastly increased. The country was prosperous and expansive and war veterans were offered the opportunity of study, many enrolling in ceramics classes at art colleges. The American Craftsmen's Cooperative Council, founded in 1943 and headed by Aileen O. Webb, sought to provide potters in America with a measure of professional identity and a means of national and international communication. The Council also helped foster a spirit of communion among the arts. The American Crafts Council published the influential magazine *Crafts Horizons* (later *American Crafts*) and organized national conferences and seminars. By 1966 *Craft Horizons* had some 30,000 subscribers, which ten years later had risen to 400,000.

Ceramists in America developed a style and approach very different from their peers in Europe, particularly in the early 1950s. Although some were influenced by the ideas and work of Bernard Leach, who made two extensive lecture tours of the country in 1950 and 1952, bringing direct experience of his ideas and ways of working, others looked more to Scandinavia or contemporary art movements. Warren MacKenzie and Alix, his wife, studied with Leach in England at the

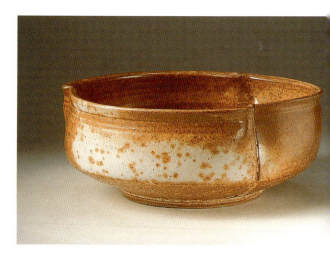

Leach Pottery (1950–2) before returning to the United States, where they set up a pottery based on Leach's ideas. On his 1952 visit Leach was accompanied by the Japanese potter Hamada Shoji and the director of the National Folk Museum of Japan, Yanagi Soetsu, their combina-

Teapot by Jeff Oestreich (USA), 1991. Stoneware, thrown and altered, reduction fired, temmoku glaze. Height 12 cm (4.8 in).

tion of practical demonstrations and mystical concepts of beauty catching the attention of many. It was during this second visit that Leach met the potter Janet Darnell, who was to become his third wife.

In America Leach, Hamada and Yanagi talked to students and potters about the aesthetic qualities of Japanese pots and Korean Yi dynasty wares, pointing out that 'regularity of form seems to call for an irregular element in decoration, and as an antithesis widens the range of expression'. Leach also referred to the living quality of Japanese country functional pottery, the subtle beauty of textured stoneware bodies and the richness of reduction firing in which pots are exposed to the flames. Although Leach's claim that Americans had no 'tap root' irritated many potters, others were drawn to his ideas as a way of helping focus an identity for studio pottery. Minnie Negoro, a student at Alfred, was particularly inspired by Leach and his advocacy of Japanese culture, for it

reflected her own interest. In 1947 she had produced a teaset, complete with bamboo handle and swiftly executed brushwork, for which she was given an award at the 12th Ceramic National Exhibition.

In addition to Leach and Hamada there were others who came from overseas who were influential in broadening the philosophy of American ceramics. Among these were Hui Ka Kwong and Elizabeth Irwin (who studied initially in China), Harue O. McVey and Henry Takemoto (b. 1930). Takemoto was born in Honolulu and rapidly developed his own style in which he decorated the surface of the clay in a bold way, using the form as a canvas. Toshiko Takeazu (b. 1929), born in Hawaii, studied under Maija Grotell and until 1968 she taught, but she gave it up to concentrate on her own work. Takaezu is influenced by Zen Buddhism, nature – particularly landscape – and Abstract Expressionism. Gradually her ceramics became less functional and more sculptural with

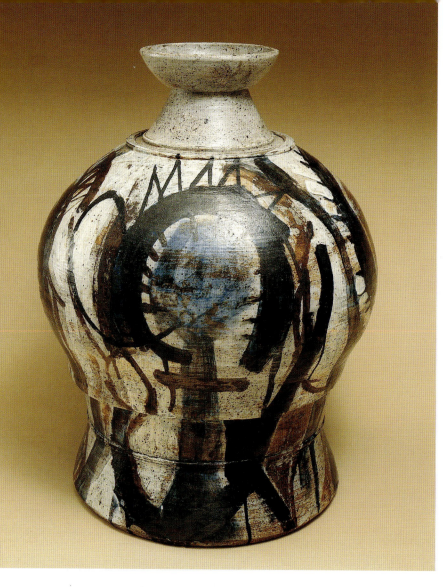

forms into sculptural structures, moving beyond the idea of vessel or container. At Otis he encouraged the students to handle the clay loosely, in an expressionist manner, allowing its qualities to play a vital part in the finished piece.

Paul Soldner (b. 1921) is also a major figure in post-war ceramics. He attended Otis Art Institute where he worked with Voulkos, pioneering the use of oil-fired kilns and fuel-efficient burners. Soldner's great contribution was the development of the raku technique on large-scale hand-built pieces, and the use of post-reduction firing. Unlike the Japanese, who allow the pot to cool in the open air after removing it from the glowing hot kiln, Soldner buried it in leaves or other organic material in a closed container, a process

Tall covered jar by Peter Voulkos (USA), 1956. Stoneware, wheel-thrown. Voulkos met Hamada Shoji and Yanagi Soetsu in 1952 and 1953, and he also got to know leading Abstract Expressionists in New York, all of whom had a profound influence on his work. Height 63.75 cm (25.5 in).

Bottle by Paul Soldner (USA), 1964. Earthenware, thrown and hand-built with painted and texture decoration over white slip, partially smoked to give both oxidized and reduced effect. Height c. 22.5 cm (9 in).

objects made out of several thrown sections joined freely together. In a desire to find out more she travelled to Japan to study more intimately the meaning of Zen, visiting several leading potters and potteries.

The most influential figure of the new movement in the 1950s is Peter Voulkos (b. 1924), who helped revolutionize the concept of the ceramic vessel. After studying painting Voulkos became involved with ceramics, eventually becoming a highly influential teacher at the Otis Art Institute in Los Angeles and later at the University of California at Berkeley. Voulkos's early ceramics consist of strongly conceived functional pieces that are powerfully thrown with minimal decoration. At the Archie Bray Foundation he met Leach, Hamada and Yanagi, and was impressed less by Leach's work than the Zen concept of wholeness and unity. At this time he also came into contact with Abstract Expressionist artists, both making a profound effect on his work. An expert on the wheel, Voulkos began to assemble his thrown

that resulted in thick smoke and a heavy reduction atmosphere. This technique, known as post-firing reduction, added a more dramatic quality, blackening the body and turning glazes containing copper into rich lustrous shades of red, orange and gold. Soldner builds his ceramic forms from thrown and slabbed units, the work often having a powerful organic quality. Many of his early pieces, decorated with figures derived from magazines and newspapers, are reminiscent of pop art.

In contrast to the restrained aesthetic of the Far East, exhibitions of Scandinavian design and the importing of contemporary pots brought other influences. The 'Good Design' travelling show sponsored by the New York Museum of Modern Art in 1949, devoted to Scandinavian crafts intended for daily use, included porcelain, earthenware and stoneware, much of it with strong, clean lines and bright glazes and uncompromisingly 'modern' in feel. Four years later the travelling exhibition 'Design in Scandinavia' introduced the work of Hertha Bengtsson, Wilhelm Kåge, Gunnar Nylund and Karl-Hary Stalhåne in addition to designs from Sweden's Stig Lindberg and Finland's Kyllikki Salmenhaara. The flowing, simple lines of Lindberg's porcelain were influential in the work of American potters such as Irwin Whitacker, Ernie Kim and Glen Nelson. A different approach was introduced through the ideas and work of Nicholas Vergette (1923–74), who left England for the US in 1958, adding to the diversity of styles and attitudes.

Ceramists were also stimulated by the sculptural work of fine artists, often making their work larger and more assertive. The work of Spanish-born potter Antonio Prieto (1912–67) alternated between utilitarian forms and sculptural constructions with bold white, black and yellow glazes standing over a hundred centimetres high. Scale was generally considered to be important if work was to have impact, with many ceramists making quite large pieces. Carlton Ball (b. 1910), who originally trained as a painter but studied ceramics with Glen Lukens at the University of Southern California at Los Angeles, often collaborated with his wife Kathryn Uhl Ball (b. 1911). They devised a method of throwing extremely tall vessels by adding thick coils of clay and then pulling the walls to the desired height.

'Sky Pot' by Jerry Rothman (USA), 1960. Stoneware, thrown and hand-built. Height 71 cm (28.5 in).

On the West Coast 'artists working with clay' responded to the new ideas about sculptural form with great energy. At the Otis Art Institute, Los Angeles, Voulkos was dynamically challenging preconceptions about what clay could or should do. Notable students who took up and developed Voulkos's ideas and produced their own abstract forms with little or no reference to the conventional vessel included Kenneth Price (b. 1935), a colourist dealing with precise form and mass, and John Mason (b. 1927), whose large outdoor pieces were influenced first by Abstract Expressionism and later by more minimalist concerns. Others who were part of the experimental group around Voulkos include Billy Al Bengston (b. 1934), who was particularly influenced by raku and Japanese Oribe wares, and Jerry Rothman (b. 1933), for whom the term 'Bauhaus Baroque' was coined to describe his blend of ornate decoration and functional form. In 1958 Voulkos moved to Berkeley and the University of California, where students included Ron Nagle (b. 1939), who makes precise, sculptural cup forms, Jim Melchert (b. 1930) who explored the horizontal format of the vessel, and Stephen DeStaebler (b. 1933), who produces large stylized figures in anthropomorphic forms.

On the East Coast a quieter revolution took place, with Alfred University and its more academic tradition acting both as a stabilizing and restraining force. Robert Turner (b. 1913), Val Cushing (b. 1931) and Ken Ferguson (b. 1938) made functional wares, experimenting with high-fired stoneware and salt-glaze. Other artists, such as David Weinrib (b. 1924) who worked at Black Mountain College, built structured slab pots. Daniel Rhodes (1911–89), who became head of ceramics at Alfred University, explored both functional and sculptural forms. Rhodes wrote a best-selling book, *Clays and Glazes for the Potter*, which along with *A Potter's Book* by Bernard Leach became a standard reference for both potters and students in the United States and Britain.

FUNK AND PUNK

Following the 1950s restlessness and exploration of new art forms came the even more frenetic 1960s and '70s. In the United States ceramics 'as a medium of expression' seemed as legitimate as painting and sculpture and, following renewed interest in the ideas of Dada and Surrealism, 'funk

'Jar in Two Volumes' by Richard Shaw (USA), 1978. Porcelain, *trompe l'oeil* sculpture of two closed books with vertically piled playing cards, cast, hand-built and printed with silk-screen images. Height *c.* 17.5 cm (7 in).

'Captain Ace' by Robert Arneson (USA), *c.* 1970. Stoneware. Height *c.* 40 cm (16 in).

art' was born of Pop. Funk is often outrageous in its imagery and crude sexual references, seeking to shock rather than please or seduce. The work is essentially sculptural in intent with much of it a response to and comment on contemporary attitudes and events. Objects are often deliberately crudely made and challenge concepts of 'good' or 'bad' and what is a legitimate use for clay. The work of David Gilhooly (b. 1943) and Robert Arneson (1930–92) is particularly significant. Typical mid-1960s sculptural objects by Arneson, a former student of Voulkos, include 'Toasties' in which fingers stick out of an electric toaster, 'Typewriter' where red lacquered fingernails replace the keys, and 'Call Girl' – a telephone with breasts. Realism and the use of everyday items – tinned foods, sexual imagery, cosmetics and the more socially provocative displays of sexual genitalia – give the work humorous, thoughtful or shocking qualities, reflecting the political and social unrest of the time. Gilhooly invented a mythical frog world in which he could legitimately satirize society and particularly its art. 'Bad taste' or even 'gross taste' was the aim of Clayton Bailey (b. 1939); many of his carefully made pieces, often with lurid, realistically modelled sexual organs, caused faces to redden and critics to deplore them as 'tasteless and obscene'.

Other funk artists did not seek such crudely stated or sensational effects but wanted to explore the boundary between illusion and reality. Their objects are often precise and technically accomplished and convey both visual and intellectual comment, which may be serious or humorous. With little interest in the traditions of studio pottery, they made use of industrial techniques such as plaster casting, highly purified white clays, smooth industrial glazes, screen-printed transfers and bright enamel colours to further refine their ideas. The ceramic sculptures of pop artist Roy Lichtenstein (b. 1925) make use of these techniques to explore themes of 'reality' and 'illusion'. For one piece he assembled a pile of commercially produced cups and saucers decorated with screen-printed dots; the cups and saucers were real but unusable, while the dots appeared to cast confusing shadows. Richard Shaw (b. 1941) is also associated with this movement: his 'Ocean Liner Sinking into Sofa' made in 1966 was one of his first 'super-realist' objects and a worthy forerunner of his other such pieces. Shaw's use of fine slip-cast forms such as books or playing cards in porcelain, assembled into still-life groups and covered with transfer (decal) decoration, has resulted in fascinating *trompe-l'oeil* pieces. Much of the success of Shaw's work lies in its expert handling of the processes of ceramics, exploiting their versatility and drawing on the traditions associated with fine porcelain and the meticulous ornateness of royal factories such as Sèvres and Meissen. Although Shaw calls on long-established decorative ceramic processes his choice of imagery is totally up to date, combining the pop elements of Warhol's soup cans with the illusionistic facade of much modern life.

Contextual art statements embodying collage, assemblage, *trompe l'oeil* and hyper-realism developed in Seattle with important contributions coming from makers such as Howard Kottler, Fred Bauer and Patti Warashina. Realism continues to be a major aspect of American sculptural ceramics ranging from the hyper-realist objects of

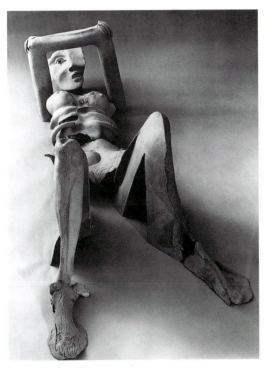

seek out sculptural qualities in their work and notable here is the large-scale figurative work of Mary Frank (b. 1933) as well as the vessel forms and sculptural installations of Ruth Duckworth (b. 1919). Duckworth, who arrived in Chicago from England in 1964, established a reputation as a thoughtful maker of container forms and as a creator of sensitive site-specific installations that make use of the plastic, soft qualities of clay.

Ceramists, like all artists, continue to be influenced by current social and economic trends. The excesses and extravagances of the 1960s and early '70s gave way to the more sombre approach of the 1970s and '80s, as economic restraint affected both educational opportunities and commercial viability. There was a general move away from

provocative, sensational work towards more decorative forms.

Despite the publicity given to a small number of ceramic artists, the backbone of American ceramics remains the production of domestic pottery for use in and around the home. Less sensational than 'funk' or 'punk' objects, the pots are skilfully made, combining both functional and decorative qualities. Artists such as Karen Karnes and Robert Turner create pots that hover on the boundary between function and decoration,

'Johan's Jacket' by Marilyn Levine (Canada/USA), 1990. Stoneware, hand-built, with metal additions. Dimensions 87.5 x 47.5 x 17.5 cm (35 x 19 x 7 in).

'Woman' by Mary Frank (USA), 1975. Unglazed ceramic. Length 245 cm (98 in).

artists such as Richard Shaw and David Middlebrook to the 'sharp-focus' realism of Canadian-born ceramist Marilyn Levine (b. 1935), whose leather jackets and clothes look totally convincing. The super-realism of Levine's handling of clay and surface finishes presents objects such as briefcases and leather jackets hanging on pegs so naturalistically modelled and finished that they truly 'fool the eye'. The detail of each seam, fastening and button-hole is meticulously observed, the texture of leather, metal and canvas faithfully reproduced. Levine's work explores the concept that things may not be what they seem, and only through touch do the 'unreal' nature of Levine's objects become apparent. Other ceramists deliberately

Two vessels by Ruth Duckworth (USA), *c.* 1985. Porcelain, hand-built. Height (tallest) *c.* 18 cm (7.2 in).

Fish vase by Walter Ostrom (Canada), 1990, thrown, altered and constructed, tin glazed. Height 23.2 (9.25 in).

Untitled square slab-built vessel by Satoshi Saito and Louise Doucet Saito (Canada), 1987. Stoneware, hand-built. Height 35.5 cm (14.2 in).

at Halifax under the direction of teachers such as Homer Lord, encouraged a deep understanding of the craft as opposed to the more decorative aspects of ceramics. After his apprenticeship at the Leach Pottery in the 1970s John Reeve returned to Vancouver where he helped foster the ideas of Zen Buddhism and its philosophical application to the making of functional pottery. Some of the concepts of minimalism and simplicity, of 'less is more', are incorporated into the work of Satoshi Saito and Louise Doucet Saito, who among other forms produce square slab-built vessels.

Other potters, reflecting the influence of West Coast American ceramics, produced objects with 'funk' elements. The American-born ceramist David Gilhooly (b. 1943), who studied marine biology before turning to ceramics, spent time in

drawing on the finest traditional work while still relating their pots and ideas to the present day.

CANADA

Unlike ceramists in the United States, many of whom were strongly affected by ideas in fine art, potters in Canada developed more slowly as influences were absorbed from the States as well as from immigrant British and overseas potters. Until the late 1960s many Canadian studio potters produced domestic tablewares influenced by the Leach-made stonewares. The opening of excellent ceramic departments in art schools, notably

Canada and inspired others to explore the fantasy worlds he created, such as the one inhabited by frogs. Harlan House's modelled sports cars and highways are decorated with low-temperature enamels and bright colours, very much in the 'funk' vogue. Realism, introduced by the work of Marilyn Levine, inspired Stanley Tanira to explore this in his models of iron stoves.

EUROPE

Studio potters on the Continent have been inspired by several broad influences. These not only include traditional work, a particular feature

Teapot by Theodor Bogler
(Germany), designed and
made at the Velten works
of the Steingut-Fabriken
Velten-Vordamm, near Berlin,
1925–6. Earthenware, tin
glazed, painted in blue and
green on a white ground.
Height 12.7 cm (5 in).

'Distacco 3' by Pompeo
Pianezzola (Italy). Hand-built.
Height 14 cm (5.5 in).

of ceramics made by many potters in France, but also oriental stonewares and porcelain, the design ideas of the Bauhaus (which took up many of the ideas of the Arts and Crafts movement) and the work and patronage of ceramic factories, many of which set up studios for individual potters. During the 1920s the concepts of form and function developed by the Bauhaus were applied to ceramics made in the factories, with many individuals working as both designers for industry and as studio potters. Many factories offered studio space where artist-potters could work privately but also make use of the technical expertise of the factory, enabling their ideas to be realized and developed. Some worked closely with technicians designing products for the factory, while others concentrated on making one-off individual pieces. Several students trained in the Rosenthal factories moved to other countries where they continued to work in similar ways. Since 1950 Rosenthal has produced a particularly adventurous range of ceramics, commissioning designs from artists such as R. Loewy and Wilhelm Wagenfield. Rosenthal opened 'Studio-Houses' in several European cities to market its own wares, as well as those of other factories and individual studio potters.

GERMANY

Between the two World Wars the design ideas of the Bauhaus made an impact in many countries, influencing the design of industrial production and individual work. In 1919 Walter Gropius (1883–1969) became head of the Bauhaus, a new institution where all the arts were to be brought together, created by the amalgamation of an existing art academy and an arts and crafts school (of which Henry Van de Velde had been head) in Weimar. Primarily the Bauhaus was conceived as a school of architecture, which included the design of objects and fittings such as furniture and lighting as well as many kinds of domestic utensils. Gropius, following many of the ideas of William Morris and the Arts and Crafts movement, developed the notion that machines should not seek to emulate the work of human hands but it was the task of the designer to discover what machines could do well. The result, sometimes called 'functionalism', swept away many ideas of fussy ornament and the designs, in comparison with what had gone before, appear clean, even austere.

So successful was the Bauhaus that even today much design is based on the principles established by the school.

As far as ceramics was concerned, several artists were engaged as teachers or 'masters', notably the sculptor Gerhard Marcks, Otto Lindig who went on to become head of the ceramics department, Theodor Bogler who became business manager of the ceramics department, and Marguerite Friedlander (later Wildenhain). Their aim was to produce functional wares in bold, simple shapes that reveal the qualities of the material, many of which were consciously based on an awareness of traditional local pottery. They were also successful in linking art and industry by designing work for industrial production, such as the designs for porcelain carried out by the Berlin and Volkstedt-Rudolstadt factories.

In Vienna the ideas of Otto Wagner encouraged the search for practical as well as pleasing work. Wagner taught that objects that did not perform their function efficiently were unsatisfactory and could not be considered beautiful. The Austrian sculptor and ceramist Michael Powolny (1871–1944) was an influential lecturer at the Kunstgewerbeschule in Vienna from 1912 until his retirement in 1936, teaching among others the ceramist Lucie Rie. Powolny is primarily associated with white tin-glazed earthenware, and also modelled figures of children and other subjects with brightly painted decoration.

In 1933 the German authorities closed the

Bottle by Karl Scheid
(Germany), *c.* 1980.
Stoneware, thrown, with resist
decoration, reduction fired.
Height *c.* 20 cm (8 in).

Bauhaus and the staff dispersed, many travelling to America, taking with them the ideals of the school. Potters both in Germany and other countries responded to the ideas of the Bauhaus in many ways. Hubert Griemert (b. 1905), who worked in the 1920s and '30s, made uncluttered shapes stemming from his adoption of the stylistic principles of the Bauhaus, developing rich, matt-glaze surfaces on strong basic forms. Glaze effects, some spectacular, some subdued but all well controlled, have become the hallmark of many German ceramics. Margarete Schott (b. 1911) focused on a small number of forms, often decorating them with iron and copper oxides to achieve rich glaze effects. Walter Popp also worked with glaze, overlapping some areas to give particular effects, and incorporating powerful brush decoration.

Many potters studied at the Werkschule für Keramik in Höhr-Grenzhausen, a workshop that specialized in the production of salt-glaze stoneware. Students include Wilhelm G. Albouts

(1897–1971) and Hedwig Bollhagen (b. 1907), who established her own workshop in 1934 at the former Hael art pottery workshop in Marwitz, near Berlin. Bollhagen made utilitarian ware alongside individual pieces with linear patterns, either painted or incised. Gisela Schmidt-Reuther (b. 1915) went on to work at the state majolica factory at Karlsruhe from 1937–40 where she made stoneware figures and animal models. Werner (b. 1920) and Annemarie (b. 1919) Schmidt-Tummeley established a workshop in the craft community founded by architect Stefan Thiersch on the island of Juist. Their work included mainly functional stoneware with often complex glazes and crystalline effects.

After the Second World War two principal concerns within ceramics can be identified – sculptural and decorative forms employing techniques such as hand-building, modelling and moulding, and wheel-thrown shapes. Karl (b. 1929) and Ursula Scheid, influenced by the ideas of Leach and Rie, made precisely thrown and well-controlled glazed stoneware and porcelain vessels. Glazes are often matt and soft in colour, but bold effects were achieved with wax resist and contrasted areas. Otto Hohlt (1889–1960) established a workshop in Katsbach in 1946 with his sons Albrecht (1928–60) and Görge (b. 1930) with the aim of applying controlled ceramic techniques in the production of pottery in traditional styles. Görge trained at the Munich Academy and at Höhr-Grenzhausen, taking over the family workshop in 1965. Together with his brother he developed a range of colourful glazes that include blue and blood red, ash glazes, and the so-called adventurine effects of golden speckles, all used on a range of thrown fine decorative forms.

Notable ceramists employing hand-building techniques include Lotte Reimers who incorporated sculptural concerns into her forms, Horst Kerstan, who under the influence of the work of the sculptor Jean Arp created a series of organic-like forms, and Beata Kuhn (b. 1927), who studied at the Werkkunstschule in Darmstadt under Margarete Schott. For a time Kuhn designed for the firm of Rosenthal in Selb, establishing her own workshop in 1957 that was shared with Karl Scheid. She later introduced more sculptural elements in her work, often using thrown components assembled into intricate overlapping shapes.

Antji Bruggeman moved in a different direction, combining thrown and hand-built forms into still-life groups, as did Johannes Gebhardt whose abstract relief pieces explore the use of the qualities of clay to crack and split. All the work is characterized by a high technical level both in the form and the glazing.

tional pitchers, jugs, bowls and plates, he manipulated, modelled and then painted on them, usually figurative or animal designs. Some purely figurative pieces of the female form were modelled or thrown and modelled, and are known as tanagras. Animals such as owls and doves were also modelled. Following the Mediterranean tradition many

Vessels by three French ceramists, *c.* 1972. Stoneware, reduction fired. Tall vase and flat-sided pot by Robert Deblander, bottle and jug by Yves and Monique Mohy, two bottles and vessel by Elisabeth Joulia. Height (tallest) 37.5 cm (15 in).

FRANCE

The aims and ideals of artist-potters working in France in the last decades of the nineteenth century continued into the 1920s and '30s, but with as great an emphasis on decoration and colour as on form. Figure modelling too became popular, and many fine artists collaborated with potters, either by learning to handle clay or more usually by decorating forms made for them. Artists associated with the Fauves created work combining great sensitivity with bold and colourful decoration.

After the Second World War there was a revival of interest in earthenware, much of it centred on the colourful traditional pots indigenous to the Mediterranean area. Pablo Picasso (1881–1973) began decorating clay vessels at the Madoura Pottery, at Vallauris in the south of France, in 1946/7, following a tradition firmly established earlier in the century of artists working with clay. Using a variety of specially made forms as well as tradi-

of the colours used by Picasso are bright and intense and his designs painterly and exuberant. In contrast to the sombre, serious qualities of work based on oriental ceramics, Picasso's pots appear fresh and lively, and inspired many potters in the 1950s. In his work with clay Picasso brought both vessel-based and modelled ceramics to new prominence, prompting other artists such as Jean Cocteau to experiment with decorated ceramic forms. As a result of Picasso's success at Vallauris a large colony of potters grew up in the area making mostly decorative vessel-based ceramics.

Other potters in France looked to different traditions, some to the refined forms and subtle glazes of oriental stoneware, others to the long-established salt-glazed stoneware, wood-fired pots made in central France in the area around the small village of La Borne near Bourges. The area has a long history of pot-making which some authorities claim can be traced to the thirteenth century but is more likely to have flourished from the sixteenth. The pottery industry produced wood-fired functional stonewares largely for a regional market. Until the early 1960s there were still some half-dozen traditional potters working in the area, throwing pots on traditional wheels and firing them in huge kilns. They produced pots for the use of the farming community in much the same way as their ancestors, but by the early 1970s these potters had all but disappeared. The elegant narrow-necked and double-handled walnut-oil bottles and wine bottles, the salting vats, the pitchers, bowls and dishes for everyday farm and kitchen, as well as modelled figures for graves and shrines, with their warm toasted body and runny ash glazes, ceased to be made.

Compositie van Twee Vormen by Jan de Rooden (Holland), 1968. Stoneware. Height 18 cm (7.2 in).

Individual studio potters are attracted to the area by the rich fired qualities and high plasticity of the local clays, the variety of effects that can be achieved, and traditional methods of firing using wood from the nearby forests. Some potters make rustic-looking tablewares, but many turned to more decorative and sculptural forms. Janet Stedman and Christine Pedley, both of whom studied ceramics in England, made jug and platter forms with rich decorative surfaces, and Yves Mohy and Elisabeth Joulia responded to the simplicity of traditional work with simple, well-considered forms.

HOLLAND AND BELGIUM

Other European countries have undergone similar sorts of development to those in Germany and France. An exhibition of French ceramics in 1913 was a profound influence, especially on the work of Hein Andrée, Chris Lanooy and Bert Niehuis. Between the wars in Holland ceramics are usually characterized by rich flowing glazes on thrown functional forms. 'De Porceleyne Fles' in Delft encouraged the making of architectural pieces on an ambitious scale.

Since the ending of the Second World War ceramics have received much official recognition with well-presented exhibitions of British and American ceramics, encouraging more enlightened liberal attitudes towards more adventurous work. Museums of decorative art have also done much to promote the work of ceramists. Some potters have looked to traditional techniques and made domestic tablewares while others such as Johnny Rolf and Jan de Rooden, based in Amsterdam, produce sculptural forms with a strong awareness of the material they use. Some potters, for example Adriana Baarspul, produce domestic pottery, but the main interest lies in sculptural forms. Jan Van der Vaart made hard-edged 'pipe' forms, while the artist Jan van de Leeuden's 'hyper-realist' cast male torsos, without arms or legs, drew on contemporary ideas in art, linking them with the classical tradition in a particularly inventive way that is part pastiche, part celebration.

Similar attitudes exist in Belgium where the work of Pierre Culot, who worked for a time as a potter at the St Ives Pottery, now makes large and strongly conceived sculptural pots, often with ash glazes. Carmen Dionyse and Oliver Leloup make more figurative pieces, all with a strong 'clay' feel about them.

SCANDINAVIA

Collaboration with ceramic factories is characteristic of much of the work produced in Finland, Sweden, Denmark and Norway. In Finland the Arabia factory, one of the largest in Europe, was established in Helsinki in 1874, and operated as a subsidiary of the Swedish firm of Rorstrand until 1914. In the early part of the twentieth century pots in the Arts and Craft and art nouveau styles were produced, notably under the artistic direction of Thure Öberg (until 1931) who adopted ideals expressed earlier by the English Arts and Crafts movement inspired by William Morris. When Arabia came under Finnish ownership the factory showed an increasing awareness of contemporary design, favouring work with clean, flowing forms.

An art department was set up in 1932 for the creation of models and decoration for handmade wares. As directors both Kurt Ekholm (1931–48) and Kaj Gabriel Franck (1945–51) encouraged studio potters to produce individual pieces making use of facilities and materials provided by the factory. Franck's pieces for everyday use relied for decorative effects on coloured glazes and include square serving dishes in the form of inverted pyramid shapes. Kyllikki Salmenhaara's thrown ceramics were carried out with verve, with throwing rings often left on the pot adding a suggestion of energy. Other artists include Friedl Kjellberg (b. 1905), who specialized in delicate

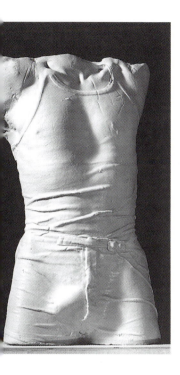

Male Torso by Jan van de Leeuden (Holland), 1977.

Vessel forms by Raija Tuumi (Finland), made at Wärtsilä-Arabia, *c.* 1975. Stoneware.

porcelain, and Aune Siimes (1909–64), noted for thin, translucent porcelain. Michael Schilkin (1900–62), the Russian sculptor and ceramic artist who worked at Arabia from 1936, was known for his animal sculptures and large relief plaques. Birger Kaipiainen (b. 1915) gained a reputation for ornamental pieces and wall panels with painted and engraved decoration. One of the most respected of the Arabia artists is Toini Muona, who joined the factory in 1931 and designed stoneware dishes and vases in simple and sometimes angular shapes decorated with mono-

chrome glazes. The work of Raija Tuumi, who contrasted areas of unglazed clay with rich glaze produced objects that combine strong textural qualities, is also notable.

Following the ending of the last war the Arabia factory maintained the production of well-designed pots based on plain, almost austere forms, often with coloured glazes. The domestic range of pots has succeeded in combining the warmth of handmade ware with the best qualities of machine production. The work of individual potters was primarily concerned with decoration as a means of breaking away from the evenness of machine production, which is one of its strongest qualities.

The Rorstrand pottery and porcelain factory (originally founded near Stockholm in Sweden in 1725), the Royal Copenhagen factory (1775) of Denmark and the Norwegian Porsgrunde factory have all played a major role in their own countries. All have been concerned with encouraging the work of individual potters within their factories. This has encouraged the development of pots often characterized by simple forms and rich decoration. Bright, rich glazes such as red and blue are often used on small areas set against dark textured unglazed surfaces on simple, often straight-sided forms. Designs, often of geometric shapes as well as stylized animals, are richly worked in relief decoration.

The Danish designer and ceramist Axel Salto (1889–1961) is one of the pioneers of sculptural ceramics in Denmark. From 1923, when he became a potter, he worked for Bing and Grøndahl and the Royal Copenhagen Porcelain Factory, where he made simple bowls with carved relief decoration in light-coloured stoneware with richly coloured glazes flowing over relief decoration. He also produced vases, utilitarian wares and sculptural pieces, believing that 'It is of greater importance for an artist to create in the spirit of Nature rather than reproduce its outer manifestation'. Nathalie Krebs (1895–1978) was influential both as a designer and potter. She first trained as a chemical engineer before joining Bing and Grøndahl where she worked with porcelain. In 1930 she set up her own workshop, Saxbo, at Herlev, producing stoneware and porcelain and aiming to achieve pure colours and simple shapes in line with functionalist ideas. In addition Krebs also

earthenware and bone china. Lindberg also made slab-built figures and slip-cast pieces in unglazed stoneware. Berndt Friberg joined the Gustavsberg factory in the mid-1930s where he made individual pieces in stoneware finished with subdued glazes.

Post-war Scandinavia saw many individual potters breaking away from the strong tradition of hand-thrown pots produced in association with industry, though some continued, such as the collective workshop 'Plus' in Fredrikstad in Norway, which also provided prototypes for industry.

Vessels by Wilhelm Kåge (Sweden), c. 1948. Stoneware, thrown and turned. Height (tallest) 22.5 cm (9 in).

Large dish by Nathalie Krebs (Denmark), c. 1935. Thrown, with flying duck applied in relief. Diameter 42.2 cm (16.5 in).

produced individual pieces such as a pear-shaped jug with the neck split and extended to form the handle and spout, a pot that was successfully exhibited in New York in 1938. Krebs also collaborated with a number of designers.

At the Gustavsberg Porcelain factory in Sweden, the artistic director Wilhelm Kåge (1889–1950) designed the 'Argenta' range of hand-thrown or moulded green-glazed vases, bowls, plates and boxes inset with typically art deco motifs of mermaids, nude female figures and flowers. He was succeeded by Stig Lindberg who produced designs for utilitarian wares, vases and bowls, with decorating techniques that included bright colours and painting of naive or surrealistic figures, or abstract patterns. These were thrown on the wheel and brought to a perfect finish through tooling and turning. Especially notable were pots that are elongated and dramatic in concept as well as sculptural pieces in stoneware,

Many individual ceramists turned to more sculptural objects with much of the work inspired by and commenting upon contemporary social and political conditions. Influences came from surrealism and pop art as well as more traditional sources such as Far Eastern ceramics. Anna-Maria Osipow in Finland and Marjatta Lahtela both explore the surrealistic qualities of form using naturalistic modelling contrasted with unlikely shapes and forms. In Norway Erik Ploen made attractive reduction-fired domestic stoneware, while Finn Hald and Dagny Hald made modelled forms, often incorporating the figure in various sorts of often complex relationships.

Many of the sculptural ceramics produced in the 1960s were issue-based, the 'message' of the piece as significant as its form and texture. Topics such as politics, pollution, the destruction of the environment and over-production were often addressed obliquely, for instance by portraying a solitary seagull. Some ceramists, concerned with the 'roots' of ceramics, looked at indigenous folk pottery, the use of local clay and the 'natural' qualities of ceramics. Catharina Kajander in Finland started using local red clay for large surreal sculptural forms, while Ulrica Hydman-Vallien in Sweden made folk-based ceramics with a humorous element. In Sweden Britt-Ingrid Persson used ceramic sculpture as a means of commenting on and often attacking consumerism as well as other aspects of contemporary society. Hertha Hillfon and Marit Lindberg-Freund

Bowl by Alev Siesbye (Denmark), 1990. Stoneware, with resist decoration, electric kiln fired. Diameter 20 cm (8 in).

'Blossom Jar' by Peter Rushforth (Australia), *c.* 1975. Stoneware, salt-glazed, thrown and ash glazed. Height 30 cm (12 in).

worked on a smaller scale and tend to comment on more human sensitivities.

In Denmark the Turkish-born potter Alev Siesbye developed a range of full, rounded forms, often covered in matt glazes in earth shades of brown, yellow, rust and beige. Later she extended her colours to include various shades of blue and turquoise. The Danish potter Lisbeth Munch Petersen (b. 1909) shared a workshop with her sister Gertrud Vasegaard (b. 1913) and subsequently worked as a designer. In the 1950s she worked at Bing and Grøndahl producing, among other forms, pierced porcelain bowls with glaze in the manner of rice-grain decoration. After running her own studio with her sister, Gertrud worked as a designer for Bing and Grøndahl, designing teasets with linear patterns. Her daughter Myre (b. 1936) set up her own studio in 1959 after designing for four years at Bing and Grøndahl.

AUSTRALIA

One of the first recorded accounts of pottery-making in Australia appeared in the *Sydney Gazette and New South Wales Advertiser* in September 1803, which advertised for earthenware. Samuel Skinner, one of the first known professionally trained potters to work in Australia, had arrived in Sydney in 1801. Two more arrived in 1819, both from the Staffordshire potteries. Typical products included jars and bottles for food, and bricks. Later sewage pipes were produced in quantity. In 1830 James King set up a workshop making water jars, cups and jugs at Irrawang, NSW, and by 1857 George Guthrie was producing bottles, jugs and jars at Bendigo, Victoria. Gradually potteries making wares for local needs were opened, mostly using clays from the area. Flowerpots, jars, teapots, filter bottles and inkpots were being made semi-industrially to supply the needs of the newly settling country. James Silcock opened his pottery in Lithgow Valley in 1879, which continued production until 1973.

One of the earliest artist-potters was Merric Boyd (1889–1959), who set up his workshop at

Murrumbeena, Victoria, in 1911, and studied ceramic techniques in Stoke-on-Trent between 1917 and 1920. Many of Boyd's ceramics are directly inspired by natural form and art nouveau and include jugs with 'tree-trunk' handles and large pots decorated with animal and human figures. Other early potters include Harold R.

Untitled still life by Gwyn Hanssen Pigott (Australia), 1993. Porcelain, thrown and turned, wood fired. Height (tallest) c. 20 cm (8 in).

sufficiency, he researched and found local materials with which to produce a range of fine wheel-thrown tablewares. These are simple in form and reflect the influence of both the Leach tradition and the great Song pots of China. His students included Gwyn Hanssen and Les Blakeborough. As a teacher at the University of New South Wales, McMeekin helped inspire young potters, and his book *Notes for Potters in Australia,* published in 1967, has been influential in helping to encourage potters to investigate indigenous Australian materials and indirectly to develop their own styles.

The establishment of art schools such as the National Art School in Sydney, New South Wales, with well thought out pottery courses, the immigration of potters trained in Europe and the increase in the number of studio potters led, in 1956, to the formation of the Potters' Society of Australia. Peter Rushforth, Ivan McMeekin, Mollie Douglas and Ivan England, all of whom produce distinctive decorative wares, were involved in the setting up of the society. Potters responded to a wide variety of influences, including oriental high-fired wares, tempting some to spend study periods in Japan. Much influence also came from the strong colours of the landscape, the starkness of desert areas and the shapes and forms of plant and animal life unique to Australia. Particularly successful is the work of Peter Rushworth, who as head of ceramics at the National Art School had a great influence on young potters. His work combines influences from medieval English wares as well as oriental pots. His strong, simple ash-glazed forms have great strength and beauty.

Organizations such as the Potters' Society of Australia, which sets up exhibitions of contemporary work and produces the society's magazine *Pottery in Australia,* do much to encourage new ideas and to spread information. International exhibitions at Bendigo stimulated a much broader interest in processes and styles, adding a useful dimension to ceramics in Australia. Many potters experimented with ceramic form, moving away from functional work towards freer interpretations of both concept and form. Notable among these are Shunichi Inone and Marea Gazzard (b. 1928), who in 1973 was appointed first chairman of the Crafts Board of the Australian Council. Gazzard makes large, coil-built sculptural forms that are

Hughan (b. 1893) who first made hand-built forms with F.E. Cox, a potter in Melbourne, and then started to produce high-fired wares after being inspired by Leach's *A Potter's Book* and the study of Chinese ceramics displayed in the National Gallery of Victoria. Additional inspiration for his stonewares came from the colours of the Australian landscape and its vast sense of scale.

A major influence on many post-Second World War potters has been the writings and philosophy of Bernard Leach, as well the pottery of Japanese Jomon or Chinese Shang wares. The symbolism of New Guinea masks and Maori totem figures have served as other important stimuli for Australian potters. Ivan McMeekin, who first trained with Michael Cardew and then ran the Wenford Bridge Pottery in Cornwall, returned to Australia in the early 1950s and set up the Sturt Craft Centre at Mittagong where he produced high-fired porcelain and stoneware inspired by Chinese Song wares. Following Michael Cardew's example of self-

intended, when grouped together, to evoke a particular environment. Decorative ware by Peter Travis and Stephen Skillitzi often reflects the influence of the Australian countryside. Vic Greenaway's work combines a strong feeling for form with the 'natural' glaze qualities associated with ash and ground igneous rocks.

NEW ZEALAND

Production of pottery in New Zealand started first with the manufacture of bricks, pipes and tiles; towards the end of the nineteenth century local potteries produced salt-glazed crocks, bottles and jars for industrial and domestic use. Luke Adams in Christchurch successfully expanded production to include cast and moulded domestic ware, while the Temuka Pottery in South Canterbury was equally capable of producing well-made wares.

Early studio potters drew support and encouragement from the ceramics industry, which they persuaded to fire their pots in their large kilns. In the period from the 1920s to the 1940s potters included Brian Gardiner, Olive Jones, Elizabeth Lissaman and Elizabeth Matheson. In 1935 Robert Field built a wood and coke kiln and ten years later started a series of pottery classes. After the Second World War there was a great surge of interest as contacts were made with the work and ideas of Bernard Leach, who visited the country in the 1960s. The New Zealand Association of Art Societies awarded travel and study grants to potters such as Len Castle and Peter Stitchbury to study abroad and to work with Bernard Leach at St Ives. They in turn took their knowledge back to New Zealand, having gained a particular view of the craft as well as increased experience and technical knowledge.

The government's severe restrictions on imported ceramics in the 1950s encouraged a strong public demand for home-produced tablewares as well as individual pieces. Potters responded to the buoyant market, though taste tended to be conservative, inclining towards browns and beige glazes. In 1962 Harry and May Davis, who had worked at the Leach Pottery in the 1930s, moved from Cornwall to set up the Crewenna pottery at Nelson, introducing the concept of self-sufficiency by searching out and using indigenous raw materials. Here they produced a range of functional high-fired stoneware very much in the Leach style. Potters such as Peter Stichbury, Barry Brickell and Mirek Smisek produced domestic pottery in substantial quantities as well as individual pieces.

Slowly other ideas were absorbed. Organic forms such as gourds and shells inspired strong shapes from Ned Grant and Len Castle. A focus for activity was the establishment of the New Zealand Potters Society in the late 1950s. The society promotes an influential annual exhibition and also started publication of the magazine *The New Zealand Potter*.

ISRAEL

Studio ceramics in Israel started in the 1930s with the arrival of Hedwig Grossman-Lehmann, often known as the 'mother of Israel's studio ceramics', followed by Paula Ahronson and Chava Samuels and then Hanna Zuntz-Charag, all from Europe. Many students studied with these ceramists and the creation of the ceramics department at the Bezalel Academy in Jerusalem in the late 1950s, together with departments set up in other colleges, affirmed the importance of ceramics as an art form in its own right.

Potters in Israel have drawn heavily on traditional ideas and forms for much of their domestic ware. Of particular interest are the smooth earth-

Dish by Barry Brickell (New Zealand), *c.* 1995. Stoneware, thrown and reduction fired.

enware forms of Zuntz-Charag. Ceramists in Israel have, however, on the whole been less concerned with producing functional ware, although many have, than with more decorative wares and sculptural forms. The large, egg-shaped vessels of Yal Gurfinkel-Pasternak, with their smooth terra-sigilatta covering and striped decoration, have great individuality, while Lydia Zavadski's 'jar sculptures' call on desert-related themes. Many

'Desert Texture' by Naomi and Nora (Israel), 1971: Naomi Bitter (b. 1936) and Nora Kochavi (b. 1934). Earthenware, hand-built. Diameter 50 cm (20 in).

new buildings incorporate decorative ceramics both on the inside and on the exterior with architectural ceramic panels. A good example is the mural by Gedula Ogen on the Ceramic Museum, Tel Aviv. Gedula Ogen also makes decorated work, much of which relates to native plant forms.

Potters such as Edith Ady and Agi Yoeli have made anthropomorphic sculptural objects with a sure awareness both of the form and the qualities of the clay. Particularly notable are the sculptural forms of Nora (Nora Kochavi) and Naomi (Naomi Bitter). They have produced a series of installations that look at history, landscape and ritual, and the interaction of human activity. Also notable is the work of Siona Shimshi, who spent

the years 1959–63 in America where she developed a way of approaching her work that can be summed up as 'openness', as well as acquiring a wide range of technical abilities. Shimshi's sculptural work touches on the 'human condition' in such pieces as 'Ten Little Angels' in which the figures grow sequentially from thirty centimetres to three metres high with the angel wings growing proportionally smaller, suggesting a lessening of our idealistic powers as we age and experience. Official recognition of the work of studio potters came in 1968 with the setting up of the Ceramic Arts Association of Israel with the support of the Ministry of Education and Culture.

AFRICA

The two major influences on the development of studio ceramics in Africa are traditional pots built by hand and fired to a low temperature, and the introduction of Western making and firing techniques and its associated aesthetic of ceramics as an art form. Traditional African pots are usually built by coiling from locally dug red-coloured clays, the surface simply decorated with incised designs, and fired either in basic kilns or in open bonfires, usually without glaze. Shapes tend to be strong and rounded to withstand the open firing, with many relating to natural forms such as gourds; pots made for ceremonial or ritual use tend to be more elaborate and ornate. Such work has inspired contemporary potters such as Isaac Olusegun Aina in Nigeria.

Studio potters from Europe travelled to Africa in the inter-war period. Other contemporary potters have combined traditional influences with oriental high-firing techniques. Kenneth Murray, who arrived from Britain in 1927 to serve as an education officer in Nigeria, recognized the skills of the local potters. Murray had worked for a short time at the Leach Pottery at St Ives and wrote long accounts of the African pottery techniques he saw. In the 1930s and '40s studio potters were invited to Africa to introduce Western technology. One of the most influential was H.V. Meyerowitz, a Russian sculptor trained in Germany who moved from South Africa to Achimota College, West Africa, where he became art master. Meyerowitz adopted Gerhard Marcks' view that 'the workshop should become the art school' and set up a production workshop that

Jar by Esias Bosch (South Africa), 1972. Stoneware, slab-built, ash glazed, reduction fired. Height 23 cm (9.2 in).

would make functional wares and also teach and develop the skills of the individual potters. The workshop produced tablewares, tiles, pipes and insulators and had the ambitious aim of fulfilling the entire needs of the country. To take charge of the technical aspects of production Harry Davis arrived in 1936, followed by Michael Cardew in 1942, both of whom had worked at the Leach Pottery. Cardew felt that the low-fired earthenwares were ill suited to modern life and introduced high-fired stoneware. After the death of Meyerowitz in 1945 the centre closed and Cardew moved to Vumé-Dugamé in present-day Ghana, eager to extend the making of stoneware, remaining there until 1948.

Local potters making traditional hand-built pots were slow to respond to the high-fired wares and the particular technical difficulties they presented. In 1950 Cardew returned to Africa at the invitation of the Nigerian government as Pottery Officer with a brief to improve the quality of 'native pottery'. Although he greatly admired the thriving indigenous pottery industry, where the wares were hand-built and fired to low tempera-

ture in bonfire firings, he introduced high temperature firings. Some of the finest traditional pots were made by Ladi Kwali using a coil-and-smooth technique. Deeply impressed, Cardew encouraged Ladi Kwali to travel and demonstrate her skills in many other countries, and her rounded bowl forms with their traditional incised decoration became internationally renowned. Indirectly Ladi Kwali helped introduce hand-building and low-firing methods in the West. She visited England on several occasions in the 1960s where she demonstrated her techniques to admiring studio potters. At Abuja in Nigeria Cardew established a Pottery Training Centre making high-fired reduced stonewares, remaining until 1965 when he returned to England.

At Wenford Bridge Pottery in Cornwall Cardew was joined by Hyme Rabinowitz who subsequently returned to South Africa to set up a workshop at Eagle's Nest, on the slopes of the Vlakkenberg Mountains, making high-fired reduction wares. One of the earliest studio pottery workshops in South Africa is that of Sammy Libermann, who trained originally at the Chelsea Pottery in London. At one point he employed a large team making functional earthenware. Esias Bosch (b. 1926), who worked in England with Ray Finch and Michael Cardew, started making earthenware decorated with Bushman motifs at his workshop at White River, Eastern Transvaal, but later changed to reduction-fired domestic stoneware decorated with powerful iron brushwork. Sculptural work by Barbara Greig touches upon more social concerns and recently potters are finding an appreciative audience for decorative work.

JAPAN

The modern studio craft movement in Japan that arose following the end of the Meiji period in 1912 challenged the hierarchy that had been established on the basis of western distinctions between the fine and applied arts. In 1927, after almost ten years of lobbying by the crafts

Water pot by Ladi Kwali (Nigeria), *c.* 1970. Stoneware, hand-built, with incised decoration of panels of crocodiles and abstract forms. Height 29 cm (11.5 in).

Bottle by Hamada Shoji (Japan), *c.* 1950. Stoneware, thrown with trailed decoration on dark glaze. Height *c.* 23 cm (9 in).

Bottle by Kawai Kanjiro (Japan). Stoneware, press-moulded, reduction fired. Height 21.5 cm (8.5 in).

community, crafts were put on an equal footing with painting and sculpture. While many of the free-thinking artists looked to contemporary western art and design movements such as art deco, constructivism and the Bauhaus for inspiration, there were others who believed that only traditional East Asian culture could provide a way forward. Japan's historical past provided the basis of the social and aesthetic ideology promoted by Yanagi Soetsu (1889–1961) and other founders of the Mingei, the Japanese Folk Craft Movement, in the 1920s. The movement played a key role in the preservation and promotion of traditional craft practices during this critical period.

Potters initially associated with the movement include Hamada Shoji (1894–1978), Tomimoto Kenkichi (1886–1963) abd Kawai Kanjiro (1890–1966) as well as the English potter Bernard Leach (1887–1979), who had learned to pot in Japan in 1911 with Tomimoto. Both Leach and Tomimoto had studied art in the West and in Japan they sought to pioneer new ways of working with clay, although both had a highly conventional Japanese training in pottery. For Leach a major concern was with the unification of Eastern and Western ideas, while for Tomimoto it was the reconciliation of the past and the present. Both concerns have continued to dominate work made in Japan. Potters such as Hamada, Kawai, Tomimoto and Rosanjin Kitaoji (1883–1959) shared a belief in the individual consciousness, while at the same time striving to maintain and even build on the work of the old masters.

Hamada studied ceramics at technical school and made pots in his spare time before moving to England with Bernard Leach to set up the Leach Pottery in St Ives. In 1924 Hamada returned to Japan, where he set up his workshop in the traditional pottery village of Mashiko, responding to the simplicity and functional qualities of the modest, traditional country wares made in the town but developing his own distinctive style. Employing local clays and materials, his work draws strongly on tradition, but interpreted with a modern edge. Tomimoto, who trained initially as an architect, brought more graphic qualities to his work and is best known for lavish porcelains with gold, silver and polychrome decoration. During the 1920s and '30s he made both blue-and-white and plain white porcelains inspired by Korean ware, under-

stated in feel and austere in appearance. In contrast Rosanjin worked freely in a variety of regional and historical styles. Shimaoka Tatsuzo (b. 1919) also responded to historical ceramics, setting up his pottery in Mashiko. Like Hamada he was a follower of the Japanese folk craft movement known as Mingei, making use of traditional forms as a basis for his work. One of his special techniques involves pressing rope into the surface of full, rounded thrown pots and rubbing cobalt into the surface before firing in a salt-glaze kiln to bring out the pattern. The cord-like decoration is inspired by the techniques of the earthenwares of the prehistoric Jomon period. Koyama Fujio (1900–75) combined aspects of historical work with forms of great simplicity, particularly in his porcelain vessels with enamel decoration.

The turmoil of the Second World War brought profound changes to Japan's social, economic and cultural landscape. Defeat and occupation triggered both renewed interest in tradition and a determination to break away from conventional concepts. The relentless decline of traditional craft production in the face of continuing industrialization prompted various responses. The government inaugurated a system of recognition for

living artists of Important Cultural Properties, the individual appointees popularly becoming known as Living National Treasures.

Closely allied with this system was the staging of the Japanese Traditional Crafts Exhibition, held annually since 1954, as well as several major competitive ceramics exhibitions, many sponsored by newspaper companies. Until 1982 the Asahi exhibition had two thematic categories, 'Topic Work' and 'Free Work', before they were amalgamated into a single category of 'Free Creation Work'. Much of the traditionally based work addresses the ceramic histories of the Far East, but often broadly interpreted rather than imitated. Suzuki Osamu (b. 1934) has looked at the vessels

'Returning to Earth' by Ryoji Koie (Japan), 1988. Stoneware, moulded, from a set of eight.

of the tea ceremony and specializes in Shino glazes, an opaque white glaze contrasting with the redness of the body on forms that are rooted in tradition. Chinese Song period porcelain celadons have offered inspiration to Miura Koheiji (b. 1933), the smooth forms covered with a delicate pale blue-green glaze and soft orange-brown crackle that makes reference to so-called *guan* (official) wares. Fine blue-and-white porcelain has also been the starting point for Yoshikawa Masamichi (b. 1946). The hand-built forms ornamented with incised decoration inlaid with underglaze blue successfully combine function and decoration. Matsui Kosei (b. 1927) makes use of the ancient technique of marblizing (neriage), from medieval Tang dynasty China, in which different coloured clays are layered together. The restrained, classical forms and intricate patterns belong entirely to the late twentieth century. Matsui's involved vessels have also been inspired by his career as a Buddhist priest.

In Kyoto an avant-garde movement calling itself the Sodeisha sprang up in 1948, founded by ceramists who included Yagi Kazuo, Suzuki Osamu (b. 1926) and Yamada Hikaru. Sodeisha artists severed ties with the rigidly formalized tea ritual aesthetics, turning away from function and purpose in art, and some entered the ceramics world eager to criticize and oppose. Their work deals with issues such as tradition in ceramics, the social conditions of the post-war period and the effects of mass destruction and nationalism, as well as sexual themes. Much of their work is anarchic, disturbing and often monumental in concept. Notable among this group are Yanagihara Mutsuo (b. 1934), Nakamura Kinpei (b. 1935), Ryoji Koie (b. 1938) and Kamota Shoji (1933–83). Nakamura's assemblies of natural and manufactured elements, often incorporating explicit sexual themes, are usually gaudily coloured and iconoclastic, referring to the confusion of the individual within modern society as well as to the conditions of national culture.

Studio Ceramics Today

FRIVOLITY, SELF-EXPRESSION, CONTENT

*The handmade object is a sign that expresses human society
in a way all its own: not as work (technology), not as symbol
(art, religion), but as a mutually shared physical life*

OCTAVIO PAZ

Three vessels by Elizabeth Fritsch (UK), 1994. Stoneware, hand-built, with painted decorations of slips and oxides, multiple firings to 1260°C. Height (tallest) *c.* 30 cm (12 in).

The 1970s heralded a major broadening of the spectrum of ceramic activity as a result of rapid development in the attitudes of artists using clay and a great expansion in the range of work. This diversity and freedom is attributable partly to the geographical and ideological decentralization of artistic authority and partly to a greater awareness of the expressive potential of clay. As barriers, rules and boundaries began to crumble, hierarchical elitism gave way to a democratization that encouraged the merging of fine art and craft and a subsequent blurring of the distinction between them. Three broad groups of ceramic production can usefully be identified: one concerned with functional, practical wares, the second with more decorative pieces, and the third with sculptural forms wherein clay is used primarily as a medium of expression. No group is discrete, all of them to some extent overlapping. In the US the broad spectrum of ceramics is often referred to as 'clay work' to avoid such potentially emotive labelling as potter, ceramist or maker.

In Britain potters/ceramists generally adopt a more pragmatic approach. The crafts as an independent form of artistic activity gained a large measure of official support with the setting up in 1971 of the Crafts Advisory Committee (later the Crafts Council of England, with Scotland and Wales having their own systems). The organization is similar to the visual arts department of the Arts Council, although smaller in size and more modest in its remit. Its broad aim then and now is the promotion of the work of craftsmen and women through a variety of means, including direct grants to individuals and craft bodies, sponsoring publications and exhibitions, and setting up a wide-ranging educational programme. The Crafts Council not only provides a welcome injection of funds but also serves to lift the status of craft, giving it proper recognition and seeking to introduce it to a wider audience. In the United States the work of the American Crafts Council and the setting up of the American Craft Museum in New York addressed broadly similar concerns, while many other countries have a variety of schemes for promoting craft.

Ceramists today are part of an ever-growing international movement with ready access to the world's historical and modern ceramics through a plethora of books, journals, photo images, videotapes, Internet contacts and travel. Publication of journals – such as *Ceramic Review* in Britain, *Ceramics: Art and Perception* in Australia, *Ceramic Monthly* and *American Ceramics* in the US and *Les Ceramique et Art du Métier* in France, and more recently *Ceramic Art* in Taiwan, *Ceramics Art Monthly* in Seoul, Korea and *Kerameiki Techni* in Greece – are crucial in helping to spread ideas and information. All have a wide remit to foster the finest ceramics, whether vessel or sculpturally

based, encouraging a broad spectrum that not only embraces the ideas of Leach and his followers and the value of function, but the clay object as sculpture. Such publications help bring an understanding of clay as a creative medium in its own right while also raising the question of whether there are distinct national characteristics in contemporary ceramics. International exhibitions in countries such as New Zealand, Italy, France and Japan also help promote the concept of ceramics as part of a growing international language.

Other significant changes have signalled both a new freedom and wider market for ceramics. The deaths of several major twentieth-century figures, including Hamada Shoji in 1978, Bernard Leach in 1979, Hans Coper in 1981, Michael Cardew in 1983 and, after a debilitating illness, Lucie Rie in 1995, were seen as marking the end of a particular era within studio ceramics. At the same time ceramics began to find a new market as leading auction houses successfully promoted the work. Since then prices have continued to rise, some dramatically, with pieces hitherto offered for sale at hundreds of pounds or dollars beginning to sell for thousands. Ceramics suddenly seemed to offer significant investment potential. New galleries opened to show the work of established potters and promote up-and-coming younger makers.

TECHNOLOGICAL DEVELOPMENTS

During the last twenty-five years rapid technological change meant more efficient machines and a wider range of ready-prepared materials. Machinery used by potters such as throwing wheels, pugmills, slab-rollers or kilns have been redesigned, with many becoming smaller in size, lighter in weight and easier to use. By far the biggest change has affected kilns, where the use of the highly effective lightweight insulating material ceramic fibre has greatly increased effectiveness. Such lightweight kilns which can quickly and easily be built and economically fired are particularly useful for potters firing raku. Firing techniques that had previously been cumbersome and difficult now became accessible and relatively easy to handle, opening up new and exciting possibilities, and potters were quick to respond. Materials have been refined or extended with high-temperature yellows and reds, and a wide range of ready prepared glazes and slips generally available.

EDUCATION

Educational institutions have also responded to the changing role of ceramics. In Britain, the ending of the old Higher Education examination system encouraged more individual, project-based work, enabling students to follow their own ideas and schemes whether making decorative pots, functional tablewares or sculptural forms. London-based art institutions such as Camberwell School of Art and Middlesex Polytechnic (now University) were particularly important in fostering new work at degree level. For post-graduate students in the UK much of the change centred around the Royal College of Art in London, where, under the direction of Professor David Queensberry, ceramic students were encouraged to explore the possibilities of clay both as a creative medium for individual expression and as a way of approaching design for industry and architecture. Tutors included the sculptor Eduardo Paolozzi and the potter/sculptor Hans Coper. Both were particularly active in fostering an enquiring attitude, posing the question 'why?' rather than 'how?'. As a result many students elected to move away from traditional working methods such as throwing to investigate handbuilding techniques or slip-casting, calling on influences as diverse as space-age rockets, toys or sardine cans. These new freedoms echoed the strong sense of individualism that had grown up in the US in the mid-1950s at such institutions as the Otis Art Institute in California, centred around the charismatic work and teaching of Peter Voulkos (b. 1924).

TRUTH, BEAUTY AND VITALITY

'One measures art by the standards of truth, beauty and vitality', wrote Bernard Leach in defining his approach to making pots, believing that the objects used in everyday life influence the quality of life of their user, an attitude that emphasizes simplicity and truth to materials. It is a philosophy that continues to hold sway in Britain and many other countries, although many tableware potters have sought to broaden and extend its interpretation. In Britain this has taken various forms such as the introduction of colour and the use of techniques such as salt-glazing for stoneware, as well as a return to the simplicity and plainness of white, undecorated shapes.

'Poppy' tablewares, designed
by Janice Tchalenko (UK),
c. 1990, and made by
Dartington Pottery, Devon,
as one of their standard
ranges. Stoneware, with painted
and applied decoration,
reduction fired. Diameter
(plate) c. 25 cm (10 in).

'Time at Yagul' by Glenys
Barton (UK), 1978, made at
Josiah Wedgwood & Sons Ltd.
Bone china, hand-printed
and unglazed, with a photo-
lithographic transfer.
Height 17 cm (6.8 in).

One of the early potters to experiment with
colour and decoration in a modern idiom is Janice
Tchalenko (b. 1942), who trained on the studio
pottery course at Harrow College of Technology
in the mid-1960s and set up a workshop in south
London making domestic pots fired to stoneware
temperatures in a gas kiln. Glazes used were the
conventional range of brown and black
temmokus, dark greens and creams, with shapes
reflecting the requirements of function and sound
making. Contact with painters such as Roger
Hilton and with ceramists like Jacqueline Poncelet
(b. 1947) and Glenys Barton (b. 1944), who had
trained at the Royal College of Art in London,
brought a new awareness of the possibilities of
ceramics. Equally, visits to the Middle East and to
France made her familiar with pottery traditions
other than those of the Far East, as did an interest
in mass-produced enamelled metal forms with
stencil decoration. With the help of a Crafts

Three vessels by Clive Bowen (UK), 1991. Earthenware, red clay with slip and clear glaze, and impressed shell decoration on the oval platter. Height (tallest) 60 cm (24 in).

Council grant she simplified her shapes and concentrated on a limited number of forms including thrown tall jugs, teapots, bowls and dishes. Tchalenko devised a decorative method of trailing glaze over the surface of a white base glaze, inspired by French medieval slip-decorated jugs but fired to high temperature to produce rich colours and a lively animation of the surface of the pot, integrating form and decoration in a new way. A collaboration with textile designer John Hinchcliffe pushed her ideas forward so that large, flat press-moulded dishes and large open bowls provided ideal surfaces for experiments with colour and pattern.

An immediate success, Tchalenko's work caught the spirit of adventure of the time, merging a bold decorative approach with technical innovation. Dartington Pottery, a small production workshop in Devon, invited her to redesign their shapes and decoration, which were to be produced using a combination of hand-throwing, jigger-and-jolly and slip-cast methods, decorated with a highly coloured painted and sponged design. Acknowledged as the work of a decorator with a facility for enlivening three-dimensional forms, Tchalenko's richly coloured and patterned pots encouraged a renewed interest in producing domestic wares among other potters, and many devised a variety of decorative styles on highly finished pieces. In France Catherine Vannier uses slip-trailing and painting on red earthenware with a white slip ground to produce colourful and lively pieces.

Other potters saw the potential for a more dec-

orative approach, adapting a variety of techniques. Andrew McGarva, who moved from England to France in the late 1980s, successfully paints elaborate but freely interpreted designs of floral motifs, animals and figures based on tin-glazed earthenware on to reduction-fired thrown stoneware forms. Clive Bowen (b. 1943) draws on the vigour of traditional English slip-decorated earthenware for his large-scale thrown pieces, decorating them with slip-trailing and brush strokes of great verve and confidence. The Danish-born potter Svend Bayer (b. 1946) worked first with Michael Cardew at Wenford Bridge, Cornwall, before setting up his own pottery in north Devon. Here he throws pots on a large scale, making garden containers, jugs, lidded jars and bowls on which the unglazed body is marked by the fly ash resulting from the wood-firing process. Bayer's work integrates Far Eastern, African and English styles with a modern sensibility.

In England Sandy Brown (b. 1946), who studied at a traditional pottery in Japan before setting up a studio in Devon, produces bowls, plates, cups and saucers freely thrown from soft clay as well as large-scale female figurative sculptures. All of Brown's ceramics are decorated with bright colours painted, splashed or trailed on to a white ground. In contrast David Garland (b. 1941), who trained as a painter, makes a limited range of domestic items in red earthenware, decorating them with bold, striking designs of deep, undiluted cobalt blue and iron brown on a white slip base. Among younger potters Nigel Lambert also works with red earthenware covered with white slip, freely painting his bowls, lidded tureens, mugs and dishes with a rich blue-black pigment, enlivening the creamy yellow background with a sense of fun and enjoyment.

In America John Glick (b. 1938), who studied at Wayne State University and Cranbrook Academy, is one of the most innovative of the new wave of studio potters producing domestic pots. He has not only developed a range of rich colours for use on plates, dishes, lidded boxes, teapots and other practical forms but has evolved ingenious making methods that combine clay slabs and extruded sections as well as forms thrown on the potter's wheel. Stylistically the work has an attractive hybrid quality with an intelligent combination of different processes, colour and decoration.

Tea service and tray by Morgen Hall (UK), 1997. Earthenware, thrown and slabbed, with applied decoration.
Height (tallest) *c.* 20 cm (8 in).

Teapot by Yasuda Takeshi (UK/Japan), *c.* 1990. Stoneware, thrown and turned, oxidized, with sancai three-colour glaze. Height *c.* 20 cm (8 in).

way. His latest pieces have completely eliminated any colour and decoration in favour of an austere creamy-white purity. The UK potter Julian Stair (b. 1955) also produces finely made and finished lidded pots, coffee cups and saucers and vases that are quiveringly minimal in their elimination of decoration. On some pieces the unglazed red-brown body is left exposed, while others highlight the contrast between white and black surfaces.

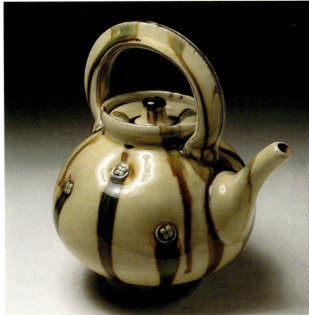

While drawing on tradition, Glick produces a lively and inventive range of shapes with surfaces ideal for decoration. His pots and his combined experimental, alternative-technology-engineering approach have had an influence on many potters around the world.

In the UK ceramists such as Will Levi Marshall and Morgen Hall produce tablewares and decorative dishes that make effective use of form and colour. Marshall, who studied at Alfred University in New York State, works at stoneware temperature and has devised a wide range of coloured glazes including purples, pinks, mauves, blues, reds and greens. Marshall's richly coloured glazes fit his forms well. Morgen Hall, an American now potting in Wales, works in red earthenware and uses modelled and slip-trailed decoration on her thrown forms to produce items such as teasets on trays in which all the pieces form a harmonious whole.

Not all potters opt for colour and action; many explore the concept of 'new minimalism' in terms of purity of colour, simplicity of form and absence of decoration. A clarity and sureness is evident in the modern equivalents of traditional shapes in the work of Yasuda Takeshi (b. 1943), the Japanese-born ceramist now living in the UK, whose thrown forms reinterpret conventional Japanese shapes in a fresh

Plate by John Glick (USA), *c.* 1985. Stoneware with applied, trailed and poured decoration. Diameter *c.* 35 cm (14 in).

Three beakers by Edmund de Waal (UK), 1997. Porcelain, thrown and turned, with pale blue celadon glaze. Height (tallest) 14 cm (5.5 in).

Two lidded containers by Byron Temple (USA), 1995. Porcelain and mixed media. Height *c.* 13 cm (5.2 in).

Equally minimal in their language are the finely thrown reduction-fired porcelain jars, bowls, teapots and cups by Edmund de Waal (b. 1966). Their soft shapes and delicate pale-blue glaze link them with the ceramics of Song dynasty China while also recalling the astringency and economy of Bauhaus design with its emphasis on strong form. Potters such as Joanna Constantinidis (b. 1927) and Karen Downing also produce ranges of porcelain tablewares such as plates, teacups and coffee mugs with white, pale cream or blue glazes that have a spartan but effective simplicity. In the US Byron Temple (b. 1936) produces a range of tableware fired in a wood-burning kiln as well as individual porcelain pieces such as lidded boxes. Temple's vigorously thrown forms are often enlivened by quick, light finger-decoration, highlighting one area and adding an element of tension to the form. In Australia Prue Venables (b. 1952) is also concerned with strong minimal form. She throws and manipulates bowl shapes in porcelain and covers them with plain, matt glaze,

in blacks, creams or whites. Her gently curving bowls and cups with their polished, almost perfect finish have none of the qualities usually associated with hand-making. Although working within a totally modern idiom, Venables shares a concern for simplicity with the more traditional but equally minimal forms of Korean potters Kim Cheekul and Dong-oh Ahn. While their austere shapes and pale celadon glaze make reference to Korean historical wares, their work has a sense of individual expression that is tellingly modern in concept.

In addition to throwing pots on the wheel, studio potters have adopted production techniques usually associated with industrial production such as slip-casting and jigger-and-jollying, using such processes to make limited runs of shapes and to produce work that does not celebrate the 'handmade'. Many potters see their work as an alternative or even in opposition to conventional lifestyles, identifying with green issues such as energy conservation, pollution and a broad range of environmental concerns, stimulating some to investigate alternative methods of firing that avoid the use of fossil fuels. Wood-firing is attractive not only because of the unique effects created by the marks of the flame and the effects of wood ash falling on the sides of unglazed pots, but, unlike fuels such as oil or gas, it is also a renewable resource. In the UK Michael (b. 1925) and Sheila Casson have built wood-fired kilns to exploit the possibilities of this type of firing, as have potters such as Jim Malone (b. 1946), Mike Dodd (b. 1943) and Phil Rogers (b. 1952). In the US Jeff Oestreich (b. 1947), who worked as an apprentice at the Leach Pottery in the early 1960s,

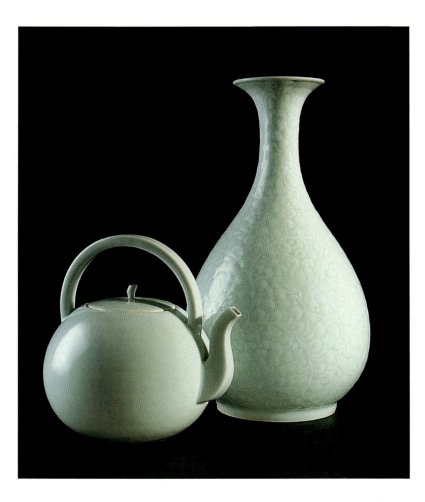

Teapot form by Kim Cheekul (Korea), 1984, and vase by Dong-oh Ahn (Korea), 1986. Porcelain, wheel-thrown. Height (tallest) 31 cm (12.4 in).

Tall bottle by Jim Malone (UK), 1992. Stoneware, thrown with black temmoku-type glaze, reduction fired. Height *c.* 31 cm (12.4 in).

Tall jug by Michael Casson (UK), *c.* 1990. Stoneware, thrown with incised decoration, salt glazed. Height *c.* 31 cm (12.4 in).

set up a pottery making well-designed functional pieces including neat, ergonomically designed teapots. More recently, Oestreich has been making decorative/functional jugs assembled from thrown components. Tom Turner (b. 1945), an American who graduated from Illinois State University in 1968, produces vigorously thrown full-bellied bottle forms, teapots and lidded jars in porcelain

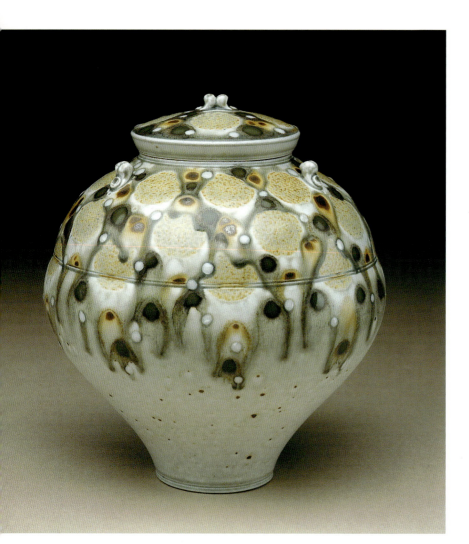

Lidded jar by Tom Turner (USA), c. 1985. Stoneware, thrown and turned, with ash-type glaze and resist decoration. Height c. 40 cm (16 in).

Straight-sided teapot by Walter Keeler (UK), 1989. Stoneware, thrown and extruded, salt glazed. Height 19 cm (7.5 in).

of eliminating fumes by 'washing' the gases given off and investigating the use of alternatives such as soda, which has proved to give excellent results.

Salt-glaze became an important element of the work of the UK potter Walter Keeler (b. 1942) in the 1970s. Attracted by the refinement and smooth perfection of eighteenth-century Staffordshire lathe-turned pots with their clean-cut profile and crisp decoration and by the more mechanical strength of metal containers such as oil cans, Keeler incorporates these qualities into his shapes and enhances them by salt-glazing. While still making pieces domestic in scale and context such as teapots, jugs and bowls, Keeler has concentrated on the idea of the form and through a series of clever manipulations has sought to emphasize 'essence' in the pieces. Teapots, though often flattened and with exaggerated spouts or handles, become elaborations of the idea yet still function as teapots. Through expert making, combining thrown and extruded sections, Keeler ensures that there is little if any evidence of the hand-making process, so the mechanical precision of the piece becomes a vital part of its quality. Sprayed layers of slips coloured with underglaze stains give mottled slate blues, greys or dark green salt-glaze surfaces with a semi-matt shine. Little or no decoration embellishes the shapes, which rely

covered with decorative ash glazes. The glazes can be quiet and austere or mottled and runny, adding dramatic tension and individual excitement to the surface.

Potters have also become interested in the possibilities of working with vapour glazing, whether the more conventional use of salt or through the use of soda which is thought to be more environmentally friendly. The vapour given off by introducing common salt or soda into the kiln at stoneware temperatures yields a thin covering of glaze that enhances the surface qualities of the clay and highlights any decoration. It is also smooth, practical and waterproof and resolves the problems of formulating and applying glaze mixtures while simultaneously referring back to traditional eighteenth- and nineteenth-century ceramics. Difficulties with pollution resulting from the salt-glazing process have prompted research into ways

Six lidded jars by Heidi and
Aage Birck (Denmark), 1983.
Stoneware, thrown and turned,
with various applied slips,
salt glaze. Height (tallest)
c. 25 cm (10 in).

Harrison have incorporated silver and ivory
fittings on to salt-glazed mugs and teapots.

Despite the problems of firing and safety, the
directness and quality of salt-glaze has caught the
attention of potters around the world. Danish
potters Heidi and Aage Birck produce thrown
pots with high domed lids that bring out the
strong qualities of salt-glaze. In the US Karen
Karnes (b. 1925) makes finely thrown pieces with
a rich texture, David Shaner (b. 1934) produces a
range of tablewares including teapots with freely
trailed slip-decoration, while Robert and Paula
Winokur have sought to integrate utility with
visual experiment. Don Reitz of Wisconsin, realizing the limitations of conventional stoneware
glazes, wanted a more direct method of decorating
and firing which would afford maximum opportunities for improvization. After many experiments Reitz developed a wide and rich vocabulary
of colours, textures and other surface embellish-
ments that give his ceramics strength and distinction. Anne Shattuck (b. 1957) has introduced
glaze stains into her salt-fired work to add a range
of muted but subtle colour on forms that include
tall handled vessels and flattened basket shapes.

entirely on their form and the salt glaze for their
success. More recently Keeler has been making
earthenware pieces such as teapots and jugs with
clear glaze splashed with coloured oxides, in the
style of eighteenth-century Whieldon-type ware.

Other notable UK potters working with salt-
glazing include Jane Hamlyn (b. 1940), Ruthanne
Tudball (both of whom make a range of domestic
tableware), Jack Doherty (who works with decorative dishes and bowls) and Sarah Walton (b.
1945). Hamlyn's salt-glazed tablewares are monumental in feel, often incorporating textured patterns and designs. Colours include soft greens and
browns. Hamlyn has also adapted some of John
Glick's forming methods into her own work. In
the 1980s her approach became more experimental, involving not only the use of extruded sections
for the walls of dishes and the like but also,
through the application of coloured slips, to introduce greens and blues into the usual limited range
of salt-glaze colours. Sarah Walton produces both
large objects such as birdbaths and high-quality
domestic tablewares, superbly crafted, which celebrate the softness of salt-glaze with its textured
surface, introducing subtle colours of greens, blues
and oranges on white-firing bodies. The pots,
lively and inventive, are enhanced with simple
clay decoration. Younger potters such as Steve

'Fiesta Basket' by Anne
Shattuck (USA), *c.* 1989.
Porcelain, thrown and
decorated, salt glaze.
Height *c.* 60 cm (24 in).

Flower vase by Janet Mansfield
(Australia), 1997. Stoneware,
wheel-thrown, wood fired.
Height 45 cm (18 in).

Large dish by Charles Bound
(UK), 1997. Stoneware,
thrown and wood fired.
Diameter 65 cm (26 in).

In Australia the vigorously thrown salt-glazed vessels of Janet Mansfield (b. 1934) achieve rich orange-reds and browns that make full use of the possibilities of the process. Sue Atkins in France added gold lustre to her richly decorated jug forms, giving them a particular exotic quality. In Japan the tradition of salt-glaze was slow to develop, although it has been used occasionally by Smimaoka Tatsuzo and more recently by other potters.

The awareness of the 'natural' qualities of fired clay in the way it responds to the great heat of the flame and smoke over a long period of time has stimulated many potters to experiment with the traditional Far Eastern technique of long slow firings in *anagama* (or single-chamber) kilns and so avoid the sophistication of complex glazes. Traditionally anagama kilns are large and often built into the side of a hill, but modern potters have improvised with ingenious alternatives though all involve long slow firings. Inside the kiln the pots are packed so that they come into as much contact with the flame and smoke and fly ash given off by the wood used for stoking the kiln as possible. One of the qualities of anagama firings is that the pieces appear to retain many of the qualities of the

freshly made pot, giving them vitality and life. The UK-born potter Patrick Sargent (1956–98), working in Switzerland, produced spectacular dishes, teabowls and jugs from his large kiln, the pieces often emerging with encrustations of the sea shells on which the pieces were placed and the dramatic markings of fly ash from the wood. The American-born potter Charles Bound, living in

the UK, also produces distinctive dishes and bottle forms, while potters in America and Australia have also explored the potential of the anagama process.

Although ceramists on the Continent continue fruitful collaborations with the ceramic industry, this has not been common in the UK or the US. However, ceramists are now beginning to look at collaborations with industry for the production of small-scale runs of particular objects they themselves design and for which they make the models. Sue Pryke, a Royal College of Art graduate, has designed a ceramic range for the international trading company IKEA and more recently has been investigating marketing her own industrially produced pieces. She has designed tableware including a lemon squeezer, mugs and lidded bowls with either bright coloured or soft earth tones that are produced by a ceramics factory. These celebrate strong, uncluttered design rather than seek to emulate a 'handmade' look, the work combining the 'feel' of clay with the crispness of industrial production.

NEW DIRECTIONS

Despite all the developments within contemporary ceramics with the move towards more sculptural and conceptual form, many potters continue to be concerned with the vessel both as an object in its own right and as a metaphor for a variety of meanings. These are usually hand-built, often by coiling, rounded in shape, and are one-off even if made as part of a series. Although such work openly acknowledges the traditions of pottery stretching to the beginnings of clay-working, it also relates easily to the modern world, making statements about material and the processes of firing and is a refreshing alternative to the increasing demands of technology. The vessel may serve as a container but may also evoke ritual or even mystical uses.

Notable vessel-makers include such established figures as Ewen Henderson (b. 1934) in the UK, who works with a combination of stoneware, porcelain and bone china, often interleaving the different bodies to build up a patchwork surface on vessel forms. For Henderson the hand-building process is an intrinsic part of the concept of his work. The forms are essentially organic in feel, some less vessel-orientated and more sculptural in

'Long Meg IV' by Ewen
Henderson (UK), 1993.
Stoneware, hand-built.
Height 90 cm (36 in).

'Grand Coquille' by Jean-
François Fouilhoux (France),
1997. Porcelain with pale blue
celadon glaze, reduction fired.
Length 48 cm (19.2 in).

Untitled by Martin Smith (UK),
1994. Terracotta, hand-built.
Height 30 cm (12 in).

concept, with the bubbled and volcanic surfaces suggesting great heat and transformation adding further elements of depth and mystery. A concern with the organic is taken in a different direction by French-born maker Jean-François Fouilhoux who constructs shallow dish forms that combine the qualities of rock and shell. Fouilhoux finishes

his pieces with a classic pale-blue celadon glaze, giving them a minimal simplicity that emphasizes form and structure.

Throughout the 1970s and '80s the Royal College of Art in London maintained its position as an important centre for the development of new ideas and for the reappraisal of the work of the potters. Elizabeth Fritsch (b. 1941), a student in the 1970s, originally trained as a musician and began working with clay with few preconceptions. Fritsch constructs her vessels using coils of clay to create rounded, flowing shapes, slowly and meticulously rubbing and scraping down the walls to make them flat and smooth. Some are symmetrical and curved, others more organic in feel. In some vessels one side may be flattened to serve as a strong contrast to the rest of the form. Decoration is a crucial aspect of her pieces, with coloured slips painted in precise patterns onto the surface to create the matt quality of fresco with abstract and geometrical designs. Geometrical rhythmic patterns, reminiscent of musical notation, produce an almost optical effect of movement and harmony. Although still aligned to the traditional pottery vessel, Fritsch's work is closely related to contemporary ideas in the visual arts.

'Blue and White Jug' by Alison Britton (UK), 1987. Earthenware, hand-built, with trailed slip and painted decoration. Height 30 cm (12 in).

Other students at the RCA responded more to the materials and techniques of industrial ceramics. Paul Astbury made futuristic-looking forms based on space-age imagery but more recently has produced more conceptually based pieces that deal with erosion and decay. Contained within enclosed damp environments are unfired clay pieces fashioned into popular forms such as horse ornaments that slowly disintegrate over time as moisture condenses and drips onto them. Geoffrey Swindell, also a student at the RCA in the 1970s, throws small porcelain bottle forms with highly decorative surfaces in lustre, pinks, greens and greys, their jewel-like intensity contrasting with the highly textured surfaces. Martin Smith (b. 1950) graduated from the Royal College of Art in the mid-'70s and first explored the vessel form in raku using effective black and white patterning. More recently Smith has constructed a series of shapes in red polished highly grogged earthenware which make reference to architecture and the forms of building without in any sense seeking to portray or replicate them directly. Silver and gold leaf applied to some surfaces adds further elements of distortion and manipulation.

Like Fritsch, Alison Britton (b. 1948) enjoys the creative possibilities of hand-building, producing distinctive vessels, many based on jug forms, with stylized images of animals and mythological figures. As a student at the Royal College of Art she started to build shapes by hand, concentrating on jugs, often constructed with faceted sides that are decorated with painted figurative stylized designs. Although her forms could be seen as functional in that all are containers, she has pushed the idea to the extent where no precise label can be applied and the jugs take on an anthropomorphic quality. The forms have grown larger and now seem more slab-like and monumental, with the shapes moving in and out in complex ways; some make more obvious reference to jugs, others have a more figurative feel, the sinuous curves echoing such parts of the body as the torso or thighs. Decoration is now more abstract with splashes of colour or trails of slip introducing elements of both freedom and tension.

Hand-building offers a means of carefully considering form without the speed involved in wheel making. The three Copenhagen-based potters Jane Reumert, Gunhild Aaberg and Beate Andersen all produce distinctive vessel forms distinguished by a minimalism of shapes with a restrained richness of decoration. Their bowls employ repeating patterns of lines and divisions of space to reveal and highlight the strength of the shapes themselves. Malene Müllertz (b. 1949), also Danish, worked as a designer for Bing and Grøndahls before setting up her own studio. Müllertz's individual hand-built forms, many of them with a strong organic presence, are decorated with geometrical patterns that both enhance and develop the shape. In contrast the vessel forms constructed in porcelain by the Dutch maker Babs Haenen (b. 1948) seem almost abstract. Her bowl-like forms have odd angles and folds that give them an almost human appearance, while more recent pieces have resonance with architectural form. Haenen's use of colours such as dark greens and pinks on forms that are soft and sensual explore the ceramic qualities of clay. Despite employing different making methods, there are similarities between Haenen's forms and those of the UK ceramist Nicholas Arroyave-Portela, who throws tall bowl-like forms on the wheel and then folds and distorts them to take on figurative qualities. Arroyave-Portela decorates his

Seven spouted containers by Malene Müllertz (Denmark), 1996. Stoneware with painted decoration.

complex forms with a semi-matt slip, which adds a soft gloss to the surface that intensifies the skin-like quality of the form.

The industrial technique of making objects by slip-casting has been taken up by potters both in Britain and the US. Such West Coast American potters as Richard Shaw (b. 1941) and Kenneth Price (b. 1935) continue to produce finely made pieces with wit and ingenuity. In Britain ceramists such as Jacqueline Poncelet (b. 1947) experimented with slip-casting bone china, which she used to produce eggshell-thin bowls and dishes which were then decorated with delicate carved patterns and designs. The same materials also enabled Glenys Barton (b. 1944) to obtain precise and clean effects on sculptural pieces, many including greatly simplified representations of the human figure, posing questions about the human role in the universe and the concept of the classical ideal. Some earlier geometrical forms were often decorated with transfer-printed patterns. More recently Barton has made portrait heads, some over-life-sized, others in delicate relief.

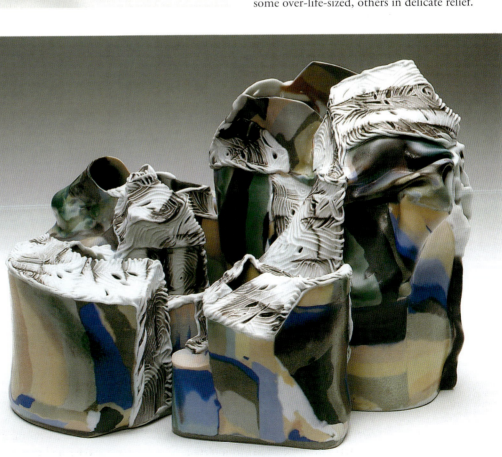

'The Happy Pavilions' by Babs Haenen (Netherlands), 1998. Porcelain, coloured clay, hand-built, translucent glaze. Dimensions 24 x 36 x 31 cm (9.6 x 14.4 x 12.4 in).

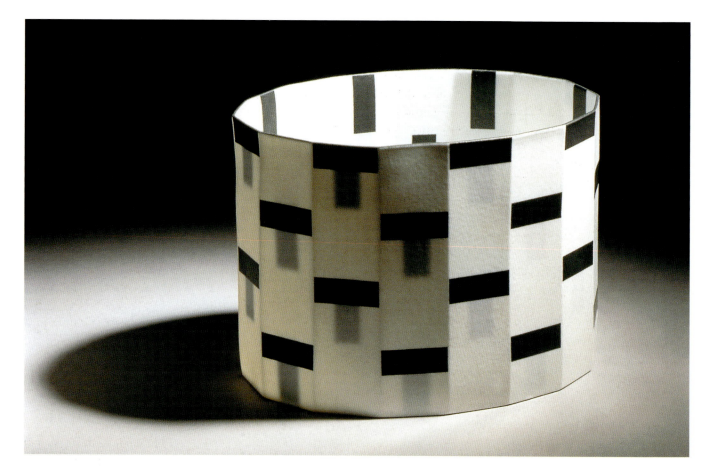

Straight-sided form by Bodil Manz (Denmark), 1997. Porcelain, slip-cast and reduction fired, with enamel decoration. Height *c.* 13 cm (5.2 in).

The potter Bodil Manz in Denmark also pushes porcelain to its limits. Manz, through slip-casting porcelain, produces fine, paper-thin bowls that are translucent and enhanced with varying degrees of colour applied to the surface. Some recall the work of artists such as Mondrian with well-defined areas of bold, bright colours such as red, black and blue. Others are more subtly shaded and patterned with soft yellows and pale terracottas used in understated rhythmical patterns. Manz's delicate pieces stand on an edge between the refinement of traditional industrially made porcelain and the work of the studio potter. Her work can be seen alongside that of others such as the Dutch maker Leen Quist, whose super-thin porcelain forms are enhanced by a minimal use of black patterning to divide and animate the shape. The Japanese potter Masamichi Yoshikawa (b. 1946) also explores the edge of minimalism with hand-built forms in porcelain with a shimmering pale-blue celadon glaze, combining elements of wit and abstraction with an intense physical prescence.

The diversity of approach in ceramics of the 1980s is nowhere better demonstrated than in the reinterpretation of ancient techniques such as fine agate. American-born ceramist Dorothy Feibleman (b. 1951), working in London, has devised a range of coloured porcelains that she uses to construct delicate bowls with spiralling agate patterns and fine jewellery inspired by that made in ancient Egypt. In Japan, the ceramist Matsui Kosei builds minimal forms using different coloured clays assembled in rich texture-patterns. Matsui's shapes relate to both the strength of natural form and the ingenious skill of the potter.

In contrast to the fineness and definition of Manz's porcelain pieces, the UK ceramist Carol McNicoll (b. 1948) has taken ceramics in a different direction, producing often intricate objects assembled from slip-cast components that include teasets and bowls, technically unorthodox but visually intriguing. After studying at Leeds Polytechnic and the Royal College of Art McNicoll set up a workshop in London making slipware items that imitate other processes and materials. Teacups and saucers, for example, may look as if they are slab-built from folded clay but are in fact slip-cast in plaster-of-Paris moulds. More complex decorative dishes with structures that echo wood or metal are made in much the same way. Pieces are cast and then assembled, either while still in the mould or subsequently. These individual forms, with their concern for the processes of ceramics, for more

Like McNicoll, Kate Malone uses a variety of making methods to produce objects that are both highly decorative and functional. The exuberant excess of Malone's one-off pieces call on both the idiosyncratic qualities of late-nineteenth-century art pottery and industrial wares featuring natural forms such as shells, fish, vegetables and fruit. One of her recurring themes is the use of encrustations of sea forms and prints of fish on watery greens, blues and yellows in evocations of the sea on giant, thick-lipped jugs. More recently she has modelled shapes based on gourds, melons and nuts, converting them into vessel forms such as jugs and bowls with richly flowing multi-layered glazes in bright yellows, reds, blues and pinks.

Large jar by Matsui Kosei (Japan), 1986. Earthenware, form built up by neriage process. Height 35.5 cm (14.2 in).

'Tutti Frutti Bumper Car Jug' by Kate Malone (UK), 1998. Earthenware, press-moulded, multiple glaze firings. Height 25 cm (10 in).

sculptural requirements and also for function, are typical of McNicoll's work. Although still made for the home and intended to serve as dishes or containers of some sort, they cross boundaries between the functional and decorative, demonstrating the adaptability of ceramics in the hands of a creative potter. McNicoll has also designed items for factory production such as vases and ashtrays that look humorously handmade. Along with bowls and jugs designed by Janice Tchalenko, these pieces have been produced for sale at reasonable prices in retail shops across Britain.

Canada has seen a rich flowering of many sorts of ceramics ranging from tableware to sculptural forms. Ceramists such as Colleen O'Reilly-Lafferty and Guy Simoneau produce tablewares that work well as decorative pieces with or without food. As Professor of Ceramics at Nova Scotia College of Art and Design Walter Ostrom (b. 1944) is both an inspired teacher and maker. Resisting the general move towards higher-temperature firings, Ostrom works with earthenware in the majolica tradition, throwing and assembling forms such as flower vases into shapes that have a resonance with

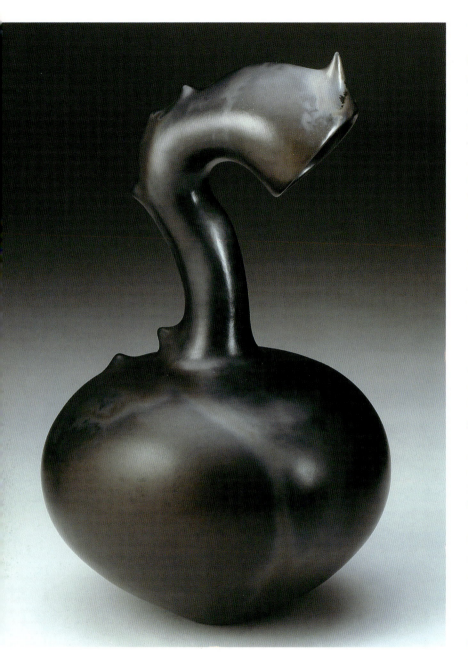

Vessel by Magdalene Odundo (UK), 1997. Earthenware, hand-built, burnished, smoke fired. Height *c.* 50 cm (20 in).

marks of which are captured on the surface as areas of black or grey in random markings. The long tradition of hand-built pots fired without glaze has inspired many potters to interpret this technique in new ways. Magdalene Anyango N Odundo (b. 1950) and Fiona Salazar (b. 1949), both of whom studied at the Royal College of Art, work with red earthenware to build up precisely controlled shapes. Odundo's monumental coiled forms relate to the traditional techniques and forms associated with Kenya and Nigeria, bringing them up to date in both form and concept. Salazar's rounded bottle forms and animal pieces, decorated with a variety of designs painted in different earth-coloured slips often on black backgrounds and highly burnished, make reference to ancient American shapes and decoration. Slow to make and finished with great care, Odundo's and Salazar's pots set up resonant echoes with the past.

The work of Jane Perryman explores similar themes. In addition to looking at African burnished pots she studied European Celtic and Bronze Age forms before coiling her bowls and jugs. These are often decorated with simple chevron patterns and are low-fired in sawdust to mark and seal the surface. In contrast Judy Trim, who graduated from Bath Academy of Art in England in the 1960s, builds a variety of large oval bowls and tall bottles, enhancing the hand-built and polished surfaces after a pit firing with rich lustres of gold and silver. The combination of the reflective surface and dark body creates objects with almost ritual intensity.

The processes of sawdust or saggar firing produce a distinctive, almost primitive mark on vessels, an aspect of firing that interests potters both because of the emotive and powerful associations of earth and fire and because they are in themselves paradoxically simple, accessible processes that also offer sophisticated possibilities. In Australia the potter Barry Hayes has devised a method of pit-firing using additions of salt and oxides such as copper to the sawdust to produce vessels with pink, grey and black markings. The work of Elsbeth Owen in the UK, Richard Hirsch and Roberta Marks in the US, and in France Pierre Bayle should also be mentioned as pushing at and exploring the possibilities of clay, fire and smoke.

The Austrian potter Gerhild Tschachler-Nagy, who spent time on America's West Coast, is par-

the history of the ware but are reinterpreted with wit and skill.

In sharp contrast to the sophistication and finesse of such precise techniques as slip-casting or press-moulding, there has been renewed interest in more ancient 'primitive' forms and processes of building vessels. These include techniques such as coiling and smoothing to create flowing, even surfaces that may be covered with a coating of a fine clay slip known as terra sigillata or burnished to give a dull shine. Such pieces are often fired with wood or sawdust to create flame and smoke, the

ticularly impressed by all the qualities obtained in the long slow wood-firing of anagama kilns. In the US she shared such a firing with American potters Tom Coleman, Nils Lou and Frank Boyden, and although she liked the effects they obtained, she was disturbed by the pollution associated with the consumption of fuel and emissions of smoke. As a result Tschachler-Nagy investigated other means of achieving similar rich effects and has successfully devised a technique of wrapping her vessels and sculptural forms in straw soaked in a salt solution.

Raku, particularly for large-scale pieces, is a technique which continues to find favour in many parts of the world, its virtually instant results and often spectacular effects bypassing the often laboured skills of conventionally fired and glazed work. In the UK the thrown and coil-built bottle and bowl forms of David Roberts (b. 1947) have made effective use of the medium in a restrained form, allowing the post-reduction process to play a significant part. In particular his large rounded vessels make use of a white crackle glaze softened by smoke patterning. Wayne Higby (b. 1943), in the US, has also pushed at conventional raku forms, developing a fascinating range of landscape bowls with intricate inlay and glaze finish. Some are broken up before firing and subsequently reassembled, giving them an archaeological appearance that paradoxically suggests both great age and modern construction.

Peder Rasmussen in Denmark also hand-builds tall vessel forms, decorating the surface with lines and odd areas of colour in an abstract way recalling some ancient, long-lost cave painting. The vessels are enhanced by a raku firing, which adds further to the mysteriousness of the objects.

Tradition and innovation are successfully brought together in the vessel forms of Japanese ceramist Matsui Kosei, whose strong forms are well able to accommodate complex patterns and textures. The Japanese ceramist Kazuhiko Sato (b. 1947) builds flat-sided vessel forms that take on great strength, the surfaces enriched by incised linear decoration that combines the sophistication of design with a powerful sense of the organic. The UK potter Jennifer Lee (b. 1955) has evolved a series of precise, rounded coil-built forms which have elements of Fritsch's skilled working in that the making appears seamless, but which are combined with aspects of Anglo-Saxon coil-built funerary vessels. Lee gives her forms a 'twist' by mixing colouring oxides into the clay. These bleed and run into adjacent areas to create overall muted effect that take on a geological quality, the soft greys, ochres and yellows recalling the colour of rocks and strata. A final burnish, adding subtlety and richness, is used to enhance the surface. Another graduate of the Royal College of Art, Lawson Oyekan, is a hand-builder who combines this technique with thrown forms to create vessels that refer to traditional African work, blending this with the

Large bowl by David Roberts (UK), 1992. Coil-built, burnished raku fired, with green glaze. Diameter 44 cm (17.5 in).

'Midsummer Bay', landscape bowl by Wayne Higby (USA), 1991. Thrown and altered, raku fired. Height 33 cm (13 in).

Vessel by Kazuhiko Sato (Japan). Stoneware, large reddish-brown narrow oval vase, with incised and inlaid decoration.

western concept of 'abstract' form. Oyekan uses the construction process as a major feature of the structure of the pieces and covers the surface with broadly painted clay slips to emphasize material and process. The vessels, in red or cream clay, are usually left unglazed, their simplicity taking on a monumental but mysterious quality.

CEREMONY AND RITUAL

The attractions of everyday, familiar items such as teapots and cups, tureens and even shoes and boots

'Cadent Teapot Diptych' by Anne Hirondelle (USA), 1988. Stoneware, reduction fired. Height 31.25 cm (12.5 in).

'Double Cooling Tower Teapot (#10)' by Richard Notkin (USA), c. 1985. Stoneware, hand-built, unglazed, incorporating a curved lightning bolt as handle and spout with a mushroom-cloud knob arising from the lid. Height 15 cm (6 in).

the finely crafted teapots of the American Richard Notkin (b. 1948). Using the precedents of the Chinese redware teapots from Yixing, Notkin builds small pots that incorporate complex narratives. These may involve a basic form such as a cube on which are modelled elements such as a skull, a nuclear explosion and dice, all assembled into a teapot barely fifteen centimetres in height. Teapots with an atomic explosion on the lid comment on the 'dance of death' involved in making and possibly using atomic weapons, while the handle in the form of jagged lightning suggests danger; all are carefully and precisely modelled. In combining social comment with surreal and often disturbing imagery of modern life and while also making functional objects, Notkin's work is a grim reminder of contemporary events beyond our own domestic concerns.

In great contrast Belinda Gabryl's teapot and cup precariously perched on tripod legs are only distantly related to their more functional relatives. The delicate vessels appear to have taken on a whirlwind life of their own and seem ready to start to move across the table. While Gabryl's teapots appear almost like prowling animals, the teapots made by American Philip Cornelius (b. 1934), though elegant to the point of parody,

prove stimulating starting points for many potters to explore the technical skills of making, and as a means of responding to the society in which they live. The teapot continues to engage potters, as much for its central role in social situations in the West and ceremonial significance in the East as for practical purposes. For potters teapots are also as a means of exploring a complex ceramic form, as they are generally thought to be one of the most challenging objects to construct because the four components – body, lid, spout and handle – must unite happily and efficiently to create a whole. In the US the work of James Lawton is notable, as are the ritualistic forms of Anne Hirondelle and Jeannie Mah's paper-thin porcelain teapots constructed from slabs.

Ritual of a different sort is evident in

'Enterprise' by Philip Cornelius (USA), 1976. Porcelain, hand-built. Height 29 cm (11.6 in).

suggest the strength and stability of soaring architectural form. With rudimentary spouts and tiny handles and lids, his pots in stoneware and porcelain are sufficiently engaging as objects in their own right, although they may still function as teapots. Other potters prefer soft, sensual form rather than powerful geometry such as the so-called Winepots made by Danish ceramist Ann Linneman. These cushion-like forms with their rounded curves and gentle colouring inviting touch and use.

For the Scottish-born ceramist Angus Suttie (1946–93) the teapot form served as a means of looking at such dark themes as death and danger, often with an autobiographical edge, as well as making innovative, involved shapes. After training at Camberwell School of Art Suttie set up his studio in central London where he made coiled and slabbed forms vaguely reminiscent of the figure, freely built in the form of teapots. Some carried written messages of love and expressions of sexual

'Involvement' by Angus Suttie (UK), 1992. Stoneware, hand-built, with glazes and oxides. Height 57 cm (22.8 in).

'Contenedor Defensivo' by
Xavier Monsalvatje Vich
(Spain), 1997. Gres esmaltado,
hierro, cobre y vidrio.
Height 20 cm (8 in).

'Dream of Montpelier' by
Adrian Saxe (USA), 1996.
Earthenware, hand-built.
Height 29.5 cm (11.75 in).

desire and are brightly coloured with earthenware glazes. In later work Suttie made use of higher-firing clays and sombre colouring on forms that appear to have an involved internal structure that in some aspects recall the hand-built 'stirrup' pots of Native Americans. Handles are constructed to resemble linking bridges or stirrups, and although architectural in feel the vessels also appear to have an organic suggestion of growth. Some forms take on an animal quality with rearing head-like features and thick, sturdy legs. Just as Suttie's work is intended to both attract and repel, the Spanish ceramist Xavier Monsalvatje Vich's 'Contenedor Defensivo' is also intended to evoke contradictory feelings. The mechanical precision of the box form, the flat walls and neat corners are far from the organic qualities of Suttie's forms. The sharp pieces of metal covering the outside of the container are apparently protecting something of great significance or worth.

For the US potter Richard Hirsch (b. 1944) it is the ceremony and ritual qualities of American Indian ceramics that serve as a source of inspiration for pieces such as the three-legged object 'Ceremonial Cup No. 46'. This intriguing form appears to have no practical function other than to be decorative and sculptural. The unglazed, softly burnished form takes on a powerful totemic quality, giving it architectural strength. Betty Woodman (b. 1930) has been inspired by the splendour of tin- and lead-glazed wares and the colours of Tang earthenware to make individual vessel forms in earthenware that combine thrown and hand-built elements. Shapes include flasks, jugs and dishes with clear glazes splashed with iron browns, cobalt blues and copper greens. More recently, Woodman's pieces have become more abstract and sculptural.

The work of the American Adrian Saxe (b. 1943) again calls on everyday familiar forms such as teapots, but also on less likely objects such as boots and shoes for his ceramics, transforming them into exotic, often bejewelled containers. Using the technique of slip-casting, Saxe creates objects that appear precious, teetering on the edge of kitsch but with sufficient control of form and surface to reflect on their presence in everyday life. In contrast Mark Pharis constructs spouted vessels which he calls Soy Bottles which are almost rugged in comparison. The curling spout and the hat-like stoppers are light-hearted and fun, making these objects both decorative and functional

POTS WITH ATTITUDE

Post-modernism has been as influential in ceramics as in other areas of visual art. It has inspired work making use of virtually any making, decorating or firing technique or historical form as a basis for

'The Dinner Party' by
Judy Chicago (USA), 1979.
Mixed media. Installation view
featuring the Virginia Woolf and
Georgia O'Keeffe place settings.
Dimensions 14.4 x 12 x 0.9 m
(48 x 42 x 3 ft).

pastiche, irony and cynicism as well as celebration. Through the use of narrative, illusion, period styles, naturalism and a confusion between function and form, all in some way represent or offer a means of reaction to aspects of modern society. The response is international, part of a universal language understood around the world. In countries such as Japan, South Korea and China an abiding theme is acknowledging and responding to the past. Here artist-potters either react against or are attracted to long and distinguished ceramic traditions. Despite the fact that ceramics has become part of an international language with a shared literature that addresses both technical and aesthetic concerns, ceramists in many counties have retained aspects of identifiable styles, which though far from being nationalistic celebrate cultural and national difference.

Concern with issues such as the environment, the cold war, the nuclear threat and sexual politics arose out of the independence movements rooted in the politics of the 1960s. One of the first to make a significant impact on an international scale

was Judy Chicago's feminist installation 'The Dinner Party'. This was completed in 1979 and toured to many cities including London (in 1984), being seen by some half a million people. The huge installation consists of a vast triangular table laid with thirty-nine place settings, each one representing a famous or significant woman. Each setting has a plate with modelled or painted decoration, a chalice, ceramic cutlery, a table napkin and an embroidered cloth depicting scenes from the woman's life, or an abstracted design referring to it. Each plate has a design that is part flower, part vagina, part butterfly. The installation also includes a series of ceramic floor tiles bearing the names of 999 notable women from history, some still well known, others long forgotten. The sculptural piece, epic in scale, took Chicago and 400 other women six years to complete. 'The Dinner Party' raises relevant questions about the nature of art and craft and shows that traditional craft materials can be as provocative and thoughtful as any conventional fine art material.

In the US and Canada ceramists have also

looked frankly at aspects of sexual politics, such as homosexuality, creating vessels that explore and celebrate sexual diversity. The Canadian Paul Mathieu uses the majolica technique of painting on tin-glaze earthenware to create images that assert and investigate sexual difference and identity. With the advent of the AIDS epidemic, some ceramists have produced moving and often monumental work that suggests both dignity and profound loss. Jason Waterworth, a student at West Surrey College of Art in the UK, produced an installation of urn-type vessels as a memorial for friends and others who have died. In his minimal sculptural pieces the US

forms stand like individuals, poignant memorials perhaps of those who are no longer here.

Realism, an abiding concern of fine artists, has been little seen in ceramics, with one of the most notable exceptions being the work of Marilyn Levine (see chapter 13). In the UK the two ceramists Nicki Smart and Lorraine Taylor, operating under the name of Penkridge Ceramics, call on the long tradition of making ceramic objects in the form of fruit and nuts that appear totally lifelike. Such objects in the form of apples, oranges and nuts were produced by porcelain factories to both demonstrate skill and serve as 'talking points'

'Garniture #2, Day (or Night)' by Paul Mathieu (Canada), 1993. Porcelain and bronze. Length 1.5 m (5 ft).

ceramist Marek Cecula touches on the way illnesses such as HIV and AIDS have been defined as much by medical attention as social concern. His highly finished clinical-like objects in pure white recall the sterility and impersonality of the clinic or hospital, the cool, white forms reminiscent of body parts. The German Daniel Kruger has produced a series of porcelain urns in classical vase-like forms onto which are attached what appear to be sheets of paper bearing screen-printed black and white images of male friends in a series that has been described as 'the dramatization of sexuality'. In sharp divergence, the British-born sculptor Andrew Lord (b. 1950) creates installations incorporating ceramic urns and handled and spouted vessels, some covered with an intense black glaze, and where split and broken during the making or firing repaired with epoxy resin and gold leaf. Lord's

when displayed on the dinning tables of the wealthy. The superbly crafted fruit and vegetables made by Penkridge Ceramics include apples, pears, artichokes, pineapples, horse-chestnuts and mushrooms, the forms exact and the colouring and surface markings totally realistic.

THE VESSEL AND THE FIGURE

After many decades of neglect the figure, whether in human or animal form, has again become an accepted subject for ceramists and sculptors. Some ceramists search for 'essence' in both finish and pose, while others want to abstract and hone down. Vladimir Tsivin (b. 1949), who has a studio in St Petersburg, creates minimal pieces based on the human torso, with influences drawn from ancient cultures such as Egypt and Greece. He works with an oval cylinder of clay, gently

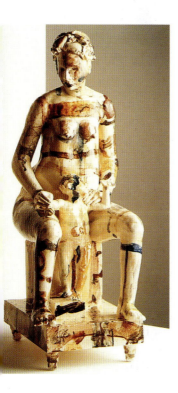

Viola Frey (USA) in her studio, Oakland, California, 1994.

'Madonna col Bambino' by Philip Eglin (UK), 1993. Earthenware, painted decoration. Height *c.* 36 cm (14.5 in).

easing and squeezing it to take on the form of the human body, more suggested and understated than real. The English ceramist Christie Brown (b. 1946) also seeks to capture some essential qualities of the human form in pieces that are near life-size in scale. Brown constructs her torsos from slabs of clay carefully shaped to suggest the form of the body in low relief. With a minimum of modelling and surface treatment, Brown's figures move successfully between abstraction and realism.

Many ceramists in the US have explored figurative work on an altogether larger scale. Viola Frey (b. 1933) builds huge figures of men, women and children that are often well over life-size, some standing more than two metres tall, and painted with coloured glazes and enamels to give them a heightened quality of realism. Frey's over life-size sculptures have a disturbing presence, their social observation offering an unflattering insight into one aspect of American society. In the UK Sean Henry (b. 1965) has modelled figures that push at the bounds of realism, his well-crafted life-sized figures appearing almost as if they may be about to walk. About his work, Henry says, 'I try to depict some essential truths. My figures are often on the edge of action – passive, but acutely aware of their surroundings, as well as their ability to affect or change them.' His figures, he says, are intended to suggest Everyman –'quirky, powerful, but not responsible for his actions'.

The US ceramist Peter Vandenberge (b. 1935) produces large coil-built portraits that mix caricature and interpretation with great fluidity. The figurative work of Judy Moonelis (b. 1953) is more expressionist and extrovert in feel, her figures suggesting the powerful and deep feelings of relationships as the couples writhe and twist, involved in some dark and secret bond, the significance of which we can only speculate. Moonelis's clinging figures, abstracted yet emotionally intense, are intensely personal and suggest a need for closeness and intimacy. In contrast Rudy Autio (b. 1926) explores the patterning and form of the figure in large, vaguely anthropomorphic vessel forms. On these he paints in a broad, bold style a complex landscape of figures in a style reminiscent of Matisse. Although Autio's figure-vessels call on a centuries-old tradition they are uncompromisingly modern in their concerns. Akio Takamori (b. 1950) works along similar lines, but combines drawing on his pots with the idea of the pot as a drawing.

Frey's concerns, like those of Moonelis, Vandenberge and Henry, are essentially humanist, offering comment on and insight into the 'human condition', not as parody or satire but as a shared and common humanity. Despite their often alarming spectacle, which may combine aspects of realism, surrealism and vulnerability, they seek to further our understanding. By contrast, the huge, matchstick-thin stoneware figures made by the US artist Robert Brady (b. 1946) take us into a different world. His tall, figurative forms, often standing some fifty centimetres tall, recall the work of the sculptor Alberto Giacometti, but in Brady's work the clay imposes its own spiky, tense structure. Brady's figures may be enmeshed in a network of support which appears both literal and emotional. The monumental heads and figurative pieces constructed by the Japanese-born artist Jan Janeko (b. 1942) who lives in the US makes sensitive use of clay and glaze for his abstract figures. The pieces also call on aspects of Western and Eastern art with great skill and ingenuity.

While the work of sculptors such as Frey and Moonelis are clearly rooted in twentieth-century art, the modelled figures of UK potter Philip Eglin (b. 1959) draw freely on other European figurative traditions. Eglin's images of subjects such as mother and child make specific reference to the maiolica wares of sixteenth-century Italy, and to the folk art traditions of eighteenth-century Staffordshire figurative ornaments. The naked female figures, whether standing or sitting, seem poised but exposed, their vulnerability emphasized by broad strokes of painted cobalt blue or the application of coloured transfers, suggesting defilement, ownership and individual identity.

The near life-sized standing figures made by the Belgian potter and sculptor José Vermeersch (1922–97), made in groups rather than as individual pieces, evoke a community in which the figures have a predestined role. The naked, semi-abstracted

Figures by Noria Mabasa (South Africa), 1990. Earthenware, hand-built.

figures are constructed in sections and subsequently joined together, then fired in a large kiln where the rich terracotta clay takes on a worn, 'experienced' quality. Vermeersch's figures inhabit their own world in which they have a collective and individual identity, suggesting isolation and alienation. The Irish-born maker Claire Curneen also models standing naked figures that suggest vulnerablity, though on a much smaller, more intimate scale. The delicate modelled skin of Curneen's figures is pierced with holes that serve to emphasize their fragility, while the detailed modelling of the hands and other parts of the body suggest that senses such as touch are still important.

The figures modelled by UK artist Jill Crowley (b. 1946) and South African ceramist Noria Mabasa (b. 1940) are just as concerned with the domestic environment of home and city as with the individual character. As a student at the Royal College of Art in the 1970s Crowley experimented

with raku, making among other forms a series of small teapots in the shapes of animals. Later she made figurative sculptures that often combine sharp observation of character with a satirical element such as her series of portrait heads of business men. Following the birth of her child Crowley made a series of over life-size limbs and hands that are baby-like and sturdy. Mabasa's doll-like figures are disturbingly like 'little people' and in their portrayal of human characteristics are eerily surreal.

In many ways animals continue to pose the greatest challenge to sculptors who perhaps wisely feel they must avoid too accurate a representation. The UK-born maker Susan Halls, now living in the US, creates various animals such as dogs and monkey heads, imbuing the creatures with life often with what only appears to be a minimal amount of modelling. Her dogs in particular appear as if they are about to walk away while continuing to look convincingly modelled in clay, while recent work evokes a mythical world peopled by creatures half human, half animal.

ABSTRACTION AND MINIMALISM

Integral to many of the broad changes taking place within ceramics is a recurring debate about status. Whether artists who work with clay, in the broadest sense, are artists or craftspeople with the corresponding differing standing of their work in terms of price and the context in which the work is shown – whether for instance, objects are exhibited in craftshops or galleries – continues to be keenly debated. Further technological developments have resulted in ready-made materials more easily available so that decorative glazes and slips can be purchased ready-prepared in tubs and painted onto clay, while colour ranges are virtually limitless. There is also ample good-quality practical and discursive literature. Computerization has also made kiln firings simpler. This element of 'de-skilling' has called into question the intrinsic need for training in technique in preference to a more ideas-based approach.

For many fine artists clay has become a 'new' material, offering undiscovered possibilities, with many painters and sculptors working in collaboration with potters. In Britain lively vessel-based work has been produced by established fine artists such as Bruce McLean (b. 1944) and John Hoyland (b. 1934), both of whom tend to work

'There was a young man…' by Grayson Perry (UK), 1988. Earthenware, press-moulded, with impressed text, oxides and transfer-printed designs. Length *c*. 31 cm (12.5 in).

with conventional vessel forms and concentrate on surface decoration rather than making. McLean decorates pressed dishes and bowls with bold, incised and painted figurative decoration and Hoyland paints large dishes and vase forms with rich, vibrant colour in abstract designs. The directness of clay has inspired sculptor Barry Flanagan (b. 1951) to constructing a series of small coil pots with the method of making incorporated as an intrinsic part of the form. UK performance artist Grayson Perry, regarded by some as the *enfant terrible* of British ceramics, makes vessel-based work which comfortably embraces the concerns of fine and applied art. Perry creates highly conventional vase forms by throwing or press-moulding, his classical vase shapes reminiscent of Ming China, serving as vehicles for a complex variety of messages and designs drawn, painted, impressed or stencilled on the surface. Primarily these are concerned with the human condition in general but also touch on such sensitive topics as transgender issues, genital fixation, nuclear war and the arms race. In the US Keith Haring (1950–90) decorated terracotta forms with his graphic figurative designs, as does the artist Frim Kess.

Others artists have been attracted to the more sculptural possibilities of clay, responding to its earthy and historical associations. Anthony Caro (b. 1924) has created both abstract sculptural forms and more recently a series of 'book' sculptures which explore the monumental qualities of the printed page; Anish Kapor (b. 1954) builds large-scale pieces that contrast matt, brightly coloured rock-like mass with the plastic, 'squeezed' qualities of clay. Tony Cragg (b. 1949), working at the Ceramic Work Centre near Amsterdam, produces clay forms that, like Kapor's, exploit the plastic, earthy aspects of the material and its ability to imitate other forms such as the casings of engines. In the UK Anthony Gormely (b. 1950) has worked with clay in various ways. Early work used painted white tin-glaze, while more recent pieces include the building of a clay army of thousands of figures, each some twenty

'Cage' by Gillian Lowndes (UK), 1996. Galvanized wire basket, bone china, shredded clay, stoneware hook. Height 23 cm (9.2 in).

'Flower' by Richard Slee (UK), 1991. Earthenware, hand-built, with sprayed colour and clear glaze. Height *c.* 20 cm (8 in).

centimetres high, forming part of a vast installation dealing with issues such as population, identity and individuality as well as the quality of clay itself.

In England Gillian Lowndes (b. 1936), who graduated from the Central School of Art in London in 1959, has sought to explore the sculptural aspects of form as well as exploit the qualities of her chosen material. Some of her early vessels were intriguingly 'woven' out of clay coils, their open form questioning popular perceptions about pots and containers. Early sculptural pieces, inspired by time spent in Africa, were made out of thin slabs of clay and wire, the forms recalling insects of unusual shape. More recent sculptures are elaborate, involved constructions that are almost totally abstract in form. The complex assemblies make use of ceramic materials – be they pieces of tile, broken cups or the metal element wire used in the electric kiln to fire the work – partly as a means of looking at the nature of the fired material and partly as metaphors for the complexity of modern life, the urban environment and the concept of waste.

'Yellow Angle, Purple Angle' by John Chalke (Canada), 1996. Earthenware/stoneware, hand-built and press-moulded, crawled glaze. Length 56.75 cm (22.75 in).

The sculptural forms of UK artist Richard Slee (b. 1946) look not to the 'human condition' but to the history of 'material culture', whether the history of ceramics or the concept of the ornament. For his decorative forms Slee uses hand-building or press-moulding, brought to a high degree of precision. Bright industrial-style glazes over careful gradations of colour enliven his pieces and provide an engaging commentary not only on the process of ceramics but also on the activity of art pottery. His shapes – a particular favourite at one point was the cornucopia, used to suggest excess and plenty and an overabundance of treats – are crisp and colourful, with the high-quality finish associated with industrial production. References in his work are not only to the classical tradition but also to elements of nineteenth-century decorative forms. Slee maintains a balance between formal beauty and a conscious vulgarity of decorative motifs, many of which knowingly reflect a nostalgia for pre-war suburbia whilst simultaneously acting as a critique of the values suburbia embodies. There is also a curious ambiguity in the plate-like objects of Canadian John Chalke. His highly textured and colourful assemblies appear to have unorthodox elements combining organic with machine-like qualities in compositions that are both highly decorative and bizarre.

The work of the Catalan potter Claudi Casanovas (b. 1956) straddles the boundaries between craft and fine art, his often large-scale forms appearing to have been hewn out of the earth itself. Rock strata have proved a potent source of

Blue soft form by Felicity Aylieff (UK), 1999. White clay body stained with aggregates. Dimensions 45 x 36 x 36 cm (18 x 14.5 x 14.5 in).

'Plat Conic' by Claudi Casanovas (Spain), 1993. Stoneware, hand-built. Diameter *c.* 60 cm (24 in).

reference for him, in particular the varying textures and qualities of different rocks sandwiched together with magma in the surrounding Catalan volcanic district of his home. Whether fashioning vast vessels or wall pieces, Casanovas is both 'individual potter and ingenious engineer', seeking to capture the essence of landscape with all its weight and strength. Ulla Viotti, a Swedish ceramist, also responds to the layering and folding of rock and landscape, often linking it to the way the body also creases. She creates large wall pieces into which she may model tiny human beings, dwarfed by the size and monumental qualities of the landscape. Responding to environmental issues and the proliferation of weapons of mass destruction, Viotti uses her work to heighten awareness and provoke response. The Finnish ceramist Pekka Pekkaari combines studio work with designing for Arabia, and in the Scandinavian tradition has a studio in the factory. Making use of available materials Pekkaari has worked with commercial bricks, slicing and carving them to create intriguing rhythmic patterns. In the UK Gwen Heeney has also collab-

orated with a brick manufacturer to create functional, sculptural forms. Using industrially made bricks Heeney cuts and models them while still plastic as components for large outdoor seating. Some, placed along the side of Cardiff Bay, are over three or four metres long and fashioned in the form of mythological animals.

The taut, hollow, hand-built forms of UK artist Sarah Radstone (b. 1955) make reference to natural rock formations and to parts of the body. With minimal surface modelling and colour, Radstone's forms stand as a metaphor for the skin that both defines and conceals. The Hungarian ceramist Imre Schrammel continues to produce engaging sculptural forms. Some with holes and jagged edges stand as evidence of pain or hurt, too nebulous to pin down accurately, yet compelling in their cry for help and defiance. The sculptural forms of New Zealand ceramist Madeline Child are equally minimal and effective. Child makes use of the soft, plastic qualities of clay to form playful, flowing wall-pieces that celebrate the qualities of the material and the way clay can create an impression of pleasure and enjoyment.

The cool, austere forms of Felicity Aylieff also have suggestions of industrial production. Using a mixture of a body based on brick clay with added glass fragments and other material, Aylieff moulds large forms which, though abstract, recall the flowing lines of nature as seen, for instance, on shells. Aylieff polishes the surfaces to give them an almost granite-like appearance, a quality that suggests great strength and solidity. Yet the forms, though often standing as high as a grown man, still appear delicate and light, evocative of both movement and rhythm.

In calling on such diverse sources as geology, natural form and manufactured objects as well as the history of ceramics, artists working with clay continue to push at and extend our understanding of the material and how it can be used to enhance and enrich the world in which we live. Clay is a material limited as much by the imagination of the artist as by its physical properties, and as such will remain a vital medium for creative work, touching the past, the present and the future.

The State of Things

*...the thought that bears the stamp of our age and our geography –
breaking up all the ordered surfaces and all the planes with which
we are accustomed to tame the wild profusion of existing things, and
continuing long afterwards to disturb and threaten with collapse our
age-old distinction between the Same and the Other.*

MICHEL FOUCAULT
The Order of Things: An Archaeology of the Human Sciences

BELOW: *Two Lidded Jars* by
Kirsten Coelho, 2009. Porcelain
with iron decoration, thrown.
Height 23 cm (9 in).

BELOW RIGHT: *Dividing* by
Frances Lambe, 2009. Stoneware.
Dimensions 38 x 38 x 8 cm
(15 x 15 x 3 in). Photographer:
Gerry Morgan.

Two major themes dominate ceramics in the twenty-first century. One is a concern with history in all its diverse forms; the other is a breaking down of the traditional barriers between art, craft and design that challenges the established categories in favour of a more fluid approach to working with clay. Potters continue to make tableware, such as the fine, cool, seductive porcelain forms of the Australian potter Kirsten Coelho (b 1966, Australia), or the amusing 'bird beakers' of Bernadette Curran (b 1974, USA); to look at the possibilities of decorative forms, as in the assemblies of objects by Frances Lambe (b 1961, Ireland) and the highly ornate forms of

Bonnie Seeman (b 1969, USA); and to explore a sculptural approach, as in the work of Barnaby Barford (b 1977, UK) or Daphné Corregan (b 1954, France). But the lines between the different areas of art, craft and design are now more blurred. This is particularly evident in the way that some ceramicists collaborate with the ceramic industry to design forms for factory production.

The challenge to perceived categories was clearly demonstrated in the UK when Grayson Perry (b 1962, UK) was awarded the 2003 Turner Prize for his hand-built and decorated pots. Like many other fine art institutions, London's Tate Gallery has been committed to the fine, rather

ABOVE: *I Was an Angry Working-
Class Man* by Grayson Perry,
2001. Glazed ceramic.
Height 56 cm (22 in).

TOP RIGHT: *Randy Racoon*
by Bernadette Curran, 2007.
Porcelain, thrown and modelled,
cone 6. Height *c.* 17 cm (6.75 in).

ABOVE RIGHT: *Teapot with
Seeds* by Bonnie Seeman, 2008.
Porcelain. Height 17 cm (6.75 in).

than the applied arts; and while Perry's vessels are
undoubtedly pots, made by Perry himself, rather
than a bevy of assistants and fabricators, they are
made by someone with unimpeachable credentials
as a fine artist. While generally dubbed 'an artist
who makes pots', rather than a potter who has
stormed the Holy Grail of the art establishment,
Perry, especially as his alter ego, Clair, conforms
entirely to the concept of a modern artist.

There is space here for only a limited
discussion of Perry's pots, but the first point to
be borne in mind is his referencing to ceramic
history, a theme he shares with some other artists.
Many of the shapes of Perry's vases are derived
from conventional and highly regarded classical
forms from Song Dynasty China. Such shapes by
Perry are not entirely 'neutral', in that they suggest
security and respectability, in part derived from
the classical Song tradition, instantly recognizable
by anyone with a passing knowledge of ceramic
history. By contrast, the bottle form serves as

a useful and comparatively unemotive vehicle
for Perry's decoration. Equally significant are
Perry's references to the long and distinguished
tradition of decorating pots with scenes that
may be mythical, sexual, social and/or political,
as evidenced by the fine pieces produced, for
example, in ancient Greece.

Like the ancient Greeks, Perry's principle
concerns revolve around shape and the content
of decoration, rather than technique. By working
with 3-D forms, Perry produces sculptural objects,
which, because of their intensity and detailed
surface-marking, demand a quite considerable
amount of study to absorb. As Perry has pointed
out, one of the reasons he chose to work with
pottery was because it was an art practice that was
generally regarded as the least acceptable fine art
form. Illustrating this point, he said it was more
difficult to come out as a maker of pots than as a
transvestite. In setting out to consciously challenge
the audience with depictions of sensational

current and autobiographical topics, Perry has found himself at the centre of the art world. His confrontational subject matter – be it child abuse, explicit sexual activity, cross-dressing or violence – is often sufficiently strong to make the eyes water.

In resisting 'the order of things', by opposing certain preconceptions with regard to clay, Perry shares a concern with artists such as Clare Twomey, Emmanuel Cooper, Marian Heyerdahl, Virgil Ortiz and Robin Best who all investigate ways in which ceramic form can question and contest perceptions of 'craft' and 'art'. In statements about their work, they make it clear that they see themselves as artists rather than makers, concerned with the visual impact of their objects rather than with issues, such as function, use or even 'truth to materials'. In *Trophy,* Clare Twomey (b 1968, UK) modelled hundreds of bluebirds out of Wedgwood's iconic blue Jasper ware. Placed in the Sculpture Court of London's Victoria and Albert Museum, visitors were invited to take the birds away, to take flight, and, in return, to send an account or an image of their new life – their new home. In using such a familiar material as the jasper body, Twomey's flock of bluebirds, a symbol of freedom, take flight in an act of participation and collaboration between artists and consumer.

Just as Twomey draws on the history of ceramics, other artists like Nicole Cherubini (b 1970, USA) and Keith Harrison (b 1967, UK) also make use of the past. In Harrison's *The Last Supper*, an installation also at the Victoria and Albert Museum, he constructed his own version of the biblical event using blocks of coloured Egyptian paste, a self-glazing body devised in the Middle East from which small, precious objects were made in bright colours. Harrison 'fired' the paste with recycled heating elements scavenged from old cookers. In the course of his 'performance', the body emitted steam and gradually changed colour – a combination of history, technology and spectacle.

For artists Felicity Aylieff (b 1954, UK), Robin Best (b 1953, Australia), Emmanuel Cooper (b 1938, UK) and Marian Heyerdahl (b 1957, Norway), the Far East is the starting point for their ceramics. Calling on the skills and techniques of traditional potters in China, Aylieff produces vast porcelain jars. Covering their surface with hand-painted or transfer decorations, she

OPPOSITE, TOP: *Trophy, Wedgwood Blue Jasper Birds, 4000* by Clare Twomey, 2006. Blue jasper clay, modelled; installation at the Victoria and Albert Museum.

OPPOSITE, BOTTOM: *The Last Supper* by Keith Harrison, 2006. Egyptian paste, heating elements, mixed media; installation at the Victoria and Albert Museum.

TOP: *Nones* by Emmanuel Cooper, 2010. Porcelain, hand-built. Height 12 cm (4.75 in).

ABOVE: *In China We Trust* (detail) by Robin Best, 2007. Porcelain, slip-cast, blue ceramic pencil. Sizes, various.

ABOVE RIGHT: *Vase, Still Life* by Felicity Aylieff, 2009. Glazed porcelain, Fencai enamel colours, hand-painted. Height 200 x 60 x 60 cm (6.5 ft x 2 ft x 2 ft).

turns them into playful, light-hearted objects, which, in their monumental scale and lively decoration, successfully unite form and surface. Much the same effect is conveyed by Robin Best's classically inspired porcelain bottle forms, transformed into precious objects through their resemblance to the classic blue-and-white wares of Ming dynasty China. Recent work by Best, started during and after a number of residencies in China, reflects the complexity of the cultural, commercial and political history of China. In the series, *In China We Trust,* Best takes the subject of cultural exchange between Asia with Europe as the underlying theme. The bottles are a picture gallery of images relating to trade, culture and commerce, while some of Best's other works carry designs inspired by each of the countries through which blue-and-white porcelain passed on its way from China to Europe, via India and the Middle East.

The fine bronzes of the Shang Dynasty, in particular the *Ku* form, used to pour wine in ritual religious ceremonies, have influenced Emmanuel Cooper's series *Nones*. But, rather than reproduce the form in ceramic by throwing on the wheel, his usual method of making, Cooper hand-builds the shape in porcelain by coiling, in this way appropriating a classical shape, while subverting it into something freer and less stately. The magnificent Chinese Terracotta Army, dating from 210 BC, inspired Marian Heyerdahl, who responded to this monumental work by an equally impressive assembly, *The Terracotta Women Project*. This vast installation re-contextualizes the Warriors by duplicating them at their original scale while changing their gender to female. At first glance the figures look similar to their male counterparts, with seemingly identical outfits, but a closer look reveals that they are no longer soldiers brandishing weapons but women – with varied expressions, clothes and hair styles – some nursing children. Strong and robust, the figures burst with pride and strength.

ABOVE: *The Terracotta Women Project* (detail) by Marion Heyerdahl, 2007. Clay, mixed media, life-sized.

BELOW: *Teabowl* by Ken Matsuzaki, 2008. Stoneware. Height *c.* 9 cm (3.5 in).

OPPOSITE TOP LEFT: *Ocean* (detail) by Natasha Daintry, 2009. Porcelain, mixed media. Photography: Matthew Donaldson.

A quieter, more subdued approach to ceramic history is taken by the Japanese potter Ken Matsuzaki (b 1950). His teabowls, slab vases and bottles follow the well-established tradition of reduction-fired ware, often used in the Japanese tea ceremony, but Matsuzaki subverts the convention by overstatement and elaboration, often applying a thick layer of glaze that fuses to the surface to create a relief effect. The result is a reworking of history, richly finished and redolent with tradition, bringing an ancient process of firing into our own time.

The way Matsuzaki responds to the ceramic heritage of his own country is shared by the New Mexican-born artist Virgil Ortiz (b 1969). His work is informed by the comment that 'The two most important elements of Pueblo life are our language and our art'. Ortiz, a member of Cochiti Pueblo, uses the tradition of painting on pots to comment on modern mores,

highlighting the contrast between painted and undecorated areas as part of the dynamic.

In his assemblies of industrially produced figures brought together in seemingly conventional tableau, Barnaby Barford creates playful, amusing objects with unsettling undertones. He uses mass-produced and antique porcelain figurines, and 'refigures' them by cutting them up, adding pieces and reassembling them in unlikely juxtapositions. There is also something playful in Daphné Corregan's sculptures. In *Two Bellies,* the dumb-bell-like form carries references to aspects of the human form, though the result can be seen as entirely abstract. Abstraction is also one of the concerns in the vessel groups brought together by Natasha Daintry (b 1966, UK). In *Ocean 09,* Daintry makes bold but sensitive use of colour, evoking a subtle but pervasive sense of movement through the use of hundreds of differently coloured slim cylinder forms.

The everyday is the subject of the sculptural installations, derived from domestic objects and furniture, by Anders Ruhwald (b 1974, Denmark). While mutated almost beyond recognition, they create an uncanny effect of functionality, conveying a sense of the familiar that lies just beyond our reach. The sculptures touch on our relationship with things that surround us, through which we understand the world and through which we want the world to understand us. The objects can be seen as, for example, 'chair', 'shelf' or 'stand'; but, with

only vague references to go on, the viewer is left to make his or her own connections with these tantalizing traces of functionality. The outcome is objects, whose meaning is not fixed but needs to be constantly negotiated.

Art and design are brought effortlessly together in the work of the artist Marek Cecula (b 1944, Poland), who practises in both the USA and Poland. Cecula moves fluently between design and art, between the ceramic artist and the ceramic industry, between traditional production of decorative art and advanced technologies of image reproduction. As a designer of tableware, he produces sleek, modern forms that contrast with his appropriation of redundant factory ware, which he stacks up and fires in a wood kiln until they fuse together, scar and distort. As a comment on the declining ceramic industry in the West, such work is both intriguing and salutary.

The work of Michael Eden (b 1955, UK) also

embodies a response to ceramic history and to the development of technologies, such as computer aided design (CAD), rapid prototyping and new materials. Eden's *The Wedgwoodn't Tureen* is a poetic investigation that makes use of rapid manufacturing (RM) and highly innovative ceramic materials to reproduce an iconic ceramic object first made by Wedgwood over 200 years ago, but in a different, although recognizable, form.

RIGHT: *Still Life* by Marek Cecula, 2005. Industrial porcelain, wood-fired. Height *c.* 12 cm (4.7 in).

BELOW: *Shelf/Lamp* by Anders Ruhwald, 2006; glazed earthenware, cord, bulb, plug. Dimensions 7 x 35 x 34 cm (2.75 x 13.75 x 13.25 in).

OPPOSITE: *The Wedgwoodn't Tureen – Tall Pink Round* by Michael Eden, 2009. Three-dimensional printing from a plaster/polymer material with unique non-fired ceramic coating. Height 40 cm (15.75 in), diameter 28 cm (11 in).

The Wedgwoodn't Tureen involves a new treatment that converts a fragile RM model into a durable product, which is coated with a non-fired, eco-ceramic layer with the same material properties as conventional ceramics. It is non-toxic, food-safe, frost-resistant, acid- and alkali-resistant and acts as a gas barrier, which can be stained with organic, inorganic or metallic pigments.

With clay as the common material used by sculptors, designers and potters, it has seemingly endless possibilities. Clay is versatile, capable of being fashioned into an endless variety of forms, and offers a malleable, cheap substance that responds quickly to the hand. Yet it is not totally neutral, but is redolent with history, and with the role of fired clay objects in daily life. As a non-precious, readily available material, it carries associations with the earth that can make it accessible and 'human'. It is such qualities that continue to attract artists to new levels of invention in the creation of objects that amaze, delight and provoke.

Glossary of Technical Terms

ALKALINE GLAZE – Glaze containing an alkaline material such as sodium or potassium in some form; can give rich turquoise colours when small quantities of copper oxide are present.

AMPHORA – Pot form used in Mediterranean countries for storing and transporting liquids; usually characterized by two handles linking the neck to the body of the pot.

ANTIMONY – Metallic element once used to make glazes opaque white.

ARABESQUE – Ornamentation derived from a mixture of formal geometric and foliage patterns, characterized by flowing linear designs of leaves and scrolls.

ARMENIAN BOLE – Fine red pigment rich in iron oxide, originating in the Near East and widely used from about the thirteenth or fourteenth century.

ASH – Remains from fired wood or other organic matter, often used in high-temperature glazes.

BARBOTINE DECORATION – Made by trailing thick slip through a fine nozzle on to the surface of a leather-hard pot.

BASALT – Fine-grained black igneous rock; a term used by Wedgwood amongst others for black unglazed ware.

BISCUIT – Pottery that has been fired once without a glaze in a biscuit firing; usually porous and relatively soft.

BODY – General term for various clays from which pots are made.

BONE CHINA – Type of porcelain, made in England from china clay, bone ash and flint; pure white and translucent.

BURNISHING – Rubbing the surface of unfired pots with a smooth tool such as a stone or a bone; the particles of clay, pressed flat and smooth, take on a dull gloss; sometimes known as polishing.

CARINATE – Pottery shape made by joining a rounded base and straight inward-sloping walls.

CELADONS – General term for oriental stonewares and porcelains with green glazes, where the colour is obtained from small amounts of iron in the glaze. Sometimes known as greenwares.

CHINA CLAY – Pure white clay, sometimes known as kaolin, of theoretically pure composition; essential for the production of fine porcelain.

CHINA STONE OR PORCELAIN STONE – Chinese material used for the manufacture of high-temperature porcelain, made from a rock composed of quartz, alkali feldspars, secondary mica and a small amount of clay; sometimes known as petuntse; Cornwall stone and Cornish stone are Western equivalents.

COLOURING OXIDES – Various metal oxides which, when painted on or mixed into a glaze, give different colours: copper oxide gives green; manganese, oxide brown or purple; iron oxide, brown or green; cobalt, oxide blue.

COMBING – Incised parallel-line decoration made by a toothed tool such as a comb.

CRAZING – Cracking of glaze to give a fine network of lines; sometimes known as crackle.

DELFT WARE – English term used originally to describe tin-glazed earthenware made in Delft, Holland; sometimes used to describe all tin-glazed ware made in England.

EARTHENWARE – General term used for pottery fired to temperatures up to 1150°C; characterized by slightly porous body in which glaze and body remain separate layers.

ENAMELS OR ON-GLAZE DECORATION – Glazes prepared in frit form to melt at low temperature, allowing a wide range of colours; painted on to a fired glaze and refired in a muffle kiln.

FAIENCE (EGYPTIAN PASTE) – Artificially made clay body prepared from clay and sand to which a fluxing agent has been added; can be moulded into small objects or pots; the surface becomes glossy when fired and, if dusted with copper oxide, turquoise. Faience is a term also used by the French for tin-glazed earthenware.

FRIT – Manufactured glaze or body material made by heating two or more raw materials together until they melt to form a glass which is then shattered, usually by pouring into cold water, and ground to powder.

GALENA – An impure lead ore used by potters to make lead glazes.

GLAZE – A smooth waterproof glossy surface usually applied to the surface of pottery to make it smooth and waterproof and also as a decorative finish.

GREEN WARE – General term for pots before they have been fired; also used for celadons.

GROG – Fired crushed pottery added to clay to make it more workable.

INCISED DECORATION – Lines pressed or cut into the surface of a pot or tile.

KILNS – Structures in which clay forms are fired until they become pottery, sometimes known as the potter's oven; more sophisticated kilns separate the fire from the chamber that holds the pots.

KWAART – Technique used by the Delft potters to imitate Chinese blue-and-white porcelain in tin-glazed earthenware, by using a clear transparent glaze over a white opaque glaze to give greater gloss and depth to the colours.

LEATHER-HARD – Term describing the midway stage between wet and dry clay, comparable to shoe leather, when the clay is sufficiently stiff to support its own weight but still pliable enough to be bent and carved, at which point turning can also be carried out on unfinished pots; sometimes known as cheese-hard.

LEVIGATION – Process of preparing clay by reducing it to liquid and then decanting the finer particles, which remain in suspension while the heavier particles sink.

LUSTRE – Colouring decoration achieved by painting metallic pigment on to a fired glaze and refiring in a reducing atmosphere, giving an iridescent effect.

MAIOLICA – General term for tin-glazed earthenware decorated with colouring oxides painted on to unfired opaque white tin-glaze.

MAJOLICA – Corruption of maiolica; a term used during the nineteenth century for moulded earthenware with relief patterns decorated with coloured glazes or maiolica tin-glaze painting.

MONOCHROME POTTERY – Usually made in one colour or with decoration painted in a single contrasting colour.

MUFFLE KILN – Protects pots from flames in a flame-burning kiln; essential for production of enamels.

NATRON – Mineral found in the Near East containing sodium oxide (Na_2O), which acts as a flux in a glaze or in faience.

OPACIFIER – Substance, usually a metal oxide such as tin oxide, which, when added to clear glazes, becomes suspended and renders the glaze opaque.

OXIDATION FIRING – Oxygen-rich atmosphere with a clean bright flame; the resulting pots are often bright coral red; iron glazes give yellow or brown (opposite to reduction firing).

PADDLE AND ANVIL – Tools often used for hand-built pottery. The anvil, often in the form of a stone, supports the pot wall inside while the paddle is beaten against the outside wall.

POLYCHROME POTTERY – Decoration painted in two or more colours, usually with coloured slips or oxides.

PORCELAIN – High-temperature ware which is white and translucent, with a body made by mixing china clay, china stone and quartz together; sometimes known as hard-paste porcelain.

POTASH – Form of potassium oxide (K_2O) found in wood-ash, which acts as a flux in glaze or faience.

QUARTZ – Form of silica (SiO_2) such as sand, which, when mixed with a suitable flux, will form a glaze; flint is a finely ground form of silica.

RAKU – A method, which originated in Japan, of firing quickly by placing pots in a glowing kiln and removing them while still at top temperature.

REDUCTION FIRING – Oxygen-reduced atmosphere; the resulting pots are often dark brown or black; iron glazes produce greens or blues (opposite to oxidation firing).

RESIST DECORATION – Part of the pot is painted with a substance such as wax, which resists any colouring pigment or glaze and therefore fires a contrasting colour.

ROULETTING – In antiquity, decoration made by allowing a tool to 'chatter' against the side of a leather-hard pot revolving on the wheel; also used to describe the pattern made by a relief-decorated revolving wheel held against a turning pot.

SAGGAR – Ceramic container in which the ware is placed during the firing for protection from kiln gases, flames or contact with other pots or loose material.

SALT-GLAZE – A thin glaze achieved by introducing common salt (NaCl) into the kiln at high temperature. The chlorine goes up the chimney as a gas and the sodium vapour reacts with the surface of the clay to form a glaze.

SGRAFFITO – Decoration scratched through a layer of slip to show the body of contrasting colour.

SLIP – Clay that has been thinned in water and sieved to make it smooth.

SLIP-CAST – Ware, usually thin-walled, made in a mould from a specially prepared clay slip.

SLIP WARE – Pots and dishes decorated with different coloured clay slips and usually finished with a transparent lead glaze.

SOFT-PASTE PORCELAIN – Made by mixing white clay with a frit or flux, such as bone ash or talc, which vitrifies at earthenware temperature to give a white translucent body; European invention produced to imitate Chinese high-temperature (sometimes called hard-paste) porcelain.

SPRIGGING – Decorating technique in which relief-moulded decoration is applied to the leather-hard pot; used extensively by Wedgwood in the production of his Jasper wares.

STONEWARE – Pottery fired to a high temperature, about 1250°C, at which the body is vitrified and the glaze and body are partially fused together.

TEMMOKU – Term used to describe black oriental glazes that break light brown on rims and ornament.

TEMPER – Coarse, non-plastic material added to clay to improve its working and firing qualities.

TERRA SIGILLATA – Pottery with an orange or red glossy surface achieved by adding a layer of finely prepared slip; made in Italy and Gaul during the Roman period and sometimes known as Samian ware.

THROWING – Art of building up pots on the fast-spinning potter's wheel using centrifugal force.

TIN-GLAZE – Glaze rendered white and opaque by the addition of tin oxide to the mixture.

TOURNETTE – Turntable device used to assist the shaping of pots by coiling.

TURNING OR TRIMMING – Process of removing surplus clay from thrown pots by returning them, when leather-hard, to the potter's wheel and trimming with a metal tool.

UNDERGLAZE PAINTING – Technique of painting colouring oxides on to unfired pottery which may or may not be subsequently glazed; used occasionally to describe the technique of painting on to unfired glaze.

Museum and National Collections of Pottery

AUSTRALIA
National Gallery of Australia, Melbourne
The Western Australian Art Gallery, Perth
Art Gallery of New South Wales, Sydney
Australia Museum, Sydney
Power House Museum, Sydney

CANADA
Canada National Museum, Ottawa
George R. Gardiner Museum of Ceramic Art,
   Toronto
Royal Ontario Museum, Toronto

FRANCE
Musée du Berry, Bourges
Musée des Arts Décoratifs, Paris
Musée d'Art Modern du Nord, Villeneuve d'Ascq

GERMANY
Hetjens Museum, Deutsches Keramikmuseum,
   Düsseldorf
Keramion, Museum für zeitgenössische
   Keramische Kunst, Frechen
Badisches Landesmuseum, Karlsruhe
Württembergisches Landesmuseum, Stuttgart

GREECE
National Museum of Greece, Athens
National Museum, Heraklion, Crete

INDIA
National Museum, Madras

ITALY
Museo Internazionale della Ceramica, Faenza
Vatican Museum, Rome
Villa Julia, Rome

JAPAN
Hakone Art Museum, Kanagawa Prefecture
Ohara Museum, Kurashiki
Shoji Hamada Museum, Mashiko
Idemitsu Art Gallery, Tokyo
Mingei-Kan (Folk Art Museum), Tokyo
The National Museum, Tokyo
Nezu Art Museum, Tokyo
Nikon Mingei-Kan, Tokyo
Ueno Museum, Tokyo
University Museum, Tokyo

NETHERLANDS
Stedelijk Museum, Amsterdam
Museum voor Stad en Lande, Groningen

Gemeente Museum, The Hague
Kuituis Museum, 's Hertogenbosch
Museum Het Princessehof, Leeuwarden
Boymans-van Beuningen Museum, Rotterdam

SWEDEN
Asiatic Museum, Stockholm
Etnografiska Museet, Stockholm

SWITZERLAND
Swiss National Museum, Zurich

TAIWAN
National Museum of Art, Taipei
National Palace Museum, Taipei

UK
Aberdeen Art Gallery
Aberdeen University Anthropological Museum
Aberystwyth Arts Centre
Buckinghamshire County Museum, Aylesbury
Ulster Museum, Belfast
Central Museum and Art Gallery, Birmingham
Museum and Art Gallery, Brighton
City Museum and Art Gallery, Bristol
Fitzwilliam Museum, Cambridge
University Museum of Archaeology and
   Ethnology, Cambridge
National Museum of Wales, Cardiff
Museum and Art Gallery, Derby
Gulbenkian Museum of Oriental Art and
   Archaeology, Durham
Huntly House, Edinburgh
National Museum of Scotland, Edinburgh
Craft Study Centre, Farnham
Art Gallery and Museum, Kelvingrove, Glasgow
Burrell Collection, Glasgow
Public Museum and Art Gallery, Hastings
Liverpool Museum
British Museum, London
Contemporary Ceramics, London
Crafts Council, London
London University College Department of
   Egyptology
Museum of London
Percival David Foundation of Chinese Art,
   University of London
Victoria and Albert Museum and Art Library
   London
Wallace Collection, London
City Art Gallery, Manchester
Laing Art Gallery, Newcastle-upon-Tyne
Castle Museum, Norwich

Sainsbury Centre for Visual Arts, Norwich
Castle Museum and Art Gallery, Nottingham
Ashmolean Museum of Art and Archaeology, Oxford
Pitt Rivers Museum, Oxford
Paisley Museum and Art Galleries
Salisbury and South Wiltshire Museum
Gladstone Pottery Museum, Stoke-on-Trent
Minton Museum, Royal Doulton Ltd,
   Stoke-on-Trent
The Potteries Museum and Art Gallery (City
   Museum and Art Gallery), Stoke-on-Trent
Wedgwood Museum, Stoke-on-Trent
Glynn Vivian Art Gallery and Museum, Swansea
Whitby Museum
City Art Gallery, York
(Museums and Galleries in Great Britain and
   Ireland, a full detailed list of museums, is
   published annually)

USA
Museum of Northern Arizona, Flagstaff
Heard Museum of Anthropology and Primitive
   Art, Phoenix, Arizona
Phoenix Art Museum, Arizona
Arizona State Museum, University of Arizona,
   Tucson
Eagle Rock Southwest Indian Museum, California
Stendahl Gallery, Hollywood, California
Los Angeles County Art Museum, California
Southwest Museum, Los Angeles, California
Mills College, Oakland, California
Pasadena Art Museum, California
San Diego Museum of Man, California
De Young Museum, San Francisco, California
San Francisco Art Museum, California
Taylor Museum, Colorado Springs, Colorado
Denver Art Museum, Colorado
Winterthur Museum of American Decorative
   Arts, Delaware
Bernice P. Bishop Museum, Honolulu, Hawaii
Chicago Art Institute, Illinois
Field Museum of Natural History, Chicago, Illinois
Oriental Institute of the University of Chicago,
   Illinois
Cincinnati Art Museum, Illinois
Krannert Museum, University of Illinois
Indianapolis Museum of Art, Indiana
The University of Iowa Museum of Art,
   Iowa City, Iowa
Wichita Art Association, Kansas
Baltimore Museum of Art, Maryland
Boston Museum of Fine Arts, Massachusetts
Peabody Museum, Harvard University, Cambridge,
   Massachusetts

Bibliography

Cranbrook Academy of Art Galleries, Michigan

Henry Ford Museum, Dearborn, Michigan

Minneapolis Museum of Art, Minnesota

Minnesota Museum of Art

William Rockhill Nelson Gallery, Kansas City, Missouri

St Louis Museum, Missouri

Prairie Museum, Grand Island, Nebraska

Maxwell Museum of Anthropology, University of New Mexico, Albuquerque

Millicent Rogers Museum, Taos, New Mexico

Museum of Navajo Ceremonial Art, Santa Fe, New Mexico

Museum of New Mexico, Santa Fe

American Museum of Natural History, New York

Brooklyn Museum, New York

Carborundum Museum of Ceramics, New York

Cooper-Hewitt Museum of Decorative Art and Design, New York

Everson Museum of Art, Syracuse, New York

The Hispanic Society of America, New York

Metropolitan Museum of Art, New York

National Museum of the American Indian, New York

Museum of Contemporary Crafts, New York

Museum of Modern Art, New York

Museum of Primitive Art, New York

Cleveland Museum of Art, Ohio

Dayton Art Institute, Ohio

Philbrook Museum, Tulsa, Oklahoma

Landis Valley Farm Museum, Pennsylvania

Philadelphia Museum of Art, Pennsylvania

University of Pennsylvania Museum, Philadelphia

Houston Museum of Fine Arts, Texas

Bennington Museum, Vermont

Shelburne Museum, Vermont

Chrysler Museum, Norfolk, Virginia

Colonial Williamsburg, Virginia

Freer Gallery of Art, Washington, DC

Henry Art Gallery, Washington, DC

Smithsonian Institution, Washington, DC

Seattle Art Museum, Washington

Milwaukee Art Centre, Wisconsin

It is only possible to identify major sources of information for a book that seeks to cover as much ground as this one. Research into the history of pottery is constantly developing and the literature is growing apace, so I have focused here on some of the latest published material generally available. Exhibition and gallery displays such as those in the British Museum indicate the range and scope of ceramics made at various times and places, and no book can substitute for actually looking at the wares in order to appreciate their textural qualities.

The single recent publication which has guided my task most clearly in revising and expanding on previous editions of this book is *Pottery in the Making: World Ceramic Traditions,* edited by Ian Freestone and David Gaimster (1997), London, British Museum Press and Washington, DC, Smithsonian Institution Press. Specific excerpts are referenced under the relevant chapter headings. *Pottery in the Making* also contains an extensive international bibliography of books and articles on ceramics.

CHAPTER ONE: EARLY BEGINNINGS

Simpson, St John (1997), 'Prehistoric Ceramics in Mesopotamia', in *Pottery in the Making,* pp. 38–43

Simpson, St John (1997), 'Early Urban Ceramic Industries in Mesopotamia', in *Pottery in the Making,* pp. 50–5

Simpson, St John (1997), 'Early Iron Age Rural Ceramic Traditions in Iran', in *Pottery in the Making,* pp. 152–7

Simpson, St John (1997), 'Partho–Sasanian Ceramic Industries in Mesopotamia', in *Pottery in the Making,* pp. 74–9

Spencer, A.J. (1997), 'Pottery in Predynastic Egypt', in *Pottery in the Making,* pp. 44–9

Spencer, A.J. and Schofield, Louise (1997), 'Faience in the Ancient Mediterranean World', in *Pottery in the Making,* pp. 104–9

Spencer, A.J. (1997), 'Dynastic Egyptian Pottery', in *Pottery in the Making,* pp. 62–7

Welsby, Derek (1997), 'Early Pottery in the Middle Nile Valley', in *Pottery in the Making,* pp. 26–31

CHAPTER TWO: THE ANCIENT WORLD

Cohen Beth (2006), *The Colours of Clay: Special Techniques in Athenian Vases,* Los Angeles, J. Paul Getty Museum

Doumas, Christos (1983) *CyckdicArt: The N.P Goulandris Collection,* London, British Museum Press

Roberts, Paul (1997), 'Mass-Production of Roman Finewares', in *Pottery in the Making,* pp. 188–93

Spencer, A.J. (1997), 'Pottery in Predynastic Egypt', in *Pottery in the Making,* pp. 44–9

Tatton-Brown, Veronica (1997), *Ancient Cyprus,* London, British Museum Press

Williams, Dyfri (1997), Ancient Greek Pottery', in *Pottery in the Making,* pp. 86–91

Williams, Dyfri (1999), *Greek Vases,* London, British Museum Press

CHAPTER THREE: THE ORIENTAL WORLD

Earle, Joe (ed.) (1986), *Japanese Art and Design,* London, V&A Publicatons

Goepper, Roger and Whitfield, Roderick (1984), *Treasures from Korea: Art Through 5000 Years,* London, British Museum Press

Harris, Victor (1997), 'Ash-Glazed Stonewares in Japan'; and 'Jomon Pottery in Ancient Japan', in *Pottery in the Making,* pp. 80–5 and 20–5.

Harrison-Hall, Jessica (1997), 'Chinese Porcelain from Jingdezhen', in *Pottery in the Making* pp. 194–9; and 'Ding and Other Whitewares of Northern China', in *Pottery in the Making,* pp. 182–7.

He Li (2008), *Chinese Ceramics: The New Standard Guide from the Asian Art Museum of San Francisco,* London, Thames & Hudson

Honda, Hiromu and Shimazu, Noriki (1997), *The Beauty of Fired Clay: Ceramics from Burma, Cambodia, Laos and Thailand,* Kuala Lumpur, Oxford University Press

McKillop, Beth (1992), *Korean Art and Design: The Samsung Gallery of Korean Art,* London, V&A Publications

Portal, Jane (1997), 'Korean Celadons of the Koryo Dynasty', in *Pottery in the Making,* pp. 98–103

Vainker, S.J. (1995), *Chinese Pottery and Porcelain: From Prehistory to the Present,* London, British Museum Press

Chapter Four: The Islamic World

Allan, James W. (1991), *Islamic Ceramics,* Oxford, Ashmolean Museum

Canby, Sheila R. (1997), 'Islamic Lustreware', in *Pottery in the Making,* pp. 110–15

Carswell, John (1998), *Iznik Pottery,* London, British Museum Press

Porter, Venetia (1995), *Islamic Tiles,* London, British Museum Press

Rogers, J.M. (1983), *Islamic Art and Design 1500–1700,* London, British Museum Press

Chapter Five: Continental European Earthenwares and Stonewares

Buckton, David (ed.) (1994), *Byzantium: Treasures of Byzantine Art and Culture,* London, British Museum Press

Gaimster, David (1997), *German Stoneware 1200–1900: Archaeology and Cultural History,* London, British Museum Press

Gaimster, David (1997), 'Stoneware Production in Medieval and Early Modern Germany', in *Pottery in the Making,* pp. 122–7

Gaimster, David and Redknap, Mark (eds) (1992), *Everyday and Exotic Pottery from Europe c. 650–1900: Studies in Honour of John Hurst,* Oxford, Oxbow Monograph 23

Gerrard, C.M. and Gutierrez, A. (1992), 'Lustreware and tin-glazed pottery from Spain: An overview of its origin and development', Medieval Europe conference, York 1992, pre-printed papers, vol. 3, pp. 145–51

Gerrard, CM. and Gutierrez, A. (eds) (1995), *Spanish Medieval Ceramics in Spain and the British Isles,* Oxford, BAR International Series 610

Hurst, J.G. (ed.) (1971), 'Red–Painted and Glazed Pottery in Western Europe from the Eighth to the Twelfth Century', *Medieval Archaeology* 13, pp. 93–105

Hurst, J.G., Neal, D.S. and van Beuningen, H.J.E. (1986), *Pottery Produced and Traded in North-West Europe 1350–1650,* Rotterdam, Rotterdam Papers VI

Hymersma, Herbert-Jan (1977), 'Guido di Savino and other Antwerp potters of the sixteenth century', *Connoisseur,* August, pp. 264–70

Kaufmann, Gerhard (1979), *North German Pottery of the 17th to the 20th Centuries,* Washington, DC, International Exhibitions Foundation

Ray, A. (1987), 'Fifteenth-century Spanish Pottery: the blue and purple family', *The Burlington Magazine,* May, pp. 343–4

Ray, A. (1987), 'Renaissance pottery in Seville', *The Burlington Magazine,* May, pp. 306–8

Thornton, Dora (1997), 'Maiolica Production in Renaissance Italy', in *Pottery in the Making,* pp. 116–21

Wilson, Timothy (ed.) (1987), *Ceramic Art of the Italian Renaissance,* London, British Museum Press

Chapter Six: Britain

Archer, Michael (1997), *Delftware: The Tin-glazed Earthenware of the British Isles: A Catalogue of the Collection in the Victoria and Albert Museum,* London, The Stationery Office

Edwards, Diana, Hampson, Rodney (2005), *White Salt-Glazed Stoneware of the British Isles,* Woodbridge, Antique Collectors' Club

Elliott, G.W. (1977), 'Staffordshire Red and Black Stonewares', *English Ceramic Circle Transactions,* vol. 10, part 2

Gaimster, David (1997), 'Regional Decorative Traditions in English Post-Medieval Slipware', in *Pottery in the Making,* pp. 128–33

Gaimster, D.R.M. (1988), 'Pottery production in the Lower Rhineland: the Duisburg Sequence *c.* 1400–1800', in Gaimster, D.R.M., Redknap, M. and Wegner, H.-H. *(eds), Medieval and Later Pottery from the Rhineland and its Markets,* Oxford, BAR International Series 440, pp. 151–72

Gaimster, David and Nenk, Beverley (1997), 'English households in transition 1400–1600: the ceramic evidence', in Gaimster, D. and Stamper, P. (eds), *The Age of Transition: The Archaeology of English Culture 1400–1600,* Oxford, Oxbow Books

Haith, Cathy (1997), 'Pottery in Early Anglo-Saxon England', in *Pottery in the Making,* pp. 146–51

Lomax, Derek W. (1995), 'Outline to Spanish Historical Background', in Gerrard, C.M. and Gutierrez, A. (eds), *Spanish Medieval Ceramics in Spain and the British Isles,* Oxford, BAR International Series 610

Nenk, Beverley (1997), 'Highly Decorated Pottery in Medieval England', in *Pottery in the Making,* pp. 92–7

Pierce, Donald (1989), *English Ceramics: The Frances and Emory Cocke Collection,* Seattle, University of Washington Press

Rigby, Val and Freestone, Ian (1997), 'Ceramic Changes in Late Iron Age Britain', in *Pottery in the Making,* pp. 56–61

Scholten, Frits (1993), *Dutch Majolica and Delftware 1550–1700 from the Edwin van Drecht Collection,* The Hague

Stephen, H.G. (1987), *Die beuralte Irdenware der Renaissance in Mitteleuropa,* Munich, Deutsche Kunstverlag

Varndell, Gillian and Freestone, Ian (1997), 'Early Prehistoric Pottery in Britain', in *Pottery in the Making,* pp. 32–7

Vincenzini, P. (1995), 'Italian Influence on Antwerp Maiolica in the 16th and 17th century', in *Monographs on Materials and Society 2,* Ceramics Cultural Heritage

Chapter Seven: European Porcelain

Boone, Mary Lou (1998), *Terre et Feu: Four Centuries of French Ceramics from the Boone Collection,* Seattle, University of Washington Press

Dawson, Aileen (1994), *French Porcelain,* London, British Museum Press

Selleck, Douglas (1978), *Cookworthy a Man of No Common Clay,* Baron Jay Publishers

Chapter Eight: American-Indian Pottery

Berlant, Tony (1983), Introduction, in *Ancient Art of the American Southwest,* New York, Hudson Press

Berrin, Kathleen (ed.) (1998), *The Spirit of Ancient Peru: Treasures from the Museo Arqueologico Rafael Larco Herrera,* London, Thames and Hudson

Davies, Lucy and Fini, Mo (1994), *Arts and Crafts of South America,* London, Thames and Hudson

Crawford, Michael H. (1998), *The Origins of Native Americans: Evidence from Anthropological Genetics,* Cambridge, Cambridge University Press

Hardin, Margaret Ann (1983), *Gifts of Mother Earth: Ceramics in the Zuni Tradition,* Phoenix, Heard Museum

Harlow, Francis H. (1978), *An Introduction to Hopi Pottery,* Flagstaff, Museum of Northern Arizona Press

Hayes, Allan and Blom, John (1996), *Southwestern Pottery: Anasazi to Zuni,* Flagstaff, Northland Publishing

Lanmon, Dwight P., Harlow, Francis H. (2009), *The Pottery of Zuni Pueblo,* New Mexico, Museum of New Mexico Press

Litto, Gertrude (1976), *South American Folk Pottery: Traditional Techniques from Peru, Ecuador, Bolivia, Venezuela, Chile, Colombia,* New York, Watson-Guptill

McEwan, Colin (1997), 'Whistling Vessels from Pre-Hispanic Peru', in *Pottery in the Making,* pp. 176–81

Peterson, Susan (1984), *Lucy M. Lewis: American*

Indian Potter, Tokyo and New York, Kodansha International

Purdy, Barbara A. (1996), *Indian Art of Ancient Florida,* Gainesville, University Press of Florida

Selser, Christopher (1981), 'Indian Ceramic Art in the American Southwest', in *One Thousand Years of Southwestern Indian Ceramic Art,* New York, ACA American Indian Arts

Spencer, Anne M. (1983), *Tempered by Time: 800 Years of Southwest Indian Pottery in the Collection of the Newark Museum,* Newark Museum

CHAPTER NINE: LIVING TRADITIONS

Barley, Nigel (1994), *Smashing Pots: Feats of Clay from Africa,* London, British Museum Press

Barley, Nigel (1997), 'Traditional Rural Potting in West Africa', in *Pottery in the Making,* pp. 140–5

Blurton, T. Richard (1997), 'Terracotta Figurines of Eastern Gujarat', in *Pottery in the Making,* pp. 170–5

Frank, Barbara E. (1998), *Mande Potters and Leatherworkers: Art and Heritage in West Africa,* Washington, DC, Smithsonian Institution Press

Hudson, Julie (1997), 'Urban Pottery Workshops in North Africa', in *Pottery in the Making,* pp. 134–9

CHAPTER TEN: MODERN AMERICA

Clark, Garth (1987), *American Ceramics: 1876 to the Present,* London, Booth-Clibborn Editions

Donhauser, Paul S. (1978), *History of American Ceramics: The Studio Potter,* Dubuque, Kendall Hunt

Hillier, Bevis (1968), *Pottery and Porcelain 1700–1914: The Social History of the Decorative Arts,* London, Weidenfeld and Nicolson

Perry, Barbara (1989), *American Ceramics: The Collection of the Everson Museum of Art,* New York, Rizzoli

CHAPTER ELEVEN: CRAFT INTO INDUSTRY

Copeland, Robert (1993), *Spode and Copeland: Marks and other relevant intelligence,* London, Studio Vista

Dawson, Aileen (1997), 'The Growth of the Staffordshire Ceramic Industry', in *Pottery in the Making,* pp. 200–5

Dawson, Aileen (1995), *Masterpieces of Wedgwood,* London, British Museum Press

Halfpenny, Pat (1997), 'Thomas Wieldon: his life and work', London, *English Ceramic Circle Transactions*

Jones, Joan (1993), *Minton: The First Two*

Hundred Years of Design and Production, Shrewsbury, Swan Hill Press

Pierce, Donald (1989), *English Ceramics: The Frances and Emory Cocke Collection,* Seattle, University of Washington Press

CHAPTER TWELVE: THE ARTS AND CRAFTS MOVEMENT

Frelinghuysen, Alice Cooney (1995), *American Art Pottery: Selections for the Charles Hosmer Morse Museum of American Art,* Seattle, Orlando Museum of Art in association with University of Washington Press

Lewenstein, Eileen and Cooper, Emmanuel (1974), *New Ceramics,* London, Studio Vista

Perry, Barbara (1989), *American Ceramics: The Collection of the Everson Museum of Art,* New York, Rizzoli

Rudoe, Judy (1994), *Decorative Arts 1850–1950: A Catalogue of the British Museum Collection,* London, British Museum Press

CHAPTER THIRTEEN: ARTIST POTTERS

Casey, Andrew (2001), *20th Century Ceramic Designers in Britain,* Woodbridge, Antique Collectors' Club

Donhauser, Paul S. (1978), *History of American Ceramics: The Studio Potter,* Dubuque, Kendall Hunt

Leach, Bernard (1978), *Beyond East and West: Memoirs, Portraits and Essays,* London, Faber & Faber

McCully, Marilyn (ed.) (1998), *Picasso: Painter and Sculptor in Clay,* London, Royal Academy

Perry, Barbara (1989), *American Ceramics: The Collection of the Everson Museum of Art,* New York, Rizzoli

Rudoe, Judy (1994), *Decorative Arts 1850–1950: A Catalogue of the British Museum Collection,* London, British Museum Press

Watson, Oliver (1990), *British Studio Pottery: The Victoria and Albert Collection,* London and Oxford, Phaidon/Christie's in association with the Victoria and Albert Museum

Wilcox, Timothy (1998), *Shoji Hamada: Master Potter,* London, Lund Humphries in association with Ditchling Museum, Sussex

CHAPTER FOURTEEN: STUDIO CERAMICS TODAY

Cruise, Wilma (1991), *Contemporary Ceramics in South Africa,* Cape Town, Struik

Dormer, Peter (1986), *The New Ceramics: Trends and Traditions,* London, Thames and Hudson

Duits, T. (1990), *Modern Ceramics in the Netherlands,* 's-Gravenhage, Stichting Keramiek

Faulkner, Rupert (1995), *Japanese Studio Crafts: Tradition & the Avant-Garde,* London, Laurence King

Janeko, Jan and Toubes, Xavier (1996), *Janjaneko,* European Ceramic Work Centre

Jones, Jeffrey (1900–2005), *Studio Pottery in Britain,* London, A & C Black

Mansfield, Janet (1991), *Salt-Glaze Ceramics: An International Perspective,* London, A. & C. Black and Radnor, Pennsylvania, Chilton Book Company

Perry, Barbara (1989), *American Ceramics: The Collection of the Everson Museum of Art,* New York, Rizzoli

Singh (1998), *The Legacy of Sardar Gurcharan Singh,* New Delhi, Delhi Blue Pottery Trust

CHAPTER FIFTEEN: THE STATE OF THINGS

Alfoldy, Sandra (ed.) (2007) *NeoCraft: Modernity and the Crafts,* Nova Scotia, Nova Scotia College of Art and Design University Press

Cecula, Marek with Kopala, Dagmara (2008), *Object Factory: The Art of Industrial Ceramics,* Toronto, Gardiner Museum

Cho, Chung Hyun, curator (2006), *Tradition Transformed: Contemporary Korean Ceramics,* Exhibition catalogue, Seoul, International Arts and Artists/The Korean Foundation

Clark, Garth (ed.) (2006) *Ceramic Millennium: Critical Writings on Ceramic History, Theory, and Art,* Halifax, Nova Scotia, The Press of the Nova Scotia College of Art and Design

Cochrane, Grace (ed.) (2007) *Smart Works: Design and the Handmade,* Sydney, Australia, Powerhouse Publishing

Cooper, Emmanuel (2009), *Contemporary Ceramics,* Thames & Hudson, London

Dietz, Ulysses Grant (2003), *Great Pots: Contemporary Ceramics from Function to Fantasy,* Madison Wisconsin, The Newark Museum/Guild

Groom, Simon (ed.) (2004), *A Secret History of Clay: From Gauguin to Gormley,* London, Tate Publishing

Hewitt, Mark and Sweezy, Nancy (2005), *The Potter's Eye: Art and Tradition in North Carolina Pottery,* University of North Carolina Press

Hildyard, Robin (1999), *European Ceramics,* London, V&A Publications

Illustration References

Photographs by the British Museum's Department of Photography and Imaging (abbreviated here as BM) are © The Trustees of the British Museum; registration numbers begin with departmental initials. Abbreviations are also given for images reproduced by courtesy of the Victoria and Albert Museum, London (V&A), the Everson Museum of Art (EMA), the archives of *Ceramic Review (CR),* and Technical Art Services (TAS).

p. 1: Courtesy © Kirsten Coelho
pp. 2–3: BM
pp. 4–5: Courtesy © Virgil Ortiz
p. 7: Photo Compte Henri Begouen, released by Jean Clottes, courtesy Janet Lever

CHAPTER ONE
p. 9: BM (OA 651; 639; 653, Dr J. Anderson collection); BM (WA 132406; 132388)
p. 10: BM (GR 1907.1–19.599, Cat. Vases A742); BM (WA 91109)
p. 11: BM (Ethno 1937.6–73); BM, (WA92215)
p. 12: BM (WA 134707; 134945; 134846)
p. 13: BM (EA 69839)
p. 14: BM; BM (WA 121749)
p. 15: TAS
p. 17: BM (WA 1924–4–16.8; 250; 251)
p. 18: BM (WA 1924–9–2.2; 3)
p. 19: BM (WA 1851–14–1.5)
p. 20: BM (WA 131819; 20)
p. 21: BM (WA 125934)
p. 22: BM (WA 129072; 135281; 131442)
p. 23: BM (WA 1913–12–16.2; 1914–4–12.1; 1915–2–18.1; 135694)
p. 24: BM (WA 132525 L78)
p. 25: BM (EA 62414)
p. 26: BM (EA 66544)
p. 27: BM (EA 62169; 59688)
p. 28: BM; Petrie Collection, University College, London (UC 17616)
p. 29: BM (EA 47996; 26636)
p. 30: BM (EA 53892); Photo Dick Wolters, Ovezande, Holland
p. 31: BM (EA 59774)
p. 32: BM (EA 35028)
p. 33: BM (OA 1873.12–10.1)

CHAPTER TWO
p. 34: BM (GR 1860.2–1.1)
p. 35: BM (GR 1863.12–44.1, Cat. Vases A344)
p. 36: BM (GR Cat. Vases A739, l 13)
p. 37: BM (GR 1873.8–20.385, Cat. Vases 85)
p. 38: BM (GR 1897.4–1.1150, Cat. Vases C416)
p. 39: TAS
p. 40: BM(GR 1959.11–4,1)
p. 41: BM(GR 1899.2–19.1)
p. 42: Burrell Collection, Glasgow Museums and Art Gallery (19/137)
p. 43: BM (GR 1912.5–22.1)

p. 44: BM (GR Cat. Vases B176)
p. 45: BM (GR Cat. Vases E140)
p. 46: BM (GR Cat. Vases D20)
p. 47: BM (GR 1885.3–16.1, Cat. Terracottas C529); BM (GR Cat. Vases H69, LB42)
p. 48: BM (GR Cat. Vases F479)
p. 49: Fitzwilliam Museum, Cambridge (GR1–1930); BM (GR 1869.2–5.4, Cat. Vases L54)
p. 50: BM (GR Cat. Vases Ml56)
p. 51: BM (GR 1862.7–12.2, Cat. Terracottas D185)
p. 53: BM (GR 1856.12–23.406, Cat. Vases K17; 1851.8–13.492, Cat. Vases K38; 1931.5–14.1)

CHAPTER THREE
p. 55: BM(OA 1913.11–21.1)
p. 56: BM (OA 1929.6–13.1); BM (OA 1959.2–16.1)
p. 57: BM (OA 1936.10–12.233)
p. 58: TAS
p. 59: BM (OA 1973.7–26.173, Seligman Bequest)
p. 60: BM (OA 1946.7–15.1, Colhurst Bequest)
p. 61: Courtesy Sotheby's, London ©1994
p. 62: BM (OA 1936.10–12.265)
p. 63: Percival David Foundation of Chinese Art, University of London (PDF A496)
p. 64: Percival David Foundation of Chinese Art, University of London (PDF 301)
p. 65: BM (OA 1968.4–22.25)
p. 66: Courtesy Sotheby's, London
p. 67: BM (OA 1960.7–28.1; 1972.6–20.1)
p. 68: Percival David Foundation of Chinese Art, University of London
p. 69: Burrell Collection, Glasgow Museums and Art Gallery
p. 70: Hastings Museum
p. 71: BM (OAF67)
p. 72: BM (OA 601; 583; 606; 1936.10–12.289; 582)
p. 73: BM (OA 1936.10–12.202)
p. 74: BM (OA 1913.10–7.1)
p. 75: BM (QA F2238, Gowland Collection)
p. 76: BM (JA 1958.10–21.2)
p. 77: Mingei Kan (National Folk Museum, Tokyo)
p. 78: BM (QAF1832)
p. 79: BM (QA 1952.11–13.1)
p. 80: Courtesy Sotheby Parke Bernet & Co., New York
p. 81: BM (OA 1972.9–19.1); BM (OA1945.10–17.507a; b)

CHAPTER FOUR
p. 82: BM
p. 83: BM(OAG. 1983.204, Godman Bequest)
p. 84: BM (WA 1923.7–25.1; 1956. 7–28.1)
p. 85: BM(OA 1930.3–10.1)
p. 86: BM(OA 1956.7–28.3, given by Sir Alan and Lady Barlow)
p. 87: TAS
p. 88: BM (OA 1951.10–9.1)
p. 89: BM (OA 1938.4–11.1)
p. 90: BM (OA 1956.7–28.2)
p. 91: BM (OA 1945.10–17.265)
p. 92: Fitzwilliam Museum, Cambridge (C148–1946)
p. 93: BM (OA 1914.3–18.1); BM (OA 1923.2–17.1)
p. 94: BM (OA G. 1983.28–4, Godman Bequest; 1931.2–17.1)
p. 95: Wallace Collection, London (C199)
p. 96: BM (OA, Godman Bequest)
p. 97: BM (OA 1924.4–23.1)
p. 98: BM (OA 1878.12–30.519, Henderson Bequest)
p. 99: BM (OA 1878.12–30.517, Henderson Bequest); BM (OA 1887.2–11.3)
p. 100: BM (OA G. 1983.395, Godman Bequest); BM (OA 1878.12–30.615, Henderson Bequest)
p. 101: BM (OA 1887.6–17.3)

CHAPTER FIVE
p. 102: BM (PRB ML2734)
p. 103: BM (PRB 1908.8–1.240)
p. 104: BM
p. 105: TAS
p. 106: BM (MLA 1969.12–7.3); BM (MLA 1855.12–1.70)
p. 107: BM (MLA 1910.2–14.12; 18; 17; 9)
p. 109: BM (MLA 1903.5–15.1; 1902.4–24.1; 1898.5–23.4)
p. 110: BM (MLA 1899.6–15.1)
p. 111: BM (MLA 1855.12–1.7; 1855. 3–13.4; 1851.21–1.4; 1855.12–1.81)
p. 112: BM (MLA 1855.12–1.96); Wallace Collection, London
p. 113: BM (MLA 1855.12–1.59)
p. 114: Museo Arquéologuo, Barcelona
p. 115: BM (MLA, Godman Collection)
p. 116: V & A
p. 117: BM (MLA G.1983.619, Godman Bequest)
p. 119: BM (MLA 1905.10–12.2)
p. 120: BM (MLA 1890.4–12.7)
p. 121: BM (MLA 1887.6–17.36); Museum für Kunst und Gewerbe, Hamburg; BM (MLA 1887.2–11.31)
p. 123: BM (MLA 1928.6–11.25)
p. 124: BM (MLA 1853.4–23.3)
p. 125: BM (MLA 1855.7–30.3)
p. 126: BM (MLA 1948.12–3.53)
p. 127: BM (MLA 1959.4–1.1)
p. 128: BM (MLA 1991.7–12.1); BM (MLA 1855.12–1.89)
p. 129: Courtesy Sotheby's, London © 1999
p. 130: Courtesy Sotheby's, London © 1999
p. 131: Museum of London
p. 132: BM (MLA 1887.6–17.43; 1855.12–1.211; 179; 138; 1894. 3–9.31; 1855.12–1.145; 1877.2–11.10; 1865.12–20.122) *p. 133:* BM (MLA 1891.11–14.1)

p. 134: BM (MLA 1854.7–26.1)
p. 137: Courtesy Sotheby's, London © 1999

CHAPTER SIX
p. 139: BM (PRB 1892.9–1.232; 1892. 9–1.240; 1958.5–6.556; WG 2285; 1893.4–26.8; P1982.1–1.86)
p. 140: BM (PRB 56.7–1.73 CRS; 1915.12–8.34)
p. 141: TAS
p. 142: Norwich Museums (CM 374); BM (PRB 145.3–20.59)
p. 143: BM (MLA 1915.12–8.192; 1856.7–1.1566; 1910.5–5.4; 1915. 12–8.191)
p. 144: Rotunda Museum, Scarborough Borough Council
p. 145: Ministry of Works; BM (MLA Archbishop 1306–9)
p. 146: BM (MLA 1899.10–5.3, B245; 1887.3–7, B246)
p. 147: BM (MLA)
p. 148: BM (MLA 1925.4–10.1; D24; D36)
*p. 749:*BM (MLAD1)
p. 150: Stoke-on-Trent Museums and Art Gallery
p. 151: BM (MLAD51; 1973.6–11)
p. 152: BM (MLA 1928.4–23.1); Hastings Museum
p. 153: Courtesy Christie's, London
p. 154: BM (MLA)
p. 155: BM (MLA); Jonathan Home, London
p. 156: BM (MLA 1887.2–10.105, Pottery Cat. F14)
p. 157: V&A; BM (MLA 1919.5–3.9, given by B.T. Hartland)
p. 158: Courtesy Sotheby's, London
p. 159: BM (MLA Franks Cat. 102); Courtesy Sotheby's, London

CHAPTER SEVEN
p. 160: BM (MLA 1887.5–16.2)
p. 161: TAS
p. 162: BM (MLA Franks Cat. 6)
p. 163: BM (MLA Franks Cat. *67*)
p. 164: BM (MLA 1923.3–14.6)
p. 165: BM (MLA Franks Cat. 136)
p. 166: Musée des Arts Décoratifs, Paris
p. 167: BM (MLA 1931.10–19.12)
p. 168: BM (MLA 1935.12–18.1; 2)
p. 169: BM (MLA Strasbourg 212)
p. 171: BM (MLA 1986.3–5.1; la); BM (MLA 1992.5–16.1)
p. 172: Courtesy The Royal Silver Room, Christiansborg Palace, Denmark
p. 173: BM (MLA 1990.5–6.7)
p. 174: BM (MLA 1938.3–14.35); Godden reference collection, Worthing
p. 175: BM (MLA 1927.4–11.1)
p. 176: BM (MLA 1923.12–18.12)
p. 177: Courtesy Bonhams, London
p. 178: BM (MLA Wore. Porcelain Cat. V119)
p. 179: Courtesy Sotheby's, London; BM (MLA Porcelain Cat. 111.35)

CHAPTER EIGHT
p. 180: Courtesy Museum of the American Indian, New York, Heye Foundation
p. 181: BM (Ethno 1951.Am.82)
p. 182: BM (Ethno 1938.10–17.16)
p. 183: TAS
p. 184: BM (Ethno 1939.Am.l7.9; 10); Peabody Museum of Archaeology and Ethnography, Harvard University (cat. no. 523)
p. 185: CR
p. 186: Private collection, photo Bobby Hansson; EMA
p. 187: Courtesy Seaver Center, Los Angeles County Museum of Natural History, photo Adam Clark Vroman, 1900
p. 188: BM (Ethno 1926.5–1.1)
p. 189: BM (Ethno 1977.Am.38.1)
p. 190: BM (Ethno 1844.7–20.971)
p. 191: BM (Ethno 1856.4–22.90); BM (Ethno 1946.Am. 19.1)
p. 192: BM (Ethno 1892.6–18.7)
p. 193: BM (Ethno 1920.2–12.5; 1919. 6–14.2; 1909.12–18.31)
p. 195: BM (Ethno Am.95.96)
p. 196: BM (Ethno 1938–20)
p. 197: Anthropological Museum, University of Aberdeen; BM (Ethno 1928.6–2.2)
p. 198: BM (Ethno)
p. 199: Museo del Banco Popular, Bogota, Colombia

CHAPTER NINE
p. 201: Photo Joy Voisey
p. 203: Photo Peter Beard
p. 204: Photo Jane Perryman
p. 205: Photo Peter Beard
p. 207: Photo Carol Ventura
p. 208: Photo Eileen Lewenstein
p. 210: Photo Peter Beard
p. 211: CR; Photo Moira Vincentelli
p. 212: BM (Ethno 1990. Am.8.33)

CHAPTER TEN
p. 214: Philadelphia Museum of Art
p. 215: Courtesy Winterthur Museum (55.109.4A)
p. 216: The American Museum in Britain, Claverton, Bath; Shelburne Museum, Vermont
p. 217: TAS
p. 218: Smithsonian Institution, J.P. Remensnyder Collection (1977.0803.9)
p. 219: Smithsonian Institution, J.P. Remensnyder Collection (1977.0803.195)
p. 220: Smithsonian Institution, J.P Remensnyder Collection (1977.0803.121)
p. 221: EMA (PC 85.68); (PC 87.101), photos © Courtney Frisse
p. 222: EMA (PC 88.20.8; 86.20.7; 86.20.9), photo © Courtney Frisse
p. 223: EMA, photo © Courtney Frisse
p. 224: EMA (PC 88.11), photo © Courtney Frisse

p. 225: EMA (PC 81.23.3), photo © Courtney Frisse

CHAPTER ELEVEN
p. 227: BM (MLA 1923.1–22.14)
p. 228: BM (MLA 1923.1–22.7)
p. 229: BM (MLA 1923.1–22.59)
p. 230: Trustees of the Wedgwood Museum, Barlaston, Staffordshire
p. 231: Trustees of the Wedgwood Museum, Barlaston, Staffordshire
p. 233: Trustees of the Wedgwood Museum, Barlaston, Staffordshire
p. 234: V&A
p. 235: BM (MLA 1786.5–27.1, Pottery Cat. 1712, given by Josiah Wedgwood)
p. 236: BM (MLA 1980.3–1.1)
p. 237: BM (MLA Pottery Cat. R30); Mason's Ironstone
p. 239: Courtesy Sotheby's, London
p. 240: Courtesy Minton Museum, Stoke-on-Trent
p. 241: Courtesy Sir Henry Doulton Gallery, Royal Doulton
p. 242: Courtesy Minton Museum, Stoke-on-Trent
p. 243: Courtesy Sir Henry Doulton Gallery, Royal Doulton
p. 244: Courtesy Sir Henry Doulton Gallery, Royal Doulton
p. 246: Courtesy Sir Henry Doulton Gallery, Royal Doulton
p. 247: CR
p. 248: CR; V&A
p. 249: Courtesy Josiah Wedgwood & Son

CHAPTER TWELVE
p. 251: Courtesy Sotheby's, London
p. 252: Courtesy Minton Museum, Stoke-on-Trent
p. 253: Fine Arts Society, London
p. 255: V&A, photo Bernard Alfieri
p. 256: BM (MLA 1980.12–7.3; 1 1945.2–4.8; 1978.7–4.8; 12; 1945. 2–4.16; 1980.12–7.2; 1978.7–4.13; 1945.2–4.20; 1978.7–4.14; 7)
p. 257: BM (MLA 1980.5–6.1; 1980. 5–5.1; 2)
p. 259: Courtesy Sir Henry Doulton Gallery, Royal Doulton
p. 260: BM (MLA 1989.11–3.1)
p. 261: Courtesy Minton Museum, Stoke-on-Trent
p. 262: Ceramic Collection, University of Wales, Aberystwyth; CR
p. 263: BM (MLA 1984.11–7.1)
p. 265: CR; EMA
p. 266: EMA (PC 62.45.2), photo © Courtney Frisse; BM (MLA 1984.11–7.2)
p. 267: CR
p. 268: BM (MLA 1984.10–10.2)
p. 269: National Museum of History and Technology, Smithsonian Institution, Washington, DC; EMA, photo Jane Courtney Frisse
p. 270: EMA (TN 132), photo © Courtney Frisse

p. 271: Ceramic Collection, University of Wales, Aberystwyth; BM (MLA 1901.4–25.1)
p. 272: Ceramic Collection, University of Wales, Aberystwyth
p. 273: V&A; Musée des Arts Décoratifs, Paris
p. 274: V&A
p. 275: BM (MLA 1986.11–2.1)
p. 276: BM (MLA 1986.3–2.1; 2); V&A
p. 277: BM (MLA 1992.6–10.1; 1992.7–14.1; 1992.6–9.1; 1992.6–8.10; 1993.10–12.2)
p. 279: BM (MLA 1987.3–1.1)

CHAPTER THIRTEEN
p. 280: Hetj ens-Museum der Landeshauptstadt, Düsseldorf, Deutsches Keramik Museum
p. 281: Courtesy Bloomsbury Workshop, London, photo Colin Mills
p. 282: Ceramic Collection, University of Wales, Aberystwyth
p. 283: CR
p. 284: CR
p. 285: Ceramic Collection, University of Wales, Aberystwyth; Winnipeg Art Gallery, Canada
p. 286: CR
p. 287: Courtesy Bonhams, London
p. 288: CR, photo Stephen Brayne
p. 289: CR, photo Stephen Brayne
p. 290: CR
p. 291: V&A; CR
p. 292: CR, photo Bob Allen; International Museum of Ceramic Art, Alfred, New York
p. 293: EMA (PC 40.331.1), photo © Courtney Frisse; Cowan Pottery Museum, Ohio; CR
p. 294: EMA (PC 59.26), photo © Courtney Frisse; CR
p. 295: CR
p. 296: EMA (PC 59.14; 64.86), photos © Courtney Frisse
p. 297: CR
p. 298: CR
p. 299: Courtesy the artist; Collection of Mr & Mrs Al A. Lippe
p. 300: CR; Courtesy the artist; Winnipeg Art Gallery, Canada
p. 301: CR; BM (MLA 1983.10–8.5)
p. 302: CR
p. 303: CR
p. 304: CR, photo Tom Haartsen
p. 305 Photo Hans Vos; CR
p. 306: Courtesy Garth Clark Gallery, New York; York City Art Gallery
p. 307: Courtesy Galerie Besson, London; CR
p. 308: Courtesy the artist
p. 309: CR
p. 310: CR
p. 311: CR; Courtesy Bonhams, London
p. 312: Courtesy Dartington Hall Trust Collection, England; CR
p. 313: V&A

CHAPTER FOURTEEN
p. 315: Courtesy the artist
p. 317: CR; Courtesy the artist
p. 318: Courtesy Contemporary Applied Arts, London, photo David Cripps
p. 319: Courtesy the artists; CR
p. 320: Courtesy Galerie Besson, London, photo Stephen Brayne; Courtesy the artist
p. 321: BM (OA 1990.1–14.4; 1986. 3–15.1); CR, photo Michael Harvey; Courtesy the artist
p. 322: CR; Courtesy the artist
p. 323: CR
p. 324: Courtesy the artists
p. 325: Courtesy Galerie Besson, London; Courtesy Fletcher Challenge, New Zealand; Courtesy Garth Clark Gallery, New York, photo Anthony Cunha
p. 326: Courtesy the artist
p. 327: Courtesy the artist; Private collection, Amsterdam, photo Frans Grummer
p. 328: Courtesy the artist
p. 329: CR; Courtesy the artist
p. 330: Courtesy the artist
p. 331: Courtesy the artist; CR; Courtesy Bonhams, London
p. 332: CR
p. 333: CR; Courtesy Contemporary Applied Arts, London, photo David Cripps
p. 334: Courtesy the artist; Courtesy Garth Clark Gallery, New York, photo Anthony Cunha
p. 335: Collection: The Dinner Party Trust, photo Donald Woodman
p. 336: Courtesy the artist
p. 337: Courtesy the artist; CR
p. 338: CR
p. 339: Courtesy the artist; Courtesy Contemporary Applied Arts, London, photo David Cripps
p. 340: CR; Courtesy Fletcher Challenge, New Zealand
p. 341: Courtesy the artist; Courtesy Galerie Besson, London

CHAPTER FIFTEEN
p. 342: Courtesy © Kirsten Coelho; Courtesy © Frances Lambe
p. 343: Courtesy © Grayson Perry; Courtesy © Bernadette Curran; Courtesy © Bonnie Seeman
p. 344: Courtesy © Clare Twomey; Courtesy © Keith Harrison
p. 345: Courtesy © Emmanuel Cooper; Courtesy © Robin Best; Courtesy © Felicity Aylieff
p. 346: Courtesy © Marian Heyerdahl; Courtesy © Ken Matsuzaki
p. 347: Courtesy © Natasha Daintry; Courtesy © Virgil Ortiz; Courtesy © Daphné Corregan; Courtesy © Barnaby Barford
p. 348: Courtesy © Marek Cecula; Courtesy © Anders Ruhwald
p. 349: Courtesy © Michael Eden

Index of Names